YEARBOOK MARITIME LAW

YEARBOOK MARITIME LAW

VOLUME I

1984

General Editor

Ignacio Arroyo

Springer Science+Business Media, B.V.

General Editor
IGNACIO ARROYO

Professor of Law, University of Barcelona. – J.D. University of Deusto, Bilbao, Spain. – LL.M. Harvard University, USA. – Doctor of Law, University of Bologna, Italy. – Diplôme de Droit Comparé, University of Strasbourg, France. – Titulary Member Comité Maritime International. – International Maritime Arbitrator, Deutsche Seeschiedsgerichtsbarkeit, Hamburg, Chambre Arbitrale de Paris.

All editorial correspondence, included book reviews, to Professor Ignacio Arroyo, c/o 'Ramos & Arroyo, Abogados', Paseo de Gracia 92, 2ª, 1ª (Gaudí-La Pedrera), Barcelona 08008, Spain. Phone (3) 215.77.11; telex 59398 FRM-E.

This issue should be cited as (1984) 1 YML

D/1986/2664/28

ISBN 978-94-017-3709-8 ISBN 978-94-017-3707-4 (eBook)
DOI 10.1007/978-94-017-3707-4

Originally published by Kluwer Law and Taxation Publishers, Deventer, Netherlands in 1986
Softcover reprint of the hardcover 1st edition 1986

Contents

III. INTERNATIONAL MARITIME ORGANIZATIONS

IV. CASE LAW

V. COMMERCIAL AND MARITIME EVENTS

VI. DOCUMENTATION

VII. BIBLIOGRAPHY

BOOKS

JOURNALS

VIII. INDEX

Foreword

I.

The importance of legal questions related to the sea is obvious to everyone. It is hardly surprising that the subjects that make up international current events illustrate the leading role played by maritime affairs. Indeed, it is no coincidence that three quarters of the earth's surface is covered by oceans. Territorial seas, exclusive economic zones, exploitation of the seabed, fishing, transport, insurance, collision, and pollution raise many unresolved questions.

On the other hand, the contrast of this importance with the modest attention that existing periodical publications merit must be underscored. Without undervaluing these publications, there has been a need for some time to create a vehicle of common expression, based on three central tenets: interdisciplinary framework, tendency towards uniform law, and both a theoretical and practical approach.

a. A framework of interdisciplinary nature seems to be relevant as it is desirable to overcome the artificial separation between public and private law. This is not the proper time to get bogged down in the traditional controversy surrounding the distinction between the various legal disciplines that have as their scope the study of one of the aspects of the sea, either the law of shipping (Seehandelsrecht) as the private law of sea trade, or the law of the sea (droit de la mer) as the international law of the oceans, or even the law of navigation (diritto della navigazione) as a specialized branch of general law; the first one is limited to the relation between private parties, the second relegated to intergovernmental relations, and the third open to all public and private activities derived from the technical fact of navigation. Our goal is something simpler: to cover, as far as possible, the entire ensemble of legal relations that arise from or are carried out on the sea. It is not our desire to solve in this manner the problem of the concept of maritime law. But we are also aware that the mere juxtaposition of the disciplines must yield before a convergent, interdisciplinary understanding. We realize that precise profiles in scientific study are tempting, but easily become mutilations of reality at least when they deal with legal sciences.

Precisely this interdisciplinary framework has been the first governing criterion of the Yearbook.

b. The international perspective has penetrated maritime law far more than any other branch of law. From the beginning of history, the interchange between peoples has been carried on by sea. Leaving aside the interpretation of the history of civilization as a battle between land and sea or, if you prefer, a fight for control of the sea, it surprises no one that the sea, as a channel of communication, has forged on the one hand the nature of relations between States, and on the other the orientation of private interests: navigators were the first merchants and sailors the discovering pioneers who changed the course of history. The conflicts that arose on these two levels of public and private interests nevertheless rest in the same historical constant: the necessity for uniformity of norms. In other words, the history of maritime law is the history of uniform uses, internationally accepted. It is therefore disturbing to accentuate, in effect, the peculiarities of domestic rules designed to regulate phenomena that are no longer domestic in character. The limitation of the territorial sea is an act of national sovereignty but is intended to limit the jurisdiction of other States. The regulation of seaborne transport can only be supranational. These and other examples illustrate the preponderance of the technique of international conventions or the generalization of the law of standard forms as peculiar sources of autonomous production of norms. This is the so-called uniform law.

If we now move from the historical approach to modern times and likewise continue to examine the distinction between public and private law, I would dare to say that the difference between maritime law and the law of the sea is that which separates renovation from consolidation. Maritime law is thousands of years old and only recently has it undergone a phase of profound revision; on the contrary, the law of the sea, as positive, codified law is in an incipient formative process that was initiated in the second half of this century with the 1958 Geneva Conferences. Notwithstanding, both processes converge before a new reality: the consideration of the volume of the sea. From a flat surface used merely for transport, we have discovered today, thanks to technological progress, an immense volume to exploit. Therefore, it is not unusual that the horizontal and vertical planes of the sea demand the apex of international uniformity. The sea has become a common neighborhood yard and it consequently needs the contribution of those scholars with a supranational perspective. This has been the second criterion for orientation of the Yearbook.

c. Together with the overcoming of public and private aspects of maritime law and its international perspective, the Yearbook tries to respond to the concrete necessities of trade, unimpaired by the demands that normally surround all scientific publications. This is perhaps the most delicate question, because it attempts to serve as a model of a specialized publication.

Within the abundance of today's legal journals there exists a variety so rich that it resists all attempts at classification. Nowadays, nevertheless, there seems to be a tendency in favor of a middle ground among the large consolidated journals who, faithful to a purified tradition, are characterized by their adherence to the traditional method: they are indebted to dogmatism and conceptualism. On the other hand, there are those publications of an informational nature. I do not think that it is bold to understand that this new attitude has grown under the protection of the first group, and it is reinforced by the insufficiency of the second. They are not wrong, those who from a practical perspective, who live the law where it collides with life, argue for the revision of the traditional method, which, anchored in the worship of categories and concepts, has sometimes brought contemporary legal science to a certain type of stalemate where words are discussed more than the human acts that express them. However, this unrestrained eagerness for information is also unsatisfactory, since in the end it encapsulates knowledge without the possibility of transcending the rapidity and immanence of occurrances. Not every decision, nor legal disposition, nor administrative act deserves attention and comment.

We are not trying to recall the debate between theory and practice, covered with precision by Savigny, since the problem disintegrates when the theoretician enunciates the general case and formulates a useful and efficient theory, and when the practical expert, resolving the concrete case, applies valid and rigorous knowledge. On the contrary, we are trying to signify that the modern lawyer cannot turn his back to reality, and construe the law with reference to philologism and dogmatism. Today more than ever it is necessary to examine the application of the law; to figure out the manner in which mankind applies, distorts, or replaces the will of the State to establish order.

From this perspective, both theoretical and practical, the Yearbook may serve as a sample of the convergence of the two most significant legal systems of western civilization. To affirm, as does Pound, that legal technique is characterized by the manner of applying the law to new situations, or in the Holmes' words, that the life of the law lies in experience, is the same as proposing the classic jurisprudence of the Roman praetor as a model. For Savigny it was, in effect, because the Roman jurists not only dominated the general principles, but also had a perfect legal vision of cases that they had to resolve. This ability to pass from the general to the concrete, and from the particular to the general is, in my opinion, the cornerstone of legal sensibility.

II.

The publication that I am honored to present to the benevolence of the reader attempts to pursue this new path, thereby breaking the watertight holds that separate tradition and modernity. It aspires to be the vanguard that opens routes of future expression, but without renouncing the investigator's patient labor, constructed upon the facts that history has given us.

The previous considerations permit the reader to situate himself in relation to the work that he holds in this hands. A publication that does not want to separate life and text. For this reason it is an open work that is offered – reiterating that well-known expression – to those who make their life a fight for justice with the law as their weapon. I would also like to indicate that the realization of the project is reflected in an obvious form; through publication, and in a constant manner: in a Yearbook. On the other hand, I believe it is safe to say that a reading of the index provides a thoroughly detailed explanation of the contents. The reader will be able to judge, in any case, if efforts have been spared.

Naturally, none of this would have been possible without the enthusiasm of all my colleagues, both Spanish and foreign, and institutions, both public and private, which have responded to my invitation to collaborate in this first volume. They have demonstrated that the solidarity that has always governed the activity of the people of the sea has not on this occasion been a mere declaration of words. I am profoundly grateful to everyone. Finally, I hope that the permanence of this efforts demonstrates the vitality of our law at the same time that it fosters the hope of continuity. This is something of which we are certain if we combine the pessimism of intelligence with the optimism of the force of will.

Prof. IGNACIO ARROYO

PART I.

ARTICLES

MARITIME LAW: AN APPROACH TO THE CONCEPT

Ignacio Arroyo*

Professor of Law at the University of Barcelona

* Professor Ignacio Arroyo is LL.B. University of Deusto (Spain), Doctor of Laws at the University of Bologna (Italy), LL.M. Harvard '75, Professor of Law at the University of Barcelona and is actually Senior Partner of 'Ramos & Arroyo', Abogados (Barcelona, Spain) and General Editor of YML.

I. Introduction

The expression 'maritime law' not only poses a question of terminology, but also defines a concept. This requires further explanation.

Maritime law has experienced, in the course of its extensive history, a bevy of alterations, many wise but others unfortunate. Analyzed from a modern viewpoint, these changes are manifestations of the fierce controversy aroused regarding the scientific determination of the concept.

When experts, case law, and sometimes even legislators insert the adjective 'commercial' into the concept, they are making a symbolic gesture that represents a change of attitude: maritime law is reduced to commercial maritime law. This produces, in other words, the substitution of navigation by trade as the criterion that delimits the material, at the same time that it is defined by its objective. This occurs in the nineteenth century codification. An analogous phenomenon, though of a different nature, occurs when the expression Maritime Law is interpreted as Navigation Law. The bounds of knowledge are widened and the autonomous nature of a new branch of law within the field is asserted. It is much more significant in the present case than in the preceding hypothesis: the substitution of Maritime Law by Navigation Law gives rise to a substantial autonomy; that is, a body of norms of a special nature exist which thus create a special system of Law, endowed with general principles capable of regulating and giving internal coherence to the material covered. Given thus, this legislative and scientific autonomy, the other levels of autonomy, jurisdictional and didactic, are no more than simple questions of political expediency. The Italian doctrine of mid-century proves this, as demonstrated by the enactment of the Code of Navigation in 1942. A range of intermediate possibilities can be found between the extremes of integration and autonomy, which, although they affect the terminological question, remain no more than simple variations, corrections or adaptations of the basic theme; that is, the conceptual problem.

1. THE STATE OF THE ISSUE

My first approach to the subject is an attempt to analyze a fundamental premise of the question under consideration: the separation of principles which, it is felt, has influenced traditional doctrine. The supports of autonomy have reduced the subject area to only one of the criteria which argue in favour of specialization, either the technical data of maritime navigation or the purpose or nature of the norms. The former definition necessarily leads to the delimitation of the goal: Commercial Maritime Law is wholly opposed to temporal Commercial Law and divorces itself from the latter since maritime navigation cannot survive in the normative body of Commercial Law. If this submission is carefully analyzed it may be observed that the criterion is confined to a problem concerning the geographical scope of application, that is, commercial maritime navigation delimits the purpose of Maritime Law, or, what amounts to the same thing, it can only be defined by its goal.[1] Therefore, the bulk of the problem consists of the subject matter to be defined, on the hypothetical facts contemplated, or on the division of a sector of reality. The nature of the arrangements or of the common or special feature of the subject are consequently alien. Naturally, the results of this thesis must necessarily be cautious, or preferably, confined to the didactive or explanatory spheres, or at the best of times, the terminological sphere. It is not surprising, therefore, that its main achievements have been gained in the harmonious construction of the content than in the creation of a special branch of law. In this context it cannot be said that an autonomous juridical system with its own norms and principles exists. The notion of Maritime Law as a collection of rules which exists to protect the continued performance of lucrative maritime business is consequently reached; where the shipowner is the subject, the merchant ship the object and the charterparty the central legal act.[2]

The second aspect mentioned, the purpose or special nature of the norms, leads to the affirmation of the existence of a special Law, an autonomous legal branch within the subject in which principles and concepts capable of scientifically structuring the subject can be detected. In this paragraph, as can easily be ascertained, emphasis is placed upon the acknowledged individuality of a group of norms whose specialized nature gives rise to an independent branch within the subject. In this context it may be affirmed that Navigation Law constitutes a departure from the common or general rule, not because it creates an exceptional regime vis-à-vis the general law, but because it develops or complements it, thus addressing itself to the peculiarities of the sectors of reality which it defines.[3] The technical data of

[1] G. Ripert, *Précis de Droit Maritime*, Paris (Dalloz), 1952, 6th ed., p. 10, n. 1, who suggests that it is not the nature of the norms which determine the scope of the subject but their objective.

[2] This notion is based on the work of J. Rubio, 'Derecho marítimo y Derecho aéreo (notas sobre la autonomía de las ramas jurídicas)' *Anuario de Derecho Civil*, 1952, p. 557.

[3] It may thus be further asserted that the autonomous nature of Maritime Law or Shipping Law demands special but not exceptional norms, although of course they are not excluded. However, it does not seem pointless to recall that the most authoritative doctrine, the distinction between both types of norms lies in the law's major or minor sphere of application in the legal relations it influences; the general law would influence all, while Maritime Law only those that have occurred on the sea or in maritime shipping, in accordance with the respective notion. In either cases, the distinguishing criterion is external to the nature of the norm; but to the contrary, the exceptional law may be distinguished from the normal law

self-sufficient transport therefore becomes an essential element of the end of the specialist principle. However, as shall be seen throughout this text, perhaps the steps taken in this direction have developed excessively, given that the demands of the system itself have created a tendency to exaggerate the distinctions which justify that autonomy. When the researcher is methodologically engaged in identifying groups of special norms, so as to deduce subsequently the general norms which structure knowledge and thus convert it into scientific knowledge, it does not appear risky to agree that the opportunity of research or independent study easily assumes the character of an autonomous branch of the law. The problems in delimiting the concept remain alive and, if it may be said, it is a question of pure chance whether the study of a branch of the law is classified as scientific. However, matters need not necessarily be so.

The previous considerations may appear familiar to those who follow closely the development of the so-called new branches of law (Labour Law, Tax Law. . .); or the temptation to surmount the issue of the concept and autonomy within the phenomenon of internal specialization may be proven, to which respond what one writer has termed Information Laws (Insurance Law, Company Law, Industrial Law, Banking Law. . .). It would, in other words, first consist of a scientific specialization followed by a corresponding normative specialization, and secondly, of a simple didactive or descriptive

---

breaks away from or separates from the general principle. Those norms that run contrary to the principles of the legal order constitute the exceptional law, also known as singular or irregular. Hence there are three important consequences that stem from this distinction: a) the exceptional norms cannot refer to a branch or complete sector of the legal order: they govern a specific relationship, and their speciality lies in the application of different criteria in solving a particular question within the same area; or better still, the contrast lies in the confrontation between fundamental rules, between one norm and another. (Pugliatti, 'Codice della navigazione e codice civile', *Rivista diritto della navigazione*, 1943–1948, p. 63, with reference to Shipping Law of a general character; Bobbio, with an analogous argument, in *Novissimo Digesto Italiano*, I, Turin 1957, pp. 605–606.) As a result of the preceding, b) some precepts of an exceptional nature may exist in the special Law, in much the same way as they coexist in the general Law (*see* generally, Enneccerus-Nipperdey, *Allgemeiner Teil des Bürgerlichen Rechts*, Bd. I (1959), 1st., p. 195), and c) the most important result is the fact that the exceptional Law is not the object of analogous application; no derogation occurs in deviating from the general principle, which is why the general principle is applied when it falls outside the facts that it was meant to regulate. This principle is expressly enshrined in Article 4, paragraph 2 of the Civil Code.

As regards the Spanish bibliography the textbooks on Civil Law (Albadalejo, Castán, Clemente de Diego, Cossío, De Castro – but with peculiar sleights that the special law denies in practice – Díez Picazo y Gullón y Lacruz) maintain this doctrine, and among the specialist works the following must be cited: Lalaguna 'Aplicación del Código civil como Derecho supletorio de otras leyes', *Revista de Derecho Privado*, 1976, pp. 598 et seq.; Montes, 'Comentario al art. 4–2 del Cód. civil', in *Comentarios a las reformas del Código civil: el nuevo titulo preliminar del código y la ley de 2 de mayo de 1975*, Madrid (Ed. Tecnos), 1977, pp. 207–239.

autonomy.[4] Nevertheless, neither the one nor the other has occurred in the field of Maritime Law, quite the contrary: born as a body of customary norms of a special nature, it subsequently disappeared into the common whole of codified Commercial Law, which, paradoxically, it has preceded in time, subsequently to be transformed into a different subject, in some cases without its special nature, and lately emerged with an assumed scientific and normative autonomy. Today, however, the retreat of the special nature of its norms may be witnessed while at the same time the scope of its content widens.[5] That is to say, historical evolution has demonstrated that the phenomenon of new laws has occurred also in this case, but in the opposite direction: normative specialization has developed into a scientific specialization and not vice versa.[6] Moreover, the first stages of scientific emancipation occur when legal autonomy loses its specialized character upon debilitation among the precepts of the Commercial Code. Perhaps it is as a reaction to the legal unification of all commercial subjects that the Maritime Law – Maritime Commercial Law dichotomy is dispensed with the Commercial Law consequently commences.

[4] See A. Sánchez Andrés, 'En torno al concepto, evolución y fuentes del Derecho bursátil en el sistema español', *Revista de Derecho Mercantil*, 1980, no. 155, pp. 8–9.

[5] This is not the proper venue to discuss whether the norms of Maritime Law enjoy historical priority over those of terrestrial Commercial Law as propounded by Goldschmidt (*Universalgeschichte des Handelsrecht*, 1891, p. 28) and Ascavelli (*Rivista diritto della navigazione*, 1950, p. 159); or whether, according to Silberschmidt ('Le droit commercial avant et après L. Goldschmidt', *Revue historique de droit français et étranger*, 1934, and Lattes, 'L. Goldschmidt e la critica recente' *Rivista diritto commerciale*, 1955, I, p. 605), the maritime and terrestrial norms have experienced a parallel development. It suffices to state that some of the most singular principles of Commercial Law and some of its more characteristic norms originate on the sea: limitation on risks and liability, the forms of association of exploitation of the commercial firm, the insurance contract. (Cf. Perdikas, 'Die Palermo Verträge und ihre Bedeutung für die Entstehung der Versicherung', *Z. Vers. Wiss.*, 1970, p. 152; ibid. 'Die Entstehung der Versicherung in Mittelalter; *Z. Vers. Wiss*, 1966, p. 429.)

[6] This is surprising since it is the exact opposite that is 'normal'. A good example of the assertion made in the text may be found in that era of history stretching from the Ordinance of the French Navy of 1681 until the first thirty years of the XIX century, and specifically at that time when Pardessus was writing. It cannot be denied that the publication of Louis XIV's Ordinance was reacting to the view that the body of the special norms ought to be contained in a single legal code in accordance with the field it regulates. As is known, the five books into which Colbert's tome is divided (Admiralty officials and their jurisdiction, seamen and ships, maritime contracts, natural harbours and coves, the police of coastal ports and fishing on the seas) give a very good idea of what their editors intended: to enunciate a body of rules governing the sea and all those activities connected with it, without distinction between private and public norms, between administrative or civil norms, between procedural or penal norms (Cf. J. Chadelat, 'L'élaboration de l'Ordonnance de la marine d'août 1681' in *Revue historique de droit*, 1964, pp. 74 and 228 who, on the other hand, shows that the legislative end-result was not the principal aim of the Ordinance; according to this author it seems that the objective was to curtail the abuses of the Admiralty and consequently to improve its organization and functioning). This classic legislative example which today may be called special law, overcoming naturally that technical obstacle contained in transferring the notion of special law to a bygone era in order to elaborate the legal science, did not receive support

It is therefore comprehensible that faced with actual evolution, which means a widening of its content and a revision of its special nature, the defenders of autonomy anxiously sought new fields of specialization, forgetting that the autonomies game is not a necessary result of special law. The object of knowledge may be widened seen though special norms may not exist, which does not prejudge the autonomous character of the subject.[7]

The reason for this phenomenon may be found, as has already been mentioned, in the confrontation, or better said opposition, between the two positions, when what really exists is a complementary relationship. This

---

however, from a separate and scientific study of the doctrine, which has been regarded by some as a mistake. The best proof of the preceding is an analysis of Pardessus' work. Pardessus' name is among the most famous maritime lawyers in history, which does not mean that he engaged in the elaboration of systematic rules nor that he was a defender of the scientific autonomy of Maritime Law. Even if it is true that the work for which he is best known is his seminal *Collection des lois maritimes antérieures au XVIe siècle* (6 vols., 1828–1845) attention must not be focussed on this work in order to prove or disprove the thesis that we contend: essentially it is a legal compilation and not a systematic study. However, the five volume work on Commercial Law (*Cours de droit commercial*, 3rd ed., 1825) and particularly the third, given over to Maritime Law, and the second on commercial contracts (*engagements commerciaux*) reveal that this great comparative lawyer and historian was far from concerned with problems of systematization and where understandably the notion of individualism or autonomy were alien to this descriptive exposition. (Cf. A. Rodière, *Traité de Droit maritime. Introduction. L'Armement*, Paris (Dalloz), 1976, no. 24, pp. 42–43.)

The same may be said about our legal history if, on the one hand, the legal body composed of the different Ordinances of the Consulates of Burgos (1538), Seville (1556) and Bilbao (1560) are taken as a starting point and, on the other hand, the first complete treatise on Spanish Commercial Law until the XIX century: *El laberinto del commercio terroestre y naval*, de Juan de Hevia Bolaños, published in Lima and Madrid in 1617 and 1619 respectively. It is not a question of drawing parallels between the various Spanish and French Ordinances on the one hand, and between the works of Pardessus and Hevia on the other; an analogy as remote as the two centuries that separate both documents and texts. What these examples help to demonstrate is that clearly scientific specialization has not resulted in legal emancipation as has occurred however, with the other new laws.

[7] The trend towards individualism as the phenomenon of autonomy is known in France coincides with the publication of the great tomes in the second decade of this century (thus, G. Ripert, *Traité de Droit maritime*, 3 vols. Paris (Collection Thaller), 3rd. ed. 1929–1930, vol. I, no. 185 et seq.; also in his *Précis de droit maritime*, Paris, 5th ed. 1952, pp. 12–13, considered his seminal work and openly opposed by Bonnecasse, *Le droit commercial maritime. Son particularisime. Son domaine d'application et sa methode d'interpretation*, Paris (Recueil Sirey), 1921, (2nd ed. 1931), in his *Traité de Droit commercial maritime*, Paris (Recueil Sirey), 1923, no. 185, and in his *Précis de Droit Maritime*, no. 113, In Italy, as is well known, the first essays on the theory of Shipping Law were written under the influence of the Commercial Code of 1882 by A. Scialoja, 'La sistemazione scientifica del diritto marittimo', *Rivista di diritto commerciale*, 1928, I, pp. 1 et seq.; *Sistema del diritto della navigazione*, Rome 1933, 3rd ed., p. 12; *Corso di diritto della navigazione*, Rome (Società Editrice del Foro Italiano), 1943, p. 17, to which the rest of the doctrine progressively adhere; thus Brunetti, *Diritto maritimo privato italiano*, Turin 1929, I, no. 3, p. 11; Dominedo, 'Teoria generale e diritto marittimo', *Rivista di diritto della navigazione*, 1936, I, pp. 21 et seq.

complementary relationship becomes apparent when it is realized that the concept of a legal subject is not a part of positive law, nor a logical nor rational element but, in that famous phrase, 'the general synthesis of the facts which the present is offering history.'[8]

In historical perspective the predominance of a trend over another at a certain period in time gathers sense, since the concept can only have a contingent effect. Alternatively, it also demonstrates the futility of the effort which seeks a concept independent from the co-ordinates of time and space. In essence, the special law derives its force from the evaluation a lawmaker makes of a part of the subject at any given moment. Supported by the special needs of a segment of social reality, it would seem more advantageous to delimit a topic divorced from general principles; without breaking away from it, however, seeking merely to complement and develop the general law. During these times in history, it would appear normal that the speciality would be reinforced through specialization, since it seems evident that the existence of norms of a different nature and purpose is the best endorsement for the emergence of a new branch of law. However, a substantially autonomous branch of the law does not always enjoy independent scientific analysis. It is not surprising therefore that the arguments for and against expanding the content of Maritime Law depend on whether one is in favour of or against its special character.[9] Hence it would not seem

[8] Professor Girón quite properly shed light on the conceptual problem of Commercial Law which I believe is perfectly applicable to Maritime Law. Cf. J. Girón Tena, 'El concepto del Derecho mercantil', *Anuario de Derecho Civil*, 1954, pp. 654 et seq.; *Apuntes de Derecho mercantil* (Introducción) Madrid (Universidad Complutense), 1977–78, pp. 12 et seq.

[9] A good example may be found in J. Rubio, op. cit., p. 560, no. 6, who in using the criterion of commercial shipping in delimiting special Maritime Law does no more than, in my opinion, diminish its content so that the application of the special (and privileged) regime is similarly reduced. The principle of the limitation of shipowner's liability consequently is inapplicable to the occupant of a ship given over to sporting or recreational activities. Shipping that is not profitable is not commercial shipping and therefore lies without Maritime Law. Professor Rubio's logic is impeccable since with his usual finesse he is demonstrating that the special law is, at least in this case, privileged law, and these needs of justice move him to curtail the scope of Maritime Law, thus applying the general principles of the order. This discrepancy does not lie, as may have already been noted, in the conclusion, with which I agree, but in the varied focus of the conceptual problem. It is my opinion that Maritime Law may be endowed with autonomy, thus no longer being special law, which is not incompatible with the extension of its content. This is made possible by the historical nature of the concept. However, when the special nature of its norms is loosened it does not appear proper to defend a scientific autonomy, at least if this last phrase is interpreted as a body endowed with special principles that generate a closed body with its own peculiar norm-generating capacity. It thus seems more appropriate to emphasise the double dimension of the autonomous nature of the branches of the law on the one hand, and the autonomous nature of the legal subjects on the other. In the former case, Maritime Law is regarded as special law; in the latter instance, Maritime Law is regarded as an autonomous subject. This particular autonomy, which cannot be understood by didactic or explanatory methods, but which can also include the scientific aspect, is naturally interpreted in its role as a scientific subject and not as a branch of the legal order. Here lies, it is submitted, the crux of the matter, because those who support scientific

exaggerated to suggest that the question of the affirmation or negation of Maritime Law vis-à-vis other branches of law is not, to a large extent, a matter of formulae or concepts, i.e., the question of the autonomy of Maritime Law is largely related to its affirmation by the specialist than of its specialization. Conversely, in other historical times the separate study of this branch of law has not been accompanied by any recognition of its special character, so that the so-called autonomous law is either interrupted or still-born in view of the lawmaker's indifference, or because the special principles themselves are in a state of crisis, or because, finally, in the 'era of their greatest triumph' they have been weakened in joining the common juridical order.

Consequently, the phrase Maritime Law as traditionally used has, depending on the age or the writers, come to have various different meanings, essentially by reference to one of these two facts: either as an organic body of norms regulating a specific category of relations; or else as a legal discipline that subjects such norms to its scrutiny. The former denotes a section of a legal order; the latter comprises one of the constituent elements of the general science of law. However, it should be borne in mind that a scientific concept which takes account of the facts must not see into this difference any significance other than two collatoral terms, in the sense that the science of Maritime Law must coincide, at least in principle, with the legal facts to which it is applied. In other words, Maritime Law may be assimilated to positive law, to statutory law or else as a particular legal science and, depending on which definition is accepted, the problem of special law or the question on delimiting the subject will be accentuated in a more direct manner.[10]

These obsrevations have constituted an attempt to illustrate the inadequacy of an exclusively explanatory study in answering the problem, since it would seem to lead in effect to a vicious circle in which the group of norms regulating navigation or maritime commerce would be known as Maritime Law, which maritime matters would be interpreted as precisely those governed by the law. It thus seems inexcusable to venture out of the purely legal field to search through economic factors and the criteria of legislative politics which have endowed it with its peculiar characteristics. The question that must be answered therefore consists of: (a) delimiting the

---

autonomy wish to see general principles illuminate that branch of the law and deduce therefrom the application of a special regime. However, the scientific autonomy of the subject is compatible with non-existence, or the relaxation of special norms, since the principles of interpretation may be found in the body of the subject, but not 'a fortiori' in that of the applicable law.

[10] This formulation that draws distinctions between branches of the law and legal subjects is a common feature of those jurists who study the general problems of the law. *See* A. Latorre, *Introducción al Derecho*, Barcelona (Ariel), 1976, 7th ed., p. 184.

legal-maritime facts in order to; (b) determine subsequently what the best method will be for discovering the objective conditions which have determined its existence, the reasons for its evolution and those which delimit its actual character.

II. The comparative law experience

2. THE PROCEDURAL PERSPECTIVE OF ENGLISH AND AMERICAN LAW: ADMIRALTY LAW

The significance of England to the formation and development of Maritime Law is not accompanied by any concern regarding the scientific definition of the concept.

When a Latin jurist analyzes English doctrine it becomes apparent that systematic planning hardly exists. The criteria employed in editing legal works, at least in this branch of the law, are not exactly methodological nor conceptual. The writers select particular subject areas, chosen by virtue of the wealth or extent of available material and on which they superimpose priciples derived from didactic requirements. The continental lawyer thus finds the literature on specific topics or monographs of greater interest, such as, e.g., carriage, charterparties, insurance, etc., than general works that are usually of little importance and the contents of which more often than not are chosen arbitrarily.[11] This is hardly surprising given the structural diversity between the Civil Law and Common Law systems which is a well known fact. This dichotomy between a system which tends to deduce general principles from the concepts and that of a system established on principles extracted from decided cases as legal facts must naturally be borne in mind in order to comprehend fully the structural arrangement of the conceptual problem of Maritime Law. The empiricism of the solutions and the absence

[11] Thus it is hardly surprising that works considered classic and worthy of citation include, for example, Scrutton, *Charterparties and Bills of Lading*, London (1st ed. 1886) and Carver, *Carriage of Goods by Sea*, London, 1885, with reference to charters and carriage. The former has reached nineteen editions (London, Sweet and Maxwell 1984, edited by Mocatta, Mustill and Boyd) and thirteen the latter (London, Stevens and Sons, 1982, third reprint edited by Colinveaux since 1952); or the two volume work by Arnould, *The Law of Marine Insurance and General Average*, London 1981, 16th ed., edited by Chorley and Bailhache. However, the books on a general theme are cited less often; as an example it need only be recalled that very few books are concerned with Maritime Law from a conceptual viewpoint on the basis of the legendary Abbot, *A treatise on the law relating to merchant shipping*, London (15th ed., edited by Aspinal and Moore, 1920); Duckworth, *The principles of marine law*, London, 4th ed. 1930, Machachlan, *A treatise on the law relating to merchant shipping*, London, 1932, 7th ed.; Chorley, *Shipping Law*, London 1947, the first edition and currently Chorley and Giles, *Shipping Law*, London (Pitman) 7th ed. 1980; R.D. Barthe, *Introduction to shipping law*, London, 1959, or the more recent R. Grime, *Shipping Law*, London (Sweet and Maxwell) 1978.

of any universal pretentions beyond the narrow confines of the particular case on the one hand, and its adaptation to the real needs of a specific case of conflict of interests on the other hand, may be easily explained when the approach is made from the common threads that characterize the Common Law; i.e., the case law system, the doctrine of binding precedent and the relevance of procedure.[12] The contrast with the reduced volume of decisions by Civil Law courts naturally justifies the greater significance to the continental legal system of conceptual organization and creativity.

Given these observations it may be submitted, without risking exaggeration, that English legal doctrine ignores one of the areas to which continental lawyers attach great importance. A brief summary of Anglosaxon literature published in the last century suffices to prove this contention. It should be noted that even the established texts omit any reference to the scope and significance of the subject.[13] This at least would appear to be the

[12] From a comparative angle, the most valuable Spanish work for understanding English private law continues to be, in my opinion, J. Puig Brutau, *Fundamentos de Derecho civil*, Barcelona, (Bosch) 1956 and his *Estudios de Derecho compavado, la doctrina de los actos proprios*, Barcelona (Ariel), 1951, and amongst the plentiful foreign literature, see the seminal work by R. David, *Les grands systèmes de droit contemporains*, Paris (Dalloz), 7th ed. 1978, pp. 321 et seq., in which a substantial part of a previous work co-written with David, Gutteridge and Wortley is reproduced, *Introduction à l'étude du droit privé de l'Angleterre*, Paris (Sirey), 1948, Walker and Walker, *The English Legal System*, London, (Butterworths), 5th ed., edited by R.J. Waler, 1980; G. Wilson, *Cases and Materials on the English Legal System*, London (Sweet and Maxwell) 1973, and as regards the United States, cf. A. Tunc, *Le droit des Etats Unis d'Amerique. Sources et technique*, Paris (Dalloz) 1955, and A.F. Farnsworth, *An Introduction to the Legal System of the United States*, N.Y. (Oceana Publications), 1963 (reprint 1968), translated into Italian and published by Guiffrè (1980).

[13] Cf. Chorley and Giles, op. cit., whose first chapter begins with the concept of a ship. However, Grime's book, op. cit., begins with a few sentences on the origins of Maritime Law and English Law in general, which have nothing at all to do with the conceptual problem. On the periphery are the numerous works on jurisprudence, the compilation of teaching materials and casebooks which for obvious reasons do not have to address this question. Generally speaking, doctrinal law journals in this field were unknown in Great Britain until the publication in 1975 of the first specialist journal: *Lloyd's Maritime and Commercial Law Quarterly*, but in no issue has a conceptual analysis yet been published. However, a brief look through the bibliography on Maritime Law of Latin legal systems proves that not only do the general works discuss the conceptual problem, either as a notion or as a definition of the subject matter, or as an autonomous subject, but rare is the article where as least one paragraph does not analyze the question of individualism. *See*, generally, Rodière, *Droit maritime*, cit. n. 1–7. Lefebvre D'Ovidio-Pescatore, *Manuale Diritto della Navigazione*, cit. n. 1–5; Schaps-Abraham, *Das Deutsche Seerecht-Kommentar und Materialsammlung*, Berlin, 1959–1962, 2 vols. 3rd. ed., edited by Hans J. Abraham, suppl. (Ergänzungsband), Berlin 1967, ch. 1; Ray, *Derecho de la navegación*, Buenos Aires (Abeledo-Perrot), 1964, ch. 1, pp. 12 et seq., Mezzera Alvarez, *Curso de Derecho marítimo*, 2 vols., Montevideo (Ed. Alcali), 1977, ch. 1, pp. 1–18; Sampaio de Lacerda, *Curso de direito privado de navagacao*, 2 vols., Rio de Janeiro (L. Freitas), 2nd ed. 1974, Introduction, pp. 15 et seq., and Garrigues, *Curso de Derecho marítimo*, Madrid, 1974, vol. 2, 6th ed., p. 503, to cite a general work of the most representative States.

case with reference to Maritime Law, paradoxically when in the rest of the world where this question has been addressed, it has enjoyed the greatest consideration of normative, jurisdictional and didactive specialization.

Seen in this context, is the Common Law experience devoid of any merit? Evidently not. What then has it contributed? Procedural requirements as distinguished from Maritime Law it is submitted. This is evidenced at first hand by secular history, and it is no stranger to the same definition of Admiralty Law. The Law of Admiralty was, in effect, the earliest suitable experience which defined the groups of customary norms and various other precepts which the Lord High Admiral applied in deciding the cases submitted to his jurisdiction. Similarly, the first written text which lists the common law and practices prior to the XV century was the Black Book of Admiralty, which is the foundation of modern English Maritime Law. Neither is it coincidental that Britain's most prized ex-colony, the United States of America, should keep using that same term to describe Maritime Law. Let us study individually each paragraph.

Although it may appear surprising, a general and comprehensive history of the Admiralty has not yet been written in England; nonetheless, the reseach that has been undertaken, even if rather fragmentary and referring usually to certain specified periods, permits us to trace an evolutionary line which suffices for present purposes.[14]

Leaving aside the effect which various medieval compilations and codes may have had (the laws of Amalfi, the Consolato del Mare, the Guidon de

[14] *See* F.M. Wiswall, *The Development of Admiralty Jurisdiction and Practice, since 1800*, Cambridge 1970, especially pp. 12 et seq., Mears, 'The History of the Admiralty Jurisdiction', in *Select Essays in Anglo-American Legal History*, 1908, vol. 2, p. 312; Laing, 'Historic Origins of Admiralty Jurisdiction in England', 45 *Michigan Law Review* (1946) 163; Thompson, *Admiralty Registrats: some Historical Notes*, 1958; Senior, 'Early Writers on Maritime Law', 37 *Law Quarterly Review* (1921) 232; Fitzgerald, 'Admiralty and Prize Jurisdiction in The British Commonwealth of Nations' 60 *Juridical Review* (1948) 106; Stinson, 'Admiralty and Maritime Jurisdiction of the Courts of Great Britain, France and the United States' 16 *Northwestern University Law Review* (1921) pp. 1 et seq., and the well-known article among scholars, Sacks, 'Conflicts of Laws in the History of English Law: A Century of Progress' 3 *New York University* (1937) 342 who although dealing with a question of private international law cites numerous bibliographical and documentary references on Maritime Law. Along with these specific articles, limited to certain eras and particular aspects, the general American works contain good summaries of the developments that occurred just as much in England as in the United States. Cf. G.W. Robinson, *Admiralty*, St. Paul (West Publishing), 1939, pp. 1–7; Gilmore and Black, *The Law of Admiralty*, Mineola (Foundation), 1957, and 1975, 2nd ed., pp. 7–9; Robertson, *Admiralty and Federalism*, 1970, 6–103, p. 35; Healy and Sharpe, *Admiralty* (Cases and Materials), St. Paul (West Publishing), 1974, pp. 1–7 whose reading, though brief, is recommended since one's attention is drawn by the precision of the introduction to a work that teaches Maritime Law through the case law system. Similarly, volume IV of E. Benedict's, *Admiralty*, 7th ed., edited by N.Y. Knauth (Mathew Bender), 1968–69, pp. 343–463, and C.J. Colombos, *The International Law of the Sea* (6th ed.), London (Longmans), 1967, nos. 10–20, contain some interesting facts.

la Mer, the Rules of Oléron, etc.)[15], historical research has demonstrated that during the XV century a maritime tribunal was established by the Lord High Admiral with jurisdiction over all civil questions of a maritime nature. As the major representative of the King in maritime affairs, the Lord High Admiral was the official of highest standing, whose competence extended principally to questions of piracy, wrecking, smuggling, blockades, enemy assistance and the policing of ports. Although the exact date of the conferment of the new judicial role is not known, it is true that during the reign of Richard II (1377–1400) the importance of the issues under his personal jurisdiction led to a debate in Parliament, with the result that this jurisdiction was limited to a thing upon the sea, and by the Tudor era it was a court endowed with exclusive jurisdiction in civil and commercial cases with reference to the law of the sea.[16] The progressive expansion and consolidation of the Admiralty courts as a special court in maritime affairs, which in addition operated without the need of the jury system and in accordance with a more flexible procedure and consequently gave rise to distrust from the Common Law courts, requires no further elaboration as the facts are well known.

[15] Jurists have discussed the influence of one or the other in the formation of Maritime Law in this country and their conclusions, under the critic's scrutiny, are rather doubtful since that influence has favoured the document or code and which has merited the attentions of the researcher. Thus, S.S. Jados cannot conceal his sympathies for the Book on the Consulate of the Sea in, *Consulate of the Sea and Related Documents*, Alabama (The University of Alabama Press), undated but 1974, pp. v. et seq. of the Introduction. Nevertheless, opinion seems to favour the Rules of Oleron as the mediaeval code that left its mark on Admiralty Law, partly because of the strategic situation of the island that gave them its name, halfway to the commercial wine route in the English Channel during the XII and XIII centuries. (J. Craeybeck, *Les vins de France aux anciens Pays-Bas* (*XII–XVIs*), Paris, 1958, pp. 84–90; Gilmore and Black, op. cit.; Healy and Sharpe, op. loc. cit. This question has been exaggerated to such an extent that it has been affirmed that 'In the same way as Commercial Law has its origins in the fairs of Champagne, Maritime Law was born in the wine trade of Aquitaine' (Lefranc), cited and modified by Rodière himself, *Traité de Droit maritime*, vol. I, *Introduction*, cit. n. 14, p. 21.

[16] A reading of the works of Mears, 'The History of Admiralty Jurisdiction', op. cit., and Laing, 'Historic Origins of Admiralty Jurisdiction in England', cit., note not only the imprecision of the date when the Admiralty registers were created but also the initial form this special jurisdiction adopted, a coincidence in the thematic origins of their jurisdiction: questions of Public Law and the Law of War (piracy, looting, and harbour police). Originating thus at the beginning of the XIV century with penal jurisdiction they would develop until they recognized civil causes, a phenomenon that occured towards the end of that century and towards the beginning of the XV century. R.G. Marsden, 'Documents relating to the law and custom of the sea', 49 *Navy Records Society* (1915); Ibid., *Select Pleas of the Court of Admiralty*, vol. I, p. XIII, which illustrates that the *Doomsday* of the Ipswich Tribunal, published in the *Rolls Series*, and those of the *Borough Roles* of Yarmouth prove the existence of port or marine tribunals – as they were known in the times antecedent to Edward III (1326–1377) – . Marsden, 'Six centuries of the Admiralty Court', 67 *Nautical Magazine*, pp. 86–88.

It appears significant, nevertheless, to emphasize this fact, however paradoxical it may seem, since it offers a good illustration of the contribution English law has made to the development of Maritime Law: the procedural aspects of the Admiralty courts have more in common with the Civil Law system than with that of the Common Law since they have become internationalized through commerce. In other words therefore, it is submitted that the longevity and continuity of the special maritime courts in England, which originated in the early XV century and which have survived to this day, was due to the quick adaptability of court procedure to the needs of the sea and maritime commerce, at the cost of distancing themselves from the procedural practices of the Common Law courts. If this had not been the case, and leaving aside the question of the possible fusion of the courts, the Admiralty courts would not have dispensed with the jury system, to the consequent detriment of procedural rapidity, and, alternatively, neither would the question of jurisdiction have been decided in their favour, thus widening the category of cases beyond the narrow confines of the law. Naturally enough, the reaction of the Common Law judges, who perceived, first, a diminution of their general jurisdiction and, secondly, a transfer of procedural practices from civil law cases, was not long in coming. This jurisdictional dispute was conducted with the aid of interpretative techniques: the phrase 'done upon the sea' was given a wide or restrictive meaning according to the type of judge adjudicating the case. The change in emphasis occurred when it was decided that contracts relating to goods of a maritime nature, but which were not performed on the sea, fell without the jurisdiction of the Admiralty, so that little was needed to deprive the special court of its jurisdictional competence.[17] However, subsequent acts deny the existence of this misguided logic. Whilst a reciprocal battle continued for over a century, during which time writs of prohibition against proceedings in Admiralty were exchanged, and with the courts of special jurisdiction clearly in retreat, the Admiralty courts won the war when, at the very least, a strengthening of its jurisdiction became unquestionable.

Hence, during the nineteenth century, two significant but apparently contradictory acts occur: one, the enactment between 1840 and 1861 of a

[17] An examination of this problem may be better noted in A. Holdsworth, *History of English Law*, 3rd ed., 1922, p. 553, which has become the classic work on the history of English Law.

[18] An analysis of this question raises some interesting points; while the development of Commercial Law underwent a process of unification in the general body of the common law, Maritime Law encountered a different experience. It seems even more peculiar when it is noted that the absorption of the *lex mercatoria* into the Common Law in the XVIII century also resulted in the disappearance of the special commercial tribunals. Thus, commercial lawyers have sought a different argument to explain the substantive survival of Commercial Law beyond that formal unification, which extends beyond jurisdiction, norms and principles. This process is expecially complex and cannot be adequately comprehended if the development of the jurisdictional system is not borne in mind, and particularly the fact of the progressive extension of the jurisdiction of the ordinary tribunals to the detriment of the special ones. (Burin des Rozières, *La distinction du droit civil et du droit commercial et le*

droit anglais, Paris, 1959, pp. 17–31; Girón, 'El concepto', cit., pp. 65–69). Initially, commercial jurisdiction founded on local privileges witnessed a restriction on its competence; subsequently, it was gradually extended until it was absorbed by that new royal Court of Admiralty. However, its disappearance did not finally take place until the XVI century, initially for the English traders and subsequently for the foreign ones, when the fiction arose that a contract must be entered into in England if it is to take place in that country. The controversy arose in the XVII century that denied the competence of the Admiralty courts in favour of the special tribunals, although the issue was not settled in their favour. The process of absorption under Lord Mansfield was completed in the XVIII century, to whom we owe, however, the achievement of a coherent system. Lord Mansfield's achievement lay in integrating the heterogeneous elements of the *lex mercatoria* until a harmonious system resulted (Gutteridge, 'Lord Mansfield, a Comparative jurist of the 18th century' in *Recueil d'Etudes sur les sources du Droit en l'honneur*, by F. Geny, Paris, III, pp. 239–246). Harmonization was accomplished by the commercialization of the common law, so that while the principle of the subject's unity is respected the needs of the traders are likewise satisfied. Thus, law applied by ordinary courts is unified, incorporating into the common law a large number of principles developed by the *lex mercatoria*, and submitting to the same norms all subjects, whether or not they are traders, nationals or aliens, and all businesses. It is interesting to note that the general process of legal nationalism that occurred in England in the XVIII century whereby the *lex mercatoria* was absorbed into the common law took place through a technique different to the one utilized by continental systems which, as is known, expediently delimits formally the commercial subject. In England, the dissolution of the *lex mercatoria* is a consequence of the absorption of the special commercial jurisdiction by the common law (David, 'La distinction du droit civil et du droit commercial en Angleterre', *Estudios homenage a Mossa*, 1961, I, p. 401; J. Rubio, *Introducción al Derecho mercantil*, Barcelona, 1959, p. 225). These unique tribunals applied the norms of the common law as well as the traditional ones of the normal law, which as we have witnessed they have always maintained, changing the formula only, a special jurisdiction based on a different procedure. It can thus be seen that as from that distant moment of absorption, the concept of Commercial Law is no longer a purely historical notion for English jurists, who consider the possibility of its antiscientific independence and its source of uncertainty and consequently reject its possibility (Girón, *Apuntes de Derecho mercantil*, cit., p. 55; J. Rubio, op. loc. cit.). It is therefore logical that other options be sought; it was therefore said that this trend was in no way an acknowledgement of the thesis of unification in the legislative sphere, at least as it is posed on the continent, but that it is the normal consequence of the British attitude towards sources, concepts and the systematic legal schemes (Girón Tena, op. ult. loc. cit.). This explains why that country's doctrine does not countenance the problem of possible autonomy, since there is a strange distinction between Civil Law and Commercial Law given that no legal texts exist that seek to pose the question of the subject's delimitation, nor of special jurisdiction, nor a scientific doctrine broaches consideration of the discipline from a general angle. Viewed from this perspective it can be understood why it is that the continental jurists are determined to prove the autonomy of Commercial Law, the existence of an independent Commercial Law for the United Kingdom, despite legislative and jurisdictional unity (Rubio, *Introducción*, cit., p. 225). Consequently, only by adopting the methodological approach of the continental lawyers may a series of norms which attend to the typical necessities of commercial traffic be noticed in the English system, and from that perspective it does not appear difficult to assert that neither legislative nor jurisdictional unity, nor the existence of delimiting norms, constitute obstacles which prevent noticing a similarity on a normative level between our system and that of the Anglosaxon. This analysis of Commercial Law, which necessitates the introduction of elements that are extraneous to the common law tradition, emphasizes in my opinion the differences regarding the conceptual problem of Maritime Law.

series of instruments with legal force[18] in which the jurisdiction of the Admiralty Court is recognized and widened; the formal dissolution of the special Admiralty courts. However, they are not phenomenons of a paradoxical or contradictory nature, but they simply have different emphasis. The first case suggests the delimitation of Maritime Law in the legislative sphere, limited to seaborne Commercial Law.[19] The second of the facts mentioned refers more to a question of form than of content, since it does not affect the eminently procedural dimension of Maritime Law. Therefore, the reorganization of the English legal system, which commenced in the last third of the XIX century and has lasted to this day, concerns basically a terminological readjustment. The disappearance of the Admiralty courts, which in 1873 were merged with those of the Common Law, thus giving rise to the Supreme Court of Judicature, cannot be interpreted as the destruction of the special jurisdictional system by the subject matter, since the facts show that a specialized division was maintained – Probate, Divorce and Admiralty Division – until its abolition in 1971 under the Administration of Justice Act 1970, in force from 1 October 1971; a specification which did not also disappear in the latest reform, which has preserved a special bench, the Admiralty Court within the Queen's Bench Division of the High Court, to which are referred the majority of maritime cases and where procedures and norms 'not yet common' are still applied.[20]

It was stated in favour of differentiated legal treatment that, along with the maintenance of a special jurisdiction of maritime courts throughout the ages, the earliest known written work is entitled 'Admiralty Law'. It certainly corroborates what has just been suggested that the source of modern English Maritime Law is to be found in a text entitled, not by

[19] 3–4 Victoria c. 65 (1840); 13–14 Vict. c. 26 (1850) and 25 Vict. c. 10 (1861).

[20] *See* P.V. Gray and V.E. Ricks, *Admiralty Practice. Third Cumulative Supplement* (*up to date to July 1, 1975*) of Vol. I, *Admiralty Practice*, by McGuffie, Fugeman and Gray, in *British Shipping Laws*, London (Stevens and Sons), 1964, and the *Supplement*, London, 1975, para. 2; R. Grime, *Shipping Law*, London (Sweet), 1978, p. 2. Note that Sections 20–24 Supreme Court Act 1981 have introduced further reforms to the Admiralty jurisdiction of the High Court. In order to put the issues raised in the main text in their proper perspective it appears necessary to have prior knowledge of the English judicial system and of its organization, the discussion of which is naturally beyond the confines of this study. However, it should be noted that at present England has a sole judicial system, or better still, based on the principle of sole jurisdiction, and founded on a single legal system, that is, a single order. Hence, a maritime order distinct from the general system does not exist, nor does independent jurisdiction, although a body of rules and procedural practices applicable exclusively to maritime actions does exist. It would be a mistake to think of the notion of maritime courts within the special jurisdiction, but it is similarly a mistake that the common or ordinary judges understand the maritime cases since, on the one hand, the lower courts can call upon a 'special' judge with expertise in the Law of the Sea to give advice and deliver judgment, as long as such an issue falls within his sphere of competence, and on the other, as we have seen, a special maritime court at the level of higher courts has been maintained: the Admiralty Court.

coincidence surely, 'Black Book of Admiralty'. Although the exact date of its edition or publication has not been determined, although its authors date it between the end of the XIV century and the beginning of the XV century, it would appear true to say that it consists of a compilation of usages, codes and practices related to the procedure then practiced by the Admiralty Courts in maritime cases.[21] Therefore, the influence of procedural question, the mode of the judge in interpreting and applying the law, was a fact of singular importance which structured, with time, the practice and procedure of this branch of the law. Numerous references may be cited to support the view that the jurists who developed this subject continued in this approach, and if in one precise moment in time it may be noticed that the English jurists are substituting the phrase Admiralty Law by Maritime Law or Shipping Law, it cannot be legitimately attributed to a distinct understanding of the subject but to a mere terminological readjustment which, as examined earlier, was a response to judicial reorganization and, more specifically, the nominal abolition of the Admiralty Courts.

Finally, as a plausible manifestation of the continuity of the process, appears the consolidation of Admiralty Law in the United States of America. Briefly, the history of American Maritime Law may be divided into three periods: the colonial era, that which ran from 1787 to 1966 and from 1966 to the present day. The first is distinguishable by the existence of British colonial courts of Viceadmiralty. The second is characterized by the constitutional recognition of Maritime Law as Federal Law, subject therefore to the exclusive jurisdiction of Federal courts. The third period is distinguished by the substitution of procedural norms in favour of the general ones of the Code of Civil Procedure.

The first period, the so-called colonial era has been deliberately prolonged for some years beyond the formal declaration of independence because on 4 July 1776, when the ties of dependence with the British Crown were finally broken and sovereign and self-governing rights were consequently established, from a personal viewpoint the year 1787 is indubitably of greater importance, when, upon the adoption of the Constitution, Maritime Law is established within the sphere of judicial competence, which encompasses 'all Admiralty cases and of maritime jurisdiction'. What occurred during this period of time may be summarized in two propositions: on the one hand, the function of the Viceadmiralty courts which, though dependent on the British Crown, operated with greater flexibility than their English counterparts since they were not subjected to the close scrutiny of the Common

[21] This appears to be the opinion of Sir Travers Twiss, who edited the work in four volumes between 1871 and 1876; cf. T. Twiss (ed.), *Black Book of the Admiralty*, London (Rolls Series No. 55), 4 vols., 1871–1876, in *Introduction* to vol. I. The first edition, in goatskin, can presently be found in the Public Records Office in London to where it was transferred in 1873, the year of its discovery following its disappearance in 1808 from the Registry of the Former Admiralty Court. A few years ago this author was able to inspect this bibliographical treasure, held to be one of the most valuable books in existence.

Law judges who, as has been noted, reclaimed their competence, and because their judgments were rarely subject to appeal in the mother country;[22] and on the other hand, following independence, the old colonies, converted into Federal states had to create their own Admiralty courts, which principally dealt with questions of maritime prize, naturally habitual after a war of independence.[23] Despite the sparse and fragmentary records that have survived, the laudable efforts of some historians have proved conclusively that it was an insignificant stage in which little more than common sense and good judgment played a role in the development of the law. It is not surprising that good faith and a natural sense of justice should form the basis of judgments when digests of cases had not yet been published and that the first book on our subject had not seen the light of day.[24]

The most fertile period, when the differentiated legal period was definitely established, is that which spans the time between the adoption of the Constitution until 1966. Its significance does not lie in its length of time, almost two hundred years, which in American historical terms is tantamount to its entire history, but precisely because it derives from positions of determined assumptions and with a determined content. Those assumptions lie in their constitutional origin, whether popular or democratic, manifestly summed up in the Federal Constitution which expresses the doctrine of the social contract and its basic assumption in self-organization as the fountain of the legitimacy of power and Law; its content is neatly summarized by the famous Article 3, paragraph 2: 'The judicial Power shall entend . . . to all Cases of Admiralty and maritime Jurisdiction'.

[22] Crump, *Colonial Admiralty Jurisdiction in the Seventeenth Century*, N.Y. 1931, 22–43; Wroth, 'The Massachusetts Vice-Admiralty Court', in the collected work by Billias (ed.), *Law and Authority in America*, 1965, cited by Gilmore and Black, cit. n. 36 and other bibliographical references.

[23] J.H. Smith, *Appeals to the Privy Council from the American Plantations*, 1950; a vast amount of material is gathered on the appeals that were lodged in this lengthy work, which illustrates the machinery of these courts and their relationship with the high-ranking Crown officials, particularly pp. 90–93 and 265 et seq.; also Wiener, 'Notes on the Rhode Island Admiralty, 1727–1790', 46 *Harvard Law Review* (1932) pp. 44 et seq.

[24] The first systematic collection of cases was published in 1801, and only covers judgments delivered between 1776 and 1779 (Hay and Marriott's *Reports*). Subsequently, in 1885, Burrell's collection was published wherein cases from 1758 to 1774 are listed. As regards the bibliography, the book by A. Browne, *Compendious View of the Civil Law and the Law of Admiralty*, published in Dublin between 1797 and 1799, has been credited as the first theoretical work in English on Maritime Law. The present author in his day (Harvard University Library) could only acquire a second edition, certainly much better known, dated London 1802, as well as the American version, published in New York in 1840. However, it is clear that Browne's book did not achieve the success nor the scope which Baron Tenterden's book accomplished at the beginning of the XIX century. Charles Abbott, as the aristocrat who wrote the *Treatise of the Law Relative to Merchant Ships and Seamen*, London 1802, was originally called, was introduced in the United States by the father of American Admiralty Law, judge Joseph Story who, as is known, edited the notes to the second edition in 1810.

This precise concept of Admiralty Law as Federal Law and, therefore, subject to the exclusive jurisdiction of Federal courts, has suffered throughout history the characteristic buffetings of a legal system based on judicial supremacy, hegemony that has made the Supreme Court a true 'indirect constituent power'.[25] It should not be surprising, therefore, that the father of Maritime Law be a judge, Joseph Story, and that a judgment, in the case of *De Lovio v. Boit*, be the starting point in the delimitation of Admiralty jurisdiction which, due to the subject matter covered, is equivalent to the notion of Maritime Law. The reader shall not be detained further by a commentary on the life and works of one of the most brilliant judges, certainly the youngest and according to his biographers the most cultered, who have graced the Supreme Court, given that it may lead to oversimplification; his most important contribution was linked to the leading case in the history of Anglo-American maritime jurisdiction.[26]

[25] This quotation is a more technical and sweetened formulation of that more daring phrase – 'The Supreme Court is the Constitution' – which illustrates that singular function of American judges, judicial review and, as is known, is the greatest American contribution to Constitutional Law: to instill in a written Constitution a higher or fundamental law that scrutinizes the validity of the laws of the legislature, which is implemented precisely through judicial review. The introduction of this principle was the achievement of subsequent caselaw itself, which interpreting the Constitutional gap on this issue, disposed of that English concept of Parliamentary sovereignty; thus the doctrine enunciated by Blackstone years back that the 'power of Parliament is absolute and without control' (cf. W. Blackstone, *Commentaries on the Laws of England*, London 1825, 6th ed., vol. I, p. 160). The earliest formulation of the doctrine of judicial review may be found in the oft-cited case of *Marbury v. Madison* 5 U.S. (1 Cranch), 137 (1803) delivered in 1803 under the direction of Chief Justice Marshall. A useful book for a correct understanding of the contribution of the Supreme Court in influencing the Anglo-American legal system is R. McCloskey, *The American Supreme Court*, Chicago 1960 (The University of Chicago Press), 260 pages, from which some ideas have been borrowed, which is preferable to the numerous reference works on Constitutional Law that the European scholars of Comparative Constitutional Law are so determined to cite.

[26] Cf. G. Dunne, *Justice Joseph Story and the Rise of the Supreme Court*, 1970; *also W.W. Story, Life and Letters of Joseph Story*, 1815, continue to be the chief sources of biographical information on this eminent republican who acceded to the Supreme Court in 1811, at the age of thirty-two. Recently, the American constitutional lawyer Bernard Schwartz has devoted a few pages of a distinguished article ('The Judicial Ten: America's Greatest Judges', *Southern Illinois University Law Journal*, 1979, no. 3), appearing as a book for the Spanish reader (*Los diez mejores jueces de la Historia norteamericana*, Madrid, Editorial Civitas, 1980, 37–45), highlighting some of his personality traits and classifying him as the author of the 'first Commercial and Maritime Law' found in his caselaw, delivered when he sat on the Supreme Court as when he was District Judge. But if Story's work in the judicial field was outstanding, his contribution to the didactic and doctrinal spheres were surely more prolific and important, until it could be said that 'if Story's figure as a judge was overshadowed by that of Marshall, he had no rival as a Law professor' (B. Schwartz, p. 43). Story's academic biography have been exaggerated to such an extent, however, that he has even been considered 'the first Law professor who occupied the deanship at Harvard' (p. 43). This is not the place to discuss Professor Joseph Story's links with the most ancient and what is traditionally considered to be among the most prestigious academic institutions in the United States, but it should be remembered that in 1853, twenty-four years after his appointment as

Story, then Federal judge of the District of Massachusetts, delivered judgment in 1815 in the case of José Manuel de Lovio, resident of Cuba, and apparently co-owner of the Spanish ship, *Esperanza*, given over to the slave trade; but what is significant is not the decision of the case – a contract of maritime insurance is subject to Admiralty jurisdiction, but the ratio decidendi in reaching that conclusion.[27] After rejecting various hypotheses in order to found jurisdiction in maritime affairs (the practice followed by the English Admiralty courts during the colonial era, or that established by the courts that succeeded them, the courts of Viceadmiralty, which considered all shipping cases independently from their place of origin), gave rise to a stylistic formula in the body of subsequent case law: maritime jurisdiction comprehends:

'all maritime contracts, torts and injuries. The latter branch is necessarily bounded by locality; the former extends over all contracts, (wheresoever they may be made or executed, or whatsoever may be the form of the stipulations,) which relate to the navigation, business or commerce of the sea.'[28]

professor, Harvard Law School did not deserve the title of Faculty, since it was not even called Harvard Law School but Dane Law School, and was experiencing some of the most precarious times of its history: exams did not exist, seminars were voluntary, there were no compulsory subjects, the requirement of academic residence was unknown and the course was limited to two years' duration, divided into three semesters, and depending on one's arrival on the commencement or end of the teaching term (J. Ph. Reid, *Chief Justice. The Judicial World of Charles Doe*, Cambridge, Mass., Harvard University Press, 1967, p. 47). However, specific studies on the history of Harvard Law School consider Christopher Columbus Langdell as the first Dean of the institution (1870–1895) whose name has also passed into the history of universal Law for having introduced the case method system as a mode of teaching. Langdell has been succeeded by eight deans: Ames, 1895–1910; Thayer, 1910–15; Roscoe Pound, 1916–36; Landis, 1937–46; Griswold, 1946–67; Bok, 1968–71; Sacks, 1972–80, and Vorenberg, 1981, whose biography may be found in succinct form in 32 *Harvard Law School Bulletin*, (1981), no. 2, pp. 16–24. For a detailed study on the history of the Harvard Faculty, *see Centennial History of the Harvard Law School 1817–1917,* and A.E. Sutherland, *The Law at Harvard*, Cambridge, Mass. (Harvard University Press), 1967.

[27] *De Lovio v. Boit*, United States Circuit Court for the District of Massachusetts, 1815, 7 Fed. Cas. 148 (No. 3776). The ship *Esperanza* was confiscated in a British vice-admiralty court in Africa for slaving, a loss that was transferred to the underwriters so that compensation could be collected. The underwriters refused to pay for a variety of reasons, namely, fraud, lack of agent's authority, and lack of insurable interest. De Lovio's agent commenced this action in admiralty in Boston, but the District Court dismissed for lack of admiralty jurisdiction, subsequently the judgment was overturned by the Federal Circuit Court for the District of Massachusetts, when Judge Story held that it did fall within maritime jurisdiction. Regrettably, no appeal was lodged with the Supreme Court, and the action was withdrawn during proceedings before the maritime division of the lower District Court to which it had been referred given the plantiff's, De Lovio, impossibility of submitting a written deposition from his residence in La Havana.

[28] The notion of locality has proven troublesome given that it is a controversial concept which has not followed a uniform jurisprudential pattern; in any case, it emphasizes the territorial or geographical links that must exist between the sea and the act. It is therefore a question of

As from that moment, the content of Admiralty Law would be feeding on the rich experience of the solution to the conflict of interests, the judge having to determine whether or not he had jurisdiction in order to subsume or not the assumed fact in the subject matter; which, on the other hand, is not surprising in a Common Law system, where legal technique is characterized by, as Pound has demonstrated, the manner in which experience is applied to new facts, or, as Holmes said, because the life of the law is in its experience.[29]

fact the assessment of which depends on judicial interpretation; thus some maritime contracts exist which inure or take place on land, in much the same way as some instances of extracontractual liability exist that occur on the sea but have no connection with maritime trade (for example, any damage to harbour installations, to ships in dry dock or in shipyards, etc., see *Chicago, Burlington and Quincy v. The W.C. Harms*, 134 F. Suppl. 636, AMC, 1955, p. 1423, S.D. Tex. 1954). On the jurisdictional clause in general, *see*: Black, 'Admiralty Jurisdiction: Critique and Suggestions' 50 *Columbia Law Review* (1950) p. 259; and the note 'From Judicial Grant to Legislative Power: The Admiralty Clause in the Nineteenth Century' 67 *Harvard Law Review* (1954) p. 1214.

[29] R. Pound, 'What is the Common Law?', in the volume *The Future of the Common Law*, Cambridge, Mass., 1937, p. 6; ibid. *Las grandes tendencias del pensamiento jurídico*, Barcelona (Spanish translation by Puig Brutau), Ariel, 1950, p. 70, centrepiece to his thesis which may be observed throughout his work; also in *The Development of Constitutional Guarantees of Liberty*, New Haven 1957; and in a more elaborate and detailed form in *The Spirit of the Common Law*, Boston 1954 (re-edition), Spanish translation by Puig Brutau (*El espíritu del 'Common Law'*), Barcelona (Bosch) (undated), pp. 173 et seq.

It is a well-known fact that Oliver Wendell Holmes, the 'great dissenter', distinguished himself, precisely outside his judicial work, as a profound scholar of the history of the Law, and from the perspective of historical analysis he published his work *The Common Law* in 1881. The citation from Holmes' text has been taken from the 1963 reprint (Harvard University Press), p. 5; cf. also, ibid. 'The Path of the Law' in *The Holmes Reader*, New York (Oceana Publications) 1955, p. 74; O.W. Holmes, 'Your Business as Thinkers', in *The Mind and Faith of Justice Holmes* (Ed. M. Lerner), 1943, p. 51.

Holmes and Pound are the leading representatives of the so-called 'American sociologial jurisprudence' who, influenced by the jurisprudence of interests of Philip Heck (*El problema de la creación del Derecho*, Spanish translation by Manuel Entenza, Barcelona, Ariel, 1961), offer more than just a method for the interpretation and application of the law. It is hardly surprising that in the cultural environment of America of the end of last century and the beginning of the present an accentuated pragmatism which held sway over the other philosophies then in vogue should also influence the Law. Thus, Holmes draws the jurists' attention to the need to abandon the traditional theoretical exercises in order to experience the needs and realities of life; but if Holmes' drive, initiative and energy stimulated legal knowledge, it was the systematic thoughts of Roscoe Pound which scientifically elaborated the current of sociological jurisprudence, thus developing a concept of law and not simply a modest technique of interpretation. It is a well known fact that the subsequent movement of 'American realists' are greatly indebted to these authors, since their theories on the suspicion of necessary change or their insistence on the uncertainty that is a feature of legal life, expressed in the fact that in a specific case that a judge must decide the jurist can only specify the possibilities open to the judge and of these merely predict which is the more notable, constitute an adaptation of Pound's moderate sociological jurisprudence in an era that gave them birth (the 1929 depression and the crisis of the system and style of American life). K. Llewellyn, 'Some Realism About Realism', in *Jurisprudence Realism in Theory and Practice* (The University of Chicago Press), 1962, p. 56; previously published in 34 *Harvard Law Review* (1931) pp. 1222 et seq.

If we now attempted to relive that experience we would find a list of cases subject to its jurisdiction, accompanied by any exceptions and doubtful assumptions. Applying the most persuasive authority to this question the following would need to be included in the definition of Maritime Law: (a) contracts for the carriage of goods and passengers, charters, repairs, ship chandling, towage, pilotage, moorage, the hiring of officers and crew members, compensation and premiums for marine insurance contracts, claims relating to collisions or other damage done to ship or cargo in navigable waters, actions arising from extracontractual liability and made subject to that jurisdiction by virtue of special law, and when damage is caused by the ship (such as accidents causing pollution); personal injuries to passengers, crew and probably any other person on board, at least while in navigable waters; claims for the death of seafaring men, either in territorial waters or on the high seas; premiums of salvage, contributions to the general average and care of the crew members; application of restrictive liability on behalf of the shipowner; proceedings regarding the mortgage and impounding of ships or repayment of loans in bulk; actions for the recovery of an impounded ship or a ship held illegally. (b) On the other hand, without the jurisdiction, although this has not always been the case, include: contracts of sale and construction of ships; the payment of premium on a charter agreement; services rendered to a dried up ship; repayment of a naval mortgage by special credit for which the law on ship mortgages makes no provision; actions for compensation and damages for the contractual failure to stipulate an insurance policy to cover the cargo; actions for damages caused by artificial islands or drilling platforms at sea. (c) Finally, grouped as doubtful cases may be included: claims arising out of quasi-contracts for maritime transactions (e.g., mistaken payment for excessive freight, or the recovery of money paid for a voyage which was never made; alternatively, the repayment of excess freight paid in advance has been held to be without the jurisdiction); agency contracts in general have also been excluded but, conversely, the management of the vessel has been included; extracontractual liability for damage caused in navigable waters, but without any maritime connection; mixed contracts: a typical example is multimodal carriage, when part of the voyage only is by sea, when the thesis of the division or autonomy of the maritime part has been maintained in order to submit the case before the special jurisdiction; extracontractual damages related indirectly with the shipping business, such as the liability incurred for inducing a third party to break a contract, and finally, in the category of doubtful assumptions is products liability.[30]

This lengthy list illustrates the need for reference to a technical dossier so lacking, from a continental perspective, in definitions or analytical accounts of which Anglosaxon jurists are so fond, and of which international conventions drafted under this influence constitute prime examples.

[30] Gilmore and Black, *The Law of Admiralty*, cit. 22 to 29, where each paragraph is supported by copious references and all the cases decided in favour of the proposition are cited.

Authoritative precedent, such as those cited in preceding paragraphs, allow certain general observations to be made. First, delimitation depends on a mixed criterion for included in the activities of seaborne trade may be found, on an equal basis, the labour relations of seafaring men, understood of course in its widest sense. Secondly, the jurisdiction of the Admiralty continues to have an expansionist tendency as is immediately recognized when, on the one hand, the doubtful categories are studied, and which are generally decided affirmatively, and on the other hand, the excluded categories which were not always treated as 'civil cases'; and such is the case, for example, with shipbuilding contracts.[31] But what is probably more interesting is that a common coincidence builds upon the foundations laid by these conclusions: the scarce usefulness of a general criterion. The identity of the assumed fact is a more significant factor than the integration of the general criterion in determining the applicabilty of Maritime Law. In questions of jurisdiction and applicable law, an adequate evaluation of the closeness or similarity of the assumed fact to precedent gives rise to a high degree of legal certainty. To the contrary, however, a pure doctrinal elaboration based on analogous assumptions provides no panacea in solving to any degree of certainty the question of the submission of a case to special jurisdiction. But we are certainly not referring to the problem of analogical interpretation in a system based on a link of legal precedent. Better still it is based on a technical-legal instrument used in order to make that application more effective. That brings us to the very issue that needs emphasizing.

Until now an attempt has been made to summarise, how successfully has yet to be determined, the significance of a constitutional principle that derogates the development and delimitation of Maritime Law to the law and the Federal courts. It may be observed throughout this evolution that the technique is genuinely procedural since the judge is called upon case after case to interpret what is meant by Admiralty jurisdiction, while at the same time he judges the problem at issue and thus the conflict of interest before him. But if seen from a different perspective it should be noted that the procedural value of this law is reinforced given the fact that the cases submitted to federal jurisdiction are considered according to a special maritime procedure. Or, in other words, when the Federal District Court pronounces that it has jurisdiction to entertain the case before it because it has a maritime aspect, the proceedings take place in a 'courtroom' or special division according to an again special procedure, adapted to the needs of maritime traffic. Finally, when the court pronounces sentence and decides the cases it is faced with a question of substantive law. The significance of this fact becomes immediately apparent when it is noted that the Constitu-

[31] Numerous judgments have upheld the requirement favourable to its inclusion while others have not, frequently depending on a terminological question which compares 'repair' to 'rebuilding'; cf. 'Admiralty Jurisdiction and Ship-Sale Contracts' 6 *Stanford Law Review* (1954), p. 540; and more recently, *Richard Bertraam Co. v. Yacht Wanda*, 447 F. 2d 966, AMC, 1971, p. 1841 (5th Cir. 1971).

tion not only legitimises a greater potential of federal jurisdiction, but provides a basis for the development of procedural Admiralty Law on the one hand, and substantive Maritime Law on the other.[32]

The third and final period into which the evolution of American Maritime Law has been divided has as its initial reference point the year 1966, a period which has not yet reached completion. The pinnacle of reform effected by the Federal Code of Civil Procedure affects the formal separation of Admiralty jurisdiction within the Federal District Courts.[33] Analyzed from an internal angle, the court structure appeared to be divided into a maritime chamber (separate side of district court), was endowed with an autonomous and independent system of distribution (docket), it enjoyed peculiar functioning norms, the oral judgment offered a singular feature (trial), all of which was manifested to the outside world through a terminology that was distinct, genuine and traditional.[34] Reform brought division to an end, cases with a maritime theme became ordinary civil actions and the provisions of the Federal Code of Civil Procedure became generally applicable, except for a few special sections for exceptional cases. Did this constitute a fundamental reform which affected the special procedural nature of American Maritime Law? According to authoritative sources, no. The unification of procedural norms has overcome, leaving aside the

[32] At this stage of the discussion some reference, however short, must be made to the federal jurisdiction shared by the States of the Union by virtue of the saving clause introduced by the Judiciary Act 1789 in the development of constitutional provision. The clause in question constitutes an exception to the general jurisdiction of the Law and of the federal courts in favour of the municipal legal system. In other words, this means that the exclusive jurisdiction of the District Courts to deliver judgment in maritime actions does not prejudice the right of a common law remedy where the common law is competent to give it (now incorporated in the United States Code Annotated, 28 U.S.C.A. §133). The clear and concise language used by the legislator raises some problems, however, for those who are not familiar with the Anglo-American system. Nevertheless, it is a question that is tangential to the subject that concerns us, which, however, does raise all the procedural complexities – once again the procedural slope of Admiralty Law – and that in a few words, has the following meaning: when the plaintiff exercises his right with an in personam claim he can file the suit in personam in admiralty or else in a Common Law court; in this case, the procedure is no longer maritime; it is a civil action, and therefore comes within the jurisdiction of the State Court or the Federal Court (but not in the Admiralty Division) if circumstances so require it; for example, diversity of citizenship, the amount of the claim, etc. This theme may be further elaborated in the textbooks – Healy and Sharpe, cit.; Gilmore and Black, cit., p. 37; Lucas, *Admiralty*, Mineola (Foundation Press) 1969, and 2nd ed., 1974; Baer, *Admiralty Law of the Supreme Court*, Charlottesville (The Michie Co.), 2nd ed., 1969, and O. Robinson, *Admiralty*, cit.

[33] Among the numerous publications stands out the chairman's Report of the Assessing Committee of the Supreme Court on the Rules of Admiralty, and the true architect of unification, Professor Currie (17 Maine Law Review (1965) pp. 1 et seq.); Powell, 'Admiralty Practice After Unification' 81 *Yale Law Journal* (1972) p. 1154.

[34] This happens, for example, with the words *libel* instead of *complaint*; *libellant* instead of *plantiff*; *respondent* instead of *defendant* and the term *lawyer* becomes *proctor* when he specializes in, works in and participates in maritime actions.

terminological question, the conduct and procedure of actions in rem which legally administered maritime liens. This requires some explanation. Briefly, the substantive law as created by case law and considered by the special proceedings remains in force in the sense that the procedural vehicle respected by reform is the procedure in actions in rem, that is to say, that used in the majority of cases because it is associated with the sale of a maritime lien. Or, in other words, unification has not affected maritime liens. Consequently, the nucleus of the nature of proceedings which necessitated a distinction between actio in personam which are brought against a responsible physical or legal person, and actio in rem which are brought against goods (the ship, cargo, a classic example, on the other hand, of the theory of the personalization of a ship) remains valid since the fulfilment of a lien must be through an actio in rem.[35]

3. THE CONCEPT OF INDIVIDUALISM IN FRENCH LAW

Individualism is to French legal theory what autonomy is to Italian legal theory. Whilst Maritime Law has distinguished itself in France by reference to individualism, in Italy autonomy has given rise to Shipping Law. But what do these phrases mean? Are they equivalent terms or do they denote different subject matters? In order to understand their scope and true significance it is necessary to explain, if only briefly, the state of the law in these settings.

Georges Ripert coined the phrase, but it had no scientific pretentions; it is a descriptive term, devoid of technical meaning: Maritime Law is not temporal Commercial Law applied to seafaring men and objects. Its contribution, therefore, has been a negative one, since it says more about what it is not rather than what it is; it gains strength by comparing itself with the terrestrial law, with which it resists identification. The father of individualism has brilliantly described the original and distinct history of the fundamentals of Maritime Law in order to reach a sensible conclusion. They originate from maritime usages and customs; their precepts are analyzed by experts; from the beginning they are written in the vernacular instead of Latin; the general custom is not invoked before the special jurisdiction of the Admiralty courts. But that originality or individualism is weakened by legal and economic factors. Included among the former are codification and commentators, who begin to apply the general principles of the Common Law until a large number of the fundamental provisions are changed or distorted. The basic and most important source, usage, is seriously affected by codification which consigns it as a secondary source. Included among the latter are the integration of seaborne trade into general commerce and the

[35] See generally, Gilmore and Black, cit., p. 35; Healy and Sharpe, op. cit., ch. II, pp. 28–196.

recognition of the merchant navy as the maritime branch of a national activity. All this leads to a conclusion favourable to a laudable originality.[36]

Authoritative sources have highlighted the fact that individualism is of little use for practical purposes, especially in addressing itself to the question of whether the rules of Common Law ought or ought not to apply.[37] However, what has not been sufficiently emphasized is the fact that its value resides in its historic view of the concept, which has acted as a curb on future speculation regarding the relationship between individualism and the special law. On the other hand, it is submitted that it would have been preferable if the definition of Maritime Law as 'that Law governing all legal relationships whose theatre is the sea and its object seaborne trade' had been carried to its logical conclusion, thus regulating issues of Private Maritime Law only as opposed to those of Public Maritime Law. That notion based on the object or the delimitation of the subject matter, and not on the special nature of the norms, foresaw that that must be urgently addressed today.

It is interesting to note that the scientific exposition of individualism is due to Bonnecasse, a staunch opponent of specialization and advocate therefore, of Maritime Law as a branch of Private Law, specifically Commercial Law. The fundamental question is this: does Maritime Law really exist as a distinct area of law? If the answer is in the affirmative, what then is its relationship with other branches of the law? The present writer distinguishes between two types of individualism: an external individualism and an internal individualism, according to whether one refers to the real and formal sources or to the physiognomy of the fundamental norms. The nonexistence of the former is beyond doubt: the sources of Maritime Law are the same as those of Commercial Law and consequently of Private Law; and that does not contradict the incidence of the different sources through-

[36] George Ripert, *Droit maritime*, Paris, I, 4th ed., 1950, nos, 52 et seq.

[37] R. Rodiere, 'Le particularisme du Droit maritime', *Le Droit Maritime Français*, 1974, no. 26, pp. 195–206. I shall not enter into the controversy regarding the validity of the thesis in the autonomous sphere, but it appears evident to me that Ripert, after emphasizing the weakening of individualism, strongly defends it in its future on two grounds. First, the general tendency of contemporary law to avoid general laws in favour of laws adapted to the various types of exploitation. Seaborne trade 'requires special legislation', given the importance of this means of transport, the living standards of seamen, the accidents and risks connected with shipping, security, the variety and distance of certain undertakings; secondly, because maritime transport is usually an international transport, which suggests that the system of conflict of laws should be substituted by uniform rules. Consequently, the terms autonomy and Speial Law feature in Ripert's work, although the specific question of the scope of this autonomy beyond the didactive and explanatory spheres is not addressed nor does he question the consequences that derive from the application of sources that are regulated by special laws (cf. Ripert, Précis de Droit maritime, Paris, Dalloz, 6th ed., 1952, no. 5, pp. 13 and 14). One must place oneself in that context, and particularly in those times – the first editions appeared in the twenties – , in order to understand that the question of special law as an autonomous branch of the legal order and as an independent subject in legal science had not been properly addressed.

out history, an otherwise contingent phenomenon. Internal individualism may be absolute or relative. In order to speak of an absolute internal individualism it would seem necessary that it consist of a web of particularly special fundamental norms; this may have occurred at some moment in history but appears to be no longer the case; the reasons for this being, on the one hand, that there are many examples of fundamental norms that have been completely transformed, or have disappeared or are in the course of disappearing (orders in bulk); and on the other hand, because of the twin movement of the extension of specifically maritime norms to the common law and fundamental norms of general law to Maritime Law (ship mortgage). Only one relative internal individualism exists, and this amounts to the adaptation of the rules of Commercial and Civil Law to the necessities of seaborne trade. This individualism does not, however, weaken the writer's thesis but strengthens it: Maritime Law is no more than a branch of Private Commercial Law which, in turn, is only a branch of general Private Law.[38]

Recently, an authoritative element of French academy has revived the old controversy, among whom is included Dean Rodière.[39] In his view, the question of individualism must be approached from an exclusively technical-legal angle, which amounts to answering two basic questions: first, whether a proper and exclusive body of rules, fundamental norms and concepts of Maritime Law exists; and secondly, the relationship between the rules enunciated by this branch of the law vis-à-vis the Common Law must be properly determined. It is submitted that the answers to both questions cannot be found in legal texts. It is necessary to analyze critically case law in order to find them. The decision of the *Cour de Cassation* in 1870, in the case of the ship *Colorado*, illustrates the inapplicability of the precepts of general Private Law since they proved incompatible with the ship's statute and consequently the application of the general principle to the effect that the guardian of an inanimate object is liable for any damage that it may cause is excluded. This and other judgments in the field of commission agencies for transport, prescription and social security allow the following conclusions to be drawn: (a) Absolute individualism does not exist; Maritime Law is not a self-contained world of rules, fundamental norms and concepts. It is based on the basic precepts of civil law (contract, liability, damages). (b) Relative individualism has no meaning in legal terms since

[38] J. Bonecasse, *Le Droit commercial maritime, son particularisme. Son domaine d'application et sa méthode d'interpretation*, Paris (Sirey) 1921, 2nd ed., 1931; *Précis de Droit maritime*, cit., no. 121; ibid., *Traité de Droit commercial maritime*, Paris (Sirey) 1923, nos. 185 et seq.

[39] Cf. essentially *Le particularisme du Droit maritime*, cit., and in his Traité, cit., Introduction, no. 29, pp. 52–53. Other authors include: E. du Pontavice, 'L'évolution récente des ventes à l'embarquement, l'affaiblissement de leur particularisme', *DMF*, 1966, p. 387; M. de Juglart, 'Le particularisme du transport de marchandises par mer en Droit interne', *DMF*, 1956, p. 1995; ibid., 'Le particularisme de Droit maritime, réformes opérés depuis 1961 en Droit français', *JCP(C.I.)*, 1970, 88540.

ultimately it is dependent on a question of originality that nobody denies because it has no meaning. In relation to the second question, it should be noted that the maritime norm takes precedence over that of the general law by virtue of the maxim *speciala generalibus derogant*. Finally, a provision of temporal law may or may not function in an area governed by maritime norms at a given time that is not provided for expressly. It cannot be a composite answer in this particular case; it will depend in each hypothetical situation on whether or not the application of the general norm contradicts the body of principles and instructions in which the lacuna has been individualized. This conclusion may be explained without recourse to a proper theoretical construction.

The serious doubts on a general theory of Maritime Law, the intelligible historical review of the reasons for individualism, the more or less terminological scope, the need to delimit the subject matter, the obsession in solving concrete issues of applicable law and the reasonable expectation of finding an adequate legislative technique to reform positive law are but some of the factors which suggest to the author the limited scope of individualism in our neighbouring country.

It is thus not surprising that France, the cradle of codified law, has proved the model for those systems that, when updating or reforming Maritime Law, have followed the trend in uncodified law. The legislator opts for special laws rather than a general code. Whether it be a rational act or whether it be imposed by the facts, it is true that reform in France commenced towards the end of the forties (1947), ambitiously at first, subsequently enshrined in a simple ossified reform of the Commercial Code, which gave rise to a change in direction ending, finally, in the enactment of a series of significant legislation, by virtue of its content, as from 1966. Volume II of the Code de Commerce, given over to seaborne trade, is composed of the following: the Act of 18 June 1966 and the enabling decree of 31 December of the same year on charterparties and carriage; the Act of 3 January 1967 and the Decree of 27 October, also of the same year on the legal status of ships; the Act of 7 July 1967 and the Decree of 19 January 1968 which redefines the regime of accidents at sea (collisions, assistance, salvage and general average); the Act of 3 July 1967 and the Decree of 19 January 1968 on the fitting out of ships, along with the Decree of 19 June 1969 on maritime sales. General provisions with legal force which complement those referred to relating to the Law of the Sea properly so-called, included that of 30 December 1968 on the continental shelf, as amended by the Act of 11 May 1977; the Act of 16 July 1976 and the Decree of 11 February 1977 creating and regulating an exclusive economic zone stretching along the territorial waters of the French Republic; the Act of 30 December 1968, as amended by that of 11 May 1977, on the exploitation of the seabed and subsoil thereof. And in the area of pollution, along with the general Act of 10 July 1976 on the protection of the environment, there have been numerous provisions of lesser authority; and the Acts which have incorporated international conventions, such as that of 27 December 1977 on the Barcelona Convention and the Act relating to incineration at sea of 7 July 1976 should also be noted.[40]

4. SHIPPING LAW IN ITALIAN DOCTRINE; THE SCOPE OF OPPORTUNITY AND VALIDITY

The merit of the Italian doctrine is to be found in its scrupolous exposition of the conceptual problem and its application to its logical conclusion, with the exception of special jurisdiction. First, there is no reference to individualism, which is an ambiguous expression of extrajuridical origin, but to autonomy which initially denotes a greater desire for precision and technical exactitude. Secondly, it does not limit its scope to the problem of the hierarchy of applicable sources, but it builds a system. Finally, the doctrinal effort is not submerged by legislative techniques, but is consummated by the enactment of a code, the 1942 Shipping Code.

A detailed exposition of the different theories prevalent in Italian doctrine lies beyond the ambit of this work, and which is strictly unnecessary as they are well-known. It seems necessary merely to note briefly the views that have attained greater consensus amongst jurists. It has already been seen how Shipping Law has been characterized as special law since it is composed of an orderly group of special norms. The legislator reaches that conclusion, evaluating at various stages a sector of reality, because existing needs require treatment different from the general norm. Thus, distinct norms and diverse principles exist from those which are professed by the common law.[41]

[40] It is not mere coincidence that the *autor intellectualis* of the five acts and five decrees of the French réform 1966–1969 has been the self-same Professor Rodière. Cf. on the numerous bibliographical references, 'Le réforme des lois maritimes: un second train de réformes concerne le statut des navires', *Bull. Transports*, 1966, no. 1, 267, p. 90; P. Chauveau, 'Rétrospective d'actualités, *DMF*, 1968, p. 4.

[41] F. Dominedò, *Introduzione al Diritto della navigazione*, Rome, 1951, p. 94. An excessive wealth of bibliographical references has recently appeared which seems to be more of a bibliographical and cultural list and selective citations, in M. Grigoli, *Sistema di Diritto della navigazione*, Bari (Cacucci Editore), 1979. In future I shall limit myself to citing only those references that are necessary for supporting the assertions made in the main text, since the general and specialist works on the subject are innumerable, so that it can be affirmed without exaggeration that in the *Rivista di Diritto della navigazione*, founded in 1935 by Scialoja himself until its recent demise in 1978, rarely did an issue not include some reference to the conceptual problem. In the other specialist journal, *Il Diritto Marittimo*, founded by Francisco Berlintrinal, the articles that govern the same topic are similarly numerous, despite its more practical and less academic inclinations. Besides the general works, treatises, textbooks, courses, lectures and notes one may also find the respective contributions of legal encyclopaedias: *Enciclopedia del Diritto*, Milan (Guiffrè), as from 1958; *Enciclopedia forense*, Milan (Vallardi), as from 1954, and the more recent *Novissimo Digesto Italiano*, Turin (Utet) as from 1957.

The specialist nature, however, is not a unique fact; autonomy completes it. Shipping Law is thus both a special law and an autonomous law; an autonomous law because it is composed of an autonomous body of rules, and not a body of autonomous rules. In this sense, and contrary to specialization, autonomy refers to a body of norms evaluated as a group and not to rules considered on an individual basis. Hence special law may or may not be autonomous. On the other hand, autonomy does not denote a system independent from the legal order. Autonomy is a historical concept derived from positive law, its existence revealing its proper position and thus establishing a fundamental discipline for a particular category of relations. However, the autonomy of Shipping Law may be analyzed from various angles: scientific, legislative and didactic. That which is evident in the Italian example is legislative autonomy, since its fundamental classification in a code, in 1942, was its greatest moment, a time which, on the other hand, coincided with the merger of Commercial Law into a single Civil Code.[42]

An important consequence emerges from this exposition: Maritime Law is defined by its goal, by the technological fact of self-sufficient transport. Shipping Law therefore governs, with its own norms, the technical facts of carriage by sea and air. The existence of an independent medium of carriage operating in a free environment defines the special nature of the legal regime; the single code, the scientific grouping of investigation and classification constitutes logical requirements of its definition by the object and technical and economic facts which it regulates. Shipping law is thus broadly defined as a body of norms which govern the subject of maritime, land and aerial transport. Strictly speaking, Shipping Law properly consists of norms that directly and particularly regulate the subject of shipping.[43]

Maritime Law is therefore indebted to Italian doctrine which managed to overcome the burden of codification by limiting its scope solely to seaborne trade. It has already been noted that the incorporation of private maritime commercial law to the Commercial Law system was as a result of the split with the old sources which the French code of 1807 represented, and specifically with the Naval Ordinance of 1681. The European codifying movement, which extended to Latin America under French and Spanish influence, experienced the same phenomenon; they limited themselves to compiling a book on the private rules of seaborne trade, excluding those of a public-administrative nature. Thus, while distinguishing the old unitary legal source, they incorporated part of that law as a branch of Commercial

[42] See generally Lefebvre–Pescatore, *Manuale di Diritto della navigazione*, Milano (Guiffrè), 1969, p. 6.

[43] Gaeta, *Le fonti del Diritto della navigazione*, Milan (Guiffrè) 1965, Ch. I, 1–33; Lefebvre–Pescatore, op. cit., pp. 4–5. A current review of the theory in Spasiano, 'Oggetto e autonomia del Diritto della navigazione: progresso della dottrina od involuzione?' in *Rivista Diritto commerciale*, 1978, I, pp. 1 et seq.; S. Carbone, 'La c.d. autonomia del Diritto della navigazione', *Riv. Dir. nav.*, 1975, p. 24.

Law. In accordance with the new principle, commerce initially gave way to the sea, so providing a vent for the controversy regarding speculation, the finality of lucrative mediation, and including peripheral activities. Specialization is not justified by commerce but by shipping. No valid reason exists for refusing to extend this principle to all forms of carriage by sea, whether those with commercial ends or those non-profitable activities (scientific, leisure, sport, fishing, etc.).[44] The crux of the matter arises when the maritime aspect (a spatial criterion) cedes to shipping, indifferent to the ends as well as to the medium in which it transpires.

However, experience suggests that the brilliant thesis formulated by Antonio Sciajola in 1933 in his work Sistema del Diritto della navigazione, has not had the effect that had been originally anticipated. If the example of Italy is excluded, where the development of the thesis has borne the expected fruit, the thesis, leaving aside doctrinal arguments, has not germinated in the legislative sphere in the rest of Europe. The European legislator has certainly not given due consideration to the notion of drafting a single code regulating the technical data of shipping, with the independence of the environment in which it develops. Without doubt, the Codice de la Navigazione is the legislative result of a doctrinal movement based on that unitary concept of the shipping phenomenon, and in which shipping and flight respond to the same principles. It is also true that certain Latin American countries, such as Brazil and Argentina, are great admirers of the Shipping Law. And it is also true that this expression, besides the problems of compatibility between shipping and flight, has given rise to a general theory of Shipping Law, as special law, which may be questioned at present for reasons of opportunity and for reasons of validity.[45]

[44] The repercussions of this theory have affected us; overcoming the letter and the spirit of the Code an important sector wants to see Maritime Law not as the law of maritime commerce, but as Shipping Law. With his usual perspicacity, Girón has explained this phenomenon demonstrating an error in outlook, since commerce is the cause but not the basis of the legal-maritime specializations; J. Girón, *La evolución de la estructura y significado económico jurídico de la empresa en el Derecho marítimo*, Valladolid 1958; V. Santos has worked with the same information, 'En torno a la delimitación del Derecho marítimo', *Estudios ofrecidos a Ignacio Serrano*, Valladolid 1965, vol. II, 437–472. This trend appears to entrench itself at least as a criterion of didactic and explanatory arrangements. Openly in favour of the maritime element, without distinction between public and private norms, are Aurelio Menéndez and Juan Luis Iglesias, 'Prólogo', in *Codigo de las Leyes Marítimas*, Madrid (BOE) 1980, p. 11.

[45] I do not intend here to embark upon a general theory of Shipping Law, although this would be the proper place to do so, as I have discussed this issue elsewhere: cf. I. Arroyo, 'Oportunidad y vigencia de la teoría general Derecho de la navigación' in *Revista de Estudios Marítimos* (Instituto de Estudios Marítimos, Buenos Aires), Vol. IX, May–September 1980, nos. 26–27, pp. 9–25. Nevertheless, my submissions have been challenged by the Argentine Professor Jorge Bengolea Zapata, 'Solre la teoría general del Derecho de la navegación (Acotaciones a un estudio crítico)', *ibidem*, nos. 28–29 (January–May 1981) pp. 43–53, who I believe will find new ideas to ruminate on throughout this work.

III. The new facts

5. A REVIEW OF INTERNATIONAL UNIFORMITY

One of the issues that is meekly accepted is the international character of Maritime Law. This international aspect has fortunately not been settled by reference to the principles of Conflicts of Law which sows a certain legal uncertainty, but by the more sophisticated process of uniform rules. In our case, as distinct from other branches of the law, the results that have been achieved in the elaboration of a uniform system of law applicable to legal relations which originate or take place upon the sea cannot be described as modest.

The historical evolution of Maritime Law is dominated by the continuity of uniformity. Its origin is customary; in modern times, as a result of international conventions. Naturally, the degree of international uniformity varies from norm to norm, and hence it appears sufficient to note as extreme examples the imperative nature of carriage as an area of study vis-à-vis contractual freedom in charterparties. However, we are witnessing a radical change in the norm generating process which is affecting traditional private Maritime Law as much as the nascent Law of the Sea. Both tread parallel courses covering the same ground: the search for a more just and economic distribution of risk, while at the same time a new economic order in the exploitation of marine resources is being established. Both have the sea in common, but view it from different perspectives; the former as space, the latter as expanse. The sea as space has served as a channel for communication and the exchange of ideas, which is tantamount to the expansion of trade. Activities that have occurred on the sea have affected commercial business, always in a linear dimension, though doctrinal rules have eventually been drafted resulting, in their most form, in the shape of Shipping Law. In this context, uniformity has been advocated by the International Maritime Organization. Alternatively, the view of the sea as expanse is a more recent phenomenon, almost yesterday's and includes the question of the codification of the Law of the Sea by United Nations' conferences, commencing in the latter half of this century. In this case, it is not the sea surface as a means of transport or as the scene of lucrative commercial activities that is of concern, but rather the exploration and exploitation of a body brimming with vast reserves of natural resoruces. In this instance unification is intertwined with the codification process taking place at the III United Nations Conference on the Law of the Sea (UNCLOS III). Unification appears to be more effective where the process of elaboration has been slow and expensive.

As regards Maritime Law, as has been shown elsewhere, uniformity in itself may not suffice when just and economic criteria are being established in the distribution of risk among the parties.[46] In other words, traditional

[46] *See* I. Arroyo, *La distribución del riesgo en el Derecho marítimo*, Madrid 1977, pp. 44–50.

Maritime Law, based on specialization, has been offering a regime that, based on the interesting notion of international uniformity, only provides, in the majority of cases, criteria for the needs of the most organized sector: that of the shipping firms. Essentially, to seek final justification of a special or privileged norm in the needs of shipping, in the peculiar circumstances in which it evolves, or in the technical details of carriage, is a suggestion that has been the subject of detailed review by the least economic part of the equation: the developing world. The crux of the new approach consists in keeping alive the vested interests which sustain the present norms. The point being made is punctuated when it is noted that the privileged situation casts a shadow over the special regime, a fact hastened by international uniformity.

The voice of the developing world has in the last decade joined in the political debate, an initiative that has become the monopoly of the International Maritime Organization. It has waged an efficient campaign in the proper forum for the elaboration and adoption of uniform rules: the United Nations Conference for Trade and Development (UNCTAD) and the United Nations Conference for International Trade Law (UNCITRAL). It is curious to note the reversal that the new policy on risk distribution has operated has coincided with developments in unification. It need only be recalled that under the recent convention on carriage of goods by sea adopted by the Hamburg Conference in March 1978, the benefits conceded to the stevedores far exceeded those of the shipowners.[47]

Until relatively recently, that is towards the end of the sixties (1968), the traditional method of elaborating the norms of private Maritime Law has been, in practice, the preserve of the International Maritime Organization. Owing to its efficient organization and the influence of its members, this private international organization, composed of a varied group of shipowners, insurers, bankers, and lawyers, had been preparing the draft texts of treaties which, once approved sought the cooperation of the Belgian Ministry of Foreign Affairs in order to convene a diplomatic conference which adopted the treaty.[48] Thus, the IMO is reponsible for virtually all international maritime conventions, international conventions which were subsequently incorporated into domestic law in accordance with their particular procedures. However, without scorning the important contribution that this

[47] Despite the short time that has elapsed since its adoption and although it has not yet entered into force, jurists have given it considerable attention, notable among the bibliography being the collective or co-written books; thus, S. Mankabady (ed.), *The Hamburg Rules on the Carriage of Goods by Sea*, Leyden-Boston (Sijthoff) 1978; *CMI Colloquium on the Hamburg Rules*, Vienna 1979; in Spain, J.A. Gómez Segade, 'El transporte marítimo de mercancías: de las Reglas de La Haya a las Reglas de Hamburgo', *R.D.M.*, 1980, no. 156, pp. 221–245; F. Sánchez Calero, *Las Reglas de Hamburgo solve el contrato de transporte marítimo de mercancias* (*Una valoración crítica*) (offprint), Barcelona (Comíté de Derecho marítimo de Barcelona) 1981, 51 pages.

[48] In its infancy, 1897, stevedores were not included in the CMI; cf. S. Dor, *Bill of Lading Clauses and the International Conventions of Brussels 1924* (*The Hague Rules*), London (Witherby) 1960, 2nd ed., p. 19.

body has made in the area of unification, it can easily be understood that a normative development to compensate for the weak position of Third World States cannot flourish in the atmosphere of a club composed of developed States, and of a tendency towards shipowners, considering in particular that these developing nations were not long ago colonial possessions and only recently achieved independence.[49]

The well known fact that the responsibilities of the maritime carrier, e.g., have been unburdening throughout history thanks to the principle of freedom of contract shall not be dwelt upon. The validity of exclusion clauses reached the extremity of contending that the carrier was safe with the legal regime of carriage of goods. This situation has been made possible by the autonomy of will, which efficiently used means that the economically stronger party will impose the most favourable terms, disregarding the law. However, the difference between Maritime Law and the other contractual subjects has not been emphasized enough: the unilateral use of the autonomy of will has not only influenced the elaboration of contracts and general clauses, but also the drafting of international conventions. Hence, it is not simply an issue of questioning the valid uniformity of this living branch of the law, an autonomous creation, which tends to distance itself from the domestic system, thus assuming a uniform character, but of those same sources of the elaboration of traditional *lex maritima*. In other words, a review affects the law in its technical sense as it does that customary *ius mercatorium* and which is in force in the shape of principles, contracts, forms, and general clauses which govern commercial relationships, and whose security and application is guaranteed by arbitral institutions. In our case, the juxtaposition of the laws of every State with self-normative law has not given rise to problems of accommodation since they share analogous foundations. Thus a greater participation of interested groups and more substantial State and supranational control over the process of elaboration appears necessary in order to secure, vis-à-vis the inequality in strength, the primacy of equity in uniform regulation. On the one hand, the progressive incursion of the necessary law has responded to these suggestions, while on the other hand, the principles of majority voting and consensus in the adoption of norms drafted by international organizations has been consolidated. It should be noted further at the same time that these goals are but complementary pieces of this new approach which, it is submitted, imposes itself by virtue of the facts as much as by logic.

[49] Note the list of conventions sponsored by the CMI, in A. Lilar et Van Den Bosch, *Le Comité Maritime International 1897–1972*, Antwerp 1972–1973. It it not surprising that given its work in favour of unification it should adjust itself as an assessor organization rather than an initiator, while it has also widened the scope of its concurrent interests; see F. Berlingieri, '*Il Comité Maritime International. Le sue origini, la sua storia, il suo futuro*', Il Diritto Marittimo, 1979, 148–156.

The growing role of the specialized agencies of the UN in the development of Maritime Law is inextricably linked to the increased participation of a growing number of States, thus reflecting a wider scope of opposing interests. This fact, and given the principle of majority vote in the adoption of resolutions which seems to lead irreversibly towards consensus, denotes a radical departure in the formation of normative will, the most plausible effect of which is compromise solutions that breathe life into the new precepts.[50] However, it does not seem worthwhile creating a new source of production if the subject is diverted either in national parliaments, through the technique of reservations or amendments in the domestic law incorporating the convention; or in the policies or documents adopted by the traffic. In order to avoid this fraudulent effect towards uniformity, treaty practice and an analysis of contemporary positive law prove that its scope is not limited to a dispositive or supplementary regime, as has happened throughout codification, but that an imperative regime is ensured, thus falling beyond the autonomy of will.[51]

6. A CRITIQUE OF THE FUNDAMENTAL NORMS

Renewal is not, however, exhausted by the new criteria of norm generation, but it lays foundations, in the same basics that justify the peculiar nature of the most representative features of Maritime Law. One is referring here to the attempts made by an influential sect of the discipline who, with the aid of the method of comparative history, have proved how the greater part of the fundamental norms responds to the desire of protecting and maintaining the privileged position of carriers or shipowners. Thus: the revision of the theory of general average (Selmer 1958, and Sánchez Andrés, 1978); the analytical study on the benefits of shipowners's liability (Girón Tena, 1959); the desuetude of the criteria which gave rise to the regime of carriage of goods enshrined in the Hague Rules (Yiannopoulos, 1962, and Arroyo, 1977); the criticism of the rhetorical principle of freedom

[50] For a concise assessment of voting patterns and procedures in international organizations *see*, Vicente Blanco Gaspar, *El voto ponderado*, Madrid (Instituto Hispano-Suso-Americano de Derecho International) 1981, p. 32; the Council of the International Seabed Authority, which adopts its decisions on non-procedural questions by simple majority vote, by a two-thirds maajority vote on substantive issues, by a three-quarters majority vote on important questions, and by consensus on extremely important issues, which in my view constitutes consideration by means other than voting.

[51] This phenomenon, far from being exclusive to Maritime Law, is part of a trend in private law in general, specifically Commercial Law, and extends not only to the Civil Law systems but also to those of the Common Law. See the interesting work on this question from a comparative angle by R. Newman (ed.), *The Unity of Strict Law. A comparative study*, vol. II: 'The Unity of Law', Brussels (Bruylant) 1978; and specifically the writings of Clive M. Schmitthoff on *ius cogens* (*strict law*) in reservation of title (pp. 18–33), of Detlev Vagts on companies (pp. 35–55) and of Minocher Sethra on contracts (pp. 57–67).

of contract which exists in charterparties (Romberg, 1970); and the crisis of the maritime conferences system (Du Pontavice, 1976) constitute good examples of this assertion.

Amongst all the principles cited, perhaps that of particular or general average has been the most criticized, as much by the right as by the left. It would not be fair to suggest that any of the criticisms have attracted a response and despite the fact that it is now more than a century since the first criticism was made, it is at its most persistent today. At the heart of the controversy lies a confrontation between, on the one hand, the principle of solidarity, which seeks a distribution of voluntary sacrifices between ships and cargo for all those involved in a maritime venture, and on the other hand, the system of risk cover added to the factor of security, which make shipping less fortuitous and liquidation speedier and more economic. But in analyzing the question from a practical angle it can be seen that the solidarity has tended to favour the shipowner rather than the stevedore, since the list of damages and costs to the ship outweighs that that benefits the cargo. That same tendency in favour of shipowners is more forcefully revealed in the constant expansion of its field of application; other jurists have already discussed ably the controversy between the doctrines of common safety and common benefit, since it seems apparent that the predominance of the latter over the former runs alongside the recognition of new costs whose distribution through general average exonerates the ship-owner from his responsibilities regarding the voyage, in distributing costs which should be taken into account in the bill of operating costs of the shipping firm. Finally, in a similar vein, the question of insurance should not be forgotten since in areas of cover and distribution it can offer the same service at a much reduced cost and time.[52]

The doctrine has not allowed the justification of the gain in limiting the liability of a shipowner to escape scrutiny. Reference is not being made to observations derivative of a technical character: a) the defects of the liability regime (the system of default, the system of real liability); b) an improvement in actuarial methods which permit liability to be insured, and c) the difficulties born of the assumptions of liability and loss of profits (personal fault, act of the shipowner, distinction between nautical and commercial faults). Neither does it concern different, and certainly secondary, issues in the consideration of the fundamental question, as questions of procedural organization are (absence of adequate procedure). The crux of the matter is tied up with those reasons that have sought to justify once again the special

[52] The central theses have been adopted from Selmer's work, *The Survival of General Average a Necessity or an Anachronism?*, Oslo (Oslo University Press) 1958, and particularly pp. 288–296; and the learned article by A. Sánchez Andrés, "Reflexiones críticas sobre la avería común', *Estudios de Derecho mercantil en homenaje a Rodrigo Uría*, Madrid (Civitas) 1978, p. 727–760. This topic has also been covered in my previously cited book *La distribución del riesgo en el Derecho marítimo*, cit., pp. 105–109.

character of Maritime Law. The concepts of remoteness and gravity of risk decrease as communications and technical progress improve. On the other hand, the image of the voyage-enterprise, inextricably linked to the fortunes of the sea, crumbles when confronted by social niceties, born precisely under the protection of limitation of liability. The shipowner does not limit his liability qua owner, but because of his status as social entrepreneur.[53]

When the question is nowadays examined from the angle of the general development of private law, it becomes apparent, and not without cause, that the trend militates in favour of the mitigating expedients of liability: the limitation of indemnity and compulsory insurance.[54] However, it appears to be overlooked that traditional Maritime Law does not acknowledge the concept of objective liability, a real budget of the limit on repairs. On the other hand, the benefit of limitation operates in the fields of contractual liability, a system of limitation by bulk or unit of the acknowledged means of transport, and of extracontractual liability, a system of global limitation under the shipowner's Convention of 1957.[55]

For those who have kept pace with the *travaux préparatoires* of the Hamburg Conference there is little to add regarding the privileged character of the regime of carriage of goods enshrined in the Hague Rules, which has brought the list of exceptions to an end, except for fire; places the onus of proof upon the carrier and raises the ceiling on limitations while at the same time the causes of loss of profit are reinforced. However, the final stage of development has not yet been reached, marked by a return to the common regime of liability *ex recepto*, the complete suppression of a catalogue of exceptions or the consolidation of a regime of liability by cause. In any case, the critical review of the Brussels Convention of 1924 has been another blow to the movement to substitute the IMO by other organizations more sensitive towards the needs of developing States.[56]

Analogous considerations to those already discussed may be applied to the question of charterparties. However, some peculiarities do exist that cannot be set aside: absolute freedom of contract vis-à-vis a certain imperative conceptual regime; the absence of uniform regulation, in contrast to the international convention on carriage of goods, and in each case economic

[53] Cf. Girón Tena, *El naviero*: *directrices actuales de su régimen jurídico*, (Bilbao) Universidad de Deusto 1959, pp. 90–132, and its bibliography, ibi cit.

[54] On this question, on which so much has been written, volume XXII of the *Archives de Philosophie du Droit*, a monograph dealing with 'La responsabilité', Paris (Sirey) 1977, and particularly the 'Introduction' by Battifol, has been a constant source of reference.

[55] I have omitted from this discussion the exception to the traditional theory of fault, that is, objective liability enshrined in the conventions on oil pollution of 1969 and operators of nuclear ships of 1962.

[56] For a detailed analysis of this question, cf. A.N. Yiannopoulus, *Negligence Clauses in Ocean Bills of Lading*, Louisiana University Press, 1962; the report of UNCTAD's Secretariat, *Secretarial Report on Bills of Lading*, 14 December 1970, Doc. No. TD/B/C.4/ISL/6; and in Spain, I. Arroyo, op. cit., pp. 44–52.

conditions leading to various forms of exploitation, are some of the issues that distinguished charters from carriage of goods. That autonomy, added to the dispositive character of the subject, has been explained by reference to the equal position occupied by the demise charter party and charterer at the time of chartering the ship. Consequently, while under most legal systems the charterer is not protected by a special norm, as opposed to the shipper, part carrier and holder of the bill of lading, to whom the law offers a series of protective guarantees to his defaulting contractual situation. Therefore, these provisions do not contain imperative norms relating to charterparties, but the rules are enforced with the issue of the bill of lading with the aim of favouring the sender and addressee of the goods. The policies make frequent use of this facility, through the inclusion of clauses and conditions into the charterparties, thus reducing legislation to a mere supplementary or interpretative role.

Recently, however, faced with this system of private regulation, typical of the law of forms, a new trend is becoming discernible which, after the principle of the equality of the parties had been put in jeopardy, calls for a compulsory discipline. This is what was previously formulated as a denunciation of the rhetorical principle of freedom of contract that flourishes in charterparties.[57]

Added to the crisis of the principle of equality arises the question of the similarity between the method of creating uniform norms for carriage with uniform clauses and standard contracts elaborated for charterparties by private organizations. Alternatively, the opportunistic and vagrant character of the owners of tramp steamers has been emphasized which, as is well known, in contrast to regular shipping lines, contract with whom they wish under their conditions, the so called roving opportunism of tramp owners, circumstances which in practice have given rise to problems regarding the identity of the shipowner, with consequent fears about economic solvency. It is therefore not surprising that the constant search for charters wherever they are to be found prevents, in the majority of cases, the maintenance of properly accredited permanent representatives or branches who guarantee the seaworthiness and other conditions of the ship which, according to the policy, it is supposed to possess. Hence, it does not appear imprudent to reach a conclusion advocating an imperative regime, prepared by an independent and representative international organization from an interna-

[57] Not only have the theoreticians jumped to the defence of this assertion: Ramberg, *Cancellation of Contracts of Affreightment on Account of War and Similar Circumstances*, Handelshögskolan i Göteborg, Gothenburg 1970, p. 416; Cufley, *Ocean Freights and Chartering*, London (Crosby Lockwood Staples) 1976, pp. 85 and 153; but also UNCTAD's Secretariat in its report on charter parties: UNCTAD, *Charter Parties*, Geneva-New York, United Nations, 1974, Doc. TD/B/C.4/ISL/13, no. 533, p. 81. Against, F. Berlingieri, 'Need for Uniformity in Contracts for Carriage by Sea', in *Congress on Contracts of Affreightment*, Lloyd's of London Press and European Transport Law, Antwerp (November 27–29, 1975), published in *Il Diritto Marittimo*, 1976, p. 5, who would be satisfied with the creation of a system for liability for damages in order to remedy the abuses of agency.

tional perspective, since practical abuses are not easily corrected by freedom of contract.

Finally, in this section some of the typical institutions of Maritime Law have been reviewed and reference has been made to the existing crisis in the system of maritime conferences. This subject is certainly much more complicated since various questions of varying degree arise which justify for the time being a different legal consideration. On the other hand, economic and political aspects, in unison with jurisdictional law, play a decisive role in the approval of or rejection of that peculiar system of cargo sharing or reservation of the flag. What is true is that the fixing of charters and the monopoly of traffic is not going to disappear in the near future, neither can one be certain that the severest criticisms of the users, principally countries exporters of raw materials, have obtained any results. A careful scrutiny of the new Code of Conduct of the United Nations, opened for signature on 1 July 1974, suffices to prove that the criticisms were not unfounded. The substitution of the principle of the free flow of shippng by that of cargo sharing contained in Rule 40-40-20 does not destroy the discriminatory nature of tariffs nor the danger of abuse of monopoly situations, but at least the conference circuit will be opened to Third World States and thus stimulate the construction of their national fleets.[58]

7. TECHNOLOGICAL PROGRESS

If the new direction taken by the international vocation and the critical review of its fundamental norms have affected its special character, the technological advances of the last decades go beyond the narrow limits that determine it. As an example, let us examine what has occurred to the ship as a concept.

In its widest sense, a ship has referred to any maritime construction destined for navigation. With this definition, most modern classifications have overcome doubts that have arisen with respect to those crafts with uses other than carriage, such as scientific, fishing or recreation. The concept of a ship as a means of transport has been shelved, and furthermore concern over crafts used in non-marine circumstances, such as navigation through internal waters, has been overcome. The doctrine of the Rules of Commercial Registry also surmounts the problem of those floating crafts devoid of means of propulsion, and although they cannot be considered ships in the technical sense of the word, they have that capability for legal purposes.[59]

[58] See generally, E. du Pontavice, 'Rapports de force économiques dans le Droit de la mer', *Droit Maritime Français*, 1976, no. 329, 268; and UNCTAD's working document: CNUCED, *La réglementation des conférences maritimes* (*Code de conduite conférences maritimes*), Doc. TD/104/Rev. 1.

[59] See Article 146 of the *Reglamento de Registro Mercantil* 1957, and the criticism by Rubio, 'Algunos comentarios al artículo 146 del Reglamento del Registro Mercantil', *Revista Crítica Derecho Inmobiliario*, 1966, 593.

The emergence of new factors, such as drilling platforms, hovercrafts, factory ships, artificial islands, submarine hotels, ports and oil pipelines, have turned the scope of the problem upside down. The ship has ceased to be the central object in Maritime Law, since it is only one of the possible constructions afloat. In other words, these technological advances cannot be fitted into a definition that regards the ship as the focal point of the system. The successive criteria of navigability and seaworthiness, combined or not to the sea, are insufficient to endow modern constructions with a special status. The ship, however widely defined, has been displaced as a qualitative element capable of attracting to its sphere of specialization the challenge of new technological achievements: it is only one of the type of constructions found upon the sea. How can the subjects of liability, insurance, contributions to general average, salvage premiums, benefit of limitation, maritime liens, asistance and towage or the regime of contracts of operating costs be applied? The application of traditional Maritime Law neither adapts to the characteristics nor to the functions. However, the reaction has not been long in coming, although for the moment the disparity of solutions takes precedence over the desired-for uniformity. This diversity affects Comparative Law as much as the specific regime in each particular case.

For example, in Norwegian law drilling platforms are assimilated to ships, but in France only as regards the effects of collisions and with the conditions that they be fixed installations. Where assimilation does take place, a special discipline is discernible in certain circumstances, among which the limits of liability is noticeable.[60]

Hovercrafts suffer a similar fate; in some cases they are assimilated to ships and in others to aircraft, the Italian legal system aligning itself with the former and the British and American systems with the latter. However, this classification is not rigid. Specifically, British law applies the Warsaw Convention for the transport of passengers and the Brussels Convention if the hovercraft carries cargo, but curiously the crew is captained by aircraft pilots and not captains of the Merchant Navy. To the contrary, the Chicago Convention excludes them from its field of application, thus falling beyond the ambit of Air Law. It is not surprising therefore, that a third view regards hovercraft as a *sui generis* category which defies classification.[61]

The conversion of ships into floating hotels, such as the liner *France*, or their transformation into floating museums, such as the *Savannah*, the first nuclear-powered merchant ship; the construction of factory ships, ordered already by waterpurifying plants and others who need vast amounts of water

[60] Reform of the Norwegian Maritime Code in 1974. Gombrii, in *Anuario Derecho Marítimo*, 1980, pp. 537-538; R. Rodière, 'Faut il réviser la definition classique du navire?' *J.C.P.*, 1977, I, 2880, reproduced in *Il Diritto Marittimo*, 1978, 175.

[61] M. Sáenz Sagaseta de Ilurdoz, 'Aerodeslizadores (Estudio jurídico de un nuevo medio de transporte', *RDM*, 1975, no 138, pp. 463–508.

(nuclear power stations); permanent drilling ships engaged in the exploration and extraction of oil in deep sea areas, or lastly, the vast tracts of oil pipelines, constitute other examples which lengthen the list of technological advances that have necessitated a review of the concept of the ship as a means of maritime transport. American caselaw, in the first of the examples cited, has classified in the special regime of seafarers those labourers injured in the course of working on floating museums, thus guaranteeing indemnity for maintenance and cure as recognized in the Jones Act. If the dangers of the sea are certainly reduced in these fixed installations, the cause of distance which in other times justified specialization disappears altogether, so that it is hardly surprising that the widening of the definition of the ship, classified solely in accordance with structure, is more a notion of equity than a true technical expedient.[62] Factory ships, the dimensions and construction characteristics of which make any assimilation to ships more difficult, despite using this expression solely in relation to its structure, or as modern Greek law does, by including auxiliary constructions and floating appliances pose other difficulties.[63]

These prior observations allow us to draw some general conclusions. It is submitted that the best solution from a technical point of view is plain recognition of the facts. To recover from a narrow definition is to search for the essential. Structure, buoyancy, size and destination count for little. These structures are on the sea, are manned, and cost a substantial amount. To defend a technological criterion means maintaining the classic definition of a ship, without altering or corrupting the concept, without the need of incorporating foreign bodies. It appears best to introduce a special regime and endow it with special status, a suggestion which, however, should not appear too remote from realization if the project of the international Convention on all appliances and exploitation systems of the sea succeeds.[64]

[62] From that perspective the judgments handed down by the American courts on the concept of the ship may be understood. For an analysis of this question, see the cases of *Off-Shore Company v. Jude Wisdom Robinson*, 266 F. 2d 769, 1950 *AMC* 2049 (5th Cir. 1967); *Vincent v. Harvey Well Service*, 441 F. 2d 146, 1971 *AMC* 2541 (5th Cir. 1971), and *Sims v. Marine Catering Service*, 217 F. Supp. 511, 1964 *AMC* 377 (E.D. La. 1963).

[63] Article 1 of the Greek Code 1958 defines a ship as a 'concave construction of a net tonnage of at least ten tons destined to navigate on the sea under its own means'. Three elements are necessary according to this classic definition: minimum tonnage, maritime navigation as the objective and self-propulsion, so that all the examples mentioned in the text lie outside the definition. The extension occurs when a new concept is introduced: the floating artefacts, which have ultimately been assimilated to ships. J. Schinas, 'L'engin flotant, un concept particulier au Droit grec', *DFM*, 1980, 45; and formerly, 'Le statut des engins óperant en mer autres que les navires en Droit grec', Athens 1978 (offprint from the journal *Revue Hellénique de Droit International* 1977).

[64] Voelckel, 'Le statut juridique des systèmes d'acquisition de donnés océaniques', in *Actualités du Droit de la mer*, Paris 1973, p. 76, cited by Martine Remond-Gouilloud in Rodière and Remond-Gouilloud, *La mer, droits des hommes ou proie des Etats*?, Paris (Pedone) 1980, p. 139.

8. THE EMERGENT LAW OF THE SEA

If the review of Maritime Law has led to a crisis regarding its role as special law, the trend towards economic equality among States has questioned the very fundamentals of the Law of the Sea. The similarities between these two processes is so apparent that they lead to the same conclusion: from a legal viewpoint, the sea has made itself available to development.

The Law of the Sea, as part of Public International Law, by the enduring history of change. It is the normal process of evolution of Public International Law. However, two very different stages may be perceived in this change: that which spans the era dating from its origins to the latter part of the XX century and that which initiated the Third United Nations Conference on the Law of the Sea (hereafter known as UNCLOS III).

The process may be described swiftly in the following terms.[65] The birth of the international maritime order flows from State practice, manifested in a series of acts of contrary nature which sought to reconcile the capture of ships with the right of free passage, posing naturally as respect for the principle of freedom of navigation. These norms, which clearly are of a

[65] A detailed account of the synthesis which I am relating may be found in any general text on the Law of the Sea or in some of the chapters dealing with this subject in books on Public International Law; J.C. Colombos, *The International Law of the Sea*, London (Longman, Green and Co.) 1959, 4th ed.; Spanish translation by J.L. Azcárraga, *Derecho internacional marítimo*, Madrid (Aguilar) 1961, whose classification reflects the coordinates of development, the first section dealing with International Law of the Sea in times of peace and the second dealing with International Law in times of war, although chronologically the reverse has been the true position; J.L. Azcárraga, *Derecho Internacional Marítimo*, Barcelona 1970; O. de Ferron, *Le Droit international de la mer*, Genève 1958 (Librairie Minard), 2 vols; D.W. Bowett, *The Law of the Sea*, Dobbs Ferry and Manchester (Oceana and Manchester University Press) 1967; R.R. Churchill and A.V. Lowe, *The Law of the Sea*, Manchester (Manchester University Press) 1983; Sh. Oda, 'New Trends in the Regime of the Sea', in 18 *Zeitschrift für Ausländisches Offentliches Recht und Völkerrecht* (1957), pp. 61–102 and 261–286; ibid., *The International Law of the Ocean and Ocean Development: Basic Documents*, Leyden (Sijthoff), vol. I, 1972, and vol. II, 1974, which although a compilation of documents does have some very useful commentaries. Amongst the numerous books on contemporary aspects of the Law of the Sea, that carried out by the British Institute of International and Comparative Law stands out, Developments in the Law of the Sea 1958–1964, London (Temple) 1965; and ibid., the six volumed New Directions on the Law of the Sea (Dobbs Ferry-New York, Oceana Publications), 1973–1977, vols. I–II: 'Documents' (1973), vol. III: 'Collected Papers' (1973), vol. IV: 'Documents' (1975), and vols. V and VI: 'Documents and Index to vols. I–IV' (1977), all edited by Churchill, Nordquist and Lay; R.J. Dupuy, *The Law of the Sea: Current Problems* (Oceana Publications, N.Y., and Sijthoff), 1974 which constitutes a good summary. In Spain one must cite the volumes edited under the direction of Ambassador Professor Antonio Poch, *La actual revisión del Derecho del mar: Una perspectiva española*, 4 vols.; the first two are comprised of articles, the third and fourth of 'Texts and documents', edited by José Antonio Yturriaga, Madrid (Instituto de Estudios Políticós, Centro de Documentación) 1974; of particular interest is the 'Introducción' by Antonio Poch and Gutiérrez de Cabiedes, vol. I, pp. 2–29.

customary origin, have since the end of the XVIII century been refined by the process of codification; until the first decade of this century it was directed towards that part of Maritime Law applicable in times of war: it is the law of naval war first propounded by the Paris Declaration of 1856 and culminating in the Hague Peace Conferences of 1899 and 1907; until the latter part of the XX century it is directed towards the Law of the Sea in times of peace. The Geneva codification process brought about a change of direction: The Hague Conference of 1930 abandoned the subject of the use of force and unsuccessfully sought to establish the first general principles on the Law of the Sea. Despite the final failure of the Conference it did achieve some important gains. The precise definition of terms and concepts, together with the strong opposing views on the issue of exploitation of resources, compensates for the rejection of the extension of the territorial sea beyond the three mile limit. Following the Second World War, as from 1948, the UN continued the task of codification, the most concrete results of which have been the three conferences on the Law of the Sea. The first led to the adoption of the four Geneva Conventions of 1958 on the Territorial Sea and Contiguous zone, the High Seas, the Continental Shelf and Fishing and Conservation of the Living Resources of the High Seas.[66] To the contrary, the second Geneva Conference on the Law of the Sea did not reach fruition. It is not surprising therefore that the unilateral acts taken by States in support of extending their jurisdiction, and given the other serious problems that were still pending – the delimitation of maritime zones, the extension of the territorial sea, strategic questions, the emergence of new concepts such as the exclusive fishing zones which guarantee the rights of coastal states to the zones adjacent to the territorial sea, environmental problems and, generally, conservation of the seas, hampered a favourable outcome to the Geneva Conference of 1960.[67] We thus reach the period of

[66] All have been ratified by Spain; see A. Menéndez and J.L. Iglesias, *Código de las leyes marítimas*, cit., p. 133 et seq.

[67] Lack of agreement on the width of the territorial sea was the factor that led to failure. The Conference adopted its decisions by two thirds majority vote, and just for the lack of one vote a compromise formula which included a maximum six mile limit for the territorial sea, a six mile contiguous zone in which the coastal State could regulate fishing, without prejudice to the historic rights of third States and the acknowledgment of a preferential right of coastal States to fish in any area of the high sea adjacent to their fishery zone failed to be adopted. See *Ministerio de Asuntos Exteriores (Oficina de Información Diplomática), III Conferencia de las Naciones Unidas sobre Derecho del Mar*, Madrid 1978 (Cuadernos de Documentación), p. 13 (edited by Lacleta Muñoz, Pastor Ridruejo and Yturriaga); D.W. Bowett, 'The Second United Nations Conference on the Law of the Sea', 9 *International and Comparative Law Quarterly* (1960) 415–435; J.P.A. François, 'La Deuxième Conférence sur le Droit de la Mer', *Nederlands Tijdschrift voor Internationaal Recht*, 1960, 249–254; *Second United Nations Conference on the Law of the Sea*, Geneva, 17 March–26 April 1960, Official Records, U.N. Publications Sales No. 60, V. 6, 176 pp.; A. Gros, 'Entre Deux Conférences sur le Droit de la Mer', en *Hommage d'une Génération de Juristes au Président Basdevant*, Paris (Pedone) 1960, 237–257.

UNCLOS III which marks a new stage and whose ultimate proposals we still await.[68]

In essence, the evolution of the general process of codification, which extends till 1973, the year in which the New York Conference convened, does not indicate a radical spirit of change.[69] They are the traditional methods of developing International Law save, logically, the important variations brought about by the passage of time. Customs that have emerged from State practice, acts which are internationally relevant vis-à-vis other States, crystallize into norms of International Law through the process of multilateral diplomatic conferences. In its formal aspect it seems as if the process perseveres without a solution to the question of continuity. But on analyzing the factors of change closely it quickly becomes apparent that we are faced with a substantive law that is different. It is still emergent law but law that breaks away completely with the past. Political, economic and technological factors have given impetus to the achievement of a new goal: the sea as common heritage of mankind. This concept is going to erode in some cases, and modify in others, the principles that govern the traditional Law of the Sea.

In the political field, decolonization, which has largely taken place in the last thirty years, is going to alter dramaticaly the distribution of power in the international community, with the most powerful States being in a minority. Until fairly recently the majority of independent States were still colonies which could not generate custom, nor were they aware of the usefulness of the principle of freedom of the seas. Classical International Law, particularly Law of the Sea, had been formulated in their absence. Their presence was unknown in the ambit of international conventions which were reserved for sovereign States; on the other hand, little did it matter to colonial possessions that they did not know the law since it applied only to sovereign States. But when the membership of the international community doubled the reaction was not long in coming. The position of the developing States would just as much affect the content of customary law as that of conven-

[68] The United Nations Convention on the Law of the Sea, The Law of the Sea: Official Text of the United Nations Convention on the Law of the Sea with Annexes and Index, London and Canberra (Croom Helm); New York (St. Martin's Press), 1983, concluded at Montego Bay on 10 December 1982, remained open for signature until 9 December 1984, by which time one hundred and fifty-nine signatures had been appended but ratified only by fourteen States (according to Article 308 the Convention shall enter into force twelve months after the date of deposit of the sixtieth instrument of ratification or accession).

[69] The preparation of UNCLOS III and the numerous problems that arose therefrom demonstrated the presence of new factors; on this development see *III Conferencia de las Naciones Unidas sobre Derecho del Mar*, cit., pp. 17 et seq.; J.A. Pastor Ridruejo, 'Consideraciones sobre la III Conferencia de las Naciones Unidas sobre el Derecho del Mar', *Anuario de Derecho Internacional III*, 1976, Pamplona (Ediciones Universidad de Navarra) 1978, pp. 282 et seq., and bibliography, ibid. cit.

tional law, considered to be excessively favourable to the developed States.[70] In addition, as a result of political independence economic development became a priority. It is evident that the developing States gave precedence to economic and social progress, and it is thus that the affirmation of the principle of State sovereignty over their natural resources is bitterly resisted by the traditional order of marine resources, based on the principle of freedom of fishing.[71] Correlative to the factors of decolonization and development, the spectacular advances made in science and technology in the area of the deep sea are demonstrating that man can live off marine resources. This concept can be encapsulated in the following phrase: the sea does not consist solely of the surface, but is a whole exploitable mass. It is not therefore a question of ensuring freedom of navigation for all nor of distributing equitably the produce of fishing, which are constantly diminishing. Today, the great debate centres round the question of discovering who and how the riches of the seabed situated in international waters are going to be exploited.[72]

[70] A criterion easily accepted by doctrine; see generally, G. Gobbi, *I Paesi dell'OUA e il mare*, Milan (Giuffrè) 1978, 7–31; Queneudec, 'La rémise en cause du Droit de la mer', in *Actualités du Droit de la mer*, Paris (Pedone) 1973, 14 et seq.; J.A. Carrillo Salcedo, 'Los Estados sin litoral y en situación geográfica desventajosa ante la revisión del Derecho del mar', in *La actual revisión del Derecho del mar*, cit., I, 155–201; R.P. Anand, 'Interests of the Developing Countries and the Developing Law of the Sea', in *Annales d'Etudes Internationales*, 1973, 13–29; G. Chouraqui, 'L'Afrique et le Droit de la mer', *Revue Juridique et Politique, Indépendence et Cooperation*, 1977, 1079–1220; 'Needs and Interests of Developing Countries', in *Proceedings of the Seventh Annual Conference of the Law of the Sea Institute*, 1972, 238 pp.; W. Pintoc, 'Problems of Developing States and Their Effects on Decisions on Law of the Sea', in *Seventh Annual Conference of the Law of the Sea Institute*, 1972, 3–13.

[71] Elisa Pérez Vera, 'Los factores económicos en el proceso de revisión del Derecho del mar', in *La actual revisión*, cit., I, pp. 69–113; E. Vargas Carreño, *América Latina y el Derecho del Mar*, México (Fondo de Cultura Económica), 1973, 17, and the Prologue by Vásquez Carrozosa, a booklet I believe to be excellent and which states with numerous documentation the state of the question in Latin American countries.

[72] All the traditionalists generally agree on this point, see generally, Tullio Treves (ed.), *La ricerca scientifica nell' evoluzione del diritto del mare*, Milan (Guiffrè), 1978, in particular R.P. Mazzeschi, *La ricerca scientifica ed il nuovo diritto internazionale del Mare*, 1973, pp. 13–29.

The potential mineral wealth to be found in the seabed is of such a magnitude that according to the experts, the world can subsist on the resources of the sea. According to published data, oil and gas exist in unquantifiable amounts; as drilling technology develops and those first couple of meters become thousands, the reserves multiply: the drill-on-shore technique is substituted for the drill-off-shore platforms. Thus, in 1975 the *National Petroleum Council* of the USA estimated that the deposits of hydrocarbons beneath the sea amount to a couple of hundred billion tons compared with the lesser amount of a hundred billion on land (cf. 'Offshore Petroleum Development and Potential', in *Maritime Studies and Management*, 1975, pp. 181–189; M. Remond, *L' Exploration Pétrolière en Mer et le Droit*, Paris (Editions Techniques), 1970, 197 pages; K.F. Gaskell, 'Exploration, Evaluation and Exploitation of Deep Water Petroleum'. Paper presented at the *Symposium on the International Regime of the Sea-Bed*, Rome, 1969, p. 20; N.A. Erenmenko (ed. al), 'Geological

That is, according to most authorities, the real issue at stake at UNCLOS III.

In embarking upon the question from this angle it is hardly surprising that the view of the new States on natural resources should give impetus to the extension of jurisdiction over the sea. If the 1958 Conference did not fulfill their aspirations, still incipient, and the Second Conference failed to resolve the problem of the extension of the territorial sea, it appears to be easily agreed that the imperative route has shattered that order created by the method of unilateral acts. The concept of the two hundred mile zone is basically a response to this. Third World States thus closed ranks in the name of solidarity, a fact culminated in the 1973 Algiers Resolution, ratified by seventy-five non-aligned States.[73]

Structure and Oil and Gas Prospects of USSR. Continental Shelf', in *American Association of Petroleum Geologist Bulletin*, 1973, vol. 57(2), pp. 235–243; M. Crommelin, 'Offshore Oil and Gas Rights: A Comparative Study', in *Natural Resources Journal*, 1974, pp. 457–500, and abundant data in the report of the U.S. Congress Senate Committee on Commerce: *The Economic Value of Ocean Resources to the United States*, Washington D.C., 1974, 109 pages (U.S. Cong., 2 sess. Committee Print). In addition, it has been demonstrated in an analysis of seawater that it contains some basic dissolved substances: potassium, sodium, magnesium, bromide, as well as heavy water, which is a raw material necessary for nuclear fusion, which makes the acquisition of uranium more likely. According to the journal *Nucleonics Week*, a uranium extractor factory constructed on the sea is operational in the Soviet Union, in Chevtchenko, on the shores of the Caspian Sea. Similarly, the sweet water obtained by desalinating plants could transform the desert into orchards in the not too distant future.

However, if these aspects are important, the wealth stored in the so-called *manganese nodules* are far more significant. As may already have been noted, they consist of minerals in the shape of potatoes found on the deep sea-bed, and which contain a number of metals, rare in the majority, in proportions higher than those found on land. Thus, they may come to contain up to 30% of manganese, 8% of iron, nickel and copper, and at times it is not uncommon to find other proportions of cobalt, zinc and vanadium. The best are situated below the depth of four thousand metres. See A. Xavier, 'The Exploitation of Deep-Sea Manganese Nodules: Progress and Prospects', in 4 *Marine Policy and Management* (1976) July, pp. 33–40; U.S. Library of Congress: Congressional Research Service. *Ocean Manganese Nodules*, edited by J.E. Mielke, on the request of the Committee President, H.M. Jackson, Committee on Interior and the Insular Affairs. United States Senate, Washington, 1976, 163 pages (U.S. Cong. 2 sess. Committee Print); J.L. Mero, 'The Great Nodule Controversy', in *IX Annual Conference of the Law of the Sea Institute*, 1975, 343–350; F.M. Auburn, 'Some Legal Problems of the Commercial Exploitation of Manganese Nodules in the Pacific Ocean', in 1 *Ocean Development and International Law* (1973), pp. 185–201.

The facts are sufficiently explicit to give rise to the pointed questioning of the validity of a traditional norm, which in applying the principle of the freedom of the high seas places this wealth at the disposal of those that occupy it since it is considered to be *res nullius*. Note, however, that the United Nations Law of the Sea Conference 1982 gives the deep sea-bed the status of common heritage of mankind.

[73] The movement in favour of the two hundred mile zone was initiated by the Latin American countries; specifically the first multilateral agreement which established the coastal State's jurisdiction over that zone was the 'Declaration on the Maritime Zone', adopted by Chile, Ecuador and Peru, in Santiago, Chile, on 18 August 1952, on the conclusion of the I

However, the principle of freedom, postulated by Grotius at the beginning of the XVI century as freedom of navigation and freedom of commerce, no longer serves as a reference point for International Law of the Sea. Authoritative works have accurately shed light on how the freedom of the high seas satisfies the needs of the great maritime powes, particularly freedom of commerce, and safeguarded the interests of the first Indian companies.[74] In other words, it deals with the question of how the free exchange between the European metropolis and the overseas possessions. This principle, recognized as a norm by the Geneva Conference 1958, has not withstood the accusations of bias from underdeveloped States. Furthermore, it is precisely the view of the sea as a mass that provides those ex-colonial powers with the best opportunities for taking advantage of the riches of the deep seabed, inaccessible for those who possess the freedom but lack the technology. Freedom of commerce which was a means of communication and exchange along the surface has been transformed into freedom to instal, explore, exploit and appropriate the riches of the sea, all of which is, naturally enough, blessed by the dogma of private property. The scope of freedom in the Law of the Sea should not delude us, since it merely accentuates economic inequalities.

The claims of Third World States are based therefore on two issues. On the one hand, they seek recognition of the right to sovereignty over natural resources, on which basis the unilateral extension of maritime zones is perceived to be legally founded, particularly the fishery zones and the two hundred mile territorial sea. On the other hand, beyond the scope of that

---

Conference on the Exploitation and Conservation of Maritime Wealth in the South Pacific (the entire text of this Declaration, which consists of six paragraphs, may be found in E. Vargas Carreño, *América Latina y el Derecho del mar*, cit., p. 123. On the significance, legal nature and consequences which the movement on unilateral declaration unleashed, *see* Gutiérrez Olivos, *Mar territorial y Derecho moderno*, Santiago de Chile, 1955; *Instrumentos nacionales e internacionales sobre Derecho del mar*, Lima, 1971, p. 212–281, and Vargos also, op. cit.; subsequently other countries joined this movement (Nicaragua in 1965, Argentina in 1966, Panama in 1967, Uruguay in 1969, Brazil in 1970 and Costa Rica in 1972).

[74] The Belgian historian Jacques Pirenne, *Les grands courants de l'histoire universelle*, Paris (1945–1957), 7 vols., has attempted to explain the history of civilization as a constant battle between sea and land, a conflict between the oceans and the continents; that is, the struggle of the maritime democracies, liberals against the continental empires, nationalist and authoritarian (the struggle of the Persian empire against the Greek world, of the Roman empire against the barbarians, of Islam against the feudal system, of the Law Countries against the Empire of Charles V, of England against the Napoleonic Empire, of the Anglo-saxon democracies against the Axis powers, of NATO against the Warsaw Pact) in the political and social order. This wider context in which the sea appears to be the basis of all relationships manifests itself in a more specific manner as the origin of the first economic liberalism which occurred in overseas trade. (Cf. the collective work *Sociétés et Compagnies de commerce en orient et dans l'océan indien (actes du huitième coloque international d'histoire maritime – Beyrouth 5–10 septembre 1966 –*), Paris (E.J. Touzot), 1970, particularly the conclusions drawn by Federico Melis, pp. 703–715.

jurisdiction, lies the creation of an international regime for the exploitation of the deep seabed under the administration of a new authority which would distribute equitably the benefits extracted from that common heritage.[75]

Compare to this the position of the industrialized nations, which although favouring the international regulation of marine resources, have a radically different concept of the organization and its distribution from that of the underdeveloped world. While the latter logically want an effective authority, endowed with sweeping powers, the true operator of the direct exploitation of the deep and distribution of its benefits, the industialized States visualize an impotent organization, with its jurisdiction limited to the administration of the concession and registration of exploitation licence. In other words, the dispute revolves around the desire of the former in postponing the commencement of operations and in conserving the riches, while at the same time their technology is modernized, vis-à-vis the impatience of the powers in not inhibiting the application of that technology to the exploitation of those deposits.[76]

[75] The speech by Ambassador Alvid Pardo, representative of the Government of Malta to the United Nations, before the First Committee of the General Assembly, where in taking account of technological progess which made the exploitation of the sea-bed at great depths feasible, the wheels of a new Convention were put in motion and a new international organization was created, the basic principles of which were the unilateral appropriation by States and the common exploitation by all Mankind. This proposal immediately resulted in the creation of the Commission on the Deep Sea-Bed and subsequently the adoption by the General Assembly of resolution 2749 (XXV) of 17 December 1970, in which the zone of the deep sea-bed beyond the reach of national sovereignty is declared to be the 'common heritage of mankind' (the text may be found in *The Official Documents of the Third United Nations Conference on the Law of the Sea* (United Nations publication).

The concept of the deep sea-bed as common heritage of mankind has been enshrined in Article 136 of the Law of the Sea Convention 1982. Furthermore, Article 137 states that no State shall claim or exercise sovereignty or sovereign rights over the deep sea-bed, nor shall such claim or exercise of sovereignty or sovereign rights be recognized, and paragraph 2 states that any minerals recovered therefrom shall only be alienated in accordance with the Convention and under the supervision of the Authority. A number of industrialized States, particularly the USA, the United Kingdom and the Federal Republic of Germany, objected to these provisions and have not signed the Convention. In addition, in August 1984 Belgium, France, Federal Republic of Germany, Italy, Japan, the Netherlands, United Kingdom and USA reached a Provisional Understanding Regarding Deep Seabed Mining, *see* XXIII *International Legal Materials* (No. 6) 1984, p. 1354. According to this agreement each of the signatories undertakes to avoid any disputes over the exploitation of deep sea-bed resources and not to grant any licences for exploitation for areas already claimed by any other signatory thereto. In addition, the agreement provides for periodic consultations on deep sea-bed mining.

[76] E. Langavant, *Droit de mer. Cadre institucionel et milieu marin* (*oceanologie-pollution*), Paris (Editions Cujas), 1979, p. 15; René Rodière-Maritine Remond-Gouilloud, *La mer*, *Droits des hommes ou proie des Etats*?, Paris (Pedone), 1980, pp. 134–136. In fact, some American and Japanese companies have, under the *Deep Sea Ventures* formula, commenced the work on collecting the nodules, and in 1974 sought diplomatic protection from the United States Government in order to exploit a deposit of 60,000 square metres somewhere in the Pacific Ocean. The wishes of these enterprises were granted with the adoption of a law on 28 June

From a technical point of view the question is inextricably linked, first, with the distribution of jurisdiction and secondly, with the procedure regarding the constitution and system for the adoption of the agreements. Those in favour want an International Seabed Authority composed of three bodies: the Authority, the Council, and the Assembly, according to which the Council will adopt the agreements by a three quarters' majority of members present and voting. This is naturally unacceptable to the industrialized States who would not possess the power of veto.[77]

The subsequent development of this rather speculative issue, whose fortune is inextricably linked to that of UNCLOS III, falls outside the general scope of this article.[78] However, I would like to make one final submission. Given the recent decisions of the United States Government – the change in the composition of the delegation, the drafting of an alternative text in which the question of resources is shelved, the general attitude defending staunchly national interests, etc. – may put in serious jeopardy the ambitious programme of the Conference, but not however, the irreversible process of reviewing the Law of the Sea. Consquently, and leaving aside the agreements achieved in an important number of subjects, the effort of eight years' work spread over ten sessions to date, excluding three other preparatory conferences by the Seabed Committee, subsequently transformed into the preparatory Commission of UNCLOS III, the participation of delegations from one hundred and fifty States and of a high number of observers from the more representative specialist organizations, and the overcoming of many difficult issues by the disparity and importance of interests, the politics of unilateralism through the absence of a working draft and the adoption of the consensus system, have left an important mark in the history of the Law of the Sea which cannot be legitimately ignored.

1980 that guarantees legal and financial resources to American companies so that the *unilateral* exploitation of the international deep sea-bed enjoys the protection of the United States Navy. However, the Carter Administration did not wish to disrupt the work of UNCLOS III and its entry into force was frozen. Cf. *Public Law*, 96, 283. But, as indicated above in n. 75 the Reagan Administration has reversed this policy.

77 Section 4 of Part XI, The Area, Articles 156–185, governs the functions of the Authority.

78 Until 1980, UNCLOS III had had ten periods of sessions: I, New York, 1973, was preparatory; II Caracas 1974, initiated the proper substantive phase, discussing as the central issue the system of exploration and exploitation; III Geneva 1975, which discussed the same question; IV New York, 1976, which drafted the single revised text for negotiation; V New York, on the composition and jurisdiction of the maritime authority; VI New York 1977, on the preceding questions plus the political issues of funding the authority; VII and VIII Geneva 1978, the seventh dealing with the creation of negotiating groups to consider the most complex issues, and the eighth nominated a Committee of Legal Experts to consider the technical details of the final provisions, and IX New York-Geneva, which examined the various reports submitted to the plenum for their examination. Accurate information of these workings may be found in the official documents of UNCLOS III, *Sessions*, U.N. Doc. A/Conf. 62. As has been indicated elsewhere the Convention was finally adopted at Montego Bay, Jamaica, in 1982.

IV. Final remarks

It has been seen how the development of the historical sources has broken with tradition various times: we have moved from a general law to the encroachment of private law principles into the codifying process.

Alternatively, it has been noted how the critical review of a large number of the fundamental norms has accentuated the privileged and contingent nature of the special law. Similarly, the diversity of the criteria employed by the doctrine, allied to the heterogeneous nature of Comparative Law, has clearly proven the difficulties inherent in elaborating a general concept, beyond the coordinates of time and space because the special law is confronted by questions of opportunity and validity. It has been shown with sufficient clarity that the wish for international uniformity as established in conventional law, as has occurred in practice, favours the organized States more than a desire for equity. It can equally be confirmed in these considerations that the change in the status quo of the international community corresponds to the irreversible participation of the new organizations in the generation of a new uniform law. And finally, the spectacular advances made in the field of technology demonstrate that the traditional notions must assume a more modest role, identifying an element, and abandoning the most ambitious project of classifying the subject matter by reference to the object or its goal.

But if any general conclusions may be drawn from these observations, it not only seems expedient but logical to affirm that the sea does not distinguish between public and private law. Thus, the classification of the subject as Law of the Sea, as an exclusive part of Public International Law, i.e., rights and duties of States, and Maritime Law as private law, i.e., relations between individuals, has lost all meaning. It does not seem possible therefore to draw up distinct legal systems to handle identical problems: pollution, the protection of the marine environment, fisheries, the exploration and exploitation of living and mineral resources, the distribution of deep seabed resources, the diminution or elimination of shipwrecks, are not altered by their passage from one regime to another; the same needs exist on the surface of the territorial sea as below it. The same conflicts continue to exist where State jurisdiction ends and freedom of the seas commences. The same problems persist where the high seas end and sovereignty begins. Why is there a need to search for different answers to similar questions?

Consequently, a constant assimilation of Public Law elements may be observed in traditional Maritime Law which, given the question of uniformity, is derived from its international vocation; the endowment of Maritime Law with Public Law principles.

The worthlessness of the system conceived on its own is a well-known fact. It is not a question of bringing to mind the usual examples of the traditional figure of the captain, endowed with public functions, an on board representative of public authority and empowered with competence in the private sphere in his role as shipowner's representative; nor does an analysis of the legal status of the ship as an exclusively mobile object, a typical principle of civil law, leaving aside administrative elements, denote an attack; nor is it a question of insisting that a review of the subject of collisions necessarily must include a study of safety at sea. It is more a question of noting the ever increasing State regulation of maritime affairs, so that in fact the submission may be made that 'carriage of goods by sea has become a matter of State'. Legislative provisions dealing with limitations on cargo, required in some cases by the needs of development and fitting out of the national fleet, and in other cases as a result of the financial system of State commerce, and finally in others in response to the preceding, either as a result of compromises reached in a conference on charters, or as a consequence of the application of the new code of conduct, are some facts that point in that direction.

Next to this fusion between norms of International and Municipal Law on the one hand and Public and Private Law on the other, we are today witnessing a positive phenomenon which resists any easy assimilation to the process of assimilation which the different branches of the law have experienced. This problem appears to be, but not without some doubts, unique to this discipline, although it naturally has elements that are applicable to the process of approximation between Public Law and Private Law, but interrelating the double connection between International Law and Municipal Law. Briefly, the increasing role of the State in the international sphere leads to the internationalization of Municipal Law. In other words, the extension of the State apparatus in the marine world and its resources augments the public sector. It is submitted that the new Law of the Sea has its origins in national legal systems. Thus, for example, when a State claims exclusive jurisdiction of two hundred miles over an economic zone, which while it denotes the extent of its sovereignty vis-à-vis other States, at the same time it augments its patrimony, that is, the public domain in the domestic order. Or to cite another example, when a State extends the limit of the territorial sea to twelve miles it is aiding the extent of public property. This is particularly the case in the latter example since the so-called economic zone recognizes sovereign rights only insofar as connected to exploration and exploitation of the natural resources of the deepsea bed and subsoil (and the superadjacent waters) while by definition the territorial sea recognizes all the authority of exclusive State sovereignty. It is, as has been eloquently put, that portion of liquid State territory.[79] Consequently, if the

[79] In addition, the phenomenon that most attracts my attention is the ignorance of the significance of the effect that the extension of the territorial sea will have, since I await with impatience for basic textbooks to university books on the geography of Spain, and including some official documents and political statements, to correct the mistake that Spain has half a million square kilometres instead of those which result from multiplying the twelve miles by the perimeter of the coast, according to the act of 10/1977, 4 January, on the territorial sea. According to this calculation, Spain has an area of approximately a million and a half square kilometres, since to the half a million land area must be added the 1,155,816 square kilometers of the surface of the territorial sea.

ordinary legisation is combined with Article 132 (2) of the Constitution, which defines public property as 'the territorial sea and the natural resources of the economic zone and the continental shelf' the submission may be better understood. This constitutional provision has therefore placed restraints on the private initiative and autonomy of the sea and of its inches in holding that this liquid mass and its marine resources are subject to public ownership. The internationalization of the Law of the Sea is not accompanied by any corresponding extension of private law in the domestic system. The major grades of sovereignty in the international sphere are resolved in favour of the patrimony of the Municipal Law. The investment of International Law principles and Public Law principles are therefore two sides of the same coin. Thus the new Law of the Sea is transformed into a platform for the new presence of the public domain; the State acquires for itself, and not for its citizens, the produce reaped from that old zone once governed by the freedom of the high seas. In conclusion, the new peaks that sovereignty has scaled are not regulated by Private Law (freedom of commerce, freedom of establishment, freedom of contract, acquisition of private property. . .) but by Administrative Law, and specifically by those principles that forbid alienation, prescription and seizure. Consequently, in the uncertain future of the Law of the Sea the State will not act in defence of private interests, even in general ones, even if the interest in the sea is a collective one, but by representing its own interests, and only in the public sphere. Given the sea's international aspect the State will be more representative of Public Administration than the citizen as an individual or as a collective group.

These observations have permitted the concept to be considered in its proper perspective, while at the same time invite a final conclusion: 'Maritime Law is that system of legal relationships that have their origin in or evolve with the sea.'

One is aware, however, that any definition is, and please excuse the pun, by definition a capricious affair. This is a dogmatic opinion which is therefore open to all the indepth revisions that appear necessary. But at the same time it provides an immutable point of departure for a study of the subject. It is necessary for us and when a stream of independent expression appears it is opportune. An attempt has therefore been made to incorporate this question in the title and frame it in plain language: *Maritime Law*. Thus, at least in the formal context, the usual approach of those jurists who are more concerned with adjectival considerations which are formulated in titles such as *A Revolution in Maritime Law*, *Tradition and Modernism in Maritime Law*, *The Evolution of Maritime Law and the Law of the Sea*, *The Review Procedure of Maritime Law*, *New Contributions of the Law of the Sea*, etc., has been abandoned.[80] In opting for this method, an attempt has been made to recapture the historical element, irreplaceable in the formulation of the concept. This testimonial to the origins, to the initial reference point, serves to explain the defence of the term Maritime Law, otherwise a secondary consideration when the questions are considered in detail and when solutions based on equity are proffered. It is a question of reclaiming the genuine formula in order to design a changing sector of reality, valid at least in the Latin and Germanic systems, inspired in Civil Law in the same manner that the Common Law system maintains tradition with respect to Admiralty Law, of a procedural nature and, as has been seen, devoid of systematic pretensions.

If the definition is analyzed in classical terms, perhaps the heady atmosphere of a fusion between Maritime Law (private) and the Law of the Sea (international and public) will be experienced in a more or less stable and appropriate atmosphere.

However, it is not simply a question of bringing into juxtaposition the internationalization of private Maritime Law with the opposite phenomenon: the infusion of private law elements into Public Law. It is submitted that it is something more radical that consists in the scientific logic of the Law being applied to the sea and the activities that take place upon it. The traditional classifications have no meaning any longer and give way to the science of Maritime Law with all its consequences and leads to some, not unreasonably, preferring to label it Marine Law. Consequently, it is the application of the substantive science of the Law to the sea and that relationships that originate with it or occur there rather than the adjective maritime that give rise to the fundamentals of a special science, which is definitely not an autonomous branch of the law. It is more than that. The barriers continue to exist because we are still far from scientific unity, which amounts to saying that the scholars of the general theory of law would give serious consideration to the special branches. It is only the application of a method of study to a new subject in the field of knowledge.

The maritime lawyer will thus have to transform himself into the jurist par excellence since his knowledge is limited to one area of the law. Today's maritime lawyer must have a profound knowledge of history in order to unravel the causes of the speciality and plan future developments; of technological advances, so spectacular as far as the sea is concerned, if he wants to follow closely those events that influence the regulation of the phenomenon; if he wishes to update his information he must be aware of the state of the international community and international affairs; and if he does not wish to propose the application of outdated laws, he must be aware of the new trends of the general law.

This then is the challenge to the jurist of the future.

---

[80] P. Chauveau, 'Le Droit maritime en revolution', in *Estudios homenaje a Joaquén Garrigues*, Madrid (Tecnos), 1971, vol II, 173; A. Polo, 'Tradición y modernismo en el Derecho marítimo', conference paper published in the *Revista Española de Derecho Marítimo*, 1966–1967, fasc. 5, p. 89; E. du Pontavice, "La evolución del Derecho del mar y del Derecho marítimo', *infra*, pp. 62, etc., or those others who assert it for opposite reasons, Rubío, 'El Derecho marítimo y el Derecho aéreo', cit. However, Vicente Santos does it out of course for the problem of delimitation, 'En torno a la delimitación del Derecho marítimo', op. cit.

A LAWYER'S VIEW OF ARBITRATION PROCEEDINGS AND COMPOSITION OF THE ARBITRATION PANEL*

HOWARD M. McCORMACK

Member of the Law Firm of 'Healy & Bailie'

* Paper presented to the VII International Congress of Maritime Arbitrators, Casablanca, 25–27 September, 1985.

Introduction

It is the purpose of this paper to discuss with the assembled Congress the position of a practicing attorney in New York who is substantially involved in maritime arbitrations as counsel and arbitrator regarding the present status of arbitration proceedings and the composition of arbitration panels in the United States. First, a disclaimer is in order in that the views set forth herein are the personal views of the author and do not necessarily reflect the views of the other maritime counsel in New York engaged in similar matters nor, the views of my colleagues and associates within the law firm. The comments in this paper are based upon the author's personal involvement in maritime arbitrations, both from the viewpoint of service as maritime counsel to a major United States industrial corporation and as counsel for both owners and charterers in arbitration disputes as well as serving as a chairman or arbitrator in maritime disputes. Essentially, this paper is the product of the author's involvement and active engagement in maritime arbitrations.

I. Time required to conclude arbitration proceedings

Although in the conceptual world, arbitration proceedings always go forward expeditiously and are concluded most promptly with a decision satisfactory to all parties, the pragmatic world of every day maritime business does not lend itself to this utopian concept. We believe it is a common ground of acceptance that there are problems with arbitration proceedings in various countries; there are quite legitimate criticisms leveled at some of the proceedings, the most common is that relating to the excruciatingly slow progress in resolution of what is rightly perceived to be an alternative solution to a long process of litigation in the Courts.

A. NEW YORK ARBITRATION PROCESS

In order to facilitate the discussion about the process of arbitration, we believe it will serve all interests to discuss briefly the arbitration procedure in New York in maritime matters. These are conducted either through the auspices of the Society of Maritime Arbitrators or before arbitrators who are themselves members of the Society.

The statutory regime for maritime arbitration in the United States is the

Federal Arbitration Act, 9 U.S.C. §1, *et seq*. The majority of maritime arbitrations are conducted without the necessity for resort to the Courts since the parties have agreed in the charter for arbitration in New York before a panel consisting of three commercial men. In some instances, the arbitration clause does not designate any limitation as to the identity or qualifications of the arbitrator. A copy of the Federal Arbitration Act is annexed to this paper and is reproduced from the Rules for Arbitration Procedures of the Society of Maritime Arbitrators (Revised, 15 September 1983).

For purposes of this discussion we will assume a typical arbitration in New York pursuant to a New York Produce Exchange Time Charter which calls for arbitration before a panel of three commercial men. Assume, for the sake of argument, that the dispute involves a claim brought by the charterer for alleged breaches of speed and fuel performance warranties of the owner and the charterer is seeking a refund or return of the charter hire and costs of fuel during the alleged excess charter period.

B. COMMENCEMENT OF ARBITRATION

The arbitration process is commenced by the charterer making a demand for arbitration to the owner outlining, in brief form, the subject of the dispute; that is, a performance claim, and nominating an arbitrator on its behalf. Since the Produce Exchange form does not give any time frame within which the owner would have to nominate its arbitrator, the criterion to be utilized is what would be a reasonable time, given the circumstances of the case. In most instances the owner would appoint its arbitrator without undue delay. To the extent that the charterer perceives that the owner is not willing to nominate an arbitrator, then it may seek recourse to the Court in accordance with Section 4 of the Federal Arbitration Act by filing a petition with the United States Federal Court in New York seeking a court order to compel the owner to proceed to arbitration.

C. RESORT TO THE COURT

In certain instances the petition, in addition to seeking an order to compel the owner to proceed to arbitration, will also requests the Court to nominate a specific person by name or someone from a defined group as an arbitrator in default of a nomination by the respondent. This is a rather unsatisfactory procedure in that the Court may ultimately be called upon to nominate as an arbitrator someone who does not necessarily have any maritime background. To obviate this possibility, it is our custom and practice in these instances to furnish the Court with a roster of the Society of Maritime

Arbitrators and request that, if the Court is to appoint an arbitrator, it be someone from that roster. In many instances, once the petition has been filed with the Court, the recalcitrant party, knowing that it may wind up having an arbitrator appointed against it that it perceives is not necessarily familiar with the maritime chartering field, will finally nominate an arbitrator.

If that is done, the parties will then usually submit to the Court a proposed form of order setting forth the identity of the arbitrator to be nominated by the respondent. The Court, thereafter, will continue to exercise jurisdiction over the matter to the extent required after the arbitration process is completed. The two arbitrators so appointed will now nominate and appoint the chairman of the arbitration panel. In most instances, the chairman will be an individual well known to the two arbitrators so appointed and, in view of the prohibition in the Produce Exchange charter, will not be an attorney. We will discuss this aspect infra, but it is our contention that, in many instances, the chairman should be appointed from one of the ranks of the maritime attorneys in the United States in order to provide a more balanced distribution between the commercial and substantial legal issues that will be raised in many arbitrations.

D. COMMENCEMENT OF ARBITRATION

Once the panel has been chosen, the chairman is charged with the duty of consulting with the parties or their counsel, if they have appointed them, in order to set up the initial hearing date. The chairman is also the one who will act as liaison with the other members of the panel in trying to schedule a hearing at a mutually convenient time.

This is the first hurdle that must be overcome in the desire to expedite the arbitration proceedings. A substantial number of arbitration panels in New York are comprised of a limited number of the same arbitrators. It is obvious that a prompt hearing is not available due to the busy schedule of the members of the arbitration panel on other cases. Most arbitration hearings in New York take place during noon hours or after normal working hours since the majority of the commercial arbitrators are fully engaged in private commercial enterprises. This, in and of itself, creates a built-in delay process in that there is a limited amount of time within which to assemble a panel of three arbitrators and two opposing counsel. It is submitted that the arbitration process could be expedited more efficiently if the hearings in certain cases could be scheduled during the workday, particularly when a number of witnesses are intended to be called and there will be a substantial amount of documents exchanged during the hearings.

E. DISCLOSURES

At the initial hearing the arbitrators make what are known as their disclosures. Succinctly put, this is a statement by each arbitrator setting forth his personal relationship, if any, with the participants in the arbitration and their counsel, and his relationships, business or social, with the other members of the arbitration panel. In general, the disclosures are designed to set forth facts that would show that the arbitrator (1) does not have any substantial business connection with the parties, (2) has no bias or prejudice and (3) has not had any dealings with the parties or counsel that could, in any way, be construed as suggesting that the arbitration award would be a product of anything other than a fair, impartial and unbiased approach.

These disclosures are the product of the United States Supreme Court decision in *Commonwealth Coatings Corp.* v. *Continental Casualty Company*, 393 U.S. 145 (1968), wherein the Court vacated an arbitration award when a member of the arbitration panel had failed to disclose that a close financial relation had existed between one of the parties and the arbitrator for a period of years. One of the grounds under the Federal Arbitration Act for setting aside an arbitration award is where there was evidence of partiality or corruption in the arbitrators. These disclosures, therefore, are designed to comply with the legal decisions which are addressed to this issue.

In essence, the disclosures if anything err on the side of more complete disclosure than may perhaps be absolutely necessary but dealings between an arbitrator and a party to the arbitration proceedings, which might create the impression of a possible bias, must be disclosed by an arbitrator, *Sanko Steamship Company, Ltd.* v. *Cook Industries, Inc.* 495 F.2d 1260 (2nd Cir. 1973). An award may not be set aside on the grounds of bias of an arbitrator where he has completely followed his obligation under the rules to disclose any circumstances likely to create a presumption of bias which he believes might disqualify him as an impartial arbitrator. *Reed & Martin, Inc.* v. *Westinghouse Electric Corp.*, 439 F.2d 1268 (2d Cir. 1971). Where an arbitrator made no attempt to hide his relationship with a corporation which had business relationships with one of the parties to the arbitration, and had in fact mentioned such corporation nine times during the hearing and the party alleging the bias had full knowledge of the arbitrator's affiliation with the corporation, the arbitration award would not be set aside on the grounds of alleged bias. *UCO Terminals, Inc.* v. *Apex Oil Company*, 583 F.Supp. 1213 (S.D.N.Y. 1984).

In order to vacate an arbitration award for evidence of partiality, the Court must find some personal interest on the part of an arbitrator, whether pecuniary or otherwise, that extends beyond any personal views on the merits of the matter before him. *Sidarma Societa Italiana di Armamento, S.p.A., Venice* v. *Holt Marine Industries, Inc.*, 515 F.Supp. 1302 (S.D.N.Y. 1981), aff'd., 681 F.2d 802 (2d Cir. 1981). Where there are facts existing which reasonably create an appearance of partiality of an arbitrator and are undisclosed, an award may be vacated. There is no need to probe the mind of an arbitrator nor to identify evidence of actual bias. *International Produce, Inc.* v. *A/S ROSSHAVET*, 504 F.Supp. 736 (S.D.N.Y. 1980), *reversed*, 638 F.2d 548, (2d Cir. 1981) *cert. denied*, 451 U.S. 1017.

F. DESCRIPTION OF CONDUCT OF HEARINGS

After the disclosures, the first hearing is generally taken up with presentation of the case on behalf of the claimant. This may or may not involve the presentation of witnesses, but it is usual in a case of this nature (e.g. performance claim) for the claimant to submit a series of documents, usually telex exchanges, or other data between the parties and an analysis by a weather service contesting the validity of the ship's data. It is also customary for counsel for the claimant to prepare a preliminary memorandum outlining the facts and highlighting the legal issues that will be considered by the panel. In many instances, this is the first time that the other side has seen some of the documents, is aware of the identity of the witness and, in general, obtains knowledge of the substance of evidence to be utilized by the claimant.

This creates an immediate dilemma with the arbitration panel in that if a witness, either fact or expert, is produced for testimony by the claimant, opposing counsel in many instances has received no prior notice of it nor has had an opportunity to learn the substance of the testimony. Counsel may then request that any cross examination of the witness be postponed until another hearing date, after being given an opportunity of reviewing the documents and exhibits. This postponement then has become the subject of substantial controversy, particularly when a witness that has been produced may have come from overseas or is a ship's officer about to return to his vessel and there is no guarantee of production of the witness in the near future.

The parties and the panel will then have to work out some method for cross examination which could well include the continuing of the cross examination by means of a deposition in the absence of the arbitration panel or scheduling a hearing date when one or other of the arbitration panel may not be present. This will not be a valid hearing unless the parties consent to go forward in the absence of one of the arbitrators. This is always a risk when an issue of credibility is involved because the written page of the transcript of the hearing is not sufficient in many instances to give the full flavor of the testimony to the arbitrators. It is the custom and practice of New York arbitrations to have a verbatim transcript kept of the hearings. In many instances this relieves the arbitrators of the tedious task of keeping notes and permits them to give their full time and attention to the evidence being introduced and to evaluate the testimony of the witnesses as it is given.

A next hearing is then scheduled, or at least attempted to be scheduled, consistent with the schedules of the arbitrators and counsel. It is at this time that it becomes most difficult to get a date than can accommodate all parties, given the short period of time during the day, that is noon time or after working hours, that is available for arbitrations. Counsel's engagements are also involved in that while they may be able to make certain commitments for new hearings, based upon their present schedule, at times they cannot adhere to them. Courts in the United States are not notoriously prone to postpone their own hearings due to the engagement of counsel in arbitration proceedings. In such cases it is a better practice for counsel to have another member of the law firm also fully involved in the arbitration process in order to obviate the necessity for seeking postponement of hearings due to the unavailability of counsel.

The next hearing will then go forward in the same manner as the initial hearing. Witnesses may be cross examined. At the end of the presentation of evidence by the claimant, it is then the obligation of the opponent to go forward with its evidence in support of its defense and, at times, in support of its counterclaim. The same procedure as the first hearing process is utilized. On major cases, it is evident that there can be a series of hearings which have inherent built-in delays since there are five separate entities to concern themselves with schedules.

After the hearings are closed, the parties then generally will supply the arbitration panel with written memoranda. These will review the facts and the law and put forth the legal arguments of the parties. Each side generally executes a simultaneous exchange of these documents so that there is no prior knowledge of the exact arguments being put forth by each side, other than those articulated during the arbitration hearings. Each side then has a period of time, usually two to three weeks, within which to submit reply memoranda, which are similar legal documents intended to be used as rebuttal to the legal arguments presented by the parties and their counsel in the first instance.

After the legal memoranda have been exchanged, the arbitration panel meets to discuss its proposed award. Counsel, of course, hope that all members of the arbitration panel come to this initial meeting for a discussion on the merits having read all the documentation and exhibits including the legal cases cited to them by counsel and, in general, are fully conversant with the issues in the case.

Once the panel has decided the issues, it is then the function of the chairman to prepare the written award. This sets forth in substantial detail the basis for the arbitrators' decision. In many instances, there is a format utilized by the Society of Maritime Arbitrators in preparing the written award. The award generally sets forth the issues in the case, the contentions of both sides and the panel's decision on each of the issues raised. The award is then sent to all parties. It is not the custom, as it is in England, for the arbitration panel to collect payment of their fees prior to issuance of the award. In many instances, the panel has already provided for security for its fees by requiring both parties to set up an escrow fund, generally with their counsel, in an amount that the arbitration panel obviously trusts will be sufficient to cover the costs and fees of the arbitrators.

It is evident from the above brief discussion of arbitration hearings that there are many potential causes of delay. A substantial cause is the inability of most commercial arbitrators to be prepared to sit as arbitrators during the entire day in that they are engaged in other full-time commercial activities. The schedules of the arbitrators and counsel are also a stumbling block, particularly if the arbitration panel is comprised of a cadre of those arbitrators who are involved in most of the arbitration proceedings in New York.

To sacrifice the fundamental concept of fair arbitration proceedings to the primary requirement of speed does not serve the urgent need for arbitration proceedings which will resolve disputes in a logical and commercially acceptable manner.

II. Legal criteria for conduct of arbitration proceedings

Courts have accepted the concept of arbitration as a commercial method of resolution of disputes between private parties. They have indicated that they must give broad leeway to an arbitrator's decision since this is what the parties bargained for. Courts have no business overruling arbitrators because their interpretation of a contract may be different from that of an arbitrator. A strict construction of the statutory requirements for vacating or overruling an award is adhered to by the Court. 9 USC §9 and 10. The goal of the United States Congress in enacting the Federal Arbitration Act was to establish arbitration as a desirable alternative to the complications and inherent delays of litigation. When arbitrators explain their conclusions in terms that offer even a barely colorable justification for the outcome reached, confirmation of the award by a Court cannot be prevented by litigants who merely argue, however persuasively, for a different result. *Andros Compania Maritima*, *S.A.* v. *Marc Rich & Co.*, *A.G.*, 579 F.2d 691 (2d Cir. 1978).

III. Consideration of evidence

An arbitration panel in the United States has wide discretion concerning introduction of evidence before the tribunal. It has full discretion to determine whether additional evidence is necessary or would simply prolong the proceedings. *Petroleum Transport*, *Ltd.* v. *Yacimientos Petroliferos Fiscales*, 419 F.Supp. 1233 (S.D.N.Y. 1976). The panel also has the duty of determining the relevancy of evidence that is brought before it. Barring a clear showing of an abuse of discretion, a Court will not vacate an award based upon improper evidence or lack of proper evidence. *Orion Shipping & Trading Company* v. *Eastern States Petroleum Corp. of Panama, S.A.*, 312 F. 2d 299 (2d Cir. 1962); *Harbor Island Spa, Inc.* v. *Norwegian American Line A/S*, 314 F.Supp. 471 (S.D.N.Y. 1970).

IV. Arbitration panels are not governed by rules of evidence

Arbitration tribunals, by their very nature, are intended to resolve commercial disputes. They are not required to, nor do they necessarily follow Rules of Evidence which would be required to be followed in the Court. They need not follow all the niceties of Federal Court procedure. They need provide the parties only with a fundamentally fair hearing. *Totem Marine Tug & Barge, Inc.* v. *North American Towing, Inc.*, 607 F.2d 649 (5th Cir. 1979); *Parsons & Wittemore Overseas Company* v. *Société Générale de L'Industrie du Papier* (*Rakta*), 508 F.2d 969 (2d Cir. 1974). Arbitration panels do, in many instances, accept hearsay evidence as they are entitled to do. As succinctly stated by one Court:

'If parties wish to rely on such technical objections, they should not include arbitration clauses in their contract.'

Petroleum Separating Company v. *Interamerican Refining Corporation*, 296 F.2d 1224 (2d Cir. 1961).

An arbitration panel may also decide that it does not wish to consider evidence on the issue of credibility; this will not be a valid ground for vacating the arbitration award. *Shearson Hayden Stone, Inc.* v. *Liang*, 653 F.2d 310 (7th Cir. 1981). In essence, an arbitration proceeding is informal in context; the common law rules of evidence are not binding. Arbitrators are empowered to conduct an arbitration fashion in any reasonable fashion. They are not restricted in any way in the introduction of evidence by witnesses or the method in which witnesses may testify. *Barker* v. *Government Employers Insurance Company*, 339 F.Supp. 1064 (D.D.C. 1972). Courts usually grant wide deference to arbitrators in their conduct of proceedings. They have discretion to exclude and sequester witnesses; they are the judges of admissibility and relevancy of evidence; they are not bound to hear all evidence tendered by the parties. Their primary obligation is to give each party an adequate opportunity to present evidence in arguments; the rules they utilize and methods to be considered are those that they may make up themselves. *Hoteles Condado Beach, et al.* v. *Union Tronquistas Local 901*, 763 F.2d 34 (1st Cir. 1985).

Parties who agree to arbitration proceedings must be content with their informalities. *Western Canada Steamship Company, Ltd.* v. *Cia de Navigacion San Leonardo*, 105 F.Supp. 452 (S.D.N.Y. 1952); *International Longshoremen's Association, AFL-CIO* v. *West Gulf Maritime Association*, 594 F. Supp. 670 (S.D.N.Y. 1984). However, this informality of arbitration must still give way to the requirement of a fundamentally fair hearing being afforded to the parties. The determination and relevance of evidence is a job entrusted to the arbitration panel; any mistake in handling this process does not necessarily constitute misconduct on the part of the arbitration panel. *Fairchild & Company, Inc.* v. *Richmond, Fredericksburg & Potomac Railroad Company*, 516 F.Supp. 1305 (D.C.C. 1981).

This wide discretion given to an arbitration panel can, in many ways, be the reason for substantial delays in the proceedings. Since the panel is not bound by the formal rules or procedures of evidence, it is required to give the parties an opportunity to be heard and present material evidence. *Ryan Walsh Stevedoring Company, Inc.* v. *General Longshoremen's Workers Union, et al.*, 509 F.Supp. 463 (E.D. La. 1981); *Wright-Bernet, Inc.* v. *Amalgamated Local Union No. 41*, 501 F.Supp. 72 (S.D. Ohio 1980). In general, they must offer the parties a fundamentally fair hearing. However, 'fundamental fairness does not require that an arbitrator must hear any and all evidence that a party must wish to offer, regardless of its length, repetitiveness or irrelevance.' *National Post Office, et al.* v. *U.S. Postal Service, et al.*, 751 F.2d 834 (6th Cir. 1985).

A panel has broad discretion to consider the evidence and may prohibit cumulative evidence. They are charged with the duty of determining what evidence is relevant and irrelevant; an error in deciding this issue must be one which so effects the rights of the party that it may be said to deprive him of the right of a fair hearing. *Fairchild, etc., supra*; *Newark Stereotypers Union No. 18* v. *Newark Morning Ledger Company*, 397 F.2d 594 (3d Cir. 1968).

V. Wide discretionary powers of panel in conducting hearings

Considering the above criteria, the panel is empowered with wide discretionary powers. It must be expected to take actions which will expedite proceedings. *Ballantine Books, Inc.* v. *Capital Distributing Company*, 302 F.2d 17 (2d Cir. 1962). It may decide whether additional evidence is necessary or would simply prolong a hearing. *Catz American Company* v. *Pearl Grange Food Exchange, Inc.* 292 F.Supp. 549 (S.D.N.Y. 1968). As part of their duties, arbitration panels may consider requests for postponement. Although an advantage of arbitration is speed and informality, an arbitrator should be expected to act affirmatively to simplify and expedite the proceedings before him. Legitimate efforts to move proceedings along expeditiously may be abrasive but are not grounds for vacating an arbitration award. *Fairchild & Company, Inc., et al., supra.* However, an arbitrary denial of a reasonable request for postponement may be a basis for vacating the award. *Tube and Steel Corp. of America* v. *Chicago Carbon Steel Products*, 319 F.Supp. 1302 (S.D.N.Y. 1970).

Since the main purpose of arbitration is the expeditious resolution of disputes, arbitrators are given very broad latitude and discretion by the Courts on this point. The Courts are extremely reluctant to interfere with arbitrators' determination of the procedural methods utilized during the arbitration proceedings. As stated above, an arbitration panel also has a duty to weigh all evidence presented, which includes post hearing briefs, in order to reach a reasoned decision. *Motor Expressman's Union* v. *Mistletoe Express Service*, 462 F.Supp. 143 (N.D. Texas 1978).

In substance, therefore, arbitration panels have almost carte blanche to conduct the proceedings in a manner designed to produce the desired results in an informal proceeding. Since arbitration panels have been given wide discretion by the Courts, this discretion should be exercised in support of expediting the hearings, keeping clearly before the panel, the basic criterion of the necessity for a fundamentally fair hearing.

VI. Suggestions for expedition of arbitration proceedings

Considering the criteria established by the Courts and the wide discretion given to arbitrators discussed above, we believe that their are a series of steps that could be taken to expedite arbitration proceedings and still retain the requirement of fundamental fairness. We recognize, of course, that a statement of general principles may not satisfy each case because of the peculiarities of the issues before the panel. Some of these concepts may be better suited to those disputes with substantial issues, material dispute of involved facts and convoluted legal concepts.

We therefore put forth the following suggestions:

1. Hearings, to the extent possible, should be held during the day or, if necessary, on weekends, particularly when witnesses are being produced from overseas. The parties are entitled to the full attention of the arbitration panel without their distraction, whether caused by business matters or due to fatigue caused by the length of the workday. In certain instances where chartering brokers are members of arbitration panels they have, unfortunately, continued to be involved in non-related Charter negotiations during recesses of the hearings or, in many instances, have been interrupted during the hearings to prepare a response to their counterpart's broker last offer within the short time frame that the offer remains open. Counsel, of course, can appreciate, at times, an emergency requiring arbitrators to conduct their own business during the hearing. Indeed, counsel themselves normally do not expect to be interrupted during the hearings unless an emergency occurs; however, we believe these interruptions to be most distracting, not only to the parties but also to the other members of the arbitration panel.

To the extent possible, however, our suggestion that hearings be held in major cases during the working day or on weekends will provide the parties and the panel with an uninterrupted period of time to conduct the hearings. We also suggest that, in the event the hearings are held in the evening, there be a time limit placed on the continuance of the hearings beyond a certain hour in order to assure the parties and the panel that they are devoting the full time and attention expected to the issues. The attention span of any individual who has worked a full day and then is involved in arbitration hearings that continue well into the late evening hours is necessarily depleted. On many hearings, witnesses have been brought in from overseas; they are required to testify during late evening hours in New York after having come a substantial distance and are subject to jet lag and fatigue. This is not the best situation for either party in which to find itself.

2. In order to eliminate some procedural activities that take place at the usual first hearing (see discussion section I.E *supra*) and permit the panel to get right into the merits of the controversy, we suggest that the panel prepare its disclosures, as discussed above, by mail prior to the first arbitration hearing. The result of this is that the initial hearing will address that issue only with regard to any additional questions that may be solicited by counsel.

3. Along these lines, we also suggest that prior to the first hearing, the panel set a deadline for the submission of preliminary documents, exhibits and legal memoranda which are to be exchanged simultaneously by the parties. This would permit the arbitration panel and counsel to have the documents that each side intends to rely upon in the preliminary hearing at least two weeks before the first hearing. The panel would then have the opportunity to review the documents and be familiar with the areas of dispute prior to assembling for the first hearing. This should, in most instances, expedite the first hearing and perhaps limit the entire arbitration to one hearing without the necessity of further hearings, once both sides have the documents and data of the other party in advance.

4. In major cases, we would suggest that each party advise the panel and opposing counsel of (a) the issues in the case, (b) the identity of the witnesses they intend to rely upon, (c) the designation of expert witnesses and the area of expertise, (d) list the documents to be relied upon and (e) prepare a list that sets forth the issues that the panel are going to be called upon to decide. This designation should also include a proposed stipulation or agreement as to undisputed facts so that the panel will be able to assess only the disputed issues without the necessity of hearing evidence that will only confirm that there are no disputes as to certain facts or issues. This is in line with the requirements of U.S. Federal Courts wherein counsel are directed to prepare a pre-trial order covering all these areas. It is designed to insure that the trial or arbitration is fully on the issues and not trial by ambush or surprise. This pre-trial order is intended to submit to the fact finder a road map of those issues that are being brought to the Court or, in this case the arbitration panel, for decision as well as giving the other side information regarding the identity and number of witnesses, and the area of expert testimony. Arbitration panels should encourage the parties to set forth as far in advance of the hearing date as possible an agreed stipulation of facts and documents.

5. We suggest that in major cases, where there have been a series of arbitration hearings spaced over a period of time and numerous exhibits introduced, the arbitration panel consider the presentation of oral argument after all legal memoranda have been filed by counsel. This argument would give each side a certain amount of time in order to highlight to the panel the position of each party. Naturally, the arbitration panel should be fully similar with all of the evidence and legal decisions cited by each party to them during the proceedings. They should be fully prepared to engage counsel or the parties in questioning as to those areas that require further clarification by the panel.

We believe that this method of review would greatly expedite the issuance of arbitration awards because the panel would have one final chance, after reviewing all the documents and evidence, of making sure that the issues and positions of all parties are fully comprehended and that each party has had a fair opportunity of presenting its position. This oral argument could be scheduled within a period of one or two weeks after the final legal memoranda have been exchanged. We anticipate that it should not be in excess of two to three hours total time but the time table for that can be regulated by the panel.

6. As of this moment, there is no deadline imposed by Courts or by the Federal Arbitration Act for the issuance of an arbitration award. The well known statement that 'Justice Delayed is Justice Denied' is equally applicable to arbitration proceedings. The parties have brought their disputes to the arbitration panel in the expectation of receiving a prompt, reasoned decision on these disputes. Any undue delay in issuing this award will not serve the interests of the parties nor the commercial rationale for utilization of arbitration proceedings. We recommend that the arbitration panel set for themselves a deadline within which the award will be issued. It may well be necessary to issue an award in the form of a truncated decision indicating the basic ruling of the panel on the merits of each issue with a more detailed explanatory reasoned award being issued in the future, if time does not permit the award to encompass all the panel's reasons within a reasonable time. We suggest a maximum period of three months within where an award should be issued. The issuance of the truncated award should probably satisfy the requirements of the Federal Arbitration Act for a final award and give the parties the satisfaction of having their disputes resolved as expeditiously as possible.

There are, of course, difficulties that must be considered, including the problem that may arise in seeking to confirm or vacate an award by the Court without detailed specific reasons as well as the possibility for misunderstanding of the succinct statement of the arbitration panel. In either event, there should be some deadline considered as reasonable by the arbitration panel within which they should issue the award. Arbitration awards that are not issued for eight to ten months after the closing of the hearings and exchange of final legal memoranda serve no ones interest. To the extent that the delay is due to the press of business of the chairman of the panel in his primary job or due to the extraordinary number of arbitrations in which the chairman may be involved, then perhaps this is time when the small group of arbitrators serving on most cases should be expanded.

7. We also suggest that arbitration panels have inherent power to impose sanctions upon the parties or their counsel for failing to meet deadlines without valid reasons. This may be the imposition of attorneys' fees in cases where the arbitration agreement permits the award of attorneys' fees; the award of arbitrators' fees solely against one party and, if necessary, the preclusion of evidence by one party, if deadlines on the production of documents or witnesses is not met. Arbitration panel tribunals, in the writer's opinion, have this inherent power as long as they adhere to the concept of a fundamentally fair hearing.

This concept does not require arbitrators to bear with purposeful delays and obstructionistic tactics by one of the parties to the detriment of the other party and the negation of the arbitration process. Although arbitration proceedings are informal, they still must be kept within the bounds of good judgment and judicious handling of the time frame.

VII. Sole arbitrators

Use of sole arbitrators in the United States has not normally been actively sought by the parties. The reason for this is undoubtedly the reluctance of two diverse interests, owner and charterer, to entrust the dispute to an individual who may be perceived to be more owner or charterer oriented. A sole arbitrator is one of the best methods of expediting arbitration proceedings but the participants utilizing this service must be convinced that they have a fair, impartial and unbiased arbitrator that will decide the issue solely on the evidence before him. There is already a procedure in the Society of Maritime Arbitrators for a simplified arbitration process before a sole arbitrator of claims not exceeding $15,000,000. A copy of this simplified procedure is annexed hereto.

The difficulty is that the limitation of the amount of the claim to $15,000,000 precludes most sole arbitration cases because of the economics involved in arbitration in the first instance. There is nothing to prevent the parties from modifying their arbitration agreement to provide for arbitration before a sole arbitrator in cases where the amount in dispute is in excess of that figure. It is submitted, in these instances, particularly where there is no basic dispute as to the facts and the sole issue is one of interpretation of the charter, a maritime attorney may be better suited to fulfill the role of a sole arbitrator. In that instance, an arbitration hearing could be held very promptly during normal working hours. The arbitrator would be able to sort out what issues of fact involved the legal issues and, in general, conduct a hearing that will permit the parties an expeditious resolution of their disputes.

The dilemma is, of course, the method of choosing the sole arbitrator, once the parties have agreed to the concept. In the absence of agreement by the parties to a specific nominee to be sole arbitrator, the issue then is how can a sole arbitrator be appointed. In this instance, we suggest the Court would be the proper forum to which the parties could go, but this in and of itself defeats the entire purpose of expedition in using a sole arbitrator. The parties must have substantial trust and confidence in the competence of the sole arbitrator to whom they are entrusting their decision.

One suggestion for the appointment of a lawyer as sole arbitrator is that if the parties cannot agree on the identity of the arbitrator, the arbitration agreement for sole arbitrator provide for the designation of a maritime attorney to be appointed from a panel of five lawyers who are members of the Arbitration Committee of the Maritime Law Association of the United States. Each party would then have the opportunity of listing their choice of each maritime attorney by ranking. The maritime attorney with the highest ranking or survivor of the designation process would then be designated as the sole arbitrator, in the absence of a specific agreement for a certain individual. This would ensure that the parties have the benefit of an arbitrator who is an experienced maritime attorney fully familiar with maritime arbitration, as this is the purpose of the Maritime Arbitration Committee of the Maritime Law Association. Certain cases are not well suited for sole arbitration if the arbitrator is a maritime attorney. Cases like calculation of laytime, determining quantities of ROB aboard vessels, stevedore damage claims, etc., are those types of cases that would be well suited for resolution by a commercial man as sole arbitrator.

It is regrettable that the use of a sole arbitrator is not more widespread in the United States. Contrary to the provisions in England, wherein if one party does not nominate an arbitrator within a certain period of time the arbitrator named by the initiating party sits as a sole arbitrator, the American process does not provide for that alternative. Resort must be made to the Court to resolve this impasse. This is one of the reasons for potential delay in completion of an arbitration panel. An agreement to arbitrate before a sole arbitrator will remove a substantial potential for built-in delays from the arbitration process. However, as arbitration is the creature of agreement by the parties, if one of the parties decides for its own purpose not to agree to a sole arbitrator, then there is no practical method for compelling arbitration in this fashion, in the absence of a specific agreement to do so.

VIII. Composition of arbitration panel – commercial men or maritime attorneys

We have already discussed the issue of use of maritime attorneys as sole arbitrators, particularly on those disputes that are specifically related to the construction of the terms of the contract or clearly are legal issues. We do not at all suggest that maritime attorneys would be a proper choice to consider a complex dispatch demurrage dispute or an assessment of the performance of the vessel's engines during a long term time charter. These matters are, undoubtedly, much better handled by commercial men who deal with these issues on a a daily basis and have the technical expertise and background to understand the process.

However, as to the composition of the usual three man arbitration panel, we suggest the possibility of utilizing maritime attorneys as the third arbitrator or umpire. This will depend upon the type of case involved. In complex cases that will involve (*1*) considerable number of witnesses, (*2*) substantial documentation, (*3*) complex evidentiary matters, and (*4*) issues as to burden of proof, then we believe that the assistance of a maritime attorney as an arbitrator will prove invaluable to the arbitration panel.

As indicated above, even though arbitration proceedings in the United States are relatively informal and do not normally adhere to the rules of evidence, disjointed proceedings and arbitrary rulings on crucial issues are not the norm. However, many maritime attorneys have had prior experience in the commercial field, as well as practical sailing experience in the Merchant Marine or in the U.S. Navy; they are also quite familiar with matters dealing with technical aspects of vessels. Their forte as attorneys, however, is legal analysis and problem solving, which is what the parties want arbitration panels to do in connection with their disputes. Maritime attorneys are quite familiar with procedural matters, the mechanics of conducting proceedings, martialing and analyzing evidence submitted by the parties, considering issues of credibility and, in general, are well suited to resolve issues and disputes brought to an arbitration panel by virtue of their education and experience.

The legal concept of burden of proof is one that unfortunately at times appears to be totally devoid from arbitration tribunals. Burden of proof has among its elements a burden of production or going forward and a burden of persuasion. Although the claimant always has the burden of persuasion, which never shifts, he may produce suffficient evidence so that his opponent's failure to adduce contradictory proof either may lead to a decision for the claimant or must lead to such a ruling. *Willingham* v. *Secretary of*

Health, Education and Welfare, 377 F.Supp. 1254 (SD Fla. 1974); It has two elements, the burden of producing evidence and the burden of persuading the fact finder. *Abilene Sheet Metal, Inc.* v. *N.L.R.B.* 619 F.2d 332 (5th Cir. 1980). E. Cleary, McCormick's Handbook of the Law of Evidence §336 (2d ed. 1972). The claimant bears the burden of providing evidence from which its claim can be established. *Compagnie des Bauxites de Guinee* v. *Insurance Company of North America*, 551 F.Supp. 1239 (W.D. Pa. 1982).

There are many instances of evidence permitted in arbitration tribunals that would never be permitted in Court proceedings. Even though arbitrations are informal, there should be some basic guidelines concerning the utilization of evidence and the weight to be given it. By virtue of the broad leeway given arbitration decisions by the Courts, arbitrators are generally extremely lenient in accepting documents and testimony concerning data that may not necessarily be within the personal knowledge of the writer or witness; in many instances the evidence involves hearsay once or twice removed. Although arbitration panels are not required to follow the rules of evidence, (see discussion section IV *supra*) there should at least be some minimal attention given to them and the burden of proof, which are designed to insure that relevant, material and competent evidence is available to the fact finders, viz, the arbitrators.

We submit that maritime attorneys would be most helpful to arbitration panels, as chairmen, in assessing the evidence and the weight it should be given or at least pointing out to the other members of the panel the pitfalls that await the unwary panel in reliance upon evidence that is so defective as to warrant immediate dismissal of a claim. We concede that an arbitration clause calling only for appointment of commercial men does not permit the utilization of a maritime attorney as an arbitrator at any time. It is only if the parties will agree to modify the arbitration clause that will permit a maritime attorney to sit as a member of the panel.

We suggest modification of the usual arbitration clauses to provide that the majority of the panel must be commercial men but that one of the members of the panel, not necessarily the chairman, may be a maritime attorney. This is an option given to the parties, not a specific requirement that there must be a maritime attorney on the panel. In certain instances, as we have indicated, there would be no practical reason for having a maritime attorney sit as a member of the panel. However, if the parties have the option to nominate a maritime attorney, they should be able to feel somewhat assured that the evidence produced by the parties, however defective, would be reviewed by an impartial, unbiased, experienced maritime attorney, who would be able to consider the weight to be given to that evidence.

IX. Conclusion

As indicated in our introduction, the purpose of this paper was to submit certain views of the writer concerning the very troublesome problem in the

United States, and elsewhere, of delays encountered in arbitration proceedings. We do not intend to exclude counsel as one of the culprits in causing delays, nor do we suggest that the use of counsel at all times during the hearings expedite them in any way. In essence, what we are saying is that there is no reason why arbitration hearings are not proceeding as expeditiously as they should and as the parties want them to do. The writer believes that the parties are entitled to an arbitration panel that is not hampered by the pressures of the commercial world in which they must deal every day when considering substantial arbitrable issues in the late evening hours or during a very short period during the lunch hour when arbitrators have to travel some distance from their daily jobs to attend the hearings.

We submit that the present method is not the best means of resolving disputes between parties. It imposes substantial burdens, both physical and mental, upon those arbitrators who are attempting to give their full time and attention to the issues submited to them but are also diverted from these activities by the pressures of their daily job. Obviously, a balance must be struck between the necessities of private employment and the availability of competent, conscientious, unbiased, experienced commercial men sitting as arbitrators. We do not suggest that we have the solution; we merely have indicated some methods that may be utilized, tempered as they may be by the issues in each case.

We have considered these issues both from the viewpoint as counsel for vessel Owners and Charterers as parties in an arbitration as well as an arbitrator. We believe that a conscientious, concerted effort by members of the arbitration community and counsel can meet the demands of the parties for a fair, impartial and expeditious arbitration. The Arbitration Committee of the Maritime Law Association is working closely with the Society of Maritime Arbitrators along these lines.

There is no ready answer to these issues but the energy and enthusiasm of those involved in maritime arbitrations convinces us that these problems will be resolved. We are delighted at being afforded the opportunity once again, after London, New York and Monaco, to exchange these thoughts with members of the International Maritime Arbitration Community.

SOCIETY OF MARITIME ARBITRATORS, INC.
26 Broadway – Room 1200
New York, N.Y. 10004

Rules for Arbitration Procedures

Adopted 12 May 1964, Revised 1 July 1974
Revised 15 September 1983

Federal Arbitration Act Governs

The United States Arbitration Act (9 USC §§1–14), hereinafter referred to as 'the Act', provides procedures for the enforcement of maritime arbitration agreements in federal courts. Its provisions govern all maritime arbitrations conducted under the auspices of the Society of Maritime Arbitrations, Inc. and the Maritime Arbitration Rules which follow shall be subordinate to the Act in the event of any conflict.

The United States Arbitration Act is reproduced below in full.

THE ACT

§1. 'Maritime transactions' and 'commerce' defined; exceptions to operation of title

'Maritime transactions', as herein defined, means charter parties, bills of lading of water carriers, agreements relating to wharfage, supplies furnished vessels or repairs to vessels, collisions, or any other matters in foreign commerce which, if the subject of controversy, would be embraced within admiralty jurisdiction; 'commerce', as herein defined means commerce among the several States or with foreign nations, or in any Territory of the United States or in the District of Columbia, or between any such Territory and another, or any such Territory and any State or foreign nation or between the District of Columbia and any State or Territory or foreign nation, but nothing herein contained shall apply to contracts of employment of seamen, railroad employees, or any other class of workers engaged in foreign or interstate commerce. 30 July 1947, c.392 §1,61 Stat. 669.

§2. Validity, irrevocability, and enforcement of agreements to arbitrate

A written provision in any maritime transaction or a contract evidencing a transaction involving commerce to settle by arbitration a controversy thereafter arising out of such contract or transaction or the refusal to perform the whole or any part thereof, or an agreement in writing to submit to arbitration an existing controversy arising out of such a contract, transaction, or refusal, shall be valid, irrevocable, and enforceable, save upon such grounds as exist at law or in equity for the revocation of any contract. 30 July 1947, c.392. §1,61 Stat. 669.

§3. Stay of proceedings where issue therein referable to arbitration

If any suit or proceeding be brought in any of the courts of the United States upon any issue referable to arbitration under an agreement in writing for such arbitration, the courts in which such suit is pending, upon being satisfied that the issue involved in such suit or proceeding is referable to arbitration under such an agreement, shall on application of one of the parties stay the trial of the action until such arbitration has been had in accordance with the terms of the agreement, providing the applicant for the stay is not in default in proceeding with such arbitration. 30 July 1947, c.392 §1,61 Stat. 669.

§4. Failure to arbitrate under agreement; petition to United States Court having jurisdiction for order to compel arbitration; notice and service thereof; hearing and determination

A party aggrieved by the alleged failure, neglect, or refusal of another to arbitrate under a written agreement for arbitration may petition any United States district court which, save for such agreement, would have jurisdiction under Title 28, in a civil action or in admiralty of the subject matter of a suit arising out of the controversy between the parties, for an order directing that such arbitration proceed in the manner provided for in such agreement. Five days' notice in writing of such application shall be served upon the party in default. Service thereof shall be made in the manner provided by the Federal Rules of Civil Procedure. The court shall hear the parties and upon being satisfied that the making of the agreement for arbitration or the failure to comply therewith is not in issue, the court shall make an order directing the parties to proceed to arbitration in accordance with the terms of the agreement. The hearing and proceedings, under such agreement, shall be within the district in which the petition for an order directing such arbitration is filed. If the making of the arbitration agreement or the failure, neglect, or refusal to perform the same be in issue, the court shall proceed summarily to the trial thereof. If no jury trial be demanded by the party alleged to be in default, or if the matter in dispute is within admiralty jurisdiction, the court shall hear and determine such issue. Where such an issue is raised, the party alleged to be in default may, except in cases of admiralty, on or before the return day of the notice of application, demand a jury trial of such issue, and upon such demand the court shall make an order referring the issue or issues to a jury in the manner provided by the Federal Rules of Civil Procedure, or may specially call a jury for that purpose. If the jury find that no agreement in writing for arbitration was made or that there is no default in proceeding thereunder, the proceeding shall be dismissed. If the jury find that an agreement for arbitration was made in writing and that there is a default in proceeding thereunder, the court shall make an order summarily directing the parties to proceed with the arbitration in accordance with the terms thereof. As amended 3 September 1954, c.1263 §19.68 Stat. 1233.

§5. Appointment of arbitrators or umpire

If in the agreement provision be made for a method of naming or appointing an arbitrator or arbitrators or any umpire such method shall be followed; but if no method be provided therein, or if a method be provided and any party thereto shall fail to avail himself of such method, or if for any other reason there shall be a lapse in the naming of an arbitrator or arbitrators or umpire, or in filling a vacancy, then upon the application of either party to the controversy the court shall designate and appoint an arbitrator or arbitrators or umpire, as the case may require, who shall act under the said agreement with the same force and effect as if he or they had been specifically named therein; and unless otherwise provided in the agreement the arbitration shall be by a single arbitrator. 30 July 1947, c.392 §1,61 Stat. 669.

§6. Application heard as motion
Any application to the court hereunder shall be made and heard in the manner provided by law for the making and hearing of motions, except as otherwise herein expressly provided. 30 July 1947, c.392 §1,61 Stat. 669.

§7. Witnesses before arbitrators; fees, compelling attendance
The arbitrators selected either as prescribed in this title or otherwise, or a majority of them, may summon in writing any person to attend before them or any of them as a witness and in a proper case to bring with him or them any book, record document, or paper which may be deemed material as evidence in the case. The fees for such attendance shall be the same as the fees of witnesses before masters of the United States courts. Said summons shall issue in the name of the arbitrator or arbitrators, or a majority of them, and shall be signed by the arbitrators, or a majority of them, and shall be directed to the said person and shall be served in the same manner as subpoenas to appear and testify before the court; if any person or persons so summoned to testify shall refuse or neglect to obey said summons, upon petition the United States district court for the district in which such arbitrators, or a majority of them, are sitting may compel the attendance of such person or persons before said arbitrator or arbitrators, or punish said person or persons for contempt in the same manner provided by law for securing the attendance of witnesses or their punishment for neglect or refusal to attend in the courts of the United States. 30 July 1947, c.392, §1,61 Stat. 669; 31 October 1951, c.665, §14.65 Stat. 715.

§8. Proceedings begun by libel in admiralty and seizure of vessel or property
If the basis of jurisdiction be a cause of action otherwise justiciable in admiralty, then, notwithstanding anything herein to the contrary, the party claiming to be aggrieved may begin his proceeding hereunder by libel and seizure of the vessel or other property of the other party according to the usual course of admiralty proceedings, and the court shall then have jurisdiction to direct the parties to proceed with the arbitration and shall retain jurisdiction to enter its decree upon the award. 30 July 1947, c.392, §1,61 Stat. 669.

§9. Award of arbitrators; confirmation; jurisdiction; procedure
If the parties in their agreement have agreed that a judgment of the court shall be entered upon the award made pursuant to the arbitration, and shall

specify the court, then at any time within one year after the award is made any party to the arbitration may apply to the court so specified for an order confirming the award, and thereupon the court must grant such an order unless the award is vacated, modified, or corrected, as prescribed in sections 10 and 11 of this title. If no court is specified in the agreement of the parties, then such application may be made to the United States court in and for the district within which such award was made. Notice of the application shall be served upon the adverse party, and thereupon the court shall have jurisdiction of such party as though he had appeared generally in the proceeding. If the adverse party is a resident of the district within which the award was made, such service shall be made upon the adverse party or his attorney as prescribed by law for service of notice of motion in an action in the same court. If the adverse party shall be a nonresident, then the notice of the application shall be served by the marshall of any district within which the adverse party may be found in like manner as other process of the court. 30 July 1947, c.382, §1,61 Stat. 669.

§10. Same; vacation; grounds; rehearing

In either of the following cases the United States court in and for the district wherein the award was made may make an order vacating the award upon the application of any party to the arbitration:

(a) Where the award was procured by corruption, fraud, or undue means.

(b) Where there was evident partiality or corruption in the arbitrators, or either of them.

(c) Where the arbitrators were guilty of misconduct in refusing to postpone the hearing, upon sufficient cause shown or in refusing to hear evidence pertinent and material to the controversy; or of any other misbehavior by which the rights of any party have been prejudiced.

(d) Where the arbitrators exceeded their powers, or so imperfectly executed them that a mutual, final, and definite award upon the subject matter submitted was not made.

(e) Where an award is vacated and the time within which the agreement required the award to be made has not expired the court may, in its discretion, direct a rehearing by the arbitrators. 30 July 1947, c.392. §1,61 Stat. 669.

§11. Same; modification or correction; grounds order

In either of the following cases the United States court in and for the district wherein the award was made may make an order modifying or correcting the award upon the application of any party to the arbitration.

(a) Where there was an evident material miscalculation of figures or an evident material mistake in the description of any person, thing, or propety referred to in the award.

(b) Where the arbitrators have awarded upon a matter not submitted to them, unless it is a matter not affecting the merits of the decision upon the matter submitted.
(c) Where the award is imperfect in matter of form not affecting the merits of the controversy.

The order may modify and correct the award, so as to effect the intent thereof and promote justice between the parties. 30 July 1947, c. 392, §1,61 Stat. 669.

§12. Notice of motion to vacate or modify; service; stay of proceedings

Notice of a motion to vacate, modify, or correct an award must be served upon the adverse party or his attorney within three months after the award is filed or delivered. If the adverse party is a resident of the district within which the award was made, such service shall be made upon the adverse party or his attorney as prescribed by law for service of notice of motion in an action in the same court. If the adverse party shall be a nonresident then the notice of the application shall be served by the marshal of any district within which the adverse party may be found in like manner as other process of the court. For the purpose of the motion any judge who might make an order to stay the proceedings in an action brought in the same court may make an order, to be served with the notice of motion, staying the proceedings of the adverse party to enforce the award, 30 July 1947, c.392, §1,61 Stat. 669.

§13. Papers filed with order on motions; judgment; docketing; force and effect; enforcement

The party moving for an order confirming, modifying, or correcting an award shall, at the time such order is filed with the clerk for the entry of judgment thereon, also file the following papers with the clerk:
(a) The agreement; the selection or appointment, if any, of an additional arbitrator or umpire; and each written extension of the time, if any, within which to make the award.
(b) The award.
(c) Each notice, affidavit, or other paper used upon an application to confirm, modify, or correct the award, and a copy of each order of the court upon such an application.

The judgment shall be docketed as if it were rendered in an action.

The judgment so entered shall have the same force and effect, in all respects, as, and be subject to all the provisions of law relating to, a judgment in an action; and it may be enforced as if it had been rendered in an action in the court in which it is entered. 30 July 1947, c.392, §1,61 Stat. 669.

§14. Contracts not affected

This title shall not apply to contracts made prior to 1 January 1926, 30 July 1947, c.392, §1,61 Stat. 669.

APPENDIX A

SIMPLIFIED PROCEDURE

RULES

1. The total amount claimed by *either* party shall not exceed $15,000,000.
2. The parties must agree to arbitrate under this procedure, waiving all other arbitral agreements.
3. The dispute shall be submitted to a single arbitrator who is to be selected by the parties from the Roster of the Society of Maritime Arbitrators, Inc. If they are unable to agree upon an arbitrator, the Secretary of the Society, after receipt of a detailed Submission Agreement, is to select from the Society Roster, the names of ten (10) Members who are well versed in the matter(s) under dispute. From this list, each party is to submit to the Secretary within seven (7) days the names of the candidates in order of his preference. The Secretary, by means of points (10 for first preference, 9 for second, etc.) will determine the Member selected on the basis of maximum points scored. In the event of a tie, the Secretary, at his discretion, will then select from the Society's Roster an Arbitrator who is well versed in the matter(s) under dispute.
4. Upon accepting the appointment, the Arbitrator shall make his disclosure by writing in accordance with Section No. 8 to the two parties.
5. Having once accepted the Simplified Procedure, the parties may only revert to Standard Procedures by the joint agreement of all parties. There shall be no more than one hearing, however, if the arbitrator finds during the course of the hearing, that the arbitration cannot be confined to a single hearing, or if subsequently, the limit on monetary amount under Rule 1 is exceeded by the presentation of additional claims during the hearing, then he may advise the parties that Simplified Procedure cannot be applied, and the Arbitration will continue on Standard Procedure with the Arbitrator acting as sole Arbitrator. The parties may jointly elect to waive oral hearings. In this event, the Arbitrator is to be so advised in writing at time of presentation of Submission Agreement.
6. A signed detailed Submission Agreement, stipulating inter alia the Simplified Procedure in accordance with these Rules, is to be presented to the Arbitrator prior to the hearing; together with a preliminary memorandum from each litigant, outlining each party's position in the dispute.
7. A stenographic record will be dispensed with unless specially requested by the parties, in advance.
8. Briefs, if desired by the parties or by the arbitrator, will be submitted not later than two weeks after the termination of the hearing or after receipt of the record (if any), whichever shall later occur. In the event

the oral hearing is waived, briefs if required, will be submitted not later than two weeks from date of presentation of the respective case.

9. The Arbitrator shall deliver his decision in writing not later than four weeks after the case is closed, circumstances beyond his control excepted.
10. Each party to the dispute will deposit $425 with the Secretary of the Society in advance of the hearing. It is understood that the Arbitrator's total fees and expenses will not exceed $800 and any unused portions will be returned when the decision is rendered. $50.00 of this sum is to be retained by the Society for its services.
11. The United States Arbitration Act (9 USC #1–14) shall govern all maritime arbitrations conducted under these Rules, which shall be subordinate to the Act in event of any conflict.
12. Except where in conflict with the preceeding Rules 1–11, the Rules of the Society of Maritime Arbitrators, Inc., as incorporated herein shall be deemed to be part of the Simplified Procedure Rules.

THE UN CONVENTION ON THE CARRIAGE OF GOODS BY SEA, 1978, HAMBURG RULES, ITS FUTURE AND THE DEMANDS OF DEVELOPING COUNTRIES*

Professor Rolf Herber

Institut für Seerecht und Seehandelsrecht; *University of Hamburg*

* Paper, delivered at a Symposion in Torún (Poland) in September 1985. The Author was President of the UN Conference in Hamburg 1978.

I. Introduction

On 31 March 1978, the UN Conference held at Hamburg adopted the United Nations Convention on the Carriage of Goods by Sea, 1978 (Hamburg Rules). The Convention was adopted by Representatives of 72 States (78 States participated in the Conference), of which 68 voted in favour, none voted against and four (Canada, Greece, Liberia and Switzerland) abstained.

During the period when the Convention was opened for signature, until 30 April 1979, the Convention was signed by 27 States. The Convention received up to now 3 ratifications and 7 accessions.

According to its final clauses it will enter into force after 20 ratifications or accessions.

The preparatory work done within UNCITRAL has taken seven years. It was initiated by a Recommendation of the International Shipping Legislation Group of UNCTAD adopted in 1971 and stating the need for examination in view to a revision of the Brussel's Convention on Bills of Lading (1924) (Hague Rules) and the Brussel's Protocol thereto (1968) (Visby Rules).

UNCTAD, which considers itself as acting mainly on behalf of the interests of Developing Countries had proposed 'to review the economic and commercial aspects of international legislation and practices in the field of B/L from the standpoint of their conformity with needs of economic development in particular of the Developing Countries and to make appropriate recommendations'.

UNCITRAL, setting up a particular working group for this topic, devoted seven years of intense work to that revision. After having been approved by UNCTAD, a draft convention was submitted to the Hamburg Conference. There, as mentioned, a large majority of States voted in favour of the New Convention.

In spite of this history and the great endeavour of all States participating in the work the Convention did, up to now, not enter into force. And there is little hope that it will do so during the years to come. To the contrary, the Visby Protocol of 1968 received, after conclusion of the Hamburg Conference, a number of ratifications. Including ratifications by Developing Countries, such as Egypt, Sri Lanka, Tonga. – After March 1978 the Visby Rules have been ratified (or adhered to) by important European Shipping States as well, namely GDR, Poland, Netherlands and Spain.

The revision of the existing maritime transport conventions has been undertaken in order to meet concerns of a great number of States. These concerns were based on various reasons. And the Conference has taken a decision on the basis of a compromise which seemed, at that time, to satisfy the great majority of delegations. Including those of the Developing Countries which might perhaps have expected even more change towards their ideas but which had accepted this solution in a spirit of compromise. The same goes for many industrialized countries.

More than seven years after the conclusion of the Hamburg Rules it may be asked why the States are so reluctant in transforming the new rules into their law. It is true, the setting in force of an international convention usually takes years if not decades. But in the present context it is not only the elapse of time which leads to the sceptical prospective for the future but even more the fact that there is still, within the industry, more of critic than of support for the new Convention. In spite of the fact and acknowledgement that the Convention solves a lot of technical problems which are not sufficiently clarified by existing law. The point of disagreement is nearly exclusively the so-called shift of liability which means that the new Convention provides for liability of the carrier in cases of fault or neglect of the master and the crew in the course of management or navigation of the ship. And the discussion sometimes gives the impression that a similar degree of emotion which before the adoption of the Convention was to be found mainly on the part of the cargo-interested countries now conducts the more shipping-oriented States.

Reason enough, it seems to me, to have a look at the history of, the reasons for and the prospect for further revision of the actual international legal system. And in particular to ask oneself whether the interests of the Developing Countries which have been considered so much involved at the beginning of the work are no longer existent so that even the most important countries among them hesitate to ratify the new Convention.

II. Reasons for revision of the present international rules on carriage of goods by sea

1. POLITICAL REASONS

When, in 1967, UNCITRAL was created it was one of its main tasks to examine the possibilities to make acceptable, if necessary, existing international Conventions to all States of the world. One of these Conventions which was outdated by the elapse of time and new technical and economic developments was the Hague Rules of 1924. This Convention certainly needed modernization after nearly half a century of existence. Such modernization, in fact, had been undertaken by the Brussel's Protocol (Visby Rules) of 1968. An attempt, which seemed to fail at least at that time.

There were many reasons in favour of revision of the Hague and even of the Visby Rules. Part of them was of a legal, part of them of an economic nature. But probably the most important incentive was a political shortcoming of the existing conventions:

It was by means of ratifications of mostly European States that the Developing States which formed part of the community of Member States to a large extent were tied to the Convention by force of a ratification by their former colonial mother country. And at the Brussel's Conference of 1968, again, the industrialized countries played the most important if not the only role.

It is understandable, therefore, that the Developing Countries were in favour of a revision of that system to which they could contribute on an equal footing. This was not only a matter of selfconsciousness but, as well, a matter of suspicion that the existing system on carriage of goods by sea was detrimental for the economy of Developing Countries. For the Hague Rules in 1924 had been adopted as a measure to stabilize the role of liner conferences by granting similar trade conditions to all participating shipping companies. And the capital-intensive sea trade provided to a large extent by liner conferences was one of the reasons which, in view of the Developing Countries, led to an unbalanced economic situation of Developing Countries in sea trade.

UNCITRAL, because of its composition taking into account all parts and legal systems of the world, seemed to be an appropriate body to carry on a revision of the Hague Rules and granting sufficient participation of countries of all parts of the world including the Developing Countries. In fact, the Developing Countries in UNCITRAL had a 2/3 majority.

2. LEGAL REASONS

It may well be that the political reasons were the most important incentive for revision. But there were legal reasons as well. The Hague Rules of 1924 did, on one hand, unify in practice the conditions of liner trading during nearly half a century. But they were, legally spoken, not an ideal convention. Basis of the 1924 Brussel's Conference was a compromise: Compulsory liability of the carrier up to certain limitation amounts was fixed for so-called commercial fault committed by the owner himself and his crew. On the other hand the owner should not be liable for fault in the navigation and management of the ship performed by the crew. This compromise originally was meant to be the first step of doing away with the liberty of shipowners to exonerate themselves by conditions incorporated in Bills of Lading. Its justification was more and more questioned: One saw its merits at the doorstep of unification of maritime commercial law, but it seemed no longer necessary to many States to preserve the privilege of carriers forever.

And, in addition, there are among the neutral provisions of the Convention a great deal of provisions which could be improved. It is normally said that the Hague/Visby Rules grant a high degree of uniformity in maritime law all over the world. This is certainly true, but many provisions of the

Hague Rules are unclear, others unjust and some of them still today widely unknown even in the Contracting States. The Hague Rules – even in the United Kingdom from where the most important elements had been brought to it – were never considered as an ideal legal instrument; they left open too many choices for national courts and were drafted in a manner which was not understandable in many Contracting States, as they had their origin in contractual clauses. And most important: The Hague/Visby Rules did not govern all elements of a contract on sea-carriage but only a few elements – certainly, however, the most important. And part of the rules contained in the present conventions, moreover, is overruled by the technical and economic development.

The main example of outdated provisions is the limitation provision. The gold clause, originally based on the pound Sterling and then transformed into Franc Poincaré by the Visby Protocol, was unable to fulfill its function any more; this problem, it is true, was solved in the meantime, after the Hamburg Conference, by a Gold Protocol to the Visby Rules accepting the Special Drawing Right (SDR). The same goes for the package or unit-limitation which was, as such, no longer able to solve problems of container transport. This point was solved as well by the Visby Rules.

But there were and are other topics which have not been remedied by the Protocol of 1968. E.g. the structure of the Hague Rules, which is based on the concept of each contract on carriage of goods by Sea being represented in a Bill of Lading; nowadays carriage of goods without negotiable document is more and more frequent. Then the particular rules on deck cargo which is a common form of transportation in container trade. The lack of rules on through- and on-carriage, of jurisdiction and arbitration clauses and of many other aspects of modern marine practice in detail. And one, perhaps most important element: The Hague/Visby Rules have taken, as already mentioned, the clauses incorporated by commercial practice into Bills of Lading. They are drafted according to requirements of Anglo-American case law. Therefore, it was difficult to apply them in civil law countries on an equal footing. In the meantime transportation conventions in other fields of law, for instance the widespread Road Transportation Convention CMR, were based on a more systematical, Roman law concept and had sustained the test of practical applicability for the sake of greater uniformity.

3. ECONOMIC REASONS

The most controversial reason was the economic one. When UNCTAD passed its recommendation for revision a study by its secretariat had been carried out investigating the economic impact of the Hague Rules. Whereas the legal inaccuracies could not, of course, be evaluated as to its economical impact exactly, it was mainly the basic political decision of the Hague Rules which formed the subject of economic investigation: The rule providing for legal exoneration of the carrier from liability for damages caused by fault or neglect of the crew in connection with the management or navigation of the ship. It seemed to be clear that such a rule was contrary to the interest of the shipper who had to insure this risk on his own. And, in addition, this situation was considered to be detrimental to the interests of the Developing Countries in particular which were considered mainly to be in a position of predominantly cargo-interested countries. It has, in the discussion, been mentioned that the Hague Rules in their origin were connected with the establishment of the present liner conference system because for such a system with permanent freight rates common conditions for transportation were necessary. And the liner conference system in particular has met the objection of Developing Countries as a means of economic power.

It was, therefore, from the beginning of the work in UNCTAD and UNCITAL an important issue for Developing Countries to do away with this exception for nautical fault. This shift of liability towards the carrier was, however, not only the aim of Developing Countries; many industrialized countries with prevailing cargo interests shared this view.

III. UN Convention on the carriage of goods by sea, 1978 (Hamburg Rules)

1. HISTORY

I need not repeat here the history which led to the Hague Rules of 1924. This Convention is now more than 60 years old. And the technical and commercial development has overruled its provisions to a large extent.

This started already immediately after the conclusion of the Convention when the Pound Sterling whch constituted the unit for calculation of the limitation figure lost its gold cover. Since then it was unclear how the £100 had to be transformed into national currencies and, therefore, the amount available for the shipper sustaining damage was different in the Contracting States.

A second element of the limitation rule became more and more dubious: the package or unit concept. In 1924 general cargo normally did consist of chests, drums and barrels. Consolidation of these goods first by pallets and then by containers took place in a progressive manner. The average value of a piece of cargo which might have been in the neighbourhood of the £100 in 1924 increased as a consequence of this development. A 40-foot-container nowadays represents a value far beyond the amount of DM 1,250. – which is the equivalent of the Hague Rules' limitation sum in the Federal Republic of Germany and which is, under our jurisprudence, still the limitation figure applicable to a full container.

There were other shortcomings as well, mainly the rule of deck cargo. And it was questioned whether the exception for nautical fault was still justified in view of the fact that the carrier, as a consequence of modern means of wireless communication, was able to control his crew at any place in the world.

After World War II, therefore, a revision of the Hague Rules seemed unavoidable. It was prepared by the CMI which had worked out the Hague Rules. The draft was submitted to a Brussel's Diplomatic Conference in 1967, which continued in 1968 and adopted the Brussel's Protocol named Visby-Rules.

This Protocol added to the Hague Rules only few changes. Main improvement was the replacement of the per-package-limitation by a combined limitation rule providing for a limitation per package or unit and a limitation per kilogram at choice of the shipper. The figures had been expressed in Poincaré Francs, a monetary unit which at that time was usually applied in international conventions and which was easily transferable into the national currencies of all countries being a member to the International Monetary Fund. Moreover, there were some changes on minor points such as the scope of application and the value of proof which the B/L represents. But there was, as suggestion of the CMI, a decision of the Conference not to accept amendments which had in mind to touch upon the basic compromise of the Hague Rules – the relatively low limitation amount and the exception for nautical fault on the one hand and the compulsory liability of the carier on the other. In spite of the desire of many delegations the CMI refused such amendments even to be discussed at the Diplomatic Conference. So the Visby-Rules were restricted to the changes mentioned above.

After that decision many States had the impression that a more global modernization of the international rules on carriage of goods by sea was necessary for the reasons mentioned already under II. They saw a chance to do such a revision within UNCITRAL which was created approximately at the same time. UNCITRAL had the task to promote unification of law and, in particular, to make existing conventions acceptable to all States of the world if they were not. This was the starting point for the UNCTAD decision which led immediately to the creation of a working group of UNCITAL to follow the UNCTAD recommendation.

This working group, under the chairmanship of Prof. Chafik (Egypt), worked out an entirely new convention. The draft was submited to UNCTAD and to all States of the world and received the approval of the great majority. Therefore it was submitted to a Diplomatic Conference under the auspices of the United Nations which was held, at the invitation of the Federal Republic of Germany, at Hamburg. There it took place in March 1978 where the United Nations Convention on Carriage of Goods by Sea, the so-called Hamburg Rules, was finally adopted.

I mentioned already the number of votes in favour of the new Convention: 68 with 4 delegations abstaining.

2. THE BASIC COMPROMISE OF THE HAMBURG CONFERENCE

One of the most controversial topics discussed during the preparatory work in UNCITRAL was whether the exception for nautical fault should be deleted or not. There were some States, few but important ones, which were very strongly in favour of retaining the apportionment of liability provided for in the Hague Rules. The reason was mainly that commercial practice was accustomed to it and any change would probably cause additional costs. Firstly, because any change of law might well amount to additional expenses. Secondly, because the attribution of liabilities foreseen in the Hague Rules was, in their view, the most effective balance of mutual obligations if not under the general ideas of justice then under the viewpoint of insurability of the risks to bear by either contractual party.

It was this element of the Hague Rules which put the whole result of the Conference in danger. Therefore it was necessary to reach a compromise which was done by a small informal negotiating group consisting of representatives of Argentina, Czechoslovakia, Ecuador, Ghana, India, Mexico, Netherlands, Norway, the Philippines, Poland, Uganda, the UK, USA, USSR. This group reached the following compromise:

The exception of the Hague Rules from liability of the carrier in case of nautical fault was deleted. On the other hand the limits fixed by the Convention per kilogram or per package or unit – according to the Visby-Rules – were fixed on a relatively low level, namely 2.5 SDR per kilogram or 835 SDR per package or other shipping unit. And, moreover, the breakability of this limitation was restricted to cases where the carrier personally acted with intent to cause damage or recklessness and with knowledge that damage would probably result. And there was another element to this compromise: The privilege of the Hague Rules that there is no liability in case of fire was maintained with the modification that in case of fire the burden of proof of fault on the part of the carrier or his servants lies on the shipper. And, lastly, it was stated expressly in a so-called 'Common Understanding', that the basis of liability was still that of fault presumed by the Convention. This seemed desirable to the shipping orientated countries because the definition of fault in the Hamburg Rules was taken from the CMR where to some extent there has been confusion as to its bearing. A question, certainly, which is more of an academic than of practical value because it seems obvious anyway that it is up to the Courts to decide to what extent they consider as proven that the carrier or his servants or agents took all measures that could reasonably be required to avoid the occurrence and its consequences.

This compromise was lastly adopted by the Conference with a great majority of 60 to 3 votes with 9 abstentions.

3. MAIN CHANGES IN RELATION TO THE HAGUE/VISBY-RULES

The shift of liability towards the carrier as mentioned above was not the only change which the Hamburg Rules contain in relation to the old conventions. It were mainly the following aspects in which differences between Hamburg Rules and Hague/Visby-Rules were decided by the Hamburg Conference:

The *scope of the convention* is broader than that of the Hague Rules. Its binding rules are applicable not only in cases where a B/L is issued. They apply if either the port of loading or the port of discharge or the place where a B/L has been issued is situated in a Contracting State. (Art. 2).

Not only the scope of application of the convention itself was extended but as well the period of custody during which the carrier is bound by compulsory rules of liability: It covers now the whole period from taking into charge of the goods until their delivery. (Art 4).

There are, in the Hamburg Rules (Art. 1) some new *definitions*. Mainly the terms 'contract of carriage by sea' and 'shipper' needed definition because their exact meaning in future is much more important since the convention does no longer restrict its applicability to cases where a B/L has been issued.

Deck cargo and *life animals* have been included into the liability regime of the convention. The former exceptions were deleted.

Damage to be compensated includes damage because of *delay*. The definition (Art. 5, §2), it is true, is rather narrow: delay occurs if the carriage is not performed within the time either expressly agreed or reasonable to require with regard to the circumstances of the case. Moreover, this liability is limited to two and a half times the freight.

The *monetary unit* is the SDR. A solution which in the meantime has been confirmed by a recommendation of the General Assembly of 1983.

The *cases where the limitation cannot be invoked* by the carrier have been defined narrower and clearer. This was meant as a certain compensation for the deletion of the nautical fault privilege.

According to the Guadalajara concept in air transportation there is, within the Hamburg Rules, an additional *liability of the actual carrier* jointly to that of the contractual carrier.

A particular rule covers situations of *on-carriage* and of *through-carriage* (Art. 11).

New rules deal with *letters of guarantee*, *notice of damage*, with *jurisdiction* and *arbitration*.

IV. Evaluation of the Hamburg Rules

1. UNDER LEGAL ASPECTS

It follows already from the description that the Hamburg Rules present advantages as to their legal concept. They have been worked out on the basis of a very thorough and world-wide study. This may sometimes have led to the consequence that legal rules based on a world-wide compromise are weaker and less clear than they should be. But on the other hand most problems of modern sea transport have been settled at all and in many cases more reasonably than before. This goes, e.g., for the scope, for the deck cargo and the liability of the actual carrier.

For example, the non-limitation of the scope to B/L is of great importance because nowadays in some relations maritime transport without issuance of a B/L amounts already up to 30–50%. The B/L sometimes causes delay in delivery and therefore is often left aside. Under the present legal system that does mean that there is no compulsory liability of the carrier under most legislations. The same goes for deck cargo which, due to the special stowage of containers, has an increasing importance for ordinary cargo.

Of legal advantage is, irrespective of its economic evaluation, the deletion of the exception of liability for nautical fault as well. It is quite obvious that responsibility of the carrier for any kind of damage caused by his servants corresponds to the law of all other means of transportation. It is, from the legal point of view, a matter of justice. And a change in international maritime law towards this general legal situation would bring maritime law more in line with the law of other means of transport.

In particular the latter aspect is of utmost practical importance: The legal regime of combined transport, particularly the answer to the question according to which rules damage occurred at an unknown part of the voyage has to be compensated is extremely doubtful. Rules on this problem are the easier to create the smaller the differences of law for the various means of transportations are. Maritime law mainly because of the exception for nautical fault and of the low limits of limitation is an extreme as to the liability rules. The increase of carrier's liability provided for in the Hamburg Rules has facilitated the preparation of international rules on combined transport immediately: already in 1980, two years after the conclusion of the Hamburg Rules, a convention on liability in case of multi-modal transport has been adopted at an UNCTAD-Conference in Geneva. Its entry in force, of course, is dependent on the previous coming in force of the Hamburg Rules which for the reason given is a condition.

Lastly the whole drafting and structure of the Hamburg Rules present, at least for a civil law lawyer, considerable advantages in relation to the Hague Rules. The Hamburg Rules follow the structure usual in other transportation conventions, mainly of the CMR.

2. UNDER COMMERCIAL ASPECTS

Whereas it seems rather clear that the Hamburg Rules present legal advantages over the present liability system it is very much debated what the economic effect of its coming in force would be.

When discussing this problem one normally takes into account exclusively the so-called shift of liability, which means the deletion of the exception for nautical fault and, in addition, the modification of the fire exception. One should, perhaps, have in mind that the other improvements brought by the Hamburg Rules may reduce the litigation cost as well. But it is true that the shift of liability may present the most important element of change.

Those States who were originally in favour of the shift of liability towards the carrier thought that the new rule would be in the cost interest of the shipper. This is very much contested by representatives of the shipping and insurance industries and by various States. The mutual reasoning is basically as follows:

If the liability of the carrier goes further than today it seems obvious, at first glance, that this is advantageous for the shipper and his (cargo-) insurer, because the insurer has to bear without possibility of recourse less damages than before. Cargo insurance premiums therefore are to decrease.

There is, however, an adverse opinion: It is argued that it is very expensive, in particular in maritime trade (which means world-wide), to recover against a sea-carrier. This would mean that the overall charge by insurance premiums on a given transport might increase: The shipper wants, as he does today, his cargo insurance, because he may not rely on the liability of the carrier. The carrier, however, being exposed to the new liability towards the shipper, has to make out liability insurance. Insurance which puts an additional financial burden first on the carrier but by means of the freight rate on the shipper as well. Because, it is argued, the recourse action of the cargo insurer against the liability insurer is difficult and expensive the premium of cargo insurance will not reduce to the same extent as the liability insurance costs money. This the more so as the cargo insurance in principle is less expensive than the liability insurance. This reason is, however, very much to question. Liability insurance in maritime trade is done by P & I-Clubs. They charge their members by calls only to the extent they really pay for damages. This would, at least in theory, mean that the carrier is charged by additional insurance costs only to the extent the shippers get paid either directly or by means of recourse put forward by the cargo insurer. So in the long run there should not be any additional amount of overall premiums. It is certain of course that there might be some slight increase during a transitional period.

On the other hand, there might not be a decrease of overall insurance costs as well. Unless the shipper decides, in view of the better legal protection, not to make out cargo insurance at all. This might happen in Developing Countries but is not possible in Industrialized Countries.

One economic change, however, would be for certain: The shift would give additional business to the liability insurer, mainly the P & I-Clubs. And it might perhaps decrease somewhat the business of the cargo insurers.

If one follows this line of thinking, it is probable that there will be neither an increase nor a decrease of overall insurance cost. One must therefore put the question whether the change is worth while. The answer may be that in case there is no disadvantage the better legal solution may take preference.

Anyway it may be doubtful whether one should give up an existing and world-wide applied legal system for the mere reason of better legal clarity.

3. STATE OF DISCUSSION ON AND ADHERENCE TO THE CONVENTION

As already mentioned the Convention has been ratified or adhered to by ten States, namely Barbados, Chile, Egypt, Hungary, Lebanon, Morocco, Romania, Tunesia, Uganda and Tanzania. It will enter into force after its tenth instrument of ratification or accession has been deposited.

The discussion is still controversial. Mainly the shipping industry and the cargo insurers are opposed to the new rules. They seem to be afraid that business would be more expensive, at least more complicated for them. The discussion has shown, however, mainly at the occasion of the CMI Colloquium in Vienna in 1979, that shipowners and insurers as well would be willing to pay the price they believe must be paid in case of a change to the new liability system, if they felt the new convention would be the only means to preserve legal uniformity. But for the moment, obviously, they do not feel this is necessary. To the contrary: After the Hamburg Conference the Visby Protocol of 1968 which did not receive much support before but came into force in 1977, was ratified (or adhered to) by many States, namely by Egypt, GDR, Poland, Netherlands, Sri Lanka, Spain, Tonga. These States obviously have drawn from the Hamburg Conference the conclusion that the new Convention probably will not enter into force soon. Therefore they may feel that the progress granted by the Visby Protocol is the utmost which can be achieved at the moment.

The discussion after the conference, in particular among interested economic circles, was more sceptical than positive. Matter of concern was the so-called 'radical change of the liability system' and its predicted consequences for the overall cost of sea-transportation. If one would try to draw a simple conclusion from the general debate it should be the following: There is some concern that the change to the Hamburg Rules might increase the overall insurance cost. One sees, in addition, the likelihood that the application and interpretation of the new provisions would need some time for adjustment and therefore would cause some temporary uncertainty. On the other hand it is mostly acknowledged that the Hamburg Rules solve sufficiently a lot of problems which maritime trade has to face nowadays and which are not provided for by the old conventions. Legally spoken the Hamburg Rules would simplify the law of carriage of goods by sea and at the same time bring it into line with the law of transportation in general, thus in particular facilitating the elaboration and adoption of common rules on combined transport. And the CMI, already in January 1979, expressed a pragmatic view when it stated that it would be preferable to stay for the reasons mentioned with the actual system which had, in principle, worked rather well. But if it would be necessary to change to the new system of Hamburg Rules in order to preserve uniformity of maritime law all over the world this could be done – under the condition, however, that the new system would entirely and at the same time replace the old one.

V. In particular: evaluation from the viewpoint of developing countries

1. DEMANDS OF THE SO-CALLED 'NEW INTERNATIONAL ECONOMIC ORDER'

The term 'New International Economic Order' is not clearly defined. The idea comes from the 'Declaration on the Establishment of a New International Economic Order' passed by the 6th Special General Assembly in 1974. This is more a catalogue of topics than a general principle. Of course, the common underlying idea is to amend the existing economic order into a new system of international economic relationship which is more – from the viewpoint of the authors – in favour of the Developing Countries.

There seem to be mainly two points which might be of importance in connection with international maritime trade: At first there is the demand to minimize restrictive business practices. The liability system of the Hague Rules, which as I mentioned was created in connection with the construction of the Liner Conference system, are considered as sort of general conditions which are in favour of the carrier. The liability rule seems to prove this by itself and by its origin. If, of course, one considers the Developing Countries as merely cargo countries and not shipping countries, this could be detrimental to them.

The second principle could be the demand for 'preferential treatment' in favour of the Developing Countries. It is valid mainly for raw material markets and may lead, if applied to maritime trade, to an even further reaching demand for not only a balance in rights and duties of the parties to a contract of carriage but for better protection of the interests of the Developing Countries.

In the course of the preparatory work within UNCITRAL as well as in connection with the work done by this UN-body in general it has been always clear and even accepted by the representatives of Developing Countries that, within the framework of international commercial law, there should not be any preferential treatment of Developing Countries. Commercial law consists of legal technical rules which try to produce a fair balance of rights and duties of either party to the contract. There is, in this context, no room for any kind of preferential treatment. The more, as a member of a Developing Country may well be party to such a contract on both sides. Developing Countries for instance are sellers as well as buyers and as well carriers and shippers of various kinds of goods. The legal rules in the field of private law at least could not define the rights of parties to such contracts according to from which country they come. Preferential treatment is a matter of public international law, of customs and of trade restrictions by State legislation. So the demand for reduction of restrictive business practices may be the only one which brings the revision of the Hague/Visby Rules in a certain context to the New Economic International Order.

2. SPECIAL INTERESTS OF DEVELOPING COUNTRIES IN SEA TRANSPORTATION?

But are there particular interests of Developing Countries in this field? It is true, Developing Countries for a long time have had mainly shippers' interests. Only few of them have commercial fleets and even fewer are able to conduct these fleets and the necessary port equipment on their own. Shipping as well as running ports with all their modern installations like for instance container terminals is a business which needs considerable amounts of capital which normally lacks a poorer country. But there are exceptions and shipping is perhaps one of the industries which may be open to the entry of Developing Countries from the point of view of know-how rather sooner than other kinds of modern industry.

It is true, in general, that the Developing Countries are mainly interested in cargo and only in the second place and increasingly in shipping.

In this context, there is one additional element to be taken into consideration: Higher liability of the carrier means more business for the liability insurers, in particular the P & I-Clubs. And possibly less business for the cargo insurers. P & I-Clubs are situated in England and in Norway. It is practically impossible for other countries, in particular for Developing Countries, to provide for liability insurance. Cargo insurance markets, however, are available in most countries of the world. Developing Countries are in the course of building them up. This may lead to the consequence that cargo countries, such as the Federal Republic of Germany in this respect as well, might be interested in having not too strong liabilities on the part of the carrier which must lead the carrier to make out better insurance and to pay higher premiums which then influence the trade rates but to bear the risk themselves and to insure against losses. This is the actual situation and it presents the advantage for the shipper that he may get his loss indemnified with his insurer and at home.

3. CONCLUSION

It follows from the few remarks that there is no particular interest of Developing Countries. They, like the industrialized countries, are merely but strongly interested in having a well balanced, practicable law of the carriage of goods by sea which takes into account the interests of both contracting parties. Any unilaterality would be detrimental to Developing States concentrating on shipping – like for instance India – likewise as to major European shipping countries.

The demand for balanced interest does not necessarily mean a legal balance. If the present rules in spite of a certain unilaterality of rights and obligations grant advantages from the economic viewpoint, because insurance is easier and therefore cheaper to make out, they could be considered as economically balanced. What counts is the overall cost of transportation which lastly will be born by the shipper in any event.

The legal improvements brought by the Hamburg Rules are an advantage in itself. First, because they tend at least in the long run – to minimize ligitation and therefore to keep transportation cheaper. Secondly, and in particular for Developing Countries, because clearer rules are easier to understand for commercial people less accustomed to common practice. And lastly, because they present the chance to sooner get reasonable rules on container transportation which is perhaps even more necessary for Developing Countries than for industrialized countries.

The economic impact of the Hamburg Rules is the same for Developing Countries and for industrialized countries. There is little likelihood that sea carriage – again in the long run – will become more expensive under the new rules. But it may well be that there is some increase of insurance premiums for the transitional period of adaptation. If such a sacrifice must be brought in favour of the global unification of law it is at the same time in the interest of Developing Countries. Because uniform law for carriage of goods is important and contributes very much to greater clarity.

It follows therefrom, on the other hand, that it would not be detrimental to the interests of Developing Countries more than to that of industrialized countries if the Hamburg Rules would not enter into force. Provided, the uniformity of law can be preserved by means of the Visby Rules it probably economically would not matter much whether there is liability for nautical fault or whether there is not. It is true, however, that other shortcomings of the Hague/Visby-System may cause even more difficulties in the future. – This seems to be the attitude of most Developing Countries as well, because a large number of them in spite of their strong attitude at the Conference did not proceed to ratification of the new Convention.

VI. Outlook

Future development is difficult to forecast. It seems, at least for the moment, that mainly for reasons of economic precaution there is greater tendency to ratify the Visby Protocol of 1968 rather than the Hamburg

Rules. We should not regret this, because even in this way the Hamburg Conference has its influence on progressive unification of maritime law.

But it seems to be doubtful whether the Hague/Visby-Rules may be sufficient for the future. As mentioned, many actual problems are not solved by them and their legal technique should be subject to improvement.

There are two more international activities which might have influence on the future of the Hamburg Rules:

Firstly, the Convention on Multimodal Transport (Geneva, 1980) can enter into force only after the Hamburg Rules, because the new liability regime in sea transportation is a condition for its application. But the pressure for the latter Convention is not very strong, because the multimodal Convention is complicated and not very appropriate for European countries with a variety of different means of transportation in daily business.

Secondly, there is a growing tendency no longer to use B/L. They have turned out in some relations to be rather an impediment than a means of facilitation of sea transport, because B/L travel too slow and their non-presence at the port of destination causes problems. To the extent that seacarriage is done under waybills, the liability regime of the Hague/Visby Rules is no longer compulsorily applicable at least in many jurisdictions. Therefore and for other reasons the CMI, at its Conference in Lisbon 1985, has set up an International Working Group to study the problems of waybills with a view to propose either conditions or a draft convention. Such a convention must deal – different from the Hague/Visby Rules – no longer with B/L but with the contract as such. This means, that it had to follow the pattern of the Hamburg Rules in this respect. And it certainly could not neglect other problems of modern seatrade such as carriage of containers on deck, through-and-on-carriage and so on. This work may present a new chance to apply some of the modern features on the Hamburg Rules. Whereas it seems to be difficult from the political angle it was highly desirable in this context to discuss again, with the experience and investigation which has been made after the Hamburg Conference the famous shift of liability and to take a second decision on it at the occasion of a new, global convention on carriage of goods by sea which is still needed but blocked by the high degree of emotion which has been set free by the Hamburg Rules as well during its preparation at the Conference as afterwards. For commerce it is not so much important how the decisions of the rules are, provided they are practicable and they are uniform.

COMPENSATION IN THE LIGHT OF THE 1984 PROTOCOLS TO REVISE THE 1969 CLC AND THE 1971 FUND CONVENTIONS

PROF. Z. BRODECKI

University of Gdansk (Poland)

Introduction

The International Conference on Liability and Compensation for Damage in Connection with the Carriage of Certain Substances by Sea adopted the Protocols of 1984 to amend the International Convention on Civil Liability for Oil Pollution Damage 1969 and the International Convention on the Establishment of an International Fund for Compensation for Oil Pollution Damage 1971.[1] Increase of the limits of the shipowner's liability was the heart of the work on the review of the 1969 CLC and the 1971 Fund Conventions. Therefore this article concentrates its attention on the problem of compensation for oil pollution damage.

1. Limitation of the shipowner's liability

1.1. THE LEGAL RIGHT OF THE SHIPOWNER TO LIMIT HIS LIABILITY

At the first stage of development of the maritime law the right of the shipowner to limit his liability was treated by doctrine as an exceptional rule from the principle of the full liability.[2] But in recent years came an important change in the maritime law proving that the number of changes leads to the changes of principle. As a matter of fact, the Convention on Limitation of Liability for Maritime Claims, 1976 has accepted the principle of limited liability.[3] Therefore the 1984 International Legal Conference did not question the legal right of the shipowner to limit his liability for all claims subject to limitation of liability for pollution damage, which was previously adopted by the International Convention on Civil Liability for Oil Pollution Damage, 1969.

[1] The 1969 Convention has been ratified by 54 states including the United Kingdom and Poland, as of 31 December 1983.

[2] The international conventions relating to the limitation of the liability of owners of seagoing ships (Brussels 1924 and 1957) provide that shipowners, and others, may limit their liability, when the loss, damage, etc., is caused . . . in specified ways. Also the national enactments of the mentioned conventions describe claims subject to limitation, e.g. the U.K. Merchant Shipping (Liability of Shipowners and Others) Act 1958 (*See*: R. Grime, Shipping Law, London 1978, p. 178) or the Polish Maritime Code, 1969 (*See*: J. Lopuski, Odpowiedzialnosc za szkode w zegludze morskiej – Liability for Damage in Shipping, Gdansk 1976).

[3] Although Article 3 of the 1976 Limitation Convention provides that the rules of this Convention shall not apply to claims for salvage or contribution in general average, claims by servants of the shipowner or salvor as well as claims for pollution damage or nuclear damage.

Therefore, the meetings of the Legal Committee of IMO and the International Legal Conference were concentrated on the problem of breakability of limits. Article 6(2) of the Protocol 1984 to the 1969 CLC which replaced Article 5(2) of the existing convention was adopted a new text in order to align it with relevant provisions in similar conventions recently adopted,[4] as follows:

> 'The owner shall not be entitled to limit his liability under this Convention if it is proved that the pollution damage resulted from his personal act or omission, committed with the intent to cause such damage, or recklessly and with knowledge that such damage would probably result.'

This imposes a heavy burden of proof on a claimant who, to exclude limitation under the 1969 CLC,[5] needs in effect only to prove the defendant's carelessness. The 1984 Protocol as amended the 1969 CLC[6] demands proof of far more reprehensible conduct.

1.2. LIMITATION FUND AS A CONDITION FOR THE SHIPOWNER'S RIGHT TO LIMIT HIS LIABILITY

A limitation fund as a condition for the shipowner's right to limit his liability was also discussed during the International Legal Conference. The development of the institution of limitation of liability shows that a limitation fund is a very controversial issue. That is because at the first stage of this development the maritime law provided limitation of liability without constitution of a limitation fund,[7] that the principle of a mandatory limitation fund (equal to the full amount of the limit, with the court where a claim is brought) was introduced,[8] and finally the Convention on the Limitation of Liability for Maritime Claims 1976 has not retained this principle providing limitation of liability without constitution of a limitation fund.[9]

[4] Particularly, Article 4 of the Convention on Limitation on Liability for Maritime Claims, 1976 dealing with conduct of limitation. This concept, formally known as wilful misconduct, seems to be an important change in the maritime law. *See*: Chorley and Giles', Shipping Law, Seventh Edition by O.C. Giles, Guildford 1980, p. 52.

[5] As well as under the Brussels Conventions of 1924 and 1957 and the national legislation enacted as a result of these conventions.

[6] Taking into consideration the concept of the 1976 Limitation Convention. See comments to this Convention by O.C. Giles, op. cit., p. 54.

[7] E.g. the International Convention Relating to the Limitation of the Liability of Owners of Seagoing Ships, 1924.

[8] By the International Convention Relating to the Limitation of the Liability of Owners of Sea-Going Ships, 1957.

[9] Article 10 of this Convention provides that 'limitation of liability may be invoked notwithstanding that a limitation fund as mentioned in Article 11 has not been constituted'. Although it is no condition for the right of limitation that a limitation fund be established, a fund may be established in the same manner as under the 1957 Convention and the legal implications of the establishment of a fund are also essentially the same.

Several delegations pointed out that the text of the 1976 Convention represents the modern tendency of maritime law to treat the insurance as a key to solve the problems of liability and compensation. They realised that the institutions of compulsory insurance and a direct action against insurers has changed the philosophy of liability and compensation.[10] They felt that, in view of the requirement for compulsory insurance imposed on the shipowner, the principle of a mandatory limitation fund – as expressed in Article V.3 of the 1969 CLC – may not be retained. Moreover – as the Director of the I.O.P.C. Fund said – the compulsory establishment of the CLC limitation fund has led to delays in the payment of compensation through the I.O.P.C. Fund.[11]

But the majority of States were against the idea of an optional limitation fund. They argued that there was always a risk that the shipowner's insurance might fail to satisfy the victim's claims in full, particularly in situations where an incident involved a large number of claims. That is why they were in favour of a system which enabled the shipowner to constitute a limitation fund even before any action for compensation had been brought against him.

Therefore, Article V(3) of the 1969 CLC was replaced by Article 6(3) of the 1984 Protocol, by the following text:

> 'For the purpose of availing himself of the benefit of limitation provided for in paragraph 1 of this Article the owner shall constitute a fund . . .'

1.3. METHODS OF MEASUREMENT

When the privilege of the shipowner to limit his liability was first introduced the value of ship and freight was taken as the measure.[12] Then a more precise method of calculation was enacted by the maritime law suggesting the ship's tonnage as the basis of the calculation.[13] In recent years, the Convention on the Limitation of Liability for Maritime Claims 1976 has retained the concept of limitation according to the tonnage of the offending ship. That is why the majority of states taking part in the International Legal Conference were in favour of retaining the ship's tonnage as a multiplication factor adopted by the 1969 CLC.

[10] This new philosophy has been shown by Z. Brodecki in a joint book entitled 'Ubezpieczenia morski' (Marine Insurance) Gdansk 1979, pp. 81–83.

[11] LEG/CONF. 6/21.

[12] It was in Britain in 1734. The 1924 Convention relating to limitation of the liability of owners and the national legislations passed as a result of this Convention (e.g. the Polish Maritime Code 1964).

[13] E.g. by the Merchant Shipping Act 1862, which has been substantially re-enacted by s.503 of the 1894 Act. O.C. Giles, op. cit., p. 50. This concept was taken into consideration by the 1957 Convention relating to the limitation of the liability of owners and the national legislations passed as a result of this Convention.

The Convention on the Limitation of Liability for Maritime Claims 1976 has retained limitation according to the tonnage of the ship but, instead of the same rate per ton payable whatever the size of the vessel, there is a sliding scale as the size increases; the limit for small ships has long been criticised as too low, seeing that they, too, can cause serious damage.[14] The same problem arose during the International Legal Conference.

The Oil Companies International Marine Forum (OCIMF) stated that in ten years' experience of claims there was no correlation between the size of a vessel and the amount of damage caused,[15] and therefore at least a minimum liability in the 1984 Protocol to the 1969 CLC for small ships should be introduced.

The argument advanced by OCIMF that small ships can, on occasion, cause sufficiently large and expensive oil pollution problems so that a mere monetary amount per ton limit would not be adequate to compensate claims – in the view of the International Maritime Committee (IMC, well known as CMI) – was not without merit; however the argument did not abandon the time-honoured and thoroughly tested tonnage system for limitation of liability.[16]

But in relation to the proposition that there is no correlation between size of a ship and size of claim, the International Group of P and I Associations (P and I) submitted statistics showing that although approximately fifty per cent of the world's tankers were under 3,000 tons in size they were responsible for a very small proportion of the total cost of all pollution claims.[17]

In spite of this argument there was wide agreement on the desirability of introducing in the revised instruments, a specified minimum liability for ships below a certain tonnage.[18] Therefore, the International Legal Conference has made an exception to the concept of limitation according to the tonnage of the ship by providing a minimum liability for small ships.

1.4. LIMITATION AMOUNTS

It was a common opinion that the limits in the compensation under the International Convention on Civil Liability for Oil Pollution Damage 1969 were insufficient. Therefore all participants at the International Legal

[14] O.C. Giles, op. cit., p. 55. The limits for small ships up to 500 tons are as follows: for death and personal injury, 333,000 units of account and for other claims – 167,000 units of account.

[15] This Organisation presented a very interesting Chart during the Informal meetings which took place in Paris. The Maritime Legal Conference had before it other statistical data submitted by the Director of the IOPC Fund, the Advisory Committee on Pollution of the Sea (ACOPS) and INTERTANKO.

[16] LEG. 50/8.

[17] LEG. 50/4/6.

[18] Some countries expressed their full support for OCIMF's position before the Conference, among others: Italy and Brazil.

Conference accepted the need for an increase in the amounts of compensation available for victims of oil spills.

The majority of speakers taking the floor in respect of limitation amounts stated that compensation payable under the 1969 CLC had reduced in real terms.[19] They recognised that inflation must have had an impact on the adequacy of CLC limits and must be taken into account when considering proposed increases.[20]

Also the cost of oil spills had been presented during the International Legal Conference by P and I Clubs,[21] INTERTANKO,[22] OCIMF[23] (representing the point of view of a person liable) and by France[24] and ACOPS[25] (representing the point of view of a victim).

Special attention was given to statistics presented by P and I Clubs, mutual insurance associations which cover the liabilities of shipowners towards third parties.[26] Tables taken from these statistics substantiate the P and I thesis that although there are undoubtedly substantial variations from one incident to another the average cost of claims is higher for larger tankers than for small tankers.

The statistics presented by France demonstrate the assumption that spill costs in current dollars have increased at a rate higher than inflation during the seventies.[27] Furthermore, the average cost of claims was higher in the second period (1977–1980) than in the first (1970–1976). It was dependent greatly on the fact that a few catastrophic oil spills occurred at the end of the seventies.

The figures included in these statistics were based on the legal concept of damage being taken from the claim records. Unfortunately, the international organizations responsible for the protection of the environment have not yet prepared any statistics estimating actual damage to the environment, which may amount to a few billion dollars in a scale of one incident. Such statistics could illustrate a real picture of the relationship between the extent of compensable damage and the extent of moral damage and answer the most crucial question of how the increasing conflict of interests[28] between the industry and the environment should be solved.

[19] Particularly a representative of France, who presented the point of view expressed in documents LEG/CONF. 6/19 and LEG/CONF. 6/36 (attached note by Professor Henri Smets of the University of Paris I).

[20] *See*: Annex 1: Selected measures of consumer price inflation; figure presented by INTERTANKO in document LEG/CONF. 6/INF.2/Rev. 1.

[21] LEG/CONF. 6/14.

[22] LEG/CONF. 6/INF. 2/Rev. 1.

[23] LEG. 49/3/8.

[24] LEG/CONF. 6/C.2/WP.4.

[25] LEG/CONF. 6/58.

[26] *See*: Annex 2: Oil Pollution Claims (Paid and Estimated Outstanding), figure presented by P and I Clubs in document LEG/CONF. 6/14, Annex as well as in LEG. 50/4/6, Annex I.

[27] The same conclusion was made by ACOPS in document LEG/CONF. 6/58.

[28] Expressed by the United Nations General Assembly Resolution of 1971 No. 2849 (XXVI) as a conflict between the development and the environment.

In the light of the above conflict of interests, the proposals providing for an upper limit of shipowners' liability of $100 million was the most rational.[29] It would guarantee almost full compensation for victims of oil pollution, by providing the 'enhanced compensation' referred to in the preamble to the draft protocol.

But there is also a conflict of interests between the developing countries and the developed countries, which in respect of compensation limits for oil pollution damage appears to be quite significant, although it usually remains undiscussed. One of the major reasons for the above is the fact that a vast number of the developing countries do not possess hard currency, and these countries in fact pay relatively higher contributions in compensation for oil pollution damage.

Taking into account the ability of a state's economy, some delegations submitted a joint document during the International Legal Conference[30] proposing, as the basis of discussion on the subject of the limitation amounts of liability and compensation under the Protocol to the 1969 CLC, the minimum liability for small ships (about $3 million for ships less than 5,000 grt. or 10,000 grt.) and the maximum liability for ships (not exceeding $30 million).

There were countries which wanted to achieve a compromise between France and the United States on one side and China, Cyprus, Greece, India, Italy, Poland as well as Japan[31] and the USSR[32] on the other side, proposing the minimum liability for small ships on the level of $3 million for ships less than 5,000 grt. and the maximum liability of shipowners on the level of $50 million.[33]

The problem of limitation amounts was discussed to the last moment of the International Legal Conference, mainly during informal meetings. In this respect the delegations of the United States[34] and France played the key role. Therefore, Article V of the 1969 CLC is replaced by the following text:

[29] As it was suggested by ACOPS. LEG/CONF. 6/58 and by the previous proposals made by France LEG. 51/10. Also the United States suggested during the Conference very high limits of liability, taking into consideration other reasons, particularly the general policy of the US Congress in this respect (shown by the nuclear law, air law, etc. of the United States).

[30] By the delegations of China, Cyprus, Greece, India, Italy, Poland. LEG/CONF. 6/C.2/WP.23. These countries also suggested that the limitation amount of liability should be $285 or 300 per ton for ships above 5,000 grt. or 10,000 grt.

[31] Japan suggested that the Protocol to the 1969 CLC should provide for a minimum liability of a $4 or $5 million for tankers less than 5,000 grt., application of a tonnage-related limit for tankers up to 100,000 grt, and $30 million for tankers of more than 100,000 grt.

[32] The USSR expressed the view that as a basis for discussion the Japanese proposal for an increase of owner's liability up to $30 million put forward during elaboration of the draft protocol was quite acceptable LEG/CONF. 6/41.

[33] E.g. the United Kingdom. LEG/CONF. 6./50. Also, Sweden presented the point of view taking into consideration a necessity to achieve a compromise. LEG/CONF. 6/30.

[34] The US presented its point of view mainly in document LEG/CONF. 6/C.2/WP.25.

'The owner of a ship shall be entitled to limit his liability under this Convention in respect of any one incident to an aggregate amount calculated as follows:
(a) 3 million units of account for a ship not exceeding 5,000 units of tonnage;
(b) for a ship with a tonnage in excess thereof, for each additional unit of tonnage, 420 units of account in addition to the amount mentioned in sub-paragraph (a);
provided, however, that this aggregate amount shall not in any event exceed 59.7 million units of account.'

2. Insurance of the shipowner's liability

2.1. COMPULSORY INSURANCE

Capacity of the insurance market seems to be a background to establish not only the high limits of liability[35] but also the compulsory insurance, equal to the full amount of the limits of liability. The second context is more important as it relates to the performance of the duties established by the international legal instrument.[36]

This capacity to absorb risk varies by class of insurance and is usually dependent on the amount of premium available in relation to the potential maximum loss exposure as well as to the actual amount of frequency of loss.

There is a danger in assuming that capacity for each separate liability can be absorbed by the marine insurance marked in isolation from the other risk (hull and cargo). That is why the International Union of Marine Insurance (IUMI) expressed its view that, although current capacity for shipowners' liability is as substantial as the P and I Clubs and their reinsurers offer a contract of liability insurance covering about $300 million per vessel per ocurrence of oil pollution, the introduction of higher shipowner's limitation corresponding with a wider concept of compensable damage[37] and a wider

[35] This problem was mainly discussed within the context of limitation amounts being introduced mainly by Sweden (LEG/CONF. 6/30) P and I Clubs (LEG/CONF. 6/14) and IUMI (LEG/CONF. 6/22).

[36] Therefore, the Polish delegation introduced this problem in the light of compulsory insurance during the Stockholm meetings from 7–11 December 1981, reported to the forty eighth session of the Commission (LEG. 48/2/2).

[37] A new definition of pollution damage took into consideration the idea of ecological damage providing that 'compensation for impairment of the environment other than loss of profit from such impairment shall be limited to costs of reasonable measures of reinstatement actually undertaken or to be undertaken'. *See*: Z. Brodecki: A new definition of pollution damage, paper prepared to be published by Lloyds.

geographic area[38] would upset the current balance and this would introduce unpredictability both as regards capacity and costs.[39]

The principle of compulsory insurance has been introduced by modern insurance law.[40] It plays also a very important function in the battle against oil pollution as the International Convention on Civil Liability for Oil Pollution Damage 1969 is concerned with the compulsory insurance against liability of shipowners.[41] This principle was not questioned during the international Legal Conference. Moreover, some speakers stressed the view that a compulsory insurance against liability of shipowners for oil pollution creates – as a matter of fact – a new philosophy of liability and compensation in maritime law.[42]

Article VII of the 1969 CLC requiring shipowners to maintain insurance or other financial security to meet the limits of liability prescribed in Article V in respect of their liability for pollution damage applies to any ship, which carries a bulk cargo of more than 2,000 tons of persistent oil. This rule was also not questioned during the International Legal Conference.[43]

This Article required further amendments to clarify to what extent the individual paragraphs also apply to those certificates which are issues for

[38] The 1984 Protocol to revise the 1969 CLC has extended the geographical scope of the convention to the Exclusive Economic Zone. A new pattern '12 miles plus 188 miles' symbolises a great economical implication which will arise when this Protocol is in force.

[39] LEG/CONF. 6/22. This document has shown the links between the limitation amounts and the notion of damage as well as the geographical scope of application, which in fact is extremely important, because it shows real changes of the liability and compensation for pollution damage. Also the concept of strict liability reflects the other aspects of a new regime established by the 1984 Protocol. The author is of the opinion that only a comprehensive study creates a background for conclusions. This idea has been shown in a book entitled: Odpowiedzialnosc za zanieczyszczenie morza (Pollution of the Sea and its Legal Consequences) Gdansk 1983.

[40] A real revolution in this respect was made by the motor insurance, being ex lege. There is also a tendency e.g. in the nuclear law to oblige a person for entering an insurance contract. *See*: Z. Brodecki, Odpowiedzialnosc za szkode w zegludze morskiej, p. 71.

[41] Also the national legislations following this Convention are based on the principle of compulsory insurance, e.g. the UK Merchant Shipping (Oil Pollution) Act 1971. *See*: Collected Papers on Marine Claims, by J. Kenneth, London 1980, p. 226.

[42] This problem was deeply discussed during the Stockholm meetings held from 7–11 December 1981.

[43] But one should realise that new definitions of 'ship' and 'oil' were adopted by the 1984 Protocol to the 1969 CLC. They are as follows:

> 'Ship' means any sea-going vessel and sea-borne craft of any type whatsoever constructed or adopted for the carriage of oil in bulk as cargo, provided that a ship capable of carrying oil and other cargoes shall be regarded as a ship only when it is actually carrying oil in bulk as cargo and during any voyage following such carriage unless it is proved that it has no residues of such carriage of oil in bulk aboard.'
>
> 'Oil' means any persistent hydrocarbon mineral oil such as crude oil, fuel oil, heavy diesel oil and lubricating oil, whether carried on board ship as cargo or in the bunkers of such a ship.'

ships not registered in a Contracting State. The problem was raised by the Federal Republic of Germany,[44] and the P and I Clubs[45] which suggested to replace the first two sentences of paragraph 2 of Article VII.

After a discussion the International Legal Conference accepted this point of view adopting the following text:

> 'A certificate attesting that insurance or other financial security is in force in accordance with the provisions of this Convention shall be issued to each ship after the appropriate authority of a Contracting State has determined that the requirements of paragraph 1 have been complied with. With respect to a ship registered in a Contracting State such certificate shall be issued or certified by the appropriate authority of the State of the ship's registry; with respect to a ship not registered in a Contracting State it may be issued or certified by the appropriate authority of any Contracting State.'

2.2. THE CERTIFICATE OF INSURANCE

It is very well known that the certificate of insurance is the instrument which provides legally valid evidence of the existence of the insurance contract and therefore great care must be exercised to ensure the accuracy and adequacy of this document.

Taking it into consideration the United Kindgom[46] and the P and I Clubs[47] suggested a pragmatic solution be adopted by the 1984 Protocol to revise the 1969 CLC and resolution to the question of certification.

The International Legal Conference adopted the 'Certificate of Insurance or Other Financial Security in Respect of Civil Liability for Oil Pollution Damage' providing a similar text as Annex to the International Convention on Civil Liability for Oil Pollution Damage, 1969. This text reads as follows:

> 'Issued in accordance with the provisions of Article VII of the International Convention on Civil Liability for Oil Pollution Damage, 1984.

[44] LEG.CONF. 6/17. The matter was considered earlier by the Legal Committee at its Twenty Seventh session (16–20 June 1975) in the context of the early days following the Convention's entry into force. A Circular Letter, No. 232, was sent by the Organisation to all members and non-members expressing the view 'that it would be more desirable and helpful if Contracting Governments were able to agree, for an interim period of at least one year from the entry into force of the Convention, to adopt as flexible and pragmatic approach as would ensure that there [was] no undue interference with the movement and operation of international shipping . . . .'

[45] LEG/CONF. 6/48.

[46] LEG/CONF. 6/50.

[47] LEG/CONF. 6/48.

Name of Ship	Distinctive Number of Letters	Post of Registry	Name and Address of Owner

This is to certify that there is in force in respect of the above-named ship a policy of insurance or other financial security satisfying the requirements of Article VII of the International Convention on Civil Liability for Oil Pollution Damage, 1984.

Type of Security ....
....
Duration of Security ....
....
Name and Address of the Insurer(s) and/or Guarantor(s)
Name ....
Address ....
This certificate is valid until ....
Issued or certified by the Government of ....
....
(Full designation of the State)
At .... On ....
(Place) (Date)

....
Signature and Title of issuing or certifying official

Explanatory Notes:

1. If desired, the designation of the State may include a reference to the competent public authority of the country where the certificate is issued.
2. If the total amount of security has been furnished by more than one source, the amount of each of them should be indicated.
3. If security is furnished in several forms, these should be enumerated.
4. The entry 'Duration of Security' must stipulate the date on which such security takes effect.'

Also a proposal for a Resolution on Certificates, prepared by a Working Group, was adopted by the International Legal Conference. It provides that:

'1. States Parties to the International Convention on Civil Liability for Oil Pollution Damage, 1969 and States Parties to the International Convention on Civil Liability for Oil Pollution Damage, 1984 issuing certificates attesting that insurance or other financial security is in force in accordance with the provisions of the respective conventions, should use the document in the form annexed to this resolution and in so far as is appropriate in each respective case, should certify that the requirements of both Conventions are satisfied.

2. States Parties to the International Convention on Civil Liability for Oil Pollution Damage, 1969 on the one side and States Parties to the International Convention on Civil Liability for Oil Pollution Damage, 1984 on the other side should mutually recognise and accept certificates issued by the appropriate authority in accordance with the provisions of the respective conventions. /. . ./.'

2.3. DIRECT ACTION

Liability insurance is a contractual relationship between the assured and the insurer, and in principle the insurer is only liable to his contract partner, the assured. But in recent years, insurance law has, however, given persons suffering damage more or less extensive rights to proceed directly against the liability insurer of the tortfeasor, the so-called 'direct action'.[48]

This new institution was introduced by the International Convention on Civil Liability for Oil Pollution Damage 1969 (implemented by national enactments[49]) which states that any claim for compensation for pollution damage may be brought directly against the insurer or other person providing financial security for the owner's liability for pollution damage.

According to the second sentence of Article VII paragraph 8 of the 1969 CLC, the defendant may, irrespective of the actual fault or privity of the owner,[50] avail himself of the limits of liability described in Article V, paragraph 1. It means that the limit of shipowner's liability is unbreakable. As the language used in the Convention was not clear enough, the International Legal Conference decided to replace this sentence by the following text:

> 'In such case the defendant may, even if the owner is not entitled to limit his liability according to paragraph 2 of Article V, avail himself of the limits of liability prescribed in Article V.

[48] S. Braekhus and A. Rein, Handbook of P and I Insurance, Second Edition, Assuranceforeningen Gard–Gjensidig–Arendal–Norway 1979, p. 118.

[49] E.g. in the United Kingdom by Merchant Shipping (Oil Pollution) Act 1971. *See*: R. Grime, op. cit., p. 225.

[50] But as regards Article V, paragraph 2 of this Convention: 'If the incident occurred as a result of the actual fault or privity of the owner, he shall not be entitled to avail himself of the limitation provided in paragraph 1 of this Article. It was mentioned above that the paragraph was replaced by the text being cited in sec. 1.1.

This was the only part of Article VII paragraph 8 of the 1969 CLC criticised, the following sentences[51] were not. Their texts have, however, provided that the insurer is responsible for the compensation being paid to the victim. If the assured owner is bankrupt (or in liquidation) the victim has a right to recognise that the compensation be paid directly to him as it should not 'disappear' in the bankrupt estate of the assured. It means that the limit of shipowners liability is unbreakable.[52]

3. The international compensation fund

3.1. AIMS OF THE FUND

'The International Oil Pollution Compensation Fund' (hereinafter referred to as 'The Fund' was established by Article 2 of the 1971 Convention with three main aims: to provide compensation for pollution damage to the extent that the protection afforded by the Liability Convention is inadequate; to give relief to shipowners in respect of the additional financial burden imposed on them by the Liability Convention, such relief being subject to conditions designed to ensure compliance with safety at sea and other conventions; and to give effect to the related purposes set out in this Convention.

During the meetings of the Legal Committee of IMO several delegations noted that the particular circumstances which had led to the introduction of a system of 'roll-back'[53] would no longer be applicable in the context of a simultaneous revision of both the Civil Liability Convention and the Fund Convention.[54] The International Legal Conference accepted this point of view, therefore, it decided to abolish the system of shipowner relief. That is why Article 2 paragraph 1 of the 1971 Fund Convention was replaced by the

[51] As well as the first sentence.

[52] But the American concept of insurance law is in this respect different. If in the insurance contract is has not been expressly stated that the limit of liability is the sum insured in cases where the owner has a right of limitation, the result may be that the insurer in a direct action will have to compensate a loss without limitation, in spite of the fact that the owner could have limited his own liability. *See*: Moudlett, 'Direct Action Statutes and Marine P and I Insurance', JMLC 1972, pp. 559–572.

[53] *See*: Official Records of the International Conference on the Establishment of An International Compensation Fund for Oil Pollution Damage, 1971, Inter-Governmental Maritime Consultative Organisation, London 1978, p. 230. The Working Group set up by the Committee of the Whole to work out a scheme on safety standards as conditions to shipowners had had extensive discussions on how a scheme could be worked out. It decided by a large majority that in working out provisions the starting point must be the ship complying with certain rules, as opposed to the flag State of the ship having given effect in its legislation to the rules to be taken into account.

[54] LEG/CONF. 6/7.

following text:

> 'An International Fund for compensation for pollution damage, to be named 'The International Oil Pollution Compensation Fund 1984' and hereinafter referred to as 'the Fund', is hereby established with the following aims:
> (a) To provide compensation for pollution damage to the extent that the protection afforded by the 1984 Liability Convention is inadequate;
> (b) to give effect to the related purposes set out in this Convention.'

In a note made by the Secretariat which contains summaries of the discussion of the Legal Committee in the course of its consideration of draft provisions for revising the 1969 Civil Liability Convention and the Fund Convention assisted by the results of informal meetings (among others the Stockholm meetings from 7–11 December 1981) it was stated that one delegation suggested deletion of Article 5 of the 1971 Fund Convention,[55] but this proposal was not adopted by the Committee. This delegation expressed the view, that the Fund should not – as a matter of fact – be a guarantor, because in the meantime the P and I Clubs had rapidly taken up the slack, moreover the Tanker Owner's Voluntary Agreement concerning Liability for Oil Pollution (TOVALOP) signed in January 1969 changed in 1978 its concept providing compensation for oil pollution damage upon the principle of strict liability (instead of the principle of fault liability) up to $160 per limitation ton, but no more than a total of $16.8 million (instead of $120 per limitation ton, but no more than a total of $10 million) and the Contract regarding an interim Supplement to Tanker Liability for Oil Pollution (CRISTAL) was signed in 1971 refunding to the owner or his insurer a certain portion of his liability persuant to the CLC or the TOVALOP scheme, namely the amount exceeding $120 per limitation ton or a total of $10 million, whichever is lower, up to $160 per ton or a total of $16.8 million if this amount is the lower.[56]

But during the International Legal Conference a majority of States realised that for the purpose of fulfilling its function under Article 2, paragraph 1(6) of the 1971 Fund Convention, the Fund shall not indemnify the owner and his guarantor for that portion of the aggregate amount of liability under the Liability Convention which is in excess of an amount equivalent to 1,500 francs for each ton of the ship's tonnage or of an amount of 125 million francs, whichever is the less, and is not in excess of an amount equivalent to 2,000 francs for each ton of the said tonnage or an amount of 210 million francs, whichever is the less provided, however, that the Fund

[55] This proposal was submitted by the Polish delegation at Stockholm being repeated during the 48th session of the Legal Committee of IMO.

[56] *See*: Z. Brodecki, Odpowiedzialnosc za zanieczyszczenie morza, op. cit., p. 176–178.

shall incur no obligation under this paragraph where the pollution resulted from the wilful misconduct of the owner himself.

Taking it into consideration the International Legal Conference decided as follows:

'Article 5 of the 1971 Fund Convention is deleted.'

3.2. THE FUNDS' COMPENSATION

The 1969/1971 Conventions give a plaintiff (P) a legal right to claim for compensation (→) against a shipowner (A) or his insurer/other guarantor (B) and the Fund (C) creating a new system of liability and compensation for oil pollution damage. It may be symbolised by the following pattern:

'P→A or B plus CP.'

a. The sole liability and compensation

In 1969 there was a question of which principle should apply to the liability of shipowner. The Conference could adopt: liability based on fault;[57] strict liability;[58] or absolute liability (including liability for damage resulting from a 'force majeure').[59] After a considerable discussion the International Convention on Civil Liability for Oil Pollution Damage, 1969 adopted the principle of strict liability.

The concept of liability introduced by the 1969 CLC was not satisfactory from a point of view of the victims as tankers (a symbol of the Second Scientific and Technical Revolution) are more dangerous than other dangerous things (being a symbol of the First Industrial Revolution). That is because this Convention provided that no liability for pollution damage shall attach to the owner if he proves that the damage resulted from a national phenomenon of an exceptional, inevitable and irresistible character, etc.

[57] This principle has a great tradition in maritime law, therefore, some delegations suggested maintenance of fault liability.

[58] *See*: Salmond on the Law of Torts, Sixteenth Edition by R.F.V. Heuston, London 1973, p. 318–341.

[59] A term 'absolute' is treated as a synonym of a term 'strict', although some writers suggested that 'strict' was a better term than 'absolute' in view of the admitted exceptions to the rule. *See*: Winfield, The Myth of Absolute Liability (1926) 42 L.Q.R. 37, 51. If we compare the rule first clearly established in *Rylands v. Fletcher* (1868) L.R. 3 H.L. 330 and the further development of British judiciary as regards liability for damage caused by 'dangerous things' with the American concept of statutory liability for ultra-hazardous activities, then one may realise that the difference between strict liability and an absolute liability deals with the problem of liability for damage arising mainly from the Acts of God, because the rule of strict liability is subject to a number of important exceptions, including the Acts of God, but the rule of absolute liability seems to create a system of liability without fault and without the exceptions.

This problem has been satisfactorily solved by the International Convention on the Establishment of an International Fund for Compensation for Oil Pollution Damage, 1971 which provides that the Fund shall be liable[60] to any person suffering pollution damage where no liability for the damage arises under the Liability Convention, mainly in case of pollution damage resulting from a natural phenomenon of an exceptional, inevitable and irresistible character.

In this connection the Polish delegation suggested that the Fund's role should be limited to situations involving 'catastrophic damages' as those which exceeded the limits of liability of the shipowner under the Liability Convention[61] or a relatively high deduction.[62] There were two main reasons for this proposal. First, the Fund has not yet been involved in cases under Article 4(1)(a) of that Convention and probably such cases would be very rare in practice. Second, this article has closed the door for 'the pollution of the sea' as a new risk of property insurance (e.g. the all-risks policy for commercial fishermen). The majority of states expressed the view that this proposal was too radical and therefore it was not adopted by the 1984 Protocol to revise the 1971 Fund Convention.

b. *The substitutional compensation*

For the purpose of fulfilling its function under Article 2, paragraph 1(a), the Fund shall also pay compensation to any person suffering pollution damage if such person has been unable to obtain full and adequate compensation for the damage under the terms of the Liability Convention, because the owner liable for the damage under the Liability Convention is financially incapable of meeting his obligations in full and any financial security that may be provided under Article VII of that Convention does not cover or is insufficient to satisfy the claims for compensation for the damage. This rule – expressed by Article 4.1(b) of the 1971 Convention – treats an owner as financially incapable of meeting his obligation and a financial security as insufficient if the person suffering the damage has been unable to obtain full satisfaction of the amount of compensation due under the Liability Convention after having taken all reasonable steps to pursue the legal remedied available to him.

Since there was no one case based on Article 4.1(b) of the 1971 Fund

[60] Article 4.1.(a) of the 1971 Convention speaks only about 'compensation' in this respect, but – from the legal point of view – the terms 'liability and compensation' are more correct, because the only Fund is liable in this case.

[61] LEG/ 48/WP.3. This delegation proposed to make a definition of catastrophic damage which exists in the context of Article 4.1.(c) as universal as it is possible.

[62] LEG/CONF/ 5/26. The proposal was as follows: 'The Fund shall incur no obligation under sub-paragraph (a), paragraph 1 if compensation does not exceed an amount of . . . million francs.'

Convention and the idea of the substitutional compensation of the Fund seems unnecessary in the light of a direct action against insurer or other guarantors, Poland suggested deletion of this.[63] But a number of delegations objected to the proposal for the discontinuance of the Fund's role as a special guarantor of the shipowner and his insurer. They maintained that, while there had been no need so far to apply this provision, it would be inappropriate to delete it and risk the creation of a gap in the existing regime. Therefore, this problem was not raised during the International Legal Conference.

c. The additional compensation

During the International Legal Conference the discussion referring to compensation paid by the Fund was concentrated on the situation where the damage exceeds the owners liability under the Liability Convention as limited pursuant to Article V, paragraph 1, of that Convention or under the terms of any other international Convention in force or open for signature, ratification or accession at the date of this Convention. That is because the institution of catastrophic damage[64] – as it is described by Article 4.1(c) of the 1971 Fund Convention – plays a very important rule in practice.[65]

In this connection the tonnage criterion for determining the amounts of liability and compensation was discussed as there is no link between the tonnage of a ship and the contribution to the Fund. For this reason Poland suggested disposing of a tonnage-linked system and – instead of it – to assign ships into one of four categories: SMALL – up to 5,000 tons; MEDIUM – from 5,000 to 7,500 tons; LARGE – from 7,500 to 150,000 tons; SUPER-LARGE – any other ships for an equal amount of compensation for each category.[66] This proposal was not introduced during the International Legal Conference because a matter of the limits of the Funds compensation (as well as the limits of shipowners liability) was discussed by the informal groups to the last days of the Conference and the progress was made in another direction.

How to share or balance financial liability between the shipping and oil industries? This crucial question was mainly discussed in the context of the Funds limits of compensation. The majority of states expressed their view that the 1984 regime of liability and compensation should keep the balance

[63] During the Stockholm informal meeting. *See* LEG/CONF. 6/7 containing summaries of the discussion of the Legal Committee of IMO.

[64] *See*: note 58. This point of view was presented by Z. Brodecki in his book entitled 'Obowiazek naprawienia szkod o rozmiarach katastrofalnych', (Compensation for Great Disasters) Gdansk 1978.

[65] *See*: LEG/CONF/ 6/C. 2/INF. 4. Summary of Incidents submitted by the Director of the I.O.P.C. Fund – Annex 3.

[66] LEG/CONF/ 6/26.

established by the 1969/1971 regime of liability and compensation in respect of oil pollution. Although this idea was not criticised, the Polish delegation stressed the view that to keep a balance of economic interest between a ship and a cargo the Conference could justify a larger multiplication factor for the Fund than for the shipowner, because by increasing the shipowners liability many cases of pollution now covered by the Fund would no longer be covered.

The representatives of the oil industry (particularly OCIMF) made an effort to prove that the capacity of the industry to cover pollution liability had markedly increased over the past decade and therefore the limitation figure for the shipowner should be sufficiently high to cover all claims except the very large claims, for which the Fund would then be available to provide supplemental cover.[67]

But the representatives of the shipowners questioned the view that the contribution of the oil industry should be limited to catastrophic cases of pollution and they also queried the suggestions which would result in a major increase in the owner's liability but only a limited addition to the liability limit to be borne by the oil industry.[68] According to OECD statistics presented by INTERTANKO the transportation cost of oil when the 1969/1971 regime of liability and compensation was established was about forty per cent of the price of oil, whereas the percentage was currently two per cent. In these circumstances – as a representative of INTERTANKO said – it would be paradoxical to reduce the oil industry's contributions and reverse the balance of the burdens against the shipowner.

Some delegations expressed the view that the amounts laid down in the CLC should not be increased to such an extent that the International Oil Pollution Compensation Fund would only intervene in exceptional cases as – according to the principle of shared responsibility – the Fund should continue to play a role in compensating victims of oil pollution damage.

The decision taken by the International Legal Conference as regards the limitation amounts shows that the oil industry lobby (being supported by the environmentalists) was more successful than the shipping lobby. Therefore, Article 4 paragraph 4 of the 1971 Fund Convention was amended as follows:

'4. (a) Except as otherwise provided in subparagraphs (b) and (c) of this paragraph, the aggregate amount of compensation payable by the Fund under this Article shall in respect of any one incident be limited, so that the total sum of that amount and the amount of compensation actually paid under the 1984 Liability Convention for pollution damage within the scope of application of this Convention as defined in Article 3 shall not exceed 135 million units of account.

[67] LEG. 49/3/8.
[68] LEG/CONF. 6/INF. 2/Rev. 1.

(b) Except as otherwise provided in subparagraph (c), the aggregate amount of compensation payable by the Fund under this Article for pollution damage resulting from a natural phenomenon of an exceptional, inevitable and irresistible character shall not exceed 135 million units of account.

(c) The maximum amount of compensation referred to in subparagraphs (a) and (b) shall be 200 million units of account with respect to any incident occurring during any period when there are three Parties to this Convention in respect of which the combined relevant quantity of contributing oil received by persons in the territories of such Parties, during the preceding calendar year, equalled or exceeded 600 million tons.'

RECOGNITION AND ENFORCEMENT OF FOREIGN ARBITRAL AWARDS IN ITALY UNDER THE NEW YORK CONVENTION OF 1958

AVV. MARIO RICCOMAGNO

Studio legale Riccomagno, *Genoa* (*Italia*)

The New York Convention[1] (hereinafter: 'The Convention') has been effective in Italy for more than sixteen years. Its impact on the former legislation on arbitration has been (and still is) substantial: this has been increasingly perceived by the requests to the Courts to give plain meaning to its provisions.

The purpose of this paper is to report on the actual conditions of application of the Convention in the Italian Courts.

I. Article 1

1. THE LIMITS OF THE APPLICABILITY OF THE CONVENTION

The Convention refers not only to commercial but also to all civil disputes. Its very large field of applicability receives only a territorial restriction inasmuch as the only awards which cannot be enforced are the 'domestic' ones (as expressly stated by Art. 1.1 of the Convention).

Domestic awards are those rendered in the same State where the recognition is sought and are not considered foreign by the law of such a State.[2]

It has been questioned whether the recognition and the enforcement under the terms of the Convention can be given to the awards settling the disputes between two Italian parties when they decided to submit the dispute between them to arbitrators abroad.

Such agreement was not considered as against the Italian rules of public order by the Supreme Court[3] which in its decisions stated that, irrespective

[1] The New York Convention of 10 June 1958, was enacted in Italy by the Law of 19 January 1968, n. 62, and came into force on 1 May 1969.

The Geneva Protocol of 24 September 1923, relating to the arbitration clauses and the Geneva Convention of 26 September 1927, for the enforcement of the foreign arbitral awards have been abrogated by the Convention in all their parts but those which are not inconsistent with the same.

Such principle already contained in Art. 7.2 of the Convention has been constantly affirmed by the Italian Supreme Court: see its judgment of 11 September 1979, n. 4746 (reported in Dir. Mar. 1980, 31) which refers to Cass. 25 January 1977, n. 361 (reported in Riv. dir. int. priv. proc. 1978, 118); Cass. 20 February 1977, n. 272 (reported in Rass. Arb. 1977, 87); Cass. 8 November 1976, n. 4082 (reported in Foro it. 1977, 1, 2756); Cass. 8 April 1975, n. 1269 (reported in Dir. Mar. 1976, 21).

[2] In Italy such domestic arbitrations fall within the provisions of the Italian Civil Code of Procedure of 1940 and the following amendments (among them are important those contained in the recent Law 9 February 1983, n. 28).

[3] Corte di Cassazione, 25 January 1977, n. 361, mentioned above: see note 1. The same interpretation has been also given by the Court of First Instance of Naples 20 November 1982, reported in Dir. Mar. 1984, 337, and by the Court of Appeal of Florence 22 October 1976, reported in Yearbook Commercial Arbitration 1978, 279.

of the nationality of the parties, the Convention applies whenever the enforcement is sought before a Court of a State other than that where the award was made.

2. 'ARBITRATI IRRITUALI' FALL INTO THE CONVENTION

In another decision[4] the Supreme Court has stated the important principle that, within the meaning of 'arbitral awards' (to which the Convention applies) are to be included those rendered in the free arbitrations ('arbitrati irrituali'). In Italy the free arbitrations are those whereby the parties concerned submit their disputes to a third party to decide without being bound by the rules of the Code of Civil Procedure on arbitration proceedings and, in the majority of cases, these follow the dictates of justice and fairness rather than those of law: the award has therefore a contractual nature whereby the arbitrators carry out a specific mandate given to them by the parties in dispute.[5]

3. THE AWARDS RENDERED IN COUNTRIES WHICH ARE NOT PARTY TO THE CONVENTION AND THEIR RECOGNITION IN ITALY

The last paragraph of Art. 1 of the Convention applies in Italy to arbitrations which have taken place in Countries which have not introduced the Convention into their legislation. It must be said that Italy has not availed itself of either reciprocity reservation or the commercial reservation contained in Art. 1, para 3: therefore such rule has no restriction.

These principles have been recently upheld by the Supreme Court in its decision of 21 February 1984, n. 1234.[6]

II. Article 2

To which norm is it necessary to refer in order to decide on the validity of the arbitration agreement

One crucial point is that of laying down the criterion under which it can be determined whether the form of the 'agreement in writing' requested by clause 2 is valid or not for the purposes of the enforcement of the award (see also clause V.1(a) of the Convention).

[4] Cass. 18 September 1978, n. 4167, reported in Dir. Mar. 1978, 671.

[5] The 'arbitrato irrituale' differs from the 'arbitrato rituale' (or 'formal arbitration') governed by the Code of Civil Procedure. Without going into details, it should be mentioned that arbitrators are necessarily bound by the basic rules of civil procedure, must decide according to the law, unless the parties have expressly given them the power to decide according to what they deem to be just and fair. The court then issues a decree which has the effect of giving the same force to the award as if it were a judgment.

[6] Reported in Dir. Mar. 1985, 39. The Supreme Court referred to its decisions of Cass. 20 December 1982, n. 7033, reported in Dir. Mar. 1983, 284; Cass. 11 February 1982, n. 836, reported in Riv. dir. int. priv. proc. 1982, 839; Cass. 11 September 1979, n. 4746, mentioned above: see note 1; Cass. 10 November 1973, n. 2969, reported in Riv. dir. int. priv. proc. 1974, 585; Cass. 27 February 1970, n. 470, reported in Riv. dir. int. priv. proc. 1970, 393.

1. THE DEVELOPMENTS OF THE SUPREME COURT

The Supreme Court with its decision of 21 February 1984, n. 1234[7] referring to its previous judgment of 14 November 1981, n. 6035[8] has stated that the formal validity of the arbitration clause is to be determined exclusively under Art. 2 para 2 of the Convention which makes it sufficient that the clause providing for arbitration abroad results from an agreement in writing including 'an arbitration clause or submission, signed by the parties or contained in an exchange of letters or telegrams'.

Such a decision, in which the interpretation of the arbitration agreement was based on the sheer wording of Art. 2 para 2 of the Convention is correct. But the Court came to such a conclusion only recently, for in the past years (more exactly in the sixties and in the seventies) it required that the validity of the form of the arbitration agreement (in most of the cases the arbitration clause) had to be determined under the law which is applicable persuant to Art. 26 of the Italian General Provisions of Law.[9]

The Court has now changed its approach to the problem and with the two cited decisions n. 6035/81 and n. 1234/84 has drawn a simpler line of construction in considering the domestic rules of conflicts superseded by the provisions of the Convention, which is immediately applicable as 'lex specialis' setting forth its own norms of uniform international character.

2. THE 'AGREEMENT IN WRITING' NEED NOT BE SIGNED BY THE PARTIES

It follows from the above that the 'agreement in writing' requested by the Convention is validly entered even if not signed by the parties, being sufficient if it results from telexes, telecopier or letters not bearing the

[7] Above mentioned: see note 6.

[8] Reported in Foro it. 1982, 1, 1640.

[9] This article provides three alternative rules of conflicts for determining the law of the 'inter vivos' acts among which is comprised the arbitration clause: (1) the law of the place where the act is made, (2) the law which governs the substance of the act, and (3) the law of the nationality of the disposing party, or of the contracting parties, if they have a common nationality. It is worth mentioning that in applying such rules of conflicts the Supreme Court (formerly expressed by Cass. 2 May 1960, n. 968, in Foro it. 1960, 1, 736; and even recently followed by Cass. 17 March, 1982, n. 1727, in Foro it. 1983, 1, 753) used to construe the arbitration clause according to the law of a Country other than Italy. In such a way it was normally excluded that the validity of an arbitration clause had to be interpreted according to the Italian law which is very strict as it provides that for such a clause to be valid, it must be specifically approved in writing (as required by Arts. 1341 and 1342 of the Civil Code) which is not necessary, usually, in the other legislations. Before the mentioned ruling of Cass. n. 968/80 the trend of the Italian Courts was stricter as the decision on the validity of the arbitration agreement was based only according to the law of the place where the enforcement was sought i.e. in Italy, the Italian law. It goes without saying how in that period the enforcement of the foreign awards was easily challenged in this Country by the defendant requesting the Court to ascertain whether the parties – very frequently aliens – failed to execute specifically the arbitration clause as it was in most of the cases.

signature of the parties.[10] It is necessary however that such documents, coming from the parties concerned, unequivocally express their intent to resort to arbitration proceedings.

3. CAN ITALIAN 'GIURISDIZIONE' BE DEROGATED WHEN THE MATTER SUBMITTED TO ARBITRATION IS CONNECTED TO AN ACTION PENDING BEFORE AN ITALIAN COURT?

The application of Art. 2 para 3 according to which a Court must refer the parties to arbitration if one of them contends the competence of the Court on the grounds that a valid arbitration agreement exists, does not, in general, cause any problem in Italy. However, some observations may be made with regard to a specific situation.

As Art. 4.3 of the Italian Civil Code of Procedure provides that a foreigner may be subjected to Italian 'giurisdizione' (which is the adjudicatory power of the Italian Ordinary Courts over alien natural persons or foreign legal persons) if the action against him is connected with another action properly pending in the Italian Court, it is still unclear whether, according to such a norm, the judges are obliged not to refer to arbitrators a dispute connected to another dispute properly pending before an Italian Court.

The Supreme Court has decided in a conflicting manner.

In a decision of 14 November 1981, n. 6035[11] it was held that Art. 4.3 mentioned applies with the consequence that the Italian Court is only competent to hear on both cases having common elements.

On the opposite the joinder of actions was denied in the following decision of 12 January 1982, n. 124.[12] Such judgment referred to an earlier

[10] Cass. 30 July 1984, n. 4537, reported in Rep. Foro it. 1984, arbitrato n. 34; *see also* Cass. 19 January 1984, n. 465, reported in Riv. dir. int. priv. proc. 1984, 583, which refers to Cass. 6 July 1982, n. 4039, reported in Foro it. 1983, 1, 736; Cass. 17 March 1982, n. 1727, above mentioned: see note 9; Cass. 11 February 1982, n. 836, above mentioned: see note 6; Cass. 14 November 1981, n. 6035, above mentioned: see note 8, which refers to Cass. 11 September 1979, n. 4746, above mentioned: See note 1; and to Cass. 25 May 1976, n. 1877, reported in Dir. Mar. 1978, 442.

[11] Above mentioned: see note 1.

The factual circumstances of this case are the following. Plaintiff was the consignee/buyer of a cargo of soya beans ascertained as damaged at the discharge in Venice. He sued before the Trieste Court the carrier, the seller and the cargo insurers: all were foreign companies and the relevant contract of carriage sale and insurance contained arbitration clauses. All the defendants challenged the 'giurisdizione' of the Italian Courts on the basis of the arbitration clause. The Court of First Instance accepted the objection, which decision was affirmed by the Court of Appeal. The plaintiff appealed to the Supreme Court which reversed holding that the arbitration clause in the charter party was not sufficiently incorporated into the bill of lading and that by virtue of the Italian principle of connexity of actions the action against the seller and the insurer had also to be tried before the Italian Courts.

[12] Reported in Rep. Foro it. 1982, 'Arbitrato', n. 40.

decision of Cass. 15 September 1977, n. 3989[13] which upheld that the criteria which are used to determine the presence of the required degree of connection must be construed more broadly than those adopted to qualify the subject matter competence in the case of joinder of domestic actions: as a consequence the Italian 'giurisdizione' is derogated by a valid arbitration clause even in the event that such a dispute is connected to that to be tried before an Italian Court. In this light if the collateral issue represented by the dispute which falls within the competence of the arbitrators is to be decided principaliter, the Italian Court has to halt the proceedings until the award is rendered.

III. Article 3

The exclusion of the possibility of a re-examination of the merits of the award in the enforcement proceedings tried before the Italian Courts

The Court of First Instance of Naples and the Court of Appeal of Messina[14] held that Art. 3 of the Convention (which provides that the award shall be recognized in accordance with the rules of procedure of the territory where the award is relied upon, under the conditions laid down in the Convention) cannot be invoked to make application of Art. 798 of Italian Civil Code of Procedure allowing a re-examination of the merits.

The Court held that such an article, as all the provisions existing in the Italian Code of Procedure setting forth the conditions for enforcing the foreign awards,[15] is not applicable anymore to the foreign awards which fall under the New York Convention, and cannot be used to introduce additional requirements and conditions to a Convention which provides itself that the foreign arbitral awards must be recognized and enforced by the Courts' sought for the 'exequatur' unless the grounds of exclusion contained in Art. 5 of the same Convention occur.

IV. Article 4

When the recognition and enforcement of a foreign arbitral award can be contended

Article 5 states when the recognition and enforcement of the foreign arbitral awards can be refused.

For their importance it is necessary to examine singulatim the different grounds provided for by paras 1 and 2 of this article.

[13] Reported in Riv. dir. int. priv. proc. 1978, 771.

[14] Decisions of 30 June 1976 and of 19 May 1976, reported in Riv. dir. int. priv. proc. 1977, 861 and 1978, 77.

[15] Art. 800 CCP and articles it recalls (796–799 CCP).

FIRST PARAGRAPH

GROUND (*A*): This proviso deals with the *invalidity of the arbitration agreement* on which some comments have already been made when examining Art. 2.

Problems of some concern may arise on the following points.

1. WHETHER AN ARBITRATION AGREEMENT, WITHIN THE MEANING OF ART. 2 PARA 2 OF THE CONVENTION, IS VALIDLY ENTERED WHEN THE PARTIES IN THE CONTRACT MADE REFERENCE TO SOME GENERAL CONDITIONS EMBODYING THE ARBITRAL CLAUSE AND CONTAINED IN A SEPARATE DOCUMENT

The Supreme Court faced the problem for the first time in 1971 with the leading case '*Ditta Miserocchi v. Agnesi SpA*'[16] in a dispute regarding a sale of corn.

The point to be decided was whether the Italian 'giurisdizione' was derogated having the parties (both Italian) in the sale contract referred to the form 27 of LCTA (London Cover Trade Association) whose Art. 32 provided for 'Arbitration in London' and recalled in its turn the form 73 of LCTA for the 'Rules of the Arbitration'.

The principle established by the Court, then followed in subsequent decisions,[17] is that the reference is valid only when it can be presumed that the parties, in making the reference to some standard terms laid down in a document other than the original contract, really intended to adopt the arbitration clause therein embodied. For the Court the only ground on which such a presumption can be based is that the incorporating contract (bill of lading or sale agreement signed by the parties) makes a specific reference to the artibration clause ('*relatio perfecta*').

An example of a valid incorporation of the arbitral clause contained in the charter party, into a bill of lading is the following term:

'All other conditions, including arbitration clause, as per c/p'

or similar.

On the opposite if the reference is made to the general terms of the c/p

[16] Cass. 13 December 1971, n. 3620, reported in Foro it. 1972, 1, 615.

[17] Most of the following decisions regarded the incorporation of the arbitration clause contained in the charter party into a bill of lading: Cass. 8 April 1975, n. 1269, above mentioned: See note 1; Cass. 14 November 1981, n. 6035, above mentioned: See note 8; Court of First Instance of Naples 20 November 1982, above mentioned: see note 3; *see also* Cass. 22 April 1976, n. 1439, reported in Foro it. 1976, 1, 1495 (regarding the reference to the Rules of a P and I Club, which included an arbitration clause, made by an insurance agreement) and Cass. 18 September 1978, n. 4167, above mentioned: see note 4, regarding a sale contract.

the reference is invalid ('*relatio imperfecta*') with the consequence that the arbitration agreement does not meet the requirements of the Convention and the 'giurisdizione' of the arbitral Tribunal is denied when the recognition of the foreign award in Italy is tried before a local Court.

An example of invalid incorporation is that deriving from the following clause:

> 'All terms, conditions, liberties and exceptions of the c/p are herewith incorporated'

It is worth remarking how the criteria adopted by the Italian Courts are stricter than those expressed by the English Courts which, prima facie, consider the arbitration clause validly incorporated in the bill of lading even if the bill of lading refers to the general terms of the c/p.

It is hoped that such an English approach to the problem will be shared not before long also by the Italian Courts, so to have less schematic judgments on this point.

The trend should be that of holding the arbitration clause valid even when the reference is made to all the general terms of the charter party but other factors (e.g. the customs of a particular trade) show that the parties intended, or at least were aware, that their disputes were to be settled by way of arbitration. A significant step towards the introduction in Italy of the Anglo-Saxon view was given by the Court of Appeal of Venice of 26 April 1983[18] which decided a dispute regarding a sale agreement between two Italian parties.

The Court ruled that when the validity of the arbitration clause must be construed in accordance to a foreign law (in that particular case the standard form the parties adopted contained a clause providing for the applicability of the English law to the contract) the arbitration clause must be adjusted as validly incorporated in the original contract even if this is not allowed according to the above outlined Italian criteria.

2. WHETHER THE ARBITRATION CLAUSE CONTAINED (OR VALIDLY INCORPORATED) IN A BILL OF LADING IS ALSO VALID AND EFFECTIVE VIS-À-VIS THE CONSIGNEE TO WHOM THE BILL OF LADING HAS BEEN ENDORSED

The Italian Supreme Court in the two significant decisions of 18 May 1978, n. 2392[19] and 11 September 1979, n. 4746[20] upheld that the endorsement of the bill of lading entitles the endorsee to exercise all the rights arising from the contract of carriage including the right to act against the carrier for the damages incurred to the cargo, and that the close linkage of

[18] Reported in Dir. Mar. 1984, 326.
[19] Reported in Foro it. 1979, 1, 158.
[20] Above mentioned: see note 1.

the arbitral clause with the other terms of the bill of lading also entitles the endorsee to avail himself of the arbitration clause.

But in such decisions the Supreme Court has maintained that condition for a valid enforcement from the shipper to the consignee of all the terms of the bill of lading (and in particular among them the arbitration clause) is that the shipper had formerly signed for acceptance the front of the bill of lading. The Court therefore requested a signature of the shipper 'for acceptance' – which is not common in the trade (where the bill of lading is signed only by the carrier/master/agent) – different from that 'for endorsement'.

The reasoning of the Court is not convincing inasmuch as it seems to forget that under Art. 2 para 2 of the Convention the arbitration clause has to be considered effective even if contained in a writing coming from one party only (and the bill of lading is a document of the carrier) but it can be ascertained or reasonably induced to presume that the other party (the shipper) was nevertheless aware of the content of all its general terms and in particular, among them, of the arbitration clause.

This now reported view, which – it must be remarked – was shown, even if impliedly, by the Supreme Court in its former judgment on the subject matter after the entry in force of the Convention[21] is now followed by most of the Italian Courts of First Instance and it is hopeful that some of the actually pending cases will come to the Supreme Court determining the overruling of the principle of the mentioned double signature of the bill of lading.

3. WHETHER THE PRODUCTION OF THE BILL OF LADING IN COURT BY THE CONSIGNEE IN AN ACTION AGAINST THE CARRIER IS PER SE A VALID ACCEPTANCE FROM THE CONSIGNEE OF THE ARBITRATION CLAUSE EMBODIED IN THE SMALL BILL OF LADING (SEE THE ABOVE MENTIONED DECISION N. 1269 OF 1975 OF THE SUPREME COURT LEADS TO ANOTHER COLLATERAL QUESTION)

Such judgment gave the affirmative answer with the result that the validity of the arbitration clause was stated and the 'giurisdizione' of the Court in front of which the consignee tried the case against the carrier (the action was a cargo claim) was denied.

Three other following decisions of the Supreme Court adopted the same view.[22]

It is worth stressing that this point is not well established in the Italian jurisprudence so far. Indeed in a ruling of 1978[23] the Supreme Court decided contrawise, upholding that if the consignee produces the bill of

[21] Cass. 8 April 1975, n. 1269, above mentioned: see note 1.

[22] Cass. 30 December 1977, n. 5756, and Cass. 30 May 1977, n. 2216 reported in Rep. Foro it. 1977, 'Contratti in genere', 117 and 118; Cass. 6 July 1982, n. 4039, above mentioned: see note 10.

[23] Cass. 18 May, 1978, n. 2392, above mentioned: see note 19.

lading in Court against the carrier he expresses the intention to have his claim adjudged on the basis of such documentary evidence by the same Court in front of which he brought the action instead of by the arbitrators. As a consequence such factual and inequivocal conduct cannot be used to decide against him denying the 'giurisdizione' of the Court on the basis of the arbitration clause in the bill of lading.

The above mentioned view of the Supreme Court seems to be followed by some Courts of First Instance which are more inclined to share the formerly reported reasoning of the Corte di Cassazione so maintaining that the arbitration clause remains valid and effective for the purposes of derogating the Italian 'giurisdizione' even in the case of production of the bill of lading in Court by the same consignee.

4. WHETHER THE AGENT ENTERING THE ARBITRATION AGREEMENT MUST BE AUTHORIZED IN WRITING

Article 1392 of the Italian Civil Code sets forth that a power of attorney has no effect unless it is conferred with the formalities prescribed for the contract which is to be made by the agent.

As the arbitration agreement must be made in writing also the authorization granted to the agent to enter it, according to Italian law, has to be made in writing.

Problems arise when the foreign principal, acting in accordance with his law, gives to his agent, often a broker, only a verbal authorization.

As the Convention contains no provisions on this regard, the Italian Supreme Court considers Art. 26 of General Provisions of Law to be applicable. Such a norm points to the law of the place where the agreement is concluded. Consequently, if according to the rules of conflicts therein set forth, the applicable law admits that the authorization to the agent need not be in writing, the arbitration agreement entered by the agent, so empowered, is valid.[24]

GROUND (B): Deprival of the right of defence of the party against which the enforcement is sought.

This ground does not cause particular problems. Italian Courts have nevertheless clarified that a party was not 'unable to present his case' where he was duly informed of the arbitration and summoned to appoint his arbitrator but nevertheless remained inactive.[25]

[24] Cass. 15 December 1982, n. 6915, reported in Foro it. 1983, 1, 2200; Cass. 25 January 1977, n. 361, above mentioned; see note 1; Cass. 8 April 1975, n. 1269, above mentioned: see note 1; Cass. 27 February 1970, n. 470, above mentioned: see note 6; App. Naples, 22 March 1980, reported in Dir. Mar. 1980, 513.

[25] Cass. 27 June 1983, n. 4399, reported in Riv. dir. int. priv. proc. 1984, 571; Cass. 28 January 1982, n. 563, reported in Dir. Mar. 1983, 743; Cass. 7 October 1980, n. 5378, reported in Dir. Mar. 1982, 67; Court of Appeal of Bari, 30 April 1984, reported in Riv. dir. int. priv. proc. 1985, 359; Court of Appeal of Naples, 20 February 1975, reported in Riv. dir. in. priv. proc. 1977, 839.

GROUND (C): Award deciding on matters not contemplated by the submissions or not falling within the terms of the arbitration clause.

Also this paragraph seems not to cause difficulties for the applications of the Convention in Italy.

GROUND (D): Irregularities in the formation of the Tribunal and in the arbitration procedure.

There is no doubt that the composition of the arbitral Tribunal and the arbitral procedure are either determined by the parties or, if this agreement is missing, governed by the law of the place of arbitration.

Some problems may arise with regard to the compatibility between the method of a proper constitution of the Tribunal (and of the following arbitration procedure) with the Italian rules of public order. They will be examined when dealing with Art. 5 para 2.

GROUND (E): Awards not yet binding or set aside or stayed by the Court of the Country where they were issued.

With some recent decisions the Italian Supreme Court has clarified that the meaning 'as become binding' of the foreign awards allows the Italian Courts to grant the enforcement even if an exequatur (leave for enforcement) of the Court of the place where the award was issued had not been obtained.[26]

Such decisions referred to the leading case '*Pagnan v. Butera*' decided by the Italian Supreme Court on 18 September 1978 (judgment n. 4167)[27] whereby it was stated that any award made abroad can be recognized and enforced once it has binding force between the parties; the Supreme Court held that the Italian free arbitrations (see para 1 above of this paper) having contractual nature fall under the Convention and consequently can be enforced under the terms of it. This dictum remains unchanged and was followed to enforce in Italy many free arbitral awards (as those of the London Maritime Arbitrators' Association which are considered free in Italy).

With particular reference to such English awards two queries can be posed.

(i) The former is whether a final arbitral award, which is still open to the ordinary means of attack under the law applicable to it, can be recognized and enforced. The answer seems to be affirmative as the Arbitration Act 1979 has not amended Sect. 16 of the Arbitration Act 1950 which sets forth that the award to be rendered by the arbitrator or umpire shall be final and

[26] Cass. 20 December 1982, n. 7033, above mentioned: see note 6; Cass. 15 December 1982, n. 6915, above mentioned: see note 24; Cass. 28 January 1982, n. 563, reported in Dir. Mar. 1983, 743; Cass. 15 April 1980, n. 2448, reported in Foro it. 1980, 1, 2164; Cass. 27 February 1979, n. 1273, reported in Dir. Mar. 1979, 188.

[27] Above mentioned: see note 4; see also Cass. 6 July 1982, n. 4039, above mentioned: see note 10; Cass. 28 January 1982, n. 563, above mentioned: see note 25.

binding as such. As a consequence if, pending the enforcement proceedings, the award is under appeal the Court of enforcement is allowed to start or to continue the relevant proceedings and – if deemed appropriate – to order to the party contending such a halt to secure the other party with a guarantee (see Art. 6 of the Convention).

(ii) A second question is, where the English award is varied on appeal, whether the award or rather the judgment of the High Court becomes enforceable.

The answer seems to be that the judgment of the High Court is subject to the exequatur: indeed Section 1, n. 8, of the Arbitration Act 1979 provides that when the original award has been confirmed or varied by the Court 'the award as varied shall have effect as if it was the award of the arbitrator or umpire'.

SECOND PARAGRAPH

This paragraph provides that the Court may refuse recognition and enforcement if the award, according to the law of its Country, deals with a subject matter that cannot be settled by arbitration or is contrary to public order.

Controversies that are non arbitrable in Italy include disputes relating to workmen's compensation and social security, matters of personal status, marital separations and all other nondispositive matters.

With particular reference to compatibility with the public order the Courts in general are somewhat reluctant on refusing the enforcement of the award on such an issue. In this light the following points have been clarified.

A. THERE IS NO GROUND FOR REFUSING THE ENFORCEMENT IF NO REASONS WERE GIVEN BY THE ARBITRATORS

This was initially upheld by three Courts of Appeal: namely those of Florence with the decisions of 22 October 1976[28] and of 8 October 1977[29] and of Genova with the decision of 2 May 1980,[30] which stated that the violation of the public order must be appreciated on the basis of the decision and not on the reasoning of the award.[31]

[28] Above mentioned: see note 3.

[29] Reported in *Rassegna dell'Arbitrato*, 1978, 161.

[30] Reported in Dir. Mar. 1981, 233.

[31] The Courts more exactly stated that the New York Convention does not provide any requirement as to the reasoning for an arbitral decision. Furthermore, as the Convention excludes a re-examination of the merits of the award, it can be inferred that the reasoning has no relevance. Moreover, the fact that the reasoning constitutes a principle of the Italian Constitution is not important because what is fundamental in Italian Law of Procedure may not be considered as such by foreign legislative and judicial authorities.

The Courts of Appeal recalled that under Angle-Saxon and U.S. law the reasoning is not required in the award.

In the following years the Supreme Court has shared the same view of the mentioned Courts of Appeal.[32]

B. THE ITALIAN COURTS HAVE ALSO RULED THAT THE ENFORCEMENT CANNOT BE REFUSED ON THE GROUNDS OF THE PUBLIC ORDER WHEN THE AWARD WAS RENDERED BY TWO ARBITRATORS OR BY A SOLE ARBITRATOR APPOINTED BY ONE OF THE PARTIES

(i) With reference to the former hypothesis some doubts may arise when considering that Art. 809, first para, of the Italian Civil Code of Procedure spells out as follows:

> 'Arbitrators can be one or more provided that an odd number of arbitrators is provided for.'

It seems therefore that the Italian public order hinders the enforcement in Italy of those foreign awards rendered by a Tribunal where an odd number of arbitrators was sitting.

A very clear decision on this issue was rendered by the Italian Supreme Court on 15 December 1982, n. 6915.[33]

The Court was requested to decide on whether an English award rendered (before the enactment of the Arbitration Act 1979) by two arbitrators (in an arbitration where, according to Sect. 8 of the Arbitration Act 1950, they agreed their decision of the merits without the previous appointment of an umpire) was consistent with the principles of Italian law.

[32] Cass. 30 October 1979, n. 5678, reported in Giust. Civ. Rep. 1979, 'Delibazione', n. 21; Cass. 28 May 1979, n. 3073, in Riv. dir. int. priv. proc. 1980, 418.

More recently the Italian Supreme Court took an almost surprising decision (Cass. 8 February 1982, n. 722, reported in Riv. dir. int. priv. proc. 1982, 829) in which it was held to be against the Italian public order an English award issued in London according to the rules of the Council of the Refined Sugar Association (before the enactment of the Arbitration Act 1979) in which, pending the proceedings, one party requested a reasoned award. The Court argued that as both parties concerned (one Italian, the other German) were citizens of Member States of the Geneva Convention on International Commercial Arbitration of 21 April 1961, it was presumable that their intention was to impliedly apply art. 8 of the said Convention which establishes the presumption that the parties are content for the arbitrators to issue a reasoned award. This judgment seems not correct. Indeed, instead of focusing on whether the parties were citizens of Member States of the 1961 Convention the Courts would have had to ascertain whether the parties, in the arbitration agreement, intended to have a London award. As England is not a party to the Geneva Convention of 1961 but only to that of New York of 1958 this Convention only had to apply. As such a Convention recalls the rules of procedure of the place where the award was issued (and in England normally the awards are without reasons) the English award, prima facie, had to be considered enforceable in Italy. It would have been then a question of fact to decide whether the parties, pending the arbitration, were looking at the reasons (which seemed unclear in those particular circumstances) instead of resorting to criteria based on presumption.

[33] Above mentioned: see note 24. Such judgment confirms the decision of the Court of Appeal of Naples on 22 March 1980, above mentioned: see note 24.

The judgment of the Supreme Court was in the affirmative and it was based on the assumption that the parties, in agreeing the short form of the arbitration clause 'arbitration to be held in London', accepted that the law governing the arbitration was the English one (where the awards rendered by a panel of even arbitrators are valid). For the Court the lack of mention of the number and powers of the arbitrators and of the rules of procedure did not invalidate the clause, because such elements, if not expressly agreed beforehand have to be determined under the law of the Country where the arbitration takes place, being sufficient that the Country in which the award is to be rendered is indicated in the clause. In such a way the principles and the provisions of Italian law become ineffective.

It is to be remarked that also in this subject matter the will of the parties prevails.

In fact the Court of Appeal of Florence on 13 April 1978[34] has stated, in a dispute based on an Exxonvoy Form 1963 (with London arbitration clause where the parties did not provide for amending clause 24 which requires that the Arbitral Tribunal is to be formed with three arbitrators), that even if English law was applicable, the composition of the Arbitral Tribunal which rendered the award was a ground for refusing the enforcement of the award since in those proceedings it was clearly rendered by two arbitrators.

(ii) The Italian Courts have held that the exequatur can be granted in Italy even if the foreign award was rendered by a sole arbitrator appointed by one of the parties, provided his impartiality was fairly guaranteed.

Deciding on the enforceability in Italy of two English awards rendered by a sole arbitrator, the Court of Appeal of Venice on 21 May 1976[35] and the Court of Appeal of Genova on 2 May, 1980[36] stated that although the Sect. 7 of the English Arbitration Act 1950 provides that the reference shall be to two arbitrators, such a norm must be construed by analogy with the other relevant sections of the Act (ss. 8 and 9) so as to permit also, in the case of a reference to three arbitrators, the appointment by a party of his arbitrator as the unique arbitrator where the other party fails to appoint his arbitrator.

Distinguishing between domestic public policy (according to which such an appointment would be invalid: Art. 829 of Italian Civil Code of Procedure) and international public policy, the Court has not deemed the appointment as a violation of fundamental principles of the Italian public order.

Moreover, the English Arbitration Act safeguards the impartiality in several ways, as, for example, Section 7 which recalls the powers of the High Court in setting aside any wrongful appointment.

[34] Reported in Yearbook Commercial Arbitration 1979, 294.
[35] Reported in Riv. dir. int. priv. proc. 1976, 851.
[36] Reported in Dir. Mar. 1981, 233.

DISPUTES CONCERNING LAY DAYS (A PRACTICAL POINT OF VIEW OF THE MARITIME ARBITRATION COMMISSION)

A.L. Makovski

Doctor of Law. Vice President of the Soviet Association of Maritime Law

TABLE OF CONTENTS:

This review of MAC practice in adjudicating disputes about demurrage and dispatch includes only those cases considered by the Commission which deal with calculation of lay days – their number, when the lay days start to run, periods excluded from lay time. Beyond this review are left many cases dealing with more general issues of liability for ships' delays – consequences of the ship's delay not connected with loading or unloading, liability for the delay in carriage of goods under liner terms, liability of the character for the delay of the ship in the port of discharge, liens on the cargo, etc.

Thus, below will follow examination mainly on these MAC lay days cases which are the result of different understanding and application of charter's provisions by the parties. Variety of such provisions, insufficiency of national legislation applicable to relations concerning lay days and complicated by 'foreign element', lack of any internationally agreed uniform rules in this regard – all of this make the study and analysis of the MAC practice in this kind of cases practically useful.

Only recently the first effort was undertaken to create for these relations such business usages which could make a contract practice as to provisions regarding lay days and demurrage to a certain extent more uniform and could help in more consistent settlement of disputes related to these provisions in various countries. In December 1980 the Charterparty Laytime Definitions 1980 approved by the Baltic and International Maritime Conference (BIMCO), International Maritime Committee (IMC), Federation of National Associations of Ship Brokers and Agents (FONASBA) and General Council of British Shipping were published.[1] Containing definitions of 31 terms and expressions used in charters to regulate parties' relations regarding lay days, demurrage and dispatch, this document, in principle, is to be applied by reference to it in a charter. It is not excluded, however, that this document, if effective enough in practice, may, in our opinion, influence to a certain degree resolution of respective disputes even in the absence of such reference. The present review contains comparison of the MAC practice with construction of some charter provisions, which is given in the above named Definitions of 1980.

I. Beginning of lay time

Three conditions should be observed in order for the lay days to start running. First, the ship should arrive to the stipulated place of loading (or

[1] CMI News Letter, March 1981, pp. 3–5.

unloading). Such place could be the port indicated in the charter (charter for port), part of the port or particular berth (charter for berth). Only that ship which fulfilled this condition may be considered as 'arrived'. Secondly, the ship has to give a notice of readiness for loading or unloading. Thirdly, at the time indicated in the notice the ship should be in fact ready to take (or, respectively, to discharge) the cargo.

In MAC practice may be found cases regarding compliance with each of these conditions.

In regard of 'charters for port' it is very important to determine when the ship may be considered as having entered the port. This question becomes acute in estuary and other ports with long boundaries, when due to congestion of the ships, part of them come to anchor far from the place where loading or unloading is going on. Foreign practice, mostly of Great Britain, from the end of the 19th century resolves disputes concerning the possibility to consider such ships as 'arrived' by determining, whether the ship entered the 'commercial zone' of the port, i.e. the place, 'where the ships usually wait for loading or unloading, being at the disposal of charterers'[2] Analogous questions arose in MAC practice in connection with the delay of the Soviet ship chartered by 'Chekhofraht' and which arrived at Calcutta to take cargo.

The ship waited for a long time for loading at anchor in Sandhez, several tens of kilometers from Calcutta. The carrier tried to prove that in the course of this delay the lay days were running because administratively Sandhez is subordinated to Calcutta's port authority. The Commission did not agree with this argument and decided that the ship could not be considered as arrived since Sandhez is not included into the commercial zone of the port of Calcutta.[3]

It should be noted that the question which arose in this case now is settled in the above mentioned Charterparty Lay Time Definitions 1980. There, the 'port' which the ship should reach in accordance with the charter in order to be considered as 'arrived' is defined as the area, where the cargo is loaded on the ships or unloaded from the ships and includes, irrespective of the distance from that area, usual places where the ships await their turn or where they are directed or should await their turn (para. 1).

The question of including into lay days of the period of waiting for berth by the ship was raised before the MAC somewhat differently in the case

[2] M. Summerskil, Lay days, Translation from English, M., 1971, p. 81. In recent years the practice of English courts has changed somewhat. As H. Tiberg writes, with reference to cases involving ships 'Johanna Oldendorf' (1973) and 'Marapha Envoy' (1977), now 'the ship should be only 'within the port' in the position when it is really at the disposal of the charterers, if she has to wait for the berth to be free. What does mean 'within the port' – he notes – is unclear, but if the place of waiting is usual, it creates the presumption of the ship being within the port' (Tiberg H., The Law of Demurrage, Third ed., L., 1979, pp. 228–229).

[3] Aleksandrova K.I. Practice of Maritime Arbitration Commission concerning disputes arising out of carriage of goods by sea, M., 1966, p. 27 (In Russian).

involving m/v '*Ivan Moskvin*' chartered to carry cargo from Arkhangelsk to Larvik (Norway). The charter, to which there was usual reference in the bill of lading, contained a provision stating that unloading time runs 'irrespective of availability of berth' (para. 4). In the port of unloading the vessel waited for berth from 18 until 25 July and, according to calculations of the shipowner – Murmansk Steamship Line, counting lay days from the date of the ship's arrival, the delay amounted to 126 hours, for which it demanded demurrage from the consignee – Norwegian firm 'Aktieselskabet Trelandfos'. The latter, rejecting the carrier's demands, alleged that the consignees informed the charterers beforehand about unavoidable long delay of the ship in Larvik and about their refusal to admit any liability for this delay.

Deciding this case the Commission pointed out that the principal issue in dispute – concerning inclusion into lay days of the time the ship waited for berth – was 'clearly regulated by the provisions of the charter. . .'. Consignees' warning about unavoidable delay of the vessel in the port of destination, 'in MAC opinion, has no relevance for the resolution of the dispute, since the ship arrived for loading in time stipulated by the charter provisions and started the voyage timely. In order to postpone the arrival and departure of the ship the bilateral agreement between the carrier and consignee was necessary. Unilateral statement of the consignee or charterer is not sufficient for the postponement'. The Commission noted also that 'by the time the above mentioned warning was made m/v '*Ivan Moskvin*' was loaded and ready to start the voyage' (Case No. 21/68).[4]

The significance of this award going beyond the problems related to lay days and demurrage is in ascertaining the important rule that charter is a contract and, hence, non-compliance with it without liability is possible only on the basis of respective agreement (compare: Art. 33, part 4 of the Fundamentals of Civil Legislation of the USSR and Union Republics). However, the Commission probably was not quite exact in the award stating that such agreement should have been concluded 'between the carrier and consignee'. Only carrier and charterer can agree to change a charter. An agreement with consignee, for whom the charter provisions are binding (as in this case), is possible only to the extent that it does not contradict to these provisions, because otherwise the carrier who has made such an agreement may become liable before the charterer.

Importance of notice of the ship's readiness for loading or unloading given by the carrier to the owner of the cargo was considered in a number of the Maritime Arbitration Commission awards.

In the case of the delay of m/v '*Physic Vavilov*' in Beirut differences between the parties touched upon, inter alia, the question of the *form of notice*. The ship arrived at the port on 19 July and on the same day at 7 a.m. handed over through the agents to the consignor written notice of readiness.

[4] Collection of the Maritime Arbitration Commission awards in disputes arising out of carriage of goods by sea. (1962–1971), M., 1973, pp. 32–33 (In Russian).

Since the consignor refused to accept it, the master of the ship on the same day at 9 a.m. sent the notice by radio. The Commission held in the award that such 'radio message. . . confirms that the notice in fact has been given to the consignor just in that time' (case 7/74).[5]

Thus, the Commission held that it is admissible to use such manner of communication for notification of the cargo owners about the ship's readiness, and, moreover, came to the conclusion that the time of getting the notice in this case coincides with the time of sending the radio message.

Generally, unless the charter provides otherwise, the notice of readiness may be made in any form, even orally. It is important only that the owner of the cargo should be really notified that the ship is ready for loading (unloading) and that this fact could be proved. If the charter provides for the necessity to give notice in writing, it means that this provision requires to give notice by any method visually reproducing words, including telegram and telex (Charterparty Lay Time Definitions, 1980, Sec. 24). It is apparent that sending a radio message that can be received by the owner of the cargo satisfies this requirement.

The consequences of giving notice after working time were considered in two awards of the Maritime Arbitration Commission.

In the first case the notice of readiness of s/s '*Dmitry Pozharsky*' was given in the port of Djakarta on 5 April at 7.30 p.m., while the working hours in this port were from 8 a.m. to noon and from 1 p.m. to 6 p.m. The carrier, basing on the fact that the notice was given on 5 April, counted the lay days from 8 a.m. on 6 April, the charterer considered the notice as given at 8 a.m. on 6 April, and calculated the lay days from 1 p.m. of that day. In the second case the master of the British ship '*Glafida*' gave notice in the port of Poti on the Holiday, 31 December, at 2 p.m. This was certified in writing by the consignee on the notice and it was also stated that the notice 'is accepted on 2 January at 8 a.m.'. Later, the carrier considered the notice as given on 31 December, and the consignee insisted on its acceptance on 2 January. Basing on this and on the charter provisions the first one calculated lay days from 8 a.m. 2 January, and the latter – from 7 a.m. 3 January.

Both cases were decided by the MAC through construction of the terms of the respective charters. S/s '*Dmitry Pozharsky*' carried the goods under Gencon charter. The Commission took into account the provision of this charter under which lay days start to run from the beginning of the next working day, if 'notice given during office hours after noon' (Clause 6)'. The Commission came to the conclusion that notice given after office hours cannot cause lay time to be counted from the beginning of the next working day and held that the time commenced, as the charterer asserted, at 1 p.m. on 6 April (case 21/62).[6]

[5] Under the circimstances of this particular case the MAC could not, however, take this notice into account to determine the beginning of the lay days.

[6] *See*: Collection of the MAC Awards 1973, pp. 12–15: Keilin A.D. Maritime Arbitration in the USSR in recent years. – Merchant Shipping and Maritime Law, Collection of articles and documents, No. 1. M., 1963, p. 21 (In Russian).

S/s '*Glafida*' was chartered under 'Baltimor' charter, where it was said that notice should be given not later than 4 p.m. (or before noon on Saturday) and lay days start to run from 7 a.m. on the next working day (Clause 8). The Commission came to the conclusion that the text of this clause does not contain any limitation concerning holidays. So, the shipowner who had given notice on the holiday, 31 December, fulfilled his obligations, and since the office of the consignees was open on that day and notice was received by them, lay days should be counted from 8 a.m. on 2 January – the next working day (case 3/65).[7]

Both awards deal with one and the same issue and both are based on the analysis of the specific charter provisions. However, construction of these provisions not based on considerations of general nature led different arbitral tribunals to conclusions which did not quite coincide. It is submitted that the question which arose in both of the above mentioned cases could not be decided without taking into account the purpose of the period that under charter provisions, ports' customs and even the legislation of some countries elapses between the filing of notice of readiness and the beginning of loading or unloading. During this so called 'free time', usually counted in hours, the owner of the cargo has to make necessary arrangements for loading (or unloading), and for that purpose it should (at least partially) include working hours. That is why the notice given on a Sunday or a holiday, or on a working day but outside of office hours, is considered, as a general rule, as given in the morning of the next working day and, thus, the beginning of lay days is respectively postponed.[8]

The award of the Commission in the Glafida case does not follow this, in our opinion, rational principle and besides that gives rise to doubts concerning the construction of the charter provisions: if the parties agreed to reduce the time for giving notice on Saturday it hardly could be assumed that they intentionally agreed on the possibility to give it on Sunday and even without any limitations as to hours.

In several awards of the Maritime Arbitration Commission the issue of *the right of the cargo-owner for the 'free-time' in the second and following ports* of loading (or unloading) was considered. The Gencon charter, under which the Panamanian ship '*Aeftrick*' was chartered to carry cargo to three Japanese ports, contained usual for this charter provision that 'time to commence at 1 p.m. if notice of readiness to discharge is given before noon, and at 8 a.m. next working day if notice given during office hours after noon' (Clause 6). The charterers used this provision to calculate lay time in the second port of discharge, where notice was given at 2 p.m. on 4 February, and believed that time commenced at 8 a.m. on 5 February. The carrier thought that the above cited provision, unless otherwise specifically provided for in the charter, is applicable only to the first port of discharge. In the course of the hearings before the Commission the charterers agreed

[7] *See*: Collection of the MAC Awards. 1973, p. 24.
[8] Tiberg H., *op. cit.*, p. 335.

to count lay time in the second port from the moment the notice was given, and the Commission, basing on this, held the carrier entitled to the respective amount of money (case No. 5/65).[9] An analogous dispute concerning discharge of the ship in several Italian ports was decided likewise.[10]

In the doctrine the charterers' waiver of right for 'free time' in ports following the first one is substantiated by the consideration that if there was already a call at one port of loading, the charterer knows that the ship had started to fulfil her obligations.[11] Hence, the charterer is able to follow further movement of the ship and to prepare for loading (unloading) in other ports. Practice of English courts follows the same way as the MAC practice, while the courts of some other countries (the USA, Belgium, Denmark) are inclined rather to give 'free time' to a charterer in each successive port.[12]

The issue of the ship's actual readiness for loading/unloading as a condition for the beginning of lay days was discussed in the course of consideration by the MAC of a number of cases, mostly in connection with the necessity for the ship to fulfil border, customs and administrative formalities, i.e. to be granted 'free practice'.

The most interesting case in this regard is the case dealing with the delay of the tanker '*Giuseppe Garibaldi*' under discharge at the port of Leghorn. This ship unloaded in two ports – Genoa and Leghorn, and the contract between the charterer and the carrier provided that at the second and following ports time would commence at the moment of the ship's readiness according to notice. Basing on this the carrier – The Black Sea Steamship Line – counted lay days at Leghorn starting from 9.35 a.m., 17 May, when the ship gave notice of readiness to discharge at that port. The charterer – V/O 'Sojuznefteexport' – believed that before the tanker '*Giuseppe Garibaldi*' was granted 'free practice', i.e. 2.10 p.m., 18 May, the ship could not be considered as ready for discharge and, accordingly, lay days should be calculated not from the moment the notice was given by the ship, but 28 hours 45 minutes later.

In the award the Commission noted that the clause providing for the lay days to start from the moment indicated in the notice of readiness does not mean that lay days start irrespective of actual readiness of the ship to discharge and deliver the cargo. Since the owner of the cargo cannot start to fulfil his obligations concerning the discharge of the ship before the carrier actually makes the ship ready to discharge, the period of time given to the owner of the cargo to fulfil these obligations (lay days) cannot start to run as

[9] *See*: Maritime Law and Practice. Information Bulletin No. 33, (171), M., 1967, pp. 63–66 (In Russian).

[10] *See*: Maritime Law and Practice. Information Bulletin No. 35, (183), M., 1967, p. 52 (In Russian).

[11] Summerskil M., *supra*, p. 97. See also Aisenstein L. Staires et surestaries en droit français et comparé. P., 1965, p. 206.

[12] Aisenstein, L., *op. cit.*, p. 206; Tiberg H., *op. cit.*, pp. 329–330.

well, unless the ship is in fact ready for unloading. An important conclusion, to which the Commission arrived on the basis of these deliberations, is that 'if the ship is not ready to discharge at the moment stated in the notice, or, in some cases, at the moment the notice was given, lay days allowed for discharge start to run only at the moment when the ship is actually ready to discharge and deliver the cargo'. In the above mentioned case the MAC held that the moment when 'free practice' is granted depends mainly on the ship (readiness of the ship's documents, etc.) and, hence, before it is granted 'the carrier, as a general rule, cannot be considered as having fulfilled his obligations to make the ship actually ready to discharge, and the ship – as ready to discharge and deliver the cargo'. Therefore, the Commission held that it was correct to count lay days from the moment V/O 'Sojuznefteexport' insisted upon (case No. 19/63).[13]

Subsequently, the same approach to the beginning of lay time, when notice had been given before the ship was granted 'free practice', was taken in the award on the case where the charterers demanded money from the owners of the English s/s '*Rodnor*'. In this case, as it was held by the MAC, 'notice cannot be considered as notice of the ship's readiness for loading since at the moment such notice was given, the ship was not in fact ready for loading.'[14]

It is important to note that the MAC, deciding whether lay days start to run when 'free practice' has not been granted, considers this issue with regard to all circumstances of the particular case. In the above mentioned case concerning the delay of the tanker '*Giuseppe Garibaldi*' the Commission by the way noted that the general rule on beginning of lay time only after 'free practice' was granted cannot be applied when its granting was 'delayed due to circumstances dependent upon the consignor or consignee, for example, due to erroneosly issued cargo documents or impossibility to get a berth to which to order the ship and which is to be provided by the owner of the cargo'. In another case dealing with the delay of m/v '*Academic Yangel*' in Latakia, the MAC held that under the provisions of the charter concluded by the parties who used 'North American Grain Charterparty 1973', notice of the ship's readiness for loading/unloading was to be given by the master without regard to getting of 'free practice'. The Commission came to the conclusion that in such case 'the beginning of lay time does not depend on granting free practice to the ship' (Case No. 64/77).

II. Duration of lay time

The majority of the cases in the MAC practice concerning the duration of lay time deals with the calculation of time on the basis of fixed rates of

[13] *See*: Collection of the MAC Awards 1973, pp. 15–19.

[14] Keilin A.D. Maritime Arbitration Commission in 1964. – Merchant Shipping and Maritime Law. Collection of articles and documents No. 4, M., 1965, p. 5 (In Russian).

loading (or unloading) per one hatch provided for in the charter or otherwise.

The most widely used in foreign practice method to determine lay time in such cases is the largest-hold method. It means that the quantity of cargo in the largest hold should be divided by the rate per hatch per day. Since it is obvious that loading/unloading operations in that hold will require the longest period of time (i.e. they limit loading or unloading of the ship) the result is accepted as lay time for the while ship. Usually this method is applied when the charter provides for the rate per day per working hatch or per workable hatch. In those cases when the charter provides just for the rate of loading or unloading per hatch per day, more frequently is used the method of multiplying this rate by the number of the ship's hatches and, then, division of the quantity of the cargo to be loaded/unloaded by the product of multiplication.[15]

The practice has been confirmed recently by the Charterparty Lay Time Definitions 1980 (secs. 8, 9) with two significant additions. The first one, relevant to both methods of calculation of lay time, provides that the hatch that can be served simultaneously by two gangs is to be counted as two hatches. The second one relates only to the largest-hold method: if such hold has not one, but two or more hatches, the quantity of cargo in the hold is to be divided by the product of multiplication of the rate per hatch per day by the number of the hatches of this hold (sec. 9).

Despite the seeming clarity of the above rules the practice of the MAC shows that application of the rates per hatch per day causes a lot of disputes.

In the case dealing with the delay of English ship '*Ospray*' the dispute between the parties arose to what hatches should be taken into account in calculation of lay days. Since the five holds vessel had ten hatches, the shipowners calculated lay time by multiplying the rate per hatch per day by ten. As the Commission noted in the award, from the documents, photos and scheme of the ship's holds, presented by the charterer – V/O 'Sojuzpromexport' – it can be seen that simultaneous operation of ten hatches was not possible, because the construction of the ship's hatches does not allow to discharge cargo simultaneously by two cranes from one hold. Therefore, the Commission did not accept the calculation of lay time presented by the shipowner and noted that 'as working hatches of the ship may be considered only hatches which allow simultaneous operation of each of these hatches'.[16]

In another case the dispute between the parties – Black Sea Steamship Line and V/O 'Raznoexport' and 'Sojuzpromexport' – concerned the determination of lay time on the basis of the clause providing that 'lay time for the ship to be calculated with regard to the number of hatches provided by the ship for operation. . . irrespective of the number of hatches in fact used'. The dispute was about the application of this clause in a situation when different holds of the ship were under loading with different cargo for which

[15] Tiberg H., *op. cit.*, pp. 428–429.
[16] Keilin A.D., Maritime Arbitration Commission in 1964, pp. 8–9.

different rates of loading were set. The Steamship Line calculated lay time in this case for each of the charterers by multiplying all five holds of s/s '*Solnechnogorsk*' by the rate of loading set for the cargo of each particular charterer. The charterers did not agree with such calculation pointing out that at first loading of the cargo of V/O 'Sojuzpromexport' (cement) went on into all five holds of the ship and later loading of V/O 'Raznoexport' cargo into holds 1, 3 and 5 started (into holds 1 and 5 – talc, into hold 3 – glass), while loading of cement into holds 2 and 4 continued. Thus, cargo of V/O 'Raznoexport' was being loaded only into three holds out of five.

In the award the MAC noted that the clause on lay days, by which the parties were guided, requires to take into account in calculating lay time all hatches provided by the ship for operation, even in case when the charterer actually used only part of them. This rule was set in the interests of the carrier in order to prevent unjustified increase of lay time when the charterer for some reasons (for example, lack of goods) refuses to load the cargo into some of the provided hatches. However, in the opinion of the MAC, 'this rule cannot be applied to the cases of simultaneous loading of different cargo into different hatches of the ship... Calculation of lay time for each kind of goods basing on the number of all hatches provided by the ship for operation, while in fact each kind of goods was loaded only into some of them, could lead to unjustified reduction of time allocated for loading of these goods'. On this ground the Commission did not accept the calculation of the Steamship Line and rejected the claim for demurrage.[17]

The above mentioned award shows that the problem of calculating lay time on the basis of the rates per day per hatch becomes more complicated when different holds of the ship are loaded with different goods, for which different rates are set, and becomes even more complicated when such goods are loaded into one and the same hold. Under such conditions 'the largest-hold method' has to be applied with some modifications. When such goods are loaded into different holds of the ship, lay time for each kind of these goods should be calculated with account taken only of those hatches through which the goods were loaded and the longest period of time is to be considered as the general lay time. When the goods with different rates are loaded into the same holds, the time required for loading in accordance with the rates of the most laborious hold, from the point of view of the quantity and composition of the goods, should be considered as lay time. Everything that was said above is applicable accordingly to discharge of cargo.

In the MAC practice also arose the question of calculation of the lay time in cases when the charter contains the clause providing for loading (or unloading) in accordance with 'customs of the port'. However, customs of the port are not applicable when they contradict the agreement of the parties. Considering one case the MAC refused to apply to calculation of lay

[17] *See*: Friedenstein Ya.B. From the practice of the Maritime Arbitration Commission on cases concerning carriage of goods and affreightment in 1958–1962. Merchant Shipping and Maritime Law. Collection articles and documents No. 1. M., 1963, pp. 36–37 (In Russian).

time a custom of foreign port, according to which Saturday counts as two thirds of the working day. The MAC based the decision of the charter that provided for the rate of discharge 'per working day' and did not make any exceptions to this clause (Case No. 16/52).

III. Periods excluded from lay time

Terms of charters providing for exclusion of certain periods from lay time that has already started to run are of various nature.

In some cases such terms reflect the agreement of the parties concerning days or hours during which loading/unloading should go on and concerning exclusion from lay time of days (hours) when loading/unloading should not take place. Such is the generally accepted clause 'Sundays and holidays excluded'. In other cases lay time does not include periods when work should be performed but in fact it cannot be performed, as a rule, due to circumstances beyond the control of the owner of the cargo. So, a clause providing for the rate of loading 'per weather working day' excludes from the count days on which weather conditions prohibit work. It is not difficult to see that the terms of the first group set time for the owner of the cargo to fulfil his obligations concerning loading and unloading, and that the second group of terms in fact decides the question of his liability for late fulfillment of these obligations, though this question is dealt with indirectly. In the practice of the MAC one can find disputes concerning application of terms of both of these categories.

In one of the cases the dispute between V/O 'Sojuzneftexport' and the Black Sea Steamship Line dealt with the clause, usual for some charters, which provided that 'Sundays and holidays not to count as lay time, unless used'. The dispute arose because in the course of discharge of the tanker '*Rava-Russkaya*' the work was performed partly on Sunday and the parties could not agree, whether to include into lay time only hours when the work was performed or the whole Sunday. Settling this case the MAC proceeded from the general rule stated in many standard forms of charters, according to which lay days include only working days and, therefore, different regulation should be considered as an exception and 'constructed very restrictively in accordance with its exact language'.

From the clause binding upon the parties and providing for exclusion of Sundays and holidays out of lay days unless used to perform work follows the reverse rule: such days, if they were used for loading/unloading, should be counted as lay days. Since the contract did not make any exceptions for hours when the work in fact was not performed, the above clause 'means that Sunday or holiday should be counted as lay day even if actually only a part of the day was used for work' (Case No. 36/62).[18]

[18] Keilin A.D., Maritime Arbitration in the USSR in recent years, pp. 22–23.

The position taken by the Maritime Arbitration Commission in this award regarding the meaning of the clause 'unless used' finds support in literature. M. Summerskil, comparing this clause with an often used in charters similar clause – 'unless used, and in such case only actually used time to count' – comes to the conclusion that in the first instance if the charterer used a part of Sunday or holiday this day, apparently, should be considered as lay day.[19] There is, however, a different construction of the clause 'unless used'.

In accordance with the Charterparty Lay Time Definitions 1980 this clause means that if the work was performed during the days not to be counted, only hours of actual work count as lay time (sec. 20).

Among cases dealing with the exclusion of bad weather periods out of lay time a dispute between V/O 'Sojuzpromexport' and Azov Sea Steamship Line should be noted, a dispute that concerned dispatch far ahead of schedule discharge of m/v '*Cherkassy*' in the port of Savona (Italy). The parties determined the duration of lay time and amount of dispatch in different ways, because the Steamship Line believed that it was wrong to exclude out of lay time the periods of bad weather when the work in this port was not performed, and the charterer insisted on such exclusion. The Maritime Arbitration Commission held that 'resolution of this issue, in the absence of other special clauses binding upon the parties, depends on duration of working day which was used to determine the rates of discharge... If the working day was determined to last twenty four hours, the periods of bad weather should not be counted as lay time irrespective of the time of day such periods occurred.' Having found that in this case the rates of discharge of m/v '*Cherkassy*' in Savona were determined on the basis of weather working day of 24 hours, the Commission held the position of the Charterer to be correct (Case No. 27/67).[20]

With exclusion from lay time of the periods during which work cannot be performed due to circumstances not dependent upon the owner of the cargo is connected from time to time arising in practice the question of possibility to exclude such periods when it is evident that all the same the owner of the cargo could not perform work for reasons he is liable for.

In the above mentioned case dealing with the delay of s/s '*Dmitry Pozharsky*' in the port of Djakarta one of the issues in dispute was the issue of exclusion out of lay time of the period from 1 p.m. until 4 p.m. on 6 April, when there was no discharge, as was stated in the time-sheet, due to bad weather conditions and absence of the cargo-owner's lighters necessary for unloading. The Maritime Arbitration Commission, having found that the rate of discharge was set 'per normal hatch per weather working day' and that the fact of bad weather conditions was not challenged, held that in such circumstances the said period should not be counted as lay time since 'the

[19] Summerskil M., *op. cit.*, p. 120.

[20] *See*: Maritime Law and Practice. Information Bulletin No. 39 (206). M., 1968, pp. 84–85; see also No. 42 (225), M., 1969, p. 50.

absence of necessary for discharge means of transportation to be provided by the stevedores of the owners of the cargo has no significant bearing on the resolution of the dispute' (case No. 21/62).

In a more detailed manner the Commission stated its view on the same issue in the comparatively recent case concerning demurrage for the delay of m/v '*Coral Maendra*' in the port of Ventspils. The dispute in this case was whether to count or not to count as lay days three days the ship waited for berth. The charterers insisted on exclusion of these three days, since the ship could not get to a berth due to bad weather and since under the terms of the charter if 'the delay in getting the ship to berth... is caused by any reason the charterer has no control of, such delay not to count as used lay time' (sec. 6). The shipowner argued that the ship could not get to berth any way because the berth was occupied by the charterer's ships and, therefore, the time lost in waiting for berth should be counted as lay time.

In the award the MAC, basing on the statement-of-facts and reference of the Ventspils hydrometeorological bureau, considered as proven that during the period of waiting for berth by the ship '*Coral Maendra*' in the port of Ventspils storm conditions were present due to which there was no piloting at all. Such circumstances – pointed out the Commission in the award – in regard of which the charterer undoubtfully 'had no control', give grounds to believe that all the time of their duration should not be considered as 'used lay time' according to sec. 6 of the charter. Moreover... the fact that the berth was occupied by other ships cannot have relevance... since irrespective of this fact there were reasons, provided for by sec. 6 of the charter, which caused impossibility of getting the ship to berth' (Case No. 56/79).

Circumstances causing exclusion of respective periods out of lay time are taken into account by the MAC only when they occur before the end of the lay time.

PART II.

COMPARATIVE LAW

ARGENTINA

JOSE DOMINGO RAY

Professor of Maritime Law, University of Buenos Aires; President of the Argentine Association of Maritime Law

RECENT CASE LAW AND RELEVANT SEMINARS IN ARGENTINA

1. Case law

a) ASSISTANCE AND SALVAGE

On 18 March 1983, the Federal Court handed down a decision in the cases '*Flota Fluvial del Estado Argentino c/Cap. y/o Prop. bq. Argos s/cobro de pesos*' and '*Raul A. Negro e Hijos S.R.L. c/Overseas* (Soc. Econ. por Acciones) s/cobro de pesos'. The Court ruled that danger is an inseparable component of assistance, such that if danger does not exist, the situation does not fall within the legal concept of assistance. Danger should be understood as a critical situation or a threat, although it is difficult to outline a general formula that encompasses every alternative that might in reality arise.

The Court of Appeal, weighing all facets of the Law of Navigation (Art. 371), reduced the amount of assistance that was previously awarded.

b) LIABILITY AND ITS CONSEQUENCES

In the case '*Frenithe S.A. c/Elma s/cobro de pesos*', also decided on 18 March 1983, the Federal Court of the Capital accepted the indisputable principle that consequences not proximately caused by a breach cannot be imputed to the breaching party. Indeed, adequate drafting of the cargo manifest is the responsibility of the carrier and he is not justified in unreasonably delaying the period of time necessary to amend his mistake. However, it would be unjust to impute to the carrier the damages that are attributable to the conduct of the claimant.

c) DELAY IN RETURN OF CONTAINER

In the decision '*Fletamar S.A.C. c/Daimaru S.A.C.I.F.I.A. s/cobro U.S.$3,414.75*', handed down on 25 March 1983, Dr. Perez Delgado, Judge of the Federal Court, posed the theory that the legal relationship between the owner of the container transporting the goods and the consignee should be analyzed in light of the norms governing bailments because of the analogy presented between these two types of contracts. The proper period of time for the renting of the container is the period necessary for transport and a few days beforehand and afterwards. The fees charged for rent do not include all the excess time utilized by the consignee and which caused losses to the owner or holder of the container.

d) PROOF OF UNFITNESS FOR NAVIGATION

The Federal Court, in the case '*Instituto Provincial del Seguro (Misiones) c/Cap. y/o otro bq. 'Patria' s/cobro de pesos*' (10 August 1983), held that the carrier had exercised 'reasonable diligence' when he offered a vessel as suitable for navigation and transport. The carrier could not be held liable when unfitness for navigation or commission of a fault by the duly qualified captain had not been proved.

e) RUNNING AGROUND. OBSTRUCTION OF A CANAL

In '*Y.P.F. c/Cap. y otros buque Maritime Challenger s/cobro ordinario de pesos*' (21 October 1983), the Federal Court of the Capital decided that the captain and shipowners should be held partially liable for the obstruction of the canal and the delay caused to the vessels of the claimant due to the running aground of the '*Maritime Challenger*' which was imputable to the negligence of the captain. The defendants were held only partially liable because the obstruction had not been total and though it had impeded the passage of one of the claimant's vessels, another one had been able to pass.

f) DAMAGES IN A SHIPYARD

The Federal Court's judgments of 25 November 1983 in the rulings '*Talleres Navales Darsena Norte S.A.C.I. y M. (TANDANOR) c/Cap. y/o Prop. Arm. bq. bandera liberiana 'Spartan Lord's s/ordinario*'', affirmed the decision of the Court of First Instance and rejected the complaint filed by the factory, in whose dock the vessel was moored. When its mooring lines broke and it went adrift, the vessel caused damage to another dock of the same shipyard.

The ruling indicated that the captain of the ship was not liable for the election of the site on the dock nor for having remained adrift, since the rupture of the mooring lines was not caused by defects in material supplied by the ship nor was the captain negligent for accepting the site assigned to him.

g) BILL OF LADING CLAUSES. VALIDITY OF 'PARAMOUNT CLAUSE'. PROTECTION AFFORDED BY THE COMMERCIAL CODE

In '*La Defensa Cia. Argentina de Seguros Generales c/Cap. y/o Prop. y/o Arm. bq.'Riverbank' s/interrumpe prescripcion*' (3 April 1984), the Federal Court of the Capital established as a doctrine the validity of the 'Paramount' clause of the bill of lading which provided that disputes should be governed by the English Law of Transport of Goods by Sea (1924), equivalent to the Brussels Convention of the same year.

The plaintiff claimed that since the transport took place in 1972, before the Law of Navigation took effect, and because it proceeded from the port of a State that was not a party to the 1924 Brussels Convention, the latter was not applicable and the case should be considered governed by the norms established in the Commercial Code, according to which the fire was not a ground for exoneration of the carrier's liability. Citing previous case law, the claimant argued that the bill of lading clauses which did not coincide with the public order provisions of the Commercial Code should be held invalid.

The Court of Appeal emphasized that the international trend towards uniformity is manifested by acceptance of the Convention, and noted that it had previously rejected the theory advanced by the plaintiff. For these reasons it ruled that the clause was valid and consequently recognized that English law provides for exoneration of liability in case of fire. The Court reasoned that the theory of nullity of these clauses received harsh doctrinal criticism, and it was later held that these clauses would only be considered void if they were arbitrarily imposed by the carrier. Those clauses which fall within the principle of equivalence of obligations and do not violate the public order must be adjudged valid.

2. Seminars

Over the past several years, the Argentine Association of Maritime Law organized various seminars in the Faculty of Law and Social Sciences of the University of Buenos Aires, with the cooperation of the University's Institute of Maritime Law.

In April of 1983, a seminar on chartering was held with the participation of members of the Peruvian Association of Maritime Law. Historical evolution, civil and common law doctrine, concepts and terminology in charterparties, and criticism of the prevailing system were discussed. In particular, topics including conditions and warranties, navigability, cancelling date, safe port and safe berth, off hire and distribution of liability in the time-charter, booking note, lay days, and the relation between the charterparty and the bill of lading in the 'voyage charter' (Gencon and Centrocon) were analyzed.

Offshore activities were the subject of a seminar held at the end of 1983. Oil drilling vessels were examined with the help of corporations involved in these operations.

The Institute of Maritime Studies also organized various seminars. In June of 1982 one was given on economic, technical, and legal aspects of containers and a second session continued work in April of 1983.

3. Doctrine

Our commentaries on the 'Colloquium of Venice' for bills of lading, organized by the International Maritime Committee in 1983, appeared in the magazine 'La Ley'. In the 1984 Lima Seminar we developed the theme of 'Fraud in Maritime Activities'.

In the National Academy of Law and Social Sciences in Buenos Aires, we discussed the topic of 'autonomies' in the various fields of legal sciences, with special reference to maritime law. The use of the term 'autonomy' and its relative character were explained.

Civil liability was also examined. On attribution of damages in contemporary law, we spoke about gross damage and the basis of the obligation for contribution.

BELGIUM

LEO DELWAIDE

Attorney at Antwerp

RECENT TRENDS IN THE DECISIONS OF THE ANTWERP COURT OF APPEALS CONCERNING MARITIME LAW (1975–1985)

The Court of Appeals of Antwerp was created in 1975. It assumed jurisdiction over maritime affairs that formerly belonged to the Court of Appeals of Brussels. After ten years of its existence, we will examine the recent trends of the maritime decisions of this new Court.

1. Jurisdiction clauses in bills of lading

The Court of Appeal of Antwerp has confirmed the trend of the traditional case law of the Court of Appeal of Brussels whereby jurisdiction clauses were declared void, as these clauses were contrary to Article 91 of the Belgian Maritime Law that included the Hague Rules, which have been declared part of public international law. Even when the jurisdiction clauses provided that a foreign court must apply Article 91 of the Belgian Maritime Law, these clauses were considered void for the reason that it was not certain that the courts would apply Article 91 as the Belgian courts would do.

This was still the position that the *Court of Appeal of Antwerp* adopted in the '*Berkshire*' decision of 25 May 1977.[1] The Court confirmed this reasoning in the case where Article 17 of the E.E.C. Convention of Brussels of 27 September 1968 was raised. This Article provides that 'if, by a written Convention . . . the parties, at least one of whom is domiciled in the territory of a contracting State, has designated a court or courts of a contracting State to decide the differences that have arisen or will arise from a particular legal relationship, only the court or courts of that State are competent' ('si, par une convention écrite . . . les parties, dont l'une au moins a son domicile sur le territoire d'un état contractant, ont designé un tribunal ou les tribunaux

[1] J.P.A. 1977–78, 31; D.E.T. 1977, 705.

d'un état contractant pour connaître des differends nés ou a naître a l'occasion d'un rapport de droit determiné, ce tribunal ou les tribunaux de cet état sont seuls competents'). The Court reasoned that the bill of lading could not be considered to be a document that is binding on the third party holder, who had never given his written consent to the jurisdiction clause, and who nevertheless enjoyed the rights of possession of the bill of lading. The Court added that Article 17 only refers to procedural rights and consequently does not apply to the rules of public order which are substantive in nature.[2]

Recently, this reasoning has suddenly collapsed. The *Berkshire* case was reversed by the Supreme Court on 2 February 1979.[3] In this decision, where Article 17 had no application, but where a 'paramount' clause established that the Swedish Courts would apply Article 91 of the Belgian maritime law, this clause was declared to be valid.

To the extent which C.E.E. Article 17 is concerned, the case law of the Antwerp Court had provoked, inter alia, vigorous attacks from authors and experts on the subject.[4] I have already called attention to the important decision of the E.E.C. Court of Justice of 19 June 1984 (Anuario de Derecho Maritimo, vol. III, p. 410) concerning the Tilly Russ affair. The decision of the Court of Luxembourg was already published in European Transport Law 1985, page 3, as well as the decision of the Belgian Supreme Court of 25 January 1985 that followed it.[5] The Supreme Court remanded the case to the Court of Appeal of Ghent for the reason that the decision of Antwerp which gave rise to the preliminary question (Article 177 of the Treaty of Rome) before the European Court of Justice did not establish if, according to Belgian law, the third party holder had succeeded to the rights and obligations of the shipper. This case will continue.

2. Bills of lading issued by the time charterer

The Court of Appeals of Antwerp has been very strict regarding shipowners, as they are considered bound by the bills of lading issued by the

[2] Arrêts TRANSONTARIO du 15 juin 1977, J.P.A. 1977–78, 40; D.E.T. 1978, 462; DUBHE du 28 février 1979, J.P.A. 1979–80, 261; MONTFERLAND du 21 novembre 1979, J.P.A. 1979–80, 346; DUTCH FAITH du 30 juillet 1982, J.P.A. 1981–82, 250.

[3] J.P.A. 1979–80, 37; voir les commentaires de L. DELWAIDE, Diez Anos de jurisprudencia maritima en el tribunal de Casacion belga (1974–1983) in: Anuario de Derecho Maritimo, vol. III, p. 409–410.

[4] PUTZEYS, J., 'Le nationalisme dans le droit international', in 'Etudes offertes à René Rodière', Dalloz, Paris 1981, p. 473–479; ZORBAS, G., 'L'effacement difficile de l'article 91 de la loi maritime belge face à l'article 17 de la Convention C.E.E. du 27 septembre 1968, Errare humanum est, perseverare diabolicum!', J.T. 1982, 521, attaques qui furent repoussées avec brio et talent (ROLAND, R., 'La clause de juridiction dans les connaissements devant l'article 17 de la Convention C.E.E. du 27 septembre 1968, retour à l'anarchie?', J.T. 1983, 301).

[5] D.E.T. 1985, p. 73—voir aussi le commentaire de l'arrêt du 19 juin 1984 par R. ROLAND: 'Le connaissement et le droit européen', R.D.C.B., 1985, 84.

time charterer.[6] All bills of lading are presumed to be signed by the master, even when they are in fact signed by the time charterer 'for the carrier' (Liverpool Bay, aforementioned) and even if for the same cargo the charterer and the master have signed different bills of lading. In the *Gold Coin* case, the master had taken the precaution of writing on the bill of lading that it was a shipment of deck cargo. Since the time charterer's agent had also issued bills of lading for the same merchandise, but without mentioning that it was deck cargo, the shipowner found himself excluded from the possibility of limiting his liability according to the Hague Rules! It is true that the charterparty provided that the charterer could have appointed the ship agents . . . .

The shipowner remained bound according to the Hague Rules, even when the charterparty contained a provision where the master is under the orders of the time charterer. Indeed, the Court held that the shipowner's liability was derived from his ownership of the vessel, as an in rem liability.[7]

In the *Ingrid* case, the Court stated that the fact that the time charterer had issued the bill of lading did not give him the right to accord extensions of the limitations period[8].

In the *Catelli* case, the suspension of the limitations period accorded by the shipowner's agent was recognized, on the grounds that the agent had acted in the name of the shipowner, which was contained in the bill of lading.[9]

The Supreme Court, in the *Stad Gent* case, indicated that the shipowner was not bound by the obligations that the time charterer or his agents undertook upon the arrival of the boat with regard to third party holders[10].

3. Deck cargo

The Antwerp Court of Appeals systematically excludes the maritime carrier from the benefits of the Hague Rules in cases of deck cargo that is not mentioned in the bill of lading, but the third party carrier is always entitled to invoke these benefits.[11] A reference to a 'long form bill of lading'

[6] Arrêts STAD GENT du 23 avril 1975, J.P.A. 1974, 428, confirmé sur ce point par la Cour de Cassation le 30 septembre 1977, J.P.A. 1977–78, 429, voir Anuario de Derecho Maritimo, vol. III, p. 409; KLAUS OLDENDORFF du 26 juin 1975, D.E.T. 1976, 76; MOSCHANTY du 5 novembre 1975, J.P.A. 1975–76, 140; WEAR BREEZE du 16 mars 1977, J.P.A. 1977–78, 8; KUIBESHEVGES du 30 mai 1979, J.P.A. 1981–82, 70; LIVERPOOL BAY du 19 novembre 1980, J.P.A. 1981–82, 210; GOLD COIN du 8 avril 1981, J.P.A. 1981–82, 129, confirmé par la Cour de Cassation le 16 septembre 1983, J.P.A. 1983–84, 135; ARMONIA du 30 septembre 1981, J.P.A. 1981–82, 457.

[7] WEAR BREEZE précité.

[8] 4 juin 1979, J.P.A. 1979–80, 338.

[9] 14 octobre 1981, J.P.A. 1981–82, 471.

[10] Anuario de Derecho Maritimo, vol. III, p. 409.

[11] Arrêts BALDUIN du 14 septembre 1977, J.P.A. 1977–78, 215, confirmé par la Cour de Cassation le 25 mai 1979, J.P.A. 1979–80, 251, voir Anuario de Derecho Maritimo, vol. III,

binds the third party only when it is established that he knew or should have known its contents.[12] This reasoning is based upon Article 66 of the Belgian Maritime Law, derived from the Ordinance of Colbert, and Article 91 A, I, c, which prohibits carriage on deck without the written consent of the shipper. It is obvious that these decisions are not in accord with today's modern techniques of maritime transport of containers. In France, new legislation has just been adopted, and similar legislation is being prepared in Belgium.

4. Validity of 'weight/quantity unknown' clauses

The reservation clauses that the carrier includes in the bill of lading when he does not know the quantity or the weight of the cargo ('weight and/or quantity unknown'; 'said to weigh'; 'said to contain') are not accepted without restriction. They are rejected when it appears that the maritime carrier had a reasonable possibility to inspect the cargo.[13] Insofar as it concerns inspection of the apparent condition of the merchandise in view of possible reservations contained in the bill of lading, it has been held that the master need only conduct a superficial inspection.[14]

5. Bulk cargo

Certain merchandise, like manioc or tapioca pellets, are loaded in very humid subtropical countries. They sometimes arrive damaged due to combustion or condensation. Even when nautical experts concede the inherent defects of the cargo, loaded in an extremely humid climate, the Antwerp Court has shown itself to be very strict with regard to the ventilation and overpacking of the hold.[15]

6. Frozen meat

It has been held that the maritime carrier must be aware of the fact that frozen meat needs to be shipped under a constant temperature of minus one degrees centigrade, and that the voyage may not exceed 20 days.[16]

---

p. 411; VESTLAND du 8 novembre 1978, J.P.A. 1979–80, 62; GOLD COIN du 18 avril 1981, précité; KARIN KEHMANN du 27 mai 1981, R.W. 1982–83, 1267 avec note L. DELWAIDE; DJURDJURA du 2 mai 1983, D.E.T. 1984, 503.

[12] Arrêt VESTLAND du 8 novembre 1978, précité.

[13] Arrêts ANCO SWAN du 5 mars 1975, J.P.A. 1974, 320, D.E.T. 1975, 465; BLANKENSTEIN du 19 novembre 1975, J.P.A. 1975–76, 145; CAP PALMAS du 18 février 1976, J.P.A. 1977–78, 453, confirmé par le Cour de Cassation le 11 mars 1977, J.P.A. 1977–78, 424, voir Anuario de Derecho Maritimo, vol. III, p. 408; KARL MARX du 26 janvier 1977, D.E.T. 1977, 833; VARDAL du 11 janvier 1978, J.P.A. 1979–80, 442.

[14] Arrêt ESTRID du 19 septembre 1979, J.P.A. 1979–80, 342.

[15] GEREMIA du 9 avril 1975, J.P.A. 1974, 424 et ARISTANDROS du 20 février 1980, J.P.A. 1981–82, 444.

[16] Arrêt RIO CARCARANA du 23 avril 1980, J.P.A. 1981–82, 81.

7. Perils of the sea

The Antwerp Court was equally rigorous when considering perils of the sea clauses. Gusts of wind of 8 to 11 during 3 days were not considered exceptional and did not constitute a cause of exoneration when the ship had been poorly maintained and there had been bad stowage.[17]

8. Towage contract

In many cases, the towage contract provides that the boat being towed is liable for damages caused to third parties. In a case of a collission caused by the fault of the tugboat, the boat being towed was ordered in solidum with the tugboat to pay damages for not having given sufficiently precise instructions and for not having exercised sufficient control over the execution of those instructions.[18] In another case, a tugboat capsized due to its own fault. Damages were caused to a ship that had to refloat it. Since the towage contract provided that the boat being towed had to pay for all damages caused to third parties, it was ordered to reimburse the tugboat for all the damages that it in turn was sentenced to pay to the boat which had rescued it.[19]

9. Conflicts of law with regard to maritime liens and mortgages

An important decision on this subject is that of 30 July 1982, concerning the case of the *Christina*.[20] In a long and detailed holding, the Court concluded that maritime mortgages were governed by the law of the flag, unlike maritime liens, which were governed by the law of the forum.

10. Liability of forwarding agents

The Court has had the opportunity several times to affirm that the General Conditions for Forwarding Agents, which contain numerous clauses of exoneration of liability, may not be used in prejudice of the rights of the party who placed the shipping order, unless they have been explicitly accepted by that party.[21]

[17] Arrêt POLLUX du 21 septembre 1977, J.P.A. 1979–80, 53; voir aussi l'arrêt CARVALHO ARAUJO du 27 juin 1979, J.P.A. 1981–82, 76.

[18] Arrêt CORNELIS van ECK, EEMHAVEN et LAURENT LETZER du 23 juin 1975, J.P.A. 1975–76, 135.

[19] Arrêt ARTHUR R, MERCANTILE TRADER et CATHERINE LETZER du 30 juin 1975, J.P.A. 1975–1976, 308.

[20] J.P.A. 1983–84, 347.

[21] Arrêts Ziegler & Cie c/La Générale de Berne du 18 février 1976, J.P.A. 1975–76, 229; Hens & Henssens et S.A. Petan & Cie C/S.A. Van Gunsteren, S.A. Transpedo et Eagle Star Insurance Cie du 13 septembre 1976, J.P.A. 1975–76, 413; ISMENE du ler décembre 1976, D.E.T. 1977, 563; KINSHASA du 11 janvier 1978, J.P.A. 1979–80, 166; AUGSBURG du 3 mai 1978, J.P.A. 1979–80, 58; TANGANYKA du 10 février 1982, J.P.A. 1981–82, 477.

The forwarding agent must safeguard the merchandise that is placed in his possession in the same manner as he would his own goods.[22] He is not liable for those forwarding agents who replace him, unless he has chosen persons who are manifestly incompetent.[23] He is no longer liable from the moment in which he has placed the cargo at the carrier's disposal within the perimeter of the ship.[24] Nor is he liable for a theft committed within a closed warehouse where the goods were stored (*Seattle* decision of 25 December 1976, D.E.T. 1977, 558). He is also not obligated to inform the party placing the shipping order when the shipping will not be done immediately.[25] Finally, there is no obligation on his part to inspect the quantity of cargo that is placed in his possession, and he has the right to reimbursement for the cargo that he advances, even if he has paid too much to the shipper because he followed erroneous instructions.[26]

11. Direct action by a third party holder against the ship's insurers

Article 20, section 9 of the Belgian Mortgage Law provides that the right of a third party or his successor in interest to receive payments for damages arising from an accident are privileged regarding the indemnity that the insurer of civil liability owes according to the insurance contract. The Antwerp Court of Appeal ruled that the third party carrier had the right to maintain a direct action against the shipper's insurers when damage to the cargo occurred.[27]

12. Refusal to deliver a bill of lading

When the merchandise has been loaded and for some reason the master refuses to deliver the bills of lading (e.g. because he claims that the cargo was paid to an agent of the charterer with whom the shipowner was in litigation over rent in arrears), this constitutes a fact that is detrimental to the third party carrier, to whom the President of the Commercial Court, acting 'en référé', ordered the master to deliver the bills of lading, but preserving his right to insert a reservation concerning the payment of the cargo.[28]

[22] Arrêts DELIA du 30 juin 1975, J.P.A. 1975–76, 209; D.E.T. 1975, 203, SILVER CLOUD du 17 février 1982, J.P.A. 1981–82, 155.

[23] Arrêt DELIA du 30 juin 1975 cité.

[24] Arrêt ATLANTA du 28 avril 1976, J.P.A. 1975–76, 155.

[25] Arrêt SERBISTAN du 4 mai 1977, J.P.A. 1977–78, 26.

[26] Arrêt TANGANYKA du 10 février 1982 précité.

[27] Arrêts SIMONE du 25 juin 1980; J.P.A. 1981–82, 451 et Hottlet c/ S.P.R.L. Vynco et Groupe Josi du 24 novembre 1981, J.P.A. 1981–82, 146. Voir aussi l'étude de S. ROLAND, 'Les droits de la victime d'un accident vis à vis de l'assureur de la responsabilité civile de l'auteur du dommage. Considérations diverses sur l'article 20, par. 9 de la loi hypothécaire', J.P.A. 1977–78, 103.

[28] Arrêts GULF FALCON des 20 février 1981, R.W. 1981–82, 2695 avec note L. DELWAIDE et du 5 mars 1981, J.P.A. 1981–82, 217.

CANADA

WILLIAM TETLEY, Q.C.*

Professor of Maritime Law McGill University Montreal, P.Q.

ANNUAL SUMMARY 1983–84
CANADIAN ADMIRALTY DECISIONS

I. Marine Insurance. II. Jurisdiction. III. Forum non conveniens. IV. Practice and procedure. V. Administrative law. VI. Carriage of goods. VII. Labour. VIII. Collision. IX. Pollution. X. Liens and mortgages. XI. Economic loss. XII. General average. XIII. Sale of a ship. XIV. Taxation. XV. Charterparties.

I. Marine insurance

1) *Triglav v. Terrasses Jewellers Inc.* [1983] 1 S.C.R. 283; [1984] *E.T.L.* 483 (*Supreme Ct. of Canada, 1983*).

The Supreme Court of Canada in a judgment which could be 'lourde de conséquences' decided that marine insurance was part of 'maritime law' and therefore within federal jurisdiction, such that the Federal Parliament, in exercising its legislative power under sect. 101 of the Constitution Act, 1867, could grand jurisdiction to the Federal Court over a marine insurance policy claim by sect. 22(2)(r) of the Federal Court Act. The Court noted that there was concurrent jurisdiction with the Superior Courts of the provinces over marine insurance but left unsaid whether the present provincial marine insurance acts were still valid and, if invalid, what 'Canadian marine insurance law' consisted of.

* The author acknowledges the assistance of Brian G. McDonough B.A., B.C.L., L1.1. in correcting, adding to, and deleting from the text.

2) *Century Ins. Co. v. Case Existological Lab.* (*The Bamcell II*) [1983] 2 S.C.R. 47, (1983) 150 D.L.R. (3d) 9, (1983) 49 N.R. 19 (*Supreme Ct. of Canada, 1983*).

The Supreme Court of Canada held that the owner of a vessel of very peculiar construction which had sunk in the calmest of weather could claim under the perils of the sea provisions of a marine insurance policy because a member of the crew had negligently permitted air to escape from the hull of the vessel. Ritchie J. speaking for the Court held that the fortuitous or unintentional incursion of sea water was foreseeable and a maritime risk and therefore a 'peril of the sea'. The decision runs contrary to the principle that for a peril of the sea to exist under a marine insurance policy there must be some outside external force and not merely a negligent act of a member of the crew.

In support of his position that negligence of a crewman was immaterial, Ritchie J. would seem to erroneously rely on *Cohen v. National Benefit Assurance Co.* (1924) 18 Ll. L. Rep. 199 at p. 202 (C.A.) which was, however, a policy covering 'all and every risk'. Ritchie J. also seems to erroneously confuse peril of the sea under a cargo policy as per *Canada Rice Mills Ltd. v. Union Marine and General Insurance Co. Ltd.* 1941 A.C. 55 (P.C.) with peril under a hull policy. Nor was there consideration of the Inchmaree clause in the decision, the respondent having formally abandoned his claim under the clause (S.C.R. at p. 55, D.L.R. at p. 14, N.R. at p. 24). *See also* D.F. and John M. McEwen—International Case Note—[1984] L.M.C.L.Q. 671.

3) *H.B. Nickerson & Sons Ltd. v. Ins. Co. of N.A.* (1983) 49 N.R. 321 (*Fed. Ct. of Appeal, 1983*).

The Federal Court of Appeal noted that, in order to claim under a marine insurance policy, an insured must show that the vessel sank due to a 'peril' insured against. If the cause is unexplained (as in this case), then the insured may demonstrate, after proving the 'clear seaworthiness of his vessel', that on the balance of probabilities a peril of the sea, although not identified, caused the loss. As the trial judge had not found evidence as to the seaworthiness of the vessel, the appeal of the insured was dismissed.

The Inchmaree clause was not invoked in this suit, either. The Inchmaree clause covers losses due to negligence of the master and crew etc., when 'no want of due diligence by the assured, the owners or managers of the vessel' had been involved.

4) *Gould v. Cornhill Insurance Co. Ltd.* (1984) 1 D.L.R. (4th) 183 (*Newfoundland Ct. of Appeal, 1983*).

A 47-foot vessel sank in a 15 mph wind when no ice was about. There was evidence, however, that the weather was rough and caused the sinking. The insurer noted the Canada Steamship Inspection certificate had expired and that there had been previous ice damage. As in *H.B. Nickerson & Sons v. Ins. Co. of N.A., supra*, the Newfoundland Court of Appeal held 'exactly what caused the sinking of the '*Samantha G*' is unknown, but there is no evidence that it was the result of unseaworthiness.'

Lack of jurisdiction was also raised, relying on *Cull v. Rose* (1982) 37 Nfld. and P.E.I.R. 476, 104 A.P.R. 476 where it had been held that the Newfoundland Supreme Court had lost its admiralty jurisdiction by the Terms of Union between Canada and Newfoundland in 1949. It was held however, in the present case that the Supreme Court of Newfoundland has jurisdiction to hear questions of maritime insurance, because common law courts, not Admiralty courts, as of 1720 had assumed settlement of marine insurance claims.

The court added that since 1970 the Federal Court of Canada has had concurrent jurisdiction over marine insurance claims in virtue of sect. 22(2)(r) of the Federal Court Act 1970.

5) *Hepburn et al. v. Fairway Life*, (1983) 57 N.S.R. (2d) 228, 120 A.P.R. 228 (*Nova Scotia Sup. Ct.*).

A 36-foot motor cruiser burned and sank off Puerto Rico. The owners escaped from the vessel but were adrift at sea for 19 days at the end of which period one of the two owners died. The surviving owner and the dependents of the deceased owner brought an action to enforce a claim under the insurance policy which covered the vessel. After waiting 6 months for payment of the claim without receiving any explanation for the delay, the plaintiffs entered a default judgment. The defendant underwriter applied to have the default judgment set aside. The Court, in dismissing the application, stated that the underwriter had not adduced sufficient evidence of an explanation for not filing its statements of defence within time that would warrant setting aside the default judgment. Furthermore, it had not adduced sufficient evidence showing that it may have had a good defence on the merits.

II. Jurisdiction

1) *Verreault Navigation v. S.I.U.* (1983) 50 N.R. 242 (*Fed. Ct. of Appeal, 1982*).

Dredging is within federal jurisdiction because of sect. 91(10) ('Shipping and Navigation') of the Constitution Act 1867. In consequence, the Canada Labour Relations Board had jurisdiction over the labour relations of not only a dredging company but its ship repairing operation, because the dredging company had not shown that its ship repairing operation was separate from the dredging operation.

2) *Seafarers' Intl. Union v. Crosbie Offshore Services Ltd.* [1982] 2 F.C. 855 (*Fed. Ct. of Appeal, 1982*).

The Canada Labour Relations Board was held to have authority to consider an application for certification of a seamen's union whose members principally transported supplies to off-shore drilling rigs. This was held clearly to be within 'Navigation and Shipping'.

The Court also held that the grant of relief under sect. 28 of the Federal Court Act was not discretionary once a case had been made out.

3) *National Harbours Board v. Saint John Shipbuilding and Dry Dock Co. Ltd.* [1982] 43 N.R. 15 (*Fed. Ct. of Appeal, 1981*).

A floating crane and its barge were held to be a 'ship' and the Federal Court was held to have jurisdiction to hear a claim in tort for damage to the crane due to the negligence of stevedores under sect. 22(2)(e), (h) or (i) of the Federal Court Act.

4) *Cull v. Rose* (1983) 139 D.L.R. 559, (1982) 37 Nfld. and P.E.I.R. 476, 104 A.P.R. 476 (*Supreme Ct. of Nfld., Trial Div., 1982*).

The Supreme Court of Newfoundland (unlike the other provincial superior courts) does not have concurrent jurisdiction with the Federal Court of Canada to hear a collision case as the Terms of Union with Canada in the Newfoundland Act 1949 failed to preserve the Admiralty jurisdiction of the Newfoundland Supreme Court when Newfoundland joined Canada.

5) *Atlantic Sandblasting & Coatings Inc. v. Marine Indust. Ltd.* [1982] 2 F.C. 883 (*Fed. Ct., Jerome J., 1982*).

A subcontractor sued a ship repair contractor who had issued incorrect and incomplete specifications for the repair of a vessel. The subcontractor also sued the ship and shipowner although it had no contract with either. It was held that there was no contractual relationship with the ship and its owner and no allegation of quasi-contract (unjust enrichment). Thus the claim was solely in tort and the Federal Court had no jurisdiction under sect. 22(2)(n) which is for contract only. Nor was there jurisdiction under sect. 22(2)(m), since the claim was not for the cost of repairs but for compensation for negligently prepared plans and specifications. The claim of the subcontractor against the ship and the shipowner was therefore dismissed.

6) *Pierson v. 706 Drilling Co. Ltd*, (1983) 146 D.L.R. (3d) 573; 41 Newfoundland & P.E.I.R. 263, 119 A.P.R. 263 (Newfoundland Sup. Ct. tr. div.); affirmed (1984) 46 Newfoundland & P.E.I.R. 269, 135 A.P.R. 269.

The Federal Court of Canada has exclusive jurisdiction in virtue of the sect. 211 of the Canada Shipping Act R.S.C. 1970, c.S-9 over wages which includes emoluments. Wages, however, do not include a claim for damages for wrongful dismissal and thus the Newfoundland Supreme Court was held to have concurrent jurisdiction with the Federal Court.

7) *Transports Insurance Co. Inc. v. The Ondine* (1983) 138 D.L.R. (3d) 745 (*Fed. Ct. of Appeal*).

The plaintiff had taken an action for damages arising from a collision between two ships. Subsequently, the defendant in the collision action sued a third party for allegedly having breached a warranty of authority to settle the plaintiff's claim. The issue before the Court was whether the Federal Court had jurisdiction over such proceedings against the third party. The Court of Appeal held that such a claim against a third party did not fall under 'Canadian maritime law' as defined in sects. 2, 22(1) and 42 of the Federal Court Act. Nor did it arise out of a claim for damages caused by a collision (sect. 22(2)(e)) or a claim on a contract of marine insurance (sect. 22(2)(r) of the Federal Court Act). The claim against the third party, in the opinion of the Court, arose out of negotiations and a contract between the defendant in the collision action and the third party, and therefore it did not fall within the Federal Court's jurisdiction.

8) *Sio Export Trading Co. v. The Dart Europe* (1983) 144 D.L.R. (3d) 182 (*Fed. Ct., tr. div.*).

A hydraulic curing press shipped from Denmark to Chicago on a through bill of lading was removed from the carrying vessel at Montreal for repairs. These were completed and while the press was being carried back by truck to the Port of Montreal for shipment on to Chicago, the press collided with a railway overpass and was considerably damaged. The trucking company was sued.

The Federal Court was held not to have jurisdiction to hear the action since the land transportation operation undertaken by the trucking company was not 'part and parcel' of the activities essential to carriage of goods by sea. Dubé J. pointed out that 'The mere fact that the vehicle was returning a container to a vessel does not by itself constitute 'a matter connected with navigation and shipping'.'

9) *Province of Newfoundland v. McNamara Corp.* (1984) 46 Nfld & P.E.I.R. 195, 135 A.P.R. 195 (*Newfoundland Sup. Ct., tr. div.*).

The Province brought a negligence action in the Supreme Court of Newfoundland when the defendant dredging company punctured a submerged pipeline. The defendant company argued only the Federal Court of Canada had jurisdiction because the cause of action was for *damage caused by a ship*. The Newfoundland Supreme Court rejected this argument, relying on sect. 4 of the Judicature Act R.S.N. 1970, c. 187 which gives the Supreme Court jurisdiction over causes of action arising within the body of the Province of Newfoundland. Whether the dredge was a ship or not was of no consequence. The Court found, however, that the defendant had conducted its dredging operations with reasonable care and that responsibility for the damage caused to the pipeline rested on the party who had laid the pipeline without accurately recording its location. The action was dismissed against the defendant.

III. Forum non conveniens

1) *The Seapearl v. Seven Seas* (1982) 43 N.R. 517, (1983) 139 D.L.R. (3d) 669 (*Fed. Ct. of Appeal, 1982*).

Pratte J. with Lalonde D.J. concurring held that it was not sufficient to show that it was more convenient to hear a case in Canada than to abide by a charterparty clause calling for arbitration in London. There had to be 'strong reasons'. He did not find them and so reversed the trial court and stayed an action taken in Quebec. Thurlow C.J. (dissenting) noted that the availability and expenses of necessary witnesses . . . heavily favours' the view that Canada (Quebec City) was the best jurisdiction as did the fact that security was available in Quebec and might not be available in the new jurisdiction.

2) *Burrard-Yarrows Corp. v. The Hoegh Merchang* [1983] 1 F.C. 495 (*Federal Court of Appeal, 1982*).

The Federal Court of Appeal abruptly dismissed an appeal in respect to foreign jurisdiction resulting from a bill of lading jurisdiction clause because the decision of the trial court to stay the action was discretionary and should not be upset 'unless it was arrived at on a wrong basis or was plainly wrong'.

3) *Yasuda Fire & Marine Insurance Co. v. The Nosira Lin* (1984) 52 N.R. 303 (*Fed. Ct. of Appeal*, 1984).

Sect. 50(1)(b) of the Federal Court Act permits the Court to stay proceedings when 'it is in the interest of justice that the proceedings be stayed.' The trial judge had relied on Ritchie J. in *Antares Shipping Corp. v. The Capricorn* [1977] 2 S.C.R. 422 at 47, that for a stay there must be 'some other forum more convenient and appropriate for the pursuit of the action and for securing the ends of justice.' The Court of Appeal nevertheless found that the trial judge had exercised his discretion on the wrong basis in granting the stay because, although there was no Canadian involvement in the dispute, it had not been shown that justice would be done between the parties elsewhere at less inconvenience and expense than in Canada. The Court relied on *MacShannon v. Rockware Glass Ltd.* [1978] All E.R. 625 at p. 630 where two conditions to justify a stay were enunciated: (a) there must be another forum where 'justice can be done at substantially less inconvenience or expense'; (b) 'the stay must not deprive plaintiff of a legitimate personal or judicial advantage which would be available to him if he invoked the jurisdiction of the English Court".

4) *Agro Co. of Canada Ltd. v. The Regal Scout* (1983) 148 D.L.R. (3d) 412 (*Fed. Ct. of Canada, Cattanach J., 1983*).

A jurisdiction clause in a bill of lading giving exclusive jurisdiction to a Japanese court was held invalid. It was noted that a Japanese court would not have considered the shipowner to be a party to a bill of lading contract and would not have given effect to an identity of carrier clause in the bill of lading. In consequence, the carrier in a Japanese court would have been relieved of its responsibility contrary to art. 3(8) of the Carriage of Goods by Water Act, R.S.C. 1970, c.C-15 which is Canada's equivalent of the Hague Rules. Because the shipper would therefore have lost certain rights available and mandatory under Canadian law, the jurisdiction clause was invalid.

IV. Practice and procedure

1) *Curbera v. Min. of Fisheries* (1983) 50 N.R. 237 (*Supreme Ct. of Canada, 1983*).

28 tons of fish were seized from foreign fishermen who were fishing illegally in Canadian waters. The Trial Court ordered 1.5 tons forfeited to the Crown but the Crown appealed and refused to return the 26.5 tons balance pending the appeal (or the proceeds of their sale as the fish had been sold by the Crown). The Supreme Court held that the Crown could retain all the fish seized or their proceeds until a final decision on the appeal had been rendered.

2) *Freighters (Steamship Agents) Co. v. The Number Four* [1983] 1 F.C. 852 (*Fed. Ct. of Appeal, 1982*).

A ship was arrested in Canada in an action *in rem* after an action *in personam* had been taken in Korea (where there is no *in rem* procedure). It was held that the suit could be continued in Canada because the *in rem* action was not identical to the Korean procedure, while the security deposited in Korea did not cover *all* the debt, i.e. the capital, interests and costs. Nor was it held to be 'vexatious' to arrest a ship a second time since the second arrest provided the plaintiff with a real benefit, i.e. a maritime lien not available in Korea.

3) *Egmont Towing v. The Telendos* (1983) 43 N.R. 147 (*Fed. Ct. of Appeal, 1983*).

The Appeal Court looked at the difficult question of having both assessors and expert witnesses at trial. The trial judge had, in accordance with the current English practice, refused expert evidence because he was assisted by assessors. The Court of Appeal concurred but noted with a certain chagrin that an appeal court could not study and weigh the advice given privately by the assessors to the trial judge, as the appeal court could have, if experts had testified.

4) *Lundqvist Rederierna A/B v. Great Northern Paper Co.* [1983] 1 F.C. 350 (*Fed. Ct. of Appeal, 1982*).

This is another judgment reminding counsel that their affidavits in support of an order to serve a writ outside the jurisdiction must be very detailed in order to be successful.

5) *Price v. Finland Steamship Co. Ltd.* (1983) 46 N.R. 372 (*Fed. Ct. of Appeal, 1982*).

The Federal Court of Appeal made an additional condition for service out of the jurisdiction. It is not sufficient that the affidavit *declare* that plaintiff has a good arguable case; rather the affidavit must *demonstrate* that there is a good arguable case.

Similarly, the affidavit in support of an application to extend the time for service of the statement of claim must not only declare difficulty in the service but must also disclose sufficient reasons to justify extending the time for service.

Finally, service on a person in Montreal who is the head of the legal department of a foreign corporation is not service on the defendant corporation, because the person in question was not in Montreal to transact any business on behalf of defendant corporation which had no place of business, agents or assets in the district, or in Canada.

6) *Islensk Kaupskip HF v. The Charm* [1982] 2 F.C. 535 (*Fed. Ct., Mahoney J., 1982*).

Plaintiff A sued Defendant B who called in C as a third party. C wished to issue a third-party notice against A, but believed it could not under Federal Court Rules 1731 and 1726 because the 'third party' (i.e. A) was already a party to the action. Mahoney J. held, however, that the first third party action (i.e. B v. C) was separate from the original action (i.e. A v. B) and in consequence C could serve notice on A under Rule 1731, but the Court elegantly suggested for clarity that the notice be entitled a 'fourth party notice'.

7) *The C.F. Todd v. The Tanu Warrior* [1982] 2 F.C. 696 (*Fed. Ct., Addy J., 1982*).

The problem faced here was to decide what delay for suit applied to a counterclaim in a ship collision in British Columbian waters. The Federal Court Act at sect. 38 stipulates that. 'Except as provided in any other act . . .' the delays for suit in any province shall apply. The British Columbia Limitation Act states that there is no time bar for a counterclaim. The B.C. Act however did not apply because the Canada Shipping Act at sect. 645(1) does provide a two-year delay for suit. Although the counterclaim had not been taken within the two years by inadvertance, the Federal Court exercised its discretionary right under sect. 645(2) to extend the time limit because, during negotiations which took place between the parties, the counterclaim was contemplated and thus the plaintiff suffered no prejudice.

8) *Jupiter Intl. Ltd. v. Dart Containerline Co. Ltd.* [1982] 2 F.C. 800 (*Fed. Ct., Walsh J., 1982*).

Plaintiff was ordered to furnish particulars within 15 days, in default of which the statement of claim would be struck and the action dismissed 'without further order'. The particulars were delivered to the bailiff but not served within 15 days. The Court nevertheless ordered an additional delay for service. The court held that the first judgment only fixed a day (15 days hence) when a final judgment dismissing the action would be pronounced and thus no *final judgment* had been rendered.

9) *Gulf v. Tug Mary Mackin* (1984) 52 N.R. 282 (*Fed. Ct. of Appeal, 1984*).

Particulars may be requested to force a party to clarify the issues raised in his pleadings and thereby enable the opposite party to prepare his case. Relied on was the English *Supreme Court Practice* 1982, Vol. 1, at p. 318 which stated the function of particulars to be:

1. to inform the other side of the nature of the case they have to meet as distinguished from the mode in which that case is to be proved;
2. to prevent the other side from being taken by surprise at the trial;
3. to enable the other side to know what evidence they ought to be prepared with and to prepare for trial;
4. to limit the generality of the pleadings;
5. to limit and decide the issues to be tried, and as to which discovery is required, and
6. to tie the hands of the party so that he cannot without leave go into any matters not included.

10) *Parmar Fisheries v. Parceria Maritima*, (1983) 141 D.L.R. (3d) 498; 53 N.S.R. (2d) 338; 109 A.P.R. 338 (*Nova Scotia Sup. Ct., tr. div.*).

A Nova Scotian exporter of fish was granted a Mareva injunction restraining the defendant from removing its ship from the jurisdiction. (Incidentally the plaintiff had also begun proceedings in the Federal Court and had caused the ship to be arrested.) After reviewing English decisions, the Mareva injunction was held to be equally available in Nova Scotia and was not excluded by the pre-trial attachment order of rule 49 of the Civil Procedure Rules nor by the arrest *in rem*. These remedies can co-exist side-by-side. The Court added that because of the necessity for speed and its *ex parte* nature, an application for a Mareva injunction need only be supported by a 'good arguable case', rather than by 'strong *prima facie* evidence'.

11) *Foley v. Ocean Drilling & Exploration Co. et al*, (1983) 40 Newfoundland & P.E.I. 427, 115 A.P.R. 427 (*Newfoundland Sup. Ct., tr. div.*).

The wife and children of a worker who died in the sinking of the offshore drilling rig Ocean Ranger took a negligence action in the U.S. against several defendants. They also issued a writ of summons and statement of claim in Newfoundland Supreme Court, without, however, serving them. Two of the defendants filed unconditional appearances and applied for an order directing the plaintiffs to deliver a copy of the statement of claim to them. The defendants, by showing that an action including discovery proceedings had begun in a Newfoundland court, hoped to convince the U.S. courts to forego jurisdiction over the prior action. The plaintiffs argued that they had the right to defer service for up to one year and that the Newfoundland action had been commenced to prevent their rights from expiring under the limitation statute. If the U.S. courts assumed jurisdiction over the action, the plaintiffs would discontinue their action in the Newfoundland Supreme Court where the award for damages would likely be considerably less than in a U.S. court. The Newfoundland Supreme Court held that the defendants could waive service and enter an appearance, and accordingly they were entitled to a copy of the writ of summons and statement of claim. The defendants had a right to expedite proceedings in order to obtain finality. Examination for discovery by the defendants should, however, be delayed pending the status of the other defendants.

V. Administrative law

1) *Thorne's Hardware Ltd. v. The Queen* [1983] 1 S.C.R. 106, (1983) 143 D.L.R. (3d) 577 (*Supreme Ct. of Canada, 1983*).

The harbour of St. John N.B. was extended geographically by an Order in Council of the Government of Canada to include private property so that the plaintiff was obliged to pay dues on entering harbour. The Supreme Court upheld the Federal Court of Appeal [1981] 2 F.C. 393, (1980) 124 D.L.R. (3d) 622, 38 N.R. 293 holding that the order had been properly enacted and in particular that harbour dues were not discriminatory even if no port services were provided to some of the payees. Further it was held that 'Decisions made by the Governor in Council in matters of public convenience and general policy are final and not reviewable in legal proceedings'.

2) *Irving Oil Ltd. v. National Harbours Bd* (1983) 46 N.R. 91 (*Supreme Ct. of Canada, 1983*).

In a judgment preceding *Thorne's Hardware Ltd. v. The Queen, supra*, the Supreme Court of Canada upheld, for almost identical reasons but in less detail, the right of the Government of Canada to extend the limits of a harbour so as to include a terminal facility built by Irving Oil and then force Irving Oil, which had never paid tolls, to commerce payment. Unsaid by the Court was the fact that the ethical question could be looked at in two ways. Was Irving Oil Ltd. discriminated against for now having to pay tolls when it did not have to do so in the past? Or was it not proper that Irving Oil Ltd. should at last pay tolls?

3) *Warwick Shipping Ltd. v. Government of Canada* (1983) 48 N.R. 378 (*Fed. Ct. of Appeal, 1983*).

Addy J.'s very complete, well-reasoned and interesting decision in first instance [1982] 2 F.C. 147 was upheld in appeal. In particular, it was held that no duty of care was owed by a servant of the Crown to individual mariners for the preparation of a chart which subsequently became misleading when a shoal developed. Nor was the Crown obliged to remove a shoal from a natural channel, which was not in its possession or control. Finally, where a buoy had been placed on a shoal rather than on its edge, the Crown was nevertheless held not responsible for the subsequent grounding of a ship since the cause was not the placement of the buoy, but the pilot unjustifiably believing the whole shoal had been dredged away.

4) *Re Coleman and The A-G Ont.* (1983) 143 D.L.R. (3d) 608 (*Ont. High Ct., 1983*).

Whether or not streams are 'navigable' is important to the riparian owners, because the stream bottom of a navigable waterway is reserved to the Crown when the original grant of land is made by the Crown of a navigable waterway. It was first noted that the right to the stream bottom is confirmed in the Beds of Navigable Waters Act, R.S.O. 1980, c.40. Secondly, navigability is adjudged as at the time of the grant (in this particular case in 1827 under George IV). Finally, to be navigable in law, the stream need only be navigable by small craft such as canoes, skiffs and rafts drawing less than one foot of water. In consequence, Bronte Creek (or Twelve Mile Creek) was held to be navigable, being 26 to 60 feet wide at various times of the year and one to five feet deep.

Henry J. provides a useful summary of the principles used in determining whether a waterway is navigable or not.

VI. Carriage of goods

1) *Domestic Converters Corp. v. Arctic Steamship Line* (1983) 46 N.R. 195 (*Fed. Ct. of Appeal, 1980*).

Goods shipped from abroad were landed at Montreal and stored in a shed owned by the Canadian Government, but operated by a stevedore/terminal operator company. Heavy snow on the roof of the shed caused it to collapse, resulting in damage to the goods. The government was found solely responsible in tort for the damage in virtue of sect. 3(1)(b) of the Crown Liability Act by both the Trial Court and the Court of Appeal.

The Appeal Court did declare that interest at 8% ordered by the Trial

Judge could only run from the date on which the action was instituted and not from the date of the mishap in virtue of sect. 35 of the Federal Court Act, sect. 3(1) of the Crown Liability Act and art. 1056(c) of the Quebec civil code, all taken together.

The Appeal Court also confirmed that bill of lading non-responsibility clauses for goods after discharge were valid in respect to damage occurring ashore without the carrier's fault after the goods had been delivered to a terminal operator.

Finally, it was held that the action against the terminal operator could not be taken in Federal Court which did not have jurisdiction but must be taken in a provincial court.

The Court of Appeal's holding as to the Federal Court's lack of jurisdiction over a claim against a terminal operator is difficult to reconcile with the Court's subsequent decision in *Miida Electronics Ltd. v. Mitsui O.S.K. lines* [1982] 1 F.C. 406. This important issue will hopefully be resolved by the Supreme Court of Canada in its much awaited decision in the *Miida* appeal.

2) *CP Ships v. Les Industries Lyon Cordways Ltée* [1983] 1 F.C. 736 (*Fed. Ct., Addy J., 1982*).

Freight was paid to a freight forwarder by a shipper in the mistaken belief that the freight forwarder was the agent of the carrier. The freight forwarder was declared bankrupt before paying the monies to the carrier and the carrier was declared to have a valid claim against the shipper for payment of the freight. To avoid having to pay again, the shipper would have had to show that the carrier authorized the agent to receive the money, or that the carrier had, by its declaration or conduct, held out the freight forwarder to be its agent, or that it was the custom of the trade for the freight forwarder to receive the payment.

3) *Cormorant Bulk-Carriers Inc. v. Canficorp Ltd.* [1983] E.T.L. 167 (*Fed. Ct., Walsh J., 1982*).

A shipper was informed by the carrier that goods shipped from Quebec City to Kuwait (in reality destined for Iraq) would cause the vessel considerable delay in discharge in Kuwait, if they were identified as transit cargo. The bills of lading therefore did not refer to transit cargo and the shipper gave the carrier a letter of undertaking that it would be responsible for any delay at Kuwait. The vessel was held up in Kuwait as a result of the goods being labelled with Iraq as destination and the Court ordered the shipper to indemnify the carrier for the delay, holding that the letter of undertaking was not a fraud despite *Brown, Jenkinson & Co. Ltd. v. Percy Dalton* [1957] 2 All E.R. 844 which had held that the parties could not enforce amongst themselves an agreement intended to defraud others. The Court held that in the present case there was no intent to defraud the Kuwait authorities, 'although it was done to circumvent their regulations'.

The distinction made by the Court, if there is one, must be very fine. The Court might have better relied on art. 1212 of the Quebec civil code which states: 'Counter-letters have effect between the parties to them only; they do not make proof against third parties'. Between the parties, however, a counter-letter might not be enforceable if the purpose was fraudulent, being contrary to art. 13 c.c. and art. 1062 c.c. (Québec) which forbids agreements which contravene public order and good morals.

4) *Norman v. Canadian National Railway*, (1983) 39 Newfoundland and P.E.I.R. 91, 11 A.P.R. 91 (*Newfoundland Court of Appeal*).

An action for damage was taken against the C.N.R. for loss of the cargo carried on its ice-breaking ferry which sank when it was holed by ice. The Court of Appeal, reversing the decision at first instance, held that the action should be dismissed because C.N.R. had exercised due diligence to make the ship seaworthy. The Court defined the test of due diligence as reasonableness in the circumstances, and noted that the ferry had been well-maintained and properly inspected. If the cause of the ferry's sinking was in fact its unseaworthiness, then the C.N.R. was exempted from liability because it had exercised due diligence under art. 4(1) of the Hague Rules (art. 4 of the schedule to the Carriage of Goods by Water Act, R.S.C. 1970 c.C-15). If, on the other hand, the cause was something other than unseaworthiness, then the C.N.R. was exculpated because the loss was the result of a peril of the sea (art. 4(2)(c) of the Rules).

It is interesting to note that the Court of Appeal stated that the list of exculpatory causes in art. 4(2) of the Rules is applicable only when the loss is caused by something other than the ship's unseaworthiness. In other words, according to this judgment, if the carrier establishes his due diligence to make the ship seaworthy, then he need not show that the cause of the loss was one of the exculpatory causes in art. 4(2)2 (For a different approach, see Tetley, *Marine Cargo Claims*, 2 Ed., 1978 at pp. 54–55).

5) *Power Construction Ltd v. C.N.R.*, (1983) 41 Newfoundland & P.E.I.R. 99, 119 A.P.R. 99 (*Newfoundland Dist. Ct.*).

The plaintiff's crane fell overboard while being loaded on to the defendant's ship. After reviewing the facts, the Court concluded that the loading operation had been carried out under the control and management of the crew of the ship, but without adequate supervision and reasonable care. The crane was lost therefore as a result of the defendant's negligence. The defendant tried to limit his liability to $500 (Can.) under art. 4(5) of the Canadian version of the Hague Rules, but the Court held that the parties had contemplated that the crane would be carried as deck cargo and accordingly the defendant could not benefit from the statutory limit of liability. The Court noted that the crane did not have to actually be conveyed over some distance in order to be 'deck cargo' within the meaning of art. 1(c). Since the plaintiff's right of recovery was not restricted to the amount specified by the Rules, the plaintiff was permitted to recover $13,753.

VII. Labour

1) *Halifax Longshoremen's Assoc. v. Nauss* (1983) 46 N.R. 324 (*Supreme Ct. of Canada, 1983*).

Two stevedores who were refused full membership in a longshoremen's union were ordered admitted to membership by the Canada Labour Relations Board which also ordered new practices in respect to job referral by the Union.

The Federal Court of Appeal had held that the Canada Labour Relations Board had exceeded its jurisdiction in dealing with specific cases of the two stevedores but this was reversed by the Supreme Court.

2) *Cargill Grain Co. v. Longshoremen* (1983) 51 N.R. 182 (*Fed. Ct. of Appeal, 1983*).

Grain was discharged by ship's crews to Cargill Grain Co. facilities and then transported by Cargill employees to storage silos and then on to customer's trucks. This latter service was not considered to be part of 'Navigation and Shipping' and therefore Cargill's grain-handling employees were held to be outside the jurisdiction of the Canada Labour Relations Board.

3) *Rose v. Marystown Shipyard* (1984) 44 Nfld & P.E.I.R. 320, 130 A.P.R. 320 (*Nfld Dist. Ct.*).

A shipyard employee was fired after ten years employment because he was drunk on the job. He took an action in damages for wrongful dismissal. The judge noted that the evidence showed that the employee was a competent foreman and that the Court must ensure that the hardship resulting from the dismissal is not unreasonable in relation to the infraction. The Court held that, though the employer was entitled to dismiss the employee, the employer should have given the employee five months notice in the circumstances. Consequently, the employee was given judgment for an amount equivalent to the salary he would have received over a 5-month period.

4) *Jacobsen v. Workers' Compensation Board* (1984) 45 Nfld & P.E.I.R. 104, 132 A.P.R. 104 (*Newfoundland Sup. Ct., tr. div.*).

The widow of a victim of the Ocean Ranger disaster claimed benefits from the Workers' Compensation Board from which she received a lump sum and monthly payments. Though she had not instituted an action, she subsequently received a settlement from her decreased husband's employer. Thereupon, the Board discontinued the monthly compensation payments. The wife appealed to the Newfoundland Supreme Court regarding this decision by the Board. Noting that the wife received from her husband's employer a full and final settlement of her claim, the Court held that sect. 61 of the Workers' Compensation Act gave the Board a broad jurisdiction to consider new evidence and redetermine a claim. The Board therefore had jurisdiction to make the decision in question and thus the Court could not set it aside.

5) *Makar v. Master of the Rivtow Lion* (1983) 140 D.L.R. (3d) 6 (*Fed. Ct. of Appeal*).

This was an appeal from a judgment of Addy J. dismissing an action for wages and an accounting under the Canada Shipping Act (C.S.A.) and for an injunction against deductions made pursuant to a collective agreement.

In first instance the judge had held that the collective agreement was the only agreement governing the seaman's relationship with his employer. Addy J. had also stated that the provisions of the Canada Shipping Act were superseded by the Canada Labour Code, R.S.C. 1970, c.L-1, as well as by the collective agreement.

Thurlow C.J., speaking for the Court of Appeal, disagreed, adding that collective agreements did not relieve the ship's owner or master of any statutory obligations arising under the *C.S.A.* The master was still required under sect. 165 to enter into an agreement with a seaman, the form and content of such articles of agreement being prescribed by sect. 167. Yet such articles had to be read as including the terms of the collective agreement, and, in the case at hand, it was clear that wages were to be paid in accordance with the collective agreement rather than by the master at the time of discharge. The Court also noted that the failure of the master to comply with the system prescribed by statute did not give a cause of action to the appellant for recovery of deductions made on his wages.

The Court also pointed out that neither a collective agreement nor an authorization given by a seaman for the deduction of certain amounts from his wages constituted an 'assignment' of wages that would not be binding on a seaman by virtue of sect. 205(1)(b) *C.S.A.* A collective agreement did not transfer to the pension fund receiving the deductions the seaman's right to sue his employer for any part of his wages. While the legal mechanism permitting such deductions was not based on an assignment, the seaman was nevertheless precluded from recovering such sums by suing his employer once they were deducted and paid over to the pension fund.

6) *Canada Labour Relations Board v. Halifax Longshoremen's Ass'n.* (1983) 144 D.L.R. (3d) 1, (1983) 46 N.R. 324 (*Supreme Ct. of Canada*).

This was an appeal by the Canada Labour Relations Board as to whether the Federal Court of Appeal had properly set aside part of an order made by the Board to remedy a breach of sect. 161.1 of the Canada Labour Code, R.S.C. 1970, c.L-1. That provision applied to trade unions who operate hiring halls, requiring them to establish and post rules on how union membership could be attained. Complainants had come before the Board seeking reform of the job referral system administered by two longshoremen's unions and also admission to these unions as full members. The Board found that the unions were unprincipled and discriminatory in the manner in which they administered the job referral system and therefore they were in violation of sect. 161.1. The Board's remedial authority under sect. 189 gave it the power to order a union contravening sect. 161.1 to comply with that provision and/or require the union to do something to counteract the consequences of its previous non-compliance. Here the Board ordered the unions to prepare and post rules for employment referral and for union membership (as specified by sect. 161.1). It also ordered that the complainants be admitted to union membership. The Federal Court of Appeal struck out the Board's second order on the ground that in making that order the Board had exceeded its jurisdiction. The Supreme Court of Canada reversed the decision of the Court of Appeal. Laskin C.J., speaking for the Court, held that sect. 189 defined the Board's remedial authority in very broad terms and that the Board had not gone beyond its jurisdiction in providing redress and protection to the complainants as individuals.

VIII. Collision

1) *Egmont Towing v. The Telendos* (1983) 43 N.R. 147 (*Fed. Ct. of Appeal, 1983*).

A vessel of 9046 tons overtook and collided with a tug. Neither vessel was keeping a proper lookout. At trial the overtaking vessel was held solely at fault for failing to keep clear in accordance with Rule 13(a) of the Collision Regulations. In appeal the overtaking vessel was held 2/3 at fault and the tug 1/3 because of its failure to keep a lookout (contrary to Rule 5 of the Regulations).

IX. Pollution

1) *The Queen v. The Sun Diamond* [1984] 1 F.C. 3 (*Fed. Ct., Walsh J., 1983*).

The *Erawan*, due to its sole fault, collided with the *Sun Diamond* and oil from the *Erawan* polluted Vancouver harbour and environs. It was held that the Crown, through the Attorney General of Canada, could take suit against the *Erawan*, whether on behalf of or in place of the National Harbours Board, or as owner of the property vested in the Crown and located in Vancouver Harbour, or because of the common law right to take action with respect to a public nuisance, thus harking back to Lord Denning's M.R.'s decision on pollution damage in *Southport Corporation v. Esso Petroleum* and the influential U.S. decision *State of California v. S.S. Bournemouth*. It was added *obiter* that the National Harbours Board had this right as well. The court noted that suit might also have been taken under s. 33(10) of the Fisheries Act.

X. Liens and Mortgages

1) *Marlex Petroleum v. The Har Rai* (1984) 4 D.L.R. (4th) 739; 53 N.R.1; (1984) A.M.C. 1649 (*Fed.C.A.*)

An American preferred maritime lien for necessaries was upheld by the Federal Court of Appeal although a Canadian necessaries claim would not have had maritime lien status. The court properly recognized the foreign contractual right as being a maritime lien and followed the principle enunciated by the Supreme Court of Canada in the *Ioannis Daskelelis*. The court also found that the Federal Court had jurisdiction to hear the claim under the general provisions of s. 22(1) of the Federal Court Act, which gave jurisdiction over claims for necessaries secured by a *maritime lien*. This jurisdiction was in addition to the court's jurisdiction under s. 22(2)(m) over claims for necessaries which were *not* secured by a maritime lien. The Court's jurisdiction *in rem* could not be based on sect. 22(2)(m) because that provision, read with sect. 43(3), required that the ship against which the action was taken be beneficially owned at the time of the commencement of the action by the person who was the beneficial owner at the time when the cause of action arose, which was not the case here. However, sect. 22(1) did provide jurisdiction over an action *in rem* for necessaries secured by a maritime lien and therefore it was not necessary that the owner of the vessel be liable *in personam* for the necessaries.

See in juxtaposition, *The M/V Leah* 729 F. 2d 971, 1984 AMC 2089 (4 Cir. 1984).

2) *Re Doucet* (1983) 42 *O.R.* (2d) 638; 150 D.L.R. (3d) 53 (*Supreme Ct. of Ont., 1983*).

A 15.75-ton yacht was registered under the Canada Shipping Act, although it was exempted from registration being less than 20 tons. A chattel mortgage on the yacht was not registered under the Canada Shipping Act. In fact the mortgage was not in form prescribed by the Canada Shipping Act and therefore could not have been registered, although the Act calls for mortgages to be registered on ships of 15 tons and over. The yacht owner was declared bankrupt and it was held that the chattel mortgage was valid against the trustee in bankruptcy because the Canada Shipping Act did not confer a special right in favour of trustees in bankruptcy as against unregistered mortgages.

3) *Ultramar Canada Inc. v. Pierson Steamship Ltd.* [1983] E.T.L. 404 (*Fed. Ct., Mahoney J., 1982*).

A tort claim for damage to a wharf and a claim for pilotage dues were both held to be secured by maritime liens. Claims for towage in the U.S. and for the services of stevedores in the U.S. (presumably because they benefitted from preferred maritime liens in the United States) were also declared to be secured by maritime liens in Canada. Necessaries supplied in Canada, however, were not granted maritime lien status, nor were harbour dues under the National Harbour Commissions Act, R.S.C. 1970, c.H-1. It is to be noted, however, that the Canada Ports Corpn. Act 1980–81–82, S.C., c.121 grants special legislative rights to a Port Corporation against ships for unpaid harbour dues.

XI. Economic loss

1) *Interocean Shipping Co. v. The Atlantic Splendour* 1984 AMC 1332 (*Fed. Ct., Dubé J., 1983*).

Economic losses were held to be recoverable without there being any physical damage to the plaintiff's ships which had been forced to wait for seventeen days because the defendant ship negligently blocked the dock at Seven Islands, Québec. In particular, Dubé held:

> My assessment of the present state of the developing jurisprudence on this vexed question of pure economic loss is that there need not be physical injury for the plaintiff to recover, provided, firstly, there was a duty owing by the defendant to the plaintiff, secondly, there was a breach of that duty, thirdly, the economic losses flowed directly from the defendant's negligence, and fourthly, the consequences were reasonably foreseeable. (at p. 1336.)

XII. General average

1) *Northland Navigation Co. Ltd. v. Patterson Boiler Works Ltd.* [1983] 2 F.C. 59 (*Fed. Ct., Collier J., 1983*).

A tug with a barge in tow during rough weather let the barge drift free whereupon it was wrecked ashore with its cargo. This was properly held to be a general average act as both tug and tow were in danger and the act was successful. The subsequent rescuing of the cargo and the barge ashore was also held to be a general average act rather than salvage. This part of the decision has been very heavily criticized in the marine insurance industry. The consternation probably lies not with the decision but with general average, which is perhaps an obsolete concept in modern times. General average arose over 2800 years ago and was a method of distributing risks at sea. With the advent of marine insurance in the last four or five hundred years, a system of risk sharing has been divised which in many cases seems more equitable. The rules of general average as well are based on concepts devised before the modern emergence of the common law rules of tort and contract and in many cases general average practices seem to have no connection with risk, responsibility or fault. A recent report of none other than the General Average Committee of the Comité Maritime International (CMI No. G.A.-1, October 1982) is extremely critical of General Average and even more indicative is the fact that the Committee was chaired by a senior executive of a London P. & I. Club, who is also a well-known member of the British Maritime Law Association.

XIII. Sale of a ship

1) *Consortium Two Thousand v. Ennis*, (1983) 39 Newfoundland & P.E.I.R. 30, 111 A.P.R. 30 (*Newfoundland Court of Appeal*).

A sea captain had offered to sell a ship which he did not own. When the sale could not be completed, the prospective buyer sued for breach of contract and fraudulent misrepresentation for which he was awarded $37,500 in special damages in first instance. These special damages were to cover amounts to be paid by the buyer to its wholly subsidiary for services in coordinating and expediting the delivery manning and chartering of the ship.

The Court of Appeal held that the payments undertaken by the buyer to its subsidiary could not be the basis for an award for breach of contract between the sea captain and the buyer because such payment undertaken by the buyer could not have been reasonably foreseen by the captain. The Court accordingly reduced the damages from $37,500 to $5,000, the latter amount to cover the buyer's expenses for traveling and inspecting the vessel.

XIV. Taxation

1) *Herbstreit v. Regional Assessment Com'n*, (1983) 38 O.R. (2d) 642; 138 D.L.R. (3d) 97.

A ship secured to land and used as a restaurant was considered to be 'land' or 'real property' subject to business assessment for the purpose of tax liability, even though at time of judgment the ship had been towed away!

XV. Charterparties

1) *Offen v. McCain Produce*, (1983) 46 N.B.R. (2d) 108, 121 A.P.R. 108 (*New Brunswick Ct. of Queen's Bench*); affirmed (1984) 49 N.B.R. (2d) 388, 129 A.P.R. 388.

A charterparty contained a clause stating 'general average and arbitration to be settled in New York'. A dispute arose with respect to demurrage and the plaintiff submitted it to arbitration in New York, resulting in an award against the defendant. The defendant, during and after the arbitration, argued that there was no jurisdiction under the charterparty to arbitrate in respect of demurrage in New York. The clause in the charterparty referring to arbitration was only meant to deal with disputes regarding general average. The Court held that the decision of the English Court of Appeal in *The Ioanna* [1978] 1 Lloyd's Rep. 238 (where the same printed clause was subject of litigation) did not apply. Rather, the Court noted that the charterparty had been made in New York, payment was to be made in New York and evidently general average was to be settled there as well. It concluded that there was nothing to show that the parties had not intended to submit disputes on all other matters to arbitration in New York.

DENMARK

ALLAN PHILIP

Professor, University of Copenhagen
Attorney and President of the Danish Maritime Law Association

NEW DEVELOPMENTS OF MARITIME LAW IN DENMARK DURING 1982, 1983 AND 1984

Legislation

a) STATUTE ON LINER CONFERENCES

The Danish parliament has in 1982 passed the necessary legislation to enable Denmark to ratify the UNCTAD Convention on a Code of Conduct for Liner Conferences in accordance with the rules of the European Community Regulation of 15 May 1979. The ratification of the Convention and the coming into force of the statute awaits, however, similar action by other EEC countries.

a) The International Rules of the road at sea, 1972, as revised by IMO by resolution of 19 November 1981 have come into force in Denmark on 1 June 1983.

b) The Danish Maritime Code contains rules on bills of lading based upon the Hague Rules 1924 as amended by the Visby 1968 protocol. However, outside the Maritime Code is found a special statute of 1937 transforming the Hague Rules 1924 into Danish law. Since the rules of the Hague Rules 1924 as modified by the Visby 1968 protocol were included in the Maritime Code in 1974, the two sets of rules have existed side by side and have been applied depending upon the respective rules of application in the 1924 convention and in the 1968 protocol.

The Danish parliament has now passed a statute authorizing the government to denunciate the 1924 Convention in its original form and thereby to terminate the statute of 1937. When denunciation takes place, the Hague Rules will only apply in Denmark as modified by the Visby protocol.

At the time of writing it is not known when denunciation will take place.

c) At the end of 1982 the Danish parliament passed a bill making a number of changes in the Maritime Code. Similar changes have been made in the other Scandinavian Maritime Codes being to a very large extent uniform legislation in each of the countries. The more important of these changes are the following:

1. The provision limiting the liability of the carrier in accordance with the Hague Rules has been changed so that a limitation based upon SDR has been substituted for the limitation based upon Poincaré francs.
2. The existing rules of the Code on transport of passengers have been changed in order that they should as far as possible be in conformity with the Athens passenger convention. However, it is not the intention to ratify that convention as it is found that the limitation of liability in the convention is too low. The Code contains higher limitation amounts.
3. The provisions of the code containing rules of global limitation of liability based upon the 1957 Brussels Convention have been replaced by provisions based upon the 1976 IMO Convention and that convention will as a result be ratified by Denmark.
4. A number of other provisions, especially in relation to limitation funds, have been revised and updated.

d) As is commonly known, at the end of 1982 the Danish parliament passed a law introducing some amendments to the Danish Maritime Code. Some of these changes related to the rules on transport of passengers in order to comply with, inter alia, the Athens Convention on transport of passengers. However, the Danish Government has not ratified the Convention, as the limit of liability is rather low. On the contrary, the Danish Maritime Code increases the limitation of liability. Now, in November 1984, a ministerial decree was issued providing for the entry into force of these amendments to the Maritime Code on 1 April 1985.

At the same time it was decided to denounce the Hague Rules in their original form on 1 March 1985. From then on only the Hague Rules as modified by the Visby Protocol will apply.

Case law

The more important cases reported in the weekly law-reports, Ugeskrift for Retsvaesen (UfR) are the following:

a) COMBINED TRANSPORT

In the case Broströms Rederi AB, Sweden v. Dansk Søassurance A/S and B&W Diesel A/S (UfR 1982 p. 398) the former undertook to carry a number of generators and other electrical equipment by ship from Gothenburg in Sweden to Jeddah in Saudi Arabia and from there to Khamis Mushait 800 km by road. The cargo was damaged during the road transport. Carriage took place under a bill of lading which contained a paramount clause making the Hague Rules 1924 applicable to the transport. Under the Danish statute transforming the Hague Rules into Danish law the carrier's liability is limited to 1,800 kr. pr. kollo. Total damage amounted to about 1.7 million Danish kroner. The limited liability would amount to 5,400 kr. The question arose whether the rules of limitation of liability of the Hague

Rules were applicable to the transport as a whole including the road transport or only to the sea transport. This question was taken out for preliminary decision.

The bill of lading referred to Jeddah as port of discharge and – in a box applied in connection with through bills of lading – to Khamis Mushait as place of delivery. In the carrier's standard conditions referred to in the bill of lading and known to the shipper reference was made to combined transport and liability was imposed upon the carrier for subcontractors.

Separate freight was agreed for the sea-carriage and the land transport respectively. The conditions expressly referred to the Hague Rules with respect to limitation of liability.

The carrier had made a sub-contract for the land transport on CMR conditions.

The court of 1st instance with 4 votes to one considered that the limitation of liability did not apply to the land transport while the Supreme Court with 6 votes to one came to the opposite conclusion. The majority found the text of the conditions so clear that there was no basis for considering that the land-transport was not covered by the limitation rule.

b) EVIDENCE. RIGHT TO SEE LOG AND MATE'S RECEIPT

In the case *VEB Deutfracht Seereederei, DDR v. Langelands Korn København A/S and others* UfR 1983 p. 372, a cargo of rapeseed was sold to be shipped August/September. The bill of lading was dated the 30th September but rumours said that the ship had sailed only on 3rd October. According to the applicable standard contract from the Grain and Feed Trade Association bills of lading must not be dated before the goods are in fact on board. The date of the bill of lading is prima facie evidence.

The price of rapeseed decreased after the 30th September and the buyers wanted to pay the new price only for the cargo. They wanted to see the ship's log and the mate's receipt in order to ascertain the precise date of receipt on board of the rapeseed.

Under Danish law of procedure generally the buyers would have the right to see the documents. However, the Maritime Code contains provisions specifically prescribing such right in respect of Danish and other Scandinavian ships but limiting it in cases of collision. The carrier contended that the right to see the documents did not exist for non-Scandinavian ships according to an e contrario interpretation of this rule but this view was rejected by the majority in the Supreme Court.

c) AS 1984 IS CONCERNED, ONLY ONE CASE OF REAL INTEREST HAS BEEN REPORTED IN THE WEEKLY LAW REPORTS, UGESKRIFT FOR RETSVAESEN (UFR):

In *Sjoforsakringsaktiebolaget Hansa v. Rederiet K/S Bres Shipping II* and *Rederiet Nielsen + Bresling*

(UfR 1984. p. 584) The shipowner carried 298 rolls of paper from a

Swedish port to Bilbao in Spain. The rolls were sold to a firm in Madrid. They were discharged in Bilbao and then transported on lorries from Bilbao to Madrid. At the time of discharge no complaints were made on behalf of the receiver. When the rolls arrived in Madrid they were all damaged. The insurance company argued on behalf of the receiver that the damage had taken place in connection with the discharge from the vessel. However, the court found that in the circumstances the burden of proof was on the receiver to show that that was so and the court did not find that the receiver was able to discharge the burden of proof.

Bibliography

The following books have been published:

a) Kjeld Rosenmeyer, *Transportret*. The book is a general textbook of the law of transport. The greater part of the book is, however, concerned with the law of carriage at sea.

b) Roger Henriksen, *The legal aspect of paper-less International Trade and Transport*. The book is a thesis on the prospects of eliminating paper documents and particularly bills of lading by use of data processing and transmission procedures in international trade and transport. It contains a general introduction describing the work in the field and an excellent discussion of all the legal aspects of the problem.

c) Bernhard Gomard and Lise Skovby, *Vejtransport af farligt gods*. The book is a monograph on the law of road transport of dangerous cargo.

d) Hardy Rechnagel, *Påtalesubjektet*. The book is a thesis for the doctor's degree. It is concerned with the question who in complex legal relationships arising where several parties are involved in arranging transport is entitled to sue the carrier. It contains an English summary.

e) Hardy Rechnagel and Anders Hjulmand, *Transport*. The book is an introduction to problems arising in connection with international transport.

f) Uffe Lind Rasmussen has published the book *Jurisdictionklausuler og Voldgiftsklausuler i Soetransportkontrakter*. It discusses the validity of jurisdiction- and arbitration clauses in maritime contracts and especially considers the relationship to legislation on bills of lading in the USA, England and Scandinavia as well as to the Hamburg rules.

It may be mentioned that Scandinavian judgments in addition to being reported in national law reports are reported in a common Scandinavian publication, Nordiske Domme I Sjoefartsanliggender. This publication also contains reports of judgments which have not been reported in the national reports but which are found to be of interest in a more specialized forum. The annual volume appears in smaller parts and the final volume appears only with much delay. In 1983 the volume with judgments from 1981 appeared and the volume from 1982 was not published until 1985.

DEMOCRATIC REPUBLIC OF GERMANY

Dolly Richter-Hannes

Institute for Foreign and Comparative Law GDR Legislation and Publications in the Sphere of Maritime Law 1984

Legislation

I. Regulation No. 2 of 12 January 1984, Concerning Maritime Traffic; Official Gazette of the GDR/Special Print No. 993/1:

1. In accordance with its Art. 35, this Regulation has been in force since its publication (22 February 1984).

2. This Regulation is based on IMO Resolution A. 464 (XII) on Amendments to International Regulations for Preventing Collisions at Sea, 1972, adopted by decision of the 12th IMO Assembly at London, on 19 November 1981.

3. The essential elements are:

- Formulation of a general duty for GDR vehicles (exceptions being vehicles of the National People's Army, of the GDR frontier troops as well as of other protection and security authorities) to cooperate in registration systems serving to ensure safety of international maritime traffic, as well as to consider meteorological recommendations as to routes;
- Modifications and additions to Annex 1 to the Maritime Traffic Regulation (International Regulations for the Prevention of Collisions at Sea, 1972, as well as special provisions concerning GDR waters);
- Modifications and additions to Appendix I of Annex 1 to the Maritime Traffic Regulation (ordering and technical details of lights and signals);
- Modifications and additions to Appendix III of Annex 1 to the Maritime Traffic Regulation (technical details of acoustic signal installations);
- Modifications and additions to Annex 2 to the Maritime Traffic Regulation (traffic signals);
- Modifications and additions to Annex 3 to the Maritime Traffic Regulation (danger warnings).

II. Convention on a Code of Conduct for Liner Conferences, of 6 April 1974, on the basis of the Announcement of 9 January 1984;
Convention: Official Gazette of the GDR/Special Print No. 1151;
Announcement: Official Gazette of the GDR II No. 2 p. 17.

III. Protocol of 1978 Relating to the International Convention for the Safety of Life at Sea, 1974, of 17 December 1978, on the basis of the Announcement of 28 March 1984;
Protocol: Official Gazette of the GDR/Special Print No. 1015/2;
Announcement: Official Gazette of the GDR II No. 3 p. 27.

1. In accordance with its Art V, this Protocol came into force in the GDR on 28 July 1983.

2. The essential elements are:

- Stipulations of the scope of application of the Protocol:
- •• The provisions of Arts II, III (b) and (c), IV, VI (b), (c) and (d), VII and VIII of the Convention become constituent elements of the Protocol;
- •• Any ship which the Protocol applies to is also subject to the provisions of the Convention (with reservation as to the modifications and additions to the Protocol);
- •• The parties shall apply the Convention and Protocol to ships of non-parties to such an extent as to secure that no preference be given to these ships.

- Modifications and additions to the Convention, in detail, concern:
- •• Chapter I, Rules 2, 6, 7, 8, 10, 11, 14, 19;
- •• Chapter II-1, Rules 1, 2, 29;
- •• Chapter II-2, Rules 1, 3, 55, 60;
- •• Chapter V, Rules 12, 19, 19-1, 19-2;
- •• adding to the Appendix of the Annex of a form of safety construction certificate for cargo ships.

IV. Announcement of 2 May 1984, concerning the International Convention on Standards of Training, Certification and Watchkeeping for Seafarers, 1978;
Convention: Official Gazette of the GDR/Special Print No. 1153;
Announcement: Official Gazette of the GDR II No. 3 p. 26.

1. In accordance with its Art. XIV, the Convention came into force in the GDR on 28 April 1984.

2. The essential elements are:

- Principles for keeping navigational and engineering watch;
- Mandatory minimum requirements for certification of masters, nautical, technical and radio officers;

- Mandatory minimum requirements for ensuring continued proficiency and updating of the knowledge of masters, nautical, technical and radio officers;
- Mandatory minimum requirements for ratings keeping navigational and engineering watch, for the certification of radiotelephone operators and lifeboat men;
- Mandatory minimum requirements for the training and qualification of masters, officers and ratings on oil, chemical and liquified gas tankers;
- Basic principles for watchkeeping in ports, and mandatory minimum requirements for watchkeeping in ports aboard ships carrying dangerous goods.

V. Regulation No. 4 on Fishing in the Fishing Zone, the Territorial Waters and Internal Waters of the German Democratic Republic, of 23 March 1984;
Official Gazette of the GDR I No. 13, p. 172.

1. In force since 1 June 1984, with the exception of Art. 3 which came into force on 1 January 1985 (Art. 3: regulation concerning fishing books).

2. The essential elements are:
- Enlargement of the facts constituting petty offences;
- Allocation of quotas in case of an allocation of species of fish of the Baltic Sea, and the granting of fishing licences according to quotas allocated; particularly regulation of government competences;
- provisions concerning the keeping of fishing books.

VI. 2nd Implementing Decree to the Act on the State Border of the German Democratic Republic of 20 December 1984;
Official Gazette of the GDR I No. 37, p. 441.

1. In force since 1 January 1985.

2. The essential elements are:
- Extension of territorial waters to 12 miles, on principle;
- Stipulation of the reservation as to the delimitation of the continental shelf or the fishing zone towards neighbouring and opposite countries;
- Formulation of the right of foreign warships or public vessels which are used for non-commercial purposes to pass through GDR territorial waters if they have to do so for arriving at or leaving their ports on direct route;
- Provisions concerning sporting boats are not affected by this Implementing Decree.

VII. Announcement of 10 August 1984 to the Protocol of the Conference of the Representatives of the States Parties to the Convention on Fishing and Conservation of Living Resources in the Baltic Sea and the Belts, Warsaw, 9–11 November 1982;
Protocol: Official Gazette of the GDR II No. 3, p. 30;
Announcement: Official Gazette of the GDR II No. 4, p. 29.

1. In accordance with para 1 of Art. XVI of the Convention, the Protocol came into force in the GDR on 10 February 1984.

2. The essential elements are:

- Modifications in connection with the establishment of fishing zones within the scope of the Convention beyond the territorial waters;
- Amendment of the competences of the International Commission for Fishery in the Baltic Sea and the Belts, particularly in connection with the management of the Baltic Sea and the Belts;
- Possibility to stop accepting a recommendation of the Commission by the states parties to the effect of the recommendation not being binding any longer;
- Duty of the states to notify the Commission of all legislative activities or agreements entered into which concern the conservation and utilization of fishery resources in the Convention area;
- Opening of the Convention to any intergovernmental integration organization;
- Stipulations concerning the admission of the EEC to the Convention;
- Statement by EEC representatives (Annex to the Convention) that obligations of the EEC under the Treaty which established it are not in conflict with obligations arising from this Convention.

Publications

1. Hahn, W.: *New Regulation for the Transport by Sea and Port-Transshipment of Packed Dangerous Goods (I)*
   in: Seewirtschaft, Berlin 16 (1984) 2, p. 72–77.
2. Hahn, W.: *New Regulation for the Transport by Sea and Port-Transshipment of Packed Dangerous Goods (II)*
   in: Seewirtschaft, Berlin 16 (1984) 3, p. 116–119.
3. Elchlepp, F.: *Disaster of the Motor Tanker 'Amoco Cadiz' – 6 Years Later.*
   in: Seewirtschaft, Berlin 16 (1984) 4, p. 165–169.
4. Trotz, N.: *On the Draft of a New Convention on Salvage*
   in: Seewirtschaft, Berlin 16 (1984) 4, p. 169–172.
5. Hahn, W.: *New Regulation for the Transport by Sea and Port-Transshipment of Packed Dangerous Goods (III)*
   in: Seewirtschaft, Berlin 16 (1984) 4, p. 176–179.
6. Kantner, G.: *Topical Aspects of Charter Parties – Remarks on the Concept and Content of War Clauses in Charter Parties*
   in: Seewirtschaft, Berlin 16 (1984) 5, p. 227–228.

7. Ley, W.: *Services with Regard to Ships and their Legal Regulation in the GDR* in: Seewirtschaft, Berlin 16 (1984) 7, p. 339–341.
8. Richter, R.: *Bills of Lading and Maritime Fraud* in: Seewirtschaft, Berlin 16 (1984) 8, p. 384–386.
9. Edelstein, H.; Kadelbach, K.: *On the New Regulation Concerning Log-Books* in: Seewirtschaft, Berlin 16 (1984) 9, p. 439–442.
10. Busch, J.; Busch, H.-J.: *The Arbitration Clause in Voyage Charter Parties* in: Seewirtschaft, Berlin 16 (1984) 9, p. 442–445.
11. Joachim, S.; Rosentreter, G.: *Legal Bases for the Establishment of Joint Ventures in Maritime Economy* in: Seewirtschaft, Berlin 16 (1984) 10, p. 487–488.
12. Hauer, A.: *On Some Questions of Limitations of Action in Maritime Law* in: Seewirtschaft, Berlin 16 (1984) 11, p. 544–548.
13. Richter-Hannes, D.; Westphal, H.: *From the Administration of Justice by National and Foreign Courts in the Sphere of Maritime Law* in: Seewirtschaft, Berlin 16 (1984) 12, p. 586–588.
14. Puls, B.: *VOLCOA – Standard Volume Contract for the Transport of Bulk Commodities* in: Seewirtschaft, Berlin 16 (1984) 12, p. 588–589.
15. Hauer, A.: *Topical Aspects of Charter Parties* in: Seewirtschaft, Berlin 16 (1984) 12, p. 590.
16. Lutze, W.: *Economic Aspects of the Application of Terms of Multi-Modal Transport in International Capitalist Container Liner Service* in: DDR-Verkehr, Berlin 17 (1984) 2, p. 53–55.
17. Richter-Hannes, D.: *Analysis of Administration of Justice in Respect of the SHSG, Part II* in: Seewirtschaft 1985, No. 2, Berlin 17, p. 92–94.
18. In 1984, the GDR Society for Maritime Law issued No. 8 of '*Contributions to the National and International Law of the Sea*', Rostock 1984 (108 pages). Being devoted to 'Legal Questions of the Protection of the Marine Environment' this edition contains the following contributions:
a) Trotz, N.: *Problems of Responsibility and Liability in the Protection of the Marine Environment, p.* 5–41;
b) Box, H.-J.: *Protection and Conservation of the Marine Environment in the Convention on the Law of the Sea from the Aspect of the Law of Treaties and Customary Law*, p. 43–76;
c) Großkopf, K.: *Controls by Coastal States for the Prevention of Water Pollution by Ships*, p. 77–91;
d) Oesau, M.: *On the Consideration of Environmental Protection in the CMI Draft of a New Convention on Salvage*, p. 93–108.
(Subjects and contents of the preceding seven copies are given in No. 8. These copies may be obtained through Buchexport und -import Leipzig or through the Society for Maritime Law).

FEDERAL REPUBLIC OF GERMANY

Prof. Dr. Rolf Herber

Institut für Seerecht und Seehandelsrecht der Universität Hamburg

RECENT DEVELOPMENT OF MARITIME LAW IN THE FEDERAL REPUBLIC OF GERMANY

Maritime Law in the Federal Republic of Germany has, during 1984, not changed considerably.

Legislation

The draft law implementing the 1976 London Convention on Limitation for Maritime Claims has been submitted to Parliament (Deutscher Bundestag) in June 1985. The legislative work consists of three draft laws, namely

- draft law providing for ratification of the 1976 Limitation Convention (Drucksache 10/3553),
- draft law of a 2nd law amending German Maritime Law (Zweites Seerechtsänderungsgesetz) (Drucksache 10/3852),
- draft law revising the Procedure on Distribution of the Limitation Fund (Seerechtliche Verteilungsordnung) (Drucksache 10/3853).

All three drafts have passed, before being introduced into Parliament, the Bundesrat which has proposed some changes – not, however, affecting the main features of the draft legislation.

The Government intends to introduce the rules on limitation of liability for maritime claims into German law by making applicable the London Convention in its original text apart from the codification of the Handelsgesetzbuch. The latter, however, will contain certain articles expressly referring to the Convention and providing for additional rules to the extent possible in §§486 to 487e. These paragraphs replace the existing limitation rules under the same numbers introduced into the Handelsgesetzbuch by the first Seerechtsänderungsgesetz (1972).

As additional rules to the Convention the following seem worth mentioning: The German draft law makes use of the faculty (art. 6 para. 3 of the Convention) to provide, when distributing the fund for priority of claims in respect of damage to harbour works, basins and waterways and aids to navigation.

Furthermore, the draft legislation makes use of a different ruling as to claims relating to wreck removal (art. 2 para. 1 lit. d) e), art. 18 para. 1.) The internal law in making use of this reservation provides for an additional fund with the same figures as those provided for property damage for these claims. This means that in cases, where an incident has caused as well property damage to third parties as claims for wreck removal, the shipowner has, in order to protect himself, to respond two times to the sums provided for in the Convention. On the other hand, he will be – contrary to actual German law – protected by the new rules against all kinds of claims presented to him for wreck removal, including claims based on administrative law.

The liability sum for small vessels (left to national legislation until 300 tons by art. 15 para. 2 lit. b) will be fixed for ships until 250 tons by providing for a limitation sum according to half of the amount provided for by the Convention as to ships of 500 tons.

The limitation of pilots, which is expressly foreseen in the 1976 Convention, will be reduced beyond the Convention by providing for a limitation amount according to a ship of 1,000 tons and, in respect to damage caused to passengers, to a ship carrying 12 passengers. This reduction corresponds to similar rules in other legislation and makes use of the possibility of national law to provide for further restriction of claims apart from the Convention.

There is one more element which merits to be mentioned in this context: Art. 15 para. 10 lit. a) mentions expressly the right of a contracting state to apply the rules of the Conventions to vessels intended for navigation on inland waterways. This rule, which – in the strict sense of public international law – is superfluous in the Convention, because every state undoubtedly has the right to apply the rules of an international Convention beyond its scope of application, is of great importance in Germany because inland navigation on the river Rhine has not only great economic importance but, until now, follows legal rules of their own which are overaged. Since the end of the last century the Binnenschiffahrtsgesetz provides for a system of limitation of liability which exposes only this ship as such (and in its actual value after the incident) to liability. Since some decades this system is subject to attempts of revision undertaken within UNIDROIT and ECE. The last attempt, an ECE Convention (CLN) of 1973, did fail. During the last months there has been discussion within the Central Commission for the Navigation on the Rhine (CCNR) in Strasbourg, to agree in common among the Rhine States (Belgium, France, Federal Republic of Germany, Netherlands, Switzerland, United Kingdom) on application of the 1976 Maritime Limitation Convention to inland navigation as well. Of course, the Convention of 1976, for the purpose of being appropriate for inland navigation law, needs some changes and amendments. This goes in particular for the limitation sums which with regard to inland navigation vessels need calculation methods different from those in maritime law. Another subject of amendments for inland navigation purposes is the limitation procedure which in inland navigation for some extent must be different. The present draft, however, does not provide for extension of the limitation rules to inland navigation. The actual limitation system in this field, as described, will therefore be retained at least for some years.

Another topic of the Zweites Seerechtsänderungsgesetz as mentioned above is the introduction of compulsory rules on liability in the carriage of passengers by sea. The rules provided for in the draft law correspond to a large extent to the Athens' Convention of 1974 without, however, proposing ratification of this convention. These rules shall be applicable to inland navigation as well, where in actual German law there are no compulsory legal rules as they are lacking now in maritime transport of passengers.

The reasons for not proposing a ratification of the Athens' Convention are mainly based on objections against the liability sums of the Athens' Convention. The government proposes a liability amount per passenger of DM 320,000.--, which corresponds to the limitation figure provided in the German law of air transportation and the Montreal Protocol of 1975 to the Warsaw Convention. The Bundesrat has proposed when commenting on the Government draft to increase this figure to DM 500,000.-- DM per passenger, which would correspond to the German law of road transportation. The Government, however, intends to retain the figure of DM 320,000.-- and the Parliament now will have to decide on the matter.

The draft legislation mentioned above does not provide for ratification of the Visby Protocol of 1968 to the Hague Rules of 1924. It provides, however, for some amendments of national German law on carriage of goods by sea by means of amendment of §660 HGB and of adding a new §607a HGB. The limitation figures of the Visby Rules shall be introduced into German national law. That means that the actual limitation according to which the carrier is liable until DM 1,250.-- per package or unit, will be changed to the rule that there is liability until DM 2,000.-- per package or unit or, at the choice of the claimant, until DM 6.-- per kg. In addition, the container clause of the Visby Rules literally will be introduced into national German law. The breakability of that rule will be restricted as well according to the Visby Rules.

Another element of the Visby Rules to be introduced into German law is the so-called Himalaya-clause according to which the master and the members of the crew enjoy to the same extent as the carrier himself the benefit of limitation. The latter rule, it is true, has been applied already by the German Supreme Court under the existing law. Different from the limitation rule and the container-clause mentioned before, which has not been applied according to the decision of the Supreme Court reported in the contribution to YML, Vol. III.

It is to be expected that the draft law will pass Parliament in the course of next year, so that ratification by the Federal Republic of Germany of the Convention may take place in the 2nd half of 1986.

Jurisdiction

After the important decisions reported to YML, Vol. III there have not been decisions of the Bundesgerichtshof (Supreme Court) of major importance in the international field.

The jurisdiction of the courts of appeal (Oberlandesgerichte) still shows that there is a lot of practical uncertainty in the legal importance of contract and documents in combined transportation. The more, as these documents very often are issued by forwarders and the bearing and obligation of a forwarder's contractual obligation mostly is unclear. German law provides for liability of a forwarder according to that of a transport operator in some cases (§§412, 413 HGB), in particular where a fixed amount of freight is agreed. The Bundesgerichtshof has spelt out this rule in various decisions. The question remains, however, which law of transport is applicable when – as in most cases – the transportation promised against expressly fixed remuneration is performed by different means of transport. Such a case recently was judged by the Oberlandesgericht Hamburg (reported in '*Versicherungsrecht*' 1984, p. 1090 f.), where a forwarder had issued a sea-Bill of Lading for a combined transport by sea and road and where the damage occurred on the road leg (between the Soviet Union and Afghanistan). The Court did not apply mandatory law of sea transportation because the B/L, which included the land transportation, did not create mandatory liability – irrespective of the fact, that land transportation was governed by the CMR. The decision shows, as mentioned, how unclear the actual legal situation in this field is and that it needs – like in other countries – some legal guidance.

Doctrine

Except for a reference to the maritime law journals in Germany such as 'Transportrecht', 'Hansa' and 'Versicherungsrecht' there is no need to mention specific books or articles during the last period of report as regards maritime law.

As to inland navigation law, which in particular with respect to limitation of liability is narrowly linked with maritime law as mentioned above, there has been an interesting publication reflecting the actual situation in inland navigation law and containing proposals for its amendment, namely:

Werner Korioth, *Die Neuregelung der Haftungsbeschränkung in der Binnenschiffahrt* (*Duisburg 1984*).

Reports on German jurisdiction in maritime cases are contained in papers reflecting speeches to the German Maritime Law Association, namely:

Emil Lau, *Neuere Entwicklungen in der seerechtlichen Rechtsprechung des Hanseatischen Oberlandesgerichts Hamburg* (Heft 51 der Schriften des Deutschen Vereins für Internationales Seerecht, Hamburg 1985).

Johannes Trappe, *Entwicklung im Charterrecht* (Heft 52 der Schriften des Deutschen Vereins für Internationales Seerecht, Hamburg 1985).

FRANCE

JEAN WAROT

Avocat à Paris. Hononary President of the French Maritime Law Association

HIGHLIGHTS IN FRENCH MARITIME LAW: LEGISLATION AND JURISPRUDENCE IN 1984

I. French legislation

1) LAW of 21 DECEMBER 1984 modifying the domestic law of 3 January 1967 on the 'Statut des navires et autres bâtiments de mer'

a) the owner of a vessel which has been abandoned in a French port cannot limit his ability towards the French Authorities in reference to the Brussels Convention of 1957 and to the French domestic law of 3 January 1967, for all expenses incurred for the removal of the vessel or of the wreck.

b) the limits of liability as fixed by the Brussels Convention of 1957 will be those stipulated in the London Convention of 19 November 1976. The new law will be enforceable when the London Convention on limitation of maritime claims will be in force.

2) LAW of 22 DECEMBER 1984 modifying the domestic law of 3 July 1967 on maritime insurance

The French Underwriters are henceforth authorized to insure the 'faute lourde' [gross negligence] of the assured and of his servants to the exception of 'faute intentionnelle' [wilful misconduct].

3) LAW of 22 DECEMBER 1984 completing the domestic law of 7 July 1967 on the 'événements de mer' [collision, salvage]

This law introduces in the domestic legislation the provisions of the

London Convention of 19 November 1976 concerning the salvors and their servants who will have the possibility to invoke limitation.

This new law will be enforceable when the London Convention will be in force.

4) COLLISIONS AT SEA

A decree dated 8 March 1985 introduces the international rule of 1972 [as fixed by O.M.I.] on 'separation of traffic'.

Any infringement of these rules will be considered as a 'delictus' as provided by the French penal and disciplinary Code.

5) PROTECTION OF FRENCH MARITIME AND COMMERCIAL INTERESTS

A decree dated 22 February 1983 has put into force the law of 23 December 1983 which is protecting French interests with regard to measures adopted in foreign countries imperiling French interests in the maritime commerce.

These texts are establishing a control upon exports and imports of goods and chartering of foreign vessels.

6) CODE DE CONDUITE DES CONFÉRENCES MARITIMES

Law of 22 May 1985 relating to the application of the U.N. Convention of 6 April 1974.

Only French shipowners trading principally and customarily under the French flag are authorized to participate in the conferences. This law contains a reference to the 'Règlement' of E.C.C. dated 15 May 1979.

II. French jurisprudence

1) RESPONSIBILITY OF PORT AUTHORITIES AND OF THE STATE IN CASE OF BLOCKADE OF A FRENCH HARBOUR BY FISHERMEN ON STRIKE

The Administrative Court of Rouen has dismissed a claim of users of the Port of Le Havre when the harbour entrance was blocked by fishing boats on the motives that:

a) the Port Authorities had not at their disposal Police forces to dismantle the blocking of boats and would not have the authority to do it:

b) the State was not responsible in consideration of the fact that it was a general strike.

[*Administrative Court of Rouen, 25 May 1984*]

Note: in similar disputes, the 'Conseil d'Etat' has condemned the State to compensate the losses suffered by the user each time the losses suffered were abnormal [Conseil d'Etat, 22 June 1984].

2) CHARTER-PARTY DISPUTE – TIME-BAR – LAW OF THE FLAG APPLICABLE

The Court of Cassation has ruled that the extinctive prescription of one year as fixed by the domestic law of 18 June 1966 [art. 4] in a charter-party dispute did not apply in international matters, i.e. a dispute between a foreign shipowner and a French charterer, in consideration of the fact that art. 3 of the same law provides:

'In international deals, the contract of affreightment is governed by the law of the vessel's flag unless otherwise agreed.'

Following the views expressed by Professor Rodière in his Treatise of Maritime law, French Courts of Appeal had ruled that the problem was to be decided by the Lex Fori in matter of time-bar, but the Court of Cassation has considered that it was a 'violation of the law' and that the time-bar as fixed by the law of the flag was applicable.

[*Court of Cassation – 20 March 1982*]

3) ARREST OF SEA-GOING SHIPS – BRUSSELS CONVENTION 10 MAY 1952 – CLAIM FOR UNPAID BUNKERS

The Court of Appeal of Rouen referring to art. 8-2 of the Convention according to which a claimant can arrest a vessel flying the flag of a non-contracting State and also to art. 3-4 of the same Convention which provides that the claimant may arrest 'such ship or any other ship in the ownership of the charterer by demise', has ruled that this arrest could take place even after the redelivery of the vessel if the arrest is made by a creditor of the owner or of the charterer or of some debtor of a maritime claim.

One should recall that under French law [Decree 27 October 1967] a ship can be arrested by 'other claimants', in French 'créanciers terrestres', i.e. for a claim whose nature is not maritime.

[*Court of Appeal of Rouen, 19 June 1984*]

4) TOWAGE CONTRACT – EXCEPTION CLAUSES IN THE TOWAGE CONDITIONS

The Court of Appeal of Rouen has ruled that the provisions of the French domestic law of 3 January 1969 on towage, i.e. art. 26 stipulating: 'Harbour towage operations are performed under the direction of the master of the vessel in tow'.

'Damage of any sort happening during the towage operations are borne by the vessel towed unless the fault of the tug is established' are 'public policy provisions' to which it cannot be derogated.

Consequently an exception clause in the towage conditions is null and void and a negligence of the master of the tug deprives her owners of any claim against the vessel.

[*Court of Appeal of Rouen, 22 March 1984*)

5) JURISDICTION CLAUSE IN BILL OF LADING GIVING COMPETENCY TO A FOREIGN COURT

Our French Courts are separated in opinion upon the validity of jurisdiction clauses.

Each time the competent Court is not clearly determined in the clause and when the clause is printed in too small type, the tendency is to decide that the clause cannot be opposed to claimants.

As a matter of fact, the matter is left at the discretion of the Court.

Lately, the Court of Appeal of Aix-en-Provence has ruled that a clause in a Bill of lading issued jointly by two different carriers and giving jurisdiction to Courts in Caracas and/or Bogota, could not be opposed to a claimant in spite of the fact that the shipper had signed the Bill of lading.

[*Court of Appeal of Aix-en-Provence, 1 September 1983*]

6) INTERNATIONAL MARITIME CARRIAGE – PARTIES NATIONALS OF COUNTRIES MEMBERS OF E.E.C.

The Court of Cassation has ruled that in addition to the compensation awarded to the receivers for losses or damage sustained by the cargo, the carrier can be condemned to reimburse to the shipper the 'subventions' ['restitutions communautaires'] granted to exporters in application of the E.E.C. Rules on export, which were lost as a consequence of the event.

The Court has decided that it was a 'damage' which could have been foreseen by the French shipowner.

[*Court of Cassation, October 1984*)

7) DAMAGE CAUSED TO A SHIP SAFELY BERTHED BY THE WASH OF ANOTHER SHIP

The Court of Appeal of Rouen has ruled that this damage was to be considered as a collision damage and compensated accordingly, as provided by the domestic law of 7 July 1967 [Chap. I: Collision].

However, the burden of proof rests upon the claimant.

[*Court of Appeal of Rouen, 14 June 1984*]

8) COMMON LAW LIENS APPLICABLE TO RADIO AND RADAR MATERIAL IN BANKRUPTCY PROCEEDINGS

French Courts have recognised that the hirer out of radio and radar material installed on board a ship could validly invoke the 'general lien' as provided by the Civil Code article 2102–3° as a guarantee for his claim in bankruptcy proceedings.

However, the judge must be satisfied that this expense has been made for the conservation of the thing.

The Court of Cassation has approved this case-law in a judgment dated *9 October 1984.*

9) VOYAGE CHARTER – GENCON CHARTER-PARTY

The Court of Appeal of Aix-en-Provence has ruled that when a shipowner invokes the benefit of clause 2, paragraph 2 which provides an exoneration of liability in case of unseaworthiness of his vessel, he must beforehand prove that he has exercised the due diligence required to maintain her in a seaworthy condition.

[*Court of Appeal of Aix-en-Provence, 28 February 1984*]

10) CLAUSE 'SAID TO BE' IN THE BILL OF LADING, AND WASTAGE IN BULK

The Court of Cassation has ruled that these mentions on a Bill of lading could be considered as a valid reserve which could be opposed to the bearer of the Bill of lading.

Moreover, in the same judgment the Court of Cassation has ruled that there must be a causation link between the loss of cargo and the wastage.

The wastage in bulk must be established in accordance with the custom at the port of destination. These customs are usually confirmed by an opinion delivered by the Chambers of Commerce.

[*Court of Cassation, 23 February 1983*]

GREECE

GR. J. TIMAGENIS LL.M., Ph.D. (Lond)

Attorney at Law, Piraeus

DEVELOPMENTS IN GREEK MARITIME LAW: LEGISLATION, CASES AND BIBLIOGRAPHY 1983–1984

Introduction

The period 1983–1984 is characterized by a serious and prolonged world shipping crisis. The main cause of the crisis is the reduction of the massive imports of earlier periods by the oil producing countries starting from the Arab countries, and extended to Nigeria and South American countries as these countries saw themselves with reduced funds at best and with heavy debts imperiling not only their own but also the world economy at worse. This reduction of cargoes resulted in excessive tonnage availability and fall in freights and ship values in turn.

Greek shipping felt this crisis more, as, in addition to the world problem, Greek owners had to face increasing competition from the Eastern European fleets and particularly the Soviet fleet, creation of national fleets by developing countries, which however small further reduced available cargoes, increased costs and an uncertainty about and from the intentions and policies of the Socialist government elected in 1981.

These problems have resulted in difficulties of Greek owners to operate their ships and repay their loans to the banks, in lay-ups, foreclosures and unemployment of seamen.

The crisis of world and Greek shipping in particular has reflected directly in the developments of maritime Law in this period. Thus, the main piece of legislation in the period concerns measures for improving the competitiveness of Greek shipping and for facing seamen's unemployment. Similarly, court cases arising from the trade of the ships (i.e. charter party disputes, cargo claims even collision or salvage cases) have been reduced and the emphasis is during the period with foreclosures, auction of ships and maritime liens. In addition to these main areas of development legislation and court cases exist in almost all the other areas of maritime law, but they are of a rather routine nature without major novelties and similarly the bibliography on maritime law during the period is relatively poor.

A. Legislation

1. INTERNATIONAL CONVENTIONS AND REGULATIONS

In 1983 Greece ratified the 'International Convention on Standards of Training, Certification and Watchkeeping for Seafarers' adopted in London in 1978 (Law 1314/1983 – Gov. Gaz. A 2/11.1.83).

In the area of marine pollution two IMO resolutions were ratified by Greece concerning technical specifications in the context of the implementation of the International Convention for the Prevention of Pollution from Ships adopted at London in 1973.

The first is IMO Resolution A 495 (XII) 19.11.81 concerning technical specifications of clean ballast tanks of tankers (Decision of the Greek Minister of Mercantile Marine No. 181053/201/84 – Gov. Gaz. B 73/13.2.84) and the second was IMO Resolution A 497 (XII) 19.11.81 concerning technical specifications for the design operations and control of the crude oil washing system (Decision of the Minister of Mercantile Marine No. 181053/96/84 – Gov. Gaz. B 224/10.4.84).

Finally, some minor amendments to the Regulations for the Prevention of Collision at Sea were ratified (IMO Resolution A 464 (XII) 15.12.81 ratified by Presidential Degree 233/83 – Gov. Gaz. A 86/5.7.83) and three bilateral treaties, the first between Greece and Morocco concerning the avoidance of the double taxation of income from the operation of ships or aircraft (Law 1343/83 Gov. Gaz. A 41/6.4.83), the second between Greece and Egypt (signed at Cairo in 1981) concerning shipping and carriage by sea and accompanied by a Protocol on Seamen (Law 1441/84 – Gov. Gaz. A 71/21.5.84) and the third between Greece and the German Democratic Republic concerning Merchant Shipping (Law 1449/84 Gov. Gaz. A 86/16.6.84).

2. MEASURES TO MEET THE CRISIS

In an effort to meet the problems arising from the shipping crisis and for the purpose of assisting the competitiveness of the Greek ship and facing the unemployment problem the Greek Government, after extensive consultations with interested parties including the Union of Greek Shipowners (UGS) and the Panhellenic Seamen's Federation, adopted Law 1376/1983 (Gov. Gaz. A 96/18.7.83) which provided for the following measures:

a. Permission to the U.G.S., subject to Minister's approval on each occasion, to conclude Collective Marine Labour agreements with Seamen's

Trade Unions of foreign countries applicable for not more than two years as of the date of the law providing among others for wages for the foreign seamen lower than those provided in the Greek Collective Labour Agreement and exemptions from the obligation of the owners to pay insurance contributions for the foreign seamen to the Greek Mariners Pension Fund (NAT) provided they comply with the social insurance scheme of the country of the nationality of the foreign seamen.

b. Possibility for the Minister of Mercantile Marine to reduce the ship complement for automated ships provided that their safety is not imperiled (The Minister issued in this respect two decisions to the effect No. 70003/6878 and No. 70005/6877 both in Gov. Gaz. B 658/21.11.83).

c. Greek ships were allowed to be manned by foreign seamen but only for lower crew and up to 30% of the ship's complement provided that no Greek seamen of the same speciality was available or willing for employment as it could be certified by the marine employment office of the Ministry of Mercantile Marine.

d. Establishment of a special fund to subsidize unemployed seamen. (In this connection Presidential Decree 29/16/24.1.84 Gov. Gaz. A 7/24.1.84 was passed fixing the requirements for considering a seamen unemployed).

e. Establishment of an obligation for owners to pay a certain amount to the above fund for each for foreign seamen employed and

f. Establishment of an obligation for owners, masters and crew that no seaman is allowed to work on board the same ship for a period exceeding 7–9 consecutive months. After the lapse of the period the seaman must take his leave and be replaced by another mariner. By this obligation of rotation it was hoped that employment would be provided to more mariners.

3. OTHER MATTERS

A number of laws, decrees or ministerial decisions have been issued in the period concerned on other matters which could be characterized in most cases as routine legislation. These regulations concern administrative matters of shipping, safety of navigations, seamen (conditions of work, wages, social security, education etc.), salvage and towage, pollution, ship financing and criminal aspects of shipping. More specifically:

a. Administrative Matters

In connection with the administration of shipping some amendments were brought to the provisions concerning the Shipping Register and the Maritime Mortgages Register (PD 26/84 Gov. Gaz. A 7/24.1.84), the change of name of ships (PD 28/84 – Gov. Gaz. A 7/24.1.84) and the form of the seamen's books (Decision of the Minister of Mercantile Marine 70056/8428/83 Gov. Gaz. B 3/9/84).

b. Safety

In the area of safety a number of decrees and regulations were issued concerning the seaworthiness of ferries (PD 33/83), fire protection of passenger ships for internal transport (PD 185/83 Gov. Gaz. A 71/8.6.83 and PD 61/84 Gov. Gaz. A 19/23.2.84), Load Lines of Ships (P.D. 399/80 Gov. Gaz. A 83/24.6.83), specially trained personnel for life rafts of passenger ships (PD 214/83 – Gov. Gaz. A 77/17.6.83) and having navigational aids (P.D. 299/83 Gov. Gaz. A 84/28.6.83).

c. Seamen

In connection with seamen a number of collective agreements were concluded fixing the wages and the working conditions for seamen. In addition, a number of regulations concerned social security matters or work conditions like the subsidies of unemployed seamen (PD 49/83 Gov. Gaz. A26/28.2.83), the organization of the special fund for the family subsidies of seamen (P.D. 213/83 Gov. Gaz. A 77/17.6.83), amendments to the regulations of the Mariners Pension Fund (P.D. 63/84 Gov. Gaz. A 20/24.2.84) and health and safety of the workers in Shipyards (P.D. 190/84 Gov. Gaz. A 64/15.5.84). Finally, in connection with the education of seamen, in addition to the relevant international convention ratified, regulations were passed for the establishment of intensive courses for the training of prospective mariners for tankers (P.D. 27/84 – Gov. Gaz. A 7/24.1.84).

d. Salvage-Towage

In this connection two Presidential Decrees were issued concerning respectively towage (P.D. 45/83 Gov. Gaz. A 24/16.2.83) and salvage (P.D. 46/83 Gov. Gaz. A 24/16.2.83) in the Greek territorial waters.

e. Pollution

In addition to the international regulations ratified by Greece within the period a number of new stations were established for the prevention and fighting of pollution of the sea (P.D. 9/84 Gov. Gaz. A 3/10.1.84).

f. Ship Financing

In connection with ships financing Decision No. 44/28.2.83 (Gov. Gaz. A. 51/22.4.83) of The (Central) Bank of Greece was issued authorizing the

Banks to grant Ship Repair Loans in Drachmas, for the repairs of ships at Greek Shipyards at a fixed interest rate provided that they are repaid within 2 or 4 years in free foreign currency.

g. Criminal Law

Finally, an important Law was passed in the area of criminal law (L. 1419/84 Gov. Gaz. A 28/14.3.84) amending the code of the Criminal Procedure for the purpose of expediting drastically the procedure for the investigation and punishment of marine fraud.

B. Court cases

As already noted Court decisions issued or reported in 1983 and 1984 cover a number of areas of Greek Law with particular emphasis to foreclosures, auction of ships and maritime liens. Indicatively a selected number of these cases follow as presented and commented by the author in the Greek/English periodical *Naftiliaki.*

1. JURISDICTIONAL/PROCEDURAL MATTERS (ARBITRATION/EVIDENCE/ ATTACHMENT OF FUNDS)

a. ARBITRATION CLAUSE ON A B/L- IDENTITY OF THE CARRIER CLAUSE- EMPLOYMENT CLAUSE- Arbitration Clause on a B/L signed by the master or an agent authorised by the master is valid. The 'Identity of the Carrier Clause' (or 'Demise Clause') is not enough by itself to make the owner of the ship the carrier

In a case of carriage by sea the receivers of the cargo and holders of a B/L signed by the master, did not pay the shipowner the freight, which according to the B/L was due at destination, on the grounds that they had paid that in advance to the charterer, who had disappeared in the meantime without paying the hire to the owners. The owner started arbitration in London for an award in connection with the freight due, on grounds that even if the receivers had paid the freight to the charterers this was not a proper payment and did not discharge them from their obligation to pay the freight to him at destination as per the B/L. On the other hand the receivers started court proceedings in Greece seeking a declaration of the court to the effect (a) that the London arbitration clause on the B/L was not valid and binding upon them, because it was not signed by both parties as the law requires but only by the master of the ship and, (b) that no freight was due to the shipowner because the receivers had agreed the carriage with the charterers, who were the carriers, as a consequence, and the receivers properly paid the freight to the charterers. The owners contended, *inter alia*, that the contract of carriage was between owner and B/L holders (receivers) because the B/L included the 'Identity of the Carrier Clause' or 'Demise Clause' i.e. a clause providing that the carrier under this B/L was the owner.

The Multi-Member First Instance Court of Piraeus held that: (a) Although the law (Code of Civil Procedure and Civil Code) requires generally that an arbitration agreement be signed by both parties, this does not apply to an arbitration clause included in a B/L signed by the master or an agent authorised by the master, because in accordance with the Code of Private Maritime Law such a B/L is proper evidence of the contract of carriage without requiring signature by both parties (i.e. owners/shippers). (b) The Demise Clause is not enough by itself to make the owner the carrier. A prerequisite for this is that the master is the servant of the owner (and not of the charterer), and this is so if under the charter party the owner has retained the nautical direction and commercial exploitation of the ship, and therefore the owner must produce evidence on these points. (c) The 'Employment Clause' in the C/P evoked by the receivers, under which the master should follow the charterers' instructions as to the employment of the ship, is rather an agreement against their views in that such a clause is a usual clause referring to the performance by the ship and its obligation under the C/P, and does not refer to nautical and navigational matters. (*Multi Member First Instance Court of Piraeus 1486/1982, Piraiki Nomologia Vol. 4, p. 164*).

Comment: No other reported case exists to our knowledge on the points dealt with by this decision. There are some earlier decisions on the 'Identity of the Carrier Clause' but from a different point of view. In those cases the receivers claimed against the charterer/carrier for loss of or damage to cargo. The charterer put up the defence that in accordance with the 'Identity of the Carrier Clause' in the B/L it is the owner who is the carrier and therefore the charterer is not responsible for the loss/damage. In those cases the Greek courts held also that the clause by itself was not enough to make the owner the carrier, and that as long as such a clause was used as an exemption of the charterer/carrier from his liability it is valid within the limits that Greek law permits limitation of or exemption from liability (e.g. for damage after the discharge of the cargo from the ship but prior to its delivery to receivers), and invalid as long as it exceeds such limits, i.e. it is partially valid and partially invalid. In the present case it is the first time that it is the owner who invokes this clause in order to claim freight from the receiver, and the court did not face the effect of the implied acceptance of the B/L both by owner and B/L holder on the binding force of the clause upon them. (This may only happen if the B/L provides for freight payable at destination and is not claused 'freight prepaid') (*Naftiliaki*, February 1983, p. 19).

b. TELEX-Probative value

In a case where a ship was released from arrest on certain conditions which included a written agreement and one of the parties alleged a modification of these conditions through a telex message, the probative value of the telex was questioned before the court on the grounds that telexes don't bear a signature as required by law for normal private documents. *The Court of Appeal of Piraeus* held that although a telex does not have a signature it has the same probative value as any other written private document (i.e. it provides full evidence of the statements included therein, but counter evidence is permitted) provided that its validity is not disputed or is proved by other means of evidence, that is it is admitted or proved, that the telex has been actually sent and received. In this case the telex provides evidence both in favour and against the sender and the receiver. (*Piraeus Court of Appeal 1455/82, Epitheorisis Naftikou Dikeou Vol. 11 (1983) p. 132*).

Note: This decision deals with a matter (the probative value of telex messages) which is of particular importance to the shipping business where the use of telex messages is extensive. The court held that a telex is evidence of the statements contained therein if it is proved or admitted that it was actually sent and received. The same view was held by implication by the Supreme Court (Plenary Session) in decision AP (Olom) 487/82 No. B 31 (1983) 58. In this connection one point should be clarified however: The courts, in holding the above view, were interpreting the provisions of the Code of Civil Procedure which concerned evidence. The solution might be different in cases where the substantive law (as compared to procedural law) like the Civil Code or Maritime Code requires a 'written private document' for a particular contract. In these cases otherwise the agreement may not be held to be concluded or proved. In the field of Maritime law two frequent contracts for which the courts require a written agreement (with signatures) are the sale of a ship and the charterparty, although a more liberal approach might not be legally inconceivable. (*Naftiliaki*, July 1983, p. 20)

c. Attachment of funds in bank accounts

In a case where a shipowner attempted to obtain an injunction for attaching the funds of the charter deposited in a bank account with the Piraeus branch of an American bank as a security for his claim for hire, the *Single Member First Instance Court of Piraeus* held among other things that because of the concept of bank secrecy established by law in 1971 these funds are not subject to attachment or any other enforcement, and that this rule applies also to funds deposited with a lawfully-established branch of a US bank because such banks should be subject to equal treatment with Greek banks and because of the equality required under the Bilateral Treaty of Friendship, Commerce and Shipping between Greece and the United States of America signed in Athens on 3 August 1951 (*Single Member Court of First Instance of Piraeus No. 1046/83, The Bulletin of the Greek Chamber of Shipping vol. 23, April/June 1983, p. 47*).

Note: (1) Often funds or other property of the defendant are in the hands of a third party. The Code of Civil Procedure (CCP) provides for the possibility of attaching such property in the hands of a third party by serving the relevant title for the attachment or the injunction upon the third party. The third party within 8 days must file a statement with the local Justice of the Peace stating whether it has the funds or other property or not. In case of an affirmative reply the funds should be paid to the claimant if he has an enforceable title, or they are kept as a security if the attachment has been effected by virtue of an injunction. In the case of a negative reply or no reply at all (which is equal to a negative reply) the claimant may challenge such reply before the Courts and possibly prove that it is not correct, in which case the third party is obliged to pay the funds to the claimant (CCP Articles 992, 1016). The most obvious case when this happens is with banks and funds deposited in bank accounts.

(2) In 1971 Legislative Decree 1059/71 established a statutory obligation of bank secrecy to the effect that (a) all accounts with Greek banks are secret, (b) all directors, managers or employees of banks who by reason of their duties hold information on bank accounts are not allowed to give any information to third parties even with the agreement of the beneficiary and in case of a breach they may be punished with imprisonment of at least 6 months, (c) these persons are not allowed to give evidence before any Court on any case concerning such matters, and (d) exceptionally bank secrecy may be lifted by decision of the Court if necessary for the investigation or punishment of serious criminal offences. The purpose of the law was to inspire a sense of confidence in prospective depositors and to encourage the depositing of funds in bank accounts.

(3) In practice the problem arose of whether this statutory secrecy prohibits the banks from making the declaration before the Justice of the Peace which is required by the Code of Civil Procedure in cases when they are served with injunctions or orders or titles aiming at the attachment of funds deposited with them by their clients.

(4) In practice banks when served with such orders file a declaration with the Justice of the Peace to the effect that because of bank secrecy they are not allowed to make a declaration as to whether they have the funds or not. The Supreme Court of Greece, in two decisions of the Plenary Session (1224/75 and 1225/75), held that the secrecy established by the law in connection with bank accounts results in effect in the impossibility of attachment. This applies, however, only to funds deposited in bank accounts and not to other property deposited with banks, e.g. share certificates etc.

(5) Most authors criticise the decisions of the Supreme Court on the grounds that the secrecy does not mean necessarily impossibility of attach-

ment of bank accounts, and that the banks may make a declaration to the Justice of the Peace because they are allowed to do so by a different provision of the law, notably the Code of Civil Procedure. However the Courts invariably follow the decisions of the Supreme Court, not because they are legally binding upon them but mainly because of the authority of the decisions of the Plenary Session of the Supreme Court. It is true that the secrecy of bank accounts and the possibility of attaching them are two different matters, but in all fairness even if the law does not refer specifically to the impossibility of attachment, the purpose of encouraging the depositing of funds with banks might be ineffective if secrecy were not to be accompanied by the impossibility of attachment. Ultimately it is a question of policy priorities rather than anything else, whether the law establishing the bank secrecy overrides the Code of Civil Procedure of vice versa, and the strictness of the law on bank secrecy and the penalties established for violation of secrecy seems to imply that the secrecy provisions should override those of the Code of Civil Procedure concerning the declaration of the third party.

(6) It should be noted however that both the law and the decisions of the Supreme Court refer expressly to Greek banks. Therefore the problem arose in practice of whether this rule of secrecy applies only to Greek banks strictly speaking (i.e. Greek banking corporations) or also to branches of foreign banks properly established in Greece and subject to Greek banking law for their operation in Greece.

(7) Court practice seemed to be uncertain for some period of time but the great majority of Courts were in favour of the view that the secrecy also applies to Greek branches of foreign banks. The best known (and perhaps the only reported) decision of an Appeal Court on this matter is the decision of the Court of Appeal of Athens No. 7060/76 (*Nomikon Vima 26.974*) holding that the same rule of secrecy should be applied also to Greek branches of foreign banks for a number of reasons, including the equality of Greek and foreign citizens so far as their civil rights are concerned both under the Constitution and under the Civil Code, and for branches of American banks because of the equality required by the Bilateral Treaty between Greece and the USA signed in Athens on 3.8.51.

(8) The First Instance Court of Piraeus, where most shipping companies have offices and bank accounts, traditionally used to hold the view in favour of the application of secrecy to foreign banks with the exception of a very few judges. At a certain period in time the practice seemed to be uncertain, but in recent months a number of decisions tend to show that the practice is standardised again in favour of the application of secrecy to foreign banks.

(9) In the mainstream of this trend lies the decision summarised above, together with another decision (*Single Member First Instance Court of Pireaus No. 691/83, Naftika Chronica No.* 1149/908 *of* 15.4.83, *p.* 29) where the Court was facing the same problem in connection with an English bank. In this case the Court held that the secrecy applies also to the branches of

banks established in a country member of the European Community for the above reasons but also because of the equality required under Article 44 of the Treaty of Accession of Greece to the EEC. (*Naftiliaki*, September 1983, p. 21)

2. SHIPS/OWNERS (TRANSFER OF SHIP/LIMITATION OF LIABILITY)

a. Transfer of ship – Liability of the buyer for debts of the seller – Requirements – A laid-up ship is not a going concern

The claimant was the owner of a small laid-up passengership under the Greek flag 50% of which was sold to S.K. for Drs 1,100,000, out of which it was agreed S.K. was to pay outstanding debts on the ship to third parties before paying the balance to the seller. The buyer (S.K.) paid the debts but he did not pay the balance, Drs 677,000, to the seller, on the contrary he even sold his share of the ship to the defendant. The claimant started proceedings against the defendant (second buyer) for the balance of the purchase price of the (first) sale, on the grounds that the defendant was responsible for such balance on the basis of Article 479 of the Civil Code.

The Supreme Court (*Arios Pagos*) held that: 1. In accordance with Article 479 of the Civil Code in case of transfer by agreement of a whole property or of a going concern, the transferee (e.g. purchaser) becomes responsible, jointly and severally with the transferor (e.g. seller), for the debts of the transferor in connection with the property or the going concern up to the value of the property transferred. 2. For the application of this rule the transferred goods must be the whole or nearly the whole of the property of the transferor and in case of transfer of a single object (like a ship) this should be the only asset or a substantial percentage of the assets of the transferor. 3. In addition, the purchaser should know that the asset transfer is the only asset or a substantial percentage of the assets of the seller. Such knowledge is considered to exist if the buyer knew at the time of the sale the general financial standing of the seller and could understand that the asset sold was the only asset or a substantial portion of the assets of the seller. 4. On the other hand a going concern as understood in the context of Article 479 of Civil Code is a group of objects including material things and rights organised in an economic unit under a single owner aiming at economic purposes and profit. 5. From the evidence before the Court, it was clear S.K., at the time of the transfer of the 50% of the ship to the defendant, was the owner of one more ship, of substantial real estate (land where a hotel was under construction), a share in a large cinema enterprise, etc., the value of which was larger than the value of the transferred share of the ship. 6. Further, a ship, when she is laid-up, is not a going concern. 7. Consequently the claim against the defendant should fail because the requirements for the application of Article 479 of Civil Code did not exist. (*Arios Pagos*

1129/1983, Nomikon Vima Vol. 32 (1984) p. 667 – President: G. Konstas, Reporting Judge: J. Premetis, Attorneys-at-Law: N. Skoulariotis, Ger. Georgatos).

Note: 1. Article 479 of the Civil Code and especially its application in the area of shipping is a peculiarity of Greek Law. The requirements of its application are clearly set out in the decision of the Supreme Court which in fact reflects an earlier crystalised practice of lower courts. What is interesting about this decision is that the legal issues involved reached the Supreme Court and that it was finally cleared that a laid-up ship cannot be held to be a going concern (although this may not be absolute especially for passenger-ships which carry out touristic tours in the summer and are laid-up temporarily for the winter). 2. Although Article 479 of the Civil Code was not originally conceived or destined for application in the case of a ship, as a single object transferred, application of 479 is widespread in shipping law because of the practice of single vessel companies for which the vessel is their only asset and consequently its transfer draws application of Civil Code Art. 479 and the knowledge of the buyer is easily proved. 3. Finally it should be noted that Article 479 of the Civil Code applies for claims of the seller, whether they are maritime liens or not, and especially in the latter case or in case that the time limit for enforcing the maritime lien against the purchaser has expired. (*Naftiliaki*, 15 September 1983, p. 11)

b. Limitation of Liability – Abandonment of Ship – Establishment of Fund – Bank Guarantee – Valuation of Ship – When limitation is not allowed

The Greek flag vessel *A.F.* completed loading a cargo of paper rolls at Rauma and Kotka, Finland by mid April 1983, for transporting to Japan. At the port of delivery substantial cargo claims arose and owners decided to limit their liability and applied to the Court of Piraeus in summary proceedings for the valuation of the ship for the purpose of establishing the limitation fund.

The Single Member of First Instance Court of Piraeus held that: (1) In accordance with Greek Law an owner may limit his liability for claims arising out of contracts concluded or torts committed by the master in performing his duties by abandoning the ship and the gross freight to the creditors. (2) Instead of this abandonment, the owner may establish a limitation fund equal to three-tenths of the value of the ship at the beginning of the voyage plus an additional three-tenths for the satisfaction of claims in respect of accidents to persons. (3) The fund includes three-tenths of the value of the ship only and not of the freight. (4) The fund is established by a declaration from the owner to the Court Clerk accompanied by a receipt showing the amount involved has been deposited with the Fund of Deposits and Loans (a public agency). Instead of this receipt a bank guarantee may be deposited. (5) Valuation of the ship for the establishment of the fund is provisionally made by the Single Member First Instance Court in summary proceedings. If there are objections the Multi-member Court resolves the issue. (6) The owner is deprived of his right to limit his liability in respect of obligations from contracts which the owner specifically approved, but in this particular case no such specific approval was proved. (7) In this particular case the ship was 17,418 gross tons, 10,146 net, 26,844dwt, had a 11,400bhp engine, was made of steel, length 175.21 m, breadth 26.62 m, depth 12.24 m, built in Sweden in 1967 and purchased by its present owners in May 1979 for $4.5m. No evidence of improvements existed and the excessive draft was a defect in that it did not allow the vessel to call at several ports. In view of these elements and taking into account the age of the ship and the market, its value by mid April 1983 should be fixed at US Dollars 2,000,000. The fund should be US Dollars 600,000 and may be established by depositing with the Court a bank guarantee. (*Single Member First Instance Court of Piraeus* (*Summary Proceedings*) *No. 2887/1983 issued November 4 – Not yet reported in Greek legal periodicals*).

3. MARINE EMPLOYMENT/MARINE LABOUR ACCIDENT

a. Marine Employment-foreign Mariners – Applicability of Greek Collective Labour Agreements

A foreign seaman was employed on a Greek-flag ship under a contract of marine employment providing, among other terms, for the application of Greek Law. In a dispute on the rights of the mariner under his contract of employment, the question was raised as to whether he may derive rights not only from the statutory rules of Greek Law, but also from those included in the Greek Collective Agreement of Marine Employment.

The Court of Appeal of Piraeus held that the reference to Greek Law includes also the collective agreements of marine employment because article 83 of the Greek Code of Private Maritime Law (KIND), as amended by article 2 of L. 451/76, provides that not only the statutory provisions but also the Greek collective agreements for marine employment apply to foreign seamen, and this provision is in full conformity with article 22 para 1 of the Greek Constitution providing for equal payment for equal work regardless of sex or other distinction. (*Court of Appeal of Piraeus 809/83 Epitheorisis Naftiliakou Dikeou Vol.* 12 (*1984*) *p. 37 – President*: *G. Vlastos*, *Reporting Judge*: *E. Petroupouleas*, *Attorney*: *A. Alykatoras*). (*Naftiliaki*, 15 March 1984, p. 11)

b. Marine Labour Law – Mariner employed in two capacities (*Cook/Steward*) *– What he is entitled to be paid?*

In a case where a mariner was employed on board a Greek ship in the two capacities of cook and steward and a dispute arose in connection with his proper payment, *the Court of Appeal of Piraeus* held that (1) An agreement under which a mariner agreed to be employed in two capacities is valid; (2) This mariner is entitled to the wages, bonus, etc. of both capacities; (3) However he is not entitled to be paid twice the amount fixed in the collective agreement for overtime as it was proved physically impossible to perform overtime duties of both capacities (*Piraeus Court of Appeal No. 197/83 Epitheorisis Naftiliakou Dikeou Vol. 11 (1983) p. 178*). (*Naftiliaki*, July 1983, p. 20)

c. Marine Labour Accident – Accident on the high seas – Applicable law – The law of the flag (majority) or the law of contract employment (minority)

A Greek mariner employed in Piraeus by the Piraeus agents of the owners on the basis of a contract expressed in the Greek language and offering his services on a vessel flying the Saudi Arabian flag fell on a stairway and suffered serious injuries while the vessel was sailing on the high seas. The mariner started proceedings and claimed compensation from the owners of the ship. In the course of the proceedings the question of the applicable law was raised.

The Court of Appeal of Piraeus held (by majority) that because a labour accident from the legal point of view is a tort, even though no fault on the part of the employer is required, it should be governed by the law of the place where it took place. As a ship on the high seas is considered to be territory of the State of the flag which she flies, in this particular case the rights of the claimant should be determined by the law of Saudi Arabia and the court should adjourn its hearing for the purpose of examining the Saudi Arabian law. One member of the Court however, in a dissenting opinion expressed the view that because the accident occurred in the performance of the contract of marine employment which in view of all relevant circumstances was governed by Greek law it was also possible to claim, the accident claim could be governed by the same law. (*Court of Appeal of Piraeus 203/1984 Epitheorisis Naftiliakou Dikeou Vol. 12 (1984) p. 255. President: G. Spinassa, Reporting Judge G. Nikolopoulos, Attorneys: G. Theoharides, N. Kairis, C. Bartsiokas*). (*Naftiliaki*, 1 August 1984, p. 11)

4. CARRIAGE BY SEA

a. Carriage by sea – Clause 'said to weigh' – When valid – Period of responsibility – Limitation by agreement – Responsibility for quantity shortfall

A cargo in bags was transported on the defendant's vessel and at the port of discharge a very small quantity of bags was not delivered compared to the quantity referred to in the Bill of Lading. The receivers began proceedings against the owners (carriers) in respect of the loss. As defence the defendants put forward: a) In accordance with the B/L the carrier was not responsible for loss or damage to cargo prior to loading or after discharge and the alleged loss occurred after discharge when the cargo was in storage in a Customs zone; b) Alternatively the missing quantity had never been loaded and the B/L was not evidence of the quantity loaded as it contained the clause 'said to weigh' and because of the large number of bags involved and the speed at which they were loaded, the master could not fully control the loading, thus the burden of proof of the number and weight of the bags loaded fell to the claimant; and c) In any event, the quantity not delivered (315 bags out of 61,728) was only 0.02% of the cargo and is a natural loss of weight and volume which is commercially tolerable and within the acceptable commercial risks of international practice.

The Multi-Member First Instance Court of Piraeus held that: 1) The clause in the B/L limiting the responsibility of the carrier to loss of or damage to cargo prior to loading or after discharge is valid and effective and since the claimant did not protest the loss at the time of delivery nor was the alleged shortage ascertained by a joint survey of the parties or by the surveyors appointed by the court, the claimant/receiver has the burden of proving both the loss and that it occurred during the period of actual transportation (the period for which the carrier is responsible). 2) For the clause 'said to weigh' to be valid and have the effect invoked by the defendants, it must be noted in writing on the B/L the reason why the master was not in a position to ascertain the actual weight of the cargo, or that the receiver must have known that a lesser quantity had been loaded and must have acted to the detriment of the carrier, for the carrier to plead using either of these two circumstances. This was not done and the defendant's relevant defence should fail. 3) The defence that loss of weight is either an inherent vice or due to the nature of the cargo applies to bulk cargoes and not to cases when the shortage involves a number of bags. Further there is no basis within the law to justify relieving the carrier of liability for non-delivery of part of a cargo in bags, however small or commercially tolerable. Therefore both the defences based on the proportionally small quantity not delivered should fail. (*Multi-Member First Instance Court of Piraeus 1624/83 Epitheorisis Naftiliakou Dikeou Vol. 12 (1984) p. 84 – President of the Court: Th. Apostolopoulos, Reporting Judge: Sp. Kolyvas, Lawyers: Ath. Theologidis, G. Arapis*). (*Naftiliaki Intelligence*, 1 April 1984, p. 11).

b. Carriage by sea – Hire not paid by charterer – Liening cargo B/L with freight prepaid – Charterer's B/L approved by master

A Greek flag cargo ship was time-chartered for a voyage of about 40–45 days duration from St Lawrence, Canada to Eastern Mediterranean ports for the carriage of general cargo at a daily hire of $3,100 payable in advance every fortnight. In performance of this charter party the ship loaded general cargo shipped in Canada by various shippers and commenced the voyage. The charterers paid one or two instalments of the hire and then stopped payment. The ship continued the voyage to the port of destination, which was in Greece, and upon arrival the owners applied to the court for an injunction ordering the arrest of all the assets of the charterers, if any, which could be located in Greece and the liening of the cargo in respect of the unpaid part of the hire. At the hearing the receivers of the cargo intervened and argued that they had paid their freight to the shippers and they were holders of Bs/L claused 'freight prepaid' and therefore the cargo could not be liened. The owner contended that the terms of the Bs/L were not binding on them because the Bs/L were not issued by the master of the ship or an agent authorised by him but were issued by charterers' agent.

The Single Member First Instance Court of Piraeus held that:

1) Under Greek law when the hire or freight has not been paid by the charterer, the carrier may lien, by court order, the cargo in respect of such claim even if this cargo belongs to a receiver who is a third party and in fact by taking delivery of the cargo the receiver becomes jointly and severally liable with the charterer for the latter's debts arising from the charter party.

2) This does not apply, however, when the receiver is a third party (vis-à-vis owner/charterer) and holds a B/L claused 'freight prepaid'. In this case the cargo may not be liened and in fact the receiver is not responsible for any claims under the C/P whether the B/L freight has been paid or not because the clause itself is binding.

3) But this is based on the requirement the B/L is properly issued. Under Greek law a B/L is properly issued if signed by the master or an agent authorised by the master. The lack of the master's signature and or of his authorisation for the issue of the B/L may be covered, however, by subsequent approval of the master, and the acceptance of the cargo on board the ship and the performance of the voyage amounts to such approval, thus a B/L issued by the charterers without the authority of the master becomes binding upon the owners.

4) As a result the arrest of the property of the charterers was allowed but not the liening of the cargo. (*Single Member First Instance Court of Piraeus No. 2089/84 Judge*: *Ch. Tritakis*, *Lawyers*: *C. Prassos*, *G. Timagenis*, *B. Kassidakis – Not reported yet in legal periodicals*).

Note: This decision moves in the mainstream of a number of other similar decisions. A point, however, which is questionable is whether the acceptance of the cargo and the performance of the voyage amount to acceptance by the master of the B/L issued by the charterers. In most cases the cargo is loaded on the basis of the C/P and the B/L is issued subsequently, consequently the master at that time has not seen the charterer's B/L or its terms. Similarly, the voyage is usually performed in compliance with the C/P, and in any event acceptance of the cargo and performance of the voyage alone may not be interpreted as acceptance of all the terms of the B/L which has not been seen by the master. It is necessary for the courts to further elaborate the requirements of approval of the charterer's B/L by the master. (*Naftiliaki*, 15 October 1984, p. 11)

c. Carriage By Sea – Container – Whether a package for the limitation of the liability of the carrier

In the case of a shipment for carriage by sea on the vessel of the defendants the relevant Bill of Lading described the cargo as one container containing 1,840 pistons No. 90226, gross weight 467 kilos. Receivers alleged that the cargo was delivered at the port of discharge in a damaged condition and claimed against the carrier. The carrier, among other defences, evoked the right of limitation of his ability to Drs 8,000 which is the limitation per package under Greek Law. *The Multi Member First Instance Court of Piraeus* held that when the contents of the container are clearly described in the B/L and thus the carrier knows what he is carrying, and consequently does not carry a container of unknown contents, then the container may not be considered to be a package and the carrier may not limit his ability accordingly. (*Multi Member First Instance Court of Piraeus No. 13/1983, Epitheorisis Naftiliakou Dikeou Vol. 11 (1983) p. 296*). (*Naftiliaki*, November 1983, p. 23)

5. SALVAGE

Salvage – Conditions for claiming salvage – Ships under the same management – distribution of salvage – claim by master on behalf of the crew

The motor vessel 'N' sailed from Chalkis with a cargo of cement for Dubai. While off the islands Kuria-Muria the vessel grounded on a coral reef and suffered underwater damage which resulted in ingress of water to the extent that the bow of the ship became submerged. The crew took to the life boats and abandoned ship but half an hour later they returned on board the vessel and contacted the office of the managers for assistance. The managers ordered the motor vessel 'M', which was under their management and was at Bombay in ballast, to assist the vessel in distress. In fact the m/v 'M' arrived close to m/v 'N' and after considerable efforts, interrupted at times because of bad weather, the cargo was transhipped. During this exercise which lasted about three days, the two ships came in physical contact and the m/v 'M' suffered damage. Subsequently the m/v 'M' accompanied the m/v 'N' from a small distance and both ships arrived safe at destination. In a case when the master of the m/v 'M', acting also on behalf of the crew, claimed salvage:

The Court of Appeal of Piraeus held: (1) For a salvage claim the following conditions should exist: (a) assistance from one ship to another ship, her cargo, freight or passengers, (b) the ship in distress to run a risk of loss which is real even if not immediate but probable, and which existed prior to salvage services and was not caused by them, (c) the salvage services to have had a beneficial result; (2) A salvage situation exists even if the two ships – that salving and that salved – are under the same management; (3) The salvage award belongs by one-half to the owner, by one-quarter to the master and by one-quarter to the crew; (4) The master is entitled to start proceedings claiming not only for his own portion of the salvage but also for that portion belonging to the crew. (*Court of Appeal of Piraeus 744/1983, President*: *G. Vlastos*, *Judge*: *J. Gegios*, *Lawyers*: *A. Bournelis*, *G. Pavlis. Epitheorisis Naftiliakou Dikeou Vol. 12* (*1984*) *p. 13*). (*Naftiliaki Intelligence*, 15 February 1984, p. 11)

6. COLLISION

Collision – Two ships at fault (tug and tow) and one innocent – Responsibility of the ships at fault vis-à-vis the innocent – Joint and multiple liability

The claimants were the owners of m/t *J*, which was anchored for more than a month by her port anchor at the southern end of the Piraeus roads anchorage. The first defendants were the owners of cargo m/v *R.M.* under Liberian flag, which anchored to the south of m/t *J* and at a distance of less than half a nautical mile. On 20.11.83 fire broke out on the *R.M.* and salvage services were offered to it by a towage and salvage company (the second defendants) through various tugs they owned which were offering their services by rotation, especially with the pumping of water out of the *R.M.* Early on the afternoon of 28.11.83 the tug on duty left for a short period and at that time the force of the wind increased to 7-8 Beaufort, and because the *R.M.* was not sufficiently anchored she dragged her anchor and her bow struck the fore part of the port side of the *J* causing her considerable damage. This incident could not be prevented by the tug which had returned but its crew did not perform effective manoeuvering for preventing the collision. The claimants asked for compensation or security from both the *R.M.* and the tug. However, the tug owners replied that because of their standard towage conditions they were not responsible for this kind of incident and any claims should be made against the *R.M.* The *R.M.*, however, contended that at the time of the incident it was a dead ship without crew on board, salvage services had not been completed and it was therefore in the hands of the salvors who were solely responsible for the incident. The claimants started proceedings for the arrest of both the *R.M.* and the tug on duty at the time of incident as a security for their claim. Among the issues brought up at the proceedings was whether the R.M. (as a dead ship) or the tug (because of the standard towage conditions) could be relieved of liability, and if not whether the tug and tow (*R.M.*) were jointly and severally liable for damages (as provided by article 926 of the Civil Code in case of damage caused by more than one wrongdoer jointly or cumulatively or successively and in the last two cases the contribution of each one of them could not be ascertained) or proportionately to the degree of their fault (in accordance with article 236 of the Code of Private Maritime law which provides that in case of collision 'If two or more ships are at fault, the liability of each ship shall be proportionate to the degree of her fault. If it is not possible to establish the proportion, or if the faults are equal, the liability shall be apportioned equally').

The Single Member First Instance Court of Piraeus held that both the *R.M.* and the tug were at fault (the *R.M.* because of insufficient anchorage, and the tug because it departed for a while and the manoeuvering carried out by its crew was not successful when it returned) and they are both jointly and severally liable. (*Single-Member First Instance Court of Piraeus* (*Summary Proceedings*) *No.* 1116/13.4.84 – *Not reported in Legal Periodicals. – Judge Ath. Kritikos – Lawyers*: *B. Kassidakis*, *N. Domvros*, *G. Albouras*).

Comments: 1) Although the court did not make any specific comment on the legal issues involved in its decision it replied by implication to all of them: a) The fact that the *R.M.* was a dead ship was not material because its crew/owners were negligent in that they had not arranged for its proper anchoring. b) The standard towage conditions have effect in relations between tug and tow and not vis-à-vis a third party and the tug was not relieved. c) Article 236 of the Code of Private Maritime Law applies when two or more ships themselves come into collision and not when two or more ships by their joint or cumulative or successive acts caused damage (by collision) to a third innocent ship, in which case article 926 of the Civil Code applies. The same solution is followed by the German, French, Belgian and English Courts.

2) A last point to be noted is that the rules of Greek Law on collision are included in the Code of Private Maritime Law (Arts 235 et seq.) supplemented by the provision of Civil Code on tort (Arts 914 et seq.). Greece has, also, ratified the Brussels 'International Convention for the Unification of Certain Rules of Law with respect to Collisions between Vessels' 1910.

3) Finally, the navigational rules for prevention of collision are included in the International Regulation for the Prevention of Collision at Sea. (*Naftiliaki*, 1 May 1984, p. 11)

7. POLLUTION

a. Pollution – Damage caused to ship by leakage of oil slops from another ship

The ship of the defendant was moored at Kyllini port on 7.1.79. While transferring oil slops from the bilges to the slop tank the chief engineer by mistake left the exit valve open and a considerable quantity of slops spilled into the sea causing pollution in the port which was cleaned up by the crew. In addition, however, the oil caused damage to the paintwork of a fishing boat moored nearby. The fishing boat had to be drydocked, cleaned and repainted. The owner of the boat sued the owners of the ship which caused the pollution.

The Court of Appeal of Piraeus held that the owners of the ship which caused the pollution are liable to pay damages to the owner of the fishing boat in respect of the cost of the dry docking, cleaning and repainting, because the damage was due to the negligence of the chief engineer, who was their servant and they are liable in respect of damage caused by their servants in the course of performing their duties. (*Court of Appeal of Piraeus 155/84, President*: *Th. Papangelopoulos*, *Reporting Judge*: *D. Soultanias*, *Lawyers*: *N. Kordis*, *G. Papadopoulos*. *Epitheorisis Naftiliakou Dikeou Vol. 12* (*1980*) *p. 224*). (*Naftiliaki*, 15 July 1984, p. 11)

b. Pollution – Limitation of liability of the owner – Establishment of the fund – Procedure – Method of calculation of the gold franc in drachmas

Greek flag m/v *I.S.* sunk on 24.2.1980 off the coast of Pylos and her cargo of 102,663 m.t. of crude oil caused extensive pollution to the coast. The owners and their P&I Club undertook the cleaning operation at their own expense. When, however, they discovered the high cost of the operation they advised the Direction for the Protection of the Environment of the ministry of Mercantile Marine that they would abandon the effort and would exercise their right to limit their ability. The ministry continued and finalised the cleaning. Subsequently the owners arranged for a bank guarantee to be issued for Drs 364,719,114 and to be deposited with the Court of Kalamata, which had jurisdiction over the area where the pollution occurred. The president of the court appointed a lawyer as liquidator of the fund and a judge of the court as the supervising judge. Subsequently, claimants registered with the liquidator included the Greek government in respect to recovering their expenses for cleaning and 239 residents of the polluted area, seeking compensation for the damage they suffered because of the pollution. The supervising judge when examining the fund ordered the owners to increase it to Drs 700m on the grounds that the original fund of

Drs 364,719,114 was not sufficient to cover the claims registered with the liquidator. Owners challenged the order of the supervising judge before the Multi-Member Court. In these proceedings a number of legal issues concerning pollution and limitation of liability were raised.

The Multi-Member First Instance Court of Kalamata held:

1) In accordance with the 'International Convention on Civil Liability for Oil Pollution' signed in Brussels in 1969 to which Greece is a party (L. 314/76), the owner of a ship is entitled to limit his liability in respect of any one pollution incident to 2,000 francs for each ton of the ship's tonnage provided this limitation fund does not exceed 210m francs.

2) The limitation may be effected by establishing a limitation fund by depositing with the competent court or authority the sum of the limitation or a bank guarantee.

3) For the limitation purposes the ship's tonnage is the net tonnage plus the addition of that deducted from the gross tonnage on account of engine room space.

4) The franc on the basis of which the limitation fund is calculated is a unit consisting of 65.5 milligrams of gold of millesimal fineness 900 and the fund will be established in the currency of the country where the fund is constituted on the basis of the official value of the currency by reference to the franc on the date the constitution of the fund.

5) In accordance with P.D. 666/82 which fixed the details for the establishment of the fund, the owner to limit his liability must submit: (a) a statement to this effect to the court clerk; (b) a certified copy of the certificate of measurement of the ship; (c) a certificate from the Bank of Greece stating the official value of the franc on the date of the issue of the certificate; (d) evidence of establishing the fund (e.g. bank guarantee); and (e) evidence that the owner deposited Drs 600,000 to cover expenses.

6) The value of the gold franc (Poincaré) should be fixed as specified in the Brussels Convention 1969, i.e. on the basis of the official value which in Greece is fixed by the Bank of Greece and not on the basis of the Warsaw Convention of 1929 which is irrelevant nor by reference to Special Drawing Rights referred to in the Protocol of 1969 because Greece is not a party to this protocol.

7) The supervising judge was wrong to ask that the fund be increased based on the registered claims because the size of the fund is calculated under the conditions of the Convention, exclusively on the basis of the ship's tonnage. In addition, the registered claims are not liquidated as the whole object of establishing the fund is to limit owner's liability and satisfy claims pro-rata.

8) As the net tonnage of the ship was 36,733.5 tons and the tonnage of the engine room 11,854.58 tons the total was 48,587.81. This should be multiplied by 2,000 (francs per ton) and then by 4.10 (drachmas per franc on the day of establishing the fund) with the result the fund should be Drs 398,420,042 (*Multi-member First Instance Court of Kalamata*, *No. 12/1984*,

Naftika Chronical No. 1174/933 of 1.5.84 President: *G. Panoutsakopoulos, Reporting Judge*: *D. Kokotinis, Lawyers*: *P. Papatheodorou, K. Assimakopoulos, G. Papangelopoulou, J. Apostolakis*). (*Naftiliaki*, 15 June 1984, p. 11)

8. INSURANCE

Insurance – Third party liability insurance – Insurance of shipowner in respect of personal injury or illness of the crew – marine labour accidents caused by aggravation of illness – mere negligence of owner's servants (crew) does not relieve insurer

The claimant shipowner had insured his ship with an insurance company in respect of liability which might arise from personal injury or illness of the crew. The ship's electrician died and his death was attributed to the fact that though he was suffering from malaria he had to work continuously for 48 hours while the ship was in the Persian Gulf. The master knew about the dead man's illness but did not have the appropriate medicines on board the ship. The owner paid compensation to the family of the deceased and claimed reimbursement from the insurers who refused payment.

The Court of Appeal of Piraeus held that: 1. The insurance policy referring to 'personal injury' and 'illness' should be interpreted as covering marine labour accidents caused by aggravation of illness. 2. The fact that the accident could be attributed to negligence on the part of the master cannot relieve the insurers because, in accordance with marine insurance law, the insurer is not relieved by the mere fact that the loss or damage was caused by negligence of the master or crew and there was nothing in the policy which was amending this rule. 3. The fact that the master did not have the appropriate medicines on board and he allowed the electrician to work despite his illness does not amount to criminal intention on the part of the master (as servant of the owner) in respect of the death, which could relieve the insurers pursuant to the terms of the policy. (*Court of Appeal of Piraeus 178/1984 – President*: *G. Spinasas, Reporting judge*: *Ch. Pampoukis, Lawyers*: *E. Paraskevas, G. Theocharidis – Epitheorisis Naftiliakou Dikeou Vol. 12* (*1984*) *p. 270*). (*Naftiliaki*, 1 September 1984, p. 11)

9. ENFORCED SALE OF SHIPS/MARITIME LIEN

a. Enforced sale of ship – Maritime Liens on ships registered under Article 13 of LD 2687/1953 – Brussels Convention 1926

A vessel registered in Greece under Article 13 of LD 2687/1953 was sold at public auction. A supplier of provisions who supplied the ship on master's orders in Germany filed a claim with the auctioneer and claimed priority over the existing preferred maritime mortgage.

The Supreme Court of Greece (Arios Pagos) in plenary session held by majority that although the supplier's claim is not covered by a maritime lien under Greek law, it should rank over the mortgage on grounds that it is covered by a maritime lien under Article 2 para 5 of the Brussels 1926 'International Convention for the Unification of Certain Rules of Law Relating to Maritime Liens and Mortgages' which, although not ratified by Greece, is applicable in this case by reference to it of the joint ministerial decision on the basis of which the ship was registered on the Greek Registry. A minority of four judges held the view, however, that the meaning of the reference of the ministerial decision is that only those claims run in priority over mortgages which are protected by maritime liens recognised both by Article 205 of the Code of Private Maritime Law and the Brussels Convention 1926. (*Supreme Court – Arios Pagos – Plenary Session, 229/83 Nomikou Vima Vol. 31 (1983) p. 1556 – President: G. Konstas, Reporting Judge: J. Grivas, Attorneys-at-Law: P. Routsakos, V. Makris*).

Comment: 1) The issue dealt with here concerns a matter that has been under dispute for several years, but with this decision of the Supreme Court it now appears to be settled and regardless of any theoretical or practical objections to the decision of the Arios Pagos the ruling is expected to be followed by lower courts. 2) Article 2 of the Brussels Convention 1926 specifying as to which claims give rise to maritime liens is as follows:

The following give rise to maritime liens on a vessel, on the freight for the voyage during which the claim giving rise to the lien arises, and on the accessories of the vessel and freight accrued since the commencement of the voyage:

(1) Law costs due to the State, and expenses incurred in the common interest of the creditors in order to preserve the vessel or to procure its sale and the distribution of the proceeds of sale; tonnage dues, light or harbor dues, and other public taxes and charges of the same character; pilotage dues; the cost of watching and preservation from the time of the entry of the vessel into the last port;

(2) Claims arising out of the contract of engagement of the master, crew, and other persons hired on board;

(3) Remuneration for assistance and salvage, and the contribution of the vessel in general average;

(4) Indemnities for collision or other accident of navigation, as also for damage caused to works forming part of harbors, docks, and navigable ways; indemnities for personal injury to passengers or crew; indemnities for loss of or damage to cargo or baggage;

(5) Claims resulting from contracts entered into or acts done by the master, acting within the scope of his authority, away from the vessel's home port, where such contracts or acts are necessary for the preservation of the vessel or the continuation of its voyage, whether the master is or is not at the same time owner of the vessel, and whether the claim is his own

or that of ship-chandlers, repairers, lenders, or other contractual creditors. (*Naftiliaki Intelligence*, 15 April 1984, p. 11)

b. Enforced sale of ship – Public auction – Deletion of the ship from Registry or recording of the change of ownership – Obligation to submit to Registrar certificates from the Seamen's Pension Fund (NAT) and tax authorities showing debts of the ship have been paid

In the standard joint ministerial decisions issued individually for each ship for its registration on the Greek Registry in accordance with Article 13 of Legislative Decree 2687/1953 it is provided that the owners of such ships may freely transfer their ships to other registries or sell them to foreign buyers, provided they submit to the Registrar a certificate from the Seamen's Pension Fund (NAT) and one from the tax authorities stating that debts on the ship have been paid, or alternatively that a bank guarantee to the amount fixed in the ministerial decision has been arranged. In a case concerning the sale of a ship at public auction the Shipping Registrar, in order to delete the vessel from the Greek Registry, required the new owners to produce certificates from NAT and the tax authorities showing the previous owner's debts had been settled or the bank guarantee. The new owners challenged this decision of the Registrar before the Courts.

The Supreme Court (*Arios Pagos*) held that regardless of its actual wording, the true meaning of the joint ministerial decision is that the certificate of NAT and the taxation authorites is required in all cases of deletion from the Greek Registry involving a change of flag of the ship including those where the owners submit an application for the change or where the vessel has been sold to foreign buyers either by voluntary sale or in a public auction or even when the beneficial ownership of the shipowning company passes to non-Greek shareholders. Therefore the case should be referred to Division D of the Court for further examination. (*Arios Pagos No. 1271/1984 – Not reported yet in legal periodicals – President*: *G. Konstas*, *Reporting judge*: *D. Stamatopoulos*, *Lawyers*: *G. Katsantonis*, *Gr. Timagenis*, *C. Doussis*). (*Naftiliaki*, 15 May 1984, p. 11)

C. Bibliography

1. BOOKS

In 1983 an important work on Maritime Law was published: Antoine M. Antapassis, 'Les Codes Maritimes Grecs', Paris, Librairie Générale de Droit et de Jurisprudence, 1983 pp. XII + 330. The book contains a translation in French of the Greek 'Code of Private Maritime Law' (Law 3816/1958), of the Legislative Decree concerning 'the Preferred Maritime Mortgages' (L.D. 3899/1959) and of the Greek 'Code of Public Maritime Law' (L.D.

187/1973.) The translation is preceded by a 100 page introduction to the codes and it is followed by an alphabetical index and a table of contents.

2. PERIODICALS

In 1983 and 1984 there were issued the respective volumes of a number of periodicals containing articles on court decision reports on Maritime Law. In this connection reference should be made to the following categories of periodicals.

a. Those specialized to Maritime Law like '*Epitheorisis Naftiliakou Dikeou*' (Shipping Law Review; abbr. END) or devoting big sections to Maritime Law like '*Epitheorisis Emporikou Dikeou*' (Commercial Law Review; abbr. EEmpD) or '*Piraiki Nomologia*' (Piraeus Jurisprudence, published by the Piraeus Bar; abbr. PN of which only the Volume for 1983 has been published to date.

b. Those referring generally to all branches of Law and containing occasionally reports on maritime court cases or articles on Maritime Law like '*Nomikon Vima*' (Legal Tribune, published by the Athens Bar; abbr. NoB), '*Armenopoulos*' (published by the Thessaloniki Bar; Abbr. Arm), '*Elliniki Dikaiosyni*' (Greek Justice, published by the Association of Judges) etc., and

c. Those periodicals which are not legal in principle, they address to commercial people in shipping but they have regular legal columns like 'Naftica Chronica' (Shipping Annuals), 'Deltion tis Naftilias' (Bulletin of Shipping, published by the Greek Chamber of Shipping), 'Naftiliaki' (published in English), 'Argo', 'Shipping Mirror' etc.

3. ARTICLES

Among the articles published in 1983 and 1984 on Maritime Law reference should be made to the following which are in Greek unless indicated differently.

a. Arvanitis, K., The written document in a series of transactions provided in the Code of Private Maritime Law – The nature and probative power of telex. (PN 5(1983) 191–203).

b. Arvanitis, K., The choice of compensation under article 16 of Law 551/1915 (concerning marine labour accidents) (END 12 (1984) 97–104).

c. Galatis, P., The Legal nature of the time charter and the problems arising therefrom; (END 11(1983) 337–341 and 385–388).

d. Gerassimou, N., The Standard Lloyd's Open Form 1980 (PN 5(1983) 86–98).

e. Harlaftis, A., Contract of Carriage of passenger by Sea (EEmpD 34(1983) 564–580).

f. Kalatzis, A., Issues relating to the responsibility under the time charter, the loading on deck and the perils of the sea. (EEmpD 34(1983) 121–126).

g. Keramefs, K., International Jurisdiction on disputes of Maritime Law at the Continental Countries and Greece in particular (NoB 31(1983)28–38).

h. Keramefs, M., Applicability of the Brussels International Convention of 10.5.1952 on the Arrest of Ships in respect of the nationality of the parties to the proceedings (PN 5(1983) 5–11).

i. Matos, L., The Legal Status of the air cushion vessels (PN 5(1983) 12–21).

j. Michaelidis, Th., The Nationality of the Ships and the question of the Flags of Convenience in International Law (END 11(1983) 1–9 and 49–59).

k. Michaelides, Th., Sister Ship Arrest in English Law (END 11(1983) 145–154).

l. Sergis, J., Theft of Cargo. (END 12(1984) 145–152).

m. Sergis, J., Registers of Ships, maritime mortgages and arrests of ships (END 12(1984) 49–61).

n. Sergis, J. Crew Complement of a foreign ship and the 'wage of the missing seaman'. (END 11(1983) 97–101).

o. Timagenis, Gr., Arrest of Ships in Greece. (in English (1984) 1 LMCLQ 90–99).

p. Timagenis, Gr., Service of Documents in Shipping Cases under Greek Law, (in English – (1984) 2 LMCLQ 275–279).

ISRAEL

Peter G. Naschitz*

Naschitz, Brandes & Co. Advocates and Notaries, Tel-Aviv

RECENT DEVELOPMENTS IN AIR LAW AND MARITIME LAW IN ISRAEL

This has been a fruitful year from the point of view of case law in Maritime and Aviation Law in Israel. A comparatively great number of judgments of authority has been given, and, although they cannot be viewed as materially changing the state of the law which has hitherto been known, it may yet be said that these judgments do accentuate the well-known rules and, in certain cases, even emerge somewhat beyond them, delineating what has so far been considered as a grey area in certain domains.

Jurisdiction clauses

Israel has so far been marked by a rather conservative approach to jurisdiction clauses and the way courts in Israel have been enforcing these clauses has been, with few exceptions, strict in the sense that the intention of the parties has been regarded sacrosanct and, only in rare instances, have the courts ventured to disregard jurisdiction clauses or refused to stay actions which have been filed in contradiction of same. The main examples in which courts proceeded to do so were, for instance, instances where the enforcement of a jurisdiction clause would have brought manifest injustice to the plaintiff as litigation in the country to which the jurisdiction clause directed him would have caused him to be time-barred in a manner that is contrary to the Hague Rules,[1] or that he would have to litigate in a hostile country where a citizen of Israel could not be expected to be treated in an

* LLB, LL.M. Partner, Naschitz, Brandes & Co., Tel Aviv, Lecturer in Maritime Law, Hebrew University of Jerusalem.

[1] C.A. 194/68, *Firemans Fund v. Enotria*, 22(2) P.D. 40.

even-handed manner, such as in Iraq.[2] Other cases where the courts were more liberal in the application of jurisdiction clauses were, for instance, when the jurisdiction clause did not single out the required venue as one being of exclusive import, or where the jurisdiction clause was unclear in its terms. In Civil Appeal 362/83, Menorah Insurance Company Limited, the ship 'Donar', 38(2) P.D., Page 505, the Supreme Court accorded jurisdiction clauses in Bills of Lading a comparatively high degree of certitude, pointing out that whenever such jurisdiction clause appeared in a bill of lading, which was standard or customary in its wording, such clause should be enforced and all other considerations existing in jurisdiction clauses in ordinary contracts, such as the doubt whether the clause should be interpreted as conferring exclusive jurisdiction or only parallel jurisdiction, should, as a rule, be disregarded.

The facts were these: The appellant was an insurance company which indemnified its insured in respect of damage which was caused in respect to a consignment of fish which was shipped on the respondent container vessel on its voyage from Germany to Israel. The appellant sued in the Admiralty Court by virtue of the right of subrogation and the action was in rem. The ship was arrested on an ex parte application, and was released from arrest only after the respondent posted a guarantee for payment of the amounts which would be awarded in the claim. The respondent applied to the Admiralty Court and moved that the order of arrest should be cancelled and that the guarantee should be returned to her and also moved to stay the proceedings in the action because of the existence of a jurisdiction clause contained in the bill of lading, directing the parties to litigate in German Courts.

The Admiralty Court granted the motions and stayed the proceedings and ordered the return of the guarantee; hence the appeal. The Supreme Court decided:-

A. The cause of action in rem in accordance with paragraph 6 of the Admiralty Court Act of 1861 (which is still valid in Israel), which widens the jurisdiction of the Admiralty Court and enables in rem actions and arrest of vessel beyond of the ordinary causes of actions founded on maritime liens which had been in existence up to that date – must be based on a bill of lading.

B. Entrance of appearance by the owners must not necessarily be accompanied by an affidavit in accordance with the Vice Admiralty Rules, 1883.

C. *1.* The object of an in rem claim based on the cause of action of damage to cargo in accordance with paragraph 6 of the Admiralty Court Act is to widen that jurisdiction of the court also over a shipowner who is resident out of jurisdiction and to enable arrest of the ship to secure the action.

2. The arrest of the ship enables the consummation of the action, but it is

[2] *Union Insurance Co. v. Moshe*, C.A. 156/60, 17 P.D. 646.

not the step which confers jurisdiction in an in rem action, but the summons addressed to the ship at the place of her being situated within the jurisdiction.

3. In view of the Vice Admiralty Rules, proceedings can be opened before the ship enters the territorial waters, provided that the writ is served on the ship in the territorial waters within six months of its issue. The order for arrest may be given – but not necessarily must be given – in the in rem action upon the issue of the writ, or at any time subsequent thereto. The arrest is not necessary for the conferment of jurisdiction or to existence of an in rem action.

4. There is no foundation to the argument that the arrest must always be given at the behest of the plaintiff as a matter of routine, without any connection to his chances to collect whatever is due to him. Still, the party moving the court for arrest must consider whether the arrest is required to confer a security on him and the matter is given to the discretion of the court.

D. In the present instance, the fact that the jurisdiction clause does not refer to a specific court in Germany does not derogate from the validity of the jurisdiction clause. From the aspect of private international law, the German courts are empowered to deal with the matter from the point of view of international jurisdiction. From the aspect of local jurisdiction – it is up to the internal German law to decide which German Court should hear the action.

1. Once an order for arrest is given, it is not necessary that the plaintiff should lose his advantage because of the existence of a foreign jurisdiction clause, even though he is bound by this clause. The court which hears the motion for stay of proceedings has the power and the discretion to decide whether the motion should be granted or whether some conditions should be imposed in connection with it. The necessity to enforce the arrest or the guarantee which was given in consideration of the release of the vessel may serve as a fundamental and even decisive reason to refuse the stay of proceedings.

2. When the stay of proceedings is based on the discretion of the court, the court which decides to stay will not leave the arrest in force, because the arrest is not intended to secure the execution of the judgment of the foreign court, but it is empowered to make the stay conditional upon the defendant supplying a suitable alternative security.

3. The question of stay of proceedings in order that these should be heard before a different forum arises not only as a result of a foreign jurisdiction clause but also in other cases, such as agreement to arbitration[3]; an argument, that the place where the action has been filed is not the convenient forum, or the argument that other proceedings already take

[3] C.A. 138/70, *Greek South American Line Shipping Co. v. Dominion* 25(1) P.D. 95; F.H. 4/71 *Dominion v. Greek South American* 25(1) P.D. 757.

place elsewhere, are all arguments which do not negate the jurisdiction of the court but only move the court to apply its discretion to decide whether it will not be just to stay the proceedings in order to compel the claimant or plaintiff to submit them before a different jurisdiction.[4]

4. Stay of proceedings because of the foreign jurisdiction clause does not vitiate the very foundation of an in rem action, and does not necessarily bring about the loss of the security or the guarantee which have been obtained as a result of the arrest.

F. The form of guarantee which is provided for under Rule 40 of the Vice Admiralty Rules in Form No. 14, does not displace an agreement of foreign jurisdiction. There is nothing to prevent the parties to agree on a different wording of guarantee or security.

G. *1.* In the present instance, the foreign jurisdiction clause in the bill of lading accords an exclusive right of jurisdiction to the German courts, and the fact that the action under reference is an in rem action and that the vessel has been arrested does not derogate from its validity.

2. The foreign jurisdiction clause does not derogate the jurisdiction of the local court, but it is up to that court to decide whether it should continue and deal with the action or stay it in order to enable its being heard in a foreign forum.

3. The rule is that the court will give effect to a foreign jurisdiction clause and will stay the proceedings which have been brought before it in breach of such stipulation, unless the plaintiff will show special good reasons why no stay should be ordered.[5]

4. Reasons of convenience only, which do not vitiate justice being done, do not justify the non-application of a foreign jurisdiction clause. Against the reasons of convenience of the party opposing the stay, the court should also bear in mind the considerations of convenience of the opposite party and, in the present instance, the hardships and expenses which will be caused to a respondent if she should bring her witnesses to Israel and prove the German law, which is the proper law of the Contract under the Bill of Lading, (as a question of fact,) including all the costs involved.

H. *1.* In a motion for arrest, as well as in any other motion which is presented ex parte and heard without the presence of the opposite party, a supreme duty of disclosure rests on the petitioner to disclose to the court any relevant fact in relation to the subject matter of the motion; should he not do so – it will be obstructing the possibility of the court to do justice.[6]

2. In the present instance, it was the duty of the appellant to disclose to the court the existence of a foreign jurisdiction clause when he applied to the court to obtain the Order or Arrest. It is not sufficient to displace this duty of disclosure, to enclose to the Petition for Arrest a photostatic copy of

[4] C.A. 435/64 *Navrom v. Hassneh* 19(2) P.D. 159.

[5] C.A. 422/64, *Zion v. KNSM*, 19(1) P.D. 303.

[6] C.A. 650/73, *Levy v. Irene*.

the bill of lading without specifically mentioning and directing the attention of the court to the fine print containing the jurisdiction clause.

The wording of the jurisdiction clause of the Bill of Lading, in the present instance, reads as follows:-

> 'The Contract of Carriage, the Bill of Lading and all disputes arising thereunder or in connection therewith shall be governed by German Law . . . and decided in the German Courts to the Jurisdiction of which the Carrier submits himself.
>
> In case the law of the country in which suit is filed does not recognize the above and said agreement on the exclusiveness of German Courts and/or the exclusiveness of the application of German Law then the Hague rules as enacted in that country shall apply.'

As will be remembered, one of the main arguments of the appellants was that the jurisdiction clause in the present instance was not of an exclusive nature, and consequently, based on previous judgments – particularly Civil Appeal 9/79[7] and Civil Appeal 433/64[8] should guide the court in deciding not to stay the proceedings as the jurisdiction of the court should be regarded as concurrent or parallel and not exclusive.

This argument was rejected mainly based on two considerations:

(*a*) The second part of the jurisdiction clause specifically speaks about the 'agreement on the exclusiveness of German Courts' and consequently – so held the court – the first part of the jurisdiction clause should be construed and interpreted in view of what is said about the exclusiveness of the German courts in the second part of the clause.

(*b*) Moreover – and here is the main innovation in this connection – the court decided that, contrary to what may be decided in ordinary cases, in cases of bills of lading, the intention of the parties should primarily be presumed to be directed to agreeing upon exclusivety rather than upon parallelism. Should the court not interpret the clause in this light, it is feared that the main intentions of the parties will be foiled.

Warsaw Convention

(*a*) In Civil Appeal 20/83, Motion for Leave to Appeal 371/83, *Dadon and Others v. Air France* and *Air France v. G. Teichner*, 38(3) P.D.785, the Supreme Court dealt with the aftermath of the famous Entebbe highjacking. As will be remembered, the main body of those highjacked sued Air France in Israel in the District Court of Tel Aviv. The main ground of claim was that Air France breached the contract by making an unscheduled stop in Athens, not drawing the attention of the passengers to the fact that on their

[7] C.A. 9/79, *Karpol v. Horowitz*, 34(1) P.D. 260.
[8] Note 4, Supra.

way to Paris they would be making a stopover there, not providing the necessary security arrangements to prevent terrorists, heavily armed and equipped with bombs and explosives, from boarding the airplane, and not taking the necessary security precautions to enable their being scanned and stopped instead of boarding the airplane virtually unabated; all this, bearing in mind the notoriously dangerous nature and character of Athens airport as a haven for terrorists and loose security arrangements. That action, which comprised 67 out of those who were on board the plane and had to undergo the appalling ordeal of being subjected to infamous activity by terrorists at Entebbe Airport, only to be saved by heroic action of the Israeli army, was ultimately settled by mutual consent and nothing further should be said in connection with same. However, there were some of the highjacked who, for some reason or other, did not join in the original lawsuit,[9] either because they were simply not aware of the necessity of suing within the prescribed period of time under the Warsaw Convention, which is valid in Israel under the Air Transport Law 1962, as repealed by the Air Transport Law 1980, or because they tried to litigate in other venues such as France and the United States – all of which actions were dismissed or otherwise ultimately unsuccessful. Such a group of disappointed litigants applied to the Tel Aviv District Court after the expiry of the two-year prescription period under the Warsaw Convention; actually a period of almost seven years elapsed till the action was initiated.

The highjacking took place in 1976. The claim was filed in 1983. Air France moved the court to dismiss the action in limine. As will be seen above, the appeal is concerned with two different actions: one filed in the Jerusalem District Court by one group of claimants and the other filed in the District Court of Tel Aviv by another group of claimants. The appeal and the leave to appeal against the two decisions were heard together. The odd result in the District Courts was that the District Court of Jerusalem allowed the motion for dismissal whilst the District Court of Tel Aviv rejected it. The main question for consideration of the Supreme Court was whether the claims were subject to the ordinary rules of limitation which exist by virtue of the Law of Limitation, 1958, or whether the courts must be guided by the special Rules of Prescription as provided for in the Air Transport Law, 1962, and the Convention for the Unification of Certain Rules relating to International Air Transport, better known as 'The Warsaw Convention, 1929'. The Supreme Court decided in favour of the Warsaw Convention and held that, in accordance with paragraph 2A of the Air Transport Law, actions which deal with air transport shall be decided only in accordance with the provisions of the Warsaw Convention, and the responsibility of the carrier shall be decided only in accordance with the rules embodied in that Convention.

(*b*) (*1*) In case of doubt of the interpretation of the Warsaw Convention,

[9] *Hernandez v. Air France*, 545 F. 2nd 279 (1976); *Karfunkel v. Air France*, 427 F. Supp. 971 (1977).

the French text should be preferred and, similarly, the interpretation given to the Convention in France should be given certain weight, although not decisive meaning, by the Court.

(*2*) Foreign jurisprudence should be available as an auxiliary instrument for the interpretation of the provisions of the Warsaw Convention, but the weight of this instrument should not be exaggerated, as the foreign courts are often guided by criteria which are specific and singular to their own system of law and no uniform approach can be gleaned from them for the solution of the problem.

(*3*) When an inconsistency exists in the wording of the Warsaw Convention, including paragraph 29(2) thereof, in relation to the extent of application of the local law, the actual intention of the parties to the Convention should be adhered to as appearing from the preparatory work (which preceded the final version of the Convention).

(*4*) When an International Convention becomes part of the Israeli law, its provisions cannot be regarded as the result of an original Israeli conception.

(*c*) (*1*) It will be incorrect to assume that the draftsmen of the Guatemala Protocol, which amended the Warsaw Convention, intended to insert a fundamental change in the wording of paragraph 17 of the Warsaw convention.

(*2*) The word 'Accident' included in paragraph 17 of the Warsaw Convention, should be given a wide construction, which includes highjacking in the ambit of the term 'Accident'.

(*3*) The term 'Bodily Injury' in paragraph 17 of the Warsaw Convention should also be given a wide meaning so that 'Mental Anguish' should be included in the term.

(*4*) The time during which passengers of an aircraft are being held by highjackers outside the aircraft should, for the purposes of paragraph 17 of the Warsaw Convention, be deemed as time which has been spent by the passengers on board the plane.

(*d*) (*1*) The wording of paragraph 14 of the Air Transport Law signifies the intention to connote a substantive prescription as distinguished from a procedural prescription only, so that the application of the Israeli Prescription Law is negated wherever paragraph 29 of the Warsaw Convention is applicable.

(*2*) Consequently, the prescription period of two years embodied in paragraph 29(1) of the Warsaw Convention is absolute and cannot be changed in accordance with the existing provisions of the local law, including the Law of Prescriptions, 1958.

Accordingly, the actions filed in both courts were dismissed in limine also by the Supreme Court. It should be mentioned that, in this specific case, the Supreme Court strongly recommended to Air France to come to an amicable settlement with the claimants. It is further worthy of mention that this case has gone through a special procedure known as 'Further Hearing' in the Supreme Court, which entails the re-hearing of the appeal before an extended panel of five justices instead of the original appellate panel of three. The judgment of the Court in the further hearing has not yet been given. In order to succeed in the re-hearing, the appellants will have to sway the opinion of at least one of the three justices who gave a unanimous judgment in the first instance of the appeal, since it is customary in the Supreme Court, when the re-hearing of the appeal is applied, that the original justices who gave the judgment in the first instance should be incorporated also in the extended panel.

Pilotage

Although being a comparatively inconspicuous subject, compulsory pilotage attracted the attention of the Supreme Court in two judgments of unusual length, depth and complexity.

Pilotage in Israel is compulsory and the regime of pilotage is regulated by an extremely concise and manifestly clear jurisdiction existing still from the date of the British mandate over Palestine, 'The Damage by Vessels under Pilotage Ordinance 1939', which is composed of only two paragraphs, the operative one of which is paragraph 2, which is worded as follows:-

> '*2.* Notwithstanding anything contained in any Ottoman Law or in any other law or ordinance, the owner or master of any vessel under pilotage, whether compulsory or otherwise, shall be answerable for any loss or damage caused by the vessel or by any fault of the navigation of the vessel.'

While this wording clearly indicates that vis-à-vis a third party it will not be the pilot but the owner and master of the vessel who will be responsible for any damage or loss caused by the vessel under pilotage, this still leaves in doubt the question whether the absoluteness of the ordinance excludes the possibility of the shipowner claiming contribution or indemnification from the pilot or his employers if the damage is caused under pilotage. There have been various decisions in the past, dealing with this problem, but it has never come to a clear ruling, mostly because the facts did not actually necessitate it. In Civil Appeal 804/80, Sidaar Tanker Corporation and Others, the Eilat-Ashkelon Pipeline Limited and the Attorney-General, 39(1) P.D., page 393, the Supreme Court, in a very lengthy judgment, which was composed in an unusual panel of five justices in the first instance of the hearing of the appeal, decided that, irrespective of the ostensibly clear provisions of the Ordinance, the regular canons of construction, and laws relating to indemnification and contribution, should apply inter partes, namely that there was nothing to prevent the master or owner from looking to the pilot or his principals for reimbursement in case their fault can be established. The report of the judgment occupies 48 pages in fine print and includes separate opinions of the president of the Supreme Court, Justice M. Shamgar, and Justices A. Barak and S. Netanyahu. The facts of the case were these: A tanker owned by Appellant No. 1 and operated by Appellant No. 2 (Zim Israel Navigation Company Limited) entered the discharge installations of the Port of Ashkelon, which is operated by Respondent No. 1 by virtue of a concession by law. The tanker was moored to the mooring dolphin and pumping of fuel into the tanker commenced. A strong wind caused the tanker to drift, the mooring ropes were broken and the loading pipes torn. At the time, the port pilot was on board the tanker. The pilot was the employee of Respondent No. 1, the Eilat-Ashkelon Pipeline Company. This company sued the appellants, namely the owners of the ship and her operators, for damages which were caused by breaking of the ropes and tearing of the pipes.

The District court allowed the action without going into the details of the facts, basing itself on paragraph 2 of the aforesaid Damage by Vessels under Pilotage Ordinance, 1939. The Supreme Court held:-

(*a*) *1.* A pilot is a person who is in charge of the transportation and pilotage of the vessel into the port up to her being anchored and moored and, similarly, in the reverse process until the ship reaches the outward pilot station.

2. A ship which is at anchor may in certain cases be considered as being under pilotage when, upon approaching the port or leaving it, it is held up because of conditions of ebb or tide or because of weather conditions or other causes of a similar nature, and it is obliged to anchor for some time in the expectation to continue the passage.

3. It is not inconsistent with a condition of pilotage for a ship to have reached its final destination and be in a stationary condition, anchored or moored inside the port, and which is not sailing or planning to weigh anchor or otherwise leave its anchorage.

4. The duty and office of the pilot should be interpreted in conjunction with the main purpose and aim of the institution of pilotage – the special knowledge and know-how in passage in the internal waters and approaches to the port or exit therefrom, when the emphasis is on the activities being made during the movement of the ship and, as an ancillary thereto – the mooring and unmooring operations. Anything beyond that should not be considered as pilotage, although the pilot may be on board.

5. The duty and role of the pilot should fit the place in which he is active. In fuel ports there are special dangers and problems in addition to those existing in an ordinary port. If these by themselves require special actions by the pilot in order to enable him to navigate the ship in a safe manner, he still fulfils his duty as a pilot.

6. A pilot who fulfils various other duties, which are not necessary or required for the duty of pilotage or navigation, does not act as a pilot. An operation of supervising the loading and unloading of tankers or the effort to prevent the tearing of hoses or pipes and, as a result thereof, perhaps preventing the pollution of the sea, is not part of the ordinary duties of the pilot.

7. In imposing an absolute duty on shipowners because of compulsory pilotage to which they were involuntarily subjected, the correct way of interpreting the definition of 'Pilotage' would be restrict it to its natural boundaries and not to extend it beyond them.

(*b*) *1.* (Following Civil Appeal 542/73, *El Yam v. Ports Authority* 30(1) P.D. 173):

The duty imposed by paragraph 2 of the Pilotage Ordinance is not one in the nature of a vicarious liability to the acts or omissions of the pilot but an absolute liability per se, namely a liability which arises even if they or their employees or the pilot were not negligent.

2. (Following Further Hearing 38/75, *El Yam v. Israel Ports Authority*, 30(2) P.D. 645):

The meaning of the first alternative in paragraph 2 of the Pilotage Ordinance is to include cases under which the ship under pilotage itself causes damage, and the second alternative in the same paragraph can also extend to places in which the damage occurs due to wilful or negligent acts in the navigation of the ship without the latter actually hitting the damaged object.

3. There is no a priori jurisprudential concept to the term 'Absolute Liability'. Its meaning varies in accordance with the context in which it appears and the purpose which it comes to serve.

4. The liability under the 'Liability for Damaged Products Law', 1980, is not an absolute liability, but a strict liability without fault, enabling various ways of defence – those provided for in paragraph 4 of this law, which include elements of fault or liability without the necessity for proof of fault. The provisions are more compatible with negative liability than with the classical concept of defence.

(*c*) *1.* The solution to the multiplicity of questions relating to the causal connection lies in the term 'Caused' in paragraph 2 of the Pilotage Ordinance. This is not a formal link only, but is of a substantive nature, as the solution to the causal questions should be found in the judicial policy which the liability comes to serve.

2. There should be a 'judicial' causal link between the ship being under pilotage and the resulting damage. The purpose of the aforesaid Ordinance is to compensate for damage which was caused by the ship under pilotage only.

3. The causal criterion in the aforesaid Ordinance is the criterion of risk. The question is: 'What is the risk which the lawmaker wanted to prevent'. In the moment that the area of the risk has been exhausted, any damaging result which falls into that area fulfils the required judicial causal risk, but nothing beyond it.

4. In accordance with this criterion, the actions of the powers of nature and the own negligence of the injured party will sever the causal link if, as a result thereof the damage comes to be of a nature which the law did not intend to compensate, at least not under the unusual term of absolute liability.

5. The rules of causation in the Civil Wrongs Ordinance express a flexible criterion, which leaves a wide scope of discretion in the hands of the judge. As for the decisive cause which may be considered as breaking the causal link, several tests have been proposed: The test of foreseeability, the test of risk and the common sense test; of the three of which the test of risk is the one most recommendable in relation to the liability which is not based on negligence.

6. The test of risk extends also to the provisions relating to the breaking of the causal link due to an unusual natural phenomenon. The negation of the causal connection shall be recognised only when part of the natural event is 'substantial', and it may be that such an event shall not negate the causal connection because it is not 'fundamental', namely – it is not to be found in the area of the risk.

(*d*) *1.* The Pilotage Ordinance does not fix any provisions in relation to indemnification between the liable parties. This reticence in the law should not be interpreted as a negative arrangement. The Ordinance simply does not deal with this question and is indifferent as to its solution. In this respect, the general principles in relation to indemnity between joint tortfeasors should be applied.

2. These principles are embodied in paragraph 84 of the Civil Wrongs Ordinance and in paragraph 56 of the Law of Contracts (General Part), 1973, and in the Common Law 'Israel Style'. The interpreter must choose between the suitable general norm from among those which are at his disposal.

3. The liability embodied in the Pilotage Ordinance is in nature and substance of a tortious nature. In the Ordinance there is no direction to apply the Civil Wrongs Ordinance, and there is nothing in the Civil Wrongs Ordinance in accordance with which its general part applies also to torts existing outside its limits.

4. However, the general part of the Civil Wrongs Ordinance should be deemed as applicable also to torts existing outside it, as long as the application of a specific doctrine embodied in its sphere should not be inconsistent with the tortious liability to which it is being sought to apply. Irrespective of which way is applied to bring us to this result, it is necessary and correct, both according to the interpretation of the Law of Contracts (General Part) and to paragraph 1 of the Law of Foundations of Justice, 1980, which again leads us to apply the provisions of the Civil Wrongs Ordinance by way of inference.

5. The definition 'Contributory Negligence' is not auspicious. The better wording should be one which explains that we are not concerned with the negligence of the injured party which contributed to the negligent behaviour of the tortfeasor, but rather an independent factor which contributed to the damage.

There is nothing to prevent the recognition of the contributory negligence of the injured party, even when the liability of the tortfeasor is not founded on the principle of fault. However, each liability should be examined on its own merits and with a view to understanding its aim and substance. There may be cases in which the object of the liability without fault is to ensure a full compensation to the injured party even if he was negligent vis-à-vis his own self. In such cases, whether it has been said expressly or whether this should be surmised from the objects of the legislation creating liability without fault, the contributory negligence of the injured party should not be taken into account.

(*e*) *1.* In the Pilotage Ordinance, the negligence of the injured party which breaks the causal connection should be considered in the framework of the Rules of Causation. The negligence of the injured party, which does not break the causal link, does not afford full defence to the tortfeasor's liability. Consequently the rules of contributory negligence as embodied in the Civil Wrongs Ordinance should be made applicable also to claims under the Pilotage Ordinance.

2. As distinguished from contributory negligence, a person who voluntarily endangers himself may not sue in tort. The fact that the liability in this case is without fault should not be deemed as preventing the injured party to endanger himself voluntarily. The test for voluntary endangering is in the consent of the injured party to bear the loss, should he be injured, to the exclusion of a claim against the tortfeasor. Such consent may come both in relation to liability based on fault and to liability not based on fault.

3. The liability under the Pilotage Ordinance is not of a cogent nature and no policy of defending the injured party from his own voluntary endangerment exists; consequently there is nothing in the Ordinance which should negate the defence of volenti non fit injuria, a defence which though non-existent in the framework of the Ordinance itself, should be found in the limits of the Civil Wrongs Ordinance.

Immediately following the monumental judgment of the Supreme Court in the above matter of *Sidaar v. Eilat-Ashkelon Pipeline Limited*, a slightly similar case was decided by the Supreme Court, though in a slightly different manner.

This is Civil Appeal 817/81, *Israel Ports Authority and Captain S. Avni*, appellants, *v. Meir Zano*, *Abraham Zvernik*, the ship '*Thebeland*', her Owners and Charterers and Captain Ian Bull (Not yet published).

This was an appeal against the decision of the Admiralty Court, in which the motion of the appellants to dismiss in limine the Third Party Notice which was sent to them by the respondents was dismissed. In the aforesaid action, the plaintiffs, Mr. Meir Zano and Mr. Abraham Zvernik, owners of two fishing boats, sued the ship '*Thebeland*' and her Owners and Charterers in rem. The claim was in respect of payment of damages for loss which was caused to their boats, according to the contention of the plaintiffs, as a result of an accident which occurred in Ashdod Port between the ship, which was under pilotage. The respondents, who were the defendants in the Admiralty Court, sent a Third Party Notice to the appellants, who are the Ports Authority and the ship's Pilot, contending that, if they were found liable for the damage to the plaintiffs, they, the Respondents, shall be entitled to be indemnified by the appellants by whose negligence the accident was caused.

The grounds of motion asking the court to dismiss the Third Party Notice were:-

(*a*) There are no Third Party proceedings in the Admiralty Court, in which special Rules of Procedure apply;

(*b*) The Admiralty Court has no power to deal with general contentions of negligence but only with contentions relating to pilotage;

(*c*) Whereas paragraph 2 of the Pilotage Ordinance, 1939, imposes an absolute liability on the shipowner and his master, the respondents are precluded, in the absence of special provisions in law or agreement, to seek indemnification of a third party in an indemnity action even if that third party brought the damages about by his own negligence.

All three contentions were dismissed by the court at first instance; however, the appeal is principally against the two latter grounds.

Justice Goldberg rejected the argument that no indemnification could be sought from a tortfeasor by way of a Third Party Notice on the basis of Civil Appeal 804/80, which has been described in detail above. The result is that the absolute liability which is imposed on the respondents to the plaintiffs in accordance with the Pilotage Ordinance does not necessarily result in the conclusion that they alone must bear the full loss, but, if they can prove fault on the part of the pilot or his employers, they may seek indemnification from him as well.

Only for procedural grounds did the court dismiss the Third Party Notice against the Ports Authority and leave it intact in relation to the Pilot himself.

Onus of proof in case of shortage of goods

(*a*) In Civil Appeal 122, 83/82, *Zim Israel Navigation Company Limited v. Hamagen Insurance Company Limited and Others*; *Israel Ports Authority v. Hamagen Insurance Company Limited*, 39(1) P.D. 640.

(*b*) The Supreme Court sat as a third instance, after having decisions by the Magistrate's Court in favour of the subrogated insurer against the ocean carrier and an appeal to the District Court sitting as a Court of Appeal resulting in the imposition of a joint and several liability on both defendants, the ocean carrier and the Israel Ports Authority, which, by virtue of law, is the exclusive body in charge of rendering stevedoring and warehousing facilities in the ports. The claim related to ten packages of steel, of which the insured received only four. It was proved that the entire cargo of steel arrived mixed with other cargoes of similar nature. The magistrate decided that, in this case, where the Hague Rules apply, the ordinary Rules of Evidence do not. Consequently, once the initial onus has been discharged by the plaintiff by showing that the ocean carrier received the entire cargo for shipment, the duty passes to the carrier to show that it delivered the cargo in the same condition. If the carrier had proved – which it did not – that he delivered the cargo in a complete condition to another party, that party would have to show what happened to the cargo in its custody. However, once the Carrier has not lifted its onus, it must bear the responsibility of what shortage resulted upon delivery of the cargo to the consignee by the Ports Authority. The District Court found that the liability should be split between the Carrier and the Ports Authority jointly and severally, on the basis of a rule that, where the loss is proved but there is no possibility of showing exactly in whose custody it occurred, the liability is joint and several.

(*c*) The Supreme Court decided that the Magistrate's Court was right. The rule that the liability is joint and several where no exact proof in whose custody the loss or damage occurred has, as a prerequisite, the requirement of proving that both parties were at fault. In other words, in order to impose joint and several liability, both parties have to be proven guilty, and only their share in the loss may remain undecided. In such a case, both parties will be held liable in equal shares. The Supreme Court further held that the Magistrate's Court was right when it decided the action in accordance with the ordinary rules of preponderance of evidence.

(*d*) All that the plaintiff had to do was to show that the goods were handed to the carrier in good condition. In this situation, the duty is on the carrier to show that the loss of the six packages occurred after their discharge from the vessel. In this case, the insurance company proved that something had happened to the cargo between the time of its loading on the ship and its discharge. While, upon being loaded, it was sorted into ten packages, at the time of discharge it was scattered, unpacked and mixed with other steel cargoes. This change in the condition of the cargo occurred, as has been proven, whilst the cargo was in the custody of Zim and before it reached the custody of the Ports Authority. In such a situation, when the cargo owner has proved that a change occurred in his cargo, while it was in the custody of the carrier, the latter has to prove that this change is in form only and that the cargo was discharged in good and full condition. This results not only from the contractual duty of the carrier in accordance with the bill of lading to deliver the same cargo which he received for carriage to the same person entitled to its receipt, but also from the duty of the Carrier as a bailee for reward.

The aforesaid examples show that, even a small country like Israel, which is highly dependent on the maritime lanes for its overseas commerce, has a varied and fascinating array of litigation which brings out interesting, and sometimes original, solutions to its complex problems of a legal nature.

ITALY

GUSTAVO ROMANELLI

Professor of Shipping Law, University of Rome

ENZO FOGLIANI

Reader in Shipping Law, University of Rome

SURVEY OF ITALIAN MARITIME LAW – 1984

1. Statutes

Not many novelties may be found in the production of last year's Italian legislation, since many statutes were meant to complete complex frameworks began earlier. On this line, several decrees containing technical provisions to align Italian law to EEC and international uniform rules have been issued. Among them, quite a number of provisions on carriage by sea of dangerous goods, and new dispositions on the procedure to get the tonnage certificate for ships longer than 24 meters (President Decree 2.2.1984, No. 46).

State financial contributions by the Italian Government to several sectors suffering from the deep economical maritime crisis were granted by another group of statutes. Among them, Law No. 396 of 27 July 1984 has extended validity to the dispositions of Law Nos. 598, 599 & 600 of 1982 which had helped to sustain the Shipbuilding Industry. Interventions in favor of shipowners were later made by Statute No. 848 of 11 December 1984.

The Parliament has also issued statutes in order to stop the serious crisis of Italian harbours. Law No. 468 of 13 August 1984 set urgent measures to cope with the difficult situation, while Law No. 859 of 20 December 1984 provided the financial resources to relieve them from their debts.

In order to save the 'Flotta Lauro' from the serious crisis which lead the Neapolitan company under 'State Controlled Administration', a new Law (the third one, No. 618 of 28 September 1984) has given a new governmental contribution to the company.

Law No. 381 of 27 July 1984 has set urgent provisions in order to save the environment; the Decree of 20 November 1984 has established a fishing reserve along the Italian territorial sea.

On international carriage by sea, the Italian Parliament authorized (on 12 June 1984, Nos. 243 & 244) the Government to ratify the protocols signed in Bruxelles on 23 February 1968 and 21 December 1979 (Visby Rules) modifying the Brussels Convention of 1924 on Bill of Lading.

2. Case law

a) ARBITRATION

Two interesting decisions of 'Corte di Cassazione' on international arbitration ruled on the New York Convention of 1958, which, even if not directly dealing with maritime law, has a great importance in this world wide kind of proceeding. The first one (19 January 1984, No. 465, *Dir. mar.* 1985, 302, annotated by La China) has punctualized the peculiar proceeding of enforcement of foreign arbitral awards in Italy, where Italian Courts can not re-open the trial on the merits of the case. It has also been stated that formal requirements on arbitration clauses are required only in accordance with the uniform rules of the New York Convention.

The second decision (21 February 1984, No. 1234, *Dir. mar.* 1985, 39) has confirmed this last consolidated position and has solved some questions on the applicability of the Conventional rules.

b) INSURANCE

The *Appeal Court of Florence* (9 March 1984, *Dir. mar.* 1985, 354) has dealt with sea carriage in containers insured under Institute Cargo Clauses – All Risks, and has stated some new principles on the burden of proof of damages.

A peculiar case following an illegal vessel arrest made by the police authority of an African Country has been solved by '*Corte di Cassazione*' (25 October 1984, No. 5437, *Dir. mar.* 1985, 45, annotated by Balestra). Costs sustained by owners to free the ship from the illegal arrest were considered covered by the Institute War and Strike Clauses – Hull, and the relevant claim recoverable from underwriters as 'value debt'.

In another case, '*Corte di Cassazione*' (27 January 1984, No. 651 *Dir. mar.* 1985, 308) has confirmed the limits of the rules on terms of the starting of prescription and has stated some rules on the burden of proof relevant to damages due to devaluation in favor of the creditor.

c) EMPLOYMENT/LABOUR

Quite interesting is the decision of *Pretura of Trieste* (5 April 1984, *Dir. mar.* 1985, 112, annotated by Enrico Lugifredi) on the discharge of a master. It has been stated that the speciality of this kind of job, and any master's behaviour which may diminish the unconditional trust in him of the owners has been considered as sufficient and legal cause for dismissing him.

Pretura of Genoa (9 March 1984, *Dir. mar.* 1985, 384) has confirmed that ship agents can not be considered as employees of the owners.

d) CARRIAGE

The *Appeal Court of Milan* (23 March 1984, *Dir. mar.* 1984, 890) has rendered an interesting decision on a case about a collect freight relevant to a maritime carriage. When not paid by the consignee, the carrier has the right to get the freight from the shipper, even if he has not exercised his lien on goods. Then, in this case, the lien is only a faculty of the carrier and not a condition to get paid from the shipper.

On the Brussels Convention of 1924 on Bills of Lading, a recent decision of '*Corte di Cassazione*' (27 April 1984, No. 2643, *Assicurazioni*, II, 1985, 10, annotated by Ferrarini) has come to contradict the commonly accepted principle (now explicitly set by the Visby rules) that a liability limit can not be applied in the case of wilful misconduct of the carrier. In this decision, dealing with an unauthorized carriage of a container on deck, the court has also substantially followed the new principles set by the Visby rules (not in force in Italy yet) on the liability limitation for containers, and has calculated the amount of limit referring once again to the price of gold on the free market.

Again on the Brussels Convention, another judgment (*Corte di Cassazione*, 5 March 1984, No. 1536, *Dir. mar.* 1985, 312) has confirmed that terms set by article 3, para 6 to bring suit against the carrier is a forfeiture and not a prescription, but may be extended by agreement of parties.

The decision No. 6298 of '*Corte di Cassazione*' (3 December 1984 *Dir. mar.* 1985, 317, annotated by Balestra) has dealt for the first time with the applicability of the Brussels convention of 1924 to bills of lading released for carriage in bulk connected with a charter party, and between parties of this last contract. The answer has been negative, since it has been stated that only the charter party may decide such kind of carriage between carrier and charterer. The same decision has also dealt with terms to bring suit against the carrier under the Italian Navigation Code.

The *Court of Milan* (13 March 1984, *Dir. mar.* 1984, 910) has once again repeated the exact definition of forwarding agent, which is often confused, in Italian Law, with the contractual carrier.

The *Court of Leghorn* (15 October 1984, *Dir. mar.* 1985, 372, annotated by Vincenzini) has stated that Certificates released by the U.S. Federal Grain Inspection Service are not conclusive as to the quality of goods, which can be proved also by any other means. This decision, the first in Italy on the matter, is very important because it is contrary to the different principle commonly accepted by English courts.

3. Bibliography

On Maritime insurance, Ferrarini, '*Le assicurazioni marittime*', 2nd vol., Giuffré, Milano, 1984 has come to complete a work which has already become a classic on the subject. This further part deals with the new contractual forms recently adopted, such as the 1983 edition of the Italian Standard Form for Goods Insurance, and the last Institute Clauses.

Migliorino, '*Il recupero degli oggetti storici ed archeologici sommersi nel diritto internazionale*', Giuffré, Milano, 1984 gives a long awaited and up-to-date survey of the international rules relevant to the submerged archeological and historical objects.

On the continental shelf and its increasing problems, Del Vecchio, '*Zona economica esclusiva e stati costieri*', Le Monnier, Firenze, 1984, provides a detailed exposition of the last developments of international law.

Scovazzi, '*La pesca nell'evoluzione del diritto del mare*', volume II, Giuffré, Milano, 1984 offers the recent history on the evolution of fishing in maritime law.

The last work of Carbone, '*Le regole di responsabilitá* del vettore marittimo', Giuffré, Milano, 1984 is an interesting survey on the liability rules of the maritime carrier, updated with the most recent case law on the matter.

A comprehensive and detailed analysis of contribution to general average is given by Pullio in his last study, titled '*La contribuzione alle avarie comuni*', Cedam, Padova, 1984.

Last but not least D'Alessio, '*Nazionalitá della nave*', Jovene, Napoli, 1984 covers the several problems arising on nationality of ship.

JAPAN

KAZUO IWASAKI

Professor of Commercial Law, University of Ehime
(Burkyo-cho, Matsuyama)

MARITIME LAW IN JAPAN DURING 1981–1983

I. Legislation: Accession of convention on limitation of liability for maritime claims, 1976

a) INTERNATIONAL CONVENTIONS

Japan ratified the Convention on Limitation of Liability for Maritime Claims, 1976 (1976 Convention) on 23 April 1982 and the Japanese Government deposited the formal instrument of accession with the Secretary-General of the International Maritime Organization on 4 June 1982.

At the time of its accession Japan has made the reservation to exclude the application of Article 2 paragraph 1(d) and (e) under Article 18 of the 1976 Convention.

In response to the accession to the 1976 Convention the 1975 Act relating to the limitation of the liability of owners of sea-going ships has been revised on 21 May 1982 and the revised 1975 Act has entered into force on 20 May 1984.

The 1975 Act was originally enacted to implement the International Convention relating to the Limitation of the Liability of Owners of Sea-going Ships done at Brussels on 10 October 1957 (1957 Convention) and revised to implement the 1976 Convention.

In this connection, the Japanese Government deposited the instrument of denunciation of the 1957 Convention with the Belgium Government on 19 May 1983 and the denunciation of the 1957 Convention took effect for Japan on 20 May 1984.

All substantial provisions of the 1976 Convention have been incorporated into the revised 1975 Act, but there remain some items which have been left by the 1976 Convention to the State Parties' domestic regulation.

b) DOMESTIC LEGISLATION

Japanese domestic regulations on the above mentioned items are as follows:

1) Although Article 6 paragraph 3 stipulates that a State Party may provide in its national law that claims in respect of damage to harbour works, basins and waterways and aids to navigation shall have such priority over other claims, the revised 1975 Act has not provided such priority.

2) According to Article 10 paragraph 1 it is provided in Article 19 of the revised 1975 Act that, where an action is brought in its Courts to enforce a claim subject to limitation, a person liable may only invoke the right to limit liability if a limitation fund has been constituted in accordance with the provisions of this Convention or is constituted when the right to limit liability is invoked.

3) Although Article 11 paragraph 1 refers to the interest on the amount for which any person alleged to be liable, it does not mention the interest rate. Article 19 paragraph 1 of the revised 1975 Act stipulates that the interest rate is 6% per annum.

4) Article 11 paragraph 2 stipulates that a fund may be constituted by producing a guarantee acceptable under the legislation of the State Party. Article 20 of the revised 1975 Act stipulates that a guarantee by a bank, a trust corporation or other financing institutions designated by the Japanese Government is acceptable.

5) According to Article 12 paragraph 3, Article 47 of the revised 1975 Act permits the right of subrogation of the persons who have paid the claim in respect of any amount or compensation which they have paid.

6) Although Article 15 paragraph 1 stipulates that each State Party may exclude wholly or partially from the application of this Convention any person referred to in Article 1 who at the time when the rules of this Convention are invoked before the Courts of that State does not have his habitual residence in a State Party or does not have his principal place of business in a State or any ship in relation to which the right of limitation is invoked or whose release is sought and which does not at the time specified above fly the flag of a State Party, revised 1975 Act does not make such exclusion.

7) In spite of Article 15 paragraph 2(a) Japan does not have any specific provision to be applied to vessels which are intended for navigation on inland waterways.

8) According to Article 15 paragraph 2(b) Article 7 of the revised 1975 Act stipulates that the limits of liability for claims not for loss of life or personal injury shall be 56,000 Units of Account for a wooden ship of less than 100 tons.

9) In spite of Article 15 paragraph 3 Japan does not have such specific provision to regulate the system of limitation of liability to be applied to claims arising in cases in which interests of persons who are nationals of other State Parties are in no way involved.

10) In relation to Article 15 paragraph 4(a) Japan does not have any national legislation to establish a higher limit of liability than that otherwise provided for in Article 6.

II. Case law

There is no case which will generate international interest in the field of maritime law, but the following which are related to international maritime arbitration and litigation will be of some interest for those who are involved in maritime law:

1. Decision of the *District Court of Osaka, 22 April 1983.*

TEXACO Overseas Tankship Ltd. (*U.K.*) *v. Okada Shipping Co., Ltd.* (*Japan*), (1983) 501 Hanrei Taimuzu 182:

1) The court found that the foreign award which was made in New York according to the arbitration clause of the time charter was under the New York Convention.

2) The court found that the defendant's counsel informed the plaintiff on 16 May 1979 that he was not the defendants' counsel hereafter and was not obliged to represent the defendant in the arbitration proceedings and also that he had not any intention to attend the scheduled hearing as the defendant's counsel.

3) The court further found that the above notice meant the intention of the defendant's counsel to resign from his duty, and that therefore the defendant's counsel had been in his position until 15 May 1979 when the above notice was given to the plaintiff.

4) The court held that the defendant had enough opportunity to present his case in the arbitration proceeding since the notices of the hearings were twice given on 18 July 1977 and 19 November 1978 to the defendant's counsel before he resigned from the defendant's counsel on 16 May 1979. The court therefore applied the New York Convention and granted the enforcement of the foreign award.

2. Decision of the *Supreme Court of 7 June 1983.*

Burroughs Corporation (*U.S.A.*) *v. Tei* (*Korea*), (1983) 503 Hanrei Taimuzu 69:

1) The plaintiff obtained a money judgment against the defendant at the U.S. District Court of Washington, D.C. and applied its enforcement at the District Court of Tokyo. The defendant rebuted that since there was no reciprocity of enforcement of foreign judgment between Japan and U.S., the U.S. money judgment should not be enforced by Japanese courts.

2) The Supreme Court supported the lower courts' decision holding that the reciprocity requirement should be regarded to have been met if the respective requirements in Japan and the foreign country for enforcement of foreign judgments did not materially differ so as to lose balance and both requirements were identical with each other in important respects, and granted the enforcement of the U.S. money judgment.

III. Bibliography

Most books and articles are written in Japanese. The following are exceptional ones which were written in English.

- Hosoi & Tsurusaki, *Arrest of vessels in Japan*, (1981) 3 *LMCLQ* 359.
- Pryles & Iwasaki, *Dispute Resolution in Australia-Japan Transactions*, The Law Book Co., Sydney (1983).

THE NETHERLANDS

VINCENT M. DE BRAUW, ADVOCATE

Partner of the Law-firm Nauta van Haersolte, Rotterdam

LEGISLATION, CASE LAW AND BIBLIOGRAPHY IN DUTCH MARITIME LAW (1982, 1983 AND 1984)

1. Legislation

Regarding new legislation relating to maritime law in the Netherlands during 1982, 1983 and 1984 the following developments may be mentioned:

(*A*) *The Hague-Visby Rules* are effective in the Netherlands as from 26 July 1982, as the following laws came into force:
  (i) The law approving the denunciation of the Hague Rules became effective as from 26 April 1983;
  (ii) the law approving the Hague-Visby Rules was enacted on 26 April 1982, so that the Hague-Visby Rules were in force in the Netherlands as from 26 July 1982;
  (iii) the law of 11 March 1981, amending the Dutch Code of Commerce for the purpose of incorporating the Hague-Visby Rules, becoming effective on 26 July 1982 as well.

  A new article 467a has been inserted in the Code of Commerce giving direct effect to the Hague-Visby Rules. In the third paragraph of this article the articles 1 up to and including 9 of the Hague-Visby Rules have been declared directly applicable to every Bill of Lading relating to the carriage of goods between ports in two different states if:
  (a) the Bill of Lading is issued in a contracting state, or
  (b) the carriage is from a port in a contracting state, or
  (c) the contract contained in or evidenced by the Bill of Lading provides that the rules of the Convention or legislation of any state giving effect to them are to govern the contract, whatever may be the nationality of the ship, the carrier, the shipper, the consignee, or any other interested person.

(*B*) *The law of 15 May 1981, regarding conversion into Dutch currency of units expressed in gold* came into force on 15 March 1982, to the effect that one franc Poincaré equals 1/15 Special Drawing Right in all conventions in which the franc Poincaré is mentioned, while 1 franc Germinal equals to 1/3 Special Drawing Right.

(*C*) *The International Convention for the prevention of pollution from ships done at London, 2 November 1973* (*Marpol*) with Protocols and Addenda I and II with Appendices together with the Protocol signed at London (17 February 1978) also with Addendum and Appendices, have been ratified by the Netherlands and came into force as from 2 October 1983.

(*D*) The Netherlands entered into *the Convention concerning the procedure of liner-trade-conferences* as per 6 April 1983. The Convention came into force on 6 October 1983.

The law on *Carriage by Sea*, which was based on this Convention came into force on 1 December 1983.

(*E*) The Netherlands ratified the *International convention for the unification of certain rules relating to the arrest of sea-going ships*, which convention entered into force for this country on 20 July 1983 and is directly applicable.

(*F*) New regulations came into force in 1984 regarding navigation and collisions (*Binnenvaartpolitiereglement*), incorporating various European rules, mainly regarding inland-navigation.

(*G*) Parts of a new code on transport-law (*Book 8 of the New Dutch Civil Code*), which will replace the present code of commerce and several other laws, and which will as well incorporate conventions to which the Netherlands are a party, have been presented to parliament. It is expected that the new code will come into force in 4 or 5 years time.

2. Case Law

The judgements referred to hereunder have been published during 1982–1984. The number (S & S . . .)* refer to the number of the relevant publication.

SUPREME COURT, 22 JUNE 1984, S & S 1984, 72:

According to Dutch law the ownership of a registered vessel is transferred

* S & S = Schip en Schade.

by registration of the deed in the Ships Register. Ownership of a vessel under construction had been transferred, before registration of the vessel itself, by the yard to its principal and subsequently by this principal to a third party. Some days later the principal did register the vessel in its own name. It was decided that such registration by an un-authorized party has no legal effect with all consequences to subsequent registrations of mortgages etc.

Questions whether equipment was part of a vessel or only part of the 'ship's appurtenances' – in which case special provisions or agreements regarding different ownership may be made – were answered as follows: *Court Leeuwarden, 28 February and 18 September 1980, S & S 1983, 25–26 'Simon'*: an echo-sounder-installation and an anchor-winch that had only provisionally been built into the vessel were not a part of that vessel, and *Court Rotterdam, 2 November 1982, S & S 1983, 27, 'Tobias'*: a radar-installation was only part of the ship's appurtenance, and not part of the vessel itself.

COURT OF APPEAL THE HAGUE, 7 SEPTEMBER 1983, S & S 1984, 28, 'PENELOPE':

In a case where clean mates receipts have been issued the carrier has to issue clean bills of lading as well, even in case after the issuing of the mates receipts, before the issuing of the bills of lading, it has been ascertained that the cargo (sugar) was full of rats.

COURT OF APPEAL THE HAGUE, 6 NOVEMBER 1981, S & S 1982, 46, 'IDA BLUMENTHAL':

A bill of lading contains an Identity of Carrier clause as well as a clause referring disputes to the Court of the principal place of business of the carrier. A claim against the German owners was dismissed by the German Courts as, according to German law, the Identity of Carrier-clause is invalid. The question was raised whether Dutch time-charterers were liable towards bill of lading holders notwithstanding the – according to Dutch law valid – 'Identity of Carrier'-clause.

It was decided that German law applied as far as that clause was considered, so that the Dutch charterers could not rely on the clause and were carrier under the bill of lading-contract.

COURT ROTTERDAM, 22 OCTOBER 1982, S & S 1983, 45, 'SANTA ISABELLA':

A bill of lading had been issued, including an 'Identity of Carrier'-clause signed after the text 'in witness whereof the charterer of the said vessel has signed . . .' with the words 'as agents to charterer only'. As it was obvious from those words that owners were not a party to the bill of lading-contract owners were not bound by the Identity of Carrier-clause.

COURT ROTTERDAM, 30 MARCH 1984, S & S 1984, 84, 'NOORDLAND':

The holder of a bill of lading which contains an identity of carrier-clause did claim against the voyage charterer, mentioned on the bill of lading as agent. It was stated that it appeared impossible for the receivers to find the identity and the address of the owners before expiration of the timebar. The charterer's P & I Club-agents could not give the relevant information regarding the identity of the owners. Under those circumstances the charterer could not rely on the identity of carrier-clause: without disclosure of the owners the charterers were found liable themselves.

COURT OF AMSTERDAM, 27 JANUARY 1982, S & S 1982, 89, 'DAVID SALMAN':

A jurisdiction-clause in a bill of lading, referring to the Courts of Korea, was declared valid, even in a case between Dutch cargo-interests and an owner domiciled in Finland.

COURT ROTTERDAM, 7 MAY 1982, S & S 1983, 1, 'KATE N.L.':

The bills of lading do not mention the name of the carrier. A bill of lading jurisdiction-clause, referring to the Courts of the country where the carrier has his principle place of business, is not valid in this case: the bill of lading does not show the name of the carrier. A jurisdiction-clause is only valid in case it is clear from the bill of lading, or anyway in case it can be established in a simple way, which court is competent to decide bill of lading -disputes.

COURT OF APPEAL OF THE NETHERLANDS ANTILLES, 11 MAY 1982, S & S 183, 12, 'GOGOFRIO':

A bill of lading stating i.a.: 'All terms, conditions, liberties and exceptions contained in the charterparty for this present voyage are herewith incorporated in this bill of lading' is not subject to the arbitration-clause in the charterparty as the relevant incorporation-clause in the bill of lading has been drawn up in general terms and does not include an arbitration-clause itself.

COURT ROTTERDAM, 5 AUGUST 1983, S & S 1984, 2, 'ULSTER STAR':

It has once more been decided that clause 2 of a Gencon charterparty is valid according to Dutch law and that an owner may as well rely on this exemption from liability clause in cases where damages to cárgo arose by faults or acts of the ship's management or owners' superintendant.

COURT OF APPEAL THE HAGUE, 3 DECEMBER 1980, S & S 1984, 123, 'EUROPEAN EXPRESS' (SIMILAR: CANTONNAL JUDGE AMSTERDAM, 14 APRIL 1983, S & S 1984, 31, 'AMSTERDAM'):

In case a vessel discharges its cargo into a shed held by the customs from where the cargo is delivered to the consignee, whilst both the carrier and the consignee lose their grip on the cargo, the burden of proof that the cargo was damaged on the moment of discharge from the vessel remains with cargo-interests.

COURT ROTTERDAM, 1 JULY 1983, S & S 1983, 117, 'BOKNIS':

Steel coils, loaded and stowed in a container by shippers, got loose and rolled during the voyage, damaging other goods as well as the vessel. A carrier who leaves the stowage of the goods to the shipper can not disculpate himself towards other cargo-interests by invoking par. 4(2) q of the Hague-Visby Rules, stating that negligent stowage by the shipper caused the damages. The carrier is liable on grounds of insufficient care for seaworthiness and stowage.

COURT AMSTERDAM, 13 JANUARY 1982, S & S 1983, 3, 'BROUWERSGRACHT':

Carriage on deck 'at shipper's risk' of cargo that had insufficiently been stowed: such insufficient stowage was gross negligence of the master, preventing owners to invoke the exception of liability for deck-cargo.

COURT ROTTERDAM, 25 NOVEMBER 1983, S & S 1984, 86, 'MARMA':

The through-carriage of magnesite by inland craft from Rotterdam to Frankfurt was only possible until some place half way in Germany where part of the cargo had to be discharged due to the low draft of water in the river. After discharge the cargo became wet by rainwater. It has been decided that the choice of an unsuitable place for storage was a fault in properly and carefully caring for the cargo; the carrier could not rely on the relevant 'before and after' -clause, nor on any other exemption from liability clause, such as a clause regarding damage by rain.

COURT ROTTERDAM, 19 MARCH 1982, S & S 1984, 13, 'WESERSAND':

The Court does once more confirm that the package limitation of the

Hague Rules, according to Dutch law, does include interest, so that no interest is due on the amount to be paid.

COURT AMSTERDAM, 13 JULY 1983, S & S 1984, 26, 'ELLI':

In case damage has been sustained in Italian lires the judgement will refer to conversion of the damage into Dutch guilders wihtout taking into account possible losses caused by differences in rates of exchange. The interest due is only awarded according to Dutch law, being 9% per annum.

ARBITRATION, 22 APRIL 1981, S & S 1982, 28, 'JUTURNA':

The amount of the overall limitation of liability does, according to Dutch law, include interests: no interest is due until the date the Court decides on the vessel's application to limit its liability.

COURT OF APPEAL THE HAGUE, 23 MARCH 1984, S & S 1984, 105, 'NEDLLOYD BAHREIN':

The newly built vessel 'Nedlloyd Bahrein' was, before delivery, being towed by the yard to the Port of Rotterdam. One of the employees of the yard, acting as master during the short shift of the vessel, forgot to check the height of the ship's derricks; the vessel collided with a railway bridge which was severely damaged. Upon asking the Court to fix the amount of the vessel's limitation of liability the railway company did argue that the collision was due to actual fault or privity of the yard as owners of the vessel.

The Court of Appeal did confirm the decision of the Rotterdam Court, being that the acting master was not a person in whom the chief management of the affairs of the company as owners of ships resides, so that the actual fault or privity of this employee could not be applied to the company.

Though the acting master did not have his master's certificates his appointment by the yard was not a serious fault of that company as, for the shifting of vessels within port, certificates for masters are not prescribed by Dutch law.

Several collisions within the Rotterdam Port areas have been dealt with.

COURT ROTTERDAM, 8 JUNE 1983, S & S 1983, 122, 'FORTHBANK':

It was decided that the collision between this vessel and a bridge was not due to any fault of the master. To decide the extent of liability of the pilot experts were appointed by the Court.

COURT ROTTERDAM, 23 APRIL 1982, S & S 1983, 7, 'GOOD LEADER':

Though the collision of this vessel with a new wharf was caused by the faults of the pilot, the exclusion of liability for such damages as enacted in the local regulations of the municipality of Rotterdam was considered to be valid and part of the pilotage-contract.

COURT AMSTERDAM, 23 JUNE 1982, S & S 1983, 70, 'OLGA-C'/'NOORDZEE':

A vessel trying to assist – without success – another (capsized) vessel is not entitled to claim for damages, sustained because an hawser came into the propellor: the exclusive applicability of the legal provisions regarding assistance and salvage render all other provisions – collision, tort, agency – inoperative.

COURT OF ROTTERDAM, 31 DECEMBER 1982, S & S 1983, 47, 'FELLOWSHIP', 22 JULY 1983, S & S 1984, 4, 'CORNELIA B VI' AND 18 NOVEMBER 1983, S & S 1984, 77, 'MARATHA MARINER':

A lien against a vessel may only be exercised within the Netherlands in case the lien exists according to the law applicable on the contract or act under which the lien arose and in case such lien would have arisen as well according to Dutch law under similar circumstances and could be exercised according to Dutch law within the Netherlands.

COURT ROTTERDAM, 29 NOVEMBER 1982, S & S 1983, 34, 'MARKA L':

Bunkers, delivered to a vessel, had been mixed with bunkers still on board, owned by time-charterers. It was decided that all bunkers were owned by time-charterers: as vessels always use some bunkers, even in port, it was not possible anymore to determine whose fuel has been used and whose fuel remains in the tanks.

COURT ROTTERDAM, 11 MAY 1984, S & S 1984, 126, 'AEGIS WISDOM':

The law governing the change of ownership of bunkers on board of a vessel at the termination of a charterparty is not the law applicable on the charterparty, but the law of the vessel's port of registry.

THE PRESIDENT OF THE COURT AT ROTTERDAM, 29 JUNE 1984, S & S, 127, 'RIVER JIMINI':

A claim for payment of hire of containers is a maritime claim (supplies) according to article 1 paragraph k of the Brussels Treaty regarding arrests of vessels, so that it was possible to arrest the vessel for this claim.

COURT ROTTERDAM, 17 JUNE 1983, S & S 1984, 14:

A forwarding agent, quoting low tariffs to shippers for sea-carriage, was not entitled to claim for a 58% rise in freight – the carrier being forced to apply conference tariffs by the conference – this notwithstanding a clause in the applicable general conditions of Dutch forwarding agents stating that increases in prices may be charged to the principal of the agent. Under the circumstances of the case the Court decided that the forwarding agent could not rely on this clause.

COURT OF APPEAL THE HAGUE, 8 JUNE 1984, S & S 1984, 99:

Stevedores/warehouse operators, where goods have been stored by the carrier, may not rely on their general conditions towards cargo receivers, claiming for damages to the goods arisen during the time of storage.

COURT OF APPEAL THE HAGUE, 19 FEBRUARY 1982, S & S 1982, 73:

The m.v. '*Noordster*' was directed by charterers to the discharging-berth where stevedores, contracted by charterers, caused damage to the vessel. The Dutch owners did claim in tort for those damages. It was decided that owners are deemed to be familiar with the usual applicability of the general conditions used by stevedores and, as owners agreed to have the vessel brought to the stevedores without objecting against the applicability of the general conditions, the stevedores were entitled to invoke such conditions including the clauses excluding their liability.

In some cases regarding shipbuilding or shiprepairs however the general conditions of Dutch shiprepairers (Cebosine) were *not* applicable by lack of explicit agreement between the parties regarding such applicability. (*Court Haarlem, 28 September 1982, S & S 1983, 54, 'Courageux' and Court Dordrecht, 15 September 1982, S & S 1983, 55, 'Atlanta').*

SUPREME COURT, 16 DECEMBER 1983, S & S 1984, 25,
'SAUDI INDEPENDENCE':

Regarding strikes on board of a vessel the law applicable on the labour-agreements has to be taken into account in order to determine whether the strike is lawful or not. The strike was forbidden in this case as the applicable Philippine law did not permit seamen to strike in the relevant circumstances.

Claims brought by seamen against the owners for wages etc., as well as several disputes regarding strikes by seamen, have been decided.

Important decisions were given by the *Court of Appeal of The Hague, 23 April 1982, S & S 1982, 79–81, 'Saudi Independence':*

Whether crewmembers have a right to strike has to be decided in accordance with the law applicable on the labour-agreements. Such law is the law of the flag of the vessel unless the labour-agreements refer to a specific applicable law. As this was the case Philippine law was applied to decide that the crewmembers were *not* entitled to strike. Owners were entitled to stop the payment of wages during the time the crewmembers were on strike, but they were not entitled to stop the supply of food.

COURT MIDDELBURG, 23 FEBRUARY 1983, S & S 1983, 65, 'BERNHARD OLDENDORFF':

Panamanian law was applied to decide whether crewmembers had a right to go on strike: as the vessel had not yet arrived at its place of destination – the strike being held whilst the vessel was anchored at Flushing-roads – the strike was illegal.

COURT ROTTERDAM, 18 DECEMBER 1981, S & S 1982, 104, 'PACIFICO':

A boycott by stevedores in England forced the owners of the vessel to sign a 'special agreement' with the International Transportworkers Federation. The question, whether this agreement, forced from the owners, was lawful, has to be decided according to the law applicable on each labour agreement, being in this case Greek law. The Court asked for information regarding that law.

3. Bibliography

In respect of the Hague-Visby Rules (mentioned under 1.A) an interesting article has been written by W.E. Haak concerning the Hague-Visby Rules and their scope of action.[1] W.E. Haak is a member of the Dutch Supreme Court.

Prof. P.J. Slot has written an article on the Convention concerning the procedure of liner-trade-conference, the law on 'Carriage by Sea' (as

[1] W.E. Haak: '*Het Gewijzigd Cognossementsverdrag en zijn werkingsomvang*', NJB, 19 June 1982 page 717/723.

mentioned under 1.D) and the relevant EEC-decree 954/79 concerning public rules for seagoing vessels.[2]

As a sequel of the inauguration speech of H. Schadee (government commissary for Book 8 concerning Maritime Law of the New Dutch Civil Code) of 1963 'Het schip en zijn schulden', or in English 'The ship and her debts', Prof. R.E. Japikse held his inauguration speech at Leiden in 1982 on 'Het schip en zijn schuldenaren' or 'The ship and her debtors'.[3] Prof. Japikse gave in his speech a thorough enumeration of all possible types of debtors and their juridicial position.

On 7 October 1982, a conference was held at Rotterdam on Maritime Law in relation to Book 8 of the New Dutch Civil Code, which is still in the process of being enacted under the direction of government commissary H. Schadee. All the lectures of this conference have been published in a booklet under the editorship of Mr F.A. van Bakelen.[4]

The full texts of important treaties and protocols in Transport Law is given in the loose-leaf volume 'Transport'. This volume contains also standard regulations such as Lloyd's Open Form, Lloyd's Average Bond, York-Antwerp Rules. Almost 100 treaties are covered in this volume, and each of the texts is reprinted in the official languages, mostly in English and French, sometimes in Spanish, German and Dutch. This volume was formerly edited by H. Schadee and is currently edited by M.H. Claringbould. It contains an up to date list of countries which have ratified the various treaties and protocols and the dates on which the treaties entered into force and the respective reservations made.[5]

Mr S. van Weeghel did publish a booklet on the changes between the Hague- and Hague-Visby Rules.[6] A leaflet on the 1910 Schrage Convention and Lloyd's Open Form was written by Mr M.L.J. Bröcher.[7]

Smaller articles were published a.o. regarding salvage,[8] the Dutch Shipping Counsel[9] and the arrest-convention.[10,11]

[2] P.J. Slot: '*Publiekrechtelijke regels voor de zeescheepvaart*', Sociaal-Economische-Wetgeving, December 1983, page 757/788.

[3] R.E. Japikse: '*Het schip en zijn schuldenaren*', W.E.J. Tjeenk Willink, Zwolle, 1982.

[4] '*Zeerecht in het licht van Boek 8 Nieuw Burgerlijke Wetboek*', teksten Vervoerrecht, W.E.J. Tjeenk Willink, Zwolle, 1983.

[5] TRANSPORT, Kluwer, Law and Taxation Publishers, Deventer.

[6] S. van Weeghel: '*De Visby Rules, wijzigingen op het cognossementsverdrag van 1924*', teksten Vervoerrecht, W.E.J. Tjeenk Willink, Zwolle, 1984.

[7] M.L.J. Bröcker: '*1910 Salvage Convention and Lloyd's Open Form under Pressure*'. Maritime Research Institute Netherlands, Rotterdam 1983.

[8] F.A.W. Bannier, '*De berger in gevaar?*', NJB (1984) 10, p. 293–298.

[9] E.J. Rosen Jacobson, '*De Raad voor de Scheepvaart, 75 jaar bijdrage aan de veiligheid ter zee*', (1984) 37, p. 1161–1163.

[10] J.P. Verheul, '*The convention relating to the arrest of seagoing ships of 1952. Some questions*'. NILR 1983, 383–386.

[11] D. Kokkini-Iatridou, '*Conservatoir beslag op zeeschepen*'. Ars Aequi 1983, katern 10, 378.

NORWAY

JØRGEN ALMELØV

Scandinavian Institute of Maritime Law, University of Oslo

NORWEGIAN LEGISLATION, CASE LAW, AND BIBLIOGRAPHY FOR MARITIME LAW IN 1982–83

1. Legislation

The last issue of this yearbook included a brief look at the standing Governmental Maritime Law Committee's draft Legislation on the 1976 Convention on Limitation of Liability for Maritime Claims, for inclusion in the Norwegian Maritime Code. Also mentioned was the incorporation of substantive provisions of the 1974 Athens Convention relating to carriage of passengers and their luggage by sea.

The draft legislation built on these two conventions has now been approved by the parliament in the form described in the previous yearbook. The provisions are incorporated in the Norwegian Maritime Code. These provisions are going to enter into force sometime in 1985, in co-ordination with the other Scandinavian countries.

In 1982, the Parliament passed new legislation that incorporates the substantive provisions of the 1972 Convention for Safe Containers. This convention is going to be ratified by Norway in the near future. The act is applicable to containers used in transport to or from Norway, or in transit through Norway. On Norwegian ships outside Norway the master of the ship can refuse to take onboard containers that do not satisfy the provisions of the Norwegian Safe Container Act or other provisions that have been passed in accordance with this act. The Norwegian act does not apply to containers specially designed for air transport. The act has not yet entered into force.

In 1983, a new petroleum law was proposed by the Petroleum Law Committee. Currently there are various Royal Decrees and other provisions on petroleum exploration, safety regulation, drilling and the like. Most of these regulations are going to be replaced by the new Petroleum law. The Parliament will probably pass the new law in the autumn of 1984.

The lack of governmental experience with petroleum activity and uncertainty about the future extent of such activities in Norway made it natural for the Parliament in 1963, and in following years, to delegate authority to come with more specific regulations in the form of Royal Decrees instead of passing an act. But today Norway has 18 years experience with exploration, 12 of which have included experience with production, since the first field, Ekofisk, started operation in 1972. The rules in force today are to a large extent more precisely described in the new act, based on nearly 20 years experience of petroleum activities.

2. Case law

During 1982–83 several cases of interest from an international perspective have been decided. The Supreme court, in 1983 Norsk rettstidende (RT) 1317, considered a problem of insurance where a fishing boat, the M/S '*Frank Erik*', sprang a leak and sank under good weather conditions. There was no possibility of establishing the reason for the leak. The boat was insured on a hull policy, that incorporated to reference the Norwegian Marine Insurance Plan of 1964 (Norwegian Plan). The insurance company, Samvirke, refused to pay any claims made by the assured under the policy. The issue the Supreme Court faced was how great a burden should be imposed on the assured to prove seaworthiness.

The relevant provision of the Norwegian Plan reads as follows: §45 Unseaworthiness.

> 'The insurer is not liable for loss that is a consequence of the ship not being in a seaworthy condition provided that the assured was or ought to have been aware of the ship's defects at such a time that it would have been possible for him to intervene.
>
> The burden is on the assured to prove that he neither was nor ought to have been aware of the defects. If the ship springs a leak whilst afloat, he has the further burden of proving that the loss is not attributable to unseaworthiness.'

The Supreme Court cited recent experience with smaller ships concerning, among other things, defects in cooling systems. The Court found that based on the evidence, the possibility of a defect in seaworthiness had not been excluded as a reason for the leakage. Furthermore the Court found that there was no evidence pointing to an external cause of the accident. The Court held for the insurance company in this case. The case demonstrates that the rule on burden of proof in section 45 of the Norwegian Plan lays a very high burden on the assured to prove that the loss is not attributable to unseaworthiness.

Another important case was decided by the Hålogaland Court of Appeal. The circumstances were briefly the following: the fishing-trawler '*Tønsnes*' damaged some fishing-nets with its trawl. In court the question was raised whether or not the trawler could limit its liability according to the provisions on limitation of liability in the Norwegian Maritime Code (chapter 10).

According to the relevant provisions in the Maritime Code section 234 subs. 2 a right to limitation could be claimed when there is loss or damage to property caused by someone onboard the ship. Subsection 3 of the same section states further that loss or damage in connection with navigation or handling of the ship could be subject of limitation.

The Court found that the casualty was caused by the mate onboard '*Tønsnes*', that the damage happened when '*Tønsnes*' was trawling, and that the ship and the trawl were one unit because they were physically connected and the trawl's movements depended on the ship's manoeuvers. Because the Court found that the ship and the trawl were one unit it saw no reason why limitation based on section 234 subs. 3 could not be applied. Court also concluded that the damage was caused by the mate's gross negligence. A majority of the court concluded further, however, that the right to limit liability is independent of the fact that the damages were caused by the mate's gross negligence, that the relevant chapter in the Maritime Code settles this matter completely and that there is nothing in the code to prevent limitation when damage is caused by gross negligence. There was dissent. Finally, court concluded that the damage to the fishing-nets constituted a single 'casualty' because it occurred as part of the same operation and it was not possible to separate the different casualties.

3. Bibliography

In 1982–83 the following books were published (in Norwegian) by the Maritime Law Foundation:

Bull, H.J., *Direct action in marine insurance*, 154 pp.

Bull, H.J. and Falkanger, T., *Introduction to Maritime Law*, 276 pp.

Askheim, L.O., Gisvold, M. and Tapper, J.K. *Contracts for Deliveries and Supplies to the Offshore Petroleum Industry in Norway*, 625 pp. (with a summary in English)

Grav, H.P., *Safety Management and Control Policy: A Study of the Safety Regulation of Offshore Oil Activity by The Norwegian Petroleum Directorate*, 224 pp. (with a summary in English).

MarIus, a law journal published by the Maritime Law Foundation, appeared with 20 issues in 1982–83. The following was published in English:

No. 86. Rønneberg, N., *Limitation of Shipowner's Liability. The Concept of 'Privity or Knowledge' in American Law*, 17 pp.

POLAND

MARIA DRAGUN

University of Copernici (Toruń)

REVIEW OF POLISH COURT DECISIONS AND MARITIME PUBLICATIONS

I. Legislation – International conventions

Poland has ratified the International Convention on tonnage measurement of ships, 1969 (Dz.U.,[1] 1983, No. 56, item 247). The instrument of ratification was deposited with International Maritime Organization on 27 July 1976. This Convention has entered into force on 18 July 1982. The pronouncement of the Polish Government on the ratification of this convention has been published in Dz.U. No. 56, item 248.

II. Judicature

In Poland judgements of the Supreme Court and also decisions of the Central Arbitration Commission are published, but the latter decisions concern only disputes between Polish socialist economic organizations. Judgements of the International Court of Arbitration for Marine and Inland Navigation at Gdynia are not published in Poland.[2] In 1982 and 1983 the following judgements of the Supreme Court concerning maritime cases were published:

1. MARITIME SALVAGE

Judgement of 29 January 1982 (III Cr 188/81) in 'Orzecznictwo Sadu Najwyższego'[3] 1982, No. 8–9, item 125:

[1] Dziennik Ustaw – Law Gazette.
[2] J. Łopuski: Nuevas aportaciones del Derecho maritimo polaco, 'Anuario de Derecho Maritimo', vol. 1, p. 557.
[3] 'Decisions of the Supreme Court'.

The remuneration for maritime salvage is due to the salvor who has proved that he had undertaken salvage operations answering the call or upon obtaining consent of the master of the salved vessel.

An acceptance of the offered assistance by the master of the ship is tantamount to the acceptance of services in answer of his express call.

The remuneration for maritime salvage is due to the salvor by law.

Towage services assume the nature of the salvage services when in consequence of their undertaking the salved vessel has been protected against the serious damage, which could not be averted by the master and the crew of the salved vessel themselves.

2. NATIONAL JURISDICTION OF POLISH COURTS

Decision of 21 December 1982 (II Cr 521/82) in 'Orzecznictwo Sadu Najwyższego', 1983, No. 9, item 136:

Under art. 1 of the Convention on deciding by arbitration of civil-law disputes relating to the economic and scientific-technical cooperation, signed in Moscow on 26 May 1972 (Dz.U. 1974, No. 7, item 37) the parties to which are Poland and Czechoslovakia, the dispute between the Czechoslovak state insurance company and the Polish Ocean Lines as maritime carrier is exempted from the jurisdiction of the Polish courts as well as the courts of other state-members of the CMEA. This applies also in case where the insurer's claim is his recourse claim following the settlement of the cargo damage caused to the person not belonging to any state-member of CMEA.

According to art. 1 of the Moscow Convention any dispute between economic organizations resulting from contractual or any other civil-law relationships that may arise in connection with the conomic and scientific-technical cooperation of the states-parties to this Convention is to be decided by arbitration and national jurisdiction of the courts of the CMEA countries is exempted in these cases.

3. PERFORMANCE OF THE CONTRACT OF CARRIAGE

The Central Arbitration Commission has issued the following decision on 31 March 1979 (IP – 1154/79), published in 'Orzecznictwo Sadów Polskich i Komisji Arbitrażowych',[4] 1982, No. 7–8, item 90a, with a note by J. Łopuski:

'An inaccessibility of the port of destination in the liner navigation is the circumstance for which the carrier is not liable and for this reason he does not bear the cost of storage at the port of loading of the cargo booked for carriage under the booking contract during the period of delay in the loading caused by an inaccessibility of the port of destination.'

[4] 'Decisions of the Polish Courts and Arbitration Commissions'.

The opinion opposed to the stand-point of the Central Arbitration Commission has been expressed by J. Łopuski in his note to this decision in which he has indicated that under general rules of law on carriage of goods by sea the risk of additional costs connected with unloading of the cargo at the port of destination is borne by the carrier, not by the shipper if no stipulation to the contrary has been inserted into the contract of carriage. In absence of such a stipulation in this case the carrier should bear the additional cost of storage of the cargo caused by the delay in loading. He has also pointed out that the liability for such damage is not governed by art. 156–160 of the Polish Maritime Code (they concern only the damage resulting from loss of or damage to the cargo in the period from its receipt for carriage until its delivery to the consignee) but by the provisions of the Polish Civil Code concerning the contractual liability (art. 471–472) which in virtue of art. 1 §2 of the Maritime Code are applicable in matters not governed by the latter Code.

III. Doctrine

A general problem discussed in 1982 and 1983 in Polish legal writings on the international law of the sea concerned questions connected with the UN Conference on the law of the sea and the international Convention on this subject which has been elaborated by this Conference.

The special volumes of such periodicals as 'Technika i Gospodarka Morska'[5] 1983, No. 3 and 'Przeglad Stosunków Miedzynarodowych'[6] 1983, Nos. 1–3 were issued which contained a number of articles on this question. The attitude of Poland to this convention has been also presented in an article by J. Symonides: *Poland and the new law of the sea*, 'Sprawy Miedzynarodowe' 1983, No. 1.[7]

With regard to the sphere of private maritime law the following questions were discussed:

a. CARRIAGE OF GOODS BY SEA

Langer, T.: *New conditions of cargo insurance against marine risk in the international trade*, 'Technika i Gospodarka Morska' 1982, No. 10; Dragun, M.: *Evolution of the unit limitation of the carrier's liability in the international maritime legislation*, 'Technika i Gospodarka Morska' 1983, No. 11; Lopuski, J.: *The leasing of the ship against a background of the evolution of international shipping relationships*, 'Problemy prawa przewozowego'[8] 1982, No. 4.

[5] 'Maritime Technique and Economy'.
[6] 'The Review of International Relations'.
[7] 'International Affairs'.
[8] 'Problems of transport law'.

The special volume of the periodical 'Problemy prawa przewozowego' 1985, No. 5 contains mainly articles on carriage of goods by sea.

b. REGISTRATION OF SHIPS

Suchorzewski, S.: *Legal problems of the registration of ships and right to a flag on the international forum*, 'Technika i Gospodarka Morska' 1983, No. 10; Rzeszewicz, M.: *A draft of the international convention on the conditions of registration of ships under the national flags*, 'Technika i Gospodarka Morska' 1983, No. 6.

c. NEW ORGANIZATIONAL FORMS OF THE POLISH SHIPPING ENTERPRISES

Pietraszek, R., Flera, W.: *Shipping joint-stock companies in the Polish Peoples Republic*, 'Technika i Gospodarka Morska' 1982, No. 6.

The following books on maritime law have been published in 1982 and 1983 by 'Wydawnictwo Morskie': Łopuski, J.: *Handy encyclopaedia of maritime law*, Gdańsk 1982 p. 159; Brodecki, Z.: *The liability for marine pollution*, Gdańsk 1983, p. 215.

SPAIN

Ignacio Arroyo

Attorney, 'Ramos & Arroyo, Abogados'

LEGISLATION, CASE LAW AND BIBLIOGRAPHY OF SPANISH MARITIME LAW IN 1984

1. Legislation

In 1984, several interesting items with regard to the development of maritime law have been produced. This is especially true in the international area. In domestic law the most important developments have occurred with regard to new regulation of liner shipping.

1. INTERNATIONAL TREATIES

Parliamentary activity has centered on the execution of multilateral and bilateral treaties, principally in the fishing sector.

a) The publication in the Official State Bulletin of 11 February 1984, of the Protocol (1979) modifying the International Convention for the unification of certain rules relating to bills of lading (1925), amended by the Visby Protocol (1968), is the most important event. It deals, in other words, with the ratification of the Hague-Visby Rules of 1968 as well as the Protocol of 1979. It is important to underline that with one sole instrument, that published in the 'BOE' of 11 February 1984, Spain has incorporated into its internal law two international instruments: the Hague-Visby Rules of 1968 and the Protocol of 1979. It can actually be said that Spain has ratified every international convention relating to bills of lading: first, the Brussels Convention of 25 August 1924; and now (1984), in one single stroke, the two modifying protocols: the Hague-Visby Rules of 1968 and the Brussels Protocol of 1979.

In addition, keeping in mind that Spain, apart from publishing the

Brussels Convention in the 'BOE' (Gazette of Madrid of 31 July 1930), also incorporated – for the second time – this treaty by adopting domestic legislation: the Carriage of Goods by Sea Act of 22 December 1949, it is understandable to question the validity of both the Act and the Convention. At the very least one might ask the following questions: Do the Protocols of 1968 and 1979, which modified the Convention of 1924, also modify the domestic law of 1949? If so, to what extent? Do they completely repeal either the law because of incompatibility, or only those articles that affect the subjects regulated in the Protocols?

Authors do not agree on the answers to these questions. For some, both in the international and the domestic area, the only instrument in force is the Convention of 1924, as published in the Gazette of 1930 with the reforms that are being introduced in 1984; in other words, with the modifications of the Protocols of 1969–1979. The domestic law of 1949 is therefore completely repealed. On the contrary, other writers believe that the Law of 1949 is still in force, repealed partially by the Protocols of 1968 and 1979 as they were published in 1984.

The Supreme Court has not passed on this question.

In my opinion, the 1949 Act is repealed only insofar as it is incompatible with the Protocols.

With regard to other matters, the ratification of the Hague-Visby (1968) and Brussels (1979) Protocols makes it unlikely for now that Spain would ratify the Hamburg Rules of 1978.

b) Fewer problems are raised by the ratification of the Brussels Protocol of 1979, which modifies the International Convention on Limitation of Liability of the Owners of Sea-going Vessels, signed in Brussels on 10 October 1957. The Convention was already in force, and incorporated into the domestic law since its publication in the 'BOE' on 21 July 1970. Now, with the publication in the 'BOE' of 9 October 1984, the Protocol of 1979 has also been incorporated, and with it the modification of the Convention.

c) Spain has ratified and also published ('BOE' of 7 November 1984) the International Convention on Standards for Training, Certification and Watchkeeping of Seamen, signed in London on 7 July 1978, which refers to problems of maritime labor regulation. The Convention entered into force both in general and in Spain on 28 April 1984, upon completion of the requirements of article XIV.1: twelve months after the date on which at least 25 States whose combined merchant fleets represent a minimum of 50% of the gross tonnage of the worldwide fleet of merchant vessels of a gross register equal or greater than 100 tons of registry sign the Convention without reservations as to ratification, approval, or adhesion. Spain deposited the Instrument of Adhesion on 11 October 1980, and now, 7 November 1984, has incorporated it into judicial regulations through publication in the 'BOE'.

d) Regarding pollution, Parliament has ratified and the 'BOE' has published the Protocol on protection of the Mediterranean Sea against pollution of a land origin, signed in Athens on 17 May 1980 (BOE 26 June 1984), without any reservations such as the ones that France adopted which excluded application in the case of a conflict with domestic law.

e) The Protocol relating to the International Convention to prevent pollution by vessels (1973), signed in London on 17 February 1978, has also been incorporated through the BOE of 17 October 1984.

f) Finally, the Convention relating to future multilateral cooperation on the fishing grounds of the Northeast Atlantic, signed in London on 18 November 1980, must be mentioned. This Convention, published in the 'BOE' of 3 September 1984, means in practice the denunciation of the precedent of 1959. Other international bilateral treaties subscribed to in 1984 are of less interest. In any case, the Convention on maritime transport between the Governments of Spain and Mexico, published in the BOE of 16 June 1984, should be mentioned.

2. DOMESTIC PROVISIONS

We refer in this paragraph to both ordinary laws and administrative regulations.

To enumerate all of them, accompanied by a brief commentary, would exceed the limits of this summary whose goal is to inform the reader of those developments of interest from the point of view of comparative law.

a) Law 22/1984, of 29 June, which modifies the legal interest rate of money. Its practical importance is evident: the interest rate was raised from 4% to approximately 12%.

b) Law 33/84, of 2 August, which deals with regulation of private insurance (BOE, No. 186, of 4 August), and as its own name indicates, reorganizes and restructures the production of all types of private insurance, including maritime insurance. This law is not one relating to the insurance contract, but rather to the production of insurance. Therefore it affects insurance companies.

c) The third and final provision, whose character as an ordinary law must be called attention to, is Law 23/84, of 25 June, on marine cultivation, which has as its scope the regulation of marine cultivation in national territory, maritime land zone, rivers, estuaries, lakes and saltwater lagoons in temporary or permanent connection with the territorial sea and exclusive economic zone.

If from the dispositions approved by the Parliament, we turn now to those approved by the Executive branch, the Decree on regular maritime transport stands out from among the others.

d) Royal Decree 720/1984, of 28 March, of regulation of liner transport. The navigation of liners in Spain represents approximately 90% of total foreign commerce in investment and consumer goods. The special characteristics of this commerce justify State intervention which guarantees its maintenance. The system of the liner code of conduct and public support or subsidies are the methods adopted by the majority of governments. The theme from the legal point of view contrasts with the principle of free market competition. Together with the code of conduct system and the aforementioned support, the Public Administration, through the Ministry of Commerce, requires the approval of the commerce, of the vessels involved, submitting the practice of the companies to 'previous administrative authorization'. Consequently, the Decree develops the system of authorizations, already established in a general way in the Protection of the Merchant Marine Act of 1956.

More concretely, the Royal Decree distinguishes the services of coastal navigation and trade from those of a regular international line. Both require previous administrative authorization for their commencement. This authorization is conceded on the basis of public character, regularity, and stability. With regard to regular lines of coastal navigation and trade, only vessels of national construction and flag are permitted. In contrast to this total ban on foreign vessels in domestic commerce, international commerce, between national and foreign ports, may be carried out by vessels of Spanish, foreign, or mixed character. The principles adopted in the decree are a manifestation of the position that Spain occupies as a member of the OECD, aligned with Group B of UNCTAD. The so called 'free flow of shipping' is the symbol of freedom of commerce and international maritime transport applied to regular liner navigation. These criteria are already contained in the current Law of 4 April 1970, concerning international maritime traffic. Finally, we must point out that of the three chapters that the UNCTAD Code of Conduct permits the administrative authorities to regulate, the Spanish Administration finds in the aforementioned provision the legal support for this decree.

II. Case law

During 1984, the Spanish Supreme Court turned its attention to the following subjects: shipbuilding contracts, maritime transport of goods, charter parties, maritime insurance, and liability for collision.

1. SHIPBUILDING CONTRACTS

The decision of 10 February 1984 is surprising. It affirms, without reservation, that the shipbuilding contract is governed by article 574 of the Commercial Code. On the other hand, it states that the liability of the shipyard is limited for the period of one year, in application of article 952, 1st Commercial Code, expressly rejecting the 15 year limitations period of article 1964 of the Civil Code.

The sentence is surprising as it changes radically the previous jurisprudential doctrine in favor of the 15 year limitations period. I have already illustrated that, from the academic point of view, the annual period of limitations is unjustifiable. It nevertheless appeared to me to be contrary to common sense and to an economic analysis of the law that the liability of the shipbuilder should last for a longer period of time than the ship which he built. We must remember in this regard that the average life of a vessel does not exceed 10 years. Nevertheless, doctrine and jurisprudence have unanimously maintained the 15 year limitations period due to the lack of applicable commercial legislation. One looked to the civil subject of building construction contracts in order to arrive at article 1964 of the Civil Code, regarding the general limitations period for personal actions. Now, this practice is drastically altered by the decision of the Supreme Court of 10 February 1984.[1]

2. MARITIME TRANSPORT

a) Inapplicability of maritime law to the land phase of transport

The *Supreme Court's 31 January 1984* decision faced various issues regarding interpretation of the subject of contracts for maritime transport of goods. On the one hand, the decision affirms that the Law of 22 December 1949 – which as is known incorporates the Hague-Visby Rules – is not applied to land transport, although there is a maritime phase included and a bill of lading has been issued. Therefore, the provisions of the Commercial Code are applied. With regard to the nature of the limitations period for the action, the Supreme Court held that the limitations period is governed by article 952 of the 2d Commercial Code, a thesis that contrasts openly with the aforementioned jurisprudence of the Supreme Court in favor of expiration when the action is brought under the Law of 1949.[2] In addition to a discussion of the maritime transport law and the limitations period, the decision of 31 January 1984, reiterates the foundation of the carrier's

[1] See Arroyo, Ignacio: *La responsabilidad quincenal del constructor de buques o el absurdo de un razonamiento jurídico correcto* in Estudios de Derecho marítimo, Barcelona (Libreria Bosch), 1985, pp. 403 to 427.

[2] See our work Arroyo, Ignacio: *Relación entre póliza de fletamento y conocimiento de embarque: la clausula de incorporación*, Bilbao (Universidad de Deusto), 1977 and formerly the decisions in Id. *Panorama del Derecho Marítimo español (1983)*, in *ADM* vol. III, Barcelona, 1984, pp. 423.

liability in light of the Commercial Code. In traditional law, this is a liability 'ex recepto'; this is to say that the carrier is responsible for damage, unless he proves an inevitable accident or Act of God.

As one may easily see, the situation is very different from the system of the Law of 1949; the carrier is responsible if at fault, but the shipper must prove the carrier's negligence. On the contrary, in the Commercial Code negligence is presumed as a consequence of the care of the goods, and only damage must be proved; from this moment on the carrier, if he wants to exonerate himself from liability, must prove the inevitability of the event.

b) Paramount Clause

In the *Supreme Court's decision of 30 May 1984*, the well-known issue of the paramount clause surfaced. This is a clause of the applicable law; more concretely, the parties either accept the application of the Brussels Convention of 1924, or the domestic law that incorporates it. It is important to realize that the binding power is not derived from the scope of the application of the Convention but rather from the express submission of the contracting parties. This is a question of freedom of contract. Consequently, although the conditions of the application of the law, or of the Convention, are not given, one may arrive at the same result of application due to the effect of the aforementioned clause. The Court ruled that the maritime transport law of 1949 applies: (i) to international maritime transport using bills of lading, and (ii) between nations that ratified the Convention and incorporated it into their domestic legislation.

In the same decision the Court dealt with the differences between a limitations period and expiration, reiterating the doctrine by which the period of expiration may not be interrupted or suspended: the right in question must be exercised within the given period of time.[3]

In particular, the Court held that the expiration period is not interrupted nor suspended by settlement negotiations, nor by the initiation of an inadequate proceeding, nor by preliminary actions. This is in contrast to the extension of time, which is permitted through express agreement of the parties.[4]

c) Maritime transport and jurisdiction

The *Supreme Court's decision of 31 May 1984* concerns the validity of the jurisdiction clause in the bill of lading. In order for this clause to be valid

[3] See previous note in Arroyo, Ignacio: *Estudios de Derecho Marítimo*, cit. 'Reseña y Comentarios de Jurisprudencia (1979–1983)', pp. 530.

[4] We already declared ourselves in favor of this apparent contradiction in Arroyo, I: *Relación*, op. cit., p. 56.

and efficient, it should be drafted in a clear and express manner. It constitutes, in effect, a derogation of the 'ius cogens' that according to procedural law provides that the judge of the place of the delivery of the goods is competent to hear the action for damages (article 62-1st LEC). Consequently, the legal criteria should be applicable unless the parties have genuinely and undoubtedly stipulated otherwise.[5]

3. AFFREIGHTMENT

a) Liability for damage to the cargo

The *Supreme Court's decision of 14 February 1984*, sheds light on the liability of the shipowner for damage to the cargo.[6] It concerned the damage suffered as a consequence of the shipwreck of the vessel due to willful wrongdoing, negligence, or unskillfulness of the captain, as provided by article 841 of the Commercial Code. In this situation the question arises as to whether only the captain, or both the captain and the shipowner, are responsible. This is an interplay of actions between the shipowner and the captain on the one side, and shippers against shipowners and captains, on the other. This factual situation is covered by article 618 of the Commercial Code.[7] The Court, with clarity worthy of applause, ruled that the shipper is entitled to interpose the action against both the shipowner and the negligent captain. This is considered an action of a third party that does not affect the action that the shipowner is entitled to bring against the captain in order to hold him responsible for his negligent conduct.[8]

b) Demurrage and inadequacies of stowage

The *decision of 28 February 1984*, gives a detailed account of a question that is not easily explained. To understand it on its own terms it is sufficient to realize that sometimes indemnization for demurrage is confused with defective stowage. The Supreme Court has had the opportunity to speak and to warn that these are two different questions, just as the actions that the same charter party might give rise to are different.[9]

[5] Cfr. Arroyo, Ignacio: '*Transporte marítimo internacional y jurisdicción extranjera*', in Revista del Colegio de Abogados de Vizcaya, 1984, noviembre–diciembre, pp. 37–43.

[6] Cfr. *Cementos Especiales S.A. c/ Mercanship, S.A.*, Vessel: 'Ramalbert', in *ADM*, vol. IV.

[7] See art. 18 et seq. Ley Penal y Disciplinaria de la Marine Mercante, y art. 703 Cod. Com, y el art. 618 n. 8, relac. arts. 574 y 586 Cod. Com y arts. 610 y 826 Cod. Com.

[8] See Gondra Romero, Jose María: *La responsabilidad personal del capitán por la custodia de las mercancías y el problema de la validez de las clausulas de exoneración de responsabilidad en el contrato de fletamento*', in Estudios al Profesor Polo, Madrid, p. 341.

[9] Cfr. Arroyo, Ignacio: *La distribución del riesgo en el derecho marítimo*, Madrid (Editoria Revista de Derecho Mercantil), 1977, 87, 93–98.

Indeed, it is important to carefully separate two aspects that are intertwined in practice. There is only one contract: the charter party; on the other side there is a complex fact situation that results in damage to the cargo. Therefore, payment of demurrage is one matter, and the liability attributed to the captain for inadequate storage is another.

From the conceptual point of view the distinction does not appear to be difficult. It is necessary to keep in mind that the 'pure' charter party which signifies the delivery of a seaworthy vessel to navigate does not exist in practice. What does exist is the charter party, by voyage or by time, for the transport of goods. The activity of navigation (making available the shipping space of the vessel) is an activity of transport. It is easily understood that the costs of demurrage constitute an aspect of the activity of navigation or shipping in the strict sense, and therefore there is no obstacle to the shipowner also being responsible for the defective stowage of the cargo; that is, of the activity of transport.

4. MARITIME INSURANCE

In the period of time covered by this article, the Supreme Court handed down three sentences concerning maritime insurance.

a) Subrogation

The *Supreme Court's decision of 13 April 1984*, involves various aspects of the general theory of contract and focuses on the right of subrogation in the insurance field. The goods suffered damage as a consequence of the failure of the ship's refrigeration system. It is a known fact that any action for damages in maritime transport gives rise to two issues: on the one hand, the liability of the carrier, and on the other, the coverage of the insurance policy. Although they are different, both questions involve similar considerations. The facts of the complaint constitute a clear example of the difficulty that sometimes results when trying to separate these two concepts. The malfunction of the vessel's refrigerators is the cause of the carrier's liability. This same fact of malfunction of the refrigerators is a loss covered by the insurance policy. In the first meaning indicated, if one demonstrates the fault or negligence of the carrier or of his servants (e.g. the captain) evidently there is liability; the shipper or receiver of the goods may make a claim for damages. The foundation of the action rests in the contract of transport; this is to say, in the bill of lading. With regard to the second meaning, the insurance contract, the coverage of the risk depends on the classification of the captain's conduct. In the case at issue, in the opinion of the insurance company, it is not because the damage was caused by the barratry of the captain. And as is known, barratry (fraud or gross negligence of the captain) is a risk excluded from coverage.[10] The Judge of First Instance, the territorial Appeals Court of La Coruña, and finally the Supreme Court ordered the insurance company to pay, as there was no barratry and the risk therefore fell within the coverage of the insurance policy.

The right of subrogation of the insurer against the party responsible for the damage is a different question. This is a right that is also recognized by the decision.

b) Proof of damage of the goods and insurance

The *Supreme Court's 17 May 1984* decision faces a situation quite similar to the aforementioned case: damage to the goods due to lack of refrigeration. Briefly, the facts can be described by saying that the claimant insured the transport of various boxes of fruit, including the risk of damage due to lack of proper temperature, through the respondent company. The vessel should have maintained adequate refrigeration to protect the cargo. The goods arrived at the port of destination, Santa Cruz de Tenerife (Canary Islands) completely spoiled, apparently due to lack of refrigeration, according to the certificate of the Maritime Commissioner. The insurance company alleged that the complainant had not proved that the damage was produced 'during the voyage' because it could have been produced before loading. The Judge of First Instance dismissed the complaint; the Appeals Court reversed the judgement, and the Supreme Court refused to hear an appeal (recurso de casacion), thereby ordering the insurer to pay indemnization for the damage.

The question revolves around knowing 'when' the damage was produced. The Appeals Court did not accept the position of the insurer, who presented a certificate of the captain who affirmed that during the voyage there was no malfunction of the refrigeration apparatus. The reasoning of the Supreme Court firmly establishes the presumption of guilt when there is merely proof of damage. The insurer has the burden of proving that the damage was produced before loading if he wants to exonerate himself from liability.

c) Deviation and insurance

The issue of whether a deviation from route exonerates the insurer from liability was the focal point of the *Supreme Court's decision of 17 September 1984*. The Judges of the three instances affirmed the liability of the insurer as the prolongation of the voyage was due to causes extraneous to the insured.

[10] Menendez, Aurelio: 'La noción de baratería en el seguro marítimo español, in *ADC*, 1970, pp. 221.

In order to understand on its proper terms the true extent of the decision, we must first examine the fact situation. The claimant (insured) obtained a maritime insurance policy for the transport of goods that were his property, traveling on his own account and at his own risk and was also the holder of the bills of lading. The merchandise was lost when the vessel sank at the entrance of the port of Cotonu (Republic of Benin). Note that the port of destination was Burutu (Nigeria), where the vessel should have arrived earlier. Nevertheless, the ship prolonged the voyage to the place where the loss occurred. The insurance company alleged in its defense that the insured had voluntarily prolonged the voyage, without the consent of the insurer, and that this constituted a broadening of the risk outside the scope of coverage of the insurance policy.

The decision has two fundamental points. First, a prolongation of the voyage is equal to a deviation from route. Second, both deviation and prolongation for causes extraneous to the insured do not exonerate the insurer from liability. In other words, the spatial scope of the coverage is automatically broadened, unless this amplification is willfully done by the insured.[11] This is, at least, the interpretation of article 756, 3d Commercial Code.[12]

5. MARITIME ACCIDENTS: COLLISION

The *Supreme Court's 13 June 1984* decision faced the issue of liability for collision. The Spanish vessel '*Chaparrudo*' was hit and sank by the Soviet vessel '*Morshank*'. At the time of the collision, the vessel that was struck worked as a pair with the fishing vessel '*Molares Alvarez*', which, although it did not suffer material damage, had to be refurbished in order to be able to work alone (without the aid of the vessel that was hit). The Spanish shipowner claimed against the Soviet shipowner for the loss of the first vessel and for the expenses of the modification of the second vessel.

The Judge of First Instance dismissed the complaint, absolving the Soviet shipowner. On appeal, the Appeals Court reversed the first decision and ordered the respondent to pay damages and costs, but in a lower amount than that requested. Both the claimant and the respondent were dissatisfied and both appealed (recurso de casacion) to the Supreme Court. Both appeals were dismissed.

If we analyze this decision from the procedural angle, it is important to realize that in a final appeal, expert evidence that was already admitted by the lower courts is not considered valid.

[11] See Goñi, José Luis: '*La aplicación de la Ley de 1949 y la desviación de ruta* (Comentario a la Sentencia del Tribunal Supremo de 21 de junio de 1980), in *ADM*, vol. I, pp. 833.

[12] art. 756. 'No responderán los aseguradores de los daños y perjuicios que sobrevengan a las cosas aseguradas por cualquiera de las causas siguientes, aunque no se haya excluído en la póliza: ... 3° Prolongación de viaje a un puerto más remoto que el designado en el seguro'.

Additionally, if we examine the decision on its merits, the Court affirmed that the doctrine of tort liability is applicable to a culpable collision. The vessel at fault is responsible for all of the 'damages' and 'costs' that result to third parties. The claim does not affect the owner or holder of the maritime company. Here, the costs of modification were a consequence of the collision, and the owner of the navigation company must be indemnified.[13]

III. Bibliography

Studies of maritime law continue to progress in Spain without interruption.

a) MONOGRAPHS

Juan Hernandez Marti, *Contrato de transporte maritimo de mercancías*, Valencia, 1984, pp. 206. This is a well written book that systematically discusses the legal discipline of maritime transport according to the Commercial Code, the Law of 1949, the Hague-Visby Rules and the Hamburg Convention of 1978.

b) ARTICLES

It is sufficient to mention the publication of *ANUARIO DE DERECHO MARITIMO*, vol. III, Barcelona (Libreria Bosch), 1984. The Yearbook has maintained its former structure and is a valuable source of information. Supervision and editing is under the care of Professor Ignacio Arroyo.

[13] Arroyo, Ignacio: '*Convenios Internacionales y derecho interno* (Especial referencia a la responsabilidad por abordaje)', *ADM* vol. II, pp. 15.

SWEDEN

Hugo Tiberg

Professor of Law at the University of Stockholm

RECENT DEVELOPMENTS IN THE SWEDISH MARITIME LAW

Legislation

The Swedish Parliament will often enact widely phrased 'frame' legislation in which the Government is frequently authorised to provide further details and to sub-delegate technical matters to a subordinate agency such as the National Authority for Shipping and Navigation. Under such powers that Authority each year issues a large number of regulations relevant to shipping. These often have mainly local interest, but the particularly wide delegation in the Government's *Pilotage* Ordinance (1982: 569) and the correspondingly wide coverage of the Authority's Pilotage Regulation (Authority's number 1985: 5) makes these provisions worthy of special notice.

The Regulation concerns all use of pilots in Swedish waters except the Trollhätte Canal and lake Vänern, where pilotage is confided to a special organization. Pilotage according to the Regulation refers to assistance by pilots in particular fairways, and under the Ordinance such pilotage is a State monopoly. Pilots can however also be used outside the special fairways, and under the Regulation foreign pilots properly licenced by states bordering the Baltic and the North Sea can be used in passage through the territorial sea, with a certain limitation for the Sound and Kattegatt. Swedish pilots are compulsory in interior waters according to a graded system, in which ships are divided according to cargoes, sizes and safety standards (double bottom ships being a special category), and where the requirements also vary for the different areas.

The Government has issued two ordinances intended to implement new provisions in the Maritime Code relating to the setting up of *limitation funds* for ships making use of their right to limit their liability – a procedure which is obligatory under section 6 of the Oil Liability Act and optional under section 240 of the Maritime Code.

Judicial decisions

The following account includes mainly cases published in the Scandinavian Maritime Cases (Nordiske Domme, ND), but also some which are not or not yet published. I have included some decisions of the sole Swedish Average Adjuster, who occupies an official position comparable to that of a court of law. The Adjuster decides not only General Average problems but other litigation concerning Marine Insurance as well.

Reported judgments below are final unless otherwise stated.

SHIPS AND RIGHTS IN SHIPS

According to section 248 of the Maritime Code a *maritime lien* is lost after one year unless before this the ship is arrested and such arrest leads to the sale of the vessel. However, for the arrest of a ship or other property the Code of Procedure requires a showing of danger that the debtor will avoid paying his debt by absconding, dissipating property or otherwise.

In *ND* 1982 p. 23 *SAILBOAT SWEDMARC 7*, a salvor claimed arrest for the sole purpose of avoiding the time-bar of his maritime lien. The Appeal Court of West Sweden agreed with the Gothenburg City Court that this was no valid ground for arrest.

It is fitting to remark that the requirement in the Procedural Code is manifestly out of harmony with the lien time-bar rule and with the 1967 Lien Convention. But a tendency to a niggardly treatment of maritime lienors is apparent in other cases too, especially in a recent decision (*5th*) *ö* 376/85 *SAILBOAT LINNEA by the Appeal Court of Skåne and Blekinge*, in which an owner's unauthorised repossession of a salved vessel was considered insufficient cause for arrest of the vessel.

PERSONNEL

In the Stockholm City Court decision (*8th div*) *DB 11/1985*, the master and mate of the passenger vessel *LINDBLAD POLARIS* were fined for *using the coast traffic zone* along the French Channel coast *instead of the traffic separation lane*. The accused had pleaded unclarity of the rules, but the court said that if they considered the rules unclear they ought to have consulted the French authorities per VHF.

In another *Stockholm City Court decision*, (*8th*) *DB 9/1983*, a ship had been unable, due to hard wind, to moore close to the quay so as to use the normal gangway, and boarding was therefore effected by means of an aluminium ladder. When the master returned from a restaurant with two girls of the crew and a visitor, the latter when climbing on board tried to give one of the girls a 'friendly pat on the back' but lost his balance and drowned. The master was charged with *negligence in keeping the vessel seaworthy*, but the court considered that the manner of boarding was the best under the circumstances, and as the first mate and the seamen's safety representative had agreed, safety measures such as nets under the ladder were impracticable. The master was acquitted.

In the *Gothenburg City Court decision (2nd div) DT 223/1984*, the Swedish Seamen's Union blockaded a Panama registered ship in the port of Norrköping in order to raise the pay of some Polish seamen on board to meet ITF standards. Under pressure of the blockade the shipowners signed a collective agreement as well as individual labour contracts incorporating the terms of the so-called *ITF agreement*. The owner refused to live up to these terms, and a new blockade ensued when the ship was later at Hälsingborg, from which she escaped at night while negotiations were in progress. The Union sued the shipowners for non-performance of the contract. The owners responded that the contract was void.

The court first determined that, although there was some evidence of Swedish interests in the ship, Panamanian law was applicable as being the law of the flag, and the fact that the lien claimed for the seamen was subject to Swedish law was irrelevant especially since there was no Swedish protection interest. In Panamanian law a contract induced by intimidation such as the present one was void, and furthermore an antecedent labour contract could be changed only by a collective agreement and by the mutual consent of those concerned. That in this case the intimidation was a recognized measure in a Swedish labour conflict did not affect this, and the Panamanian rules were not manifestly contrary to Swedish public policy. The Union's claim failed.

The judgment is not final, and an appeal is pending before the Appeal Court of West Sweden.

CARRIAGE OF GOODS BY SEA

In *ND* 1983, p. 105 *INGA* the Appeal Court for West Sweden considered the validity of an *arbitration clause*. An oil carriage agreement contained a reference to the terms of the Exxonvoy 69 charterparty, and the bill of lading – in the charterer's hands – referred to the 'charterparty' without any date or other individualising factor. The Exxonvoy charter contains a clause providing for arbitration in 'London/New York (strike out one)'. The City Court considered that this excluded its jurisdiction, but the Appeal Court reversed, on the ground that although it might be deduced that London would be the intended place of arbitration, there is a general interest in arbitration clauses being clear, and in the case at bar the claim was subject to a one-year time-bar which could easily be surpassed since arbitrators in London or New york might well consider themselves incompetent.

COLLISIONS AND OTHER DAMAGE TO SHIPS

The *Svea Appeal Court decision* (*15th div*) *DT 48/1984 VINIA-RUTHERSAND*, concerning a *fog collision* between a Swedish wine carrier and a German bulk ship, turns largely on the credibility of witnesses. The collision was witnessed on the radar of a nearby training ship, but the reports of the three ships were in conflict, and the court in evaluating them attached particular importance to the fact that *Vinia* alone had plotted her radar course and had a plotting diagram of this. The immediate cause of the collision was that *Ruthersand* mistaking *Vinia* for another ship seen on the radar veered starboard into meeting *Vinia*, while *Vinia* though prevented by the other ship from veering starboard, kept her speed too long. In substance the court held that (1) it was a fault of both the colliding vessels to proceed through the fog at full or nearly full speed (rules 6 and 19), (2) that *Vinia* being the first to notice the other should have slowed down earlier than she did, (3) that the radar watch on *Ruthersand* was insufficient under rules 5 and 7B, no plotting being performed, and that on the balance of these considerations the ships were equally to blame.

The *Stockholms City Court's decision* (*8th*) *DT 51/1985 JOSÉ MARTI* is a follower to the Supreme Court TSESIS decision discussed in the foregoing Spanish issue of this yearbook. The case concerns shipowner liability for *oil pollution* and State liability for *misleading charts* and other deficient navigational aids. The Soviet tanker *José Marti* under passage through the Stockholm Archipelago struck an 11 m shoal which caused damage to the vessel and a considerable oil spill. The State sued the shipowner for cleaning costs, and the shipowner sued the State for the damage to the ship.

Under the Oil Liability Act and Convention the shipowner bears strict liability for oil pollution from the ship with an exception, under section 3, for i.a. the State's failure to properly maintain navigational aids. According to the TSESIS decision the State conceded that charts were a navigational aid in the sense of the proviso but denied that there had been negligence.

The situation differed from the TSESIS case in that the chart was not inaccurate, but at the most misleading. The 11 metre shoal was close outside the ten-metre curve but between an 18 and a 19 metre sounding on the chart, and the owners contended that these figures were representative of the depths in the vicinity so that the navigator had a right to assume that the bottom sloped steeply outside the ten-metre curve to a depth of this order. The court denied that this was a proper way to read a chart, and denying also certain other allegations of negligence on the State's part concluded that the shipowner was solely liable for the oil pollution. As concerned the ship damage, however, the Court considered that when in 1961 the normative depth of the channel had been increased to 12 metres, the charting authorities, who were at the time aware of the 11-metre shoal, should have marked it on the chart to forestall the rather likely mistake that those responsible for the conduct of the *José Marti* had committed in this case.

This failure to mark the shoal was relevant to the ship damage question and rendered the State liable for that damage to the extent of one quarter.

An appeal is pending before the Svea Appeal Court.

SALVAGE

In the *Stockholm City Court decision* (*8th*) *DT 65/1985 KARLSHAMN*, the Soviet submarine U-137 had illicitly entered into a Swedish military zone in interior waters and had there grounded on a shoal. Since the Russians refused to employ any but Russian salvage ships, the Swedish military authorities decided to drag the vessel off the shoal and for that purpose engaged the tug *Karlshamn*, belonging to the nearby city of Karlshamn. In its final bill to the Soviet State, Sweden claimed certain compensation for costs among which were towage costs at the standard *towage* tariff. But the City as owner of the tug claimed *salvage* reward from the State, on the alternative grounds that the State had ordered a salvage service which the City had performed and that the State had neglected a duty it owed to the City of claiming salvage from the Soviet State.

The court found that the submarine had been unable to get off without assistance, that the waters in the area are difficult to navigate, that the shoal was exposed to SW winds, and that the salvage was performed in very bad weather with tempestuous winds and extremely low water, and also that in spite of the submarine's very strong build, there was an imminent risk of damage to the inner hull and of leakage of battery acid. The court further observed that the Soviet State was in no particular situation as far as salvage was concerned and that the Swedish navy's duty under international law to turn it away did not affect or mitigate any claim for salvage. Since the State had ordered an operation which had all the outward characteristics of salvage, it must pay salvage money.

The decision has been appealed to the Svea Appeal Court.

ND 1982 p. 23 and the unreported decision ö 376/85 by the Appeal Court of Skåne and Blekinge (5th) have been considered above under Ships and rights in ships.

PROCEDURE AND FORUM

Section 336 subsection 1 provides that special *Maritime Courts* have exclusive jurisdiction over litigation and indictments concerning matters dealt with by the Maritime Code. In *ND* 1982 p. 21 the *Supreme Court of Sweden* determined that a contractual claim for loss of cargo by a shipping company against a terminal company was not of this nature, even though maritime rules might affect the decision. Similarly, to the author's knowledge, the Karlshamn City Court, which is not a maritime court, has properly taken up a case concerning the City's possible liability for damage to a vessel through grounding on an unmarked shoal in the port; that case was, however, never decided but settled out of court.

ND 1983 p. 106 concerning the validity of an arbitration clause has been considered above, under Carriage of goods by sea.

MARINE INSURANCE

The disaster of the Greek ship *Deifovos*, which sunk outside Narvik in Norway because of unseaworthiness and the shifting of her cargo of iron ore concentrate has given rise to a number of procedures in different countries. In *ND* 1982 p. 108 the Swedish Average Adjuster considered the effect of a policy covering the time charterer's interest described as 'insured value up to' a certain amount. The insured claimed that this was a *valued policy*, under which the insurer must pay the indicated value unless proved to be grossly in excess of the real loss, while the insurer said it was an open policy with a stated limit. The Adjuster concluded that the insurer ought to have expressed the matter more clearly and that the policy should therefore be considered as a valued one.

The dispute was later settled amicably by the parties.

ND 1983 p. 46 *Bristol* concerns the *coverage of inventory* under a fishing vessel's policy. The policy purported to cover 'boats, implements or other objects of relatively lasting nature which are generally used on ships of the kind or in the trade in question'. This is similar to the coverage of the Marine Insurance Plan though without the latter's exception for fishing appliances, and the Average Adjuster took this as an indication that this particular policy covered fishing appliances.

A boat owner claimed compensation under a motorboat insurance on the ground that his engine had overheated through '*collision*', the water intake having become clogged by seaweed, and 'collision' being a covered circumstance under the policy. The insurer challenged the characterisation of the incident as a 'collision' and also pleaded an exemption for damage due to overheating, which under the policy was payable only if caused by an accident expressly covered, i.e. grounding, collision (in a real sense), stranding, capsizing or sinking.

In *ND* 1983 p. 58 the Average Adjuster agreed with the insurer that the incident was excepted under the conditions. Concerning the 'collision' character of the incident, the Adjuster drew attention to a decision by a previous Adjuster in which overheating caused by a plastic bag clogging the water intake was denied the character of a 'collision'. The Adjuster pointed out that the earlier decision had met with criticism, and that he himself might be prepared to regard some cases of contact with floating objects as having such a sudden and unforeseen character that they could be properly assimilated to stranding cases and compensated as such.

ND 1983 *p.* 41 *Tribel* concerns *short delivery* of a cargo of steel plate cuttings, insured under English Institute Cargo Clauses (FPA) 1963 with the additional clause: 'Incl. theft, pilferage and *non-delivery*, shortage and/or loss in excess of one percent franchise (always deductible)'. It appeared that the shortage was due to misdelivery to another party, who refused to surrender the surplus alleging lack of quality.

The Average Adjuster said that according to principles recognized in English law 'non-delivery' in connection with theft and pilferage is not a particular risk but merely means that the underwriter has the burden of proving that the loss does not depend on theft/pilferage. Moreover, this part of the clause refers only to loss of an entire cargo. On the other hand 'shortage' is applicable and applies to quantity losses, and the underwriter must therefore pay for shortage in excess of 1%.

NAVIGABLE WATERS

The *Supreme Court decision of the 13 March 1984 No. DB7* reported in last year's issue of the Spanish yearbook has now appeared in the official reports *NJA* 1984 on p. 236. However, the decision has been challenged on several grounds in a similar later case concerning three joint actions against Danish citizens who had unwittingly brought their boats into Swedish *semi-restricted* areas permissible for foreigners but not for their boats. The Karlshamn City Court in its judgment DB 9/1985 in a decision which appears to be contrary to the preceding precedent acquitted all the accused, but an appeal has been brought to the Appeal Court for Skåne and Blekinge, and judgment upon that Appeal is presently pending.

Bibliography

Kurt Grönfors, *Inledning till transporträtten* (1984) is a short (100 pages) introduction to the law of transportation intended for students. It covers some general transport principles, the carrier's liability for loss and damage to goods, documents used for general cargo, some notes on insurance and a brief survey of certain other problems.

Maritime Fraud (1984) is a collective volume in English, presenting the speeches of the rapporteurs at the 5th Axel Johnson Colloquium on Maritime Law held at Hässelby in 1982. Authors are Eric Ellen from London, Lars Gorton, Lorenz Zetterman and Hugo Tiberg from Stockholm, Hans Peter Michelet and Hans B. Thomsen from Oslo, Jan Schultsz from Amsterdam and Kurt Grönfors (editor) from Göteborg, and the articles cover a wide range of subjects concerning the disturbing accrescence of the rather varying crimes affecting maritime transport which are commonly described as Maritime Frauds.

Marius (Oslo) continues to publish short articles on maritime subjects in a simple form. Swedish articles of specific interest might be Deutgen's article on straight bills of lading (1985) and Aspström/Karlsson's article on salvage and wreck removal (1983).

The *Göteborg Law Institution's Series* publishes occasional articles on maritime law in a similarly simplified form. Nr 6 by Robert Hallberg (1985) concerns the importance of ship classification for the concept of seaworthiness.

Svensk Juristtidning (*Swedish Law Journal*, Stockholm) 1982–1985 contains an extended discussion of immunity problems in connection with the intrusion of the Soviet submarine U137 into Swedish waters. Participants have been Gustaf Petrén 1982 p. 647 and 1984 p. 68, Carl Axel Petri 1983 p. 132, Rolf Lindholm 1984 p. 321 and 1985 p. 333, Ove Bring 1985 p. 68, Anders Axlund 1985 p. 72, Ingrid Delupis 1985 p. 162 and also in American Journal of International Law 1984 p. 53.

UNITED KINGDOM

STEVEN J. HAZELWOOD

Lecturer in Law and Member of the Centre for Maritime Law and Policy, UWIST, Cardiff

A BRIEF REVIEW OF DEVELOPMENTS IN THE LAW OF SHIPPING OF THE UNITED KINGDOM 1983–84

Case law

(a) 'ACTUAL FAULT OR PRIVITY' SUCH AS TO DEPRIVE A SHIPOWNER OF THE RIGHT TO LIMIT LIABILITY

In the case of The '*Marion*',[1] the House of Lords delivered a judgment of great interest to shipowners and their legal advisers and particularly their P. and I. Clubs, when refusing a shipowner the right to limit liability under the Merchant Shipping Act, 1984 (as amended by Merchant Shipping (Liability of Shipowners and Others) Act, 1958).[2]

In March 1977, the '*Marion*', owned by the plaintiff and managed by the company 'F.M.S.L.' came to anchor off the coast of North-East England. When the vessel attempted to weigh anchor it was unable to do so because she had fouled a pipeline. It transpired that this pipeline connected a mainland terminal to the Ekofisk Oil Field, one of the most productive oil fields in the North Sea. The owners of the pipeline and others claimed for the damage to the pipeline in a figure exceeding U.S.$25m. The total liability of the plaintiffs if able to limit their liability would have been in an amount of approximately U.S.$950,000. It was not surprising, therefore, that the owners should seek a decree entitling them to limit their liability. The issue between the parties turned on whether the plaintiffs, in order to obtain a decree limiting their liability, could establish that the damage to the

[1] [1984] 2 *Lloyd's Rep*. 1.

[2] These statutes are consistent with the Convention Relating to the Limitation of Liability of Owners of Seagoing Ships, 1957.

pipeline occurred without their actual fault or privity under the relevant Acts of 1894 and 1958.[3]

The plaintiffs admitted that the damage had been caused partly by the negligence of the Master of the '*Marion*' in anchoring too close to the pipeline by reason of the fact that he was not aware of its existence because he was using a chart published in 1953 with corrections up to 1959; that is, long before the exploitation of oil in the North Sea and the laying of pipelines. Up-to-date charts did mark the position of pipelines and such a chart was available in the chartroom of the '*Marion*' but never referred to. Also the managing director of the ship's manager-operator had failed to ensure that there was brought to his notice a Safety Inspection Report from the Liberian Marine Inspectorate of 1976 which stated that navigational charts for trade of the vessel had been omitted for several years.

The Court was required to decide three issues. First, what action should have been taken by 'F.M.S.L.' as reasonably prudent ship managers to ensure that the vessel was supplied with up-to-date charts? Secondly, could the owners establish that any failure on their part was not directly responsible for the casualty? Thirdly, if it were established that there was fault on the part of 'F.M.S.L.' was that fault a fault for which the company was liable on the basis of respondant superior or was it the fault of somebody for whom the company was liable because his actions could be regarded as the actions of the company itself.

In the court of first instance, the Admiralty judge, Sheen, J., decided that the casualty took place without the actual fault or privity of the plaintiffs and that they were, therefore, entitled to a decree of limitation of liability.[4] The Court of Appeal disagreed with this finding and held that the plaintiffs had not established that the casualty was caused without their actual fault or privity.[5] The matter came to be finally resolved by the House of Lords and their decision has caused some surprise and concern to shipowners, ships' masters, P. and I. Clubs and shipping lawyers.

The House of Lords decided, first, that since the case of the 'England'[6] it was no longer sufficient for shipowners to merely appoint a competent

[3] Section 503 of the Merchant Shipping Act, 1894, as amended by the Merchant Shipping (Liability of Shipowners and Others) Act, 1958, Section 2(1), provides, as far as relevant, as follows:

> 'The owners of a ship British or foreign, shall not where . . . any of the following occurrences take place without their actual fault or privity . . . (d) where any loss or damage is caused to any property . . . or any rights are infringed through the act or omission of any person (whether on board the ship or not) in the navigation or management of the ship . . . or through any other act or omission of any person on board the ship . . . be liable in damages beyond the following amounts . . . (ii) in respect of such loss damage or infringement as is mentioned in paragraph . . . (d) of this subsection . . . an aggregate amount equivalent to 1000 gold francs for each ton of their ship's tonnage.'

[4] [1984] 2 *Lloyd's Rep*. 52.

[5] [1983] 2 *Lloyd's Rep*. 156.

[6] [1973] 1 *Lloyd's Rep*. 373.

master and thereafter leave all questions of safe navigation, including obtaining and observing up-to-date charts, to the master and then to claim that they had discharged their responsibility.[7] Their Lordships decided that it was the duty of the managing directory of 'F.M.S.L.', to whom management of the vessel had been wholly delegated, to ensure that he or one of his staff exercised an adequate degree of supervision of the master in obtaining and keeping up-to-date charts and the managing director had failed to perform this duty. Moreover, such a failure to have a system of supervision constituted actual fault of the plaintiffs.[8] Secondly, it was decided that the managing director was also at fault in failing to ensure that he was kept informed of developments such as the Liberian Report.[9] In consequence there were two elements of actual fault of the plaintiffs and they were not, therefore, entitled to a decree of limitation of liability.[10]

(b) WHETHER CONSIGNEES WERE PARTIES TO A CONTRACT IN THE BILL OF LADING AND, THEREFORE, LIABLE FOR DEMURRAGE

In the case of the '*Miramar*',[11] the House of Lords was required to consider incorporation clauses in a bill of lading as related to the Exxonvoy 1969 charter party. In 1980 the plaintiffs had voyage chartered their vessel to the charterers on the terms of the Exxonvoy form which provided for, inter alia, laytime and demurrage. A cargo of diesel oil was shipped on the vessel covered by a bill of lading prepared on the form stipulated for use in conjunction with the Exxonvoy charter. The bill of lading provided that freight was payable as per charter-party and contained the following clause:

> 'This shipment is carried under and pursuant to the terms of the Charter dated 19 May 1980, between [the plaintiffs] and [the charterers] . . . Charterer and all terms whatsoever of the said charter . . . apply to and govern the rights of the parties concerned in this shipment.'

In attempts to discharge the diesel oil substantial demurrage became due under the charter. The plaintiff owners made demands that this should be paid by the charterers or by the defendant consignees. The plaintiffs purported to exercise a lien by withholding delivery to shore tanks until an agreement between the plaintiffs and defendants was reached when delivery was eventually made.

[7] [1984] 2 *Lloyd's Rep.* 1 at page 4, see also, t''*Norman*' [1960] 1 *Lloyd's Rep.* 1; The '*Lady Gwendolen*' [1965] 1 *Lloyd's Rep.* 335.

[8] [1984] 2 *Lloyd's Rep.* 1 at page 7.

[9] ibid. at page 8.

[10] ibid., at pages 8 and 9.

[11] Miramar Maritime Corporation v. Holborn Oil Trading Ltd. (The '*Miramar*') [1984] 2 Lloyd's Rep. 129.

The issues before the court were as follows: (a) were the consignees personally liable, as parties to the contract contained in the bill of lading for demurrage computed in accordance with the charter? (b) if the plaintiffs had no contractual claim against the defendants were they nevertheless entitled to exercise a lien on the cargo in respect of the demurrage under the charter? (c) were the plaintiffs entitled to recover either by virtue of a direct contractual right or through the medium of the lien clause and the agreement to discharge between the plaintiffs and defendants? At first instance, Mustill, J. held that the charterers alone were liable for the demurrage. The Court of Appeal agreed with this view of affairs. The House of Lords confirmed the decisions of the lower courts and reached the following conclusions. Firstly, in the vast majority of clauses in the charter there were express references to contractual rights or obligations of 'the charterers' under that description and there was no reason in business to include within that expression the terms 'the consignee' or 'holder of a bill of lading' and that would be so even if the whole of the Exxonvoy charter form had been set out verbatim in the bill of lading.[12] Secondly, every reference to 'the charterer' by that designation in the Exxonvoy charter would make perfectly good sense when incorporated verbatim in the bill of lading if it meant the person designated as 'the charterer' in the charter-party and no one else.[13] Finally, the House of Lords decided that where in a bill of lading there was included a clause which purported to incorporate the terms of a specified charter-party, there was not any rule of construction that clauses in that charter-party which were directly relevant to the shipment, carriage or delivery of the goods, and imposed obligations upon the 'charterer' under that designation, were presumed to be incorporated in the bill of lading with the substitution of or inclusion in the designated 'charterer', the terms 'consignee of the cargo' or 'bill of lading holder'.[14]

(c) THE JURISDICTION OF THE ENGLISH ADMIRALTY COURT IN THE FACE OF A MORE NATURAL FORUM

In the case of the '*Abidin Daver*'[15] the House of Lords was called upon to decide whether the English Admiralty Court or the Turkish Courts was the more appropriate forum for hearing an action in respect of a collision in the Bosphorus. The judgments delivered by their Lordships provide an informative guide as to the considerations which should be used in deciding whether or not a case should be heard in the English Admiralty Court when the parties and the locus in quo have no geographical links with England.

Following a collision between the plaintiff's vessel and defendant's vessel

[12] ibid., at pages 132–134.
[13] ibid., at pages 134.
[14] ibid., pages 134, 5.
[15] [1984] 1 *Lloyd's Rep.* 339.

both parties claimed the other was at fault and commenced proceedings; the defendants applied to the Sariyer District Court for the detention of the plaintiff's vessel and commenced proceedings in the Turkish Court claiming damages. Later the plaintiffs issued a writ in England which was served on a sister-ship of the defendant's vessel. The defendants applied for a stay of those proceedings on the ground that there was another jurisdiction which was clearly more appropriate than England for the trial of the action. At first instance, the Admiralty Judge, Sheen, J. decided that the action between the parties could be much more conveniently tried in the District Court of Sariyer and that the plaintiffs would not suffer any juridicial disadvantage from such a trial and therefore justice demanded that the action in England should be stayed. The Court of Appeal took a different view and decided that if the English action was stayed the plaintiffs would be deprived of the juridical advantage of pursuing their claim here as plaintiffs in the English Admiralty Court and having control of the action rather than merely counterclaiming as defendants in Turkey and the plaintiffs should, therefore, be allowed to come to this country to resolve their dispute.

The House of Lords reinstated the first instance decision. It was decided that on the evidence not only was Turkey the country with which the claim had its closest connections, but also that the natural and appropriate forum from the point of view of convenience and expense was also Turkey.[16] Furthermore, the House of Lords decided that Sheen, J. had correctly considered the principles according to which he was obliged to exercise his discretion and had taken into account all the correct considerations and had not taken into account any wrong matters, indeed his decision was correct and was arrived at by applying the correct principles.[17]

Bibliography

The following texts are only a few of the titles to have appeared during the period of 1983–84 which are of interest to both the student and practitioner of shipping law. Firstly, a new work called '*Maritime Law of Salvage*' was published by Stevens & Son. The author of this very readable and informative work is one of England's leading barristers, Mr. Geoffrey Brice Q.C. In addition to being one of Her Majesty's Counsel, Mr. Brice is also a Member of the Panel of Lloyd's Salvage Arbitrators and is, therefore, highly qualified to offer his views on the law of salvage. In a little over 500 pages the book deals with conceptual and practical aspects of salvage and includes an interesting chapter on the Lloyd's Form of Arbitration. The

[16] ibid., at page 346, per Lord Diplock.

[17] ibid., at pages 346 (per Lord Keith of Kinkel), 349, 50 (per Lord Brandon), and 352, 3 (per Lord Templeman).

work contains Appendices with useful documentation such as all relevant statutes, conventions and a copy of the Lloyd's *Open Form of Salvage*, 1980. The book is an essential text to anyone wishing to understand the modern law of salvage.

Another new text which appeared during this period is '*Butterworth's Insurance Law Handbook*' edited by the industrious and prolific Professor E.R. Hardy Ivamy and published by Butterworths. The work contains no commentary, but is a compilation of relevant statutes, statutory instruments and other materials relating to the whole area of insurance law. Although much of this handbook may not be of direct interest to shipping lawyers it does contain all relevant provisions in the area of marine insurance including all five Lloyd's Acts from 1871 to 1982. In addition the following statutes are contained in the book: Marine Insurance (Gambling Policies) Act 1909, Third Parties (Rights against Insurers) Act 1930, Marine and Aviation Insurance (War Risks) Act 1952, Merchant Shipping (Oil Pollution) Act 1971, Insurance Companies Act 1982. To have all statutes relevant to English marine insurance in one place with a copios index is of great utility.

Other works published during the year include the following: '*Time Barred Actions*', by Kaj Pineus and Hans G. Röhreke which is based on information supplied by the Comité Maritime International and provides an up-to-date account of the prescription and limitation periods in over 40 countries. The same authors have written '*Limited Liability in Collision Cases*' which provides an account of the extent to which a shipowner can limit his liability for collision damages under whichever limitation convention applies. These two works are published by Lloyd's of London Press Ltd. who also published the following works of interest: '*Shipbrokers' Manual, Volume 1*' by the Institute of Chartered Shipbrokers, London; '*Marine Claims Handbook*' (4th Edition) by N.G. Hudson; '*Shipbroking and Chartering Practice*' (2nd Edition) by R. Ihre *et al.*

Others

In 1983 a revision took place in one of the most popular sets of standard towage conditions – The United Kingdom Standard Conditions for Towage and Other Services (1974). The new 'U.K. Standard Conditions for Towage and Other Services (Revised 1983)' do not differ markedly from the older form except as to a major change in Clause 4. Under the 1974 version it was provided under Clause 4 (a)(iii) that the Tugowner would not be responsible for or be liable for 'any personal injury or loss of life howsoever and wheresoever caused including personal injury or loss of life of the master and/or crew of... and/or any person on board the tug or tender'. This provision is omitted from the 1983 version of the Conditions which means that Tugowners cannot now exclude their liability for loss of life or personal injury. The old conditions would have conflicted with the provisions of the

English statute called the Unfair Contract Terms Act 1977 which provides that any term in a contract which allows a party to the contract to avoid liability in respect of loss of life or personal injury is unfair and consequently void. The new Clause 4 in its entirety provides as follows:

'4. Whilst towing, or whilst at the request, either expressed or implied, of the Hirer rendering any service of whatsoever nature other than towing:-

(a) The Tugowner shall not (except as provided in Clauses 4(c) and (e) hereof) be responsible for or be liable for

(i) damage of any description done by or to the tug or tender; or done by or to the Hirer's vessel or done by or to any cargo or other thing on board or being loaded on board or intended to be loaded on board the Hirer's vessel or the tug or tender or to or by any other object of property.

or

(ii) loss of the tug or tender or the Hirer's vessel or of any cargo or other thing on board or being loaded on board or intended to be loaded on board the Hirer's vessel or the tug or tender or any other object or property:

or

(iii) any claim by a person not a party to this agreement for loss or damage of any description whatsoever:

arising from any cause whatsoever, including (without prejudice to the generality of the foregoing) negligence at any time of the Tugowner his servants or agents, unseaworthiness, unfitness or breakdown of the tug or tender; its machinery, boilers, towing gear, equipment, lines, ropes or wires, lack of fuel, stores, speed or otherwise and

(b) The Hirer shall (except as provided in Clauses 4(c) and (e)) be responsible for, pay for and indemnify the Tugowner against and in respect of any loss or damage and any claims of whatsoever nature of howsoever arising or caused, whether covered by the provisions of Clause 4(a) hereof or not, suffered by or made against the Tugowner and which shall include, without prejudice to the generality of the foregoing, any loss of or damage to the tug or tender of any property of the Tugowner even if the same arises from or is caused by the negligence of the Tugowner his servants or agents.

(c) The provisions of Clauses 4(a) and 4(b) hereof shall not be applicable in respect of any claims which arise in any of the following circumstances:-

(i) All claims which the Hirer shall prove to have resulted directly and solely from the personal failure of the Tugowner to exercise reasonable care to make the tug or tender seaworthy for navigation at the commencement of the towing or other service. For the purpose of this Clause the Tugowner's personal responsibility for exercising reasonable care shall be construed as relating only to the person or persons having the ultimate control and chief management of the Tugowner's business and to any servant (excluding the officers and crew of any tug or tender) to whom the Tugowner has specifically delegated the particular duty of exercising reasonable care and shall not include any other servant of the Tugowner or any agent or independent contractor employed by the Tugowner.

(ii) All claims which arise when the tug or tender, although towing or rendering some service other than towing, is not in a position of proximity or risk to or from the Hirer's vessel or any other craft attending the Hirer's vessel and is detached from and safely clear of any ropes, lines, wire cables or moorings associated with the Hirer's vessel. Provided always that, notwithstanding the foregoing, the provisions of Clauses 4(a) and 4(b) shall be fully applicable in respect of all claims which arise at any time when the tug or tender is at the request, whether express or implied, of the Hirer, his servants or his agents, carrying persons or property of whatsoever description (in addition to the Officers and crew and usual equipment of the tug or tender) and which are wholly or partly caused by or arise out of the presence on board of such persons or property or which arise at anytime when the tug or tender is proceeding to or from the Hirer's vessel in hazardous conditions or circumstances.

(d) Notwithstanding anything hereinbefore contained, the Tugowner shall under no circumstances whatsoever be responsible for or be liable for any loss or damage caused by or contributed to or arising out of any delay or detention of the Hirer's vessel or of the cargo on board or being loaded on board or intended to be loaded on board the Hirer's vessel or of any other object or property or of any person, or any consequence thereof, whether or not the same shall be caused or arise whilst towing or whilst at the request, either express or implied, of the Hirer rendering any service of whatsoever nature other than towing or at any other time whether before during or after the making of this agreement.

(e) Notwithstanding anything contained in Clauses 4(a) and (b) hereof the liability of the Tugowner for death or personal injury resulting from negligence is not excluded or restricted thereby.'

USA

JOHN D. KIMBALL*

Partner, Healy & Baillie, New York (N.Y). Case Editor, Journal of Maritime Law and Commerce

NEW DEVELOPMENTS IN UNITED STATES MARITIME LAW 1984

I. Legislation

The Shipping Act of 1984[1] was signed into law by President Reagan on 20 March 1984 and significantly reduced the regulation of carriers under United States law. The express purposes of the Act are to minimize government intervention and regulatory costs; to provide an efficient and economic system of ocean transport; and to encourage the development of an economically sound United States flag liner fleet.[2] Among other things, the Act provides antitrust immunity for the collective setting of rates and other collective actions by carriers, and modifies the government review procedure for multicarrier agreements.[3]

The Longshoremen's and Harbor Workers' Compensation Act[4] was comprehensively amended in 1984. Among other things, the amendments limit the jurisdiction of the Act by extending the list of exempted occupations; clarify the law relating to third-party liability of contractors; permit certain claims of indemnity against LHWCA employees; provide compensation to victims of occupational disease; and provide for the creation of a special fund by employers and carriers to cover certain claims.[5]

* The author gratefully acknowledges the assistance of his associate, LeRoy Lambert, Esq., in the research of the cases discussed.

[1] Pub. L. No. 98–237, 98 Stat. 67, 46 U.S.C. §1701 *et seq*. The effective date of the Act was 18 June 1984.

[2] 46 U.S.C. §1701.

[3] For a detailed analysis of the Act, see J. McConnell, *The U.S. Shipping Act of 1984* (1985); Friedmann and Devierno, *The Shipping Act of 1984: The Shift from Government Regulation To Shipper Regulation*, 15 J. Mar. L. & Comm. 311 (1984).

[4] 33 U.S.C. §901 *et seq*.

[5] For a detailed summary of the amendments, see Report of Committee on Stevedoring and Terminal Operations, Maritime Law Assoc. of the United States reprinted in *The MLA Report* 8114 (Document No. 656, 1 February 1985).

II. Court decisions

(a) ADMIRALTY JURISDICTION

In 1982, the Supreme Court held that there was admiralty jurisdiction of claims arising from a collision between pleasure boats on navigable waters.[6] In 1984, two circuit courts of appeal extended this holding to include accidents involving a pleasure boat and a swimmer, emphasizing that navigation of a vessel now appears to be the crucial factor in determining the existence of admiralty jurisdiction.[7]

The Second Circuit re-affirmed a Supreme Court ruling from 1854[8] that admiralty jurisdiction does not extend to claims under steamship 'general agency' contracts, even if those contracts concern ocean shipping.[9] The Court stated that an overruling of the Supreme Court decision would be welcome, but held that this can be done only by the Supreme Court itself.[10]

(b) ARBITRATION

In New York, consolidated arbitrations are common between parties such as an owner, charterer and sub-charterer of the same vessel when disputes common to all parties exist. The power of the Court to compel consolidated arbitration in the absence of the consent of the parties had been in doubt, although decisions in the Second Circuit have leaned towards allowing consolidation in certain cases.[11] The Ninth Circuit declined to follow the Second Circuit on this issue and held that it had no authority under the United States Arbitration Act[12] to order consolidation without the consent of the parties involved.[13] Thus, there appears to be a split in two leading U.S. appellate Courts on this issue.

In a case involving the Convention for the Recognition and Enforcement of Arbitral Awards, the Second Circuit held that allowing post-award, pre-judgment interest was proper in a proceeding to confirm a London arbitration award, even though this was not part of the award itself.[14] The

[6] *Foremost Insurance Co. v. Richardson*, 457 U.S. 668, 1982 AMC 2253 (1982).

[7] *Oliver v. Hardesty*, 745 F.2d 317, 1985 AMC 630 (4th Cir. 1984); *Medina v. Perez*, 733 F.2d 627, 1985 AMC 627 (1st Cir. 1984).

[8] *Minturn v. Maynard*, 58 U.S. 477 (1854).

[9] *Peralta Shipping Corp. v. Smith & Johnson (Shipping) Corp.*, 739 F.2d 798, 1985 AMC 989 (2d Cir. 1984).

[10] 1985 AMC at 999.

[11] *See Compania Espanola de Petroleos, S.A. v. Nereus Shipping, S.A.*, 527 F.2d 966, 1975 AMC 2421 (2d Cir. 1975), *cert. denied*, 426 U.S. 936 (1976).

[12] 9 U.S.C. §§1–14.

[13] *Weyerhaeuser Co. v. Western Seas Shipping Co.*, 743 F.2d 635, 1985 AMC 30 (9th Cir. 1984).

[14] *Waterside Ocean Navigation Co. v. International Navigation Ltd.*, 737 F.2d 150, 1985 AMC 349 (2d Cir. 1984).

Court found that the English courts, had they been asked to confirm the award, would have awarded such interest. The Court saw no reason not to allow interest in view of the 'Convention's overriding goal of promoting the enforcement of awards.'[15]

The American rule as to attorney's fees, i.e., that each party bears its own attorney's costs, was affirmed in an arbitration pursuant to the arbitration clause of the commonly used New York Produce Exchange form.[16] The Panel awarded the prevailing party in the arbitration its attorney's fees; the losing party moved to vacate this portion of the award in district court. Finding that the clause does not provide on its face for such an award and that the proof of any custom to the contrary was insufficient, the court vacated the award of attorney's fees.[17]

(c) CARRIAGE OF GOODS BY SEA

The United States Carriage of Goods By Sea Act defines 'carrier' to include 'the owner or the charterer who enters into a contract of carriage with a shipper.[18] When a particular voyage involves a chain of charterers, it often is difficult to determine who is the COGSA carrier vis-à-vis the holder of a bill of lading. In *Dow Chemical Pacific Ltd. v. Rascator Maritime S.A.*,[19] the court took issue with cases holding that an expansive interpretation of COGSA was not justified and held that a more restrictive view was necessary. Accordingly, the court held that neither an intermediate time charterer nor the owner assumed any responsibility as a COGSA carrier vis-à-vis a bill of lading holder who had arranged for shipment with the last charterer in the chain.

Differences between the Fifth and Ninth Circuits arose over the burden of proof in cases involving the Fire Statute.[20] In *Westinghouse Electric Corp. v. M/V Leslie Lykes*,[21] the Fifth Circuit rejected the Ninth Circuit's view that the burden of proof is on the carrier to show that it exercised due diligence to provide a seaworthy ship as a precondition to invoking the fire exception. Instead, the shipper must prove that the fire was caused by 'design or neglect' of the owner.[22]

[15] 1985 AMC at 354. *See generally* Case Note, 16 J. Mar. & L. Comm. 126 (1985).

[16] *Sammi Line Co. v. Altemar Navegacion S.A.*, 1985 AMC 1790 (S.D.N.Y. 1985).

[17] *Id.* at 1791–92.

[18] 46 U.S.C. §1301(a).

[19] 594 F. Supp. 1490, 1985 AMC 523 (S.D.N.Y.) 1984.

[20] 46 U.S.C. §182.

[21] 734 F.2d 199, 1985 AMC 247 (5th Cir. 1984). *Compare Sunkist Growers, Inc. v. Adelaide Shipping Lines, Ltd.*, 603 F.2d 1327, 1979 AMC 2787 (9th Cir. 1979), *cert. denied* 444 U.S. 1012 (1980).

[22] 1985 AMC at 257.

(d) CONSTITUTIONALITY OF SUPPLEMENT RULES

Supplemental Rules B (maritime attachment) and C (maritime arrest) have weathered every constitutional attack at the appellate level during the past several years.[23] The First Circuit, in *Trans-Asiatic Oil, Ltd. v. Apex Oil Co.*,[24] became the most recent court to uphold the constitutionality of Rule B, concluding that due process claims should be reviewed 'in light of the process actually received, not the theoretical minimum under Rule B.'[25] In light of these decisions and amendments to the Rules, which became effective on 1 August 1985, this issue would appear to be finally settled and these traditional admiralty procedures may be resorted to without the threat of a long and expensive court battle over their constitutionality.

(e) DAMAGES

Requests for and awards of punitive damages, outside the traditional context of seamen's actions for maintenance and cure, are becoming more frequent in the United States. In *Protectus Alpha Navigation Co. v. North Pacific Grain Growers, Inc.*, the court awarded the plaintiff (in addition to $9,077,760 as compensatory damages for the loss of its ship) $500,000 in punitive damages, finding that the actions of the defendant's employees in casting off a burning ship from the vicinity of a grain elevator while firefighters were on board were 'unconscionable'.[26]

A frequent problem in non-admiralty cases is whether a plaintiff in a tort case may recover its 'economic loss', such as the loss of profits from the use of the product, even though there was no physical damage to other property. The traditional view is that such losses are not recoverable in tort. The issue has surfaced recently in admiralty in a number of circuits.[27]

The Ninth Circuit considered the problem in *Emerson G.M. Diesel, Inc. v. Alaskan Enterprise*.[28] The lower court held that a manufacturer of diesel engine component parts was strictly liable to a fishing vessel for damages ($254,000) due to an engine malfunction at sea. The damages were based on the cost of repairs and the loss of profits during the sixteen day wait for the

[23] *See generally* Culp, *Charting a New Course: Proposed Amendments to the Supplemental Rules for Admiralty Arrest and Attachment*, 15 J. Mar. L. & Comm. 353, 357–58 & nn.20–21 (1984); Schwartz, *Due Process and Traditional Admiralty Arrest and Attachment under the Supplemental Rules*, 8 Mar. Law 229 (1983).

[24] 743 F.2d 956, 1985 AMC 1 (1st Cir. 1984).

[25] 1985 AMC at 10.

[26] 585 F. Supp. 1062, 1984 AMC 2641 (D. Ore. 1984), *aff'd.* ___ F.2d ___, 1985 AMC ___ (9th Cir. 1985). Punitive damages may also be available in a personal injury action based on unseaworthiness. *Kopczynski v. Jacqueline*, 742 F.2d 555, 1985 AMC 769 (9th Cir. 1984) (citing *Dyer v. Merry Shipping*, 650 F.2d 622, 1981 AMC 2839 (5th Cir. 1981)).

[27] *See generally* Scowcroft, *Economic Loss in Admiralty: A Reexamination of Foundations*, 16 J. Mar. L. & Comm. 267 (1985).

[28] 732 F.2d 1468, 1985 AMC 2069 (9th Cir. 1984).

repairs to be completed. No other property damage occurred; no one was injured.

In affirming the lower court, the Ninth Circuit opinion noted the general rules in non-admiralty cases barring recovery of such losses in a tort action.[29] The court further noted, however, that admiralty is different, especially with regards to fishing vessel owners and commercial fisherman.[30] Moreover, the court saw no reason to make a distinction based on whether negligence or strict liability was the basis for recovery.[31] Finally, the court found that the traditional land-based rule was riddled with exceptions; that the economic loss suffered in this case was no different than personal injury or property damage; and that manufacturers were in the best position to predict the ramifications from failure of their products and insure themselves accordingly.[32]

The Eleventh Circuit also faced the issue, likewise in the context of a failed engine on a commercial fishing boat.[33] The lower court (in this case, a jury) found for the plaintiff on the basis of negligence, not strict liability. The manufacturer's main argument was that the traditional rule was based on the sound policy of preserving the operation of warranties and leaving 'the disappointment of commercial expectations' to the law of sales.[34] Citing earlier precedent,[35] the court rejected 'such a rigid separation of the law of sales and law of torts.'[36]

In other decisions, however, Circuit Courts have maintained the traditional rule and denied claims for economic loss.[37]

(f) WRECK ACT

The United States Wreck Act[38] obliges the owner of a sunken vessel to mark and remove it so as to lessen the chance of future accidents. If the

[29] 1985 AMC at 2074.

[30] *Id.*

[31] *Id.* at 2075.

[32] *Id.* at 2077–78.

[33] *Miller Industries v. Caterpillar Tractor Co.*, 733 F.2d 813, 1984 AMC 2559 (11th Cir. 1984).

[34] 1984 AMC at 2563.

[35] *Jig the Third Co. v. Puritan Marine Insurance Underwriters Corp.* 519 F.2d 117, 1976 AMC 118 (5th Cir. 1975).

[36] 1984 AMC at 2563. *Accord Ingram River Equip., Inc. v. Pott Industries, Inc.*, 756 F.2d 649, 1985 AMC 2062 (8th Cir. 1985) ('economic loss' recoverable in maritime tort based on negligence).

[37] *East River S.S. Corp. v. Delaval Turbine, Inc.*, 752 F.2d 903, 1985 AMC 913, (3d Cir. 1985) (*en banc*) (no recovery for economic loss in admiralty unless defect creates an 'unreasonable risk of harm to persons or property other than the product itself'; *State of Louisiana v. M/V Testbank*, 752 F.2d 1019, 1985 AMC 1521 (5th Cir. 1985) (no right to recover for economic loss in the absence of physical damage to a proprietary interest).

[38] U.S.C. §409.

owner does not do so, the vessel is deemed abandoned and the owner's duty falls to the United States. If the owner was not negligent in the original sinking, and yet the wreck was neither marked our removed, who is liable to a subsequent plaintiff whose vessel was damaged when it struck the wreck?

This question arose in *Nunley v. M/V Dauntless Colocotronis*.[39] A barge sank in 1974 due to the negligence of several parties (the 'upriver defendants'). The owner of the barge was without fault in the sinking. The wreck was neither marked nor removed, and, three years later, it was struck by another vessel. Procedurally, the matter was before the court on an appeal from a lower court's judgment on the pleadings that the upriver defendants could have no liability on any set of facts to either the owner of the wreck or to the present plaintiff.

The lower court based its ruling on the language of the Wreck Act and a long line of Second Circuit cases.[40] According to the lower court (and the two dissenters in the Fifth Circuit opinion[41]), the Wreck Act makes the failure to mark or remove a wreck the sole proximate cause of a subsequent collision with the vessel as a matter of law. Technically, the Fifth Circuit's reversal of the lower court means only that a majority of the appeals court was able to imagine sets of facts (e.g., if the owner was not shown to have been negligent in failing to mark) where the upriver defendants could be liable in whole or in part to the present plaintiff. Practically, however, the opinion represents a divergence from the earlier Second Circuit cases.[42]

(g) LIMITATION OF LIABILITY

A question which has arisen with some frequency is whether in a collision between foreign vessels in foreign waters or on the high seas, United Courts should apply the U.S. Limitation of Liability Act[43] or the foreign limitation law. Two decisions issued in 1984 dealt with this question. In *Matter of K.S. Line Corp.* (*The Swibon*),[44] the District Court in Alaska held that Korean law applied in determining the limitation fund of a Korean vessel in a collision with another Korean vessel on the high seas. In *Matter of Compania Gijonese de Navegacion S.A.* (*The Cimadevilla*),[45] the District Court in New York held that United States law applied in the case of a collision between a Spanish vessel and a Panamanian flag vessel in Spanish waters. What distinguished the two cases? In *The Swibon*, the Court held that

[39] 727 F.2d 455, 1984 AMC 2920 (5th Cir. 1984).

[40] *See* 1984 AMC at 2929 n.7 (citing cases).

[41] 1984 AMC at 2938–42.

[42] 'To the extent the Second Circuit holds the owner liable, whether negligent or not in failing to mark, we disagree.' (1984 AMC at 2930).

[43] 46 U.S.C. §§183–89.

[44] 596 F. Supp. 1268, 1985 AMC 722 (D. Alaska 1984).

[45] 590 F. Supp. 241, 1985 AMC 1469 (S.D.N.Y. 1984).

Korean law of limitation was substantive, whereas the Court in *The Cimadevilla* held that the Spanish law on limitation of liability, adopting the Brussels Convention, was procedural in nature.[46]

III. Publications

Noteworthy publications in 1984 included McCune, *The Asbatankvoy Charter*; Van Wyck and Carpenter, *The Radar Book*; Marton, *Tanker Operations*.

[46] For a detailed study of the cases, see Case Note, 16 J. Mar. L. & Comm. 117 (1985).

VENEZUELA

LUIS COVA ARRIA

Professor of Maritime Law at the Universidad Central de Venezuela, Caracas, member of the International Maritime Committee, and main partner of the lawyer's office Luis Cova Arria & Asociados

PANORAMA OF THE MARITIME LAW IN VENEZUELA DURING 1984

Although commercially active, the maritime activity remains juridically at a standstill as in previous years.

1. Legislation

With respect to 1984, it must be remarked:

1.1. LAWS

Law approving the resolutions (containing the amendments to the Convention for the Establishment of the Intergovernmental Maritime Organization) A.358 (IX) of 14 November 1975; A.371 (X) of 9 November 1975; A.400 (X) of 17 November 1977; and A.450 (XI) of 15 November 1979, Official Gazette No. 3.323, Extraordinary Issue of 18 January 1984, in which the Convention's and Organization's name are changed to its present title, 'Agreement for the Establishment of the International Maritime Organization' and 'International Maritime Organization, (IMO)'.

1.2. RESOLUTIONS

Resolution No. 185 of the Ministry of Transportation and Communications, as of 25 September 1984, which provides that any Venezuelan registered fishing vessel anchored in any Venezuelan port assigned to the National Institute of Ports, shall pay any services rendered according to rates preferential to those of the standard rate system.

2. Jurisprudence

As to jurisprudences on maritime matters for 1984, the following were dictated:

2.1. The Supreme Court of Justice of Venezuela in a suit brought by a Venezuelan insurance company against a foreign shipowner corporation with respect to a claim for indemnification of damage (loss of transported goods) deriving from a subrogation, decided:

For evidencing the existence of an insurance contract in virtue of which the payment permitting the subrogation was made, an instrument (policy), whether public or private, is sufficient. It was further decided that the policy was submitted to the suit neither to be opposed to the defendant nor to derive any action therefrom but to show a contractual relation between the plaintiff and the insured company. In other words, from the suit the plaintiff claims no rights in any way depending on the reality of said insurance contract, into which the plaintiff states to have entered, and even juridically it may be said that the subrogation, which the plaintiff claims to be in its favor, might have occurred regardless of its condition as insurer. It would be sufficient that as a third party, the insurer had made a compensation payment. It was further determined that the remission to a foreign law on which both parties agreed in Clause 3 of the bill of lading, declaring as applicable law the Unites States of America, 16 April 1936 Carriage Of Goods by Sea Act (COGSA) as valid since it is not contrary to public order.

2.2. Judgment as of *4 October 1984*, of the *Supreme Court of Justice of Venezuela* (*Court of Civil Cassation*).

Suit for the collection of bolivars begun by a Venezuelan shipping company against an Argentinian company, caused by damages to the former during the performance of a sea towing contract between both companies. Due to controversies between the parties as to the jurisdiction applicable to the lawsuit, the Court of Civil Cassation declares unfounded the exception of declinatory plea of jurisdiction for incompetence and litis pendencia opposed by the defendant, since the Court considers the contractual clause on which the declinatory plea is based as not valid through the interpretation of a principle of the Venezuelan law, implied in the Article 318 of Bustamante's Code, which provides that, 'whenever a special jurisdiction shall be chosen in a contract, the chosen law shall correspond to the nationality or domicile of any of the parties'.

2.3. Judgment of the *First Superior Court on Civil and Mercantile Matters of the Judiciary Circuit of the Federal District and State of Miranda, as of 4 October 1984.*

Lawsuit for a cargo claim on which a Venezuelan insurance company files a suit for the collection of bolivars to a foreign company, through its shipping agent in Venezuela, on the grounds that the defendant caused damages to a cargo (due to poor stowage) insured by the plaintiff. Upon request by the plaintiff, the court decided to reinstate the lawsuit because said lawsuit remained paralyzed during more than eight consecutives hearings due to the lack of proceedings by both parties.

3. Doctrine and bibliography

The only publication on Maritime Law in Venezuela in 1984 was the '*Revista de Derecho Marítimo*' (the Maritime Law Review), which represents a great effort by the Venezuelan Maritime Committee, i.e., the Venezuelan Association of Maritime Law.

Its contents can be summarized as follows:

3.1. DOCTRINE

In this area the following articles were published.

3.1.1. 'The Passenger Contract in the Venezuelan Law' by Dr. Rene De Sola, President of the Political and Administrative Court of the Supreme Court of Justice.

3.1.2. 'The United Nations Agreement on the International Multimodal Transportation of Goods' by Oscar Villegas.

3.1.3. 'Comments on the Law of Naval Privileges and Mortgages' by Carlos Matheus Gonzàlez.

3.1.4. 'Responsibility and Insurance for Pollution' by Omar Franco Ottati.

3.1.5. 'A Contribution to the Venezuelan Bibliography on Maritime Law' by Dr. Luis Corsi, Judge of First Instances on Mercantile Matters.

3.2. JURISPRUDENCE

Some of the judgments mentioned above appeared briefly described along with some others corresponding to the 1982–1984 period

3.3. LEGISLATION

The laws and resolutions described above were reviewed in this publication.

3.4. GENERAL INFORMATION

The Review included the contents of two International Conventions, namely:

3.4.1. The Code of Conduct of Maritime Conferences (1974).

3.4.2. The United Nations Convention on the International Multimodal Transport of Goods (1980).

No other publication on Maritime Law is known to have been published in 1984.

PART III.

INTERNATIONAL MARITIME ORGANIZATIONS

A.

INTERGOVERNMENTAL ORGANIZATIONS

UNCTAD

THE WORK OF UNCTAD IN SHIPPING LEGISLATION

SUMMARY: *1. Preliminary. – 2. The United Nations Convention on a Code of Conduct for Liner Conferences. – 3. United Nations Convention on International Multimodal Transport of Goods. – 4. The Ad Hoc Intergovernmental Group on Maritime Fraud. – 5. The United Nations Convention on Conditions for Registration of Ships. – 6. Marine Insurance (Hull and Cargo). – 7. Mortgages and Liens. – 8. Harmonization of Maritime Legislation in Developing Countries.*

1. Preliminary

In the past issues of a similar publication we have given a synthesis of UNCTAD activities in the field of maritime law since the creation of the Working Group on International Shipping Legislation by the Committee on Shipping by Resolution 7 (III).* We will now report on the follow-up of the activities of the secretariat during 1984.

2. The United Nations Convention on a Code of Conduct for Liner Conferences

Since our last report seven more States have ratified or acceded to the Convention, namely, Saudi Arabia, Denmark, Norway, Sweden and the United Kingdom. The United Kingdom accession includes also those of Gibraltar and Hong Kong. During the whole of 1984 the UNCTAD secretariat organized seminars and workshops to explain in detail the contents of the Code and the way in which to implement its provisions. These seminars took place in Mexico City and Santo Domingo.

Also the Committee on Shipping at its eleventh session, which took place from 19 to 30 November 1984, requested the UNCTAD secretariat to prepare an in-depth report regarding the implementation of the Code and

* *See*: *Anuario de Derecho Maritimo*, ed. Prof. Ignacio Arroyo, vols. I, II and III (Barcelona, Bosch), 1980–1984.

also the secretariat was requested to continue its efforts on technical assistance and support to developing countries in the implementation of the Code.

3. United Nations Convention on International Multimodal Transport of Goods

Since our last report two more States have become Contracting Parties to this Convention, namely Malawi, who acceded on 2 February 1984, and Senegal who ratified on 25 October 1984, making a total of four Contracting Parties. There is still a need for twenty-six more countries to ratify the Convention for it to come into force.

4. The Ad Hoc Intergovernmental Group on Maritime Fraud

A special session of the *Ad hoc* Intergovernmental Group to consider means of Combatting All Aspects of Maritime Fraud Including Piracy, was held under the auspices of UNCTAD from 6 to 17 February 1984. This Group was convened at the request of the Government of Lebanon on 20 October 1979, who suggested that IMCO (as IMO was then called) and UNCTAD should take all effective measures to prevent and suppress criminal barratry and unlawful seizure of ships and their cargoes. The IMCO Assembly in Resolution A.461(XI) requested the IMCO Council to provide for a study on the subject and the Council, in its turn, decided to establish an *Ad hoc* Working Group to study the nature and provisions of maritime fraud and the legal administration and other actions that would have been taken by States, international organizations or other interests concerned. The *Ad hoc* Working Group met in Paris on 24 and 25 November 1980, under the auspices of the International Chamber of Commerce. Following the ninth session of the Committee on Shipping of UNCTAD in September 1980, a mandate was given to the UNCTAD secretariat to undertake a study on maritime fraud connected with Bills of Lading, Charter Parties, Marine Insurance and General Average. The UNCTAD secretariat prepared an in-depth study for submission to the Group, called 'Review and Analysis of Possible Measures to Minimize the Occurrence of Maritime Fraud and Piracy'.

The *Ad hoc* Intergovernmental Group adopted unanimously a Resolution in which it called on all the parties concerned to acquire better knowledge and information on the potential exposure to maritime fraud, recommend the States members of UNCTAD to tighten their respective legislation to ensure that effective measures would be available to prevent maritime fraud and ask the secretariat to prepare further studies on:

(a) the feasilibity of the administrative and legal procedures of prosecuting authorities in co-operating at the investigating stage with the prosecuting authorities of other States with a view to improving as appropriate the effectiveness of these procedures, as well as to identify other possible means of international co-operation such as the jurisdiction of States and extradition;

(b) formulation of a set of guidelines to be recommended to the international banking community of the States members of UNCTAD for use by all parties concerned, bearing in mind, *inter alia*, the International Chamber of Commerce anti-fraud protective measures;

(c) feasibility of a banking super-service scheme;

(d) to what extent any minimum standards for professional qualifications of shipping agents may contribute to combating maritime fraud and whether such standards could be used as non-mandatory guidelines for the qualifications required;

(e) the possible implications for maritime fraud or failure of shipping agents to provide sufficient financial standards based on specific cases where such implications have occurred;

(f) availability for interested parties of information relating to shipping operations and the adequacy of the existing system of collecting and disseminating such information at the international level, including an economic and commercial assessment with a cost-benefit analysis of the extent to which ship-related information not already available is needed to combat maritime fraud.

These reports have already been finalized by the secretariat and will be available for the second and final meeting of the *Ad hoc* intergovernmental Group which will now take place from 23 October to 1 November 1985.

5. The United Nations Convention on Conditions for Registration of Ships

The first session of the United Nations Conference on Conditions for Registration of Ships was held at the Palais des Nations, Geneva from 16 July to 3 August 1984. This Conference was convened in pursuance of General Assembly Resolution No. 37/209 which was unanimously adopted on 20 December 1982, and in which it was decided that such Conference should be convened in 1984. This Resolution of the General Assembly followed after a long period of work within the UNCTAD secretariat. Way back on 9 August 1974, the Committee on Shipping of UNCTAD unanimously adopted the Resolution 22(VI) on Economic Co-operation in Merchant Shipping in which consideration was given to the economic consequences for international shipping of the existence or lack of a genuine link between vessel and flag of registration as explicitly defined in international conventions in force and requesting the UNCTAD secretariat to undertake an examination of this matter as soon as possible.

Pursuant to the resolution the UNCTAD secretariat prepared a report entitled 'Economic consequences of the existence or lack of a geniune link between vessel and flag of registry' (TD/B/C.4/168 and Add.1 and Corr.1). This report analysed the economic considerations as well as the legal aspects of the genuine link, and included a comparison of the economic features of the open-registry system, on the one hand, and of national flag systems, on the other.

In view of the complexity and importance of the issues raised in the UNCTAD secretariat report, the Committee on Shipping on 22 April 1977 adopted decisions 33 (VIII), which called for the convening of an *ad hoc* intergovernmental working group to consider the question. This Working Group, at its first session, in February 1978, adopted a unanimous resolution stating that 'the expansion of open-registry fleets has adversely affected the development and competitiveness of fleets of countries which do not offer open-registry facilities, including those of developing countries'.

The report of the Working Group on its first session was submitted at the fifth session of UNCTAD in Manila in May 1979. After considering the open-registry issue, the Conference adopted resolution 120 (V) by majority vote. This resolution took note of the desire of many countries to phase out open-registry operations and requested further studies in respect of the repercussions of phasing out open registries as well as regarding the feasibility of establishing a legal mechanism for regulating the operations of open-registry fleets during the phasing-out period. It also requested the reconvening of the Working Group for the purpose of considering these studies on the phasing out of open-registry operations.

The *ad hoc* Working Group accordingly held its second session in January 1980. It could not reach agreement, however, on the question of the phasing out of open registries and the matter was referred back to the Committee on Shipping, which decided in 1980 in its resolution 41 (IX) to hold a special session devoted entirely to the open-registry question.

At this special session, which took place in 1981, the Committee adopted resolution 43 (S-III) by majority vote, recommending the convening of a conference of plenipotentiaries to consider the adoption of an international agreement on conditions for registration of ships. The resolution also recommended the convening of an intergovernmental preparatory group (IPG) which would be responsible for proposing a set of basic principles concerning the conditions upon which vessels should be accepted on national shipping registers and which should, *inter alia*, apply to: (a) the manning of vessels; (b) the role of the flag countries in the management of shipowning companies and vessels; (c) equity participation in capital; and (d) identification and accountability of owners and operators. It was agreed further that the intergovernmental preparatory group should recommend to the conference of plenipotentiaries: (a) measures to protect the interests of labour-supplying countries, especially developing countries; (b) any additional measures needed for ensuring full jurisdiction of the flag State over vessels which fly its flag, and should also recommend to the conference of plenipotentiaries a time-frame for the registration of vessels in conformity with the basic principles of the international agreement. The IPG was also to recommend procedures for reporting on and review of the implementation of the international agreement.

The Intergovernmental Preparatory Group adopted a composite text which contained alternative phrasings on such key issues as manning of ships; the role of flag countries in the management of shipowning companies and vessels, and equity participation in capital. While there was general agreement on the need for ensuring a genuine link between a vessel and the State of its registry, there were differing views as to what the elements of the link should be and as to whether the international agreement should be of a mandatory nature.

In November 1983, the Preparatory Committee further discussed the set of basic principles which the Group had adopted and decided that it had sufficiently advanced its work for it to be used as a basis for the holding of a plenipotentiary conference. The Committee decided to annex to its report the text proposed by the Chairman on manning, management and equity and the proposal submitted by the USSR on behalf of States members of Group D in relation to the preparation of a draft international agreement on the conditions for registration of ships. All three texts are contained in the Preparatory Committee's report (TD/RS/CONF/3-TD/RS/CONF/PC/4). The Conference also had before it a communication from the United Kingdom of Great Britain and Northern Ireland submitting a proposal on behalf of Group B (TD/RS/CONF/5 and Corr.1).

The United Nations Conference on Conditions for Registration of Ships ended its first period of sessions with a large measure of agreement being reached on the elements that should be included in an international agreement concerning the conditions under which vessels should be accepted on national shipping registers. In the resolution it was agreed that a resumed session should take place from 28 January to 15 February 1985.

At this session it was agreed in principle that, in accordance with the provisions of the United Nations Convention on the Law of the Sea, there must exist a genuine link between a State and the ships flying its flag and also that flag States must exercise effective jurisdiction and control over ships flying their flags, in administrative, technical and social matters.

6. Marine Insurance (Hull and Cargo)

The Working Group on International Shipping Legislation met at its tenth session from 24 September to 5 October 1984, at the Palais des Nations, Geneva, to finalize the work on marine insurance which has been undertaken since 1979, and also to start work on maritime liens and mortgages as requested by the Committee on Shipping.

The Model Clauses were finalized at the tenth session, all delegations having reached consensus, but at the closing session it was noted that despite the overall accuracy of the texts there were some changes of an editorial nature that needed to be made in order that consistency could be achieved throughout the text. In view of this the Working Group adopted the text of the Model Clauses on Marine Hull and Cargo Insurance on the understanding that corrections to them would be communicated in writing to the secretariat and the corrected text would be examined by the competent experts during the eleventh session of the Committee on Shipping. The Committee on Shipping met from 19 to 30 November 1984, but unfortunately, no decision was made on the Marine Insurance Model Clauses as there were no experts available on the subject during the meeting. They were therefore referred to the next Trade and Development Board, which met in March 1985, for its approval.

7. Mortgages and Liens

The Tenth Session of the Working Group also dealt, on a preliminary basis, with the problem of mortgages and liens. The delegates had before them the report by the UNCTAD secretariat entitled 'Preliminary Analysis of Possible Reforms in the existing international regime of maritime liens and mortgages' (TD/B/C.4/ISL.48) which was not intended to be a comprehensive analysis of these issues. It was noted that a major concern of governments, especially of developing countries, was the need to facilitate ship financing for the acquisition of ships and it was commonly accepted that the best guarantee available was the ship itself by way of mortgage. Thus, a study in this field was considered to be essential for any possible international action to be taken to improve the availability of ship financing to developing countries. On the other hand, it was also considered by delegates that some of the maritime liens related principally to the safe and efficient operation of the ship and in that light the expertise of the IMO was required in order to make a full analysis of the problem. At that session it was reported to delegates that an agreement had been reached by the UNCTAD and IMO secretariats on the allocation of expertise, in order to avoid duplication of work and to facilitate effective co-operation between both secretariats on a subject in which both secretariats had a legitimate interest. It was further agreed that it would be useful to take account of the work of the CMI in this field. The CMI convened a general conference in May 1985, which was held in Lisbon, and at which they produced draft revisions on the existing Convention on Maritime Liens and Mortgages of 1967 and the Convention on Arrest of Sea-going Ships of 1952.

8. Harmonization of Maritime Legislation in Developing Countries

The UNCTAD secretariat has continued to give its support to various developing countries, on request, to harmonize their maritime legislation. The exercise has been carried out in Peru, in connection with IMO and the Peruvian Maritime Law Association to up-date their commercial code in the chapters related to maritime law. An exercise along the same lines has been undertaken in the countries of West and Central Africa and also UNCTAD has co-operated in the existing work on guidelines for maritime legislation in the ESCAP region.

Ricardo Vigil
Chief Legal Officer, Shipping Legislation Division
Geneva, UNCTAD

UNCITRAL

THE WORK OF THE UNITED NATIONS COMMISSION ON INTERNATIONAL TRADE LAW, 1984–1985*

SUMMARY: *1. Introduction. – 2. UNCITRAL model law on international commercial arbitration. – 3. International payments. – 4. Use of automatic data processing in international trade. – 5. Liability of operators of transport terminals. – 6. Endorsement of Uniform Customs and Practice for Documentary Credits. – 7. New international economic order: industrial works contracts. – 8. Training and assistance in the field of international trade law.*

1. Introduction

Several of the Commission's activities during the period 1984 and 1985 will be of interest not only to persons concerned with maritime transport, but also to those concerned with commercial transactions in which maritime transport may be involved. The principal achievement of the Commission during this period was the adoption in 1985 of the UNCITRAL Model Law on International Commercial Arbitration. Also in that year, the Commission adopted a recommendation designed to help reduce certain legal obstacles to the use of automatic data processing in connection with documentation and other aspects of international trade transactions. During the period under review, work progressed within the Commission and its Working Groups on a number of ongoing projects, including the draft convention on international bills of exchange and international promissory

* This article is a sequel to S.R. Katz, 'El trabajo de la Comisión de las Naciones Unidas para la Unificación del Derecho de Comercio Internacional (1982–1983)', *Anuario Derecho Marítimo*, vol. III, Madrid, p. 555 (hereinafter referred to as 'UNCITRAL 1982–1983'); K. Sono, 'El trabajo de la Comisión de las Naciones Unidas para la Unificación del Derecho del Comercio Internacional', *Anuario Derecho Marítimo*, 1982, Madrid, p. 391 (hereinafter referred to as 'UNCITRAL 1981'); and K. Sono, 'El trabajo de la Comisión de las Naciones Unidas para la Unificacion del Derecho Mercante durante 1979–1980', *Anuario Derecho Marítimo*, 1981, Madrid, p. 597 (hereinafter referred to as 'UNCITRAL 1979–1980').

notes, the preparation of legal guides on electronic funds transfers and on contracts for the construction of industrial works, and the formulation of uniform legal rules relating to the liability of operators of transport terminals. In 1984, the Commission endorsed the recent revision of the Uniform Customs and Practice for Documentary Credits, produced by the International Chamber of Commerce. Throughout the period the Commission pursued its program of training and assistance in the field of international trade law. The seventeenth session of UNCITRAL was held in New York from 25 June to 10 July 1984 and the eighteenth session was held at Vienna from 3 to 21 June 1985.

2. UNCITRAL Model Law on International Commercial Arbitration[1]

Most legal systems contain laws regulating the conduct of arbitration proceedings within their jurisdictions. However, in many cases these laws have been developed principally to govern arbitration proceedings concerning domestic matters. They often do not provide a satisfactory legal framework for the conduct of international arbitration proceedings. The UNCITRAL Model Law on International Commercial Arbitration was adopted by the Commission at its eighteenth session in 1985.[2] It is designed to serve as a guide to national legislators in revising and modernizing their national laws relating to arbitration so as to take into account the particular features of international commercial arbitration and the needs of the parties in such proceedings. It is also designed to harmonize national laws on this subject so that parties will be able to choose a mutually convenient and desirable location in which to conduct their arbitration proceedings, without having to be concerned about the possibility of special problems of uncertainties arising from the arbitration laws prevailing in that particular location.

The UNCITRAL Model Law provides a suitable framework for the conduct of arbitration proceedings in international commercial matters. Under the Model Law, parties to a dispute would have broad scope to agree upon the rules of procedure which will govern their arbitration proceedings by, for example, incorporating by reference such rules of procedure into their contracts. In situations in which parties fail to agree upon procedural rules governing the arbitration or some aspect of it, Model Law would assist by providing solutions which would be applicable in such cases. Thus, the conduct of the arbitration proceedings would not be hindered by a failure of the parties to agree on particular procedural rules. Perhaps most important-

[1] *See* UNCITRAL 1982–1983, p. 558.

[2] Report of the United Nations Commission on International Trade Law on the work of its eighteenth session (*Official Records of the General Assembly*, *Fortieth Session*, *Supplement No. 17* (A/40/17)), paras. 11–333.

ly, the Model Law contains provisions on recognition and enforcement or arbitral awards which would apply irrespective of the country where the award was made. The important factor in this context would be whether or not an arbitration was international.

The UNCITRAL Model Law is the latest in a series of substantial contributions by UNCITRAL in the area of international commercial arbitration. In 1976, for example, the Commission adopted the UNCITRAL Arbitration Rules.[3] These rules have rapidly gained international acceptance and are now used in a wide variety of international commercial contexts.

3. International payments

The Commission is currently working on two projects concerned with the law relating to international payments. In one of these projects, the Commission is seeking to unify the law relating to international negotiable instruments. In the other project the Commission is preparing a legal guide on electronic funds transfers.

(a) DRAFT CONVENTIONS ON INTERNATIONAL NEGOTIABLE INSTRUMENTS

There exist in the world two principal systems of law governing negotiable instruments, one represented by the Geneva Conventions of 1930 and 1931, and the other represented by negotiable instruments legislation in England and the United States. Not long after its creation in 1966, the Commission recognized that disparities existed in the way these two systems dealt with various issues, and that even within the systems complete unification of law had not been achieved. The disparities among rules of different legal systems gave rise to various difficulties in practice. The Commission therefore embarked on work designed to reduce the problems arising from the co-existence of these systems. In one facet of this work, the Commission undertook the preparation of a draft convention to unify the law relating to bills of exchange used in international transactions, and later decided that

[3] Report of the United Nations Commission on International Trade Law on the work of its ninth session (*Official Records of the General Assembly, Thirty-first Session, Supplement No. 17* (A/31/17)), para. 57 (reproduced in *Yearbook of the United Nations Commission on International Trade Law*, Vol. VII: 1976, (United Nations publication, Sales No. E.77.V.1), part one, II, A). (The UNCITRAL Yearbook is hereinafter referred to as '*Yearbook* . . . (year)'). The UNCITRAL Arbitration Rules have also been reproduced in booklet form: the English text is in United Nations publication, Sales No. E.77.V.6 while the Spanish text is in Sales No. S.77.V.6. The United Nations General Assembly has recommended the use of the UNCITRAL Arbitration Rules in the settlement of disputes arising in the context of international commercial relations, particularly by reference in the Rules in commercial contracts: General Assembly resolution 31/98 of 15 December 1976.

the scope of the draft convention should be extended to cover international promissory notes as well. The rules would apply only to international transactions where the drawer of the instrument opted for the application of the rules. Subsequently, the Commission decided also to prepare a draft convention to unify the law relating to international cheques.

The task of preparing the draft conventions was assigned by the Commission to its Working Group on International Negotiable Instruments. The Working Group completed its preparation of the two draft conventions in 1981.[4] As is customary in the preparation of legal texts by the Commission, the draft conventions were circulated to governments and international organizations for their comments. During the seventeenth session of the Commission in 1984, the Commission engaged in a review of many of the provisions of the draft Convention on International Bills of Exchange and International Promissory Notes, and that draft is now being revised by the Working Group in accordance with those deliberations. It is expected that a final draft will be submitted to the Commission at its nineteenth session in 1986 for its consideration. The Commission decided to postpone work on the draft Convention on International Cheques, and to take a decision as to further work on that draft Convention after completion of the work on the draft Convention on International Bills of Exchange and International Promissory Notes.

(b) ELECTRONIC FUNDS TRANSFERS[5]

The other project of the Commission in the area of international payments deals with the transfer of funds by electronic means. The Commission is preparing a legal guide on electronic funds transfers, which will deal with the legal problems arising from such funds transfers in order to provide guidance for legislators or lawyers preparing rules governing particular funds transfer systems. At its annual sessions in 1984 and 1985, the Commission considered the draft chapters of the legal guide which had been prepared by the Secretariat.[6] The draft legal guide will now be distributed to Governments and interested international organisations for their comments. It will then be revised by the Secretariat in light of the comments received, and

[4] The draft Convention on International Bills of Exchange and International Promissory Notes as adopted by the Working Group is contained in UNCITRAL document A/CN.9/211. A commentary on the draft convention is contained in UNCITRAL document A/CN.9/213. The draft Convention on International Cheques as adopted by the Working Group is contained in UNCITRAL document A/CN.9/212 and Corr.1 (Spanish only). A commentary on the draft convention is contained in UNCITRAL document A/CN.9/214.

[5] *See* UNCITRAL 1982–1983, p. 559.

[6] The draft chapters are contained in UNCITRAL documents A/CN.9/250 and Adds. 1–4, and A/CN.9/266 and Adds. 1–2.

submitted to the nineteenth session of UNCITRAL in 1986 for consideration and possible adoption.

4. Use of automatic data processing in international trade

In addition to its work in the field of electronic funds transfers, the Commission has undertaken active consideration of the use of automatic data processing techniques in international trade, and problems which could arise in the law relating to these techniques. One aspect of this work has related to the treatment of computer records under rules of evidence in national legal systems. In considering this subject at its eighteenth session in 1985, the Commission found that requirements in the rules of evidence of various legal systems that documents be signed or that they be in paper-based form constitute an obstacle to the use of computers and of computer-to-computer telecommunications in international trade. Furthermore, existing rules of evidence are based upon traditional paper-based means of documenting international trade, and this could create obstacles to the use of automatic data processing in international trade. Because of the benefits to international trade resulting from the use of automatic data processing, the Commission decided to recommend to Governments and international organizations elaborating legal texts relating to trade that they review the rules within their competence concerning automatic data processing with an end towards eliminating unnecessary obstacles to its use in international trade.[7]

5. Liability of operators of transport terminals[8]

In 1984, the UNCITRAL Working Group on International Contract Practices began work on formulating uniform legal rules relating to the liability of operators of transport terminals. The objective of the Commission in this project is to create a unified international legal regime for the liability of these non-carrying intermediaries in respect of goods involved in international transport, which would be in harmony with the legal regimes governing the carriers of goods. Preparatory to the drafting of legal rules, the Working Group engaged in an exchange of views concerning the principal legal issues arising in this area.[9]

[7] Report of the United Nations Commission on International Trade Law on the work of its eighteenth session (*Official Records of the General Assembly*, *Fortieth Session*, *Supplement No. 17* (A/40/17)) para. 360. The background study by the Secretariat on which the Commission's recommendation was based is found in document A/CN.9/265.

[8] *See* UNCITRAL 1982–1983, p. 560.

[9] *See* UNCITRAL document A/CN.9/260.

6. Endorsement of Uniform Customs and Practice for Documentary Credits

The Uniform Customs and Practice for Documentary Credits, published by the International Chamber of Commerce, has made a significant contribution to international trade by unifying the rules and practices relating to letters of credit, and thus facilitating the use of letters of credit in international trade transactions. In 1983, the International Chamber of Commerce issued its latest revision of the Uniform Customs and Practice, which takes into account modern developments in trade documentation, such as transport documents, automatic data processing and the standby letter of credit. As it has done with previous versions of the Uniform Customs and Practice, the Commission, in 1984, endorsed the latest revision and recommended its use in transactions involving the establishment of a documentary credit.[10]

7. New international economic order: industrial works contracts[11]

The UNCITRAL Working Group on the New International Economic Order has, during the period under review, made significant progress in its preparation of a legal guide on drawing up international contracts for the construction of industrial works. This legal guide will discuss the many complex issues in connection with such contracts and propose solutions to these issues in order to assist parties in drafting contracts which are balanced and equitable. The Working Group considered at its sessions during 1984 and 1985 several draft chapters prepared by the Secretariat.[12] The Working Group is now in the final stages of its drafting of the legal guide. When it is completed, the draft legal guide will be submitted to the Commission for its consideration and adoption.

8. Training and assistance in the field of international trade law

The Commission has an active programme of training and assistance in the field of international trade law. This programme is designed to promote world-wide awareness of international trade law in general, and of the

[10] Report of the United Nations Commission on International Trade Law on the work of its seventeenth session (*Official Records of the General Assembly, Thirty-ninth Session, Supplement No. 17* (A/39/17)), para 129.

[11] *See* UNCITRAL 1982–1983, p. 560, UNCITRAL 1981, p. 399, and UNCITRAL 1979–1980, p. 600.

[12] *See* UNCITRAL documents A/CN.9/247, A/CN.9/259 and A/CN.9/262.

activities and contributions of the Commission in this field. It is intended to be of particular benefit to lawyers and businessmen from developing countries. As one element of this programme, the Commission sponsors symposia and seminars on various topics within the field of international trade law, usually on a regional basis and in collaboration with other organisations active in this field. Staff members of the UNCITRAL Secretariat participate in these symposia and seminars.

As another element of the training and assistance programme, the International Trade Law Branch of the United Nations Office of Legal Affairs, which serves as the Secretariat of UNCITRAL, accepts recent law graduates, and sometimes law students who have nearly completed their legal education, as interns in the Branch for periods of two or three months. In addition, the International Trade Law Branch accommodates scholars in the field of international trade law who wish to make use of the library and other facilities of the Branch in connection with their own research projects.

Both of these elements of the training and assistance programme were actively engaged in during the period under review.

Stephen R. Katz
Legal Officer, International Trade Law Branch
Vienna, United Nations Office of Legal Affairs

Annex

STATUS OF CONVENTIONS ELABORATED BY UNCITRAL (AS OF 30 JUNE 1985)

The following multilateral instruments have been elaborated by UNCITRAL and adopted by Diplomatic Conferences. The status of each instrument, as of 30 June 1985, is indicated.

(*a*) Convention on the Limitation Period in the International Sale of Goods (New York, 1974)[13]

signatures only:	10[14]
ratifications:	4[15]
accessions:	4[16]
ratifications or accessions necessary to go into force:	10

(*b*) United Nations Convention on the Carriage of Goods by Sea, 1978 (Hamburg)[17]

signatures only:	24[18]
ratifications:	3[19]
accessions:	7[20]
ratifications, acceptances, approvals or accessions necessary to go into force:	20

[13] U.N. document A/CONF.63/15 (*Official Records of the United Nations Conference on Prescription (Limitation) in the International Sale of Goods* (United Nations publication, Sales No. S.74.V.8)). (The text of the Convention may also be found in *Yearbook* . . . 1974, part three, I, B). *See also* Commentary on the Convention on the Limitation Period in the International Sale of Goods, prepared by the Secretariat pursuant to a request by the Conference, U.N. document A/CONF.63/17.

[14] Brazil, Bulgaria, Byelorussian SSR, Costa Rica, German Democratic Republic, Mongolia, Nicaragua, Poland, Ukranian SSR, USSR.

[15] Czechoslovakia, Ghana, Hungary, Norway.

[16] Argentina, Dominican Republic, Egypt, Yugoslavia.

[17] U.N. document A/CONF.89/13, annex I (*Official Records of the United Nations Conference on the Carriage of Goods by Sea* (United Nations publication, Sales No. S.80.VII.1)). (The text of the Convention may also be found in *Yearbook* . . . 1978, part three, I, B).

[18] Austria, Brazil, Czechoslovakia, Denmark, Ecuador, Finland, France, Germany, Federal Republic of, Ghana, Holy See, Madagascar, Mexico, Norway, Pakistan, Panama, Philippines, Portugal, Senegal, Sierra Leone, Singapore, Sweden, USA, Venezuela, Zaire.

[19] Chile, Egypt, Hungary.

[20] Barbados, Lebanon, Morocco, Romania, Tunisia, Uganda, United Republic of Tanzania.

(*c*) United Nations Convention on Contracts for the International Sale of Goods (Vienna, 1980)[21]

signatures only:	17[22]
ratifications:	4[23]
accessions:	3[24]
ratifications, acceptances, approvals or accessions necessary to go into force:	10

(*d*) Protocol amending the Convention on the Limitation Period in the International Sale of Goods (Vienna, 1980)[25]

accessions:	3[26]
accessions necessary to go into force:	2[27]

[21] U.N. document A/CONF.97/18, annex I (*Official Records of the United Nations Conference on Contracts for the International Sale of Goods* (United Nations publication, Sales No. S.81.IV.3)). (The text of the Convention may also be found in *Yearbook* . . . 1980, part three, I, B).

[22] Austria, Chile, China, Czechoslovakia, Denmark, Finland, German Democratic Republic, Germany, Federal Republic of, Ghana, Italy, Netherlands, Norway, Poland, Singapore, Sweden, USA, Venezuela.

[23] France, Hungary, Lesotho, Yugoslavia.

[24] Argentina, Egypt, Syrian Arab Republic.

[25] U.N. document A/CONF.97/18, annex II (*Official Records of the United Nations Conference on Contracts for the International Sale of Goods* (United Nations publication, Sales No. S.81.IV.3)). (The text of the Protocol may also be found in *Yearbook* . . . 1980, part three, I, C).

[26] Argentina, Egypt, Hungary.

[27] Pursuant to Article IX (1) of the Protocol, the 1974 Limitation Convention and the 1980 Sales Convention must both be in force before the Protocol can enter into force.

IMO

ACTIVITIES OF THE INTERNATIONAL MARITIME ORGANIZATION (IMO) DURING 1984

SUMMARY: *1. Issues of a general nature. – 2. New developments regarding IMO Conventions. – 3. Summary of the principal provisions of the International Convention on Standards of Training, Certification and Watchkeeping for Seamen of 1978 (STCW 1978). – 4. IMO legal activities.*

1. Issues of a general nature

On 31 December 1984, the number of IMO members rose to 127 plus an associate member (Hong Kong). The process of making the IMO a universal organization continued during the year with the incorporation of two new members: Vietnam (21 June), and Brunei Darussalem (31 December).

On 10 November 1984, the amendments approved by the organization's Assembly in 1977 and 1979 entered into force. On this date the Committee on Technical Cooperation was created, and the organization's Council changed its number of members to 32.

2. New developments regarding IMO Conventions

The most important event in this area was clearly the entry into force of the Convention on Standards of Training, Certification and Watchkeeping for Seamen of 28 April 1984. Due to the importance of this Convention, a detailed analysis will be included in Section 3 of this report.

We now turn to developments concerning other IMO Conventions.

A. AMENDMENTS OF 1981 TO THE INTERNATIONAL CONVENTION ON SECURITY OF HUMAN LIFE AT SEA OF 1974 (SOLAS 1974)

In November of 1981 the Committee on Maritime Security adopted, in accordance with Article VIII(b)(iv) of the Convention, amendments to Chapters II-1, II-2, III, IV, V and VI of the Annexes which contain the

Rules of the SOLAS Convention of 1974. The Committee determined, in accordance with Article VIII(b)(vii)(2) of the Convention, that the amendments will enter into force on 1 September 1984, unless a determined percentage of States whose merchant fleets represent not less than half of the worldwide gross register object before 1 March 1984.

B. AMENDMENTS OF 1981 TO THE PROTOCOL OF 1978 RELATING TO THE INTERNATIONAL CONVENTION ON SECURITY OF HUMAN LIFE AT SEA (SOLAS PROT 1978)

The Committee on Maritime Security also adopted in November of 1981 amendments to Rule 29(d)(i) of Chapter II-1 of the Protocol. These amendments entered into force on 1 September 1984.

C. AMENDMENT OF 1973 TO THE CONVENTION ON FACILITATION OF INTERNATIONAL MARITIME TRAFFIC OF 1965 (FAL 1965)

On 2 June 1984, the amendment to Article VII of the Convention entered into force. This amendment adopts the simplified amendment proceeding recommended by the IMO Facilitation Committee.

In October of 1984, the Facilitation Committee met to consider the amendment of Article VII(3) of the Convention. The Committee requested that the IMO hold a conference at the beginning of 1986 to consider several amendments designed to increase the employment of data processing technicians by eliminating provisions in the Annex to the Convention that impede their hiring.

D. 1983 AMENDMENTS TO THE CONVENTION ON SECURITY OF CONTAINERS OF 1972

The Committee on Maritime Security, in accordance with Article X(2) of the Convention, adopted amendments to Annexes I and II of the same. In accordance with Article X(3) of the Convention, the amendments entered into force on 1 January 1984.

E. INTERNATIONAL CONVENTION ON MARITIME SEARCH AND RESCUE OF 1979 (SAR 1979)

The conditions for the entry into force of this recent IMO Convention were fulfilled on 22 June 1984, and the Convention will enter into force on 22 June 1985. In view of these circumstances, a summary of the provisions of this important instrument will be included in the 1985 report.

F. 1984 AMENDMENTS TO THE ANNEX TO THE PROTOCOL OF 1978 RELATING TO THE INTERNATIONAL CONVENTION TO PREVENT CONTAMINATION BY SHIPS AT SEA, 1973

In September of 1984, the Committee on Protection of the Marine Environment adopted, in accordance with Article 16(2) of the Convention, amendments to the Annex to the Protocol of 1978. These amendments will enter into force on 7 January 1986, if there is no objection from the required number of States.

3. Summary of the principal provisions of the International Convention on Standards of Training, Certification and Watchkeeping for Seamen of 1978 (STCW 1978)

The STCW of 1978 is the first attempt to establish universal minimum professional standards for seamen. Previously, the standards of training, certification, and watchkeeping for officers and sailors were set by each government, without taking into account the standards applied in other countries. Standards and proceedings were therefore very different in spite of the fact that maritime transport is the most international of all industries.

The Convention prescribes minimum standards that the contracting parties are obligated to comply with or to surpass. In the majority of developed maritime countries the standards are often more rigorous than those stipulated in the Convention. Nevertheless, in some countries standards are not so elevated. Through ratification or acceptance of the Convention a government is obligated to apply and enforce its provisions. Therefore, the entry into force of the Convention will serve to elevate standards worldwide.

In order to enter into force, the Convention had to be ratified by 25 countries whose combined merchant fleets represent a minimum of 50% of the gross tonnage of the worldwide fleet. This requisite was completed on 27 April 1983 and the Convention entered into force one year later on 28 April 1984.

An especially important characteristic of the Convention is that it is applicable to ships of States who are not parties when they visit ports of States who are parties to the Convention. Article X prescribes that parties will apply methods of inspection to all ships in order to insure that ships of non-contracting States do not receive treatment that is more favorable than that accorded to ships of contracting States. As this might create difficulties for ships of non-contracting States, it is hoped that the number of contracting States will increase considerably in the near future. As of 1 May 1985, STCW had been accepted by 41 countries whose fleets represent 71% of the gross tonnage of the worldwide fleet.

The Convention also incorporates a proceeding of 'tacit acceptance'. Under this proceeding, amendments to the Convention or to its Annex may be approved by the IMO Maritime Security Committee, which has been broadened to include all of the contracting parties, some of whom could not be members of the IMO. The amendments to the Annex will normally enter into force at the end of two and one-half years following the datę on which they were sent to all the contracting parties for acceptance, unless, within a set time, they are rejected by a third of the parties or by a number of parties whose combined merchant fleets represent 50% of gross worldwide tonnage. Previously, in order to amend a Convention, the amendments had to be accepted by two-thirds of the contracting parties. In practice, this condition took years to fulfill, and due to its cumbersome nature, some amendments never entered into force.

The technical provisions of the Convention are contained in an Annex which is divided into six chapters on the following subjects: I. General provisions; II. Captain and officers section; III. Machinery section; IV. Radiocommunications section; V. Special requirements for tanker crews; VI. Sufficiency of management of lifeboat embarcations.

4. IMO legal activities

The most important of these activities in 1984 was clearly the International Conference on liability and indemnification of damage derived from maritime transport of certain goods.

a) RESULTS OF THE DIPLOMATIC CONFERENCE OF APRIL–MAY 1984

The International Conference was held on 30 April–25 May 1984, in compliance with the decision adopted by the Council and the Assembly. Its goal was to examine the adoption of a convention on liability and indemnification related to maritime transport of dangerous and potentially dangerous goods (SNP Convention) and also adoption of conventions designed to revise respectively the Convention on Civil Liability of 1969, and the Fund Convention of 1971. 69 States were represented at the Conference, as well as representatives of the United Nations and observers of five intergovernmental organizations and 24 nongovernmental organizations.

With respect to the SNP Convention, the Conference decided, due to lack of the necessary time, to postpone consideration of the issue to a future date.

As to the revision of the Convention on Civil Liability of 1969, and the Fund Convention of 1971, the Conference adopted the following instruments: 1) the 1984 Protocol to amend the International Convention on Civil Liability for damage caused by oil pollution, 1969; and 2) the 1984 Protocol to amend the International Convention on the creation of an international fund for indemnification of damage caused by oil pollution, 1971.

The 1984 Protocols are open for signature from 1 December 1984 until 30 November 1985. While many countries have signed the Protocols, at the date of this report there had not been any ratifications. The United States, the world's principal importer of oil, has firmly supported the adoption of the Protocols. If, as is expected, the United States ratifies the Protocols, their future seems assured.

b) SUMMARY OF THE ACTIVITIES OF THE LEGAL COMMITTEE

Since the time of the Diplomatic Conference, the Legal Committee has had two groups of sessions, one in December of 1984, and the other in March of 1985. The most important question on the Legal Committee's agenda is the subject of salvage, particularly the revision of the Convention on Maritime Salvage and Rescue, 1910, and related matters. The Committee continued its deliberations on this issue, based on the draft convention prepared by the International Maritime Committee (CMI) and documents presented by various governments and interested organizations.

Mandatory salvage

The Committee discussed the necessity or convenience of introducing a system of mandatory salvage in which a seaside State would have the right to compel a foreign ship to undertake salvage measures designed to avoid damage to the environment of such State. The majority of the delegations recognized that the seaside States do not possess this right by virtue of any Convention currently in force. Nevertheless, they were not convinced that the practical necessity of a mandatory salvage system had been demonstrated, as the present system was seen to be satisfactory. Therefore, the Committee decided that debate on this question should be considered closed.

Scope of application of the Intervention Convention of 1969

Several delegations indicated that the adoption of the Protocols of 1984, designed to amend, respectively, the Convention on Civil Liability of 1969, and the Fund Convention of 1971, raised the question whether some of the provisions of the International Convention relating to Intervention on the High Seas in cases of Oil Pollution Casualties (Intervention Convention of 1969) should be revised, especially with regard to the suitability of the term 'connected interests' used in Article I of the Convention. The Committee decided to examine this question again in the future in light of all opinions and proposals that might be presented.

Remuneration and indemnification

The Committee studied the issue of whether coastal States should provide remuneration directly to the salvager who has acted in accordance with the instructions of that State. It was decided to examine this and related questions on the date when the Committee discusses the Convention for the third time.

Legal status of the 1973 Protocol relating to the Intervention Convention

The Committee noted that of the 48 States who were parties to the Intervention Convention of 1969, only 18 had become parties to the 1973 Protocol to the Convention. It invited the non-contracting States to examine, as soon as possible, the ratification or adherence to the Protocol.

Provisions relating to notification

The extent to which the provisions being elaborated by the Committee on Protection of the Marine Environment, regarding the notification of environmental disasters to interested coastal States, fall within the framework of the provisions of salvage adopted by those States, was studied. The question of whether additional or different provisions are required was considered. The deliberations were based on IMO documents relating to the pertinent provision of Protocol I of MARPOL 1973/79 and its corresponding directives. The IMO Secretary provided additional information.

It was decided that duplication of rules and directives should be avoided, and therefore that it would not be advisable to establish a different system of notification exclusively for salvage. The Committee concluded that the provisions of Protocol I of the MARPOL Convention 1973/78 (as amended) and of the draft of the directives related to the notification of incidents involving dangerous substances would also comply with the requirements of incidents that necessitate salvage operations. In this regard, the Committee took note of the fact that 35 States were parties to the 1978 MARPOL Protocol, and that the merchant fleets of these States represented approximately 78% of total world merchant marine tonnage.

Various proposals concerning the amendments to Protocol I and to the draft of the directives were examined. These proposals involve the scope of application regarding the ships that must notify interested parties of incidents (Article 1.1 of Protocol I of MARPOL 73/78 and paragraph 2.1 of the draft proposals), the preparation of reports (paragraph 4.3 of the draft proposals), and the clarification of circumstances which involve a 'probable discharge' (Article 2 of the Protocol and paragraph 2.2 of the directives).

Several other related provisions were also proposed, including:

– a provision through which the captains of both the ship in peril and the ship rendering assistance would be obligated to provide reports to the coastal State involved; and

– a provision specifying that both the ship rendering assistance and the ship being assisted must provide detailed reports on progress made in the salvage operations.

The Committee took note of these proposals and requested the Marine Committee to keep in mind the points of view expressed therein, as well as those contained in the proposals formulated by the Legal Committee. It also invited all interested governments to make any observations or suggestions that might make Protocol I and the revised directives more responsive to the need for notification and information regarding salvage operations.

Maritime liens and mortgages

Another important question involving the future activities of the Legal Committee was considered in the 53rd group of sessions while discussing relations with UNCTAD. This is the issue of maritime liens and mortgages.

The Legal Committee noted the decision of the Council relative to the recommendation of the Secretary General on the proceeding that he will follow in the IMO and the UNCTAD regarding the question of maritime liens and mortgages. Of particular interest was the fact that the Council had approved the proceeding agreed upon between the IMO Secretary General and the UNCTAD Secretary General, provided that it were also approved by the UNCTAD Maritime Transport Commission (this Commission approved the proceeding in November of 1984).

It was also noted that the CMI would not make a decision concerning the question of maritime liens and mortgages until its May, 1985 conference. However, a report on the CMI's work in this area was presented by its President, Mr. Francesco Berlingieri.

In light of these factors, the Legal Committee decided to examine the question again at its 55th group of sessions, at which time it will consider all relevant information and make decisions or formulate recommendations to the Council or to the Secretary General.

Mario Valenzuela
London, Legal Office, IMO

OECD

THE ORGANIZATION FOR ECONOMIC COOPERATION AND DEVELOPMENT AND MARITIME TRANSPORT IN 1984

SUMMARY: *I. Introduction: Global perspectives. – II. Highlights of the Report by the Committee on Maritime Transport – 1. Worldwide excess of tonnage. – 2. Matters relating to the United Nations: a) UN Convention on a Code of Conduct for Liner Conferences. – b) UN Convention on Multimodal Transport of Goods. – c) UN Convention of 1978 on Transport of Goods by Sea (Hamburg Rules). – d) UN Convention on the Law of the Sea. – e) UN Convention on Conditions for Registration of Ships. – 3. Fleets of the OECD member states. – a) Size and age of the fleets. – b) Personalia.*

I. Introduction: Global perspectives

The operation of ships, despite the general improvement in the situation of the member nations of the OECD and the increase in demand, has not been profitable due to a strong excess of tonnage in the sectors of oil, bulk cargo vessels, and container ships. If the panorama appears less gloomy for liquid and dry cargo, the construction of a large number of high-capacity containerships makes it likely that competition will increase in the sector of transport of general goods.

Due to this situation, countries have been eager to adopt measures concerning distribution of trade and national flag restrictions and the OECD, through its Committee on Maritime Transport, dedicated a large part of its efforts to fighting against these types of laws, particularly in North and East Africa, Southeast Asia, and the Pacific. The Working Group of the Committee followed these events closely and succeeded, to a certain extent, in coordinating common steps among various member States. The Group also continued to observe trade between member States and the maritime companies of those countries with State-run trade.

During the year, the Special Group of the Committee on International Organizations served as a meeting place for the formulation of common positions before CNUCYD and affiliated organizations. In general, the 11th session of the Commission on Maritime Transport, which has begun to apply the resolution of the 6th CNUCYD of 1983, was carefully prepared, particularly regarding the distribution of trade for bulk transport, the effective implementation of the UN Convention on a Code of Conduct for Liner Conferences, and the works in progress on international maritime legislation and multimodal transport. The Group discussed the common position adopted by the member States in the 1st session of the Diplomatic Conference on Conditions of Registration of Vessels. It also encouraged measures tending to reinforce liability and impede operation of ships that do not conform to the norms, but it continued to firmly oppose the adoption of mandatory rules involving the nationality of the crew, the location, and the capital.

With regard to the Committee itself, it dedicated most of its time to the elaboration of a project of recommendation that will be submitted to the OECD Council. This project contains the common principles for a maritime policy of the member States, having as a goal the maintenance of free circulation of ships for general and bulk goods within both the interior and exterior of the OECD zone. The project also seeks to establish directives on competition by regular liners in order to assure shipping companies of freedom to operate outside the system of liner conferences.

The list of direct or indirect tax or financial assistance that the member States have granted to maritime companies was completed. Additionally, a computerized data bank on maritime trade in the OECD zone, classified according to the carrier's flag, has been established. Finally, consultations have been held with both TUAC and BIAC concerning the most important problems of maritime transport, such as competition by State-run liners.[1]

II. Highlights of the Report by the Committee on Maritime Transport

The 31st Annual Report on Maritime Transport, drafted by the committee of the same name, deals with the most relevent events of 1984 and the first few months of 1985 in this field. It is divided into five chapters and a statistical annex.

1. THE WORLDWIDE EXCESS OF TONNAGE

During 1984, the registered worldwide fleet decreased by approximately 1% of deadweight tons. The conversion into scrap of tankers (19.8 million deadweight tons) was 20% less than the 1983 figure due to the stabilization of worldwide oil trade, and excess capacity in this sector has decreased

[1] *Activités de l'OCDE en 1984 – Rapport du Secrétaire Général –*, OCDE, Paris, 1985, pp. 26–27.

slightly. Nevertheless, this excess still represents approximately 60% of demand. The demolition of ships affected some 4 million deadweight tons in the dry bulk sector, but was compensated by the delivery of more than 14 million deadweight tons of new ships. While this excess tonnage is worrisome, the reduction of laid up tonnage during the year is encouraging.

With regard to freighters, the high level of deliveries of load cargo freighters has been the most notable element. It is estimated that the world containership fleet grew almost 11% in 1984, and is expected to grow up to 12% in 1985. Due to the fact that an insignificant amount of tonnage is forecast for demolition, a growth of capacity greater than the increase in worldwide trading of manufactured products is forecast.[2]

2. MATTERS WITHIN THE SCOPE OF THE UNITED NATIONS

a) UN Convention on a Code of Conduct for Liner Conferences

The Federal Republic of Germany and the Benelux countries are the only OECD member States that adhere to the UN Convention on a Code of Conduct for Liner Conferences, which entered into force on October 6, 1983. Several other member States made known their intention to ratify or adhere to the Convention, particularly Japan, Finland, Sweden and Norway.

The Common Market countries have either already ratified or will ratify the Convention according to EEC Rule 954/79, adopted in March, 1979. As contracting parties, they have declared or will declare upon adhesion their hope that all parties to the Convention follow its objectives and provisions as well as those contained in the Resolution on companies adopted in 1974 by the Conference of Plenipotentiaries. It was decided that companies outside of the liner conferences should be allowed to freely compete with companies who are members of these conferences. The entry into force of the Code of Conduct for Liner Conferences and of EEC Rule 954/79 reflects the concern of the EEC and OECD countries over the advance of uncontrolled protectionism.

Competition by State-run companies, especially those of the U.S.S.R., continues to worry a certain number of western nations and shipowners. Due to the persistent nature of this problem, the EEC decided to extend until the end of 1986 the vigilance that it maintains over the activities of the State-run companies in the commercial routes that link Europe with East Africa, Central America and the Far East. Other countries have used a different approach by attempting to establish a modus vivendi with the Soviet companies in question.[3]

[2] *Les Transports Maritimes, 1984*, OCDE, Paris, 1985, p. 16.

[3] In relation to this Convention: Vigil, R.: 'Las actividades de la UNCTAD en el campo de la legislación marítima internacional', Anuario de Derecho Marítimo, Vol. III, 1985, pp. 549–550; Martinez Puñal, A.: 'La Organización de Cooperación y Desarrollo Económicos y

b) UN Convention on Multimodal Transport of Goods

This Convention will enter into force 12 months after 30 States have become contracting parties. At the end of 1984, only Mexico, Chile, Malawi and Senegal had ratified it and Morocco, Norway and Venezuela had signed it.[4]

c) UN Convention of 1978 on Transport of Goods by Sea (Hamburg Rules)

At the end of 1984, the following States had ratified or adhered to this Convention: Egypt, Uganda, Tanzania, Tunisia, Barbados, Morocco, Romania, Chile, Lebanon, and Hungary. It will not enter into force until 20 States have become contracting parties.

d) UN Convention on the Law of the Sea

This Convention, adopted on 30 April 1982, establishes in great detail the system of law applicable to all of the world's oceans. By 10 December 1984, the date upon which it was closed to new signatures, 159 States had already become signatories. This is a record number for an international convention. Due to their objections to the provisions concerning extraction of minerals from the seabed, the United States, the United Kingdom, and the Federal Republic of Germany have not yet signed. The Convention will enter into force 12 months after the date on which the 60th instrument of ratification or adhesion has been deposited. By December of 1984 only 14 instruments had been deposited and none of them came from an industrialized country.[5]

During the last period of sessions, the Conference on the Law of the Sea

---

los Transportes Marítimos', *Ibid.*, pp. 591–592; Pueyo Losa, J.: 'La actividad de la Comunidad Económica Europea ante el Derecho Marítomo', *Ibid.*, pp. 618–619; Ademuni-Odeke: 'Implementing the UNCTAD Code of Conduct: the UK Merchant Shipping (Liner Conferences) Act, 1982', *Marine Policy*, Vol. 8, January 1984, pp. 56–63; Sturmey, S.G: 'Les taux de fret et le Code de conduite des conférences maritimes', *Journal de la Marine Marchande*, 66, 5 avril de 1984, p. 682–687; *Id.*: 'Administering the Code of Conduct', *Marine Policy*, Vol. 8, July 1984, pp. 203–216; Scheinvar, I.: 'El Código de conducta de las conferencias marítimas: significado y perspectivas', *Comercio Exterior*, Banco Nacional de Comercio Exterior (México), Vol. 34, septiembre 1984, pp. 899–909; Wijffels, R.H.: 'The Dispute Settlement Machinery on the Liner Code of Conduct: a Legal Jungle', *European Transport Law*, Vol. 19, no. 4, 1984, pp. 451–467; Conférence des Nations Unies sur le commerce et le développement (CNUCED): du code de conduite des conférences maritimes', SI/42/84, *La Semaine Internationale*, 3 du décembre 1984, p. 7.

[4] In relation to this Convention: Vigil: *op. cit.*, pp. 550–551; Martinez Puñal: *op. cit.*, pp. 592–593.

[5] In relation to this Convention: Dupuy, R.J.: 'La Convention sur le droit de la mer et le nouvel ordre économique international', *Impact: Science et Societé*, no. 3–4, 1983, pp. 336–347;

adopted a resolution on the establishment of a Preparatory Commission of International Authority over the Seabed, responsible for extraction of minerals from seabeds located outside of national jurisdictions, and on an International Court of the Law of the Sea. The Preparatory Commission held its second session from 21 March to 13 April 1984 in Kingston, Jamaica, and sessions were resumed on 13 August until 15 September of the same year. The subject of regulation of concurrent claims dominated the session. A group of industrialized countries, including signatories (Benelux countries, France, and Japan) and non-signatories (United States, United Kingdom, Federal Republic of Germany, and Italy) concluded a provisional agreement among themselves which specified that they would abstain from intervention in each other's seabeds. This provisional agreement, together with the Soviet Union's unwillingness to negotiate with private seabed exploitation consortiums, caused great controversy at the meetings and therefore no progress was made towards the regulation of concurrent claims. For the same reasons, little progress was made regarding specific questions surrounding the formation of the International Authority over the Seabed, particularly 1) the effects of seabed exploitation on the producer developing States; 2) the creation of the enterprise that will act in name of the Authority; 3) the completion of the Code on exploitation of the Seabed; and 4) the creation of a court to hear litigation that might be caused by application of the Convention.

In the latter part of 1984, a new effort was made to resolve cases of concurrent claims among the four nations who are signatories of claims procedures regarding exploitation of the seabed (U.S.S.R., Japan, France, and India). However, a mechanism to examine concurrent claims by private exploitation consortiums and States still does not exist.[6]

Caflisch, L.: 'La Convention des Nations Unies sur le droit de la mer adoptée le 30 avril 1982', *Schweizerisches Jahrbuch für Internationales Recht*, Vol. 39, 1983, pp. 39–104; Mateesco-Matte, M. 'Quelques remarques en marge de la Convention de Montego Bay (Jamaique) sur le nouveau Droit de la Mer – Du 'patrimoine commun de l'humanité' au patrimoine national des Etats riverains', *Annuaire de Droit Marítime et Aérien*, Vol. VII, 1983, pp. 17–41; Pastor Ridruejo, J.A.: 'La Convención de 1982 sobre el Derecho del Mar y los intereses de España', *Cursos de Derecho Internacional de Vitoria-Gasteiz 1983*, cf Vitoria, 1984, pp. 69–103; McDorman, T.L.: 'The 1982 Law of the Sea Convention: The First Year', *Journal of Maritime Law and Commerce*, Vol. 15, no. 2, April 1984, pp. 211–232; Treves, T.: 'Problemas generales del Derecho Internacional a la luz de la Convención de las Naciones Unidas sobre el Derecho del Mar', *Cursos de Derecho Internacional de Vitoria-Gasteiz 1984*, Vitoria, 1985, pp. 17–62; Pueyo Losa: 'La indeterminación del nuevo Orden Jurídico-Marítimo Internacional: Reflexiones sobre el caracter consuetudinario de la Zona Económica Exclusive y el valor de la Nueva Convención sobre el Derecho del Mar', *Revista Española de Derecho Internacional*, Vol. XXXVII, no. 2, 1985.

[6] 'La Commission préparatoire du droit de la mer ouvre une nouvelle session de quatre semaines a Kingston', WS/1172, *Revue de la Semaine*, 23 mars 1984, pp. 7–8; 'ONU: Commission préparatoire de l'autorité des fonds marins', SI/29/84, *Id.*, 20 août 1984, p. 2; 'Deuxième semaine de réunion de la Commission préparatoire de l'Autorité Internationale des Fonds Marins et du Tribunal du Droit de la Mer', SEA/160, 30 août 1984, pp. 1–5.

e) UN Conference on Conditions for Registration of Ships

This Conference met in Geneva from 16 July to 3 August 1984 in its first session, and later continued from 28 January to 16 February 1985. Between these two sessions, the President of the Conference, Mr. Fadika (Ivory Coast), undertook a vast program of consultation concerning the key problems that required solution. When the sessions resumed, Mr. Fadika deposited a document containing a summary of the points of agreement and disagreement among the diverse participants in the negotiations, but was unable to deliver an official compromise position.

This document turned out to be very useful. The Group of 77 elaborated its own compromise position, which was similar to that of Group B, and in which it was recognized that the adoption of a series of rigorous conditions on recruitment of crewmembers and management of ships ran the risk of creating difficulties. The Group of 77 remained faithful to its position, believing it necessary that the nationals of the flag State be at least in part owners of the ship or constitute a part of the crew.

The third session was held in July of 1985, and further progress was made. The final session will take place early in 1986.

3. FLEETS OF THE OECD MEMBER STATES

a) Size and age of the fleets

Due to the decrease of the fleets of the OECD member States, which has mainly affected the oldest ships, the age of the OECD fleet in its entirety is slightly lower than that of the worldwide fleet. This observation is especially true for the non-bulk fleet, where the oldest and least sophisticated vessels are found under the flags of the free registration and the developing countries. Among the principal fleets of the OECD, that of Belgium is quite modern, with 80% of its tonnage being less than 10 years old and having an average age of 7 years. The fleets of Sweden and Australia are similar. On the other hand, the fleets of Canada and the United States are the oldest. Even if the fleets of the Great Lakes (which have an average age of, respectively, 20.1 and 23.9 years) are not considered, the fleets of these two countries have an average of 15.4 and 16.4 years. Among the oldest fleets, they are followed by that of Greece (13.7 years) and Turkey (13.2 years).

b) Personalia

The number of seamen in almost all of the OECD countries has decreased. The greatest decreases are found in the United Kingdom, Denmark, the Benelux countries and the United States, reflecting for the most part the decrease in tonnage and in the number of flagships of these States. Turkey and Austria are the only nations that experienced an increase. The Turkish fleet increases 46% since 1981, and the Austrian fleet tripled during the same period.

The general contraction of fleets has been accompanied by a tendency to reduce the number of persons employed in each ship. The EEC Commission reported that total tonnage of member States doubled between 1960 and 1980, but the number of seamen decreased from 376,000 to 254,000. The President of the Norwegian group DYVI has stated that the average crew size has decreased from 25 or 30 men to 14, and may decrease to only 5 by the end of this century. Japan is working to decrease crew size, and in the United States, crews and unions are collaborating in a public program endowed with 1 million dollars designed to reduce the number of crew-members.

This reduction in crew size seems to be the only solution, if recruitment of crew members from low-cost countries is to be avoided. During the end of 1984, these questions frequently faced shipowners and unions; at the same time, differences were also centered in demands for salary increases, causing a series of conflicts in Germany, Denmark, Greece, Japan, United Kingdom, and Norway. In the latter country, proposals recommending aid for the transition to other flags and employment of foreign nationals, after encountering fierce opposition by unions, were recalled in April 1985 in order to be reexamined. In the EEC, the Commission has been repeatedly requested to apply a policy permitting shipowners to offer salaries and working conditions that would attract citizens of these countries. This option would be supported by protectionist mechanisms that would isolate European maritime transport and would be contrary to the general policy of free competition. The Commission, resisting these pressures, states that it opposed the concept of economic linkage with regard to recruitment of crewmembers.

By the end of 1984, the fleets of Australia, Austria, Belgium, Denmark, Greece, the Benelux countries, Norway, the United Kingdom, and Sweden employed at least 10% of foreign nationals. On the contrary, in the United States, Portugal, Spain and Turkey, all crewmembers were required to be nationals. In Japan, shipowners prepared to fight against competition by their immediate neighbors – Taiwan, Korea, and the Phillipines – countries in which the cost of crewmembers is lower and which are in favor of employment of foreign crews. It is clear that it will be increasingly difficult to choose between the reduction of crews, the utilization of foreign crew-members, or the transfer of ships to another flag.

Antonio Martinez Puñal
Professor of International Law
University of Santiago de Compostela Law School, Spain

B.

NON-GOVERNMENTAL ORGANIZATIONS

IMC

ACTIVITIES OF THE INTERNATIONAL MARITIME COMMITTEE IN 1984

SUMMARY: *1. Unification of maritime law. – 2. 1985 IMC International Conference. – 3. IMC Assembly, 6 April 1984. – 4. IMC Report on the Draft International Convention on Salvage. – 5. International seminars concerning maritime law. – 6. Personalia.*

1. Unification of maritime law

During the past several years the IMC has been studying methods to achieve greater unification of maritime law. The Committee has worked with individual countries and with U.N. organizations such as IMO, UNCTAD, and ESCAP.

In 1984, the Committee assisted ESCAP in the preparation of a model maritime code for Asian countries. It drafted and revised chapters on several subjects of private maritime law, and when this work was completed a meeting of the Group of Experts was held at the ESCAP headquarters in Bangkok from 12–16 November 1984. The experts reached agreement on the texts of all the chapters, including those on contracts of affreightment, maritime liens and mortgages, and limitation of shipowner's liability. Final editing is now in progress and the new code should be ready in 1985.

2. 1985 IMC International Conference

During its 9 September 1984 meeting the Executive Council announced that the agenda of the 23rd IMC International Conference, to be held in Lisbon from 19–25 May 1985, will include the subjects of arrest of sea-going ships, and maritime liens and mortgages. There will also be meetings of the two International Subcommittees on the subjects of compensation for damages in collision cases, and uniform rules on sea waybills.

3. IMC Assembly, 6 April 1984

The Assembly elected the following new honorary members: Professor Michel de Juglart, France; Mr. Panayotis Sotiropoulos and Mr. George Rediadis, Greece; Mr. P. J. Smith, Mr. F. Lynn, and Mr. B. McGovern, Ireland; Mr. Manuel Quiroga Carmona, Peru; and Professor Ignacio Arroyo Martinez, Spain. Plans were announced to create a regional association for maritime law in West Africa. The Working Group announced its intention to set up an 'IMC International Fund' to receive contributions with the goal of U.S. $300,000 from intergovernmental and governmental bodies, insurers, shipowners, banks, and law firms.

Finally, information was submitted to the Assembly on the status of several IMC works now in progress. With regard to maritime liens and mortgages, the President, Mr. Berlinghieri, reported on the meeting held by the International Subcommittee on 4 and 5 April 1984. He noted that the changes to the 1967 Convention which had been suggested by a number of national associations had been considered during the meeting. He also stated that during the 5th April joint meeting of the International Subcommittees on Maritime Liens and Mortgages and on Arrest of Ships, the problem of coordination between the two conventions was discussed. A majority agreed that better cooperation was needed, but that it was better to have two separate conventions.

In the area of arrest of ships, Professor Schultsz reported that suggestions have been made to increase the number of maritime claims and to replace the list of maritime claims with a general wording that included all claims of a maritime nature. He also mentioned other issues under discussion, including that of whether a claimant should be entitled to arrest a vessel for claims against the bare boat charterer of the vessel.

Professor Gronfors informed the Committee on matters relating to sea waybills. Standard conditions for international terminal operators was the subject of Dr. Reme's report to the Assembly. It was decided that preparation of the conditions should be postponed until UNCITRAL finishes drafting the International Convention on Operators of Transport Terminals.

Mr. Warot reported on the present status of work in the area of compensation for damages in collision cases, and Mr. Muller discussed private international maritime law.

ESCAP Guidelines on Maritime Legislation figured in Mr. Berlinghieri's report. A meeting to revise the guidelines will be held in Bangkok in December 1984. ESCAP is also involved in the preparation of a model maritime law for the Phillipines including sections on mortgages and liens, limitation of shipowner's liability, and carriage of goods. Additionally, the

People's Republic of China has requested ESCAP's assistance on a series of seminars on maritime law to be held in China in 1984 and 1985.

Finally, Mr. Pineus reported that the revised edition of the study on time bars would appear shortly.

4. Draft International Convention on Salvage

The disastrous 'Amoco Cadiz' oil spill of 1978 prompted the IMO Legal Committee to prepare a report on the legal implications of the incident. This report was completed in September of 1978 and discussed several aspects of salvage in great detail. Questions were raised concerning whether the law of salvage as contained in the 1910 Brussels Convention should be rewritten, or whether a completely new convention should be prepared.

In March 1979, the IMC offered IMO its assistance in the field of salvage, particularly regarding new rules to cover situations of oil pollution. In June 1979, the IMO Legal Committee requested that the IMC review the private law principles of salvage. The IMC set up an international subcommittee under the chairmanship of Professor Erling Selvig of Norway in September 1979. A report was prepared for the IMC's 22nd International Conference on 24–29 May 1981. The final draft of this report was overwhelmingly adopted by the National Maritime Law Associations. It is now being submitted to the IMO for consideration.

5. International seminars concerning maritime law

The IMC was presented at seminars organized by various associations. At the Meeting of the UNCTAD Ad hoc Intergovernmental Group to consider Means of Combatting all Aspects of Maritime Fraud, including Piracy, held on 6 February 1984, the IMC Venice Recommendations were taken into account. IMC submitted papers to IMO at the Diplomatic Conference on the Revision of the Civil Liability Convention and the Fund Convention and on a Convention on Carriage of Noxious and Hazardous Substances by Sea. Finally, the IMC also participated in the 1984 International Maritime Arbitration Organization's activities designed to enhance arbitration under the ICC/IMC Maritime Arbitration Rules.

6. Personalia

The following became new Presidents of member associations in 1984: Graydon S. Staring, 2 Embarcadero Center, San Francisco, CA 94111, new President of the Maritime Law Association of the United States; Per-Erik Hedborg, new President of the Swedish Association of International

Maritime Law; Dr. Guillermo Sarmiento Rodriguez, new President of the Colombian Association of Maritime Studies; Dr. Jose Joaquim de Almeida Borges, Portuguese Commission of International Maritime Law.

The new address of the Peruvian Association of Maritime Law is as follows: Association Peruana de Derecho Maritimo, Calle Cjacarilla No. 485, San Isidro, Lima 27, Peru, telephone 41-4414, 41-2847, telex 25634 PE NAFRISA.

Ignacio Arroyo
Titulary Member of IMC

BIMCO

ACTIVITIES OF THE BALTIC AND INTERNATIONAL MARITIME CONFERENCES IN 1984

SUMMARY: *1. New charterparties. – a. Nipponcoal. – b. Proposed revision of Norgrain charter. – 2. New charterparty clauses. – a. Bimchemtime. – b. Model clauses for tankers. – 3. BIMCO relations with UNCTAD. – a. Maritime fraud. – b. Charterparties. – 4. Disputes. – a. Fire in vessel's hold. – 5. Documentary Council activity. – 6. Personalia.*

1. New charterparties

a. NIPPONCOAL

The Documentary Council adopted, at its 9 November 1983 meeting, the final draft of the 'Nipponcoal' Coal Charter Party. This document had been the subject of discussions between the Documentary Council and the Documentary Committee of the Japan Shipping Exchange, Inc. of Tokyo.

The Council felt that the document was a fair one and a great improvement over the usual coal charter forms used in trading with Japan. It is believed that it may serve as a model for an international coal charter. The broad involvement of charterers, receivers, steel companies, power stations, and important Japanese consumer concerns has been praised.

b. PROPOSED REVISION OF NORGRAIN CHARTER

The North American Grain Charterparty 1973, known as 'Norgrain', was issued in 1973 by the Association of Ship Brokers and Agents Inc. of New York after discussions with various interested groups including the Federation of National Associations of Ship Brokers and Agents (FONASBA), the Chamber of Shipping of the United Kingdom (presently the General Council of British Shipping – GCBS), the North American Export Grain Association (NAEGA), and BIMCO. The parties agreed that the charter should be reviewed occasionally to conform to changes in the structure of the grain trade.

In 1980, BIMCO suggested that the parties should meet to consider certain revisions of the charter regarding port inspection, water pollution, and fumigation. Several meetings were held in New York in 1980 and 1981, and a number of changes to the Norgrain charter were agreed upon.

However, NAEGA announced in 1983 that it would not agree to any changes in the 1983 charter. BIMCO and the other parties believed it necessary to maintain the status of the Norgrain charter as one supported by NAEGA, and it was therefore decided to postpone the October 1983 meeting until such time as NAEGA could be persuaded to join in talks. For these reasons, the 1973 charter is still the one 'recommended' by the parties mentioned above.

2. New charterparty clauses

a. BIMCHEMTIME

The need for uniform chartering documents with standard terms and conditions has arisen in recent years due to the rapid growth of the chemical industry, the resulting demand, and the consequent increase in the number of vessels on the market. Therefore in 1979, the BIMCO Documentary Council published a voyage charterparty for the chemical trade called 'Bimchemvoy' Standard Voyage Charter Party for the Transportation of Chemicals in Tank Vessels. In spite of the effects of the worldwide recession on the chemical industry, the 'Bimchemvoy' Charter is being increasingly used.

Soon afterwards, BIMCO was requested by chemical trading companies to formulate uniform chartering terms for the time charter business. The Documentary Council decided to set up a subcommittee to deal with the problem of drafting a uniform time charterparty for vessels that carry chemicals in bulk. This uniform charterparty was necessary because shipowners often found themselves forced to accept one of the large oil companies' time charter forms, which were designed for oil rather than chemical tankers.

The subcommittee completed its work in 1983 after consulting interested groups. In November 1983, the BIMCO Documentary Council officially adopted the Uniform Time Charter Party for Vessels Carrying Chemicals in Bulk, known as 'Bimchemtime'. This new charter employs the 'box-layout' system with separate Part I and Part II, and includes a technical specification of the vessel to be annexed to the charter.

The central purpose of the new charter is to compel all amendments and special provisions to be made in Part I, thereby leaving Part II unaltered. This allows the parties to be flexible during negotiations and to later include in Part I those special terms that have been agreed upon. The new document also contains important clauses regarding condition of vessel/adjustment of hire, drydocking, compliance with regulations, liens, and war risks.

b. MODEL CLAUSES FOR TANKERS

INTERTANKO, the International Association of Independent Tanker Owners, has published 'Tanker Chartering Clauses', which discusses problems encountered in drafting certain chartering provisions, especially those involving novel or irregular situations not included in standard clauses. These include late payment and demurrage, bunker quality, environmental and safety conditions, and crude oil washing.

The publication also examines port safety in light of the new international safety guide for tankers and terminals (ISGOTT). The question of war risks insurance, while discussed by INTERTANKO's documentary committee, is not the subject of a new model provision, since it is already contained in the 'Intertanktime 80' clauses.

3. BIMCO relations with UNCTAD

a. MARITIME FRAUD

From 6–17 February 1984, an UNCTAD Ad Hoc Intergovernmental Group met in Geneva to discuss ways of combatting all aspects of maritime fraud, including piracy. BIMCO attended the meeting and delivered both oral and written statements.

BIMCO stated that, in order to protect their image, reputation, and trustworthiness, shipowners must make intensified efforts to reduce incidents of fraud and piracy. The work of the International Maritime Bureau (IMB), which has resulted in a decrease in reported incidents, was commended. BIMCO has cooperated and exchanged information with the IMB.

Additionally, BIMCO felt that the issue of armed robberies against ships should be left with the International Maritime Organization (IMO) for further action, including a possible International Conference on the issue of Piracy and Armed Robberies Against Ships.

BIMCO declared that before UNCTAD mounts a total program to suppress maritime fraud, the users of international maritime transport and the shippng industry must be consulted to determine whether maritime fraud related to international trading cannot be more efficiently encountered by commercial entities.

The BIMCO paper that was submitted to the meeting discussed the following topics and proposals: a central registry for bills of lading; 'secure' bills of lading; a register of authorized signatures; stamped signatures on bills of lading; part shipments, revocable credits, and bank guarantees; conditions of registration of vessels; monitoring of ship movement; tightening of procedures by governments concerning the sale of goods; improved supervision of free trade zones; establishing a checking scheme; improvement of port security; establishment of an international ship information registry; proposed number system for ships; uniform minimum standards concerning shipping agencies' financial qualifications; and piracy and armed robbery against ships.

b. CHARTERPARTIES

Charterparties were on everyone's mind during a visit of BIMCO's President, Mr. Eduardo Bages, and Executive Committee Chairman, Mr. Lund, to the UNCTAD Secretariat's Shipping Division in Geneva in 1984. The visit was designed to establish greater cooperation between BIMCO and the UNCTAD Secretariat, particularly regarding BIMCO's expertise in drafting charterparties.

Mr. Lamine Fadika, the Marine Minister of the Ivory Coast, discussed his feelings on the state of the shipping industry with the BIMCO delegation.

Finally, the UNCTAD Secretariat informed BIMCO that it would continue to rely on the input offered by private assocations within the shipping industry, and that BIMCO in particular would be consulted on subjects such as charterparties and maritime fraud.

4. Disputes

a. FIRE IN VESSEL'S HOLD

BIMCO advised the parties in the following dispute: during cargo loading at port, the vessel's hold caught fire due to spontaneous combustion of the cargo in one of the holds. The charterparty at issue was the NYPE Charter. The charterers claimed that under clause 15 of the charterparty, they were entitled to put the vessel off-hire for the lost time caused by the fire. The owners disagreed, alleging that the word "fire" in clause 15 signified a fire to the vessel's hull, machinery, and equipment, and that the charterers could not put the vessel off-hire when the fire was not caused by the fault of the owners or crew.

The BIMCO Office first stated that this was a case of first impression, as it was not aware of any awards or judgments involving cargo fires on time chartered vessels. Furthermore, it believed that liability for fire and ensuing loss of time did not necessarily fall upon the time charterers merely because they supplied the vessel. To the contrary, clause 16 of the charterparty, which immunized both parties from liability for fire, and clause 15, suspending payment of hire for fires expressly mentioned in the clause, were applicable. The word 'fire' in clause 15 was not limited to 'vessel's parts', nor to 'fire on board'. (I BIMCO Bulletin 7529, No. 333, 1984).

5. Documentary Council activity

A meeting of the Documentary Council was held on 14 November 1984. It was attended by representatives of brokers, INTERTANKO, and FONASBA, among others.

The Council completed the first draft of the Proposed Standard Transportation Contract for Heavy and Voluminous Cargoes ('Heavycon'). After consideration of amendments, the document will be distributed to trade interests for their input. The Council also considered two proposed standard international towage agreements which were drafted after consultations among representatives of the International Salvage Union (ISU) and a Documentary Council subcommittee. Final drafts will hopefully be ready in 1985. Lastly, BIMCO pointed out the danger of using obsolete war risk clauses, several of which were drafted as far back in time as 1935, and are totally inadequate for modern conflicts such as the hostilities in the Persian Gulf.

6. Personalia

The BIMCO Secretary General, Mr. W. Moller Sorensen of Denmark, retired effective 1 April 1984. Mr. Sorensen, who joined BIMCO in 1953, spent most of his life in the shipping industry. He had a distinguished career as both a businessman and a BIMCO member.

Ignacio Arroyo
Matthew Schreiber

UNIDROIT

THE ACTIVITY OF UNIDROIT IN 1982 AND 1983

SUMMARY: *1. Introduction. – 2. Liability of international terminal operators (the warehousing contract). – 3. Civil liability for damage caused by hazardous cargoes. – 4. Pleasure navigation. – 5. Agency in the international sale of goods. – 6. Progressive codification of international trade law. – 7. The leasing contract. – 8. The factoring contract.*

1. Introduction

In the course of 1982 and 1983 Unidroit continued its work not only in the field of maritime law but also in other areas falling within the general compass of international trade law. A summary of the progress made in respect of each subject is given below. In addition, the Institute pursued its policy of maintaining close links with the principal organisations responsible for the unification of maritime law such as IMO, UNCITRAL, UNCTAD and the CMI, while the Secretariat of Unidroit also played an important role in the International Conference on the Harmonisation of the Maritime Law of African Countries held in Venice in May 1982.

2. Liability of international terminal operators (the warehousing contract)

In accordance with a decision taken by the Governing Council of Unidroit at its 61st session in 1982 the Secretariat communicated the preliminary draft Convention on the liability of international terminal operators to interested circles for observations and the replies received formed the object of study by a restricted group of members of the Governing Council which met on 2 and 3 May 1983 under the chairmanship of the Swedish member, Professor Kurt Grönfors. The other members of the group were Professor Diamond (United Kingdom), Professor Enderlein (German Democratic Republic),

Professor Farnsworth (United States of America), Professor Loewe (Austria), Professor Parra-Aranguren (Venezuela) and Judge Plantard (France). Most of the amendments made to the text were of a drafting character and the title was changed to read: 'Preliminary draft Convention on operators of transport terminals (OTTs)'. One important change of substance however was constituted by the decision to delete the draft final clauses prepared by the Secretariat on the ground first that it was premature to determine the precise character which any future instrument containing the rules might assume and secondly that if the form of a convention were ultimately to be chosen then the formulation of the final clauses would depend upon the forum in which the convention would be adopted. Notwithstanding this general policy decision, it was decided to maintain the provision (Article 13) relating to the unit of account in which the limitation of the liability of the OTT should be expressed and to substitute for the language taken from the Hamburg Rules a provision corresponding to that recommended by United Nations General Assembly Resolution 37/107 of 16 December 1982. In view of the close link between this provision and the possibility of instituting a revision mechanism, and this without prejudice to the form of the future rules, it was also considered useful for the sake of completeness to include an Article Y concerning the revision of the limitation amounts and unit of account, once again based on the model recommended in General Assembly Resolution 37/107.

At its 62nd session in May 1983 the Governing Council approved the text of the preliminary draft Convention on operators of transport terminals as drawn up by the Secretariat on the basis of the decisions of the restricted group of members of the Council at its meeting held on 2 and 3 May 1983. The Council also reiterated the wish already expressed in its Resolution 61 (2) that the Secretariat should seek to give maximum exposure to the draft and authorised it formally to transmit the draft to UNCITRAL should the latter make such a request.

At its 16th session, held in Vienna from 24 May to 3 June 1983, the United Nations Commission on International Trade Law (UNCITRAL) decided to include the topic of liability of international terminal operators in its work programme, to request Unidroit to transmit its preliminary draft Convention to the Commission for its consideration, and to assign work on the preparation of uniform rules on this topic to a Working Group. The Commission deferred to its next session the decision on the composition of the Working Group. The Secretariat was requested to submit to the Commission at its next session a study of important issues arising from the Unidroit preliminary draft Convention, and to consider in this study the possibility of broadening the scope of uniform rules to cover storage and safekeeping of goods not involved in transport. The Secretariat of Unidroit has communicated the text of the preliminary draft Convention to the Commission pursuant to its request.

3. Civil liability for damage caused by hazardous cargoes

The Unidroit Committee of Governmental Experts for the preparation of uniform rules relating to liability and compensation for damage caused during the carriage over land of hazardous substances held four sessions in the period 1982 to 1983 in the course of which it completed the first reading of the preliminary draft articles for a Convention on civil liability for damage caused during carriage of dangerous goods by road, rail and inland navigation vessels.

The draft articles are modelled to a very large extent on the IMO draft articles for a convention on liability and compensation in connection with carriage of hazardous and noxious substances by sea (the draft HNS Convention). In particular they make provision for a channelling of the liability under the draft Convention to the carrier on the grounds that he is the person most easily identifiable by the victim, a strict liability regime with limited defences, a limitation of the carrier's liability to amounts which can be broken only in highly exceptional circumstances as well as an obligation for the carrier to take out insurance and to constitute a limitation fund in order to benefit from the limitation of liability.

The basic principles underlying the initial text prepared by the chairman of the committee have to a large extent been maintained although a number of qualifications have been proposed to the principle of channelling liability to the carrier, to the strict liability regime, to the virtually unbreakable character of the limitation amounts and to the obligations to take out insurance and to constitute a limitation fund.

In particular, at the committee's fifth session held in October 1983, moves were made to alleviate the carrier's liability under the draft Convention in those cases where he neither knew nor ought to have known of the dangerous character of the goods and where the operations of loading and discharging the goods were performed under the responsibility of another person and the incident causing the damage occurred during the performance of such operations. These proposals will be discussed in further detail at the sixth session of the committee, to be held from 22 to 26 October 1984, that is to say after sufficient time has elapsed to assess the results of the IMO Diplomatic Conference for the adoption of the draft HNS Convention.

Some thirty States are now actively involved in the work of the Unidroit committee, together with observer representatives from the interested intergovernmental and non-governmental organisations. It is anticipated that the committee will complete its work in the course of 1985.

4. Pleasure navigation

As announced in Volume II of the Annuario de Derecho Maritimo (page

415), Unidroit's draft Convention on civil liability for damage caused by small craft was forwarded to the Economic Commission for Europe and it was considered by the Group of Experts on River Law of the Working Party on Inland Water Transport at its sixth session, held in Geneva from 26 to 28 October 1981.

It emerged from the discussions of the Working Party that a majority of States represented at the session considered that there was little need for such a Convention at the present time and that there was above all no justification for a liability regime of the kind contemplated by the draft which was not based on the principle of fault. Criticism was also levelled in some quarters at the absence of provisions dealing with compulsory insurance while other representatives were strongly opposed to the introduction of the requirement of compulsory insurance in this field, primarily for administrative reasons. In these circumstances the Group decided not to embark on a detailed discussion of the provisions of the Convention, pending a decision by the competent organs of the Economic Commission for Europe as to whether work should be continued on the draft.

The matter was referred back to the Working Party on Inland Water Transport which, at its 26th session, held in Geneva from 8 to 12 November 1982, noted that a majority of the representatives present at the above-mentioned meeting of the Group of Experts on River Law had expressed doubts as to whether such a convention should be prepared under ECE auspices, and the Working Party consequently took the view that there was no need to continue the work for the time being. The only support for a continuation of work on the draft Convention came from the representative of Hungary who stressed its importance in view of the increase in waterway tourism, although at the same time he believed that its application should be limited to pleasure craft and not to small craft in general.

The Governing Council of Unidroit took note of these developments at its 62nd session in May 1983 as well as of the fact that certain States such as Austria and Italy have adopted, or are moving in the direction of adopting, legislation which contains solutions similar to those for which provision is made in the draft Convention. The Council therefore authorised the Secretariat to transmit the text of the draft Convention on civil liability for damage caused by small craft and the accompanying Explanatory Report to the Governments of the member States of Unidroit with the expression of the wish that they take account of the principles contained in the draft Convention when proceeding to any revision of their law on the subject.

5. Agency in the international sale of goods

A Diplomatic Conference for the adoption of a Convention on agency in the international sale of goods was held in Geneva, at the invitation of the Swiss Government, from 31 January to 17 February 1983. Fifty-eight States participated in the Conference, amongst which not only all the most important Western countries but also the Soviet Union, China and many other Socialist countries. There was in addition a wide participation from Third World countries. The head of the Swedish delegation, Mr. K. Grönfors, was elected President of the Conference, which also elected as its Vice-Presidents Mr. M. J. Bonell (Italy), Mr. A. Fajardo-Maldonado (Guatemala), Mr. D. Kimbembé (Congo), Mr. O. V. Koschevnikov (U.S.S.R) and Mr. C. Liu (China). The work of the Committee of the Whole was presided over by Mr. P. Widmer (Switzerland), that of the Final Clauses Committee by Mr. L. Sevón (Finland), that of the Drafting Committee by Mr. E. A. Farnsworth (U.S.A.) and that of the Credentials Committee by Mr. H. Hausheer (Switzerland). The Secretary-General of the Conference was Mr. M. Evans, Deputy Secretary-General of Unidroit, who also exercised the functions of Rapporteur to the Committee of the Whole.

The new Convention is based on a draft worked out by Unidroit, after years of preparatory study in which the most eminent jurists from the main legal systems took part. Its purpose is to lay down a uniform regulation of those cases where a person has the authority (or purports to have the authority) to conclude on behalf of another person a contract for the international sale of goods (cf. Article 1, paragraph 1 and Article 2, paragraph 1).

The new Convention, approved unanimously at the Geneva Conference, is open to signature until 31 December 1984 (Article 22). It will enter into force when ratified by ten States (Article 33). There are many reasons for welcoming ths new set of rules. They achieve a satisfactory compromise between the difference which traditionally exist between the Civil Law and Common law systems in regard to agency. The fact should also be borne in mind that there already exists among a number of European countries a uniform regime relating to the international sale of goods (cf. the Hague Uniform Laws of 1964), and with the entry into force in the near future of the Vienna Convention of 1980, the matter should become the subject of uniform rules at universal level: as it is a well-known fact that it is common for international sales to be concluded through an agent rather than by the parties directly, it is easy to see how the new Geneva Convention may usefully be incorporated into, and complete, the uniform law regime established by the Hague Uniform Laws of 1964 (and now by the Vienna Convention of 1980).

The Convention has, to date, been signed by Chile, the Holy See, Italy, Morocco and Switzerland.

6. Progressive codification of international trade law

In the course of four sessions, held between February 1974 and April 1978, a Steering Committee set up by the President of Unidroit prepared the first two chapters of a projected international trade law Code, dealing respectively with the formation and interpretation of contracts. These texts, with an accompanying explanatory report prepared by the Secretariat of Unifroit, were considered by an enlarged group, the Study Group on the progressive codification of international trade law, at a meeting held in Rome in September 1979. The Group requested the Secretariat to revise the texts in the light of the proposals for amendment and the new suggestions made. The Group also agreed that the next chapter of the Code should deal with the problem of validity of contracts in general, in which connection it was considered that the work already carried out by the Institute in this field could serve as a starting point and that, in the future draft, specific rules on the validity of general conditions and standard forms of contracts should be added. As to the proposed chapters on performance and non-performance of contracts, the Group requested the President of Unidroit to set up special sub-committees for their preparation.

Two meetings of an informal Working Group were subsequently held, the first in Copenhagen in 1980 and the second in Hamburg in 1981, at the second of which the Group considered two preliminary studies prepared by members of the Group. The first of these aimed at the clarification and completion of the existing Unidroit draft of a law for the unification of certain rules relating to validity of contracts of international sale of goods of 1972 so as to adapt it to the requirements of international commercial contracts in general while the second investigated the possibility of dealing in the framework of the future Code also with the problem of illegality of international commercial contracts. The first study, prepared by Professors Drobnig and Lando, included a number of new provisions as compared with the 1972 Unidroit draft so as to cover important questions such as unequal bargaining power, gross unfairness and the right of adaptation, while in addition the remaining part of that draft was revised in the light of recent developments in international legislation and case-law. The draft rules on 'Prohibitation and licence requirements' prepared by Professor Maskow and Dr. Andrae on the other hand constitutes the first attempt to deal with the question in a general and systematic manner at international level.

Following consideration of the two draft sets of rules by the Study Group at its second session, held in Rome in April 1982, two further meetings of the informal Working Group were held in 1983, at Louvain-la-Neuve and Rome respectively. At the first of these meetings the Group had before it the texts of the three draft chapters relating to formation, interpretation and validity of contracts as revised following the discussions at the two meetings of the Study Group. A number of new ideas were put forward at the meeting of the Informal Working Group which called for further revision of the chapter on validity, thus permitting the finalisation of the first three chapters of the draft. The meeting was also informed of the preparation of a study and draft articles on hardship by Professor Maskow and of a preliminary study on performance by Professors Rajski and Fontaine. At the Rome meeting the informal Working Group revised certain provisions of the chapter on public prohibitions and permission requirements in the light of the reservations expressed by a number of members of the Governing Council during its 62nd session in May 1983.

7. The leasing contract

At its 56th session in May 1977, the Governing Council of Unidroit decided to set up a study Group with a view to the preparation of uniform rules on the leasing contract.

Three sessions of the Study Group were held in Rome in November 1977, in February 1979 and from 30 September to 2 October 1980 under the chairmanship of the Hungarian member of the Governing Council, Professor László Réczei, who had alrady chaired the restricted exploratory Working Group of the Governing Council. The preliminary draft uniform rules worked out by the Study Group were then given wide exposure by the Secretariat, in particular at symposia organised in New York and Zürich in 1981 and at the First World Leasing Convention held in Hong Kong in January 1983, at which the draft was introduced to bankers, businessmen and practising lawyers having expertise in international leasing. On the basis of the discussions at these meetings, the Secretariat and the Chairman of the Study Group prepared a revised draft of the rules for consideration by the Study Group at its fourth session to be held in Rome in March 1984.

The principal features of the preliminary draft uniform rules drawn up by the Study Group are their characterisation of the *sui generis* form of leasing transaction in which it is the user rather than the owner who chooses both supplier and equipment and their enshrinement of this *sui generis* character in *sui generis* legal consequences framed with its particular characteristics specifically in mind. Thus the uniform rules confer on the user a direct independent right of action for damages against the supplier in respect of any loss or damage sustained by him as a result of non-delivery, late delivery or the delivery of defective equipment. They establish the lessee's right to reject a tender of the equipment which is not made within a reasonable time after the delivery date stipulated in the supply contract (or, if none, within a reasonable time after the making of that contract) or which otherwise fails in a material respect to conform to the terms of the supply contract. Both these rights are novel creations in favour of the lessee, as they would normally inure to the lessor as owner of the equipment; their conferment on the lessee in the *sui generis* leasing situation is justified by the fact that it is the lessee who chooses both supplier and equipment. The uniform rules, subject to certain exceptions, on the other hand give the lessor a general immunity from the contractual and tortious duties that would ordinarily flow from his ownership of the equipment, given that his ownership in the *sui generis* form of leasing is stripped of virtually all the normal attributes of legal ownership and that the technical responsibility for the equipment chosen, and therefore the physical risks associated with its use, cannot reasonably be laid at his door.

It should, however, be borne in mind that the uniform rules are in no way intended to be an exhaustive regulation of the legal problems arising in respect of this *sui generis* transaction but merely to provide a basic, largely permissive legal framework to which the parties would then be free to add in accordance with the particular requirements of each transaction. This was felt to be particularly important in the case of a transaction to which all the parties are businessmen, consumer leasing having been excluded from the outset.

At its third session, the Study Group agreed to limit the scope of the uniform rules to specifically international leasing situations. As regards the question of which factors should determine whether or not a given leasing transaction should be treated as international for the purposes of the uniform rules, it was decided to exclude the impact of the supplier's principal place of business and rather to take the principal places of business of the lessor and the lessee as the decisive factors for this purpose. However, the fact that the uniform rules are cast in the form of an international Convention and are stated to apply specifically to international leasing situations should not be seen as prejudicing the final form which it may be decided to give to the uniform rules. The principal objective of these rules has all along been the establishment of a basic legal framework cast with the particular characteristics of the *sui generis* form of tripartite leasing transaction specifically in mind, so as to distinguish it once and for all from the various classical contractual schemata within the comfortable logic of which it has hitherto in general been the tendency to try to accommodate it. There has been agreement from the outset within the Study Group that, notwithstanding the enormous potential of leasing at the cross-border level, true cross-border leasing will not really take off until such time as there is a greater degree of legal certainty regarding the treatment of leasing transactions at the purely domestic level. Given the dearth of domestic legislation addressed to this problem, it is likely that for some time to come the uniform rules will accordingly have a greater impact as the basis of domestic legislation than as legislation addressed specifically to international leasing.

8. The factoring contract

At three sessions held in Rome in February 1979, April 1981 and April 1982, a Study Group chaired by the Netherlands member of the Governing Council of Unidroit, Professor Jean-Georges Sauveplanne, considered a number of problems related to international factoring operations and at the close of its third session it approved the text of a set of preliminary draft rules on certain aspects of international factoring.

One of the principal features of the draft rules is the affirmation of the commercial or professional character of the receivables which the supplier undertakes to assign to the factor on a continuing basis by way of sale or security. As consideration for the assignment, the factor provides certain services such as financial, the maintenance of accounts, collection of receivables and protection against credit risks. The international character of the factoring contract is based on the fact that it relates to receivables arising from a contract for the sale of goods or provision of services between parties whose places or business are situated in different States, with the rider that if a party has more than one place of business, his place of business for the purpose of the provision is that having the closest relationship to the contract of sale and its performance. Since it is the original sales contract which confers on the contract of factoring its international character, the proposed rules also apply to successive assignments between several factors, even though their places of business are situated in the same State.

With a view to encouraging factoring operations, the assignment of receivables by the supplier to the factor, including in certain circumstances future receivables, will be effective notwithstanding any agreement between the supplier and the debtor prohibiting such assignment. The factoring contract of any assignment made pursuant to it may validly provide for the transfer to the factor of all or any of the supplier's rights under the contract of sale, including any provision in such contract reserving title to the supplier.

The factor is further protected by a provision to the effect that he shall not, by reasons only of transfer of title to goods to him, incur liability to a third party for loss, injury or damage caused by the goods. On the other hand, he may be held liable if he sells or otherwise disposes of the goods to a person who is not the supplier or another factor or the debtor.

Another important feature of the rules is that they are intended to apply only in relation to factoring contracts pursuant to which notice of assignment of the receivable is to be given to the debtor. It is also provided that for the assignment to be effective against the debtor the notice must be given to the debtor in writing and reasonably identify the receivables which have been assigned and the person to whom the debtor is required to make payment. The notice must contain a statement that the assignment is governed by the uniform rules. Furthermore the notice is effective only in relation to a receivable arising under a contract concluded at or before the time the notice is given.

On the other hand, when the factor claims payment of a receivable arising under a contract of sale, the debtor may set up against the factor all defences of which the debtor could have availed himself under the contract if such claim had been made by the supplier. The debtor may also exercise against the factor any right of set-off, in respect of claims existing and available to the debtor at the time the debtor received notice of the assignment, against the supplier in whose favour the receivable arose. However, non-performance or defective or late performance of the contract of sale by the supplier does not entitle the debtor to recover money paid by the debtor to the factor except in the cases mentioned above.

Finally a debtor in good faith who has no reason to know of any other person's right to payment of a receivable and who pays the factor pursuant to a notice of assignment given by the supplier or by the factor with the supplier's actual or apparent authority will be discharged *pro tanto* of his liability even though the receivable had not been validly assigned to the factor by the supplier or the right to payment of the receivable was vested in a third party.

The Group was, in addition, of the opinion that it was not advisable at the present time to attempt to regulate the content of contracts between factors and suppliers or to lay down rules governing contracts between factors as these appeared to be areas where the contracts which are used by the practitioners and their customers seemed to give satisfaction. Nor does the draft seek to determine the validity of the factoring contract which is to be decided by the law applicable to that contract.

Similarly, the Group ultimately abstained from providing in the rules a solution to the problem of priorities, i.e. competing claims of a factor and a third party, both of whom have rights over the receivables assigned by the supplier, since it did not seem possible to lay down a substantive uniform rule, given the wide difference in national law. Moreover, the search for a conflict rule led to fairly clear solutions but on a detailed examination each of these was shown to present drawbacks.

At its 62nd session (May 1983), the Governing Council adopted the text of the draft uniform rules as prepared by the Study Group and instructed the Secretariat to communicate the text and the accompanying Explanatory Report to Governments for observations with a view to deciding the next steps to be taken.

Riccardo Monaco
Rome, President of Unidroit

ISF

ACTIVITIES OF THE INTERNATIONAL SHIPPING FEDERATION 1983/84

SUMMARY: *1. Relations with other international organisations. – a. IMO. – b. ILO. – c. UNCTAD. – d. ICSW. – 2. Arabian Gulf.*

The International Shipping Federation, which celebrated its 75th anniversary in 1984, represents national shipowner associations in twenty-eight countries, whose members account for more than 50% of the world's merchant fleet. It is concerned with the promotion and protection of its members' interests in all matters relating to the employment and safety of seafarers.

1. Relations with other international organisations

a. IMO

ISF has for many years been closely associated with the International Maritime Organisation (IMO), where it enjoys official consultative status, and takes an active interest in all aspects of its work which have a direct effect on seafarers. The most significant personnel-related event within IMO during the last two years has been the entry into force, on 28 April 1984, of the Convention on Standards of Training, Certification and Watchkeeping (STCW). ISF was closely involved from the outset in the development of this Convention, and its ratification by thirty seven major maritime nations throughout the world is evidence of the great importance which is attached to it. ISF continues to be involved with the IMO Sub-Committee responsible for standards of training and watchkeeping, where recent work has included the revision of the 1975 Document for Guidance on maritime training, discussions on the interpretation and implementation of the STCW Convention, and procedures for the development of model training courses.

Another debate within IMO which is of considerable current importance to the international shipping community relates to the future role of the radio officer on merchant ships. New technology in the form of the Future Global Maritime Distress and Safety System is forcing IMO to re-examine the requirements for personnel in this area, and ISF is closely involved in this work. The outcome of discussions on this subject will to a considerable degree determine the extent to which new technology will be able to be used to full advantage by the international shipping industry in the future to increase efficiency and utilise manpower most cost effectively.

b. ILO

The principal focus of recent ISF activity within the International Labour Organisation (ILO) has been the Joint Maritime Commission (JMC) which was held in Geneva during 1984. This is the bipartite shipowner/union body which meets between sessions of the full ILO Maritime Conferences to consider matters of current importance and determine agendas for those Conferences. As a result of the JMC's deliberations, items for discussion at the forthcoming Preparatory Technical Maritime Conference (1986) and Maritime Conference (1987) will include the issues of seafarers' welfare, health protection and medical care, and social security provisions. In its role as co-ordinator of the shipowner group within ILO, ISF will have an important part to play in determining the outcome of deliberations on these questions over the next two years.

In the wider ILO scene, Convention No. 147 on minimum standards for merchant shipping has now been ratified by eighteen countries, and ISF has consistently expressed its disappointment at the lack of progress in securing its wider acceptance worldwide. ISF considers Convention No. 147 to be the only realistic basis for ensuring a safe and acceptable working environment for seafarers, and will continue to press in the international forum for its more widespread adoption.

c. UNCTAD

The most active debate within the United Nations Conference on Trade and Development (UNCTAD) from the shipping industry's point of view has been on the subject of conditions for registration of ships. The outcome of this debate, which began as an attempt to curb the operation of open registers, will be of considerable significance for ISF members. ISF has therefore taken an active part in the proceedings in an attempt to avert the international prescription of manning nationality requirements which would unreasonably inhibit shipowners' essential operational flexibility. At the time of writing the outcome is uncertain although there are signs that a more pragmatic document may be emerging.

d. ICSW

The International Committee on Seafarers' Welfare (ICSW) is an ILO-affiliated body made up of representatives of shipowners, seafarers and welfare agencies, whose objective is to ensure that the particular welfare requirements of seafarers throughout the world are adequately provided for. ISF provides the shipowner representation on the Committee, and its work during 1983–84 has included the problem of abandoned seafarers, ship to shore communication facilities, and the provision of welfare facilities in ports. This last item can be expected to have a significant influence on similar discussions in the forthcoming ILO Conferences.

2. Arabian Gulf

ISF has been greatly concerned at the number of attacks on merchant shipping in the Arabian Gulf which have occurred as a result of the Iran/Iraq conflict, and in June 1984 sent a message of concern to a meeting of world leaders in London. It has subsequently further condemned attacks on shipping in the area in a Resolution jointly adopted with the Seafarers' Group at the Joint Maritime Commission of the ILO (September 1984) and in a joint ISF/International Chamber of Shipping message to the Secretary-General of the United Nations. Regrettably, these expressions of concern appear to have done little to minimise the problems faced by ships trading in the Arabian Gulf, and the attacks continue.

D. A. Dearsley
Secretary, ISF (London, August 1985)

INTERTANKO

IMO 1984 PROTOCOLS ON OIL POLLUTION LIABILITY

SUMMARY: *1. Evolution of the existing oil pollution compensation regime – CLC and FC. – 2. TOVALOP and CRISTAL. – 3. The 1984 IMO Protocols. – 4. Revision of 1984 limits. – 5. Definition of ship. –
6. Definition of oil. – 7. Definition of pollution damage. – 8. Geographical scope. – 9. Entry into force. – 10. The phased-in approach – A possible problem may arise?*

1. Evolution of the existing oil pollution compensation regime – CLC and FC

In 1967 the Torrey Canyon grounding in the English Channel resulted in serious pollution of the English and French coasts. This case revealed the inadequacy of the then existing compensation arrangement for pollution damage and prompted the United Nation agency, IMO, to adopt the Civil Liability Convention of 1969 (CLC) and the Fund Convention 1971 (FC), to ensure that pollution victims receive adequate compensation. Realizing that it would take some time before the conventions would come into effect, the private shipping industry set up TOVALOP (Tanker Owners Voluntary Agreement concerning Liability for Oil Pollution) as an interim measure in 1968 to reimburse governments for oil pollution clean up costs. Several major oil companies said that they were prepared to reimburse owners for the extra insurance cost, but this compensation was later withdrawn when TOVALOP was firmly established.

During the preparatory discussions, governments expressed concern about the inherent potential of crude oil for causing pollution. While some countries argued for total liability of the tanker owners, many others demanded that oil cargo interests should accept the major or even full responsibility. A resolution was passed at the CLC conference recommending that an international fund should be set up to relieve the tanker owners of the liability under CLC.

In 1971 the oil industry successfully argued that owners had already voluntarily accepted part of the liability by signing TOVALOP. Thus only in cases where this would not be enough to compensate claimants, supplementary compensation would be provided by the FC. The result was, therefore, that the CLC and FC were based on a sharing of liability between tanker owners and cargo interests. This solution reflects the special nature of crude oil and its inherent potential for causing serious pollution damage in contrast to other bulk cargoes such as coal, grain etc., and the principle was expressed in very clear language in the convention's text. The CLC which was adopted in 1969 and took effect in 1975 related tanker owners liability to ships' tonnages at US$ 160 per ton to a maximum of US$ 16 million per casualty. Tanker owners were required to obtain insurance cover for their maximum liability.

The FC was adopted in 1971. When the FC entered into force in 1978, the total compensation available under CLC and FC was US$ 36 million per casualty, and 'the sharing concept' had entered into force.

With reference to the resolution passed by IMO, part of the shipowners liability was then taken over by the Fund through a 'roll back' system and tanker owner's maximum liability was in fact then set about US$ 10 million per incident. The Fund is financed by contributions from oil importers within member states based on their respective volume of imports. Provisions were made in the FC for the fund's liability to be subsequently increased. So far there has been one increase bringing the fund's maximum liability to a total of US$ 54 million per incident. (The figures mentioned here are approximate figures which are dependent upon exchange rate fluctuations.)

Up to 1982, 68% of the cost of all oil spills have been paid by tanker owners who are liable regardless of whether the incident was caused by any fault of theirs or not.

2. TOVALOP and CRISTAL

As already mentioned, TOVALOP is a private compensation scheme for oil pollution damage. It originated from the determination of a number of tanker owners, including the major oil companies (who also own tankers) to take constructive action to provide immediate compensation to victims of oil pollution damage. Tanker owners were aware of the fact that the traditional maritime law and practice did not provide adequate means for reimbursing national governments which incurred expenditures to avoid or mitigate pollution damage.

In the event of negligent discharge of oil or where oil pollutes or causes grave imminent danger of pollution to coast lines, TOVALOP reimburses the national governments concerned up to a maximum fo US$ 100 per gross registered ton of tankers discharging the oil or a maximum of US$ 10 million, whichever is less. If the owner himself helps to remove the oil, his cost in effect results in prorating the government's claim where the combined cost exceeds this limit. *TOVALOP was intended to be an interim measure until the time that all governments through IMO had agreed and implemented an international convention.*

The oil companies established CRISTAL in 1971 (Contract Regarding an Interim Supplement to Tanker Liability for Oil Pollution). CRISTAL is thus a voluntary agreement between various oil companies to provide compensation by topping up shipowner's liability under TOVALOP, and thereby placing victims of oil pollution damage in a better position.

CRISTAL compensation will apply to an incident if the oil cargo is owned or deemed to be owned by a member of CRISTAL and the tanker involved is owned or bareboat chartered by a party to TOVALOP who acts in compliance with his obligation under that agreement. In the cases where the claimant is or should be able to obtain compensation for pollution damage elsewhere, no compensation is payable under CRISTAL. Only if, after taking all reasonable steps, the balance of the claim is unsatisfied, the claimant may then turn to CRISTAL. The supplementary compensation goes up to a total or US$ 36 million per spill incident.

The limited exposure of CRISTAL is also related to a decision in 1978 when a change was made to avoid small claims being channeled to CRISTAL. Tanker owners took upon themselves a minimum liability through TOVALOP of US$ 1 million regardless of the size of the tanker. This was a considerable concession particularly from owners of small tankers, as no such provision was found in CLC. CRISTAL on its side agreed to apply the topping up of shipowners' liability under local law in excess of CLC limits, also in the territorial waters of countries which had not ratified CLC. This is usually referred to as 'the worldwide application'.

However, oil companies were not happy with the outcome of the 1984 diplomatic conference (see next chapter), and subsequently decided to reduce CRISTAL's exposure by abolishing 'the worldwide application'. This amendment substantially reduced the value of CRISTAL for tanker owners. 'The worldwide application' was regarded as giving some real protection. Tanker owners found themselves with an even higher minimum liability, despite the fact that the most important part of the oil industry's contribution had been unilaterally withdrawn.

3. The 1984 IMO Protocols

Following the Amoco Cadiz incident and strong inflation it became clear in the early 1980's that the compensation available for oil pollution was in need of a revision. Accordingly a Diplomatic Conference was held at IMO

Headquarters from 30 April to 25 May 1984. Sixty-nine countries were represented with two more sending observers; while there were also representatives from two UN agencies and observers from five intergovernmental and from 24 non-governmental organisations, including INTERTANKO.

During this conference, INTERTANKO devoted its efforts in particular to demonstate that there was no need to establish a high minimum liability for tanker owners. This would have been very costly for owners of small tankers and our arguments were supported by the statistics made available by the P & I Clubs.

On 29 May 1984 INTERTANKO reported as follows to its members on the new Protocols agreed in IMO:

'Minimum liability on the tanker owner US$ 3 million – up to 5000 gross tons, then US$ 420 per ton up to a maximum of US$ 60 million plus contributions from cargo giving total packages of US$ 150 million to be increased to US$ 200 million (when/if both U.S.A. and Japan ratify new conventions).'

This should be compared with –

1) INTERTANKO's proposal – minimum liability US$ 1 million plus, then US$ 360 per ton up to US$ 30 million with a total package of US$ 150 million and

2) The last OCIMF proposal – minimum liability on tanker owner of US$ 50 million to be increased with US$ 1000 per ton up to US$ 100 million plus contributions from the cargo amounting to a total package of US$ 15 million.

. . . .

The argument of the oil side that the oil companies only should be liable in cases of catastrophies has been rejected, it is expressly stated in the preamble to the new Fund Convention:

'THE STATES PARTIES TO THE PRESENT PROTOCOL (ARE) CONVINCED THAT THE ECONOMIC CONSEQUENCES OF POLLUTION DAMAGE RESULTING FROM THE CARRIAGE OF OIL IN BULK AT SEA BY SHIPS SHOULD CONTINUE TO BE SHARED BY THE SHIPPING INDUSTRY AND BY THE OIL CARGO INTERESTS.'

4. Revision of 1984 limits

Under normal circumstances a new revision would not be likely before the end of the century. However, based on experience regarding inflation, a simplified amendment procedure was adopted and laid down in the Protocols. Once they are accepted, changes may be incorporated after 18 months, unless notification of objections are received from one-fourth of the contracting states – the so called tacit acceptance. However, a two-thirds majority of the contracting states meeting in IMO's Legal Committee will be needed to amend the figures.

INTERTANKO, in a submission to IMO in September 1983 stated:

> 'When acting on proposals to amend the limits in the future according to the agreed text of the new conventions, INTERTANKO suggests that special account should be taken of the relationship between the limits in the two conventions so that safeguards are included in the future to retain the balance between the contributions of the two parties, the tanker owners and the oil industry.
>
> A future revision of the limits in the new CLC should also be accompanied by a revision of the limits in FC. INTERTANKO is concerned that if no such safeguards are included, there may be pressure to upset the mentioned balance which may result in undesirable lengthy discussions of no interest to the victims of oil pollution damage.'

The new rules include a safeguard to this effect stating that IMO's Legal Committee, when amending the limits, shall take into account the relationship between the limits in the new CLC and new FC.

The rules furthermore imply that no revision can take place less than 5 years from the date the convention was opened for signature. This means that no change in limits is possible before 1 December 1989. Under the simplified amendment system, no limit may be increased by more than 6% p.a. from the date the Protocol was opened for signature.

5. Definition of ship

The main issues concerning the definition of ship were whether unladen tankers should be covered, the circumstances in which combination carriers should be included and whether the CLC definition should be accepted for the Fund as well as the Civil Liability Conventions. The adopted text is as follows for both the CLC and Fund:-

> ''Ship' means any sea-going vessel and sea-borne craft of any type whatsoever constructed or adapted for the carriage of oil in bulk as cargo, provided that a ship capable of carrying oil and other cargoes shall be regarded as a ship only when it is actually carrying oil in bulk and during any voyage following such carriage unless it is proved that it has no residue of such carriage of oil in bulk aboard.'

6. Definition of oil

The main issue was whether non-persistent oil should be covered by the Protocols. Less important questions were the inclusion of the description 'hydrocarbon mineral' oil and of whale oil in the definition. A small majority of states were against the inclusion of non-persistent oil and it was concluded that non-persistent oil should not be covered. Whale oil was not included in the final definition while there was a clear majority for inclusion of 'hydrocarbon mineral'. The adopted definition reads as follows for both the CLC and Fund Conventions:-

> ''Oil' means any persistent hydrocarbon mineral oil such as crude oil, fuel oil, heavy diesel oil and lubricating oil, whether carried on board a ship as cargo or in the bunkers of such a ship.'

7. Definition of pollution damage

At the Conference, as at earlier meetings of the IMO Legal Committee and intersessional groups, the definition of pollution damage proved to be a very difficult issue. The adopted text for both the CLC and Fund Conventions is:-

> ''Pollution damage' means:-
> (a) loss or damage caused outside the ship by contamination resulting from the escape or discharge of oil from the ship, wherever such escape or discharge may occur, provided that compensation for impairment of the environment other than loss of profit from such impairment shall be limited to costs of reasonable measures of reinstatement actually undertaken or to be undertaken.
> (b) the costs of prevention measures and further loss or damage caused by preventive measures.'

The expression 'loss of profit' in the second definition was questioned by several delegations, but the definition was adopted following votes in which about 60 per cent favoured this alternative.

8. Geographical scope

The question of extension of the geographical scope from the territory and territorial sea to the Exclusive Economic Zone (EEZ) or even beyond, was always likely to be a contentious issue in view of the provisions regarding the jurisdiction of coastal states contained in the UN Law of the Sea Convention. The requirement that any change in the Conventions required a two-third majority of states present and voting in plenary, as well as a simple majority of parties to the Conventions, means that the issue was in balance to the end. Many traditional maritime countries were opposed to extension beyond a 12 mile territorial sea on the assumption that the Protocols would provide that measures to prevent or minimise pollution in the territorial sea could be taken anywhere. This was supported by the TOVALOP observer who quoted experience of oil spills over the past six years and data from the Federation's data bank to support his view, which was shared by all industry interests. A considerable majority of countries, however, favoured extension to the EEZ and there was a risk that if this was blocked by the states parties to the Conventions, some of the countries favouring extension would vote against the adoption of the Protocols which also needed a two-thirds majority. There was also a possibility that the CLC and the Fund Convention might have different geographical coverage, because there were fewer parties to the latter. Finally, the following definition was adopted for the CLC by a vote in plenary of 38 to 18 with 6 abstentions (which just achieved a two-thirds majority as abstentions are not counted for this purpose) and a majority of 19 to 14 with 3 abstentions of the parties to the Convention.

> 'The Convention shall apply exclusively:
> (A) to pollution damage caused:
> (i) in the territory, including the territorial sea, of a Contracting State, and
> (ii) in the exclusive economic zone of a Contracting State, established in accordance with international law, or, if a Contracting State has not established such a zone, in an area beyond and adjacent to the territorial sea of that State determined by that State in accordance with international law and extending no more than 200 nautical miles from the baselines from which the breadth of its territorial sea is measured;
> (B) to prevent measures, wherever taken, to prevent or minimize such damage.'

The same definition was adopted for the Fund Convention by a somewhat larger majority, with several countries which had previously opposed it voting in favour or abstaining in the interests of consistency between the two Protocols.

9. Entry into force

The new CLC will enter into force twelve months after 10 states, including 6 states each with not less than 1 million grt. of tankers have ratified the Convention. There are some 24 countries with more than 1 million grt: Liberia, Japan, Greece, Norway, USA, UK, Panama, France, Spain, USSR, Italy, Denmark, Saudi Arabia, Singapore, Cyprus, Bahamas, Federal Republic of Germany, Brasil, Kuwait, Finland, Sweden, India, Iraq and Netherlands.

The new FC will enter into force 12 months after 8 states have ratified – the total compensation will then be US$ 135 million, but when ratifying states in a preceding year have imported a total quantity of 600 million tons, then the total compensation available to victims will be US$ 200 million per casualty. This presupposes ratification by both the United States and Japan. The 'triggering device' was suggested by the United States – and as the final maximum figure on Shipowner/Fund also was in line with the U.S. proposals, one may hope for U.S. ratification (despite the negative attitude of the U.S. in the past to other maritime conventions).

The crude oil import of some key countries in 1983 were: U.S. 198 m.t. – Japan 177 m.t. – Netherlands 40 m.t. – Spain 42 m.t. – U.K. 31 m.t. – France 71 m.t. – Federal Republic of Germany 65 m.t. – Italy 77 m.t.

The votes on the CLC Protocol as a whole were 48 in favour, none against but with 16 abstentions. The comparable figures for the Fund Protocol were 44, none and 21. Among those abstaining in both cases were Japan, Liberia, the Federal Republic of Germany, the German Democratic Republic, the Bahamas, Greece and Panama.

The next stage is signature of the Protocols which cannot be commenced until the end of 1985 when texts are available in six languages including Arabic. The inclusion of an authentic Arabic text was agreed after an intervention from INTERTANKO.

10. The phased-in approach – A possible problem may arise?

Up to the time when both the new FC and CLC are fully applicable, there will be a soft introduction to the new system. A four stage implementation plan includes four stages from the present CLC/FC (Stage 1) to the revised FC/CLC (Stage 4). In stage 2, the new CLC will be brought into play to the extent compensation from the old CLC/FC is not satisfactory; new CLC tops up old FC. Stage 3 presupposes all four systems in operation simultaneously. This is required because not all CLC and FC States will have ratified the new rules when they come into force. This so-called 'phased-in system' closes any gap in time between the two compensation systems and was supported by INTERTANKO and was the transitional system which was favoured by the Conference majority.

During the discussion in the preparatory meetings it had become clear that unless there are provisions to the contrary, the new CLC may serve for a long time as a top layer on the old FC. The reason is that some important

States may be tempted to ratify the new CLC only as the increased compensation available through the new CLC may be seen to be satisfactory. Undoubtedly it will take some time before the new Protocols enter into force. The oil companies have made suggestions for a new private compensation scheme (PLATO). However, PLATO's figures and the way liability is to be shared between tanker owners and the oil companies differ substantially from the compromise agreed in IMO after long and detailed considerations.

Tormod Rafgård
General manager, INTERTANKO, Oslo

FIATA

ACTIVITIES OF THE INTERNATIONAL FEDERATION OF ASSOCIATIONS OF FORWARDING AGENTS (FIATA) DURING 1984

SUMMARY: *1. Introduction. – 2. Spring Meetings in Zurich. – 3. Official FIATA Recommendation of 6 April 1984, concerning the position to take with regard to the Convention on Multimodal Transport. – 4. New expression of the limitation of liability (in SDR's) in the FIATA FBL Document. – 5. The FIATA FBL Document in the Rules of the International Chamber of Commerce (ICC, Paris). – 6. 'Forum' on Maritime and Combined Transport in Tokyo, 15 October 1984: 'Consolidation: Present and Future.'*

1. Introduction

FIATA, the International Federation of Associations of Forwarding agents, is an organization composed of some 35,000 national companies whose function consists in 'organizing transport' – operating and connecting the diverse components of the 'chain of transport'. Their clients are shippers, manufacturers, and exporters, and they are also involved in contracting and coordinating all of the components which, at one time or another, must participate in the process: carriers, customs agents, insurers, merchants, consignees, etc.

FIATA was founded in 1926 and has its headquarters in Zürich. Its current president is Mr. Parikh (India) and the current Secretary General is Dr. Gyssens (Belgium). The work of FIATA is done by nine commissions: Judicial, Customs, Trains, Highways, Maritime and Combined Transport, Air Transport, Development of Commercial Activity, Professional Formation, and Public Relations, in addition to the ad hoc work groups that are formed for specific subjects.

In this article we will summarize the activities of FIATA in the area of maritime and multimodal transport during the course of the year 1984.

2. Spring Meetings in Zürich

The Commission on Maritime and Combined Transport met on 2 April in Zürich, thereby opening the work sessions that FIATA holds each year in the Spring. Due to the absence of Mr. J. A. Bernion, President of the Commission, Mr. D. Liesenfeld welcomed the participants.

The subject of the meeting was the studies of the Group of UNCTAD Experts on Rules and Fares for Containers in Multimodal Transport. For the first time in this Group, someone has been named as a representative of the forwarding agents and their interests. Mr. Schimmelpfeng, Director of the Hamburg Association of Forwarding Agents, has assumed this position. The Group has attempted to standardize and simplify the rules for the establishment of rates for container services. It has also discussed the following subjects: freight and costs, delivery of merchandise, treatment by carriers of containers provided by both the carrier and the user, and demurrage.

Everyone who is related in some way to transport activities was warned to follow closely the development of the UNCTAD proposals, since the decisions that will be made in Geneva will affect them.

The members of the Commission were informed of the program of the 'Forum' (or Round Table) entitled 'Consolidation: present and future', that would take place in the Regional Conference of Tokyo on 15 October 1984.

3. Official FIATA Recommendation of 6 April 1984, concerning the position to take with regard to the Convention on Multimodal Transport

Since the Convention on Multimodal Transport (Geneva, 24 May 1980) is strongly related to the Hamburg Rules, FIATA recommends against ratification of the Convention until the Rules enter into force, as for the maritime portion of transport the Multimodal Transport Operator's (MTO) liability limit would be higher than his possibilities of recovery (from the maritime carrier). It does not seem reasonable that the liability limit of the contractual transporter should exceed that of the de facto transporter.

Experts from many countries do not see the necessity for this new Convention, as they prefer the 'network' system adopted in the Uniform Rules for a Document of Combined Transport issued by the International Chamber of Commerce (ICC, Paris). More importantly, the total cost of liability insurance of the MTO, together with cargo insurance, would excessively raise the cost of transport in relation to the price of the product transported. We must also consider Article 4 of the Convention, which states: '. . . each country has the right to regulate multimodal transport'. For these reasons, FIATA recommends against ratification of the Convention at this time.

4. New Expression of the Limitation of Liability (in Special Drawing Rights) in the FIATA FBL Document

In the aforementioned Spring Meetings in Zürich, a modification of the text of the General Conditions printed on the back of the FIATA FBL Document was adopted in order to avoid mistakes in the limit of liability which – except for the declaration of value – affects the forwarding agent in his operations. During these meetings, it was also decided to bring up to date the monetary unit in which the liability limit is expressed.

Specifically, the reference to '30 Gold Francs' was substituted by that of '2 Special Drawing Rights' (SDR or DTS, in English or French, respectively) per gross weight kilogram of lost or damaged merchandise. These SDR's are those of the International Monetary Fund. They are a more stable unit of currency than others previously used, and they are generally used today in international trade operations.

5. The FIATA FBL Document in the Rules of the International Chamber of Commerce (ICC, Paris)

The FIATA FBL Document, which is a bill of lading (or consignment note) negotiable for combined or multimodal transport, is now expressly mentioned in the Uniform Rules and Uses Relating to Documentary Credits, of the International Chamber of Commerce.

Concretely, Article 25.d of Publication no. 400, which entered into force on 1 October 1984, states: 'Except for a contrary stipulation in the credit, banks will reject a transport document issued by a forwarding agent, unless such document is a FIATA combined bill of lading or the document indicates that it has been issued by a forwarding agent acting as a transporter or as a concrete transport agent'.

Two years ago, the ICC Commission began the work of revision of the Uniform Rules and Uses Relating to Documentary Credits. FIATA was represented in those meetings by Dr. J. Van Alsenoy, at that time President of the Commission of Legal, Documentary, and Insurance Matters (of which the author is Technical Adviser).

6. 'Forum' on Maritime and Combined Transport in Tokyo, 15 October 1984: 'Consolidation: Present and Future'

A 'Forum' or Round Table on maritime and combined transport took place at the meetings held in October in Tokyo, under the presidency of Mr. J. A. Bernion and with the participation of Mr. K. Matsuura (General

Director of Omori Kaisoten Ltd.), Mr. Tan Kay Hock (Vicepresident of the Association of Singapore Forwarding Agents), Mr. James F. White (Secretary of the FIATA Commission on Maritime and Combined Transport), Mr. Masanori Shono (General Director of Mitsui O.S.K. Lines Ltd.), and Mr. Masahisa Tamura (Vicepresident of the Committee of Combined Transport of the Japanese Council of Users). After the reading of reports, a colloquium among the participants took place.

In conclusion, the president emphasized that the containerization of consolidated goods is a labor that requires the specialization of the forwarding agent. This has occurred over the course of many years: compared to the maritime carrier, the role of the forwarding agent has become that of a consolidator. Containerization has increased the utility of the services of the forwarding agent, thereby reinforcing his position in the market.

This has two consequences. The first is that if the forwarding agent wishes to totally integrate himself into the chain of transport, he must find ways to offer the user a better and more efficient service. This is only possible if the agent has adequate facilities, or through broad cooperation between agents. The second consequence is of an economic nature, counting on cooperation and understanding between different carriers whom the forwarding agents employ. In short, the most important factor is to maintain the dialogue between all of those who form the chain of transport.

Francisco-Jose Sanchez Ortiz
Adviser to the Legal Commission of FIATA
Member of the Institute of International Transport Law
Attorney, Madrid

PART IV.
CASE LAW

INTERNATIONAL CASE LAW HIGHLIGHTS

by

IGNACIO ARROYO and MATTHEW SCHREIBER*

'Ramos & Arroyo', Abogados, Barcelona

SUMMARY: I. – ARBITRATION: *1.* Enforcement of Foreign Arbitral Award. Validity of Arbitral Agreement. Choice of Law. Effect of Voluntary Default of a Party on Arbitration Proceedings. NY Convention on Recognition and enforceability arbitral awards. (Spanish Supreme Court, 11 February 1981, *Rederiaktiebilaget Gustaf Erikson v. Eurofrio Alimentos Congelados*). – *2.* Enforcement of Foreign Arbitral Award. NY Convention, 1958. Effect of Default on Enforcement of Award. (Spanish Supreme Court, 17 June 1983; *Ludmila Shipping Co. v. Maderas G.L.S.A.*). – *3.* Whether Cause of Action merged in Arbitration Award (Queen's Bench, United Kingdom, 1984: *Richard Adler (T/A Argo Rederei) v. Soutos (Hellas) Maritime Corporation and Another*, '*The Argo Hellas*', 1 Lloyd's Rep. 296, 2 Lloyd's Mar. Comm'l. L.Q. 341, 1984). II. – ARREST: *4.* Arrest of Vessel and Construction of the Brussels Convention 1952 on Arrest of Seagoing Vessels. (The President of the Court of Rotterdam, The Netherlands, 29 June 1984; Vessel '*River Jimini*'). – *5.* Claim for unpaid bunkers. Interpretation of the Brussels Convention of 10 May 1952 on Arrest of Vessels. Art. 8-2°. (Court of Appeal of Rouen, France, 19 June 1984). – *6.* Arrest of Vessel and Arbitration. Action in rem for damage to cargo. Jurisdiction of Admiralty Court to authorize arrest. Discharge of security for vessel. (Court of Appeal, United Kingdom, 1984: *The Andria now renamed Vasso*, 2 WLR 570; sub. nom. *The Vasso*, 1 Lloyd's Rep. 235, 2 LMCLQ, 334, 1984). – *7.* Norwegian salesform construction and arrest of vessel. Indemnity Clause. (House of Lords, UK, 1984, *The Barenbels*, The Financial Times, 13 June 1984, 4 LMCLQ, 553, 1984). III. – BILL OF LADING: *8.* Proceedings brought against stevedore for damage caused to container. Whether stevedore could rely on protection afforded to carriers in bill of lading. (Court of Appeal of New South Wales, Australia, 1984: *Godina and Another v. Patrick Operations Pty. Ltd.*, 1 Lloyd's Rep. 333, 2

* Ignacio Arroyo, Professor of Law, University of Barcelona, Senior Partner 'Ramos & Arroyo', Abogados, Barcelona.
Matthew Schreiber, J. D. University of California at Berkeley. 'Ramos & Arroyo', of counsel.

LMCLQ 343, 1984). – *9.* Incorporation Clause. Arbitration by reference. Intention of the parties (Court of Appeal, United Kingdom, 1983: *Skips A/S Nordheim v. Syrian Petroleum Co.* (*The Varenna*), 2 Lloyd's Rep. 592, 2 LMCLQ 194, 1984). – *10.* Demise Clause. Himalaya Clause. Liability. (The Federal Court of Canada, Vancouver, 1984: *Weyerhouse Cy. e.o. v. Anglo Canadian Shipping Cy*; *M.S. Liberian Statesman*, 20 European Transport Law 309, 1985). IV. – CONTRACT OF CARRIAGE BY SEA: *11.* International Maritime Carriage Parties that are Nationals of EEC member countries. (French Supreme Court – Cour de Cassation, France, October, 1984, 'Le Droit Maritime Français', 1985). V. – CHARTER-PARTY: *12.* Safe port. Iran–Iraq war. Cancellation of charter-party. (United Kingdom Court of Appeal, 1984: *Uni-Ocean Lines Pty Ltd. v. C-Trade S.A.* (*The Lucille*), 1 Lloyd's Rep. 244, 2 LMCLQ 350, 1984). – *13.* Construction of New York Produce Exchange Charter-Party Form. Appeal of Arbitrator's Award. (House of Lords, UK, 1984: *Antaios Compañia Naviera S.A. v. Salen Rederierna A.B.* (*The Antaios*), 3 WLR 592, 4 LMCLQ 547, 1984). – *14.* Baltime charter-party. Exemption from liability. Interpretation of charterparty language. (The House of Lords, UK, 1984, *Tor Line A.B. v. Alltrans Group of Canada Ltd.* (*The TFL Prosperity*), 1 WLR 48, 2 LMCLQ 196, 1984). – *15.* Repudiatory breach of charter contract. Innocent party's demand for performance. (*Clea Shipping Corporation v. Bulk Oil International Ltd.*, '*The Alaskan Trader*', 2 Lloyd's Rep. 645, 3 LMCLQ 378 (1984), Court of Appeal, UK, 1984). VI. CHOICE OF LAW: *16.* Bill of lading clause. Forum non conveniens. Stay of Action. (Admiralty Court, UK, 1984: *Dubai Electricity and Others v. Islamic Republic of Iran Shipping Lines*, '*The Arya K*') VII. – FORUM NON CONVENIENS: *17.* Determination of proper forum. Lloyd's Standard Marine Policy. Jurisdiction to order service in Kuwait. Whether England proper forum. (House of Lords, UK, 1983: *Amin Rasheed Shipping Corporation v. Kuwait Insurance Co.*, '*The Al Wahab*', 2 Lloyd's Rep. 365, 1 LMCLQ 171, 1984). VIII. – HAGUE-VISBY RULES: *18.* Contractual Limitation of Liability. Transhipment. (House of Lords, UK, 1984: *Mayhew Foods v. Overseas Containers Ltd.*, 1 Lloyds Rep. 317; 2 LMCLQ 202, 1984). IX. – JURISDICTION CLAUSE: *19.* Bill of lading jurisdiction clause. Foreign tonnage limitation. Hague/Visby Rules construction. (House of Lords, UK, 1983: *The Hollandia*, 1983 A.C. 565). –*20.* Bill of lading clause on jurisdiction. Foreign tonnage limitation. Hague/Visby Rules (Court of Appeal, UK, 1984: *The Benarty*, 1984, 2 Lloyd's Rep. 244; 4 LMCLQ 545, 1984). – *21.* Stay of Action for damages. Exclusive jurisdiction clause. Choice of forum. (Queen's Bench, UK, 1984: *The Pia Vesta*, 1 Lloyd's Rep. 169; 2 LMCLQ 337, 1984). X. – LIMITATION OF LIABILITY: *22.* Choice of Law. United States Limitation of Liability Act. Brussels Convention regarding Limitation of Liability. (USA District Court for the Southern District of NY: *Matter of Compañia Gijonesa de Navegacion S.A.*, Vessel '*The Cimadevilla*'; 590 F Supp. 241, 1885 American Maritime Cases (SDNY

1984)). – *23.* Interpretation of Merchant Shipping Acts 1894–1984. Fault or Privity of Shipowner. Failure to supervise effectively. (House of Lords, UK, 1984: *Grand Champion Tankers Ltd. v. Norpipe A/S*, 2 WLR 942, 3 LMCLQ 363 (1984); Vessel '*The Marion*'). – XI. SHELF (DELIMITATION OF CONTINENTAL SHELF): *24.* Article 62 of the Statute of International Court of Justice. Right of a Third State to intervene. Determination of when a third Party is affected by an ICJ Decision (International Court of Justice, The Hague, 21 March 1984: *Libyan Arab Jamahiriya v. Malta*).

1.

SUPREME COURT OF SPAIN

11 February 1981

ARBITRATION

ENFORCEMENT OF FOREIGN ARBITRAL AWARD. VALIDITY OF ARBITRATION AGREEMENT. CHOICE OF LAW. EFFECT OF VOLUNTARY DEFAULT OF A PARTY ON ARBITRATION PROCEEDINGS. NEW YORK CONVENTION ON RECOGNITION AND ENFORCEABILITY OF FOREIGN ARBITRAL AWARDS.

Rederiaktiebilaget Gustaf Erikson v. Eurofrio Alimentos Congelados, S.A.

Vessel 'Jarsoe'

AUTHORITIES CITED: New York Convention on Recognition and Enforceability of Foreign Arbitral Awards.

FACTS: A contract for affreightment of the GENCON type was entered into between a Finnish shipowner and a Spanish charterer who agreed to carry 600 tons of frozen fish in the vessel to be transported to Port Harcourt, Finland. The contract provided for a fine of U.S. $1800 per day of demurrage and contained an arbitration clause. Disputes arising from the contract were to be resolved in London by arbitration. Each party would name an arbitrator, who would then name a third arbitrator, who in turn would have the deciding vote.

The cargo was delivered after a delay of 70 days, and the shipowners claimed damages pursuant to the contract of U.S. $121,650. The shipowner named an arbitrator, but the Spanish company failed to respond to any of the three notifications sent via a Spanish notary. Following English arbitration law, the umpire awarded the claimant the damages that he claimed, plus interest and arbitration fees.

The Spanish company refused to pay the damages awarded, and the claimant sought to enforce the award in Spain. The Spanish company raised several defenses. It alleged that the claimant's lawyer lacked the power of attorney to represent him before the arbitrator, and that the arbitration agreement was invalid. It also claimed that the New York Convention on Recognition and Enforceability of Arbitral Awards was inapplicable to the case, because the Convention had been ratified after the arbitration proceedings had been commenced. Finally, the company argued that the arbitrator's decision was invalid because it was based on grounds of default.

HELD: Enforcement of the English arbitration award was granted. The Court dismissed all of the Spanish company's defenses. It declared that under the 'locus regit actum' principle there was no defect in the claimant's lawyer's power of attorney, because its granting was governed by Finnish rather than Spanish law.

The Court further reasoned that the standard to apply as to the validity or non-validity of the agreement was not the 1953 Spanish law on domestic arbitration, but rather the New York Convention, under which the agreement was perfectly valid. The New York Convention was indeed applicable, since at the time enforcement was sought, both Spain and Finland had ratified the Convention.

The Court concluded by stating that the Spanish company had received proper and punctual notification of the proceedings and had chosen to ignore them. This constituted a refusal to abide by the contractual commitments that the company had freely and voluntarily accepted, and the Court refused to sanction such a showing of disregard and contempt for the fundamental principles that govern international commercial relations.

2.

SUPREME COURT OF SPAIN

17 June 1983

ENFORCEMENT OF FOREIGN ARBITRAL AWARD

NEW YORK CONVENTION OF 1958. EFFECT OF DEFAULT ON ENFORCEMENT OF AWARD.

Ludmila Shipping Co. v. Maderas G.L.S.A. (A.T.S. 17 June 1983)

Vessel 'Ludmila C'

AUTHORITIES CITED: The New York Convention of 1958.

FACTS: A GENCON type of contract, signed in Spain, was entered into between the owners of a ship, the '*Ludmila C*', and the charterer, a Spanish company. The ship was registered in Limasol, Cyprus. The parties agreed on the chartering of a cargo of wood from the port of Corinto, Nicaragua, to a destination at Santander, Spain. The charter-party provided for liability for dead freight and contained a clause stating that arbitration was to be held in London in the event of any disputes.

When the ship arrived at Santander, there was a dispute concerning dead freight, and the parties agreed to settle their differences in London by arbitration pursuant to the charter-party. The shipowners notified the charterer, via public notary, of their wish to submit the dispute to an Arbitrator. The charterer replied that he was willing to pursue an out-of-court settlement provided that it be conducted pursuant to the Spanish law of arbitration. In other words, the respondent wanted to be drawn up to that end by public document, while at the same time denying the claimant the authority to be represented due to insufficient power of attorney. In view of the charterer's actions, the claimant shipowner instituted the arbitration proceedings by notifying the Spanish company and forwarding all the pertinent documents. No answer or acknowledgement was received from the Spanish company.

The sole arbitrator granted an award, a copy of which was forwarded to the defendant. Soon afterwards the shipowner presented the foreign award to the Spanish Supreme Court for recognition and enforcement.

The respondent raised the following defenses: a) insufficient power of attorney; b) the arbitration clause inserted in the charter-party was null and void according to the Spanish Arbitration Act of 1953; c) the award was granted due to the default of the respondent, which denies the 'exequatur'; and finally d) the award should not be recognized because the designation of the arbitrator and confusing wording of the arbitration clause were inconsistent with Spanish law.

HELD: The Supreme Court dismissed all of the respondent's defenses and granted enforcement of the award. It stated that under the 'locus regit actum' principle, the power of attorney was perfectly sufficient.

The Court reasoned that the arbitration clause in the charter-party must be examined under the New York Convention of 1958, which as a last resort concerning this issue looks to the law of the country where the award is granted. Moreover, this rule is consistent with the Spanish Arbitration Act of 1953, in light of the obvious clarity of the arbitration clause and the manifest will of both parties to submit their disputes to arbitration.

The Court continued by noting that the main reason to deny enforcement of an award of this type is that a party was rendered defenseless, not that the award was granted by default. In the present case, the defendant was not rendered defenseless.

Finally, the Court held that the defense of public order, which was raised on the ground of defects in the arbitration clause and the designation of the arbitrator, was not available. The submission to the London arbitrator was clear and correct and in no way counteracted the Spanish public order, especially since the New York Convention forms a part of this order.

3.

QUEEN'S BENCH, UNITED KINGDOM

1984

ARBITRATION

WHETHER CAUSE OF ACTION MERGED IN ARBITRATION AWARD.

Richard Adler (T/A Argo Rederei) v. Soutos (Hellas) Maritime Corporation and Another. (The Argo Hellas), 1 Lloyd's Rep. 296, 2 Lloyd's Mar. Comm'l. L.Q. 341 (1984)

Vessel 'Argo Hellas'

FACTS: Pursuant to a charter-party agreement, the plaintiff owners let their vessel *Argo Hellas* to the charterers for a ferry service between Greece and Syria. The agreement included an arbitration clause and also provided for the inclusion of a letter of guarantee of the performance of the charter to be given to the owners, and such a letter was subsequently included.

Two years later, an addendum to the agreement was made, which provided that the charterers would cover their brokers regarding their claim for commission for the period from redelivery to 31 December 1980, and the owners would likewise cover their brokers. An arbitration clause was included in the agreement that was similar to the one contained in the charter-party.

After the vessel had been redelivered only one instalment of hire was paid under the incorporated agreement. The plaintiffs commenced arbitration proceedings against the Hellas, and the arbitrators published an award in favor of the plaintiffs. However, the defendants refused to honor the award.

The plaintiffs then sued the defendants in court for the same amounts that were found owing in the arbitration award. The claim was for sums due under the incorporated agreement. It was also made under the guarantee and by the owners as trustees for commission due to the charterer's brokers.

The defendants alleged that the claim on the incorporated agreement was barred because the owners' cause of action had merged with the arbitration award. They further argued that the guarantee did not apply since the addendums had been signed by the defendants' president and chief executive in his capacity as president of Hellas.

HELD: Judgment was given for the plaintiffs. Under the circumstances there was no merger of the cause of action in the award because the liability on the defendants' side was not joint and because the cause of action having been in debt and not in damages did not merge with the award, nor was the award of interest part of the cause of action to which it related. An award of debt in contrast to an award of damages did not operate as a bar to further proceedings. Here the award merely ascertained the amount of Hellas' indebtedness under the incorporated agreement.

Furthermore, if a plaintiff elected to proceed against only one of several defendants there was no reason why he should not be entitled to proceed against the others later notwithstanding the award in the first matter, merely because in that matter the defendant had no power to ensure that the others were joined in the same proceedings.

Finally, where Hellas and the defendants had a joint interest in procuring a settlement of the charter-party dispute, the words of the agreement should rightly be interpreted to mean joint liability.

4.

THE PRESIDENT OF THE COURT OF ROTTERDAM, THE NETHERLANDS

29 June 1984

ARREST OF VESSEL

INTERPRETATION OF BRUSSELS CONVENTION REGARDING ARREST OF VESSELS.

Vessel 'River Jimini'

HELD: A claim of payment for hire of containers is a maritime claim according to Article 1, paragraph k of the Brussels Convention regarding arrest of vessels, so that it was possible to arrest the vessel for this claim.

5.

COURT OF APPEAL OF ROUEN, FRANCE

19 June 1984

ARREST OF SEA-GOING SHIPS

CLAIM FOR UNPAID BUNKERS. INTERPRETATION OF BRUSSELS CONVENTION OF 10 MAY 1952.

HELD: Article 8-2 of the Brussels Convention of 10 May 1952, provides that a claimant may arrest a vessel flying the flag of a non-contracting State. Article 3-4 of the same Convention provides that the claimant may arrest '. . . such ship . . . or any other ship in the ownership of the charterer by demise'. The Court of Appeal interpreted these articles to signify that an arrest of a vessel flying the flag of a non-contracting State may take place even after the redelivery of the vessel if the arrest is made by a creditor of the owner or of the charterer or of some debtor of a maritime claim.

6.

COURT OF APPEAL, UNITED KINGDOM

1984

ARREST OF VESSEL AND ARBITRATION

ACTION IN REM FOR DAMAGE TO CARGO. JURISDICTION OF ADMIRALTY COURT TO AUTHORIZE ARREST. DISCHARGE OF SECURITY FOR VESSEL.

The Andria now renamed Vasso, 2 W.L.R. 570; sub. nom. *The Vasso*, 1 Lloyd's Rep. 235, 2 Lloyd's Mar. Comm'l. L.Q. 334 (1984)

Vessel 'The Vasso'

FACTS: The respondents' vessel *Andria* carried the appellants' cargo of calcium ammonium nitrate in bulk from Lisbon to Antwerp pursuant to a bill of lading dated 1 February 1979. The appellants claimed that during the voyage the cargo was damaged by water or contaminated by rust and pieces of wood. They brought proceedings against the respondents in England and secured a writ in rem, but this writ was not served because the vessel did not come within the jurisdiction.

The parties negotiated and entered into an arbitration agreement on 24 April 1981. The respondents were not informed that proceedings in England has been brought against them earlier.

In July 1981, the respondents sold *The Andria* to other shipowners who renamed her *The Vasso*.

The Vasso entered English waters in August of 1981. The appellants informed the respondents that they would have the vessel arrested unless a security in the amount of D.M. 330,000 plus interest and costs, were provided for the claim of cargo damage. The respondents replied that they had no interest in the vessel since they had sold it, and that at any rate the appellants had no right to take any action against the vessel because the matter had been submitted to arbitration. The appellants then obtained an arrest warrant and had the vessel arrested. The respondents posted the security that had been requested in order to secure the release of the vessel.

In March of 1982, the respondents petitioned the Admiralty Court for a declaration stating that there was no jurisdiction to maintain an action in rem against *The Vasso*, and that the vessel should not have been arrested and that the security should be released.

HELD: Under the circumstances the issuance of the writ to arrest the vessel was an abuse of process and therefore the security must be released. Under British law, the Admiralty Court had jurisdiction to authorize the arrest of a ship when the plaintiff's only purpose was to obtain security for an award in arbitration proceedings. The fact that the dispute between the parties fell within the scope of an arbitration agreement did not preclude one of them from bringing an action to arrest the vessel. However, in this case the Court's jurisdiction to arrest a ship for an action in rem was improperly exercised for the purpose of providing security for an award which might be made in arbitration proceedings because the purpose of the exercise of the jurisdiction was to provide security in respect of the action in rem and not in any other proceedings. This was especially true here where the affidavit sworn to obtain the warrant of arrest did not make any mention of the arbitration proceedings.

7.

HOUSE OF LORDS, UNITED KINGDOM

1984

ARREST OF VESSEL

NORWEGIAN SALEFORM CONSTRUCTION. ARREST OF VESSEL. INDEMNITY CLAUSE.

The Barenbels, The Financial Times, 13 June 1984, 4 Lloyd's Mar. Comm'l. L.Q. 553 (1984).

Vessel 'The Barenbels'

FACTS: In November of 1980, the sellers sold the vessel *Barenfels* to the buyers. The Norwegian Saleform contract provided the following standard guarantee and indemnity clause: 'The sellers guarantee that the vessel, at the time of delivery, is free from all encumbrances and maritime liens or any other debts whatsoever. Should any claims which have been incurred prior to the time of delivery be made against the vessel, the sellers hereby undertake to indemnify the buyers against all consequences of such claims.'

The buyers renamed the ship *Barenbels*. In 1982 it called at Umm Said in Qatar. The seller owed a debt to the Qatar National Shipping Company, and that company succeeded in having the courts of Qatar arrest the *Barenbels* pending the posting of security for the debt. The buyers provided the security, and the ship was released.

The buyers claimed in arbitration that the sellers were liable for the security posted pursuant to the indemnity provision of the Saleform contract.

HELD: The arbitrators awarded the buyers indemnity. Their decision was upheld by the House of Lords, who stated that the guarantee clause conferred worldwide protection against encumbrances and liens recognized by any national law. Furthermore, under the guarantee the vessel was free from arrest for *any* debts incurred by the sellers, not merely those debts connected to the vessel sold.

8.

COURT OF APPEAL OF NEW SOUTH WALES, AUSTRALIA

1984

BILL OF LADING

PROCEEDINGS BROUGHT AGAINST STEVEDORE FOR DAMAGE CAUSED TO CONTAINER. WHETHER STEVEDORE COULD RELY ON PROTECTION AFFORDED TO CARRIERS IN BILL OF LADING.

Godina and Another v. Patrick Operations Pty. Ltd., 1 Lloyd's Rep. 333, 2 Lloyd's Mar. Comm'l. L.Q. 343 (1984)

FACTS: A Russian carrier shipped plaintiff's furniture from Genoa to Sydney. The bill of lading provided that 'The Merchant undertakes that no claim shall be made against the carrier or against any servant, agent or sub-contractor of the Carrier which imposes or attempts to impose upon any of them any liability whatsoever in connection with the goods . . .'

The furniture was unloaded at Sydney during a period of heavy rains and one of the containers in which the furniture was found was inadequate to withstand the weather. The plaintiff filed a statement of claim against the stevedore, who sought to rely on the immunity granted in the bill of lading.

HELD: The plaintiff's claim was dismissed. The Court held that the bill of lading was broad enough to provide that whatever type of benefit this contract purported to obtain for the carrier, also in its capacity as agent for the stevedore, obtained for it and it obtained it as against the consignee and persons claiming under her. Therefore, the proper construction was that the bill of lading provided immunity and protection for the stevedores in addition to the carriers.

9.

COURT OF APPEAL, UNITED KINGDOM

1983

BILL OF LADING

INCORPORATION CLAUSE. ARBITRATION. INTENTION OF PARTIES.

Skips A/S Nordheim v. Syrian Petroleum Co. (*The Varenna*), 2 Lloyd's Rep. 592, 2 Lloyd's Mar. Comm'l. L.Q. 194 (1984).

Vessel 'The Varenna'

FACTS: The bill of lading entered into by the parties contained the following incorporation clause: '. . . all conditions and exceptions of which charter-party including the negligence clause are deemed to be incorporated in Bill of Lading'. A dispute arose between the parties, and the defendant claimed that the Bill of Lading incorporated the arbitration clause contained in the charter-party.

HELD: The Court of Appeal held that the arbitration clause was not incorporated into the bill of lading through the incorporation clause. An arbitration clause was not an 'exception' or 'condition' as provided by the incorporation clause, and earlier cases had set a precedent that the clear meaning of words in cases such as this should be employed. It is presumed that the parties intended this clear meaning to apply.

10.

FEDERAL COURT OF CANADA, VANCOUVER

1984

BILL OF LADING

DEMISE CLAUSE. HIMALAYA CLAUSE. LIABILITY.

Weyerhouse Cy. e.o. v. Anglo Canadian Shipping Cy. (*M.S. Liberian Statesman*), 20 European Transport Law 309 (1985)

Vessel 'M.S. Liberian Statesman'

HELD: The word 'Carrier' as used in the Hague Rules encompasses a charterer who contracts for carriage with the shipper as well as an owner. Under the demise clause in this case there is no contract of carriage between the holders of the bills of lading and the charterers. The demise clause is valid and governs when the charterers performed the services of a carrier. Under this reasoning the owners rather than the charterers were liable for cargo claims.

11.

COUR DE CASSATION, FRANCE

October 1984

CARRIAGE

INTERNATIONAL MARITIME CARRIAGE. PARTIES THAT ARE NATIONALS OF E.E.C. MEMBER COUNTRIES.

HELD: In addition to the compensation awarded to the receivers for losses or damage sustained by the cargo, the carrier can be condemned to reimburse the shipper for 'subventions' ('restitutions communautaires') granted to exporters in application of the E.E.C. Rules on exports which were lost as a consequence of the event.

12.

COURT OF APPEAL, UNITED KINGDOM

1984

CHARTER-PARTY

IRAN–IRAQ WAR. CANCELLATION. SAFE PORT.

Uni-Ocean Lines Ltd. v. C-Trade S.A. (*The Lucille*), 1 Lloyd's Rep. 244, 2 Lloyd's Mar. Comm'l. L.Q. 350 (1984)

Vessel 'The Lucille'

FACTS: In a charter-party dated 14 July 1980, the owners let their vessel *Lucille* to the charterers. The charter-party provided that the vessel was at the disposal of the charterers for 'lawful trades' between 'safe ports'. On 21 July the charterers ordered the vessel to proceed to Costanza to load a cargo of bagged cement for carriage to Basrah.

The vessel arrived at the Shatt-al-Arab anchorage on 25 August but was forced to wait there until 20 September because of congestion at Basrah. On 20 September, the charterers ordered the vessel to proceed to Basrah. The cargo was fully discharged on 23 October but the vessel was unable to leave because it was trapped in the Shatt-al-Arab waterway by the war between Iran and Iraq. On 25 September, the charterers advised the owners that they were cancelling the charter under the safe port provision of the charter-party, though at that time discharge of the cargo was still continuing.

The disputes between the owners and the charterers centered around whether the owners were entitled to be indemnified against loss and damage sustained due to the trapping of the ship, and whether the charterers were entitled to exercise their right to cancel the charter.

HELD: The charterers had breached the safe port provision of the charter by allowing the ship to proceed to Basrah when there was a foreseeable risk that the vessel might become trapped in the surrounding waterways. Furthermore, the charterers were not entitled to exercise their right to cancel the charter.

13.

HOUSE OF LORDS, UNITED KINGDOM

1984

CHARTER-PARTY

CONSTRUCTION OF CHARTER-PARTY. NYPE CHARTER-PARTY FORM. APPEAL OF ARBITRATOR'S AWARD.

Antaios Compañia Naviera S.A. v. Salen Rederierna A.B. (*The Antaios*), 3 W.L.R. 592, 4 Lloyd's Mar. Comm'l. L.Q. 547 (1984)

Vessel 'The Antaios'

FACTS: The vessel *Antaios* was chartered on a three-year time-charter. The charter-party consisted of a NYPE form, clause 5 of which provided:

'Failing the punctual and regular payment of the hire or on any breach of this charter-party the owners shall be at liberty to withdraw the vessel from the service of the charterers without prejudice to any claim they may otherwise have against the charterers'.

Well into the charter period, the owners attempted to withdraw the vessel upon learning that the charterers had breached the charter-party by issuing inaccurate bills of lading. The owners' right to withdraw was disputed by the charterers. The dispute was referred to arbitration as set forth in the charter-party. The owners claimed that the words 'any breach' in the charter-party meant any breach whatsoever, including issuing inaccurate bills of lading.

HELD: The arbitrators held that the owners were not entitled to withdraw the vessel. They interpreted the words 'any other breach of this charter party' to signify only those breaches which constituted repudiations. Furthermore, the owners were required to exercise their right of withdrawal within a reasonable time, and here they had not done so. The arbitrators reasoned that the charter-party should be interpreted in harmony with the commercial purpose of the contract. In their opinion, the owners' construction was unreasonable, uncommercial, and contradictory to the purpose of the NYPE form.

The House of Lords upheld the arbitrators' decision as to the construction of the charter-party. It also stated that as a general rule, leave to appeal an arbitration decision should not be permitted '. . . unless the judge considered that a strong prima facie case had been made out that the arbitrator had been wrong in his construction'.

14.

HOUSE OF LORDS, UNITED KINGDOM

1984

CHARTER-PARTY

BALTIME. EXEMPTION FROM LIABILITY. INTERPRETATION OF CHARTER-PARTY LANGUAGE.

Tor Line A.B. v. Alltrans Group of Canada Ltd. (*The TFL Prosperity*), 1 W.L.R. 48, 2 Lloyd's Mar. Comm'l. L.Q. 196 (1984)

Vessel 'The TFL Prosperity'

FACTS: The plaintiffs chartered the vessel *TFL Prosperity* from the defendants. The 1939 Baltime charter-party form was used. This form contains a 'responsibility and exemption' clause which purports to broadly exempt owners from liability. The parties agreed in writing on a certain height of the main deck. It was later found that the true height of the main deck was less than that agreed, and the umpire awarded the charterers damages. The owners appealed, claiming that they were not liable because of the protection afforded by the 'responsibility and exemption' clause.

HELD: The owners were held to be liable. The liability for breaching the clause containing the description of the deck was not excluded by the 'responsibility and exemption' clause. If the clause were to be interpreted in the way in which the owners desired, the charter would be excessively one-sided, and this could not have been the intention of the parties.

15.

COURT OF APPEAL, UNITED KINGDOM

1984

CHARTER-PARTY

REPUDIATORY BREACH OF CHARTER CONTRACT. INNOCENT PARTY'S DEMAND FOR PERFORMANCE.

Clea Shipping Corporation v. Bulk Oil International Ltd. (*The Alaskan Trader*), 2 Lloyd's Rep. 645, 3 Lloyd's Mar. Comm'l. L.Q. 378 (1984)

Vessel 'The Alaskan Trader'

FACTS: The defendant chartered the *Alaskan Trader*, an oil tanker, for a two year period in October of 1979. In October of 1980 the ship's engine suffered serious malfunctions and the ship was laid up for several months of repair. Due to a poor market for oil, the charterers informed the plaintiff owners that they no longer wished to use the vessel. Ignoring this warning, the plaintiff owners spent $800,000 on repairs and then told the charterers that the vessel was again ready for their use. The charterers refused to accept the vessel.

After the charter period had expired, the dispute was heard by an arbitrator, who held that the owners had no absolute right to require the charterers to continue their hire of the vessel, but that the charterers were liable in damages for breach of contract.

HELD: The arbitrator's decision was upheld by the Court. The judges reasoned that the defendant's actions constituted a repudiatory breach, and in such a situation a plaintiff could only demand actual performance if he could perform alone. To hold otherwise would be to condone economic waste.

16.

ADMIRALTY COURT, UNITED KINGDOM

1984

CHOICE OF LAW

FORUM NON CONVENIENS. BILL OF LADING. STAY OF ACTION

Dubai Electricity Company & Others v. Islamic Republic of Iran Shipping Lines (The Arya K)

Vessel 'The Arya K'

FACTS: The defendants contracted to carry 61 steel drums of electric cable for the plaintiffs. The bill of lading provided that the carrier could choose, in the event of a dispute, between German, Iranian, or British law. When the goods were damaged, the plaintiff filed an action in England. The defendants petitioned to stay the action on the ground that the bill of lading authorized them to choose the forum, and that they chose Germany, and alternatively that the doctrine of forum non conveniens applied to the English action.

HELD: The Court dismissed the petition to stay the proceedings. The choice of law clause in the bill of lading was so broad as to be invalid under British law. Furthermore, England was not an inconvenient forum because the defendants administered their European business from London and therefore no great difficulty or expense would be involved.

17.

HOUSE OF LORDS, UNITED KINGDOM

1983

FORUM NON CONVENIENS

DETERMINATION OF PROPER FORUM. LLOYD'S STANDARD MARINE POLICY. JURISDICTION TO ORDER SERVICE IN KUWAIT. WHETHER ENGLAND PROPER FORUM.

Amin Rasheed Shipping Corporation v. Kuwait Insurance Co. (*The Al Wahab*), 2 Lloyd's Rep. 365, 1 Lloyd's Mar. Comm'l. L.Q. 171 (1984)

Vessel 'The Al Wahab'

FACTS: The plaintiffs insured their vessel against war and marine risks with the defendants Kuwait Insurance Company (KIC). The policy was almost identical to the statutory Lloyd's Standard Marine policy. While the insurance policy was in force, the vessel was confiscated after it entered a Saudi Arabian port by authorities of that nation. The vessel was never released, and the plaintiffs claimed against the insurance policy. However, the KIC refused to pay. The plaintiffs obtained an ex parte order in England to serve notice of commencement of proceedings in England on the defendants KIC in Kuwait. The KIC sought to set aside the order, claiming that Kuwait, rather than England, was the proper forum for the action.

HELD: The order to serve notice of commencement of proceedings in England was set aside. The House of Lords first ruled that the proper law of the contract contained in the policy was English law, and that there was jurisdiction to order service of process of the writ in Kuwait. However, before a foreign defendant is compelled to appear before a British court, the Court must consider the type of dispute and the practical problems involved, such as local knowledge, whether witnesses are available, what type of evidence they possess, and the expense involved in travel to a foreign forum. In this case, the Court was not convinced that justice could not be obtained at a reasonable cost in the Kuwaiti courts.

18.

HOUSE OF LORDS, UNITED KINGDOM

1984

HAGUE-VISBY RULES

CONTRACTUAL LIMITATION OF LIABILITY. TRANSHIPMENT.

Mayhew Foods v. Overseas Containers Ltd., 1 Lloyd's Rep. 317, 2 Lloyd's Mar. Comm'l. L.Q. 202 (1984)

FACTS: The plaintiff poultry producers contracted the defendant carriers to transport poultry pieces in a refrigerated container from Uckfield, Sussex, to Jeddah, Saudi Arabia. One clause of the contract stated that the Hague-Visby Rules applied, but another clause limited liability to an amount lower than that provided under the rules. Such a limitation of liability is prohibited under the rules.

The carrier shipped the poultry parts to Le Havre, discharged them, and about a week later loaded them on another ship destined for Jeddah. The temperature control was not properly maintained at some point of the journey, and the poultry arrived damaged. The degree of the carrier's liability was in dispute.

HELD: The carrier was liable in accordance with the terms of the Hague-Visby Rules. The Rules did not apply to carriage or storage before the port of shipment or after the port of discharge. In this case, however, the Rules were in effect from the time of loading at Shoreham to the time of discharge at Jeddah. Transhipment and storage during this period of time did not serve to rid the defendants of liability.

19.

HOUSE OF LORDS, UNITED KINGDOM

1983

JURISDICTION CLAUSE

BILL OF LADING. STAY OF ACTION. FOREIGN TONNAGE LIMITATION. HAGUE-VISBY RULES.

The Hollandia, (1983) A.C. 565

Vessel 'The Hollandia'

FACTS: A clause in a bill of lading between the parties gave exclusive jurisdiction over disputes to the Netherlands, a country which would apply a lower package or unit limitation than that contained in the Hague-Visby Rules. On these grounds, the defendant applied for a stay of an English action filed by the plaintiff.

HELD: The application was denied. English courts were required to apply the Hague-Visby Rules as having the force of law. Under these Rules, the jurisdiction clause in the bill of lading was null and void. There were no other valid grounds for staying the action.

20.

COURT OF APPEAL, UNITED KINGDOM

1984

JURISDICTION CLAUSE

BILL OF LADING. STAY OF ACTION. FOREIGN TONNAGE LIMITATION. HAGUE-VISBY RULES.

The Benarty, (1984) 2 Lloyd's Rep. 244, 4 Lloyd's Mar. Comm'l. L.Q. 545 (1984)

Vessel 'The Benarty'

FACTS: A dispute arose between the plaintiff and the charterer. The relevant bills of lading gave exclusive jurisdiction to the courts of Indonesia, where a lower overall tonnage limitation would be applied to the claim. This would have produced a lower maximum monetary liability than that of the package or unit limitation of the Hague-Visby Rules. As in *The Hollandia*, the defendant applied for a stay of an English action filed by the plaintiff, because the defendant's probable liability would be lower if judged by Indonesian courts.

HELD: The application to stay the British action was granted. After considering the relationship of the original Hague Rules to domestic and international tonnage limitations, the Court stated that the reasoning of *The Hollandia* could not be applied because Article VIII of the rules expressly preserves 'the rights and obligations of the carrier under any statute for the time being in force relating to the limitation of the liability of the owners of sea-going vessels'. The exclusive jurisdiction clause was therefore an essential part of the contract, and would not be disregarded simply because of a less favorable tonnage limitation in the foreign forum.

21.

QUEEN'S BENCH, UNITED KINGDOM

1984

JURISDICTION CLAUSE

STAY OF ACTION FOR DAMAGES. EXCLUSIVE JURISDICTION CLAUSE. CHOICE OF FORUM.

The Pia Vesta, 1 Lloyd's Rep. 169, 2 Lloyd's Mar. Comm'l. L.Q. 337 (1984)

Vessel 'The Pia Vesta'

FACTS: On 28 July 1981, the defendants issued a bill of lading acknowledging that the plaintiffs' container had been shipped on board the vessel *Pia Vesta* at Ipswich for carriage to Freetown, Sierra Leone. The bill of lading contained a clause providing that '... any dispute arising under this bill of lading shall be decided in the country where the carrier has his principal place of business, and the law of such country shall apply'. The defendants were the carriers, who had their principal place of business in Denmark. Under the Hague-Visby Rules the limit of the defendant's liability would be 2300 Pounds Sterling.

The plaintiffs claimed damages when the defendants did not deliver the container. The defendants submitted to the British Court's jurisdiction only in order to prevent the arrest of one of their vessels in British waters. On 3 May 1983, the defendant's Danish insurance company issued a letter of guarantee. The defendants then applied to stay the British action on the ground that the action should have been brought in Denmark rather than in England.

HELD: The defendants' motion to stay the action was denied. The defendants could not claim that the Admiralty Court had no jurisdiction because they had instructed solicitors to accept service of the writ in rem and the letter of guarantee was clearly a violation of the agreement contained in the bill of lading and it therefore constituted an agreement to litigate in England. The Court would exercise its discretion by refusing to grant a stay because the amount claimed was a very small sum and neither party would wish to incur the expense entailed by forcing witnesses to travel long distances. Under the circumstances the Court believed that the defendants did not really want a trial in Denmark but had applied for a stay merely to achieve a tactical advantage.

22.

UNITED STATES DISTRICT COURT FOR THE SOUTHERN DISTRICT OF NEW YORK

1984

LIMITATION OF LIABILITY

CHOICE OF LAW. UNITED STATES LIMITATION OF LIABILITY ACT. BRUSSELS CONVENTION REGARDING LIMITATION OF LIABILITY.

Matter of Compañia Gijonesa de Navegacion S.A., 590 F. Supp. 241, 1885 AMC 1469 (S.D.N.Y. 1984)

Vessel 'The Cimadevilla'

HELD: United States law applied in the case of a collision between a Spanish vessel and a Panamanian flag vessel in Spanish waters, because the Spanish law on limitation of liability, having adopted the Brussels Convention concerning limitation of liability, was procedural in nature.

23.

HOUSE OF LORDS, UNITED KINGDOM

1984

LIMITATION OF LIABILITY

INTERPRETATION OF MERCHANT SHIPPING ACTS 1894–1984. FAULT OR PRIVITY OF SHIPOWNER. FAILURE TO SUPERVISE EFFECTIVELY.

Grand Champion Tankers Ltd. v. Norpipe A/S, 2 W.L.R. 942, 3 Lloyd's Mar. Comm'l. L.Q. 363 (1984)

Vessel 'The Marion'

FACTS: The vessel '*Marion*', while dropping anchor near Hartlepool, disturbed a submerged oil pipeline. Claims for the resulting damage exceeded U.S. $25,000,000. The accident took place because the shipmaster used an out-of-date nautical chart instead of an up-to-date chart which did mark the pipeline. The shipowners sought to invoke the Merchant Shipping Acts to limit their liability to U.S. $982,292.06.

HELD: The owners were denied the right to limit their liability. The necessary fault or privity of the owners was found in their failure to maintain effective supervision. This occurred in two ways. The first was the failure to conduct an effective program to keep the charts on board up-to-date, whether by replacement or correction. The second was the failure of the managing director to take note of a marine inspectorate report that referred to the unsatisfactory condition of the ship's charts.

24.

INTERNATIONAL COURT OF JUSTICE, THE HAGUE

21 March 1984

DELIMITATION OF CONTINENTAL SHELF

ARTICLE 62 OF THE STATUTE OF THE INTERNATIONAL COURT OF JUSTICE. RIGHT OF A THIRD STATE TO INTERVENE. DETERMINATION OF WHEN A THIRD STATE IS 'AFFECTED' BY AN ICJ DECISION.

Libyan Arab Jamahiriya v. Malta

AUTHORITIES CITED: Article 62 of The Statute of the International Court of Justice.

FACTS: On 26 July 1982, the Libyan Arab Jamahiriya (Libya) and the Republic of Malta (Malta) submitted a dispute concerning the delimitation of the continental shelf between the two States to the International Court of Justice (ICJ). Italy sought to intervene in the case under Article 62 of the Statute of the ICJ, which provides for intervention by a State which considers that it has an interest of a legal nature which 'may be affected' by the decision in the case. Italy argued that it did not wish that the Court delimit its own continental shelf, nor did it want the Court to resolve any disputes that it might have with either Libya or Malta. Italy merely wanted the Court to 'safeguard its legal interests'. Both Libya and Malta opposed Italy's application for intervention.

HELD: Italy's application for permission to intervene was denied. The Court found that if Italy was allowed to intervene, then the Court would be compelled to determine Italy's rights with respect to the disputed continental shelf area. This would involve an entanglement of the Court in disputes between Italy and one or both of the other parties. A resulting decision would not merely 'affect' Italy's rights, reasoned the Court, but would recognize or reject them. The jurisdiction of the Court, according to the ICJ Statute, is based upon the consent of the parties. Because neither Libya nor Malta consented to submit their disputes with Italy to the Court, there was no basis for jurisdiction over these disputes and therefore the Court had no authority to hear them. Italy's rights were adequately safeguarded by Article 59 of the ICJ Statute, which provides that 'The decision of the Court has no binding force except between the parties and in respect of that particular case.'

PART V.

CURRENT INTERNATIONAL EVENTS

* Formation of Uruguayan Maritime Law Association

With the assistance of prominent maritime law attorneys in Uruguay, the Uruguayan Maritime Law Association has been formed. The Association was admitted as a member of the International Maritime Committee during the 25 May 1985 session.

* Denunciation of 1957 Convention on Limitation of Liability of Owners of Sea-going Ships

The Convention on Limitation of the Liability of Owners of Sea-going Ships (Brussels, 10 October 1957), which entered into force on 31 May 1968, was denounced by the following countries during 1983–1984: Japan: 19 May 1983; Denmark, Finland, Norway, and Sweden: 1 April 1984; United Arab Republic: 8 May 1984.

* Accession to 1926 Convention on Maritime Liens and Mortgages

The Convention for the unification of certain rules relating to Maritime Liens and Mortgages (Brussels, 10 April 1926), which entered into force on 2 June 1931, was acceded to by Cuba on 21 November 1983.

* Ratification of and Accession to 1956 Convention on Arrest of Sea-going Ships

The Convention for the unification of certain rules relating to Arrest of Sea-going Ships (Brussels, 10 May 1952), which entered into force on 24 February 1956, was ratified by the Netherlands on 20 January 1983. It was acceded to by Cuba on 21 November 1983.

* Ratification of and Accession to 1969 Convention on Oil Pollution Liability

The Convention on Civil Liability for Oil Pollution Damage (Brussels 29 November 1969), which entered into force on 19 June 1975, was ratified by Australia on 7 November 1983. It was acceded to by the following States in

1983: Vanuatu: 2 February 1983; Sri Lanka: 12 April 1983; United Arab Emirates: 15 December 1983. The Convention will be modified when the IMO Protocol adopted in 1984 concerning oil pollution liability enters into force.

* Accession to 1971 Fund for Compensation for Oil Pollution Damage

The Convention on the Establishment of an International Fund for Compensation for Oil Pollution Damage (Brussels, 18 December 1971), which entered into force on 16 October 1978, was acceded to by the following States in 1983: Fiji: 4 March 1983; Sri Lanka: 12 April 1983; United Arab Emirates: 15 December 1983. The Convention will be modified when the new IMO Fund Convention adopted in 1984 enters into force.

* 1974 Athens Convention on Carriage of Passengers and their Luggage by Sea is Near to Entry into Force

As of January 1984, the Athens Convention Relating to the Carriage of Passengers and their Luggage by Sea (Athens, 13 December 1974) needed only one more ratification to enter into force. The Athens Convention establishes a regime of liability for damage suffered by passengers and their luggage. It has been ratified by nine States as follows: Tonga, Yemen, German Democratic Republic, United Kingdom, Liberia, Spain, U.S.S.R., Argentina, and the Bahamas. It will enter into force 90 days after being ratified by 10 States.

* Ratification of and Accession to the 1978 'Hamburg Rules'

The United Nations Convention on the Carriage of Goods by Sea (30 March 1978), commonly known as the 'Hamburg Rules', was acceded to by Lebanon on 4 April 1983. It was ratified by Hungary on 5 July 1984. The Convention has not yet entered into force.

* Ratification of UNCTAD Convention on Multi-Modal Transport

The UNCTAD Convention on Multi-Modal Transport has been ratified by Mexico, Chile, and Senegal.

* Ratification of 1968 Protocol on Bills of Lading

The Protocol to amend the International Convention for the unification of certain rules relating to Bills of Lading, as modified by the Amending Protocol of 23 February 1968 (Brussels, 21 December 1979), which entered into force on 14 February 1984, was ratified by the following States during the 1983–1984 period: Belgium, 7 September 1983; Sweden, 14 November 1983; Norway, 1 December 1983; Poland, 6 July 1984; and Finland, 1 December 1984. The following States acceded to the Protocol during that period: the British Territories of Bermuda, British Antartic Territories, Virgin Islands, Caimans, Falkland Islands and Dependencies, Gibraltar, Hong Kong, Isle of Man, Montserrat, Caicos & Turks Islands, 20 October 1983; Denmark, 3 November 1983.

* Adoption of 1984 IMO Protocols on Oil Pollution Liability

Prompted by the Amoco Cadiz oil spill and high worldwide inflation, a Diplomatic Conference was held at IMO headquarters from 30 April to 25 May 1984, to discuss a new system of compensation for oil pollution. Sixty-nine countries were represented and two more sent observers. There were also representatives from two United Nations agencies and observers from five intergovernmental and 24 non-governmental organizations.

Among the issues discussed was the degree of liability to be borne by tanker owners and by the oil industry. The conference adopted a Protocol which stated that both the shipping industry and the oil industry should be held liable for the economic consequences of pollution damage resulting from the carriage of oil in bulk at sea by ships. The Protocol provides for a minimum liability of the tanker owner of three-million United States dollars for cargoes of up to 5000 gross tons, and, above this amount, for liability of 420 United States dollars per ton up to a maximum of sixty-million United States dollars. In addition, contributions from cargo will provide a total figure of 135 million United States dollars, to be increased to 200 million United States dollars when both the U.S.A. and Japan ratify the new conventions adopted in the protocols. These 1984 limits may be revised under a simplified amendment procedure adopted in the Protocols. A two-thirds majority of the contracting States meeting in IMO's Legal Committee is necessary to amend the figures. However, an amendment may not be adopted if notifications of objection are received from one-fourth of the contracting States. Furthermore, the rules imply that no revision can take place less than five years from the date the convention was opened for signature. This means that no change in the liability limits is possible before 1 December 1989. Under the simplified amendment system, no limit may be increased by more than 6% per annum from the date the Protocol was opened for signature.

Some other issues that were discussed concerned the definition of 'ship' – whether unladen tankers should be included, whether combination carriers should be covered, and whether the Civil Liability Convention of 1969 (CLC) definition should be accepted for the Fund Convention (fund to compensate victims of pollution) as well. The following text was adopted for both the CLC Protocol and the Fund Convention: ''Ship' means any sea-going vessel and sea-borne craft of any type whatsoever constructed or adapted for the carriage of oil in bulk as cargo, provided that a ship capable of carrying oil and other cargoes shall be regarded as a ship only when it is actually carrying oil in bulk and during any voyage following such carriage unless it is proved that it has no residue of such carriage of oil in bulk aboard.'

As regards the definition of oil, the main issue was whether non-persistent oil should be covered by the Protocols. Both the CLC Protocol and Fund Convention adopted the following definition: "Oil' means any persistent hydrocarbon mineral oil such as crude oil, fuel oil, heavy diesel oil and lubricating oil, whether carried on board a ship as cargo or in the bunkers of such a ship'.

'Pollution damage' was defined as 'loss or damage caused outside the ship by contamination resulting from the escape or discharge of oil from the ship, wherever such escape or discharge may occur, provided that compensation for impairment of the environment other than loss of profit from such impairment shall be limited to costs of reasonable measures of reinstatement actually undertaken or to be undertaken; and the costs of prevention measures and further loss or damage caused by preventive measures.'

The geographical coverage of the Conventions was a highly contested issue. It was finally agreed that the Conventions would apply to pollution damage caused in the territory, including the territorial sea, of a contracting State, and to the exclusive economic zone of a contracting State.

The new Civil Liability Convention Protocol will enter into force twelve months after 10 States, including six States each with not less than one-million grt. of tankers have ratified it. The new Fund Convention will enter into force 12 months after eight States have ratified it. The total compensation will then be 135 million U.S. dollars, but when ratifying States in a preceding year have imported a total quantity of 600 million tons, then the total compensation available to victims will be 200 million U.S. dollars per casualty. This presupposes ratification by both the United States and Japan.

* Domestic Pilotage Ordinances Passed in Sweden

The Swedish National Authority for Shipping and Navigation, pursuant to the Pilotage Ordinance enacted by the Swedish Parliament in 1982 (1982:569), issued a Pilotage Regulation (Authority no. 1985:5) in 1985 that will have a broad impact on pilotage in Sweden. The Regulation involves all uses of pilots in Swedish waters except the Trollhatte Canal and Lake Vanern, where pilotage regulation is entrusted to a special organization. Pilotage as defined by the Regulation is assistance by pilots in particular fairlanes, and under the ordinance such pilotage is a State monopoly. However, pilots can also be used outside the special fairlanes, and the Regulation provides that foreign pilots properly licensed by States bordering the Baltic and the North Sea can be used in passage through the Swedish territorial sea, except for a certain limitation concerning the Sound and Kattegatt. It is compulsory to use Swedish pilots in interior waters according to a graded system in which ships are classified according to cargoes, sizes and safety standards (double bottom ships being a special category), and where the requirements also vary according to the location involved.

The Swedish Government also issued two ordinances intended to implement new provisions in the Maritime Code related to the setting up of limitation funds for ships making use of their right to limit their liability. This is a procedure which is obligatory under Section 6 of the Oil Liability Act and optional under Section 240 of the Maritime Code.

* New United States Legislation Reduces Domestic Regulation of Carriers and Alters Harbor Workers' Compensation

The Shipping Act of 1984 was signed into law by President Reagan on 20 March 1984, and significantly reduced the regulation of carriers under United States law. The Act is designed to minimize government intervention and regulatory costs, to provide an efficient system of ocean transport, and to promote the development of an economically competitive United States flag liner fleet. The Act provides antitrust immunity for the collective setting of rates and other collective actions by carriers, and modifies the government review procedure for multicarrier agreements.

The Longshoremen's and Harbor Workers' Compensation Act was comprehensively amended in 1984. Among other things, the amendments limit the jurisdiction of the Act by extending the list of exempted occupations; clarify the law relating to third-party liability of contractors; permit certain claims of indemnity against LHWCA employees, provide compensation to victims of occupational disease, and provide for the creation of a special fund by employers and carriers to cover certain claims.

* The International Shipping Federation is Active in 1984

The International Shipping Federation, which celebrated its 75th anniversary in 1984, represents national shipowner associations in 28 countries, whose members account for more than 50% of the world's merchant fleet. It is concerned with the promotion and protection of its members' interests in matters relating to the employment and safety of seafarers. The ISF has for many years been closely associated with the International Maritime Organization (IMO), where it enjoys official consultative status and takes an active interest in all aspects of its work which have a direct effect on seafarers. The most significant personnel-related event within IMO during the last two years has been the entry into force, on 28 April 1984, of the Convention on Standards of Training, Certification and Watchkeeping (STCW). ISF was closely involved from the outset in the development of this Convention, which has been ratified by 37 major maritime nations throughout the world.

The ISF has also been active in the International Labor Organization (ILO). ISF was present at the meeting of the Joint Maritime Commission (JMC) which was held in Geneva during 1984. The JMC is the bipartite shipowner/union body which meets between sessions of the full ILO Maritime Conferences to consider matters of current importance and determine agendas for those conferences. As a result of the JMC's deliberations, items for discussion at the forthcoming Preparatory Technical Maritime Conference (1986) and Maritime Conference (1987) will include the issues of seafarers' welfare, health protection and medical care, and social security provisions. In addition, ILO Convention No. 147, which was supported by the ISF, has been ratified by 18 countries as of August 1985.

The International Committee on Seafarers' Welfare (ICSW) has also been the target of ISF activity. The ICSW is an ILO-affiliated body composed of representatives of shipowners, seafarers and welfare agencies, whose objective is to ensure that the particular welfare requirements of seafarers throughout the world are adequately provided for. ISF provides the shipowner representation on the Committee, and its work during 1983–84 has included the problem of abandoned seafarers, ship to shore communication facilities, and the provision of welfare facilities in ports. This last item can be expected to have a significant influence on similar discussions in the forthcoming ILO conferences.

In addition, the ISF has been greatly concerned at the number of attacks on merchant ships in the Arabian Gulf which have occurred as a result of the Iran–Iraq conflict, and in June 1984 sent a message of concern to world leaders in London. It subsequently further condemned attacks on ships in that area in a Resolution jointly adopted with the Seafarer's Group at the Joint Maritime Commission of the ILO (September 1984) and in a joint ISF–International Chamber of Shipping message to the Secretary-General of the United Nations. Unfortunately, these expressions of concern have not prevented continuing attacks on ships in the Arabian Gulf.

* France Adopts Domestic Legislation Affecting Liability, Maritime Insurance, Collision and Salvage

A variety of legislation affecting maritime trade and commerce was adopted in France during 1984.

The Law of 21 December 1984, modifying the domestic law of 3 January 1967 on the 'Statut des navires et autres bâtiments de mer', provides that the owner of a vessel which has been abandoned in a French port cannot limit his liability towards the French Authorities in reference to the Brussels Convention of 1957 and to the French domestic law of 3 January 1967, for all expenses incurred for the removal of the vessel or of the wreck. This new law also states that the limits of liability as fixed by the Brussels Convention of 1957 will be those stipulated in the London Convention of 19 November 1976. It will be enforceable when the London Convention on limitation of maritime claims will be in force.

The Law of 22 December 1984, modified the Law of 3 July 1967, on maritime insurance. The law authorizes the French underwriters to insure the 'faute lourde' (gross negligence) of the insured and of his servants with the exception of 'faute intentionelle' (willful misconduct).

Another Law of 22 December 1984, completed the domestic law of 7 July 1967, on the 'événements de mer' (collision and salvage). This law introduced into the domestic legislation the provisions of the London Convention of 19 November 1976, concerning the salvors and their servants who will now be able to invoke the limitations contained in the London Convention. The new law will be enforceable when the London Convention enters into force.

A decree dated 8 March 1985, introduced the 1972 IMO rule on 'separation of traffic'. The decree provides that any infringement of this rule will be considered a 'delictus' as defined by the French Penal Code.

The Law of 22 May 1985, concerns the application of the U.N. Convention of 6 April 1974. This law states that only French shipowners trading principally and customarily under the French flag are authorized to participate in the conferences. The law contains a reference to the 'Reglement' of the E.C.C. dated 15 May 1979.

* The German Democratic Republic Passes Domestic Legislation in the Sphere of Maritime Law

The International Convention on Standards of Training, Certification and Watchkeeping for Seafarers of 1978 entered into force in the German Democratic Republic (GDR) on 28 April 1984, in accordance with the Announcement of 2 May 1984.

Regulation No. 2 of 12 January 1984, concerning Maritime Traffic entered into force on the date of its publication (12 January 1984). This Regulation is based on IMO Resolution A. 464 (XII) on Amendments to International Regulations for Preventing Collisions at Sea of 1972, adopted by decision of the 12th IMO Assembly at London on 19 November 1981. The regulation provides for the formulation of a general duty for GDR vehicles (with the exception of vehicles of the National People's Army, of the GDR frontier troops, and those of other security authorities) to cooperate in registration systems designed to ensure safety of international maritime traffic, as well as to consider meteorological recommendations as to routes. It also contains modifications and additions to various annexes and appendices of the Maritime Traffic Regulation which concern technical details of lights, acoustic signal installations, traffic signals, and danger warnings.

Regulation No. 4 on Fishing in the Fishing Zone, the Territorial Waters and the Internal Waters of the German Democratic Republic, of 23 March, 1984, entered into force on 1 June 1984, with the exception of Article 3 which entered into force on 1 January 1985. The essential elements of the Regulation are the following: an increase in the number and type of acts that constitute petty offenses; the specification of fishing quotas for fish of the Baltic Sea, and the granting of fishing licenses according to the quotas allocated, should enforcement become necessary; and provisions concerning the maintenance of fishing records.

The 2nd Implementing Decree to the Act Concerning the Borders of the German Democratic Republic of 20 December 1984, entered into force on 1 January 1985. The Decree provides for the extension in principle of German territorial waters to 12 nautical miles. It also contains a stipulation of the reservation concerning the delimitation of the continental shelf and the fishing zone with neighboring countries. A formulation of the right of foreign warships or public vessels used for non-commercial purposes to pass through GDR territorial waters if they must do so in order to arrive at or depart from their ports on direct route is also included.

* Amendments to the International Convention for Safe Containers Enter into Force

Several amendments to the International Convention for Safe Containers of 1972 (CSC) entered into force on 1 January 1984. The amendments were adopted in July 1983, by the Maritime Safety Committee of the IMO.

The CSC has two principal goals. One is to promote safety in the handling and transport of containers by specifying standardized test procedures and strength requirements. The other is to facilitate international container transport by producing standard regulations applicable to all types of transport, thereby avoiding the problems that occur when different national standards are used.

The main purpose of the new amendments is to allow governments to implement programs of continuous examination of containers instead of periodic examinations as required by the original convention. The examinations are designed to discover any dangerous defects in containers. They are to be performed whenever a major repair, refurbishment, or on-hire/off-hire interchange takes place and must in any case be performed at least once every 30 months.

* Important International Maritime Conventions Enter into Force in Spain

Several international maritime conventions were given effect in Spain in 1984. Three of these conventions have had an important effect on Spanish law concerning carriage of goods by sea and limitation of shipowners' liability. Both the Brussels Protocol of 23 February 1968, amending the International Convention for the unification of certain rules of law relating to Bills of Lading (the Hague-Visby Rules) and the Brussels Protocol of 21 December 1979, amending the Convention as modified by the 1968 Protocol were incorporated into Spanish domestic legislation by their publication in the Official State Bulletin (B.O.E.) of 3 February 1984.

The Protocol to amend the International Convention relating to the Limitation of the Liability of Owners of Sea-going Ships (Brussels, 21 December 1979) was published officially and entered into force in October of 1984.

In addition, the IMO London Protocol of 1978 relating to the International Convention for preventing Pollution from Ships of 1973 was ratified in Spain on 22 June 1984, and entered into force on 6 October 1984, with the exception of Annexes III, IV and V.

* 1979 Protocol to Amend 1957 Convention on Liability of Owners of Sea-going Ships Enters into Force

On 6 July 1984, Poland deposited with the Belgian Minister of Foreign Affairs its instrument of ratification for the Protocol Signed at Brussels on 21 December 1979, to Amend the International Convention Relating to the Limitation of the Liability of Owners of Sea-going Ships of 10 October 1957. Because this was the final ratification that was required, the Protocol entered into force on 6 October 1984. The countries bound by the Protocol as of that date are the following: United Kingdom, Ireland, Portugal, Spain, Belgium, Australia, and Poland.

* Dramatic Growth of Chinese Merchant Fleet

The Chinese government has announced a plan to increase its merchant fleet by more than two-thirds of its present size over the next five years. The greatest increase in the development of the fleet will take place in the number of container ships to be constructed.

* Sharp Increase in World Capacity of Oil Tankers

Finn Engelsen, a Norwegian expert in matters of oil, has published figures showing a dramatic increase in the global fleet of oil tankers. In June of 1985, the fleet had increased by 24 million deadweight tons and has reached the figure of 74 million deadweight tons. This spectacular increase, given the excess capacity of oil tankers that already existed, upsets the balance between supply and demand for the year 1986.

The increase is due to two principal reasons: the increase in petroleum production in countries that are not members of OPEC, and the decrease of 3% of the amount of oil that was consumed in the countries of the OECD.

According to Engelsen, the necessary capacity for the transport of crude oil can be figured at 37 million tons deadweight. Any other tankers that are employed find themselves in this situation due to inefficiencies of commercial practices that are not optimum.

* UNCTAD Adopts Resolution on Maritime Fraud

An UNCTAD Ad Hoc Intergovernmental Group met in Geneva on 6–17 February 1984, to consider means of combatting maritime fraud and piracy. As a result, the Ad Hoc Intergovernmental Group adopted a resolution on maritime fraud.

The resolution recommended that UNCTAD member States examine and, if appropriate, tighten their respective legislations to ensure that effective measures are available to prevent maritime fraud and to investigate such fraudulent acts and to prosecute persons who commit such acts of fraud, including taking necessary actions to avoid illegal sale of goods. It highlighted the need for improved transportation, handling, storage and document procedures, and stressed the necessity of effective regional cooperation between States including effective enforcement of their national legislation and bilateral or multilateral treaties.

The resolution specifically requested the Trade and Development Board to instruct the UNCTAD secretariat to prepare in-depth studies on several important topics including the following: formulation of a set of guidelines to be recommended to the international banking community of the member States of UNCTAD for use by all parties concerned, bearing in mind the International Chamber of Commerce anti-fraud protective measures; feasibility of a banking super-service scheme; to what extent any minimum standards for professional qualifications of shipping agents may contribute to combatting maritime fraud and whether such standards could be used as non-mandatory guidelines for the qualifications required; and the possible implications to maritime fraud of failure of shipping agents to provide sufficient financial standards based on specific cases where such implications have occurred.

In regard to bills of lading, the resolution urged the relevant international and commercial organizations to develop studies on the following matters: feasibilty of a central registry for bills of lading; elaboration of a scheme to develop secure bills of lading in order to avoid forgery; possibility of reduction in the numbers of bills of lading, or their replacement by another document; possibility of adoption of stamping procedures to replace the Master's signature; and revision of the practice of inserting a clause in the charter party giving the charterer the right to issue a bill of lading on behalf of the Master.

* The International Convention on Search and Rescue has Entered into Force

The International Convention on Maritime Search and Rescue of 1979 entered into force on 22 June 1985. The Convention was adopted in 1979 and is designed to facilitate cooperation between governments and those participating in search and rescue operations at sea by establishing an international search and rescue plan. The Convention was ratified by the last of the fifteen required States in June 1984.

* Albert Lilar 1984 Prize

The Board of the Albert Lilar Foundation has awarded the 1984 Prize of the Foundation to Professor Edgar Gold of the Dalhousie Ocean Studies Programme, Halifax N.S., Canada, for his book 'Maritime Transport'.

* Foreign Limitation Periods Act of 1984 Enacted in United Kingdom

The English Courts have traditionally treated limitation statutes barring the plaintiff's remedy as procedural and those extinguishing his right as substantive. Acting on the recommendation of the British Law Commission's Report on Classification of Limitation in Private International Law, the British Parliament enacted the Foreign Limitation Periods Act of 1984. This Act provides for all foreign limitation laws to be treated as substantive, regardless of how they are characterized by foreign law.

* Chinese Army Helps Manage Congested Ports

China has solicited the assistance of the Chinese Army in order to attempt to reduce the congestion of the principal Chinese ports, which have proven themselves incapable of handling the increase of 39.5% in 1984 of foreign trade.

PART VI.

DOCUMENTATION

Uniform Customs and Practice for Documentary Credits (1983)*

A. General provisions and definitions

Article 1

These articles apply to all documentary credits, including, to the extent to which they may be applicable, standby letters of credit, and are binding on all parties thereto unless otherwise expressly agreed. They shall be incorporated into each documentary credit by wording in the credit indicating that such credit is issued subject to Uniform Customs and Practice for Documentary Credits, 1983 revision, ICC Publication No. 400.

Article 2

For the purposes of these articles, the expressions 'documentary credit(s)' and 'standby letter(s) of credit' used herein (hereinafter referred to as 'credit(s)'), mean any arrangement, however named or described, whereby a bank (the issuing bank), acting at the request and on the instructions of a customer (the applicant for the credit),

(i) is to make a payment to or to the order of a third party (the beneficiary), or is to pay or accept bills of exchange (drafts) drawn by the beneficiary, or

(ii) authorizes another bank to effect such payment, or to pay, accept or negotiate such bills of exchange (drafts),

against stipulated documents, provided that the terms and conditions of the credit are complied with.

* The Council of the International Chamber of Commerce formally adopted the text on 21 June 1983. The UCP 1974/1983 revision comes into force on 1 October 1984. *See*. ICC Publication No. 400.

The ICC adopted the first version of UCP at its 7th Congress of Vienna, 1922. The 1983 revision was prepared by the Working Group of ICC in June 1980. The ICC Banking Commission finalised the text on 6 June 1983 and finally the Council adopted the present text.

As a document of world-wide importance banks in more than 165 countries operate these rules relating to the most useful way of payment in export trade. Likewise UCP sets out to achieve the new documents in shipping.

Article 3

Credits, by their nature, are separate transactions from the sales or other contract(s) on which they may be based and banks are in no way concerned with or bound by such contract(s), even if any reference whatsoever to such contract(s) is included in the credit.

Article 4

In credit operations all parties concerned deal in documents, and not in goods, service and/or other performances to which the documents may relate.

Article 5

Instructions for the issuance of credits, the credits themselves, instructions for any amendments thereto and the amendments themselves must be complete and precise.

In order to guard against confusion and misunderstanding, banks should discourage any attempt to include excessive detail in the credit or in any amendment thereto.

Article 6

A beneficiary can in no case avail himself of the contractual relationships existing between the banks or between the applicant for the credit and the issuing bank.

B. Form and notification of credits

Article 7

a. Credits may be either
   (i) revocable, or
   (ii) irrevocable.
b. All credits, therefore, should clearly indicate whether they are revocable or irrevocable.
c. In the absence of such indication the credit shall be deemed to be revocable.

Article 8

A credit may be advised to a beneficiary through another bank (the advising bank) without engagement on the part of the advising bank, but that bank shall take reasonable care to check the apparent authenticity of the credit which it advises.

Article 9

a. A revocable credit may be amended or cancelled by the issuing bank at any moment and without prior notice to the beneficiary.
b. However, the issuing bank is bound to:
   (i) reimburse a branch or bank with which a revocable credit has been made available for sight payment, acceptance or negotiation, for any payment, acceptance or negotiation made by such branch or bank prior to receipt by it of notice of amendment or cancellation, against documents which appear on their face to be in accordance with the terms and conditions of the credit;
   (ii) reimburse a branch or bank with which a revocable credit has been made available for deferred payment, if such branch or bank has, prior to receipt by it of notice of amendment or cancellation, taken up documents which appear on their face to be in accordance with the terms and conditions of the credit.

Article 10

a. An irrevocable credit constitutes a definite undertaking of the issuing bank, provided that the stipulated documents are presented and that the terms and conditions of the credit are complied with:
   (i) if the credit provides for sight payment – to pay, or that payment will be made;
   (ii) if the credit provides for deferred payment – to pay, or that payment will be made, on the date(s) determinable in accordance with the stipulations of the credit;
   (iii) if the credit provides for acceptance – to accept drafts drawn by the beneficiary if the credit stipulates that they are to be drawn on the issuing bank, or to be responsible for their acceptance and payment at maturity if the credit stipulates that they are to be drawn on the applicant for the credit or any other drawee stipulated in the credit;
   (iv) if the credit for negotiation – to pay without recourse to drawers and/or bona fide holders, draft(s) drawn by the beneficiary, at sight or at a tenor, on the applicant for the credit or on any other drawee stipulated in the credit other than the issuing bank itself, or to provide for negotiation by another bank and to pay, as above, if such negotiation is not effected.
b. When an issuing bank authorizes or requests another bank to confirm its irrevocable credit and the latter has added its confirmation, such confirmation constitutes a definite undertaking of such bank (the confirming bank), in addition to that of the issuing bank, provided that the stipulated documents are presented and that the terms and conditions of the credit are complied with:
   (i) if the credit provides for sight payment – to pay, or that payment will be made;

(ii) if the credit provides for deferred payment – to pay, or that payment will be made, on the date(s) determinable in accordance with the stipulations of the credit;
(iii) if the credit provides for acceptance – to accept drafts drawn by the beneficiary if the credit stipulates that they are to be drawn on the confirming bank, or to be responsible for their acceptance and payment at maturity if the credit stipulates that they are to be drawn on the applicant for the credit or any other drawee stipulated in the credit;
(iv) if the credit provides for negotiation – to negotiate without recourse to drawers and/or bona fide holders, draft(s) drawn by the beneficiary, at sight or at a tenor, on the issuing bank or on the applicant for the credit or on any other drawee stipulated in the credit other than the confirming bank itself.

c. If a bank is authorized or requested by the issuing bank to add its confirmation to a credit but is not prepared to do so, it must so inform the issuing bank without delay. Unless the issuing bank specifies otherwise in its confirmation, authorization or request, the advising bank will advise the credit to the beneficiary without adding its confirmation.
d. Such undertakings can neither be amended nor cancelled without the agreement of the issuing bank, the confirming bank (if any), and the beneficiary. Partial acceptance of amendments contained in one and the same advice of amendment is not effective without the agreement of all the above named parties.

Article 11

a. All credits must clearly indicate whether they are available by sight payment, by deferred payment, by acceptance or by negotiation.
b. All credits must nominate the bank (nominated bank) which is authorized to pay (paying bank), or to accept drafts (accepting bank), or to negotiate (negotiating bank), unless the credit allows negotiation by any bank (negotiating bank).
c. Unless the nominated bank is the issuing bank or the confirming bank, its nomination by the issuing bank does not constitute any undertaking by the nominated bank to pay, to accept, or to negotiate.
d. By nominating a bank other than itself, or by allowing for negotiation by any bank, or by authorizing or requesting a bank to add its confirmation, the issuing bank authorizes such bank to pay, accept or negotiate, as the case may be, against documents which appear on their face to be in accordance with the terms and conditions of the credit, and undertakes to reimburse such bank in accordance with the provisions of these articles.

Article 12

a. When an issuing bank instructs a bank (advising bank) by any teletransmission to advise a credit or an amendment to a credit, and intends the mail confirmation to be the operative credit instrument, or the operative amendment, the teletransmission must state 'full details to follow' (or words of similar effect), or that the mail confirmation will be the operative amendment. The issuing bank must forward the operative credit instruments or the operative amendment to such advising bank without delay.
b. The teletransmission will be deemed to be the operative credit instrument or the operative amendment, and no mail confirmation should be sent, unless the teletransmission states 'full details to follow' (or words of similar effect), or states that the mail confirmation is to be the operative credit instrument or the operative amendment.
c. A teletransmission intended by the issuing bank to be the operative credit instrument should clearly indicate that the credit is issued subject to Uniform Customs and Practice for Documentary Credits, 1983 revision, ICC Publication No. 400.
d. If a bank uses the services of another bank or banks (the advising bank) to have the credit advised to the beneficiary, it must also use the services of the same bank(s) for advising any amendments.
e. Banks shall be responsible for any consequences arising from their failure to follow the procedures set out in the preceding paragraphs.

Article 13

When a bank is instructed to issue, confirm or advise a credit similar in terms to one previously issued, confirmed or advised (similar credit) and the previous credit has been the subject of amendment(s), it shall be understood that the similar credit will not include any such amendment(s) unless the instructions specify clearly the amendment(s) which is/are to apply to the similar credit. Banks should discourage instructions to issue, confirm or advise a credit in this manner.

Article 14

If incomplete or unclear instructions are received to issue, confirm, advise or amend a credit, the bank requested to act on such instructions may give preliminary notification to the beneficiary for information only and without responsibility. The credit will be issued, confirmed, advised or amended only when the necessary information has been received and if the bank is then prepared to act on the instructions. Banks should provide the necessary information without delay.

C. Liabilities and responsibilities

Article 15

Banks must examine all documents with reasonable care to ascertain that they appear on their face to be in accordance with the terms and conditions of the credit. Documents which appear on their face to be inconsistent with one another will be considered as not appearing on their face to be in accordance with the terms and conditions of the credit.

Article 16

a. If a bank so authorized effects payment, or incurs a deferred payment undertaking, or accepts, or negotiates against documents which appear on their face to be in accordance with the terms and conditions of a credit, the party giving such authority shall be bound to reimburse the bank which has effected payment, or incurred a deferred payment undertaking, or has accepted, or negotiated, and to take up the documents.
b. If, upon receipt of the documents, the issuing bank considers that they appear on their face not to be in accordance with the terms and conditions of the credit, it must determine, on the basis of the documents alone, whether to take up such documents, or to refuse them and claim that they appear on their face not to be in accordance with the terms and conditions of the credit.
c. The issuing bank shall have a reasonable time in which to examine the documents and to determine as above whether to take up or to refuse the documents.
d. If the issuing bank decides to refuse the documents, it must give notice to that effect without delay by telecommunication or, if that is not possible, by other expeditious means, to the bank from which it received the documents (the remitting bank), or to the beneficiary, if it received the documents directly from him. Such notice must state the discrepancies in respect of which the issuing bank refuses the documents and must also state whether it is holding the documents at the disposal of, or is returning them to, the presentor (remitting bank or the beneficiary, as the case may be). The issuing bank shall then be entitled to claim from the remitting bank refund of any reimbursement which may have been made to that bank.
e. If the issuing bank fails to act in accordance with the provisions of paragraphs (c) and (d) of this article and/or fails to hold the documents at the disposal of, or to return them to, the presentor, the issuing bank shall be precluded from claiming that the documents are not in accordance with the terms and conditions of the credit.

f. If the remitting bank draws the attention of the issuing bank to any discrepancies in the documents or advises the issuing bank that it has paid, incurred a deferred payment undertaking, accepted or negotiated under reserve or against an indemnity in respect of such discrepancies, the issuing bank shall not be thereby relieved from any of its obligations under any provision of this article. Such reserve or indemnity concerns only the relations between the remitting bank and the party towards whom the reserve was made, or from whom, or on whose behalf, the indemnity was obtained.

Article 17

Banks assume no liability or responsibility for the form, sufficiency, accuracy, genuineness, falsification or legal effect of any documents, or for the general and/or particular conditions stipulated in the documents or superimposed thereon; nor do they assume any liability or responsibility for the description, quantity, weight, quality, condition, packing, delivery, value or existence of the goods represented by any documents, or for the good faith or acts and/or omissions, solvency, performance or standing of the consignor, the carriers, or the insurers of the goods, or any other person whomsoever.

Article 18

Banks assume no liability or responsibility for the consequences arising out of delay and/or loss in transit of any messages, letters or documents, or for delay, mutilation of other errors arising in the transmission of any telecommunication. Banks assume no liability or responsibility for errors in translation or interpretation of technical terms, and reserve the right to transmit credit terms without translating them.

Article 19

Banks assume no liability or responsibility for consequences arising out of the interruption of their business by Acts of God, riots, civil commotions, insurrections, wars or any other causes beyond their control, or by any strikes or lockouts. Unless specifically authorized, banks will not, upon resumption of their business, incur a deferred payment undertaking, or effect payment, acceptance or negotiation under credits which expired during such interruption of their business.

Article 20

a. Banks utilising the services of another bank or other banks for the purpose of giving effect to the instructions of the applicant for the credit do so for the account and at the risk of such applicant.

b. Banks assume no liability or responsibility should the instructions they transmit not be carried out, even if they have themselves taken the initiative in the choice of such other bank(s).
c. The applicant for the credit shall be bound by and liable to indemnify the bank against all obligations and responsibilities imposed by foreign laws and responsibilities imposed by foreign laws and usages.

Article 21

a. If an issuing bank intends that the reimbursement to which a paying, accepting or negotiating bank is entitled shall be obtained by such bank claiming on another branch or office of the issuing bank or on a third bank (all hereinafter referred to as the reimbursing bank) it shall provide such reimbursing bank in good time with the proper instructions or authorization to honour such reimbursement claims and without making it a condition that the bank entitled to claim reimbursement must certify compliance with the terms and conditions of the credit to the reimbursing bank.
b. An issuing bank will not be relieved from any of its obligations to provide reimbursement itself if and when reimbursement is not effected by the reimbursing bank.
c. The issuing bank will be responsible to the paying, accepting or negotiating bank for any loss of interest if reimbursement is not provided on first demand made to the reimbursing bank, or as otherwise specified in the credit, or mutually agreed, as the case may be.

D. Documents

Article 22

a. All instructions for the issuance of credits and the credits themselves and, where applicable, all instructions for amendments thereto and the amendments themselves, must state precisely the document(s) against which payment, acceptance or negotiation is to be made.
b. Terms such as 'first class', 'well known', 'qualified', 'independent', 'official', and the like shall not be used to describe the issuers of any documents to be presented under a credit. If such terms are incorporated in the credit terms, banks will accept the relative documents as presented, provided that they appear on their face to be in accordance with the other terms and conditions of the credit.
c. Unless otherwise stipulated in the credit, banks will accept as originals documents produced or appearing to have been produced:
   (i) by reprographic systems;
   (ii) by, or as the result of, automated or computerized systems;

(iii) as carbon copies;
if marked as originals, always provided that, where necessary, such documents appear to have been authenticated.

Article 23

When documents other than transport documents, insurance documents and commercial invoices are called for, the credit should stipulate by whom such documents are to be issued and their wording or data content. If the credit does not so stipulate, banks will accept such documents as presented, provided that their data content makes it possible to relate the goods and/or services referred to therein to those referred to in the commercial invoice(s) presented, or to those referred to in the credit if the credit does not stipulate presentation of a commercial invoice.

Article 24

Unless otherwise stipulatd in the credit, banks will accept a document bearing a date of issuance prior to that of the credit, subject to such document being presented within the time limits set out in the credit and in these articles.

D.1. Transport documents (documents indicating loading on board or dispatch of taking in charge)

Article 25

Unless a credit calling for a transport document stipulates as such document a marine bill of lading (ocean bill of lading or a bill of lading covering carriage by sea), or a post receipt or certificate of posting:

a. banks will, unless otherwise stipulated in the credit, accept a transport document which:
   (i) appears on its face to have been issued by a named carrier, or his agent, and
   (ii) indicates dispatch or taking in charge of the goods, or loading on board, as the case may be, and
   (iii) consists of the full set of originals issued to the consignor if issued in more than one original, and
   (iv) meets all other stipulations of the credit.
b. Subject to the above, and unless otherwise stipulated in the credit, banks will not reject a transport document which:
   (i) bears a title such as 'Combined transport bill of lading', 'Combined transport document', Combined transport bill of lading or port-to-port bill of lading', or a title or a combination of titles of similar intent and effect, and/or

(ii) indicates some or all of the conditions of carriage by reference to a source or document other than the transport document itself (short form/blank back transport document), and/or

(iii) indicates a place of taking in charge different from the port of loading and/or a place of final destination different from the port of discharge, and/or

(iv) relates to cargoes such as those in containers or on pallets, and the like, and/or

(v) contains the indication 'intended', or similar qualification, in relation to the vessel or other means of transport, and/or the port of loading and/or the port of discharge.

c. Unless otherwise stipulated in the credit in the case of carriage by sea or by more than one mode of transport by including carriage by sea, banks will reject a transport document which:

(i) indicates that it is subject to a charter party, and/or

(ii) indicates that the carrying vessel is propelled by sail only.

d. Unless otherwise stipulated in the credit, banks will reject a transport document issued by a freight forwarder unless it is the FIATA Combined Transport Bill of Lading approved by the International Chamber of Commerce or otherwise indicates that it is issued by a freight forwarder acting as a carrier or agent of a named carrier.

Article 26

If a credit calling for a transport document stipulates as such document a marine bill of lading:

a. banks will, unless otherwise stipulated in the credit, accept a document which:

(i) appears on its face to have been issued by a named carrier, or his agent, and

(ii) indicates that the goods have been loaded on board or shipped on a named vessel, and

(iii) consists of the full set of originals issued to the consignor if issued in more than one original, and

(iv) meets all other stipulations of the credit.

b. Subject to the above, and unless otherwise stipulated in the credit, banks will not reject a document which:

(i) bears a title such as 'Combined transport bill of lading', 'Combined transport document', 'Combined transport bill of lading or port-to-port bill of lading', or a title or a combination of titles of similar intent and effect, and/or

(ii) indicates some or all of the conditions of carriage by reference to a source or document other than the transport document itself (short form/blank back transport document), and/or

(iii) indicates a place in charge different from the port of loading, and/or a place of final destination different from the port of discharge, and/or
(iv) relates to cargoes such as those in containers or on pallets, and the like.

c. Unless otherwise stipulated in the credit, banks will reject a document which:
(i) indicates that it is subject to a charter party, and/or
(ii) indicates that the carrying vessel is propelled by sail only and/or
(iii) contains the indication 'intended', or similar qualification in relation to
– the vessel and/or the port of loading – unless such document bears an on board notation in accordance with article 27(b) and also indicates the actual port of loading, and/or
– the port of discharge – unless the place of final destination indicated on the document is other than the port of discharge, and/or
(iv) is issued by a freight forwarder, unless it indicates that it is issued by such freight forwarder acting as a carrier, or as the agent of a named carrier.

Article 27

a. Unless a credit specifically calls for an on board transport document, or unless inconsistent with other stipulation(s) in the credit, or with article 26, banks will accept a transport document which indicates that the goods have been taken in charge or received for shipment.
b. Loading on board or shipment on a vessel may be evidenced either by a transport document bearing wording indicating loading on board a named vessel or shipment on a named vessel, or, in the case of a transport document stating 'received for shipment', by means of a notation of loading on board on the transport document signed or initialled and dated by the carrier or his agent, and the date of this notation shall be regarded as the date of loading on board the named vessel or shipment on the named vessel.

Article 28

a. In the case of carriage by sea or by more than one mode of transport but including carriage by sea, banks will refuse a transport document stating that the goods are or will be loaded on deck, unless specifically authorized in the credit.
b. Banks will not refuse a transport document which contains a provision that the goods may be carried on deck, provided it does not specifically state that they are or will be loaded on deck.

Article 29

a. For the purpose of this article transhipment means a transfer and reloading during the course of carriage from the port of loading or place of dispatch or taking in charge to the port of discharge or place of destination either from one conveyance or vessel to another conveyance or vessel within the same mode of transport or from one mode of transport to another mode of transport.
b. Unless transhipment is prohibited by the terms of the credit, banks will accept transport documents which indicate that the goods will be transhipped, provided the entire carriage is covered by one and the same transport document.
c. Even if transhipment is prohibited by the terms of the credit, banks will accept transport documents which:
   (i) incorporate printed clauses stating that the carrier has the right to tranship, or
   (ii) state or indicate that transhipment will or may take place, when the credit stipulates a combined transport document, or indicates carriage from a place of taking in charge to a place of final destination by different modes of transport including a carriage by sea, provided that entire carriage is covered by one and the same transport document, or
   (iii) state or indicate that the goods are in a container(s), trailer(s), 'LASH' barge(s), and the like and will be carried from the place of taking in charge to the place of final destination in the same container(s), trailer(s), 'LASH' barge(s), and the like under one and the same transport document;
   (iv) state or indicate the place of receipt and/or of final destination as 'C.F.S.' (container freight station) or 'C.Y.' (container yard) at, or associated with the port of loading and/or the port of destination.

Article 30

If the credit stipulates dispatch of goods by post and calls for a post receipt or certificate of posting, banks will accept such post receipt or certificate of posting if it appears to have been stamped or otherwise authenticated and dated in the place from which the credit stipulates the goods are to be dispatched.

Article 31

a. Unless otherwise stipulated in the credit, or inconsistent with any of the documents presented under the credit, banks will accept transport documents stating that freight or transportation charges (hereinafter referred to as 'freight') have still to be paid.

b. If a credit stipulates that a transport document has to indicate that freight has been paid or prepaid, banks will accept a transport document on which words clearly indicating payment or prepayment of freight appear by stamp or otherwise, or on which payment of freight is indicated by other means.
c. The words 'freight prepayable' or 'freight to be prepaid' or words of similar effect, if appearing on transport documents, will not be accepted as constituting evidence of the payment of freight.
d. Banks will accept transport documents bearing reference by stamp or otherwise to costs additional to the freight charges, such as costs of, or disbursements incurred in connection with, loading, unloading or similar operations, unless the conditions of the credit specifically prohibit such reference.

Article 32

Unless otherwise stipulated in the credit, banks will accept transport documents which bear a clause on the face thereof such as 'shippers load and count' or 'said by shipper to contain' or words of similar effect.

Article 33

Unless otherwise stipulated in the credit, banks will accept transport documents indicating as the consignor of the goods a party other than the beneficiary of the credit.

Article 34

a. A clean transport document is one which bears no superimposed clause or notation which expressly declares a defective condition of the good and/or the packaging.
b. Banks will refuse transport documents bearing such clauses or notations unless the credit expressly stipulates the clauses or notations which may be accepted.
c. Banks will regard a requirement in a credit for a transport document to bear the clause 'clean on board' as complied with if such transport document meets the requirements of this article and of article 27(b).

D.2. Insurance documents

Article 35

a. Insurance documents must be as stipulated in the credit, and must be issued and/or signed by insurance companies or underwriters, or their agents.

b. Cover notes issued by brokers will not be accepted, unless specifically authorised by the credit.

Article 36

Unless otherwise stipulated in the credit, or unless it appears from the insurance document(s) that the cover is effective at the latest from the date of loading on board or dispatch or taking in charge of the goods, banks will refuse insurance documents presented which bear a date later than the date of loading on board or dispatch or taking in charge of the goods as indicated by the transport document(s).

Article 37

a. Unless otherwise stipulated in the credit, the insurance document must be expressed in the same currency as the credit.
b. Unless otherwise stipulated in the credit, the minimum amount for which the insurance document must indicate the insurance cover to have been effected is the CIF (cost, insurance and freight . . . 'named port of destination') or CIP (freight/carriage and insurance paid to 'named point of destination') value of the goods, as the case may be, plus 10%. However, if banks cannot determine the CIF or CIP value, as the case may be, from the documents on their face, they will accept as such minimum amount the amount for which payment, acceptance or negotiation is requested under the credit, or the amount of the commercial invoice, whichever is the greater.

Article 38

a. Credits should stipulate the type of insurance required and, if any, the additional risks which are to be covered. Imprecise terms such as 'usual risks' or 'customary risks' should not be used; if they are used, banks will accept insurance documents as presented, without responsibility for any risks not being covered.
b. Failing specific stipulations in the credit, banks will accept insurance documents as presented, without responsibility for any risks not being covered.

Article 39

Where a credit stipulates 'insurance against all risks', banks will accept an insurance document which contains any 'all risks' notation or clause, whether or not bearing the heading 'all risks', even if indicating that certain risks are excluded, without responsibility for any risk(s) not being covered.

Article 40

Banks will accept an insurance document which indicates that the cover is subject to a franchise or an excess (deductible), unless it is specifically stipulated in the credit that the insurance must be issued irrespective of percentage.

D.3. Commercial invoice

Article 41

a. Unless otherwise stipulatd in the credit, commercial invoices must be made out in the name of the applicant for the credit.
b. Unless otherwise stipulated in the credit, banks may refuse commercial invoices issued for amounts in excess of the amount permitted by the credit. Nevertheless, if a bank authorised to pay, incur a deferred payment undertaking, accept, or negotiate under a credit accepts such invoices, its decision will be binding upon all parties, provided such bank has not paid, incurred a deferred payment undertaking, accepted or effected negotiations for an amount in excess of that permitted by the credit.
c. The description of the goods in the commercial invoice must correspond with the description in the credit. In all other documents, the goods may be described in general terms not inconsistent with the description of the goods in the credit.

D.4. Other documents

Article 42

If a credit calls for an attestation or certification of weight in the case of transport other than by sea, banks will accept a weight stamp or declaration of weight which appears to have been superimposed on the transport document by the carrier or his agent unless the credit specifically stipulates that the attestation or certification of weight must be by means of a separate document.

E. Miscellaneous provisions

Quantity and amount

Article 43

a. The words 'about', 'circa' or similar expressions used in connection with the amount of the credit or the quantity or the unit price stated in the credit are to be construed as allowing a difference not to exceed 10%

more or 10% less than the amount or the quantity or the unit price to which they refer.

b. Unless a credit stipulates that the quantity of the goods specified must not be exceeded or reduced, a tolerance of 5% more or 5% less will be permissible, even if partial shipments are not permitted, always provided that the amount of the drawings does not exceed the amount of the credit. This tolerance does not apply when the credit stipulates the quantity in terms of a stated number of packing units or individual items.

Partial drawings and/or shipments

Article 44

a. Partial drawing and/or shipments are allowed, unless the credit stipulates otherwise.

b. Shipments by sea, or by more than one mode of transport but including carriage by sea, made on the same vessel and for the same voyage, will not be regarded as partial shipments, even if the transport documents indicating loading on board bear different dates of issuance and/or indicate different ports of loading on board.

c. Shipments made by post will not be regarded as partial shipments if the post receipts or certificates of posting appear to have been stamped or otherwise authenticated in the place from which the credit stipulates the goods are to be dispatched, and on the same date.

d. Shipments made by modes of transport other than those referred to in paragraphs (b) and (c) of this article will not be regarded as partial shipments, provided the transport documents are issued by one and the same carrier or his agent and indicate the same date of issuance, the same place of dispatch or taking in charge of the goods, and the same destination.

Drawings and/or shipments by instalments

Article 45

If drawing and/or shipments by instalments within given periods are stipulated in the credit and any instalment is not drawn and/or shipped within the period allowed for instalment, the credit ceases to be available for that and any subsequent instalments, unless otherwise stipulated in the credit.

Expiry date and presentation

Article 46

a. All credits must stipulate an expiry date for presentation of documents for payment, acceptance or negotiation.

b. Except as provided in Article 48(a), documents must be presented on or before such expiry date.

c. If an issuing bank states that the credit is to be available 'for one month', 'for six months', or the like, but does not specify the date from which the time is to run, the date of issuance of the credit by the issuing bank will be deemed to be the first day from which such time is to run. Banks should discourage indication of the expiry date of the credit in this manner.

Article 47

a. In addition to stipulating an expiry date for presentation of documents, every credit which calls for a transport document(s) should also stipulate a specified period of time after the date of issuance of the transport document(s) during which presentation of documents for payment, acceptance or negotiation must be made. If no such period of time is stipulated, banks will refuse documents presented to them later than 21 days after the date of issuance of the transport document(s). In every case, however, document must be presented not later than the expiry date of the credit.

b. For the purpose of these articles, the date of issuance of a transport document(s) will be deemed to be:

 (i) in the case of a transport document evidencing dispatch, or taking in charge, or receipt of goods for shipment by a mode of transport other than by air – the date of issuance indicated on the transport document or the date of the reception stamp thereon whichever is the latter;

 (ii) in the case of a transport document evidencing carriage by air – the date of issuance indicated on the transport document or, if the credit stipulates that the transport document shall indicate an actual flight date, the actual flight date as indicated on the transport document;

 (iii) in the case of a transport document evidencing loading on board a named vessel – the date of issuance of the transport document or, in the case of an on board notation in accordance with article 27(b), the date of such notation;

 (iv) in cases to which Article 44(b) applies, the date determined as above of the latest transport document issued.

Article 48

a. If the expiry date of the credit and/or the last day of the period of time after the date of issuance of the transport document(s) for presentation of documents stipulated by the credit or applicable by virtue of Article 47 falls on a day on which the bank to which presentation has to be made is closed for reasons other than those referred to in Article 19, the stipulated expiry date and/or the last day of the period of time after the date of issuance of the transport document(s) for presentation of documents, as the case may be, shall be extended to the first following business day on which such bank is open.

b. The latest date for loading on board, or dispatch, or taking in charge shall not be extended by reason of the extension of the expiry date and/or the period of time after the date of issuance of the transport document(s) for presentation of document(s) in accordance with this article. If no such latest date for shipment is stipulated in the credit or amendments thereto, banks will reject transport documents indicating a date of issuance later than the expiry date stipulated in the credit or amendments thereto.
c. The bank to which presentation is made on such first following business day must add to the documents its certificate that the documents were presented within the time limits extended in accordance with Article 48a of the Uniform Customs and Practice for Documentary Credits, 1983 revision, ICC Publication no. 400.

Article 49

Banks are under no obligation to accept presentation of documents outside their banking hours.

Loading on board, dispatch and taking in charge (shipment)

Article 50

a. Unless otherwise stipulated in the credit, the expression 'shipment' used in stipulating earliest and/or a latest shipment date will be understood to include the expressions 'loading on board', 'dispatch' and 'taking in charge'.
b. The date of issuance of the transport document determined in accordance with Article 47(b) will be taken to be the date of shipment.
c. Expressions such as 'prompt', 'immediately', 'as soon as possible', and the like should not be used. If they are used, banks will interpret them as a stipulation that shipment is to be made within thirty days from the date of issuance of the credit by the issuing bank.
d. If the expression 'on or about' and similar expressions are used, banks will interpret them as a stipulation that shipment is to be made during the period from five days before to five days after the specified date, both end days included.

Date terms

Article 51

The words 'to', 'until', 'till', 'from', and words of similar import applying to any date term in the credit will be understood to include the date mentioned. The word 'after' will be understood to exclude the date mentioned.

Article 52

The terms 'first half', 'second half' of a month shall be construed respectively as from the 1st to the 15th, and the 16th to the last day of each month, inclusive.

Article 53

The terms 'beginning', 'middle', or 'end' of a month shall be construed respectively as from the 1st to the 10th, the 11th to the 20th, and the 21st to the last day of each month, inclusive.

F. Transfer

Article 54

a. A transferable credit is a credit under which the beneficiary has the right to request the bank called upon to effect payment or acceptance or any bank entitled to effect negotiation to make the credit available in whole or in part to one or more other parties (second beneficiaries).
b. A credit can be transferred only if it is expressly designated as 'transferable' by the issuing bank. Terms such as 'divisible', 'fractionable', 'assignable' and 'transmissible' add nothing to the meaning of the term 'transferable' and shall not be used.
c. The bank requested to effect the transfer (transfering bank), whether it has confirmed the credit or not, shall be under no obligation to effect such transfer except to the extent and in the manner expressly consented to by such bank.
d. Bank charges in respect of transfers are payable by the first beneficiary unless otherwise specified. The transfering bank shall be under no obligation to effect the transfer until such charges are paid.
e. A transferable credit can be transferred once only. Fractions of a transferable credit (not exceeding in the aggregate the amount of the credit) can be transferred separately, provided partial shipments are not prohibited, and the aggregate of such transfers will be considered as constituting only one transfer of the credit. The credit can be transferred only on the terms and conditions specified in the original credit, with the exception of the amount of the credit, of any unit prices stated therein, of the period of validity, of the last date for presentation of documents in accordance with Article 47 and the period for shipment, any or all of which may be reduced or curtailed, or the percentage for which insurance cover must be effected, which may be increased in such a way as to provide the amount of cover stipulated in the original credit, or these articles. Additionally, the name of the first beneficiary can be substituted

for that of the applicant for the credit, but if the name of the applicant for the credit is specifically required by the original credit to appear in any document other than the invoice, such requirement must be fulfilled.

f. The first beneficiary has the right to substitute his own invoice (and drafts if the credit stipulates that drafts are to be drawn on the applicant for the credit) in exchange for those of the second beneficiary, for amounts not in excess of the original amount stipulated in the credit and for the original unit prices if stipulated in the credit, and upon such substitution of invoices (and drafts), the first beneficiary can draw under the credit for the difference, if any, between his invoices and the second beneficiary's invoices. When a credit has been transferred and the first beneficiary is to supply his own invoices (and drafts) in exchange for the second beneficiary's invoices (and drafts) but fails to do so on first demand, the paying, accepting or negotiating bank has the right to deliver to the issuing bank the documents received under the credit, including the second beneficiary's invoices (and drafts) without further responsibility to the first beneficiary.

g. Unless otherwise stipulated in the credit, the first beneficiary of a transferable credit may request that the credit be transferred to a second beneficiary in the same country, or in another country. Further, unless otherwise stipulated in the credit, the first beneficiary shall have the right to request that payment or negotiation be effected to the second beneficiary at the place to which the credit has been transferred, up to and including the expiry date of the original credit, and without prejudice to the first beneficiary's right subsequently to substitute his own invoices and drafts (if any) for those of the second beneficiary and to claim any difference due to him.

Assignment of proceeds

Article 55

The fact that a credit is not stated to be transferable shall not affect the beneficiary's right to assign any proceeds to which he may be, or may become, entitled under such credit, in accordance with the provisions of the applicable law.

Inter-Club New York Produce Exchange Agreement*

(As Amended May 1984)

Preamble

Memorandum of Agreement (herinafter referred to as 'the Agreement') as to the apportionment of liability for cargo claims arising under the New York Produce Exchange Charter between Assuranceforeningen Gard, Assuranceforeningen Skuld, The Britannia Steam Ship Insurance Association Limited, The Liverpool and London Steamship Protection and Indemnity Association Limited, The London Steam-Ship Owners' Mutual Insurance Association Limited, Newcastle Protection and Indemnity Association, The North of England Protecting & Indemnity Association Limited, The Standard Steamship Owners' Protection and Indemnity Association Limited, The Standard Steamship Owners' Protection and Indemnity Association (Bermuda) Limited, the Steamship Mutual Underwriting Association (Bermuda) Limited, The Sunderland Steamship Protecting & Indemnity Association, Sveriges Angfartygs Assurans Forening, The United Kingdom Mutual Steamship Assurance Association (Bermuda) Limited and The West of England Ship Owners Mutual Protection and Indemnity Association (Luxembourg) (hereinafter together referred to as 'the parties').

(1) Application and Interpretation of the Agreement

Subject to the undermentioned conditions the formula as set forth in Clause 2 shall apply in respect of Charters on the New York Produce Exchange form entered into after the 1 June 1984.

(i) It shall be a condition precedent to settlement under the Agreement that the cargo claim, including any legal costs incurred thereon, shall have been property settled or compromised and the cargo carried under a bill or bills of lading incorporating the Hague or Hague-Visby Rules or containing terms no less favourable. Ex gratia settlements made for business or other reasons where there is no legal liability to pay the claim shall be borne by whom the payment is made and for the purpose of this Agreement no regard shall be had to such payments.

* The NYPE Time Charter 1946 has raised in the past a number of disputes regarding the apportionment of liabilities between the parties of the contract. One of the most controversial issues was in connection with time bar limitation. To solve this problem an Agreement has been reached.

(ii) (a) For the Agreement to apply, the cargo responsibility clauses in the New York Produce Exchange Charter must not be materially amended. A material amendment is one which makes the liability for cargo claims, as between Owners and Charterers, clear. In particular the addition of the words 'and discharge' in Clause 8 shall not be deemed to be a material amendment.

(b) However the addition of the words 'and responsibility' with reference to the words 'under the supervision' in Clause 8 together with the addition of the words 'cargo claims' in the second sentence of Clause 26 shall render the Agreement inoperative. The addition of these two amendments, or the addition only of the words 'cargo claims' in Clause 26, without any other material provision in the Charter shall mean that Owners shall bear all cargo claims subject to Charterers' contribution under the Berth Standard of Average Clause/Charterers' Contribution Clause (1971), if applicable.

(c) If the only material amendment is the addition of the words 'and responsibility' with reference to the words 'under the supervision' in Clause 8, it is agreed by the parties hereto that it shall mean that the apportionment of cargo claims as set out in Clause 2 shall be varied in the following manner:–

Claims for loss of or damage to cargo due to unseaworthiness and claims for condensation damage resulting solely from improper ventilation	100% Owners
Claims for damage (including slackage/ullage) due to bad stowage or handling, and claims for condensation damage resulting otherwise than from improper ventilation. . .	50% Owners 50% Charterers
Except as provided in the second paragraph of Clause (2), short delivery claims (including pilferage) and claims for overcarriage	50% Owners 50% Charterers

(iii) The Agreement shall apply regardless of the place of Arbitration or the legal forum and whether or not the Charter contains a Clause Paramount incorporating therein the Hague-Visby Rules and/or the Berth Standard of Average Clause (otherwise known as the General Standard of Claim Clause/Charterers' Contribution Clause (1971)).

(iv) Any claims pursued under this Agreement by or on behalf of either Charterers or Owners should be notified to the other party in writing as soon as possible but in any event within two years from the date of discharge or the date when the goods should have been discharged, failing which any recovery shall be deemed to be waived and time barred. Such notification should record bill of lading details and the nature and amount of the claim.

(v) Where the Charter contains the Berth Standard of Average Clause/ Charterers' Contribution Clause (1971), such clause is to be applied after liability has been apportioned in accordance with Clause (2) or Clause (1)(ii)(c) as the case may be and Charterers' contribution under such clause shall be per cargo voyage and not per bill of lading or parcel of cargo notwithstanding anything to the contrary contained therein.

(vi) Where Sub-Charters are involved the Agreement, unless the parties hereto otherwise agree in any specific case, shall be applied in stages starting with the party who first settles the cargo claims. For example in the case of a single sub-charter, if the cargo claims are settled by the Sub-Charterers, the said claims shall first be apportioned between the Sub-Charterers and the Charterers in accordance with the Agreement, the Charterers being treated for the purpose as if they were the 'Owners', the balance falling to Charterers' account thereafter being apportioned between the Charterers and Owners in accordance with the Agreement.

(vii) The Agreement is not binding on Members but in all cases the parties will recommend without qualification its acceptance to Members.

(2) Apportionment of Cargo Claims

In all cases where the Agreement applies cargo claims shall be apportioned as hereunder:-

Claims for loss of or damage to cargo due to unseaworthiness . . . . 100% Owners

Claims for damage (including slackage/ullage) due to bad stowage or handling . . . . 100% Charterers

Except as provided in the succeeding paragraphs of this clause, short delivery claims (including pilferage), claims for overcarriage, and claims for condensation damage . 50% Owners
50% Charterers

As regards short delivery and overcarriage claims, where there is clear and irrefutable evidence that the shortage or overcarriage, as the case may be, was due to act, neglect or default on the part of Owners' or Charterers' servants or agents, then the party whose servants or agents were at fault shall bear the claim in full. Thus if there is corroborated eyewitness evidence that the shortage was due to pilferage by a stevedore, the claim will fall

100% to the account of Charterers, but if by a crewmember, then 100% to Owners, subject in the latter case to Charterers' contribution under the Berth Standard of Average Clause/Charterers' Contribution Clause (1971).

Claims for condensation damage shall be apportioned as provided in the first paragraph of this clause, except where there is clear evidence that the damage was due solely to bad stowage in which event such claims shall fall 100% to Charterers' account but where there is clear evidence that the damage resulted solely from improper ventilation, such claims shall be borne 100% by Owners.

(3) Extension of Agreement

It shall be open to the parties to apply in whole or in part the Agreement if they so desire notwithstanding that it is not strictly applicable by reason of any of the matters set forth in Clause 1.

(4) Duration

The Agreement shall continue in force until varied or terminated. Any variation to be effective must be approved in writing by all the parties but it is open to any Association to withdraw from the Agreement on giving to all the other parties not less than three months' written notice thereof, such withdrawal to take effect at the expiration of that period. After the expiry of such notice the Agreement shall nevertheless continue as between all the parties, other than the party giving such notice who shall remain bound by and be entitled to the benefit of this Agreement in respect of all cargo claims arising out of charters commenced prior to the expiration of such notice.

For example if the Standard Association gave written notice of withdrawal from the Agreement on the 1 January 1985, it would be bound to apply the Agreement in respect of cargo claims arising out of the charters commenced at any time on or before 31 March 1985.

(5) Operation

Nothing herein contained shall affect any settlement already concluded between the parties to this Agreement.

UNCTAD Resolution on Maritime Fraud*

(Geneva, 17 February 1984)

'*The Ad hoc Intergovernmental Group* to consider means of combating all aspects of maritime fraud, including piracy;

Recalling resolution 144(VI) on UNCTAD activities in the field of shipping, unanimously adopted on 2 July 1983, by UNCTAD at its sixth session,

Recalling also resolution 49(X), paragraphs (a) and (b), of 25 June 1982, in which the Committee on Shipping decided to establish an *Ad hoc* Intergovernmental Group to consider Means of Combating all Aspects of Maritime Fraud, including Piracy,

Convinced that the various aspects of such problems highlight is importance, which affects all countries in the world,

Recognizing that due to the complexity of subject matter all the relevant measures which might contribute to reduce the consequences arising from it should be studied in depth, by international organizations and/or by commercial parties,

Bearing in mind the study presented by the UNCTAD secretariat entitled 'Review and Analysis of Possible Measures to Minimize the Occurrence of Maritime Fraud and Piracy', several opinions and suggestions which have been presented by the delegations during this session,

Welcoming the work of the other United Nations specialized agencies, such as the International Maritime Organization, intergovernmental organizations and non-governmental organizations in combating maritime fraud and piracy,

Considering that the existing guidelines may be regarded as premises from which the subject matter should be developed,

1. *Calls* on all parties concerned to acquire better knowledge and information on the potential exposure to maritime fraud in connection with international trade and to take the necessary precautions to avoid maritime fraud;

2. *Recommends* that member States of UNCTAD should examine and, if appropriate, tighten their respective legislations to ensure that effective measures are available to prevent maritime fraud and to investigate such fraudulent acts and to prosecute persons who commit such acts of fraud, including taking necessary actions to avoid illegal sale of goods;

* An UNCTAD Ad Hoc Intergovernmental Group met in Geneva from 6 to 27 February 1984, to examine legal measures of combating maritime fraud and piracy. Although IMO has pursued its work, YML reproduces the UNCTAD Resolution.

3. *Recommends* that the Trade and Development Board should invite all member States interested in international trade to consider adoption of UNCTAD's and other organization's suggestions involving, *inter alia*, improved transportation, handling, storage and document procedures;

4. *Requests* that the Trade and Development Board recommend the member States to deal with acts of piracy, taking into consideration the need to improve regional cooperation between States including effective enforcement of their national legislation and bilateral or multilateral treaties;

5. *Requests* the Trade and Development Board to reconvene within the existing resources the intergovernmental Group in 1985 for a second session to finalize its work and to include in the work programme of the Committee on Shipping on its twelfth session all outstanding work from the second session of the intergovernmental Group and for that session to transmit its report to the Committee on Shipping;

6. *Requests* the Trade and Development Board to instruct the UNCTAD secretariat to prepare, without additional financial implications for UNCTAD, and in full collaboration with the appropriate intergovernmental organizations and non-governmental organizations and the commercial parties concerned, in-depth studies to be submitted to the second session of the intergovernmental Group on:

- the feasibility of the administrative and legal procedures of prosecuting authorities in cooperating at the investigating stage with the prosecuting authorities of other States with a view to improving as appropriate the effectiveness of these procedures, as well as to identify other possible means of international cooperation such as the jurisdiction of States and extradition,
- formulation of a set of guidelines to be recommended to the international banking community of the member States of UNCTAD for use by all parties concerned, bearing in mind, *inter alia*, the International Chamber of Commerce anti-fraud protective measures,
- feasibility of a banking super-service scheme,
- to what extent any minimum standards for professional qualifications of shipping agents may contribute to combating maritime fraud and whether such standards could be used as non-mandatory guidelines for the qualifications required,
- study the possible implications to maritime fraud of failure of shipping agents to provide sufficient financial standards based on specific cases where such implications have occurred,
- availability for interested parties of information relating to shipping operations and the adequacy of existing systems of collecting and disseminating such information at the international level, including an economic and commercial assessment with a cost-benefit analysis of the extent to which ship related information not already available is needed to combat maritime fraud;

7. *Requests* the Trade and Development Board:

(a) to invite the relevant specialized international and commercial organizations to continue and develop studies in cooperation with UNCTAD as appropriate, taking into consideration the United Nations recommendations and documents which are relevant in this context on:

- feasibility of a central registry for bills of lading,
- elaboration of a scheme to develop secure bills of lading in order to avoid forgery,
- possibility of reduction in the numbers of bills of lading, or their substitution by another document,
- possibility of adoption of stamping procedures, to replace the Master's signature,
- revision in the practice of inserting a clause in the charter party giving the charterer the right to issue a bill of lading on behalf of the Master,
- impact on prevention of maritime fraud or the elimination, wherever possible, of the use of letters of indemnity/guarantee in conjunction with failure to insert reservations on bills of lading.

(b) to instruct the UNCTAD secretariat to report on the status of these studies to the second session of the Intergovernmental Group;

8. *Calls upon* the Trade and Development Board to urge the UNCTAD secretariat [within available budgetary resources], and other relevant international, governmental and non-governmental organizations to provide and intensify their training and education schemes on measures of combating maritime fraud and piracy.'

PART VII.

BIBLIOGRAPHY

A. BOOK REVIEWS

ARROYO, Ignacio: *Estudios de Derecho Maritimo*, Barcelona (Libreria Bosch, Ronda Universidad 11) 1985, pp. 654.

Professor Ignacio Arroyo, Professor of Commercial Law at the University of Barcelona, is a well-known figure in the international arena, among other reasons for being the founder and director of the 'Anuario de Derecho Maritimo'. The book that we review is an example of his conception of Maritime Law: it encompasses traditional maritime law (Seehandelsrecht) as well as the law of the sea (Seerecht). Consequently, studies of both public and private international law are found.

Together with its interdisciplinary nature, the second characteristic of the work is that it is written from a perspective that is both theoretical and practical. The prologue tells it all – fifteen years of university research and teaching along with another five years of professional practice as an attorney explains the methodology employed. The reader will find, in effect, a rigorous and academic treatment of selected topics without losing sight of the practical application of the law.

With regard to the contents of the book, its comprehensiveness stands out. It contains ten monographic studies on the most relevant themes of maritime law and law of the sea. The first study is dedicated to the 'Origin and evolution of the concept of maritime law' (pp. 31 to 101). Special emphasis is placed on the analysis of comparative law: systems of civil law (Germany, France and Italy) compared with systems of common law (England and United States). In other words, how to compare each judicial system, with its own methodology, to the concept of maritime law.

The second study refers to 'Organizations related to maritime trade' (pp. 102 to 184). This is an original study as it is the first time that the function and achievements of the totality of international maritime organizations, both governmental and private, has been examined.

'The rights of fishing grounds in the EEC and in the UN Conference on the Law of the Sea' (pp. 184 to 228) is a topic of public international law. As its name indicates, it poses the problem of the regulation of fishing in community law regarding the position of Spain, a new member country, and the existence of fishing conventions signed by Spain with third countries. A final reference is made to fishing in the UN Convention of 1982.

The fourth study, 'The distribution of risk in maritime law' (pp. 229 to 340), is a complete essay of almost 110 pages. It examines the various institutions of maritime law (chartering, transport, collision, salvage, gross average and all types of maritime insurance) from the point of view known as 'economic analysis of law'. In other words, the author questions the law in force in light of the 'justice' and 'economy' of distribution among the affected interests.

'International conventions and domestic law: special reference to liability for collision' is the fifth study published (pp. 341 to 402). It approaches the problem of the incorporation of international law into domestic law. More concretely, it poses the problem of which law is applicable to a collision in national waters. Is the International Convention or the domestic law (Commercial Code) applied? The debate is important from the international point of view because the same question is posed with regard to many regulations. It is also interesting for other maritime institutions (not only collision) because the problem is analogous when considering double regulation (national and international).

In continuation, the study on 'Liability of the shipbuilder' (pp. 403 to 427) represents the novelty of an application, for the first time, at least in Spain, of the economic analysis of law to an institution of maritime law: the limitations period of the liability of the builder. According to judicial theory the period is fifteen years. This conclusion, although correct, is absurd because the average life of a ship does not exceed ten years. The theory and concepts of the traditional methodology are shattered by the economic analysis of law.

'Relation between the charterparty and the bill of lading' (pp. 427 to 502) studies the connections between both documents and above all the legal nature of the charterparty compared to the bill of lading as a negotiable instrument. Special reference is made to the incorporation clause, by virtue of which the holder of the bill of lading often finds himself surprised by the manner of description of the charterparty, as the bill of lading is in fact incorporated into the charterparty.

The study on 'Maritime transport and the jurisdiction clause' approaches the problem of the validity of this clause when submitted to foreign courts. The author criticizes, with well-founded reasons, the posture of Spanish case law which opposes these clauses when they provide for foreign jurisdiction.

It is worthwhile to highlight the ninth study, 'Commentary of case law' (pp. 519 to 569) because it systematically expounds the maritime law decisions handed down by the Supreme Court and the Territorial Courts from the promulgation of the Constitution in 1978 until 1983. Along with this review there is a commentary by the author.

Finally, it is highly useful, and we should congratulate Professor Ignacio Arroyo, for his initiative in including the complete Spanish bibliography of works published on maritime law. The void of information concerning sources of knowledge in this field is filled by the final study, 'Sources of knowledge regarding Spanish maritime law. Evaluation and bibliographical summary.'

The work is completed by abundant and valuable indexes.

VICENT VIVES
University of Madrid

ARROYO, Ignacio: *Anuario de Derecho Maritimo*, vol. 1, Editorial Karpos, SA, Madrid, 1981, XXVII and 1074 pp. plus 10 pp. Index, Soft Cover.

This constitutes the first volume of a Spanish yearbook on Maritime Law, edited by Professor Ignacio Arroyo of the Autonomous University of Barcelona. The launch of such a yearbook was partially attributable to the significance that the sea has always had for a maritime nation such as Spain and the absence of a specialist journal in the field of Maritime Law. Its scope is intended to be wider than for academics and students; it hopes also to be of use to practitioners and judges and it hopes to influence reform in the law.

The yearbook does not intend to enter the controversy of drawing what are perceived to be artificial distinctions between the various legal disciplines, be it Maritime Law or private commercial law, or the Law of the Sea as Public International Law; on the contrary, its aim is interdisciplinary, to discuss those issues that originate or take place upon the sea, both from a conceptual and practical viewpoint. In this sense an attempt is made to redefine Maritime Law beyond the parameters of private commercial law to cover any subject dealing with the sea. This is facilitated by the fact that Maritime Law possesses an international character and because it is not simply concerned with the sea as a medium for commerce.

The yearbook is divided into ten sections, being a variety of articles and other features one usually expects to find in such works, namely, Spanish practice and cases of Maritime Law during the year 1979–80; current news and developments regarding Maritime Law, international organizations and conferences, book and journal reviews, and a compilation of conventions and national legislation on maritime affairs.

The first section is composed of a series of articles of a conceptual nature. Thus, for example, Professor Arroyo writes on the development of Maritime Law in different legal systems, drawing comparisons with English, American, French and Italian law, and evaluating the contribution of international organisations to Maritime Law and the Law of the Sea. In his view, the Anglo-American tradition of Maritime Law, particularly the English element, suffers from a lack of systematic planning and is piecemeal. The common law does not recognise a field of Maritime Law properly so-called, but has been arrived at virtually by trial and error, a combination of admiralty and commercial caselaw. Professor Arroyo believes the codes of the civil law systems to be eminently preferable in that they provide an overall structure delimiting the subject.

Professor Emmanuel du Pontavice writes on the evolution of the Law of the Sea and Maritime Law analysing whether this evolution has been prompted by the developing States and whether it constitutes a revolution; while Judge Nagendra Singh, President of the International Court of Justice, writes on the responsibility of flag States, which include the obligations and duties of States in relation to shipping on the high seas, jurisdiction and protetion, the freedom of the seas, sovereign immunity, and sovereign equality.

The second section is composed of articles of a more varied nature, some concerned with certain specific issues. Thus some, like that of Professor José Juste Ruiz examines the effects that the new Law of the Sea on fisheries will have on Spain, while others, like that of José Antonio de Yturriaga, examines the legal principles governing pollution caused by the exploration and exploitation of the deep seabed from an international aspect.

The third section comprises a panorama of Comparative Maritime Law in nineteen countries from the Americas and Europe. Thus Professor F.J.J. Cadwallader writes a brief section on developments in Maritime Law in the United Kingdom during 1979–80; Nicholas J. Healy of the University of New York does likewise for the United States; and Jean Warot on developments in France.

Section IV is composed of a series of notes on the work of international organizations relating to Maritime Law, for example, UNCTAD, UNICITRAL, IMCO, IMC, EEC.

The appearance of the Spanish yearbook is certainly to be welcomed. The standard of Scholarship is high and contains much useful information which may appear difficult to obtain elsewhere. Unfortunately, its marketability in the English-speaking world must be limited by the fact that the yearbook is wholly written in Spanish, a language with which the vast majority of English speakers are sadly unfamiliar. However, this appears to have been a conscious decision of the editor to promote the Spanish language in view of the importance of Spanish in the international community.

GINO J. NALDI
University of East Anglia (*UK*)

PINEUS, Kaj: *Time-Barred Actions* (*International Maritime Law*), Lloyd's of London, London, 1984, pp. 151.

Kaj Pineus, the author of *Time-Barred Actions*, is an attorney, general adjuster, and a well-known international maritime consultant based in Sweden. He is quite familiar to members of the Comité Maritime International, having served for many years as its Vicepresident and reporter, and is also recognized in international maritime circles.

Because of the importance of the presence or absence of a time-bar (known alternatively as prescription, limitation of action, or laches) in a maritime action, the Comité Maritime International prepared a detailed questionnaire on the subject. This questionnaire was forwarded to National Associations throughout the world, and their replies were edited and presented in the book.

The entire world has adopted the basic principles that a claim will lapse due to the passage of time. This is rooted in the desire to put a definitive end to litigious matters. When claims become old, vital evidence often vanishes. Parties are entitled to feel secure in their belief that claims will be prohibited after a certain amount of time passes. It would be unfair to permit a plaintiff to raise a claim after evidence necessary to its defense has disappeared.

Of course, the critical aspect of being aware of time-bar rules depends on the length of time that they provide for. If the time-bar period is short, e.g. one or two years, then ignorance of its existence may well be decisive. On the other hand, an eight or fifteen year period is sufficiently long to allow the ill-informed attorney to dispatch his duties effectively.

Another important question is that of how to prevent the time-bar period from expiring. In some countries, according to the author, the parties may agree voluntarily on an extension, as long as this is done after the claim arises. Some form of court order is often required to stop the time-bar. Most jurisdictions will not accept a simple reminder to the debtor. In particular circumstances, a court may lengthen the time bar period on its own motion, without the consent of the parties.

What are the effects of an interruption or suspension of the time-bar period? Certain countries provide for a new time-bar period of the same length as the original one. Under other systems of law, the time-bar period starts running immediately after the interruption terminates.

The work is divided into two parts. In part I, the author indexes the replies by subject. In part II, the answers received from each country are printed in their entirety. The topics covered include the following situations: collision damage, oil pollution damage, salvage remuneration, freight under a charter-party or a bill of lading, demurrage, loss or damage under a marine insurance policy, and contribution to general average. Also included are: claims against a carrier by sea in respect of loss or damage to goods, passenger's injury or death, loss or damage to passenger's luggage and vehicles, loss or damage to cargo carried in combined transports, and claims by third parties against shipowners. The author also examines the point of time from which the different time bars start to run, and whether claims secured by maritime liens become time-barred simultaneously with the lien.

Time-Barred Actions is a highly useful work in which the author accomplishes his informational objectives. As every practitioner knows, the question of time-bars is the first to be examined in any maritime case and is often decisive regarding the determination of whether, how, and when to bring suit. The study covers a broad variety of topics applicable to every country and provides practical information. The format is well-chosen and the organization is effective.

The book is ideal for quick reference, valuable as a starting point when a brief answer is needed. However, as this publication is not a treatise, the author did not attempt to thoroughly analyze each country's peculiar legal treatment of the many different maritime actions in which time-bars have played an important role. This clearly cannot be achieved in the brief space of 151 pages. Therefore, the reader must not expect all of his questions to be answered, and should keep in mind that detailed or complex inquiries must be researched by an experienced practitioner.

PROF. IGNACIO ARROYO
University of Barcelona

SHARP, David J. and SPICER, W. Wylie: *New Directions in Maritime Law 1984*, Toronto, Carswell Stevens, 1985, pp. VI + 254.

This volume contains twelve papers that attorneys and academics prepared for the New Directions in Maritime Law Conference of 1984 at Halifax, Nova Scotia, which was co-sponsored by the Maritime Law Section of the Canadian Bar Association, the Faculty of Law of Dalhousie University in Halifax, and the Canadian Maritime Law Association. During its biennial meetings, this Conference chooses subjects deemed to be currently important to those involved in maritime law. The conflict of laws in maritime law was the major topic chosen for the 1984 Conference. Other areas discussed include the role of government in the provision of salvage services, and the impact of computer technology on shipping documents.

With regard to the editors, DAVID J. SHARPE is a Professor of Law at the National Law Center of the George Washington University in Washington, D.C. W. WYLIE SPICER is an attorney with McInnes, Cooper & Robertson in Halifax, Nova Scotia.

The first paper is entitled 'A Course Change to Starboard: New Directions in Maritime Conflict Resolution in the United States'. It was written by HAROLD K. WATSON, a partner in Liddell, Sapp, Zivley, Brown & LaBoon of Houston, Texas, who has published articles in The Journal of Maritime Law and Commerce, the Houston Law Review, the Louisiana Law Review, and the Maritime Lawyer. The paper covers the wide spectrum of case law regarding American maritime conflict as well as legislative actions, and includes predictions of future trends.

The author discusses subject matter jurisdiction, personal jurisdiction, choice of law, and appropriate forum. Judicial and legislative beliefs about the proper role of American law and courts in determining disputes of international dimension are examined, as well as a historical survey of the development of American maritime conflict law.

'One if by Land, Two if by Sea: Old Directions in Maritime Law' was written by VAUGHAN BLACK, Assistant Professor of Law at Dalhousie University. The author explains that many problems regarding conflict of laws arise because of the very general language used in statutes, regulations, and judicial opinions. He then sets out a framework for geographically complex cases, in terms of selection of jurisdiction and the interpretive approach. Current conflict of law problems, contractual choice of law problems, and personal injury actions all form a part of this paper.

DAVID W. ROBERTSON, the author of 'Conflict of Laws and Forum Non Conveniens Determinations in Maritime Personal Injury and Death Cases in United States Courts' is an Albert Sidney Burleson Professor of Law at the University of Texas and the author of more than 30 articles on personal injury and maritime law. Topics of the paper include the following: transnational maritime personal injury and death litigation in the United States federal courts; subject matter and personal jurisdiction; defenses based on choice of law and forum non conveniens; judicial development of maritime choice of law principles in seamen's injury cases; forum non conveniens issues in transnational maritime injury cases; traditional or 'blue water' seamen: the post-Rhoditis choice of law and forum non conveniens jurisprudence; injury and death claims by foreign offshore workers; maritime accidents injuring non-seamen; aviation and other maritime injury cases.

The fourth paper, 'Conflict of Laws and Personal Injury in the Eastern Canadian Offshore: The Aftermath of the Arctic Explorer and Ocean Ranger Sinkings', was written by MICHAEL F. HARRINGTON, an attorney with the firm of Stirling and Ryan in Newfoundland. The paper examines from a Canadian viewpoint the conflict of laws problems arising from injury and wrongful death claims. Subjects covered include: Canadian workers' compensation schemes; choice of law problems; remedies available to oil rig employees and their dependents in the courts; and defenses to forum shopping by claimants in jurisdictions outside of Canada.

ELLIOTT B. NIXON, a partner in Burlingham Underwood and Lord, wrote 'Limitation of Shipowners' Liability Under U.S. Law – Does Any Other Law Apply?' Mr. Nixon briefly reviews the historical development of United States law in this area and then poses two critical questions: what is the practical application of the term 'privity or knowledge', and whether foreign law may determine the amount of the shipowner's limitation fund. Recent decisions as to applicable law are discussed. The essay is completed by sections on international conventions and future legislation.

Foreign and Canadian charterers and shipowners may often limit their liability for property damage, personal injury, and wrongful death claims that arise due to the actions of maritime personnel, ship navigation, or management if they can demonstrate that they were without 'actual fault or privity'. 'Shipowners' Limitation of Liability and the Canadian Conflict of Laws', by SEAN HARRINGTON, a partner with McMaster Meighten in Montreal, analyzes the conflict of laws problems that present themselves when Canadian and foreign laws collide. The author does not neglect to mention the role played by the 1976 Convention on Limitation of Liability for Maritime Claims, which has not yet entered into force.

'Maritime Liens and Rights In Rem in United States Law' is the title of the paper written by Professor DAVID J. SHARPE, the well-known co-editor of 'Cases and Materials on Admiralty'. Professor Sharpe outlines the differences between the maritime lien laws of the United States and the other maritime countries, owing in substantial part to the fact that the U.S. is not a party to either the 1952 International Convention Relating to the Arrest of Sea-Going Ships, or the 1926 International Convention For the Unification of Certain Rules Relating to Maritime Liens and Mortgages. Professor Sharpe points out that the U.S. recognizes far more liens than most other nations, and that U.S. admiralty courts possess jurisdiction over foreign as well as domestic ship mortgages on ships that have been arrested in U.S. ports. He does not foresee major changes in the American system in the near future.

W. TETLEY, the author of 'The Law of Conflicts and Maritime Liens: The United States, Canada, the United Kingdom and France', is a professor of law at McGill University and a past president of the Canadian Maritime Law Association. Conflict of maritime laws results, according to Mr. Tetley, from the failure of modern international conventions to cover all aspects of maritime law. Among the many topics covered in this lengthy study are the following: categories of conflicts; processing a conflict problem; recognition of foreign law; choice of law regarding contract liens in the United States; Canadian decisions on choice of law of contract liens; contract liens and conflict of laws in the United Kingdom; and conflict of laws in France.

The ninth paper is entitled 'The Changing Face of Documentation in the Carriage of Goods', by A. R. ELLIOT, Ph.D and President of COSTPRO. It deals in large part with efforts to establish electronic networks for tracking the shipment of goods between countries. The author presents a brief history of trade facilitation efforts, and speaks of the growing use of electronic messages. He surveys activities on the Canadian and international scenes, and closes with a section on intercompany and international trade document interchange trends.

'When Bits Replace Bills, What Shall the Law Byte On? Legal Consequences of Automating Carriage Documentation', is a paper on automation by HUGH M. KINDRED, Professor of Law at Dalhousie University. This informative piece contains sections on automating bills of lading, receipts for goods, contracts of carriage, and documents of title.

DAVID G. HEBDEN, a solicitor with the London firm of Thomas Cooper and Stibbard specializing in salvage litigation and arbitration, drafted the eleventh paper on 'The Role of Government in Marine Salvage: An International Perspective'. This work focuses on the practical aspects of salvage. It summarizes the salvage systems in France, Turkey, and other countries, and examines the role of the navy in salvage. Current issues such as government and the low-valued vessel and cargo are also discussed.

The title of the last paper, 'The Role of Government in the Provision of Salvage Services: a Canadian Perspective', is self-explanatory. It was written by PETER M. TROOP, Assistant Deputy Attorney General, Admiralty and Maritime Law, Department of Justice in Ottawa. This comprehensive study of Canadian law deals with salvage claims by and against the Crown, the Crown as a volunteer, and the role of government in search and rescue as compared to the role of government in salvage.

This book is highly recommended. Generally speaking, it contains a series of well-researched and written papers. However, every collection of this nature contains writings of varying quality. From a practical viewpoint, the volume is more useful for academics than for practitioners.

MATTHEW SCHREIBER, Esq.
J. D. University of California, Berkeley
(Ramos & Arroyo, Abogados, Barcelona)

B. BOOK NOTICES

HAGBERG, Lennart (Ed.): *Arrest of Vessels*, Deventer (Kluwer), 2nd edition, 1984, pp. 114.

This publication will cover the most important subjects of an arrest of vessels in some 50 countries.

Topics covered are a.o.: type of claims, security, power of attorney, enforcement of order of arrest, court hearing, sister ships, time element, conventions, bail by defendant, appeal by defendant, claims for damages, etc.

HAGBERG, Lennart (Ed.): *Mortgage on Vessels and Registration of Vessels*, Deventer (Kluwer), 1983–4, 2 vols. pp. 754.

The aim of this new volume III of the series is to give the practising lawyer and insofar as mortgages on vessels are concerned also the bankers an overall view of the legal requirements for the registration of vessels and the registration of mortgages on vessels and in particular the legal effects of a valid mortgage on a vessel. So far as the registration of vessels is concerned the emphasis is on the type of vessels which can be registered, the qualifications for ownership and the necessary paper work.

On the subject of mortgages great care has been taken to define exactly the requirements for creating a valid charge. The pre-requisite for a mortgage to take action against the vessel to enforce a mortgage is of course that he has a valid mortgage. The mortgage systems vary of course country by country. It can be here mentioned that according to the laws of Thailand all modes of transport are treated in the same manner. Accordingly ships and other vehicles such as camels, elephants, oxen or other beasts of burden can be mortgaged.

When evaluating a security a banker or other lender must know exactly the priority of his security. Because of that the system of priorities is explained in great detail country by country. Finally in this context the rules governing enforced sales of vessels are explained in some detail for those countries which are not included in Volume II of the Series.

Lastly the system of registration of rights in respect of vessels under construction has been described in particular for those countries which have incorporated the rules of the 1967 Convention relating to Registration of Rights in respect of Vessels under Construction or have similar rules in their national systems.

MANKABADY, Samir (Ed.): *The International Maritime Organization*, London (Croom Helm Ltd.), 1984, pp. 372.

This volume takes a comprehensive look at the work of the IMO in its 25th year. Topics covered include: protection of the marine environment; navigation; IMO's structure and status in the international community; cargo and containers; construction and design of vessels; training and technical assistance; and trade and transport. Among the 16 different authors are attorneys, academics, and international organization representatives. Special attention is paid to IMO's role regarding international conventions.

The Law of the Sea (*Official Text of the United Nations Convention of the Law of the Sea with Annexes and Index*), Beckenham, Kent (Croom Helm Ltd.), 1983, pp. 211, and pp. 32 Index.

This is simply a hardcover reproduction of the 1982 Law of the Sea Convention. However, it contains an excellent index that makes it easy to work with.

BOLTON, Rita V. and BRYAN, F. J.: *Marine Transport: A Guide to Libraries and Sources of Information in Great Britain*, London (Library Association Reference and Marine Librarian's Association), 2nd edition, 1983, pp. 60.

This directory lists over 100 libraries and other organizations which possess substantial amounts of information on maritime transport or related subjects including navigation, oceanography, meteorology, shipbuilding, and telecommunications.

HERMAN, Amos: *Shipping Conferences*, London (Lloyd's of London Press Ltd.), 1983, pp. 213.

The author of this book attempts to analyze the shipping conference system and compare the attitudes of the major English speaking shipping powers, the U.S., Australia, India, and the United Kingdom, towards their regulation. International codes for conferences are also extensively discussed.

The book's chapters cover, among other subjects, passenger conferences, containerization, cost structures, international institutional developments, shippers' councils, and loyalty agreements. The UNCTAD and CENSA codes are reprinted in the appendices.

SINGH, Nagendra: *International Maritime Law Conventions*, London (Stevens & Sons), 1983, 4 vols., pp. 3302.

This work is comprised of a thorough collection of treaties cross-indexed in various ways. The respective titles of the volumes are Navigation; Safety; Training, Employment and Welfare and Environment; and Maritime Law. Titles of the major cross-indexes are: Safety; Employment, Welfare and Status of Seamen; Environment; Law of the Sea, Landlocked States, Ports, Canals and Straits; Private Maritime Law, Miscellaneous Conventions and International Organizations.

O'CONNELL, D. P. and SHEARER, I.A (Eds.): *The International Law of the Sea* (Volume II), Oxford (Clarendon Press), 1984, pp. 524.

The writings of the well-known maritime law scholar Professor O'Connell have here been compiled and edited by Professor Shearer. The reader will find detailed studies of subjects such as civil, criminal, and curial jurisdiction, the EEC and the continental shelf, pollution control, economic warfare at sea, nationality of ships and shipping regulation, and piracy. The 1982 Law of the Sea Convention is thoroughly analyzed.

WARING, Anne: *Charterparties, A Comparative Study of South African, English and American Law*, Cape Town (Juta & Co. Ltd.), 1983, pp. 353.

In this book, the author extensively examines South African maritime law. She then compares it to its American and English counterparts. Historical outlines, commentary, and conclusions are included.

BRICE, Geoffrey: *Maritime Law of Salvage*, London (Stevens & Son), 1983, pp. 318, pp. 221 Appendices and Index.

Mr. Brice, using an approach that is both theoretical and practical, broadly covers topics related to the law of the salvage, including the Civil Jurisdiction and Judgments Act of 1982, the Merchant Shipping Acts, the CRISTAL and TOVALOP agreements, and the United Kingdom Standard Conditions for Towage.

McDORMAN, Ted, BEAUCHAMP, Kenneth, and JOHNSTON, Douglas: *Maritime Boundary Delimitation*, Lexington, Mass., U.S.A. (Lexington Books), 1983, pp. 156.

This work is an annotated bibliography of writings on boundary delimitations between overlapping claims, seaward limits of coastal zones, and other types of delimitation. Each entry includes an annotation and is cross-indexed to a list of authors. The appendix provides a regional list of bilateral delimitation agreements.

C. TITLES RECEIVED

ADEMUNI-ODEKE: *Protectionism and the future of international shipping*, Martinus Nijhoff, Dordrecht, 1984, pp. 27 + 427.

ANAND, R. P.: *Origin and development of the Law of the Sea*, Martinus Nijhoff, The Hague, 1983, pp. 249.

ANTAPASSIS, A. M.: *Les Codes Maritimes Grecs*, Librairie Générale de Droit et de Jurisprudence, Paris, 1983, pp. 7 + 330.

ANTONINI, Alfredo: *L'Obbligazione Contributiva Nelle Avarie Comuni*, Vol. 1, Padova. Ed. Cedam, 1983, pp. 118.

ANTONINI, Alfredo: *L'Obbligazione Contributiva Nelle Avarie Comuni*, Vol. 2, Padova. Ed. Cedam, 1983, pp. 132.

ANTONINI, Alfredo: *Bills of Lading Law*, Fairplay Publications, London, 1982, pp. 72.

ANTONINI, Alfredo: *The Hamburg Rules*, Fairplay Publications, London, 1981, pp. XII + 163.

ANTONINI, Alfredo: *Hague Rules Law Digest*, Fairplay Publications, London, 1981, pp. IX + 90.

ANTONINI, Alfredo: *Shipping and the Law*, Fairplay Publications, London, 1982, pp. 251.

BELTRAN MONTIEL, Luis: *Curso de derecho de la navegacion 4 ta. reimpresion*, Astrea, Buenos Aires, 1983, pp. 526.

BENEDICT: *Admiralty*, *Carriage of Goods by Sea*, Vol. 2, 7th Ed., Matthew & Bender, New York, 1983.

BENEDICT: *Admiralty*, *Treaties and Related Documents*, Vol. 6, 7th Ed., Matthew & Bender, New York, 1983.

BENEDICT: *Admiralty*, *Marine Insurance*, Vol. 7, 7th Ed., Matthew & Bender, New York, 1983.

BES, J.: *Fletamentos y terminos de embarque* (*Traduccion castellana de S. Vriarte y Jarraondo*) 7th Ed., Anave, Madrid, 1982, pp. XXVIII + 506.

BOURGON TINAO, L. P.: *Los puertos Francos y el Régimen especial de Canarias*, Instituto de Estudios de Administración Local, Madrid, 1982, pp. 818.

CARBONE, S. M.: *Le regole di responsabilità del vettore marittimo* (*Dall'Aja ad Amburgo attraverso la giurisprudenza italiana*), Giuffre Editore, Milano, 1984, pp. 210.

CHRZANOWSKI, Ignacy: *An Introduction to Shipping Economics*, Fairplay Publications, London, 1985, pp. VIII + 131.

CODICE DELLA NAVIGAZIONE: A. Giuffre Editore, Milano, 1984, pp. 568.

CORTES, Luis Javier: *Póliza Flotante y Seguro en abono*, Publicaciones del Real Colegio de España, Bolonia, 1984, pp. 236.

DE ROOY, Frans P.: *Documentary Credits*, Kluwer, Deventer, 1984, pp. 12 + 266.

DRIVER, Peter: *Lloyd's Marine Equipment Guide 1985*, Lloyd's of London Press Ltd., London, 1985, pp. 354.

DUPUY, René (Ed.): *La Gestion des ressources pour l'humanité: le Droit de la mer*, Martinus Nijhoff, The Hague, 1982, pp. 433.

ECHEVERRIA RIVERA, L. E.: *El Transporte Marítimo*, Aranzadi, Pamplona, 1983, 2nd Ed., pp. 298.

FAIREN GUILLEN, Víctor: *Importancia de los Tribunales Consulares: El Consulado de mar de Valencia*, Cámara de Comercio, Industria y Navegación de Valencia, Valencia, 1984, pp. 20.

FERNANDEZ-ARMESTO, J.: *Los créditos documentarios irrevocables, en las Reglas y Usos Uniformes revisiones de 1974 y 1983 y en el Derecho español*, La Voz de Galicia S.A., La Coruña, 1984, pp. 446.

FERRARINI, S.: *Le assicurazioni marittime*, Vol. II, *La nuova disciplina convenzionale*, Giuffre Editore, Milano, 1984, pp. 163.

GARCIA, Arcadi: *Llibre del Consolat de Mar, Estudi Jurídic*, Vol. III 1, Fundació Noguera/Fundació Vives Casajuana, Barcelona, 1984, pp. 299.

GARCIA, Arcadi: *Llibre Del Consolat de Mar, Diplomatari*, Vol. III 2, Fundació Noguera/Fundació Vives Casajuana, Barcelona, 1984, pp. 373.

GARCIA Y SANZ, A. y FERRER Y MALLOL, M. T.: *Assegurances i canvis marítims medievals a Barcelona*, Vol. I and Vol. II, Institut d'estudis Catalans, Barcelona, 1983, pp. 757.

GIBNEY, R. F.: *Container Lines: The Strategy Game*, Lloyd's of London Press Ltd., London, 1984, pp. 87.

GRIGOLI, M.: *Diritto della Navigazione*, Utet, Torino, 1982, pp. 684.

HARDY IVAMY, E.R.: *Encyclopedia of Shipping Law Sources (UK)*, Lloyds of London Press Ltd., London, 1985, pp. 19 + 658.

HAUSER, W.: *The Legal Regime for Deep Seabed Mining under the Law of the Sea Convention*, Alfred Metzner Verlag, Frankfurt/Main, 1983, pp. 211.

HERMAN, A.: *Shipping Conferences*, Lloyd's of London Press, London, 1983, pp. 255.

HERNANDEZ MARTI, J.: *Contrato de transporte marítimo de mercancías*, Valencia, 1984, pp. 206.

HILL, D. J.; MESSENT, A. D.: *CMR: Contracts for the International Carriage of Goods by Road*, Lloyd's of London Press Ltd., London, 1984, pp. 32 + 283.

HOLDERT, H. M. C.; BUZEK, F. J.: *Collision Cases – Judgments and Diagrams*, Lloyd's of London Press Ltd., London, 1984, pp. XVII + 190.

IHRE, R.; GROTON, L. a.o.: *Shipbroking and Chartering Practice*, 2nd Ed., Lloyd's of London Press Ltd., London, 1984, pp. 298.

INSTITUTE OF CHARTERED SHIPBROKERS: *The Shipbroker's Manual*, Vol. 1, Lloyd's of London Press Ltd., London, 1983, pp. 167.

LAURENCE, C. A.: *Vessel Operating Economies*, Fairplay Publications, London, 1984, pp. VIII + 60.

LEFEBVRE/PESCATORE: *Manuale di Diritto della Navigazione*, Giuffre Editore, Milano, 1983, pp. 930.

LEVY, J. P.: *La Conférence des Nations Unies sur le Droit de la Mer*, Ed. A. Pedone, Paris, 1983, pp. 152.

LOPUSKI, Jan: *The Polish Maritime Code*, Wydawnictwo Morskie, Gdańsk, 1985, pp. 538.

LLOYD'S NAUTICAL YEAR BOOK, 1984: Lloyd's of London Press Ltd., London, 1984, pp. 607.

MacGREGOR, David R.: *Merchant Sailing Ships 1775–1815*, Conway, London, 1985, pp. 224.

MBANEFO, Louis Nnamdi: *Nigerian Shipping Laws*, Professional Books Limited, U.K., 1983, pp. XCIV + 1055.

Miscellaneous: *Propos sur le Noveau Droit de la Mer* (Colloque), Ed. A. Pedone, Paris, 1985, pp. VIII + 120.

Miscellaneous: *Seminario de Buenos Aires de 1980, La responsabilidad del transportador de mercaderías por agua*, Giuffre Editore, Milano, 1983, pp. 16 + 393.

OCDE: *Expérience de la gestion des zones de pêche nationales*, OCDE, Paris, 1984, pp. 177.

OFICINA DE LAS NACIONES UNIDAS: *Glosario de Transporte Maritimo, Ingles–Español*, Servicio de idiomas, Ginebra, Term/34 Abril de 1985, pp. III + 366.

ORGANIZACION INTERNACIONAL DEL TRABAJO: *Convenios y recomendaciones sobre el trabajo marítimo*, Oficina internacional del Trabajo, Ginebra, 1983, pp. 208.

ORTEGA TORRES, Jorge (Com.): *Código de Comercio de Colombia*, Temis, Bogotá, 1984, pp. 823.

PELAEZ, Manuel J.: *Cambios y seguros marítimos en derecho catalan y balear*. Studia Albornotiana, Publicaciones Real Colegio de España, Bolonia Zaragoza, 1984, pp. XLV + 274.

PINEUS, K.; ROHREKE, H. G.: *Limited Liability in Collision Cases*, Lloyd's of London Press Ltd., London, 1984, pp. 5 + 23.

PINEUS, K.: *International Maritime Law Time Barred Actions*, Lloyd's of London Press Ltd., London, 1984, pp. 7 + 157.

POST, A. M.: *Deep-sea Mining and the Law of the Sea*, Martinus Nijhoff, The Hague, 1983, pp. XXIII + 358.

QUERCI, Francesco Alessandro, Ed.: *Nuovi Ruoli per il sistema marittimo portuale negli anni'80*, Quaderni della Revista Trasporti, 7, Riassetto del porto di Venezia, Padova, Cedam, 1982, pp. 124.

REYNAUD, A.: *Le plateau continental de la France*, Librairie Générale de Droit et de Jurisprudence, Paris, 1984, pp. 15 + 431.

RODIERE, René (ed.): *Traité de Droit Maritime*, I. Assurances Maritimes, Rodiere, René, II. Ventes Maritimes, Calais-Auloy, Jean, Dalloz, Paris, 1983, pp. 599 + X.

ROSE, Francis: *The Modern Law of Pilotage*, Sweet & Maxwell, London, 1984, pp. 138.

SCOVAZZI, T.: *La pesca nell' evoluzione del diritto del mare*, Giuffre Editore, Milano, 1984, pp. 11 + 297.

SINGH, Nagendra: *International Maritime Law Conventions*, *Navigation*, Vol. 1 (British Shipping Laws), Stevens & Sons, London, 1983, pp. XVII + 978 + 60.

SINGH, Nagendra: *International Maritime Law Conventions*, *Safety*, Vol. 2 (British Shipping Laws), Sweet & Maxwell, London, 1983, pp. XXVII + 1876 + 60.

SINGH, Nagendra: *International Maritime Law Conventions, Training, Employment and Welfare; Environment*, Vol. 3 (British Shipping Laws), Sweet & Maxwell, London, 1983, pp. XXVII + 2621 + 60.

SINGH, Nagendra: *International Maritime Law Conventions, Maritime Law*, Vol. 4 (British Shipping Laws), Stevens & Sons, London, 1983, pp. XV + 677 + 60.

SLABOTZKY, A.: *Grain Contracts and Arbitration for Shipments from the United States and Canada*, Lloyd's of London Press Ltd., London, 1984, pp. VII + 105.

SLOGGETT, J. E.: *Shipping Finance*, Fairplay Publications, London, 1984, pp. VIII + 116.

TIRADO SUAREZ, Francisco Javier: *Ley Ordenadora del Seguro Privado* (Exposición y crítica). Publicaciones de la Universidad de Sevilla, Sevilla, 1984, pp. 317.

TREVES, Tullio: *La Convenzione delle Nazioni Unite sul Diritto del Mare del 10 diciembre 1982*, Giuffre Editore, Milano, 1983.

VENTRIS, F. M.: *Bankers' Documentary Credits*, 2nd ed., Lloyd's of London Press Ltd., London, 1983, pp. XXI + 350.

VOSKUIL, C. C. A. and WADE, J. A.: *Hague-Zagreb, Essays 4 on the Law of International Trade*, Martinus Nijhoff, The Hague, 1983, pp. 396.

D. JOURNALS

ANUARIO DE DERECHO MARITIMO (Volumen III, 1984)

RICARDO MÓNACO, UNIDROIT: La actividad UNIDROIT durante el período 1982–83 *631*
FRANCISCO-JOSÉ SÁNCHEZ ORTIZ, FIATA: Actividades de la Federación Internacional de las Asociaciones de Transitarios en 1983 *643*
IGNACIO ARROYO, AEDM: La Asociación Española de Derecho Marítimo (1982 y 1983) *649*
JUAN VICINTE PUENTE, ANAVE: La Asociación de Navieros Españoles: 1983 *653*
IGNACIO ARROYO, Reseña de legislación marítima (enero-diciembre 1982) *659*
IGNACIO ARROYO, Reseña de legislación marítima (enero-diciembre 1983) *665*
CESÁREO GUTIÉRREZ, ALFONSO L. CALVO Y ROSA RIQUELME, Práctica española de Derecho Internacional Marítimo (1982–1983) *679*
IGNACIO ARROYO: Reseña de las Sentencias y Autos del Tribunal Supremo dictados durante 1982 y 1983 *742*
IGNACIO ARROYO: Reseña de las Sentencias de las Audiencias Territoriales dictadas en 1983 *927*
FRANCISCO RAMOS MÉNDEZ, Arbitraje internacional: Confirmación de la doctrina jurisprudencial (Comentarios a los Autos del TS 24 de marzo y 3 de junio de 1982 y 14 enero, 10 mayo y 17 junio de 1983) *989*
IGNACIO ARROYO, Transporte marítimo internacional y jurisdicción extranjera. La necesaria reforma de un criterio jurisprudencial (Anotaciones críticas a la sentencia de la Audiencia Territorial de Barcelona de 22 de octubre de 1980) *995*

ASSICURAZIONI (1984)

SERGIO FERRARINI: Le nuove condizioni inglesi di assicurazione marittima corpi, 1984, fasc. 2, pp. 89.
CLAUDIO L. DAVEGGIA: Forme contrattuali dell'assicurazione marittima stradale, 1984, fasc. 5, pp. 360.

CMI NEWS LETTER (1984)

BONASSIES, P.: Summary of recent French case law. March, 1984.
BERLINGIERI, Francesco: New avenues to unification of Maritime Law. December, 1984.

EUROPEAN TRANSPORT LAW (1984: vol. XIX)

IWASAKI, Kuzuo: Japanese court's competence/Jurisdiction for international litigations. nr. 5, p. 559.
TETLEY, William: Highlights from Canadian maritime jurisprudence. June, 1984.

IL DIRITTO MARITTIMO (1984: vol. LXXXVI)

GUSTAVO ROMANELLI, I problemi attuali delle gestioni portuali, no. 32 (1984) *3*
UGO MARCHESE, Evoluzione delle infrastrutture portuali e dei loro modi di finanziamento, no. 32 (1984) *11*
LORENZO COLAUTTI, Le strutture dei porti italiani; come e perché si è giunti all'attuale posizione di ritardo tecnologico, no. 32 (1984) *32*
FRANCESCO BERLINGIERI, Modelli di gestione portuale, no. 32 (1984) *44*
GIANFRANCO LEGITIMO, Modelli di gestione e produttività dei porti, no. 32 (1984) *78*
FRANCESCO ALESSANDRO QUERCI, Gestioni e lavoro portuale: spunti critici per un nuovo modello organizzativo, no. 32 *96*
RENATO MATTEUCCI, La riforma delle gestioni e del lavoro portuale per il rinnovamento produttivo dei porti, no. 32 *106*
GUIDO DE VITA, Gestioni portuali e rapporti con l'armamento pubblico, no. 32 (1984) *112*
EGIDIO ORTONA, Gestioni portuali e rapporti con l'armamento privato, no. 32 (1984) *119*
EGIDIO ORTONA, 'Gestioni portuali: problemi e prospettive'. Conclusioni dell'Istituto di diritto della navigazione dell'Università di Roma, no. 32 (1984) *129*
ROBERTO CAGLIOZZI, Aspetti della gestione dei trasporti pubblici nelle aree urbane e metropolitane, no. 32 (1984) *132*
ANNIBALE D'ORO, La legge quadro francese per i trasporti interni. In particolare il trasporto aereo, no. 32 (1984) *153*
FRANCESCO ALESSANDRO QUERCI, Spunti per la fondazione di un moderno piano aeroportuale italiano, no. 32 (1984) *3*
EUGENIO SPASIANO, Distinzione dei porti, demanialità ed enti di gestione, no. 33 (1984) *19*
GIUSEPPE FONTANELLA, L'economia del trasporto pubblico con riferimento specifico alle autolinee di competenza statale, no. 33 (1984) *28*
MARCO POLASTRI MENNI, Trasporto ed appalto: problemi di qualificazione, no. 33 (1984) *53*

ENRICO VINCENZINI, Il soccorso in mare nel diritto marittimo romano, no. 33 (1984) *60*
ALBERTO LASSANDRO, L'ordinamento del trasporto aereo internazionale, no. 33 (1984) *63*
BENITO PAGNANELLI, Politica assicurativa nei trasporti aerei, no. 33 (1984) *75*
NICOLETTA MACCAFERRI, Considerazioni in materia di competenza territoriale in tema di lavoro nautico (nota a ord. Pret. Bari 18 marzo 1981, n. 439, e Cass. S.U., 11 novembre 1982, n. 5944), no. 33 (1984) *80*
FRANCESCO ALESSANDRO QUERCI, I significati e gli aspetti programmatici organizzativi della legge 979/1982, no. 34 (1984) *3*
FRANCESCO SANTORO, Il punto sulla politica dei trasporti della C.E.E, no. 34 (1984) *14*
GIORGIO CONETTI, L'impresa di trasporto nella normativa comunitaria, no. 34 (1984) *46*
ALESSANDRO CAGNOLI, L'impresa di trasporto nella normativa italiana, no. 34 (1984) *56*
FRANCESCO PAOLO SGARRO, Sulla gestione delle imprese di navigazione, no. 34 (1984) *67*
ANGELO RIZZO, Esperienze e prospettive di aziende di trasporto operanti in Italia, no. 34 (1984) *89*
ARNALDO CHISARI, I principali dati emergenti dal conto nazionale trasporti 1982, no. 34 (1984) *98*
LEOPOLDO TULLIO (a cura di), Portolano di giurisprudenza (Cass. 14 dicembre 1984 n. 6570; Pret. Salò 1 settembre 1983; Cass. 3 novembre 1983 n. 6470), no. 34 (1984) *101*

JOURNAL OF BUSINESS LAW (1984)

POWLES, D.: Maritime fraud, January, 1984, 31
McCLELLAN, A.: Choice of jurisdiction clauses under the EEC judgments Convention, September, 1984, 445

JOURNAL OF MARITIME LAW AND COMMERCE (1984)

ALEX L. PARKS, The New London Hull Clauses *Vol. 1, p. 1*
MICHAEL J. O'KANE, Accidents in the Canal: Perspectives on the Claims Structure of the New Panama Canal Act *Vol. 1, p, 29*
WILLIAM TETLEY, Waybills: The Modern Contract of Carriage of Goods by Sea (Part II) *Vol. 1, p, 41*
KAZUO IWASAKI, A Survey of Maritime Arbitration in New York *Vol. 1, p. 69*

WILLIAM L. PECK, The Pennsylvania Rule Since Reliable Transfer *Vol. 1, p. 95.*

RICHARD A. LIDINSKY, Jr. and ROBERT E. HELLAUER, Jr., American-Canadian Cross Border Container Traffic: Innovation or Cargo Diversion? *Vol. 1, p. 103*

MICHAEL KOCH, The Antarctic Challenge: Conflictintg Interests, Cooperation, Environmental Protection, and Economic Development *Vol. 1, p. 117*

MICHAEL CONANT, The Commerce Clause, the Supremacy Clause and the Law Merchant: Swift v. Tyson and the Unity of Commercial Law *Vol. 2, p. 153*

ALEX L. PARKS, Recent Developments in Admiralty and Marine Insurance Law *Vol. 2, p. 179*

WILLIAM TETLEY, Liens for Towage Freight *Vol. 2, p. 199*

TED L. McDORMAN, The 1982 Law of the Sea Convention: The First Year *Vol. 2, p. 211*

GEORGE F. CHANDLER III, A Comparison of 'COGSA', the Hague/ Visby Rules, and the Hamburg Rules *Vol. 2, p. 233*

PETER A. FRIEDMANN and JOHN A. DEVIERNO, The Shipping Act of 1984: The Shift from Governmental Regulation to Shipper 'Regulation' *Vol. 3, p. 311*

DIANA G. CULP, Charting a New Course: Proposed Amendments to the Supplemental Rules for Admiralty Arrest and Attachment *Vol. 3, p. 353*

WILLIAM TETLEY, Assignment and Transfer of Maritime Liens: Is There Subrogation of the Privilege? *Vol. 3, p. 393*

ECKART J. BROEDERMANN, China and Admiralty – An Introduction to Chinese Maritime Law and U.S.-Chinese Shipping Relations *Vol. 3, p. 419*

DOUGLAS A. JACOBSEN and JAMES D. YELLEN, Oil Pollution: The 1984 London Protocols and the AMOCO CADIZ *Vol. 4, p. 467*

W. WYLIE SPICER, Canadian Maritime Law and the Offshore: A Primer *Vol. 4, p. 489*

PAUL S. EDELMAN, *Forum Non Conveniens*: Its Application in Admiralty Law *Vol. 4, p. 517*

ECKART J. BROEDERMANN, China and Admiralty – An Introduction to Chinese Maritime Law and U.S.-Chinese Shipping Relations *Vol. 4, p. 539*

LE DROIT MARITIME FRANÇAIS (1984)

CLAUDE DOUAY, Les sanctions en matière de pollution dans la zone économique exclusive *3*

MICHEL ESPAGNON, Remarques sur le concours des actions nées du vice caché ou de la non-conformité du navire en cas d'acquéreurs ou d'utilisateurs successifs *67*

LLOYD'S MARITIME AND COMMERCIAL LAW QUARTERLY (1984)

Table of Cases

USA

Italy

France

United Kingdom

Maritime Arbitration Commission

Canada

Great Britain

Denmark

France

Greece

Norway

Poland

Spain

Ships' Names